A History of American Psychology

Works by A. A. Roback

The Interference of Will-Impulses
Behaviorism and Psychology
Psychology with Chapters on Character Analysis
Roback Mentality Tests for Superior Adults
Comprehension Tests
Scientific Ingenuity and Juristic Aptitude Tests
The Psychology of Character
A Bibliography of Character and Personality
Popular Psychology
Jewish Influence in Modern Thought
Personality: The Crux of Social Intercourse
Business Psychology
Self-Consciousness, Self-Treated
Curiosities of Yiddish Literature
I. L. Peretz: Psychologist of Literature
Behaviorism at 25
The Psychology of Common Sense
—Sense of Humor Test
The Story of Yiddish Literature
Contemporary Yiddish Literature
Apologia Pro Vita Yiddicia
William James
A Dictionary of International Slurs
Destiny and Motivation in Language
Psychorama: A Psychological Analysis
The Jew in Modern Science
Personality: In Theory and Practice
Freudiana
History of American Psychology
Di Imperye Yidish
History of Psychology and Psychiatry
Der Folksgaist in der Yidisher Shprakh (The Genius of the
    Yiddish Language)
—Aspects of Applied Psychology and Crime

A. A. ROBACK

HISTORY OF

AMERICAN

PSYCHOLOGY

New, revised edition

COLLIER BOOKS, New York

COLLIER-MACMILLAN LTD., London

TO THE OBSCURE AND FORGOTTEN
WHO WERE EITHER PREMATURELY CUT OFF
BY A CRUEL FATE
OR WHOSE FEEBLE VOICE COULD NOT BE HEARD
ABOVE THE DIN OF THEIR MORE DYNAMIC
COLLEAGUES
THIS VOLUME IS DEDICATED
AS A COMMEMORATIVE TRIBUTE

Preface to the Collier Books Edition

THREE YEARS AFTER the publication of this work, copies were unavailable. For the past few years want announcements appeared continually in the trade journals, and to the best of my knowledge not even a used copy has ever turned up in the bookstores around Harvard Square, in Cambridge. This shows that the subject appealed to the educated reader and that academic interest in the historical matter of American psychology is in the ascendant.

Were it not for technical reasons, a second edition should have been on the market soon after the first was exhausted. The lapse of a decade made it necessary to revise a number of passages and to add a dozen new chapters on the men who contributed significantly to the science, and a supplementary essay discussing the more recent developments.

In his favorable review of the book in the *American Journal of Psychology*, Professor Edwin G. Boring nevertheless intimated that the author showed some partiality toward Harvard. This exception should hardly have been taken by a Harvard professor of psychology, especially as he tells us in his own autobiographical sketch why he declined invitations of appointment to other universities, and cited Titchener, the coryphaeus at Cornell, who spoke of Harvard as the strongest center for psychology in the United States.

It is possible, naturally, that the author, with his Harvard associations, would have turned his attention more to the men he had known himself. After an analysis of the situation, the conclusion must be drawn that, as a rule, Harvard has— at least since James—attracted, both as teachers and as students, the most productive minds in psychology. Even men like Thorndike and Tolman, who received their laurels elsewhere, nevertheless did gain their apprenticeship at Harvard. However, in order to obviate, or at least lessen the charge, the supplementary chapters contain more sketches of non-Harvard psychologists and discussions of their work. Other chapters were amplified and brought up to date.

It is interesting to list the cavils of reviewers, even though with two, at most three, exceptions they were all laudatory of the book as a whole. From the nature of the criticism one might well infer the particular bias, the area of interest, and perhaps, too, the temperament of the reviewer. Again, the wisdom inherent in the famous fable of the miller, his son, and the ass comes to mind, capped by the trite saw "there is no accounting for tastes." It would be in order to deal with each of the objections briefly, if only to show how subjective they are, exposing, as they do, the specific preoccupation of the critic.

Let us begin with the criticism in the introduction to the Japanese translation of the work, that it has not delved into the social, political, and economic conditions of the country so as to account for the rise of certain ideas and movements in American psychology. Professor Benami evidently supposes that economic recessions, unemployment, the behavior of the stock market, the cold war, the tactics of the un-Americanism committee in the Senate, and so on, influence the course of psychology, e.g., engender functional psychology or cause the spread of psychoanalysis, or bring into being behaviorism or Gestalt psychology.

Even if such influences were probable, correlating them would be a matter of idle speculation. Certainly it is true that were there at the time better opportunities for scholars in Ireland, Scotland, or Germany, Witherspoon, McCosh, or Rauch would not have come to the United States, and if the Nazis had not obtained the upper hand in Germany or ceased their Judenrein policy, the Gestalt and psychoanalytic schools would not have been so well entrenched here. The vast commercial and industrial ramifications in this country could not but have fostered an elaborate network of applied psychology; and clinical psychology has been affected both by the peculiar hustle and bustle and the affluence in general of Americans.

Great historic events, such as the Civil War, were discussed in relation to the decline (or rise) of academic activity, but it would take an ideologist of the Marxian-Lenin school to attempt linking psychological schools or movements with socioeconomic conditions or changes. These attempts, based on unwarranted assumptions, would be bound to miscarry, and would only occupy space very much needed for actual exposition and interpretation of what is on record.

A more reasonable observation is that of Professor Boring, who points out that in the last analysis the history turns out to be geopolitical because so many of the men discussed in these chapters were born abroad. Less pertinently, he wonders why psychoanalysis, the product of Vienna, figures in a history of American psychology.

The answer, it would seem, is obvious. The geopolitical argument applies to practically every sphere of American civilization. Were we to take it seriously, there could be no history of American music, or of American linguistics, American anthropology (the most eminent anthropologists were born abroad), American art, etc. The question is, of course, what work had been accomplished by these men in the United States, and how they affected the fortunes of American psychology. As to psychoanalysis, there can be no contesting that it has taken hold in this country, branching out in various directions, more than anywhere else, including the land of its birth. Not only Freud, but every one of his dissident associates, has found brilliant and devoted disciples here.

While the vivid biographical sketches of the shapers of American psychology have been appreciated and praised by practically every reviewer, there has been heard a lone dissenting voice wondering what biography has to do with the scientific groundwork of psychology. This misgiving may be met by the ordinary finding that in the case of scientific history, one must know something about the originator, inventor, or exponent. A discussion of theory devoid of references to personal equation would not only prove arid but might also lead to confusion.

It was Goethe who wrote the oft-quoted lines

> *Wer den Dichter will verstehen,*
> *Muss ins Dichters Lande gehen.*

Now if it is true that in order to understand the poet, we must study his country, his habitat, may we not urge, by the same token, that if we wish to understand the art or science of a country, we must know something about the men who helped fashion it? Would it not be proper to turn Goethe's couplet conversely into something like this:

> *Wer des Landes Kunst will verstehen*
> *Muss den Künstler selbst ersehen?*

Of a captious nature is the contention that the history of American psychology prior to William James is not worth taking into account. One may surmise that the reviewer was a physiologist for whom anything outside of laboratory experimentation is of no value whatever. We have heard such an opinion uttered by Professor J. McKeen Cattell, but that was a long time ago during the early days of the "revolution." In the past half-century, psychology has become less militant and more understanding. We realize now that two and one-half centuries of psychological experience cannot be totally ignored. It is gratifying to report that experimentalists like Professor Boring and Sir Frederic C. Bartlett have expressed a similar opinion. The former writes: "Roback's account of this period is clear and informative, and we are fortunate to have it in English so easy to read . . . and we owe him our gratitude."[1] According to Bartlett, "To one reader, at any rate, the story of the beginnings 'In the Dominion of Physics and the Empire of Theology' is in many ways the most interesting part of this entire volume. It was high time that somebody should tell us more, in a readable and concise manner, about the earlier developments. This Dr. Roback has now done and done well."[2]

As for Professor Boring's criticism, "he seems to have no feeling that the historian should try to suppress his value-judgments," I plead guilty, but fortunately a staunch advocate, in the person of Sir Frederic Bartlett, comes to my defense in his review in the *British Journal of Psychology* with the observation "When, as with great gusto he often does, Roback introduces his own predilections and views, it is perfectly clear that for the time being the descriptive historian is being replaced by the historical thinker or commentator. And whether the reader agrees with these interpretations and reflections or not, they add a lot to the fun and excitement of reading."

Actually, I wonder whether there exists such a creature as a descriptive historian, in the strict sense of the word, unless a computer, a HISTORAC, be devised to chronicle data only. But that is just the difference between the mechanical and naive chronicler and the sophisticated yet reliable historian. We cannot think of a single historian, whether Mommsen, Gibbon, Parkman, certainly not Treitschke, nor Toynbee, yes, not even Boring, who has succeeded in concealing his feelings and preferences.

Other issues that have been queried by reviewers will be dealt with at relevant junctures in the text. Considering the

[1] *American Journal of Psychology*, 1953, vol. 66, p. 654.
[2] *British Journal of Psychology*, 1953, vol. 44.

extent of the period, as well as of the material, they are both few and minor points.

In the present edition, a number of quotations from the early treatises were omitted and other passages were condensed. About a third of the book consists of new material dealing with a dozen men, only referred to or cavalierly treated in the first edition, and about sixty pages are devoted to developments in the science during the last decade. The Bibliography has also been added, covering publications within the last decade or so.

A. A. ROBACK

Cambridge, Massachusetts
May, 1963

Preface to the First Edition

HISTORIES OF SCIENCE in general, or of a specific science, are not of such recent institution as is commonly supposed. Aristotle, and especially Diogenes Laertius, and to some extent Sextus Empiricus, may be said to have been the historians of philosophy in antiquity; and philosophy, then, we must bear in mind, included all science. They were not, however, historians from choice or with an avowed purpose. Rather were they epitomizers of views which had preceded their own, and thus, they found themselves impelled to look into the past. As philosophy, however, gradually split up into the various sciences, and as each science became more and more specialized, pursuing an individual objective, there emerged a new need, *viz.*, to cultivate perspective. The farther away we are from the beginnings, the more requisite becomes the historical sense, which is not given to the scientist or philosopher as such. The creative scientist is not likely to be the best historian, although there is nothing to preclude such a double function. It is most probably a matter of temperament.

It stands to reason that the oldest sciences would be the first to receive historical treatment. Mathematics has had its full quota of historians as compared with physics or chemistry. Psychology, as a young science, cannot boast of many historians. F. A. Carus seems to have been the first to attempt a history of psychology, but his *Geschichte der Psychologie* (1808) a book of 771 pages, is of course a history of the psychological portion of *philosophy*. Carus has had several successors in Germany: Siebeck, Dessoir, and Klemm. In France, Th. Ribot's name is associated with this top branch of psychology. England has never been strong in history. She lives too much in the present. Not that she failed to produce historians of philosophy or science. Even Bertrand Russell is a good example of such, but as historian he cannot begin to compare with Russell as philosopher.

It is curious that of all countries, the United States and Canada should have brought forth half a dozen or more books dealing with the history of psychology. We might have expected young peoples to slur history. It takes maturity to appreciate the past. An adolescent will not sit down to write memoirs, even if he had a host of experiences to relate. In the USSR, all history seems to have begun with the October Revolution, although recently there has been a good deal of preoccupation with the more remote past, the period of Alexander Nevsky and Ivan Grozny, but the decades preceding Bolshevik rule appear to be dealt with either as a gap or a smudge.

In the United States, the prescientific period of psychology has fared rather badly. It was simply taken for granted that the science here began with William James's *Principles of Psychology*. Even G. S. Brett, himself a philosopher, showed no sympathy nor patience with the older psychology, which was taught prior to the experimental era. On the other hand, J. W. Fay, who took it upon himself to rectify the injustice, and performed a genuine service in writing his book, *American Psychology before William James*, outstanding both as to scholarship and style, leaned too much in the opposite direction, and because of his overweening loyalty to his subject, he was disposed to discover in a large number of ordinary observations some significant anticipation or adumbration of a later finding by Freud, Lloyd Morgan, Thorndike, *et al.* He would cite unnecessarily the opinion of this or that writer on his newly-found luminary, meanwhile failing to bring out the purport of the latter's main thesis. Fay did much good spade work in an area sorely neglected, but frequently did not perceive the striking passages which revealed the difference between one author and another. Too often, a monotonous sameness runs throughout the various expositions of the earlier period.

The period beginning with James has been regarded as contemporary enough to be treated in current psychologies, which set out to be handbooks of the systematic schools. Patches of lacework here and there often take the place of the long thread which is expected to run throughout the history. Both Baldwin's and Pillsbury's histories are too sketchy and brief, traversing thousands of years in about 300 pages. Boring's *History of Experimental Psychology* is a history in full sense of the word—true, occasionally lost in details, but perspective and genealogical orientation are its merits; and Boring, of course, is thoroughly familiar with the issues, from the very roots.

The fact, however, is that Boring's *magnum opus* is not a

history of American psychology. Justified by its title, it ignores the non-experimental productions although one wonders why psychoanalysis and its offshoots are included. Then, too, since it includes *all* empirical psychology, of both continents, it cannot, even in the ample proportions to which it has grown, encompass the whole of the American contribution for the past fifty years or so, even longitudinally considered.

The present volume is an attempt to bridge the gulf between the pre-experimental and experimental epochs, and to fill in the gaps, to some extent, in both the too brief and the deliberately circumscribed histories of psychology. It is needless to state that no historian can hope to be satisfied with his work, particularly in a first edition. The question as to what to introduce and what to eliminate out of the hundreds of books examined is always an ordeal. There was something akin to a qualm when it was decided to omit references to this or that author of the earlier period. Naturally, as we were approaching our own generation, when psychological books were appearing in the scores and even in the hundreds every year, the problem solved itself by the decision that a companion volume alone could do justice to the specific contributions in the various departments and branches which have grown so luxuriant within the past half a century. To a certain extent I have tried to accomplish this in the one thousand-page / *Present-Day Psychology* (Phil. Lib.).

With a country like the United States and a period of history which necessitates migration in advanced age, as in the case of the refugees from Nazi terror, the further problem cropped up as to whether a man like L. William Stern, who became the leading psychologist in Germany before the advent of Hitler, could be included as an American, after his escape to this country. This was decided in the negative, in view of the fact that during his brief sojourn at Duke University, Stern did not produce anything which would have entitled him to a place in such a history, and his great achievement in Germany cannot count for the record here. His "intelligence ratio," which came to be known as the "intelligence quotient," however, did influence the whole course of testing. Something similar may be said about Karl Bühler.

It may be of some interest to the reader that according to the original project, this history was to contain about 50,000 words. The fact that it has almost tripled in size and now requires, in addition, a companion volume to deal with specific contributions, is a tribute to American achievement in this area of science.

My chief acknowledgement is due to the Harvard University library.

A. A. ROBACK

Cambridge, Massachusetts
February 25, 1952

Table of Contents

17

PART IV
Growth of Branches

PART I

IN THE DOMINION OF PHYSICS
AND THE EMPIRE OF THEOLOGY

Chapter 1

Introduction

THREE CENTURIES, even in a cultural, and not a geological, perspective, is a comparatively short period, and yet what strides have been made during that time in every branch of science! Mathematics, astronomy, physics, chemistry, physiology, anatomy, biology, geology, philology, economics and psychology—they have all had their birth in different centuries, perhaps even ages, yet their progress took a similar course in each case, mounting in complexity and gaining in solidity, despite occasional upheavals and revaluations, and at the same time allowing of *rapprochements* between two or more separate sciences, so that these borderlands become sciences in their own right, until the material grows too cumbersome for any one scientist to survey.

It is thus a relief to have to deal with a circumscribed subject like American psychology, which encompasses a period of only three hundred years. One could naturally enlarge, even within such scope, so as to fill a voluminous work, if the psychological content is unduly stressed, and the publications of the hundreds of authors are discussed in some detail.

History not Merely an Enumeration of Events

We must realize, however, that the purpose of the volume is not to build up a systematic psychology nor to examine its foundations. Our task is rather to trace the development of the science in the United States and Canada from its early beginnings, to show what changes have taken place through the decades, and, if possible, why. It is necessary, then, to dwell on the events which have shaped our present-day psychology; for in history, the guiding star is time, and the diachronic course, rather than the synchronic, is more consistent with our plan, considering its scope.

Histories of psychology (whether general or specific) have been variously conceived. Ribot, *e.g.*, would dwell almost exclusively on the particular men who contributed to the science: James Mill, Alexander Bain, John Stuart Mill,

Herbert Spencer, Samuel Bailey. A series of chapters dealing with their books would constitute a history of British psychology.

Others like Baldwin, Dessoir, and Brett have either followed the transitions of ideas and movements, such as idealism, naturalism, empiricism, materialism (which is the usual pursuit in philosophy), or else, like Klemm, have taken up each topic such as sensation, perception, association, etc., separately, so that the history of psychology becomes a history of the various items which go to make up general psychology. This procedure might be likened to the writing of a history of a particular country by giving historical accounts of the most important cities in that state.

Artificialities

The dubious feature of such histories is that they are not likely to reveal any *motifs* for the course which the science has taken. The changes, particularly, in the histories devoted to systems, schools, and points of view, show no progression, but a zig-zagging, or shuttling; and, just as in general histories, one often merely gains the impression that "history repeats itself." In ordinary or typical history, however, at least the events in themselves are instructive, if not always significant.

In a sense, it may be considered artificial to parcel off a special territory, even if it is our native land, and restrict our efforts to describing the development of a given science in this particular country. Is French psychology any different from German psychology or British psychology? To be sure, different topics may have been stressed here or there, but from the historical approaches we have had thus far, we would be hard put to relate just what these differences consist in, especially as comparative analysis has been most scant.

Even, however, if France, Germany, Scotland, England, and Italy can be proven to have developed psychologies of different casts, which may well be, the fact remains that within the tradition of these several countries, little variety can be recorded. It is as if a giant tree in each of these kept shooting forth more and more branches. The branches, while differing in size, sturdiness, and in shade, all stem from the same root. Slight exceptions will be found at rare intervals, but on the whole, it may be said, this represents the situation, even if we are cognizant of the differences of opinion, sometimes violent as in the case of Stumpf and Wundt, in Germany, or between Charcot and Bernheim, in France. Naturally temperaments may clash even in the same family, and both personal as well as collective reasons or, better, causes, may account for the dissidence and discrepancies.

A True Melting Pot

It is in America that the historical torch could be held up with greater results; for the influences have been wide and many. From the very start, this country was destined to become a crucible, and within the past seventy years, American psychology has become the product of a vast international processing, which has rendered it colorful, broad, and vigorous, from the constant fresh infusion of new blood. In this respect, no other country can compare with the United States.

Nor do we mean to say that because of the numerous factors which constitute American psychology, it lacks an original strain, and is therefore devoid of independence. It must be borne in mind that whatever the substances that have been placed in it, the crucible itself possesses properties of its own which must affect, to some extent, the melting; and no doubt, too, some of the ingredients, at least, are of the same composition. We shall see later that the foreign elements in the crucible, in themselves, are moulded accordingly, and that there is a certain determinism in the whole process, not a mere blind chance. There are affinities and aversions, attractions and repulsions, amalgamations and separations operating ostensibly for scientific purposes, yet dynamically veered through human foibles, which scientists and administrators have in common with farmers, laborers, and businessmen. Purely historical incidents are at work, too, in bringing about certain results perhaps on a different continent. Let us only visualize what Nazi brutishness has done for science in the United States and also other countries.

It goes without saying that a history of psychology, even on a larger scale, cannot attempt to shed light on the whole nexus of happenings; for much is fraught with speculation. We can never be certain of the interpretations, for all the circumstances surrounding the facts cannot be known even to the most painstaking historian; and the danger of turning out a historiosophy of American psychology instead of a history is too great in this connection. At the same time, the neglect of origins displayed heretofore has been a real handicap in understanding the significance of American psychology.

THE ROOTS OF OUR TRADITION

If we ask wherein does the growth of science here differ from that in Germany or France, the first answer that will occur to the average educated man is likely to be "Tradition." It is taken for granted that since the country is young, the mode of thought, or perhaps mould of thought, has not yet had the time to harden and take definite shape. In a measure this is true, but it is often forgotten that the Puritan settlers themselves did bring with them a definite tradition, that they were, in many instances, Oxford and Cambridge bred; and that their adventurous spirit and non-conformism constituted the backbone of their tradition, something which set them off from the European intellectuals.

Secondly, pioneer life imposes certain conditions, mainly restrictions, which are bound to alter the expected course. He who builds a house cannot enjoy the comforts and leisure of those who simply occupy the dwelling which stands ready for their use. Add to the cares and planning, the anxieties connected with the rigors of frontier existence amidst all sorts of dangers, not the least being hostility of the natives. Remoteness from other educational centres, and therefore virtual isolation, would be a further handicap in the spread of learning; while the dearth of instructors in a new country must have halted the academic development even of New England, New York, and Virginia, not to mention the less organized states.

On the other hand, these very conditions would foster a spirit of defiance and promote a practical attitude which can be discerned in the whole tenor of American science, and which marks it off from German or French tradition as self-sufficient, stable, and more or less incorporative. If necessity is the mother of invention, then we might anticipate in America a multiplicity of inventions, and perhaps fewer discoveries. By the same token, the theoretical would be subservient to the practical, and the "how" would be crowding out considerations of the "what" and the "why."

We must further recognize that in the early phases of American organization, particularly in the New England States, religious leaders held sway over the community.

Clergymen were the teachers as well as the preachers, and since philosophy was held to be the companion, if not the handmaid, of theology, and psychology was regarded as a branch of philosophy, they would naturally be looked up to as the psychologists of the day. A doctor of divinity might be the incumbent of half a dozen or more chairs, from mathematics to Hebrew, and thus, it would be almost physically impossible to do full justice to any one subject. Indeed, it is astonishing to find how much these clergymen, often administrators, too, were able to accomplish in the way of turning out systematic textbooks.

Had the original set-up continued indefinitely, American psychology would, indeed, have been doomed to sterility. Fortunately, it had made other than religious contacts; and by the middle of the nineteenth century, the medical profession had begun to invade our science. Various exchanges with England and Scotland brought new views to these shores, and before the end of the nineteenth century, importations from abroad, preceded by the pilgrimages of American students to German and French universities, infiltrated into the congealing psychological tradition of at least the east, rendering it more fluid and receptive.

The stream of European psychologists who were invited to teach or conduct research in psychological laboratories reached its peak during the Nazi regime, but the first wave, in the '90's, was of greater consequence for the growth of American psychology; for not only were the men who arrived then actually sought, instead of merely being accepted, but they became potent leaders in their respective institutions and in the field as a whole, bringing up a generation of able investigators and teachers. We thus not only profited from the added slants supplied by foreign psychologists but gained much through the individuality of scientists who were able to impress their charges with their forceful personalities.

Other Determining Factors

To what extent social, political, and economic happenings were responsible for the present status of psychology can scarcely be ascertained. It may be reasonably supposed that wars in the past have interfered with the normal course of education; and psychology, therefore, in common with the other theoretical disciplines, like philosophy, with which it was affiliated, either marked time or declined, but the two world wars undoubtedly gave it an impetus in the direction of research, contributed to its growing prestige and aided in the vast expansion and consolidation of the American Psychological Association so as to become one of the most powerful professional groups in the world.

For all that, it is no secret that until quite recently, at least, American psychology was not treated very seriously abroad. Indeed, an undue amount of disdain, if not contempt, toward the prescientific psychologists in this country appears in the casual expressions of our historians, who apparently thought that to read an earlier textbook than James's was sheer waste of time, and lacking the information, they were wont to make short shrift of their predecessors' efforts. We may come across psychologists who were not even aware that courses in psychology, although not necessarily under that name, were offered in most American universities prior to 1890, when William James published his *Principles of Psychology*.

As to the reputation of American psychology in Europe, I may relate that in 1930 when I paid a visit to 59 rue de Varenne, it did not take long before the affable and enthusiastic Pierre Janet gave me somewhat of a jolt by declaring that *"Les Américains—ils ont des édifices magnifiques, des laboratoires impressives—mais de psychologie—"* and this was accompanied by the characteristic French shrug and hand wave, which might mean anything from resignation to utter hopelessness.

The Germans have perhaps not been so outspoken, yet up to the Congress at Yale in 1929, they were scarcely less patronizing. Wilhelm Wundt, true enough, might have read American monographs, if only to cite them in his *Grundzüge*, but, as a rule, whatever was achieved on this side of the Atlantic carried little weight. Translations of American psychological works into French or German have been a rare occurrence, and it has been simply taken for granted that nothing fundamental could come out of the "land of the dollar." Even England, where psychology for long was not allowed its proper berth, has, conscious of her glamorous names in the past, been reluctant to acknowledge American superiority in this field.

At the present writing, it may be somewhat premature to assert that the hegemony in psychology belongs to the United States, but when we cast about for a place exhibiting greater activity in research projects in a diversified range of topics, it would be impossible for us to discover it elsewhere, especially after the impoverishment of Europe in every way, and the enrichment of the United States in the number and quality of proven scientists.

Chapter 2

In the Nebulous Colonial Days

ALTHOUGH THE HISTORY of a science should begin with the first glimpse of productiveness, nevertheless, in the case of American psychology, it might be impracticable to draw a line between educational and scientific productiveness, unless our sketch is to commence with the first results of actual laboratory experimentation; and even then who is there to say that these results were actually productive?

We cannot afford to forgo the almost 250 years during which psychology was taught, as if this period were a temporal vacuum. Hence it is just as well to date the history from 1640, when Henry Dunster, a young clergyman, educated in England, established the regular curriculum of the ramshackle boarding school which later was to become the greatest university in America.

It was a nebulous period in more than one sense. Charles Dickens, had he known the lurid details, might have incorporated some of the incidents, like the embezzlement by the steward, Eaton, his sadism, as in flogging an innocent assistant to the point of unconsciousness, or the niggardliness and gross neglect by his wife, who starved the students—into some of his pathetic children's tales (*Oliver Twist, Nicholas Nickleby*). The fifteen to twenty students who constituted the early population of Harvard College did not have an attractive programme of study. Hebrew and Aramaic, Greek and Latin, metaphysics, logic, and physics, mathematics and astronomy, supplemented by theology and ethics, was the daily pabulum. Rhetoric was perhaps looked to as a diversion from the solemn and irksome tasks which were imposed upon those boys, in their early teens, who must have received hazy notions of a great many things.

Their teacher was for the most part the President who, in addition to being an administrator, was perhaps two-in-one, for he took on the duties of a dean and often would continue his preaching as well. His specialty was Hebrew, "Chaldee" or Aramaic, and Syriac, but for a time at least, he was practically the whole faculty; for tutors were scarce, and when some young graduate was found available, it was not long before he accepted something more lucrative, like a call to a church or a chaplaincy; for let us not forget that the community was primarily religious and that in 1640, when the whole of Massachusetts, possibly all New England, could boast of one lawyer, about 25% of the people in the embryo commonwealth were connected, in one capacity or another, with the church.[1]

It is to the credit of the Pilgrim fathers that only 22 years after the landing of the Mayflower—and with the college closed down during the year 1639-40, after the Eaton scandals—nine students were graduated as bachelors in 1642. It is also fortunate that Henry Dunster, a man of parts, carried on as first President, when Harvard was just a toddler and helpless, combining the duties of a fund raiser, schoolmaster, and manager of a press, among others.

It is well to note that although Dunster was, by profession, a clergyman, and therefore might be expected to employ his efforts in the matter of seeking books for the library, on behalf of theology, religion, and biblical subjects, including Hebrew and Aramaic, he nevertheless petitioned the New England Confederation, in 1647, to supply the deficiency in law, physics, philosophy and mathematics.[2]

That he cherished his firm convictions on matters of religion is evident from the fact that he was forced to tender his resignation when the state and clergy took a serious view of his expressed opposition to infant baptism. Such was the state of affairs about 300 years ago, and it was out of this atmosphere that sound scholarship and genuine science were later to unfold before the eyes of the world.

Textbooks in the Philosophical Disciplines

Since Harvard was modelled after the British universities (it does not matter whether it was Cambridge or Edinburgh, as S. E. Morison, Harvard's own historian believes) one might have supposed that the textbooks, even in the seventeenth century, would have all been imported from England, even if the great period in English philosophy was yet to come. It may come as a surprise, then, to learn that almost every text was of a foreign origin. In philosophy alone, we

[1] J. Chaplin: *Life of Henry Dunster,* Boston, 1872, p. 32.
[2] S. E. Morison: *The Founding of Harvard College,* Cambridge, 1935, p. 269.

have the compendia of Burgerdijk and Heereboord, Dutchmen; Kechermann, a German; Maccovius, a Pole; Bartholin, a Dane; Pavone, an Italian, and Suarez, the famous Spanish Jesuit, not to mention Peter Ramus, the celebrated lecturer at the University of Paris. In other words, the sources composed an *internationale*, such as is not to be found even in our own day, when the language difficulty acts as a snag.

It must be realized, however, that in the seventeenth century, the aura of Aristotle united most schools, and that Latin, the universal language of instruction, made every book of a serious nature, no matter wherever published, accessible to every student. The approach was scholastic, and the three "philosophies," *viz.,* physics, logic, and metaphysics were taught in dogmatic fashion through a system of ready-made definitions or propositions, and logistic or syllogistic inferences, divorced from experience, but resting on speculation and wishful thinking.

True to the mediaeval tradition, psychology came under the head of physics, but to set it off from mere inanimate matter and its properties, the soul was treated in a special division of physics, called *pneumatics* or *pneumatology*, which included matter about the angels too. It was much later that psychology became a nestling of philosophy and remained so until recently in American universities.

Psychological Theses

To what extent psychological questions figured in the teaching programme may be seen from the theses which the candidate for the bachelor's degree was to defend, and the *quaestiones* which the master candidates were required to dispute on. Since the fire of 1764 destroyed the records, we are indebted to the thoughtfulness of Sir William Osler who, on finding copies of the original commencement programmes for a number of years in the Hunterian Museum of the University of Glasgow, sent photostats of them to President Lowell, which are now available in the archives room of the Widener Library. Apparently others were recovered from various sources, since in Morison's *Founding of Harvard University*, and in the second volume of his *Harvard University in the Seventeenth Century*, a number of commencement sheets are reproduced.

Even as early as 1642, we find among the physics theses, two of a psychological nature:

Anima non fit ex traduce.
The mind does not originate out of a graft (on body).
Vehemens sensibile destruit sensum.
A vehement sensation destroys the sense.

Apparently these two propositions are regarded as infallible, to be proved like a geometrical theorem. The first, of course, relating to the primordiality and simplicity of the soul, was inculcated into the minds of youngsters, as a support to the religious creed. The theory of emergent evolution, even if we introduce consciousness in place of soul, would run counter to the principle enunciated in the first thesis. On the other hand, the second thesis may be based on experience, and is acceptable today when expressed in the form that a violent stimulus is apt to impair the sense organ.

The following are further theses of a psychological order under the rubric of physics, according to year, barring those which have not been recovered.

Physics 1643
In uno corpore non sunt plures animae.
One body does not harbor a plurality of souls.
Anima est tota in toto, & tota in qualibet parte.
The soul is wholly in the entire body and in any part of it.
Status animae in corpore est naturalissimus.
The soul has its most natural seat in the body.
Visio fit receptione specierum.
Sight consists in the reception of visual forms.
Phantasia producit reales effectus.
Fantasy produces real consequences.
Primum cognitum est singulare materiale.
The first thing known consists of a single substance.

1646
Anima nil patitur a corpore.
The soul is unaffected by the body.
Operatio animae pendet a corpore.
The functioning of the soul depends on the body.
Vita est unio formae cum materia.
Life is the union of form and substance.
Synteresis[3] fundatur in intellectu.
Conscience is grounded in the intellect. [A.A.R.]

---

[3] The term *synteresis,* or synderesis which the scholastics employed, connotes that mental power which affords us the knowledge of right and wrong. It corresponds to the moral intuition.

1653

Nulla anima est forma animati.

No soul consists of the form of an animate being.

Destructa quavis anima compositum perit.

The destruction of any soul entails that of the composite.

Anima rationalis est divisibilis.[4]

The rational soul is divisible.

Voluntas sequitur non obsequitur dictamini intellectus.

The will follows, but is not subject to, the dictates of the intellect.

Voluntas movet sensus internos imperio tantum politico non despotico.

The will moves the internal senses by a rule that is similar to that of civil law rather than to that of a despot.

The issues to be debated by the candidates for the master's degree are put in the form of a question like

An anima rationalis sit forma hominis.

(Whether the rational mind dwells in a human body)

Psychology as based on Formal Logic

On superficial examination of the theses and *quaestiones*, it will be noted that the propositions recur again and again in different form. They are practically stereotypes, and seem to have served the twofold purpose of indoctrinating students with beliefs, or else truisms, acceptable to the church of that period, and, further, of initiating a mental exercise which might or might not disclose the calibre of their intellect. The argumentation was not calculated to add one iota to our knowledge, although at rare intervals an ingenious turn might be discerned in the reasoning.

As we proceed to the year 1708, the number of theses listed in physics reaches 37, and here we find such propositions as

Color is not given in the dark

The rational mind acts in an inorganic manner

The rational mind is created and ingrained (*infunditur*) at conception

Among the theses for that year, we are likely to find *animae rationales sunt aequales*—striking because of its social

[4] It would seem that this thesis was thrown in to be defended as a sop to the public, eager for excitement. The soul is supposed to be indivisible.

and political implications; for is this not the very foundation of democracy? On the other hand, among the *quaestiones* to be argued by the higher-degree candidates are such issues as whether the rational mind is created, or whether thought prevails over material forces. (The word "*superet*" may be interpreted as "prevails," "transcends," or "is superior to," or "surmounts"; and, therefore, in our day, might present some semantic difficulty, which apparently did not exist then; for the occasion was one of proclaiming, in syllogistic form, the triumph of mind over matter.) There was no doubt of the issue. It was only a question of verbal approach and perhaps, too, of delivery. From the frequency of the particular or specific disputations, one might even call it a recitation.

It may, perhaps, be interjected that the *more geometrico* method was honored by no less a genius than Spinoza, who thought of it as the only one which permits of conviction, but let us not forget that he brought infinite substance and ideas to the method, which, when discounted, after we have admired it to our heart's content, still leaves us with the precious insights that the great mind has bequeathed us.

Certainly the stock propositions which summed up the teaching of psychology at Harvard, up to the first decade of the eighteenth century at least, cannot impress us as productive. So great was the momentum of scholasticism, and so isolated were the colonists in Massachusetts from the great European centres that the works of the trail blazers in the philosophical and scientific firmament: Bacon, Hobbes, Descartes, Spinoza, Leibniz, Pascal, Newton, Locke, Van Helmont were scarcely known to the professors of Harvard, through the incumbency of ten presidents. It was thanks to Brigden, who had received his A. B. in 1657, that the names of Copernicus, Galileo, Kepler, and Gassendi were mentioned, for the first time, in an exposition of Copernican astronomy, "which is the earliest extant scientific essay by a Harvard graduate."

For all this, it was necessary to bring to light the abortive endeavors of academic psychology during the seventeenth century, since, as Morison rightly observes, "Higher education in the United States begins with the books that Harvard students read, the theses that they defended . . ."[5]

[5] S. E. Morison: *Harvard University in the Seventeenth Century,* vol. II, p. 416.

Other Institutions

Trying times, wars which at one period took a terrible toll of Massachusetts youth—it is estimated one-tenth of those of fighting age were killed in the war with Philip alone—the decline of Harvard in the latter part of the seventeenth century, together with the forced resignation of President Hoar, in 1674, after he had laid out plans almost modern in scope, made it doubtful whether the institution would survive. Even the presidency went begging, and no one qualified was anxious to accept the invitation. Small wonder that no other college had been projected for the whole new territory, until 1693, when the College of William and Mary was founded as a boarding school, in far-off Virginia. Between the founding of Harvard and the next institution of learning in the United States lies a long stretch, both geographically and temporally.

In spite of the glamorous names associated with the college, the King and Queen of England, whose land grant and additional funds from quit-rents in Virginia helped establish the institution, George Washington and ex-President Tyler, the College of William and Mary did not prosper, and was destroyed several times by incendiary fires, the last time, by drunken American soldiers, in 1859. To this day it has remained a small college.

The founding of Yale, in 1692, at first as a collegiate school at Saybrooke, which was transferred to New Haven in 1716, when Samuel Johnson became one of its early tutors, marks an event in the cultural life of New England, on a par with the founding of Harvard, and under a more auspicious star, considering the financial and religious difficulties of the latter during its early years. In 1740, Princeton, then known as the College of New Jersey, and in 1746, the University of Pennsylvania were established, while Columbia made its debut as King's College in 1754. The same year saw the opening of Brown in Providence.

Struggle Between Old Dogmas and Progressive Ideas

No longer were the colonists a mere handful. The academic sector with half a dozen colleges in fairly close communication with each other was, now that the country was more viable, bound to produce results. Streams of immigrants, many of them educated, brought a new supply of teachers with fresh ideas, while frequent travel to England on the part of American educators, mainly administrators, enabled them to take advantage of the most recent findings in the mother country. The time, however, had not yet come for throwing off the shackles of a scholastic system pervaded by theological dogma, thus throttling all progressive thinking.

In the early history of Harvard alone, for instance, theological preoccupation had played havoc with the smooth running of the institution. Henry Dunster, as we have seen previously, was forced to resign as President because he opposed infant baptism, while his successor, Charles Chauncy came perilously close to losing the office, just as he had lost most of the members of his Church when he was a clergyman, because he insisted on the baptism of practically neonates, even in wintry weather; and Chauncy, let it be understood, was probably the most brilliant mind in New England. Toward the end of the seventeenth century, William Brattle, another shining light of the day, who served as acting President while Increase Mather was in England, was compelled to leave by reason of his liberalism.

Psychological Subject-Matter in Early Eighteenth Century

It was William Brattle who gave us the first digest, in Latin naturally, of what was taught at Harvard in logic, with a sprinkling of psychological facts, as they were then known. In the sixty pages, in the form of a catechism, the students are supplied with the answers to a number of questions supposedly in accordance with Cartesian principles. The psychological questions in this Logic of Brattle bore on topics like imagination, memory, primary and secondary perception, relations, etc. Several illustrations will suffice to give the reader an idea of the method:

Quando dicitur Mens pure—Intelligere?
When is the mind said to be in a state of pure understanding?
Cum Rem percipit cujus nullum extat in cerebro vestigium
When it perceives something of which there is no trace in the brain.

Quando dicitur Mens imaginari?

When is the mind said to be imagining?

Cum Mens non ad ipsam Rem externo sensui praesentem sed at Phantasma sive vestigium cerebro impressum se applicat.

When the mind is directed not to the thing itself which is presented to the external sense but to a fancy or trace of an impression in the brain.

Another exhibit, much in the style of Brattle's, is the summary which Samuel Johnson made of the physics he had assimilated by the time he was eighteen, when he assumed his duties as tutor at Yale, which had just graduated him. Physics, as we have seen above, included all that belonged to nature; and the soul is one type of spirit, which, in its turn, is part of created nature. Thus to the question: "What is spirit?" we have the ready answer: "Spirit is an immutable, living and intelligent nature." In a subsequent proposition we have the word "immutable" superseded by "willing." To the question: "How many kinds of spirits are there?" the answer is "two: (a) angel, and (b) the rational soul." The spirit possesses faculties: life, intellect, and will, and embraces species, like humans and animals. The latter have a soul too, an irrational one, while plants possess a vegetative soul, with a number of functions like digestion, excretion, nutrition, and growth.

The sensitive soul governs sensation, appetite and motion. The five senses constitute the external senses; the internal senses include judgment, reflection, imagination and memory. Under appetite we have emotions, movements, and such physiological processes as the beating of the pulse and breathing.

Defects of the Educational System

This account, brief as it is, suffices to warrant a glimpse of the psychology taught in our two greatest institutions, some 250 years ago. Psychology then was not part of metaphysics. It was a department of physics, but while physics had already at the time some illustrious innovators, who gave the world experimentally tested laws, psychology was at the mercy of theological doctrine, manipulated through rule-of-thumb, formally denominated logic. It was the safest method for the zealots of that period. If psychology is handed down to us on a golden catechistic platter, then what need is there for seeking more information? The definitions, vague and hazy, as they were, made sense to the students of the time, and saved them the bother of thinking, although the situation today in some of the definitely partisan schools is not much better. A definition like, "Life is the act of the vivifier in the vivified by the union of both" is no better than the famous definitions and explanations in Molière's *Le Malade Imaginaire* and *Le Médecin Malgré Lui*, but the students are a bit more critical nowadays.

It is clear that no empirical science could advance on the basis of postulates and definitions or logical derivations alone. So long as psychology remained the succubus of theology, as was the case throughout the seventeenth century and during the early decades of the eighteenth century, it could only rest on the accepted authority of the past. The stimulus of dissenting voices had not yet reached these shores. Even Bacon's *Advancement of Learning*, published in 1605, not to speak of Hobbes's *Human Nature* (1650), and Locke's great *Essay* (1690), appear to have been unknown until the eighteenth century. We shall see, in the next chapter, how here and there, a searching mind would stumble upon a true pillar and discover it to be a beacon as well, guiding his course and even the destiny of the science at stake. To such a mind, "it appears" as Thomas Hobbes, one of the first semanticists in modern philosophy, has put it three centuries ago, "how necessary it is for any man that aspires to true knowledge to examine the definitions of former authors; and either to correct them where they are negligently set down, or to make them himself."

Cotton Mather, Pastoral Psychologist (1663-1728)

Although psychology, in a scholastic vein, was taught at Harvard since about 1640 under the aegis of physics and under the name of "pneumatics," because the soul was a sort of breath, according to the Bible, such psychologists as could be found in New England were anonymous. The first one to have given utterance to some observations on the subject would naturally have been a divine; for the clergyman would be the most influential member in a community that came into being on a religious principle, or perhaps as a result of a religious conflict.

In Puritan New England, toward the end of the seventeenth

century, no one had come to be regarded with greater deference, if not awe, than Cotton Mather, whose father, Increase Mather, had already established a reputation as an effective preacher and historian of sorts.

Like the son of an eminent surgeon or jurist who continued the family tradition with greater aplomb than his progenitor, Cotton Mather began to take on the aura of an oracle; having previously wavered between the medical profession and the ministry, he affected a knowledge that other divines could not claim. He was alert enough to keep up with the European trends, and dabbled in medicine, so that he was thought of as something of a scientist, especially after prescribing various medications which were the panaceas of the day—a bag of saffron worn over the heart, or a drink of whey infused with epithymum, or the standby, hellebore. He knew the efficacy of mercury in the treatment of venereal disease, but feared the medicine's side effects, or, perhaps, the self-indulgence which would follow upon the disease's successful treatment.

He was realistic enough to consider the body as a machine that needs regulation, but harped upon the Hebrew term *Nishmat-khayim* (vital spirit) which he supposed to be a mediator between the rational soul and the corporeal mass. In Jewish lore it is, of course, simply the soul.

Not unlike the German Heinroth, who lived a century later, he believed that the cause of disease was sin, ever reverting to the first sin of the original human couple.

Aside from his observations, repeated in various of his widely reverberating sermons and bearing on the mind-body relationship, he had included a chapter on melancholy in his theologico-medical treatise labeled *The Angel of Bethesda*, which entitles him to be regarded as the first articulate American psychologist with a clinical interest. It was not until half a century later, however, when Samuel Johnson, also a divine, but an academic philosopher as well, brought out a compendium based on Locke's essay, that psychology found a foothold as a subject *per se* which could be treated systematically in spite of its involvement with philosophy and theology. The *obiter dicta* of Cotton Mather, nevertheless, afford us a glimpse of the more cultivated mind of the day, which was not, however, beyond taking stock in the absurdities of witchcraft, that culminated in the hanging of the Salem women branded as *succubae* of the Devil.

In most of his numerous sermons, which served as the

radio and TV of the day in colonial New England, especially as they would appear later in pamphlet form, Mather managed to introduce some observations which could be considered psychological and which must have particularly impressed the listeners.

Chapter 3

The Secularization of Psychology

SAMUEL JOHNSON (1696-1772) the eighteen-year-old tutor at Yale, who already had compiled a miniature encyclopedia for his own use, of the knowledge circulating up to 1714, was destined not only to play a great part in the history of American education, but by virtue of his writings, contacts, and personal influence, became even more than Jonathan Edwards, his glamorous contemporary, the mouthpiece of American philosophy. His chief work, *Elementa Philosophica*, was published in 1752, but in 1715, when he was only nineteen, he had already laid out his far-flung plans for a logic and a system of psychology, or pneumatology, *i.e.*, the study of spirits or "created intelligences."

Samuel Johnson—First of the Line

It was shortly before this that, according to his own testimony, he "fell in with a copy of Lord Bacon's *Instauratio Magna*, and purchasing it immediately . . . lost no time in devouring its contents." We are further apprised that he "found himself like one at once emerging out of the glimmer of twilight into the full sunshine."[1]

The book, however, which exercised a powerful grip on the youthful mind of the subsequently first President of Columbia University or King's College, as it was then called, was John Locke's *Essay on the Human Understanding*. In his revised *Encyclopedia* (1715), Johnson shows to what extent he had benefited from the perusal of Locke's work, *e. g.*, the statement, "All ideas come into the mind either by sensation or reflection," a dictum which runs counter to the tenet, held up to then, of innate ideas. The term "idea" is understood in the very broad Lockian sense, which permits the fetus in the womb to experience ideas (warmth, hunger). Sometimes, in his succinct statements, Johnson expresses him-

[1] E. E. Beardsley: *Life and Correspondence of Samuel Johnson*, N.Y., 1874, p. 6.

self more felicitously than Locke, *e.g.*, when the latter says, "But our ideas being nothing but actual perceptions in the Mind, which cease to be anything when there is no perception of them, this laying up of our ideas in the repository of the memory signifies no more, but this that the mind has a power, in many cases, to revive perceptions which it has once had, with this additional perception annexed to them—that it has had them before,"[2] Johnson writes "The soul has a power to continue the idea for a while under its view and this may be called *retention*. Again it has a power whereby after the disappearing of an idea, it can recollect and call it to mind again. Now the capacity of the mind to do this is its *memory* and the actual doing it is its *remembrance*, which differs from the first apprehension of the idea only in this, that the mind now perceives it with a consciousness of having perceived it before."[3]

There is a prevision in Johnson, as in differentiating between memory and remembrance, which is quite modern, even if he still clings to the "soul" as the *fons et origo* of all mental operations. He makes a distinction between attention and intention, the latter involving a more intensive application, and he employs the term *apprehension* which Locke avoids, although he follows him in the serial treatment of judgment and reason with apprehension (in Locke, *perception*), and in many other respects. The plastic mind of the 19-year-old philosopher has been able to assimilate a new system in the space of a year. He was not yet willing to discard all of his former scholasticism. Indeed, it has probably stood him in good stead in the endeavors to formulate his newly-acquired knowledge, and it may have been also instrumental in fitting him for the conversion to the spiritual idealism of Bishop Berkeley whose acquaintance he had made during the latter's visit to America.

First Comprehensive American Textbook

Samuel Johnson's scope was broad. He covered in his *Elementa Philosophica* (1752) which may be regarded as the first American textbook on the subject, a large number of miscel-

---

[2] Locke: *Essay on the Human Understanding,* Chapter X.

[3] S. Johnson: Logic; cited in H. W. Schneider's *Samuel Johnson,* vol. 2 (philosophy), p. 223. The italics are not in the original passage.

laneous topics in a more or less ordered manner, embracing not only philosophy and ethics but also psychology, and paving the way for a better approach to child psychology and pedagogy. He was extraverted enough to know people, and his calling as a clergyman did not prevent him from adopting a more liberal attitude than was wont, in that period, toward life and letters, including of course philosophy. If he speaks of a "kind of intellectual light within us whereby we not only know that we perceive the object, but directly apply ourselves to the consideration of it . . . which I conceive of as it were a medium of knowledge as sensible light is of sight" deriving it from the "universal presence and action of the Deity," he is still within the tradition of the day. Even such a circumspect thinker as Locke would introduce, on occasion, a teleological argument to show how the whole mental set-up has been arranged by God for the benefit of man.

It is difficult for us to understand the purposive approach of the theologically minded during that period. Psychology existed for the sake of logic, and logic for the sake of God. In his illuminating introduction to the second volume of the comprehensive biography, H. Schneider tells us that the pastor of the Old South Church in Boston, Samuel Willard, who was Vice-President of Harvard College at the time he preached his famous sermons, asked in one of them (on a Sunday in 1724), "What is the chief end of Man?" and answered in catechistic fashion, "Man's chief end is to glorify God," adding as a mere sequel, "and enjoy Him forever."

The value relations of the various disciplines would inevitably be guided by such considerations as: Wherein does a particular study serve to hasten or to intensify this glorification? And the "science or art of thinking or meditation," as Johnson defines it, would naturally bring us closer to our goal.

When we consider that the whole *Logic* of Johnson, which is divided into ten very brief chapters, contains no more than about 25 pages, we can understand that the part dealing with the psychological elements would be limited to but a few pages. The *Elementa Philosophica*, which came out in 1752 (about 25 years after the *Logic*), a more ambitious work, in that it might constitute a book of some 200 pages, also made reference to psychological matters, in connection with epistemology (*e.g.* consciousness is defined as "our perception of objects *ab intra*, or from reflecting or turning the eye of our mind inward, and observing what passeth within itself") and morals ("the nature of man, his excellencies and imperfections"). Johnson was not the man to specialize. He was rather the urbane, precise, and versatile thinker, who wished to cover all knowledge. He even published a Hebrew grammar toward the end of his days.

The fact that he was an executive and had a charming address must have had its counterpart in his writings, which remind us of the gracefulness found in Berkeley's dialogues. That is true especially of Johnson's *Raphael or the Genius of the English America*. There is not the slightest trace of pedanticism in any of Johnson's works; and there is a forward-moving rhythm about his prose which may have been instrumental in the success which his books enjoyed over a long period.

The Fiery Revivalist Takes a Hand

In Jonathan Edwards (1703-1758) we have a philosopher of an entirely different type. In a sense, he may be contrasted with Johnson. He, too, was precocious, entering Yale College at 13, and at once becoming wrapped up in philosophy. At the age of 14, he read Locke's *Essay* with greater delight "than the most greedy miser finds when gathering up handfuls of silver and gold from some newly discovered treasure." He was steeped in the natural philosophy of Newton, and at 23 he became a tutor at Yale, but after two years of teaching, he joined his grandfather as pastor at Northampton, Mass. It was here that this crusader, for whom even his mother's father was too liberal, became a force to be reckoned with, attracting through his fire-and-brimstone sermons the more emotional people while, by the same token, alienating some of the more worldly-wise elements, until his resignation became necessary. A month before his untimely death, as a result of inoculation against smallpox, he was chosen President of Princeton College, as successor of his deceased son-in-law, Aaron Burr.

Jonathan Edwards stands out as probably the most colorful personality in early American theology and philosophy. By many he is rated as the chief thinker in the Colonies prior to the Revolution. That he was a subtle logician there can be no doubt, that he has left a deeper impress on American thinking than his older contemporary, Samuel Johnson, can scarcely be gainsaid, but most likely the halo around his name derives from his zealous championship of certain religious tenets, which led to considerable polemics and unrest in the most active part of New England. It was primarily as a preacher, a revivalist, that he wielded such prodigious influence. In an era of stormy petrels, he seemed to be about the stormiest, and waxed strong in grappling with high-placed enemies, who finally succeeded in driving him from his parish but not in crushing his perfervid spirit; for living as a missionary among the Indians at Stockbridge, Mass., he wrote several fundamental treatises, including the famous *Inquiry into the Freedom of the Will* and *The Affections*, both in the domain of psychology. His works enjoyed several editions, the first complete edition in ten volumes having been brought out by his great-grandson.

Freedom of the Will

To understand Edwards' aim, it is essential to keep in mind that since the early colonial days, theology was gradually losing its stranglehold on the life of the people. The doctrine of Arminius that man was free to choose, in opposition to the ironclad predestination dogma of the Calvinists, was beginning to make its inroads into New England theological circles. Edwards' grandfather was ready to accept into the realm of grace those who qualified on the principle of faith. Worshippers would hold it an injustice to be damned in spite of their good conduct only because it was so decreed by an omniscient Deity. It was a matter of despair for the majority to know that their own will had nothing to do with the consequences of their actions.

It was left for Jonathan Edwards to admonish the discontented and stem the tide of rebellion; and once he failed to carry conviction through his thunderous sermons, he decided to convey his message in a closely reasoned disquisition. The irony of it was that in his determinism, he uses virtually the same arguments as Hobbes and Spinoza, whose very names should have been anathema to him. Whereas, however, they rest their case after they prove, to their own satisfaction, that every act of volition is determined by some motive, Edwards traces this determinism back to the will of God. This seems to be the counterpart, in volition, of Berkeley's notion that all objects are merely God's ideas (*esse est percipi*). Thus we are to believe that human choice is only the will of God.

The keen dialectician, which Edwards incontestably was, worked up his argument in a logical discourse, very much after the fashion of an expert jurist. An edited series of excerpts (for the sake of brevity) from his chief work will serve as the best illustration of his method and style.

With respect to that grand inquiry, What determines the will? It is sufficient to my present purpose to say, it is a motive, which, as it stands in the view of the mind, is the strongest, that determines the will. By *motive* I mean the whole of that which moves, excites, or invites the mind to volition, whether that be one thing singly, or many things conjunctly. . . .

Whatever is a motive, in this sense, must be something that is extant in the view or apprehension of the understanding, or perceiving faculty. Nothing can induce or invite the mind to will or to act any thing, any further than it is perceived, or is in some way or other in the mind's view: for what is wholly unperceived, and perfectly out of the mind's view, cannot affect the mind at all. It is most evident that nothing is in the mind, or reaches it, or takes any hold of it, any other wise than as it is perceived or thought of. . . .

And I think it must be allowed by all that every thing that is properly called a motive, excitement, or inducement to a perceiving, willing agent, has some sort and degree of *tendency* or *advantage* to move or excite the will, previous to the effect, or to the act of the will excited. This previous tendency of the motive is what I call the *strength of the motive*. . . .

That whatever is perceived or apprehended by an intelligent and voluntary agent, which has the nature and influence of a motive to volition or choice, is considered or viewed as good . . . And therefore it must be true, in some sense, that the will is always as the greatest apparent good is. . . .

I use the term *good* as of the same import as *agreeable*. To appear good to the mind, as I use the phrase, is the same as to *appear agreeable*, or *seem pleasing* to the mind. . . .

Many acts of volition have some remote relation to an object that is different from the thing most immediately willed and chosen. Thus, when a drunkard has his liquor before him, and he has to choose whether to drink or no, the proper and immediate objects about which his present volition is conversant, and between which his choice now decides, are his own acts; in drinking the liquor or letting it alone; and this will certainly be done according to what, in the present view of his mind, taken in the whole of it, is the most agreeable to him. If he chooses or wills to drink it, and not to let it alone, then his action, as it stands in the view of his mind, with all that belongs to its appearance there, is more agreeable and pleasing than letting it alone. . . .

If he wills to drink, drinking is the proper object of the act of his will; and drinking, on some account or other, now appears most agreeable to him, and suits him best. If he chooses to refrain, then refraining is the immediate object of his will, and is most pleasing to him. If in the choice he makes in the case, he prefers a present pleasure to a future advantage, which he judges will be greater when it comes, then a lesser present pleasure appears more agreeable to him than a greater advantage at a distance. If, on the contrary, a future advantage is preferred, then that appears most agreeable and suits him best. And so still the present volition is as the greatest apparent good at present is.[4]

What Edwards attempts to do in this steep climb is to show that although we are free to choose that which we desire, we are not free to desire. That has been thrust upon us. It is evident that as Edwards proceeds in his reasoning, it becomes more and more difficult for the reader to check on all his moves, particularly as the language is too quaint and savors of legal phraseology. How differently Spinoza achieves his purpose by the use of the plainest and most concise diction.

The Hitch in the Argument

Edwards takes it for granted that there are only two departments of the mind: (1) understanding, or as we would call it, cognition (2) volition and affection; in other words that

[4] J. Edwards: *The Freedom of the Will,* Part I., Section 2.

will deals with what is present while *desire* governs what is absent. It was reserved for later writers to make of the mind a tripartite function, relegating the feelings, desires, emotions and sentiments to a different category. In so doing, it was thought the whole deterministic philosophy was refuted and the day saved for the freedom of the will, which the bulk of theologians and ethicists require in order to attach responsibility to the individual.

Austere and preoccupied with the afterworld, this gloomy prophet considered the psychology of will and affection as an instrument for the confirmation of Calvinistic theology, which was beginning to yield in favor of more latitudinarian views, even Deism and Socinianism, later to be known as Unitarianism. Inexorable in his attitude toward his fellows, and in his own outlook on life, he had experienced the unkindness of fate, for in addition to the continual conflicts on matters of doctrine and practice with his congregation, which led to a precarious existence, requiring his family to sell at fairs homemade laces and other articles, he lost two sons-in-law, whom he highly regarded; and this before he was 55, when death took him, but he was fortunate in his numerous descendants, who have been mentioned in many books on heredity and eugenics, as proof of the validity of the gene theory.

A Psychoanalytic Adumbration

If Edwards has unwittingly helped the cause of the non-religious by his consistent fight on behalf of determinism, Freud might have revelled in his sermon entitled "Men Naturally God's Enemies," in which he seems to have anticipated the psychoanalytic belief that because of the hostility of the boy toward the father, who is a rival for the affection of his mother, there is a tendency always to kill the leader, who represents the father. Freud's account of religion is set forth in at least three books and many articles. The theme recurs especially in his last work, *Moses and Monotheism*, which assumes that the Jews killed Moses, on the same unconscious principle.

To return to Edwards, it is strange that he should look upon his flock as God's foes. It is possible that there was identification here, in Freud's sense, and that he felt that most of the Church members would have him supplanted by a more genial pastor. Perhaps that is why whenever a penitent came to him for communion, he would not be inclined to accept his protestations without reproving him severely. In the sermon mentioned, he tells us what the poor suppliant would be expected to hear and answer to:

> "You object against your having a mortal hatred against God, that you never felt any desire to kill him. But one reason has been that it has always been conceived so impossible by you, and you have been so sensible how much desires would be in vain, that it has kept down such a desire. But if the life of God were within your reach, and you knew it, it would not be safe one hour."

That Edwards should employ such strong words as "kill" and "mortal hatred" with reference to God is perhaps more symptomatic than might be admitted at first blush.

That a religious fanatic and an outspoken atheist would share a point of incidence is illustrative of the French saying *Les extrèmes se touchent*. The fact is that the American divine and the Austro-Jewish psychoanalyst were united by a common heritage, and probably Freud's forbears in Moravia were just as mystically inclined as Edwards, who even obliterated the principle of personal identity to the point of making us all guilty of Adam's sin. This state of continuity of man in God's action is analogous to the recurrence theory of Freud, and above all is not Freud *the* determinist *par excellence*, in fact, the first *over*determinist in psychology?

Psychology of Conversion

A phase of Edwards' endeavors which has been totally ignored is his contribution to religious psychology. Edwards had cherished the fond hope that something great would be coming to pass in the New World, and that New England was to be the favored place, and possibly that he was chosen to be the one to show the way to others in preparing the people for the great event.[5] His enthusiasm was contagious, and in Northampton, which, as he tells us in a letter of about 30,000 words, harbored then about 200 families, "We have about

[5] "But we are evidently a people blessed of the Lord! And here in this corner of the world, God dwells, and manifests his glory." "Narrative of Surprising Conversions," in *Works of President Edwards* (1st Am. ed.), vol. III, p. 80.

620 communicants, which include almost all our adult persons." The "great awakening" is how the phenomenon of wholesale conversion has been referred to, for not only in Northampton did the revivalist spell seize the inhabitants ("about the same number of males as females") but also in neighboring villages, like South Hadley and Suffield.

Edwards may or may not have been a psychologist in our sense of the word. He nevertheless produced psychological phenomena which were of some consequence, and what is more, he was the first, at least in America, to probe the state of mind of those who had fallen under his spell. Among the 200 families living in Northampton there were no doubt scores who were highstrung and even definitely neurotic. Not far away, in Salem, nineteen persons were hanged and one was pressed to death about 40 years earlier, because of the hysterical tendencies of the victims and the inciting sermons of Cotton Mather.

Fortunately New England, although too late, learned its lesson, and the Salem murders will forever remain a stigma against the names of the instigators and judges, in spite of apologists like G. L. Kittredge and Barrett Wendell. In Northampton, the preaching of Edwards, by his own testimony, elevated the minds of his listeners to the point of seeking salvation. It apparently became an obsession with some of the invalids and maladjusted. The case of Abigail Hutchinson, presented in great detail, is particularly interesting; that of a four-year-old child less so, but the individual differences which Edwards sets down as belonging to the pre-conversion and actual conversion periods, the reasons given for the awakening, as well as the aims to be attained by the communicant, are of great importance for the student of religious psychology.

Edwards was not always successful. His success was credited to God; his failures, naturally to the devil. The first half of the year 1735 had been a banner season, but even in a village and more than 200 years ago, suicidal impulses began to manifest themselves. "A poor weak man . . . being in great spiritual trouble was hurried with violent temptations to cut his own throat, and made an attempt, but did not do it effectually." . . . "In the latter part of May, it began to be very sensible that the spirit of God was gradually withdrawing from us and after this time, Satan seemed to be mor⸱ let loose, and raged in a dreadful manner. The first instance wherein it appeared was a person's putting an end to his own life by cutting his throat." This man had been hopelessly melancholic, and evidently was tainted from birth, since his mother had a similar end, but according to Edwards, "the devil took the advantage and drove him into despairing thoughts."

What, however, is strange about Edwards' narrative is the fact that

After this, multitudes in this and other towns seemed to have it strongly suggested to them and pressed upon them to do as this person had done.

And many that seemed to be under no melancholy, some pious persons, that had no special darkness or doubts about the goodness of their state, nor were under any special trouble or concern of mind about any thing spiritual or temporal, yet had it urged upon them, as if somebody had spoken to them, *"Cut your own throat, now is a good opportunity."*

Jonathan Edwards, steeped in religious lore and acting as an apostle to the backsliding New Englanders was, to adapt a title of Molière's, a *psychologue malgré lui*. His treatises on the will and the religious affections contain some provocative observations, but he was also an applied psychologist in the sphere of religion, and might have functioned occasionally as a psychotherapist, considering his work a success, even if the patient died as a result of the treatment; for it was not the body but the soul that had real meaning for him. . . . The course of academic psychology was not affected by him, but his views were discussed avidly in the eighteenth century by the intellectuals of his day—clergymen, of course, as professors *per se* were practically non-existent then.

Let us now see how psychology fared at Harvard at about this time and up to the Revolution.

Psychology Neglected at Harvard

The Cartesian philosophy came to Harvard through William Brattle's compendium based on Legrand's *Institutio Philosophia Secundum Principia R. Descartes*. William Brattle was a tutor there from 1685 to 1697, and the 60-page fascicle called *New Logic* was used as text, first in manuscript, and then in printed book form, from 1735 until the middle of the eighteenth century, along with Henry More's *Enchiridion Ethicum*, and Heereboord's *Meletemata*. Some psychology is contained in all three books, but during that period, it was not recognized as a discipline in itself, but rather as fragments needed to bolster the metaphysical and ethical principles, through logical inference.

It was not until 1766, that the specialization in teaching began at Harvard. Up to then, a tutor might teach all the subjects. Having been assigned a certain number of students, he was expected to be responsible for their education throughout the four years of college, and then start with a fresh flock. The first official appointee in philosophy was Simeon Howard who was tutor only from 1767-1770. He, like most of his short-termed successors, turned to the ministry. Now and then, a tutor would graduate into the law profession or enter politics. Actually, the first permanent tutor in philosophy was Levi Hedge (1766-1844) appointed in 1795. The duties of the tutors did not consist in lecturing but in examining the students on their recitations.

Brattle's adaptation of Legrand was thought of as so great an antidote to the purely scholastic works in logic that for more than half of the eighteenth century, it was the required text, but in 1742, *i. e.*, more than 50 years after its publication, Locke's *Essay on the Human Understanding* is officially introduced in the curriculum, and in 1767, Watts's *Logic* began to supplement and then supersede Brattle's compendium.

The practice of "learning by heart" appears to have been prevalent even in the early nineteenth century when Levi Hedge, who had by this time been promoted to the first professorship in philosophy at Harvard, expected his students to regurgitate, word for word, the material of his textbook in logic, which it had taken him, with the assistance of some members of his family, fourteen years to write. Hedge's *Elements of Logic* first brought out in 1816, went through half a dozen editions, at least, the last in 1845, and compares favorably with its predecessors. Hedge, believing that a "brief description of the leading powers and operations of the mind is essential as a propaedeutic," included six small chapters of a psychological nature, *viz.*, (a) perception (b) consciousness (c) attention (d) abstraction (e) association of ideas and (f) analysis.

Harvard Intrenched in Logic

Logic appears to have been the subject especially stressed at Harvard. To this very day it occupies the centre of the philosophical programme.[6] The more idealistic touch was gained from Henry More; but significantly enough, Berkeleyan spiritualism, which wielded such influence during the first half of the eighteenth century at King's College in New York, thanks to Samuel Johnson, and the College of New Jersey (Princeton) because of S. Stanhope Smith, and even at Yale, not to mention clergy affiliations, like Jonathan Edwards' predominant interests in spirits and the Spirit who is the basis of our being and acting (willing)—had not seeped into Harvard's academic activities. Whether it was from a too realistic foundation, congregational hardheadedness, or a skeptical attitude in regard to Irish achievement, the Harvard overseers and tutors stuck to Locke and Watts, transferring their loyalty afterwards to the Scottish School. The elegant style, ingenuity, (especially, as in his *New Theory of Vision*) and charming presence of the Bishop of Cloyne obviously did not compensate for the extreme conclusions which he held in regard to the nonexistence of matter.

It may readily be seen that prior to the Revolution, Harvard had not progressed along psychological lines, primarily because of the lack of specialization in teaching, but also because of the conservative policies and matters of organization, which required so much attention then. Its political and religious contacts, too, were, to some extent, impeding factors, preventing concentration on the purely educational system. As the period of unrest was approaching, Harvard being in the midst of the discontented area, the effect on both teachers and students could hardly have been beneficial. Some of the buildings had been used as barracks; classes for a time met at Concord, and even after the War of Independence had been won, it took some years before conditions had become stabilized.

[6] At the present revision, its star, with the gradual evanescence of the Whitehead tradition, has begun to wane.

Chapter 4

Scotch Realism Comes to America

IT MAY BE puzzling that while Harvard was clinging to Locke and older authors, the new College of New Jersey (later Princeton) should have taken to the Common Sense School, which originated in Scotland, while in Philadelphia, where The College of Pennsylvania had been founded, and in New York, where Samuel Johnson was at the helm of King's College (Columbia) Berkeleyan views predominated. For that matter, Princeton, too, was not able to avoid it, since the philosophy tutor, S. Stanhope Smith had come under its influence through the senior tutor, Periam.

The explanation may be threefold. An element of chance may have entered in, too. The constitutions of the above-mentioned colleges were as different from one another as the make-up of the community and the temperaments or outlooks of the founders. Cambridge had been a Congregational centre; Princeton and its environs were Presbyterian in denomination. The stronghold of Presbyterianism was in Scotland. When the trustees of the College of New Jersey, then in Newark, cast about for a president, a few years before the War of Independence, they chose Scottish-born-and-trained John Witherspoon (1722-1794) who had had some teaching experience in Belfast. Witherspoon, later a signer of the Declaration of Independence, was an able organizer. Arriving in 1768, he at once began to steer the academic ship, and introduced in place of the Berkeleyan doctrine, which had just begun to make headway there, the works of Reid and Beattie, and finally wrote his own textbook, *Lectures on Moral Philosophy,* which contained much on psychology, particularly, the emotions.

What Is Scotch Realism?

Let us first see wherein the Scotch school differs from the English. The latter, as is evident from the works of Bacon, Hobbes, and Locke, was strictly empirical and methodological, stressing the theory of knowledge. The English philosophers were chiefly concerned with origins. Such inquiries led, in the case of Berkeley, if he may be classed with the English, to a reluctant skepticism, which resolved itself in a theological idealism, and in Hume, though he was Scotch, to a whole-hearted skepticism. There were only sensations, so far as we can be certain, and the self, or what others would designate as the soul, was merely a bundle of sensations. The Scotsman, David Hume, was the most consistent philosopher, because he was rock-bottom in his methodology and approach. His predecessors did not choose to draw the ultimate consequence which his subtlety demanded. Hence, if Berkeley was an idealist, grounding his ideas in God, Hume simply was a phenomenalist or sensationalist, letting the matter rest at that, although in everyday living he followed the dictates of common sense.

The Scotch dynasty beginning with Francis Hutcheson (1694-1747) and running through a full century and a half, with acute thinkers like Thomas Reid (1710-1796). Dugald Stewart (1753-1828), Thomas Brown (1778-1820), and the most gifted of the school, Sir William Hamilton (1788-1856), stood for common sense in philosophy. Our senses, according to them, do tell us much about the world that is acceptable at face value, and where discrepancies arise, our senses can be relied on to iron out the wrinkles. The whole method of introspection was developed by these Scottish philosophers who, for the most part, set down rules of observing their own consciousness and analyzing their experiences in a fashion that was hitherto unknown. They were the armchair psychologists on a large scale, and their long suit was analysis. Similarly, in ethics they started with certain intuitions which, they maintained, were self-evident, as against those who would cite illustrations to prove that there are no such first principles, and that morals were a matter of custom or pretense.

"To argue from common sense," writes William Hamilton, "is nothing more than to render available the presumption in favor of the orginal facts of consciousness,—and *that is by nature necessarily believed to be,* truly *is* . . . The argument from common sense therefore postulates, and founds on the assumption—that our original beliefs be not proved self-contradictory."[1] Hamilton cites a formidable array of philosophers as supporters of the common sense point of view.

[1] *Philosophy of Sir William Hamilton* (ed. by A. O. Wight), 6th ed. N.Y. 1860, p. 226.

The prestige of the Scottish school carried into foreign lands, especially since English philosophy was beginning to decline about then. In France, Victor Cousin, known for his deft eclecticism and charming style, and Jouffroy, a direct and clear thinker who wrote elegantly, became the French patrons of the philosophy, the latter translating some of Reid's works, and lending his vocal support to the Scotch School.

It must not be supposed that Scottish realism is all of one piece. True, Thomas Reid and Dugald Stewart in general agree, or to put it differently, the latter may be considered a disciple of the former. Thomas Brown, however, whose medical training might have given him a bit of an advantage, took Reid to task on many occasions; and his own philosophy brought him closer to Locke, and, were he not so religious-minded, he might even have leaned toward Hume's skepticism. Brown, nevertheless, is still in the tradition of the Common Sense School, of which he was one of the ornaments, both because of his lyric style and his gift of synthesis. Had he not died at the age of 42, his contribution to psychology might have been considerable, for it was he more than any of the other members of the School who had bent his efforts along the investigation of the mind. Sir William Hamilton was more metaphysical in his approach, having been influenced by German thinkers, and subjected Brown to scorching criticism, which helped to remove him from the pedestal upon which he had been placed in Scottish circles.

In the philosophy of common sense, psychology (or the philosophy of the human mind or of the intellect, as it was variously called) held a central place, but seldom would it be treated as a separate discipline. Moral philosophy, metaphysics, and even logic would be bound up with it. In general, psychological material was held to be the basis of all three, and the ultimate object was to build up a foundation for theology. The idea of God, of the infinite, of perfection, were all grist to the philosophical mill, and it took decades before the strands were taken apart.

Princeton Becomes the Psychological Centre

When Witherspoon arrived in the United States, his attention became engaged in an assortment of activities. He was a busy churchman, his opinions commanding respect in Presbyterian council halls; he was absorbed in the promotion of the College of New Jersey, and he also began to take an interest in politics. He still found the time to teach a course in moral philosophy. Witherspoon was the man of affairs rather than the creative scholar, and he seemed to be conscious of his limitations; for under no consideration, was he willing to have his lectures published, although students were expected to take down a transcript. When a printer started to set the lectures in type, the author threatened him with a lawsuit. These lectures, delivered between 1768 and 1794, were finally printed posthumously in 1800, and reprinted in 1912. Since Witherspoon had destroyed his original manuscripts, in the knowledge that they were not adequate, at least without elaboration and revision, several of the students' transcripts were used in the redaction of the volume, which is as the author intended it to be, a compendium.

Of the sixteen lectures, only the first three are of a psychological nature, and deal very briefly with reason and instinct, the three "faculties" of the mind, the understanding, the will, and the affections, with a brief analysis of the passions, desire, and aversion, and a discussion of internal sensation (sense of beauty, sense of harmony, sense of proportion, sculpture and poetry, and finally a sense of moral good and evil *i.e.*, the moral sense, which is the cue for his course of lectures). Leading up to the doctrine that there is nothing certain or valuable in moral philosophy, but what is perfectly coincident with the Scriptures: "Where the glory of God is the first principle of action arising from the subjection of the creature —where the good of others is the great object of duty, and our own interest the necessary consequence,"[2] the author at once makes it plain that his first interest is theology.

Witherspoon will be remembered as an outstanding administrator, as one who steered the course of the Presbyterian Church in America, as an American patriot and legislator, but his sphere of influence was not academic, although as an educator, he must have left a lasting impress on his students, for one reason, because his lectures were not wrapped in a barrage of speculation. His observations were not only marked by common sense; they were direct and to the point. The delivery was just as it might have come from a director at a meeting of a businesss corporation. The *pros* and *cons* were adduced, but he himself served as the moderator.

[2] J. Witherspoon: *Lectures on Moral Philosophy* (ed. by V. L. Collins), 1912, p. 141.

S. S. Smith—First Environmentalist and Social Psychologist

Of a different calibre was his son-in-law, Samuel Stanhope Smith (1750-1819), who, as we have seen, had come under the influence of Berkeleyanism, of which Princeton was promptly purged with the advent of Witherspoon as President, in 1768. Smith, too, subsequently became President of the College of New Jersey, and so far as the Scottish philosophy is concerned, followed in the footsteps of his predecessor, who was also his father-in-law. Like him, he was a clergyman and possibly more devout—one of his published sermons dealing with the reasonableness of fasting—but in Smith, we have a more or less original mind which, in a sense, has anticipated the views of Franz Boas, the anthropologist, and Ellsworth Huntington, the anthropogeographer. In fact, he may be looked upon as the first environmentalist to have marshalled an array of facts in support of his theory.

As professor of moral philosophy, it devolved upon him to give the course of lectures which his deceased father-in-law had offered. Instead of a compendium of less than 150 pages, his lectures (1812) constituted two volumes, diffusely entitled "The Lectures Corrected and Improved which have been delivered for a series of years in the College of New Jersey on the Subject of Moral and Political Philosophy," of which the first was devoted to psychology. Smith is more expansive than Witherspoon, covers many more topics, and while his father-in-law was somewhat careless in references and spelling of names, Smith is meticulous. His definitions of habit, instinct, propensity, and the will are precise and some may still, with slight modifications, be adopted today. Sentiment, *e.g.*, is defined as an "emotion of the mind relative to good or evil, present in ourselves or others. It produces a state of feeling rather predisposing to action in a certain direction, than exciting to any immediate effort." That he was familiar with the nervous system is evident not so much from these lectures as from his elaborate essay in anthropology, which he read before the American Philosophical Society in 1787, and which was published in 1789, both in Philadelphia and London, under the title *An Essay on the Causes of the Variety of Complexion and Figure in the Human Species*— a piece of research which has been overlooked in the histories of the mental and social sciences.

A Sociological Pioneer

It was in this little volume that Smith set himself the task of proving that the human race was descended from one couple, presumably Adam and Eve, but that the varieties according to color and other physical characteristics were due to climate and other physical conditions. Toward the end, we find a brilliant polemic against Lord Kaims, who was of the opinion that man originated in different species, and that these were so constituted as to survive only in their own areas. Whether Smith's thesis was inspired by Montesquieu or occurred to him independently does not much matter; for the merit of his essay consists in the rigid method which he adopts, in his vast fund of information, his acute first-hand observations, and in his scientific reasoning. When we reflect that 160 years ago, sociology was not even dreamed of, it surely would not be an exaggeration to rank Smith as a pioneer in that special field, whether his conclusions are acceptable today or not.

Smith first notes the gradation in complexion as practically proportioned to the latitude of the country, and is careful to add that temperature is not a function of distance from the sun, that there are secondary causes which correct and limit the solar influences, *viz.*, elevation of the land, vicinity to the sea, nature of the soil, state of cultivation, course of winds, and a good many other conditions. Smith goes into great detail explaining not only the shades of color taken on by the numerous peoples and tribes, but even differences in the constitution of the hair and expression of the face.

> Every object that impresses the senses, and every emotion that rises in the mind, affects the features of the face—the index of our feelings, and contributes to form the infinitely varied countenance of man. Paucity of ideas creates a vacant and unmeaning aspect. Agreeable and cultivated scenes compose the features, and render them regular and gay. Wild, and deformed, and solitary forests tend to impress on the countenance an image of their own rudeness. . . .

> The want of interesting emotions leaving its muscles lax and unexerted, they are suffered to distend themselves to a larger and grosser size, and acquire a soft unvarying

swell that is not distinctly marked by any idea. A general standard of beauty has its effect in forming the human countenance and figure. Every passion and mode of thinking has its peculiar expression; and all the preceding characters have again many variation, according to their degrees of strength, according to their combinations with other principles, and according to the peculiarities of constitution or of climate that form the ground on which the different impressions are received. As the degrees of civilization, as the ideas, passions, and objects of society in different countries, and under different forms of government are infinitely various, they open a boundless field for variety in the human countenance.[3]

Environmentalists have in Smith a valiant protagonist, who thought that even "the figure, the color, and properties of the horse are easily changed according to the ruling taste, *e.g.*, out of the same strain the Pennsylvania Dutch raised large and heavy horses while the Irish bred a lighter and smaller animal, and horses will be black, white or bay, in accordance with the fashion of the day by choosing horses of the desired color to supply the studs." Our author is at pains to show that human nature is more plastic than are other organisms and that civilized man is far more adaptable than the primitive to the rigors of life.

Human nature, much more pliant, and affected by a greater variety of causes from food, from clothing, from lodging, and from manners, is still more easily susceptible of change, according to any general standard, or idea of the human form. To this principle, as well as to the manner of living, it may be, in part, attributed that the Germans, the Swedes, and the French, in different parts of the United States, who live chiefly among themselves, and cultivate the habits and ideas of the countries from which they emigrated, retain, even in our climate, a strong resemblance of their primitive stocks. Those, on the other hand, who have not confined themselves to the contracted circle of their countrymen, but have mingled freely with the Anglo-Americans, entered into their manners, and adopted their

[3] S. S. Smith: *An Essay on the Cause of the Variety of Complexion and Figure in the Human Species,* 1789, pp. 54-55.

ideas, have assumed such a likeness to them, that it is not easy now to distinguish from one another people who have sprung from such different origins (pp. 73-74).

The variety of hair conditions is accounted for in this manner.

The sparseness of the African hair is analogous to the effect which a warm climate has been shown to have on other animals. Cold, by obstructing the perspiration, tends to throw out the perspiration matter accumulated at the skin in an additional coat of hair. A warm climate, by opening the pores, evaporates this matter before it can be concreted into the substance of hair; and laxness and aperture of the pores renders the hair liable to be easily eradicated by innumerable accidents.

Its curl may result in part, perhaps, from external heat, and in part from the nature of substance or secretion by which it is nourished. That it depends in a degree on the quality of the secretion is rendered probable from its appearance on the chin, and on other parts of the human body. Climate is as much distinguished by the nature and proportion of the secretions as by the degree of heat. Whatever be the nutriment of the hair, it seems to be combined, in the torrid zone of Africa, with some fluid of a highly volatile or ardent quality. That it is combined with a strong volatile salt, the rank and offensive smell of many African nations give us reason to suspect. Saline secretions tend to curl and to burn the hair. The evaporation of any volatile spirit would render its surface dry and disposed to contract, while the center continuing distended by the vital motion, these opposite dilatations and contractions would necessarily produce a curve, and make the hair grow involved. This conjecture received some confirmation by observing that the negroes born in the United States of America are gradually losing the strong smell of the African zone; their hair is, at the same time, growing less involved, and becoming denser and longer (pp. 36-38).

It is apparent that Smith does not think the Africans or any other race as originally inferior but attributes the handicaps to climate and other external conditions. He points out, from his own experience, the difference between Negroes in the South laboring in the field, and those working as domestics among the whites.

"It is well known," he tells us in a footnote, "that the Africans who have been brought to America are daily becoming, under all the disadvantages of servitude, more ingenious and susceptible of instruction. This effect, which has been taken notice of more than once, may, in part perhaps, be attributed to a change in their modes of living, as well as to society, or climate" (p. 81).

Smith's textbook, with its survey of the sensations, affections, perceptions, imagination and will, is greatly indebted to his Scottish predecessors, Reid, Stewart, Brown, Campbell, and Beattie. He may have made a better selection here and there; he may have been more felicitous in his phraseology occasionally, although, in general, it would be an occasion for anyone to excel the writers mentioned in diction or metaphor. Brown, particularly, who prided himself as much on his verse as on his philosophy, was scarcely to be outdone in that respect. What, however, gives us a real insight into Smith's scientific status and mental outlook is the little-known essay on the causes of the variety of human complexion and figure, which was read in Philadelphia before the Philosophical Society.

Scottish Philosophy at Harvard

Princeton, *i.e.*, The College of New Jersey, as it was still called, was during the days of the Revolution and decades afterwards, the citadel of the common sense school in the United States. Harvard, because of its definitely English ties, did not evince such interest, until Levi Hedge (1766-1844) was intrenched there as professor of logic and metaphysics, and later as Alford Professor of Natural Religion, Moral Philosophy, and Social Polity. From 1820 to 1827, he used not only Locke's *Essay*, but also Stewart's *Philosophy of the Human Mind*, and Brown's *Lectures on the Philosophy of the Human Mind*.[4] In fact, he brought out his own edition of Brown's comprehensive work, and his penned annotations may still be seen in the copy reposing in the Houghton Library of Harvard.

[4] B. Rand: "Philosophical Instruction in Harvard University," etc., *Harvard Graduates' Mag.* 1928-29, vol. 37.

Perhaps more inclined to Scottish realism was Hedge's successor, James Walker (1794-1874), who took over Hedge's chair which had been vacant for six years, in 1838. In his day, there was much more to choose from both in France and in Germany, and he did introduce a more balanced philosophical curriculum, yet he used Stewart's *Elements of the Philosophy of Mind* and Reid's *Essays on the Intellectual Powers of Man*, which he himself edited and abridged, and another Scottish text which found favor in this country about a century ago, *viz.*, Abercrombie's *Inquiries concerning the Intellectual Powers*, which was edited in the United States by John Abbot, and published as a school text in 1833, an abridgement of the author's *Treatises on the Human Mind*. This text was reprinted and revised, more than once, and its vogue stemmed from the fact that Abercrombie, being a physician, and not a metaphysician, still less a theologian, approached the subject from an empirical and even a practical angle, and the editor, by omitting the medical aspects, made it still more serviceable as a handbook for sophomores or even freshmen. In this respect, it resembles one of our twentieth-century textbooks with special emphasis on the abnormal. We thus see that Scottish philosophers and psychologists moulded the student mind in the United States and stimulated the teachers to write their texts in a similar vein.

Chapter 5

Philadelphia in the Foreground

HITHERTO, THE PART which Harvard, Yale, Columbia, and Princeton played in the early advancement of psychology has become evident, but even if Philadelphia was somewhat late in developing as an academic centre (for the College there which, afterwards in conjunction with the University of the State of Pennsylvania, came to be known as the University of Pennsylvania was not founded until 1740) it would not be likely that the city of William Penn, David Rittenhouse, and Benjamin Franklin, the "Cradle of Liberty" as it is sometimes referred to, would lag behind other American cities. It was, as a matter of fact, at the time of the Revolution that Philadelphia shone with its institutions and luminaries, and let us not forget that its American Philosophical Society was until recently not only the first but also the foremost learned society in the country. It may still rate as the most prestigious.

Benjamin Rush—First Medical Psychologist

The first Philadelphian to have contributed to our science was Benjamin Rush (1745-1813) a many-sided man who became the ornament of the medical faculty of the young College of Philadelphia, and is regarded as the father of American psychiatry, his likeness serving as the seal of the American Psychiatric Association. His broad training, especially in Scotland, had brought him in contact with many fields; and though he occupied the first chair in chemistry in the United States, his chief interest perhaps lay in correlating the physical with the mental in medicine. Among the topics which he discusses in his *Medical Inquiries and Observations* are "An Inquiry into the Influence of Physical Causes upon the Moral Faculty," "An Inquiry into the Relation of Tastes and Aliments to each other," and "An Account of the State of the Body and Mind in Old Age," which may be taken as the first step toward geriatrics. His *Course of Lectures on the Institutes and Practice of Medicine* also contains at least two chapters and scattered observations dealing with psychology, *e.g.*, his emphasis on the need of the physician to make himself familiar with the working of the mind, which takes him into the sphere of psychotherapy.

Rush was perhaps more self-confident than original, but he must receive credit for a certain far-sightedness, in addition to his bent for social reforms. A very capable observer, he reached conclusions too quickly. Madness to him was due to spasms in the blood vessels of the brain, and akin to fever. For physical ailments he recommended bleeding and purges, always looking for a single involvement rather than a complication. His place in American psychiatry will be reverted to in a separate brief *History of Psychology and Psychiatry*. As regards general or normal psychology, his classification of the faculties and operations is no different, except in details, from those of his predecessors. Among the faculties he includes the "principle of faith, will, the moral faculty, conscience, and the sense of Deity."[1] Despite his medical training, he opens his work on the diseases of the mind with a prayer to God that "nothing hurtful to my fellow-citizens may fall from my pen and that this work may be the means of lessening a portion of some of the greatest evils of human life."

His selection of the so-called operations of the mind as sensation, perception, association, judgment, reasoning, and volition, with others, like attention, reflection, contemplation, wit, consciousness, and the like as "nothing but modifications of the five principal operations that have been mentioned" at once shows up the weakness of the armchair psychologist, who lumps things without any justification. Why should consciousness be subordinate to association or judgment? Why should imagination be a faculty and association an operation? In those days, however, the bricks were taken ready-made and placed wherever it suited the mason.

Suggests Psychophysical Parallelism and Neural Action

In a further passage we discover that "all the operations in the mind are the effects of motions previously excited in the brain, and every idea and thought appears to depend upon a motion peculiar to itself. In a sound state of the mind, these motions are regular, and succeed impressions upon the brain with the same certainty and uniformity that perceptions succeed impressions upon the senses in their sound state."

Presumably Rush here almost stumbles upon the discovery

[1] B. Rush: *Medical Inquiries and Observations on the Diseases of the Mind* (fifth ed.), 1835, p. 7.

of nerve impulses, and also discerns the parallelism between a mental state and a nerve process, but the explanation is inchoate.

Rush gathered his data most assiduously, and left no stone unturned to prove that insanity is an arterial disease, but many of his illustrations might well have been anecdotal, if not mythological. His prowess lay in offering definite suggestions as to what to give in specific cases, in which he seemed never at a loss. It were strange, if some wag had not made some remark to the effect that "Benjamin rushed in where angels fear to tread." In any case, Rush was a fearless champion of his convictions on many matters, not only medicine, but government, and politics, temperance, and abolition. He even went so far as to impugn anonymously George Washington's qualifications as a military leader, after his first few defeats. Withal, Rush was a humanitarian and a practical idealist, a fighter as well as a scientist.

James Rush, one of his sons, entered the precinct of psychology more directly than his father, but as he belongs to a different period, it would be in order to present the men first whose teachings intervened between father and son.

Another Philadelphian to attain a certain prominence in the early history of American psychology was Frederick Beasley (1777-1845) a clergyman who had received his education at the College of New Jersey, chiefly under S. S. Smith, and had, therefore, come under the influence of the Scottish School at its peak, but was later, after he had become Provost of the University of Pennsylvania and Professor of Moral Philosophy, impelled to reject it as being of a piece with the "intellectual fooleries and skeptical impieties of Mr. Hume," and so he sat down to write his own *Search for Truth in the Science of the Human Mind,* the first volume alone of which appeared in 1822, a tome of 561 pages. In this volume, which purports to follow in the footsteps of Locke, showing wherein Reid and his Scottish associates erred in their interpretations, Beasley, the conservative Episcopalian priest, is still inclined toward using the old term "pneumatology" which, however, he explains as the "science of the human mind."

Somehow, Philadelphia has made no dent in the psychological world although the first professorship in psychology was established at the University of Pennsylvania. The Rush period was its only glorious opportunity.

Chapter 6

The Age of Independent Textbooks

IT IS OF NOTE that what textbooks were written in philosophy, which up to that time included psychology, prior to the nineteenth century on this side of the Atlantic, showed a decided leaning upon the works of English and Scotch philosophers, as if the United States were an intellectual satellite of the British Isles. Whether the Revolution had something to do with it or not, it so happens that less dependence is evinced by American writers on philosophy and psychology during the period following the War of Independence, and furthermore, psychology is gradually liberated from its philosophical suzerainty, so that it can stand on its own feet.

Benjamin Rush, Benjamin Franklin, and David Rittenhouse were among the first to proclaim the self-sufficiency of the former colonies in matters intellectual. Oxford, Cambridge, London, Greenwich, and Edinburgh surely were great centres of learning and research, but there was something which the growing American universities could impart to the greyheads on the other side. Sometimes the new guide would not even be a member of a college staff. England was not unfamiliar with such circumstances; for most of her major philosophers had been other than university professors.

In the United States those who were following philosophical and psychological pursuits were still of the clergy even as late as the last decades of the nineteenth century, theology, philosophy, and psychology forming a sort of delectable trinity for such minds. Geographically, these pioneers were not confined to the large centres. They sometimes not only came from villages or townships, but even lived there, while producing lasting works. They might choose to remain in comparative obscurity instead of shining in an executive capacity while abandoning their life of contemplation.

Asa Burton Makes a Start on his Own

An independent thinker who was destined to play a part in the annals of American psychology was the clergyman, Asa Burton (1752-1836) who preferred carrying on as a preacher in the Vermont village of Thetford to serving as President of Middlebury College; and from his activities in church matters, it might be inferred that he would have been an able administrator.

Burton, whose sermons were above the usual level in logical development if not in delivery, and whose courses at the theological seminary were a combination of philosophy and theology, or perhaps theological teachings studded with philosophical and psychological aperçus, looked upon the latter as an introduction to divinity. He was quite blunt in the declaration that "Whatever opinions respecting the mind he may advance which do not agree with experience, with facts, and the word of God are to be rejected."

Neither Locke, nor Kant, nor Berkeley, and least of all Hume, was to him an authority to be weighed against what seemed to him obvious from his own experience, combined with the Scriptural tradition; and although he tells us that he had made a careful study of English, French, Scotch and German philosophers, it is more likely that he was too impatient with any of them to cultivate an open mind, even if some of the salient points might have seeped into his system. At any rate, his *Essays on Some of the First Principles of Metaphysics, Ethics and Theology,* which appeared in 1824, the fruit of many years of teaching, is outstanding not only because of its clarity and directness of style, but for the many modern notions which it contained in shadowy form.

In the first place, Burton opposed Edwards' bipartite division of the mind, himself adopting three faculties, *viz.,* understanding, taste, and will, taste of course, presiding over the feelings, which to him are reduced to pleasure and disgust; and since the feelings are the mainsprings of action and determine the qualities of right and wrong, Burton regards the faculty of taste as paramount. What the Bible calls "the heart," Burton terms *taste*; and its many operations embrace primary, secondary, and malignant affections.

Burton may still be regarded as an offshoot of the Scotch realists; and in spite of his seemingly dogmatic manner, he succeeds in disentangling a number of the main issues dealing with the functions of the mind.

A Definitive Textbook

Shortly afterwards, in 1827, a more ambitious text appeared —*Elements of Intellectual Philosophy,* four years later to be expanded into the two-volume *Elements of Mental Philosophy* which, in a sense, was influenced by Burton, but rounding out the system and adding hundreds of illustrations from history, travel, biography, and fiction, to which the more circumscribed Burton had no access. The author, Thomas C. Upham (1789-1872) was also a clergyman, but since he actually taught philosophy at Bowdoin College, there was to be no encumbrance with or subservience to theology, as in the case of Burton.

Upham had been called to Bowdoin, partly to counteract the Kantian influences which were beginning to permeate the lesser schools, unprotected by the dominant British-imbued presidents, who had a penchant for philosophy and psychology. He found himself, however, drawn to German philosophy, without committing himself wholeheartedly to its metaphysical principles or conclusions, and at one time, he was on the point of resigning because of a misunderstanding between him and the administration, but he weathered the (inner) storm most successfully, and his textbook, which, incidentally, contains very few references to Kantian psychology, as also his subsequent works on special topics, like the will or mental aberrations, were highly regarded not only in this country but abroad as well, particularly in England. Edition after edition came out, and even several years before William Janes brought out his *Principles of Psychology,* there appeared, in 1886, a new printing of Upham's *Elements of Mental Philosophy.* The author had been dead fourteen years. Without doubt, Upham's *Elements of Mental Philosophy* was the classic text prior to James's great work. It was comprehensive, systematic, well-knit, and written in a graceful style, although, at times, perhaps in periodic, long-flowing sentences too rhetorical for the purpose of the student. We shall have occasion to see later what constituted the advance in James's approach and scope.

Improvements and Enlargements

Upham showed progress in (a) discarding the term "intellectual" philosophy, which was the Scotch brand name for psychology and adopting "mental" instead, and (b) adding to the original two departments *viz.,* intellect and the sensibilities, which according to him, even in the third edition of 1839, constituted the whole of psychology, a third—the will. In

Volume I, he discusses "intellectual states of external origin" and "intellectual states of internal origin" and in Part III "Imperfect and Disordered Intellectual Action." In the second volume, which is a tome of 705 pages, he develops his views on the affections, showing first the relation of the intellect to the sensibilities, and then classifying the latter. Under the natural or *pathematic* sensibilities, he takes up the nature of the emotions, the various classes, the desires, the instincts, the appetites, propensities, malevolent and benevolent affections, and habits. In the second part, he treats of the moral sensibilities or conscience, adducing proofs of a moral nature in man, the relation of reasoning to the moral nature, the nature of moral beauty and moral sublimity. The feelings of moral obligation are then gone into at length: the nature of obligatory feelings, the uniformity of action, the immutability of moral distinctions, topped by a chapter on moral education. In five subsequent chapters, he presents the abnormal psychology of what he calls "sentimentive action" *i.e.*, the affections, with a fund of sound advice to those *in extremis*. The third division of the volume is devoted wholly to the will. A number of dubious laws of the will are here alluded to rather than formulated, and argument follows upon argument to prove that "the will has its laws."

To show what Upham does in a single chapter, it might be expedient to reproduce the section captions dealing with the propensities, a term which William McDougall resorted to in his *Energies of Men,* in order to appease the anti-instinctivists. Upham's propensities are instincts in the older sense, as the topics listed below indicate.

Contents of a Single Chapter

General remarks on the nature of the propensities
Principle of self-preservation, or the desire of continued existence
Of the twofold action of the principle of self-preservation
Of curiosity, of the desire of knowledge
Further illustrations of the principle of curiosity
Of the twofold operation and the morality of the principle of curiosity
Imitativeness, or the propensity to imitation
Practical results of the principle of imitation
Of emulation considered as a propensive principle

Of approbativeness or the desire of esteem
Of approbativeness or the desire of esteem as a rule of conduct
Of acquisitiveness, or the desire of possession
Of the moral character of the possessory principle
Of perversions of the possessory desire
Of the desire of power
Facts in proof of the natural desire of power
Of the moral character of the desire of power
Veracity, or the propensity to utter the truth
Of the twofold action of the propensity to truth
Propensity of self-love, or the desire of happiness
Of selfishness as distinguished from all self-love
Modifications of selfishness; pride, vanity, and arrogance
Reference to the opinions of philosophical writers

Since Upham in this part of the book was attempting to do what McDougall, with greater equipment, although with scarcely more analytic power, tackled almost a century later, a sample of the earlier endeavor will suffice to give us an idea of Upham as a prospector in this region, as well as a stylist.

When, in all ordinary cases, the resentful feeling shows itself, we variously denominate it by the terms resentment, hostility, anger, hatred, indignation, and the like, but there are some modifications of the feeling, distinguished either by excess or diminution, or in some other way, which may be regarded as possessing a distinctive character. One of these is peevishness or fretfulness; a species of malevolent passion which, probably with more frequency than its decided manifestations, interrupts the peace and happiness of life.

Peevishness differs from ordinary anger in being excited by very trifling circumstances, and in a strange facility of inflicting its effects on everybody and everything within its reach. The peevish man has met with some trifling disappointment (it matters but little what it is), and the serenity of whole days is disturbed; no smiles are to be seen; everything, whether animate or inanimate, rational or irrational, is out of place, and falls under the rebuke of this fretful being.—Anger, in its more marked and decided manifestations, may be compared to a thunder-shower, that comes dark and heavily, but leaves a clear sky afterward. But peevishness is like an obscure, drizzling fog; it is less violent, and lasts longer. In general, it is more unreasonable and unjust than violent anger, and would certainly be more disagreeable, were it not often, in consequence of being so disproportioned to its cause, so exceedingly ludicrous.

One of the most frequent forms of resentment is envy. By this term we are accustomed to express that ill-will or hatred which has its rise from the contemplation of the superiority of another.

*   *   *   *   *

Another of the marked modifications of resentment is revenge. By the spirit of revenge, as we sometimes express it, we generally understand a disposition, not merely to return suffering for suffering, but to inflict a degree of pain on the person who is supposed to have injured us, beyond what strict justice requires.[1]

Character and Society

Under the heading of "Foresight of the Conduct of Masses of Men and Nations," Upham digresses into sociological territory, *e.g.,* statistics relative to mail, financial estimates, crime, a subject which, as is well known, Buckle later made one of the foundations of his materialistic conception of history. Upham was by no stretch of the imagination inclined toward materialism, but in this connection, he held a similar view: "All these things conclusively evince that the actions of men, whether considered individually or in masses, are not placed beyond the reach of some forms of law, and are not left to mere chance or accident."[2]

Fay cites passages from Upham revealing anticipations of mental set, individual differences, introversion and extraversion, rationalization, the emergence of suppressed desires in perverted forms, and the James-Lange theory of emotions; and he even sees a "Thorndikean touch" in such a statement as "Our moral principles, however correct they may be, will be of little value to us, unless thay are put to practice by being

[1] T. C. Upham: *Mental Philosophy* (1875), vol. II, pp. 202-205.
[2] T. C. Upham: *Loc. cit.,* p. 546.

incorporated into the daily and hourly series of living acts."[3] However, while one is ready to concede that Upham was an unusually astute observer, there is no need of turning him into a genius living a century ahead of his time. Much of what Fay quotes has been said in one form or another by Upham's precursors, *e.g.*, Milton's "Il Penseroso" and "L'Allegro" represent the introverted and extraverted types. La Bruyère in his Phédon and Giton, even more in detail, limns these contrasts, and as to the injunction with a "Thorndikean touch," surely Aristotle's view of habit ($\xi\xi\iota\varsigma$) comes just as close. One contribution of Upham's which Fay apparently overlooks is a solid section on the psychology of character toward the end of the second volume, probably the first treatment of the subject in a psychological textbook.

[3] J. W. Fay: *American Psychology before William James* (1939), p. 106.

Chapter 7

German Influences

By 1840, SCOTTISH realism and English empiricism were beginning to feel the competition of German transcendentalism. In some instances, the German mode of thought came to the surface through immigrants or sons of immigrants from Germany. In other cases, native Americans became imbued with the teachings of Kant, Fichte, and Hegel, through their British disciples. Coleridge, particularly, was a force in that direction.

One of the most remarkable pioneers in our field was Frederick Augustus Rauch (1806-1841). While still in his twenties, he became *extraordinarius* at the University of Heidelberg, where he was slated for promotion to a full professorship in metaphysics, but his expression of solidarity with the fraternities opposing the government made it necessary for him to seek employment in the United States.

At first he taught music and German at Lafayette College, and then qualified for the ministry, and became professor in Biblical literature at the German Reformed Theological Seminary at York, Pa. Later he became organizer and first president of Marshall College, in 1836. We must remember that this checkered career, after a hectic period in Germany, was behind a man of thirty!

In 1840, there appeared his first book in English, *Psychology or a View of the Human Soul including Anthropology*, in which he was to give the "science of man a direct bearing upon other sciences, and especially upon religion and theology." A second edition "revised and improved" came out posthumously, in 1841, the first edition having been exhausted in a very few weeks after its publication.

Psychology Receives Its Proper Name

Rauch's book was the first in America to have had for its title "Psychology," instead of the hackneyed "mental philosophy" or "intellectual philosophy" which is of Scotch provenance. Moreover, Rauch had brought to his task the fruit of his vast reading—particularly Continental *belles-lettres*. For him, as for Kant, anthropology and psychology constitute a double field dealing with the mind of man. As Rauch explains, "The present work is, as far as the author knows, the first attempt to unite German and American mental philosophy."[1] Under anthropology, he takes up the relation of the organism to the environment, and what might be considered today ecological considerations. He notes national differences, he brings up questions of sex differences, goes into the subject of temperament, does not ignore the genetic approach, and after an account of sleep and dreams, and a few pages on abnormal states, he concludes with a stimulating chapter on the power of the mind over the body, purporting to show how the thoughts and feelings tend to mould the contour of the face and form its expression.

In the second part, *i.e.*, the strictly psychological, he deals with self-consciousness (in the German, not our popular, sense) and personality, and here he is disclosed to us as probably the first personalist who wrote in English. For, more than a century ago, he held that "the *person* is not only the centre of *man* but also the centre of nature."

The idea of personality, as may be easily seen, includes that of independence of every thing that is not itself. It rests upon itself, and as it is the centre of all in man, so it is the centre of nature around, for it is not only conscious of itself, but conscious of all other things. If by self-consciousness it inclines to itself, taking an inward direction, by consciousness of other things, it takes an outward direction, one away from itself. And in this light we have yet to view personality.

The *person* is not only the centre of *man,* whose radii and periphery are all the activities of body and soul and by which all of them are *pronounced,* that is through which they sound, *personant,* but it is also the centre of nature, the echo of the universe.

What nature contains scattered and in fragments, is united in the person of man. Every isolated feeling, every solitary sound in nature is to pass through man's person-

[1] F. A. Rauch: *Psychology, or A View of the Human Soul,* 1840, p. v. (preface).

ality, and to centre in it. His personality is the great, beautiful, and complete bell, that announces every thing, while nature contains only parts of it, the sounds of which are dark and dull.[2]

Semeiotics and Semantics

Among the other topics which Rauch has fructified with his independent thinking are language and religion. He may be regarded as a pioneer in semantics, or at least semeiotics, which is more general, as is apparent from the following passage.

The term *semeiotic* is not found in the English language. It is of Greek origin from the word σημεία sign . . . Every thing in nature, upon which man may impress his will, must suffer itself to be used by him as a sign. Even rivers may become the signs of boundaries. Yet the more susceptible a thing is of receiving a mark from the hands of man, the better it is qualified for a sign. Thus, the staff in the hand of Agamemnon, "which sent forth no leaves, and retained no life, after the knife cut it from its trunk and peeled and smoothed it," is the sign of power; so the hickory pole with its flags is a sign, intelligible to all the citizens of the Union. The signs of semeiotic imagination are contained either in space or time, either in rest or in motion, and may be thus classified: Signs in *space* have different forms, yet they are not to be valued by their forms, but by what they indicate. The cockade, the flag, which indicates a nation's ideas of its liberty, and which though at rest themselves may cause the greatest commotions, as the flag when unfurled and waving in the air, are of more importance than the most showy sign before a tavern. The signs that are only in space are innumerable: those that I make in a book while reading it, in my walks, and those made by private individuals in their gardens or houses, used by companies on their seals, by nations in the uniform of their soldiers, etc. At first these signs had a meaning in themselves, but this meaning was gradually lost, and semeiotic imagination used them for whatever purpose it pleased.

*   *   *   *   *

[2] F. A. Rauch: *Loc. cit.*, p. 189.

When, on the other hand, the sign is something which exists only in *time,* it must be always in motion. The numerous signs that belong to the art of expressing thoughts by the motions of the body, have been already alluded to in Part I, Chapter III, to which the reader is referred. Other signs are: rockets discharged in the air; the waving of a handkerchief; the hoisting of a flag, etc. These are all of them for the eye, and must be noticed at the very moment, when they are in motion. Imagination is more rich, however, in the signs it produces for the ear. Sounds become signals. Clapping the hands may indicate applause; hissing, disapprobation. The same sounds may affect us in the most different ways, and these different effects depend wholly on the meaning we attach to them. . . .

Next in rank are organical sounds, or such as are produced by the organs of man; hence sounds of instruments, the trumpet, flute, etc. The sounds of the trumpet govern the motions of a body of cavalry, those of the flute are fitted for the expression of love. Whistling is likewise a signal, but a signal of uncertain character. The watchman in pursuit of a thief makes use of it, and so does the thief.

Finally, articulate sounds must serve as signs. But what sounds are *articulate?* Those produced by *articulos,* by the tongue, teeth and lips; those, therefore, that are formed by all of them. The sounds of animals differ from those of instruments; the latter are based in the vibrations of bodies, the former rest in the voice. . . . Yet while the voice of the animal is superior to the sounds of instruments, the voice of man is superior to that of animals; for it is capable of producing the word (pp. 249-251).

Suggestive as all which Rauch presents happens to be, the textbook nevertheless has its faults. In the first place, he lacks the precision and clarity of men like Burton and Upham and their British predecessors. His terms are occasionally confusing as may be seen from the quotation which follows:

When I hear a fine melody for the first time, I have a *sensation* of it; but when afterwards, without hearing it, it floats in my mind, I have a *perception* of it. Or when I experience hunger, I may have a perception of food, though it be not present, but when I eat, I have a sensation of it. The animal has perceptions as well as man. The hunter's dog dreams, and pursues in his dream the hare or the stag. The dog, when near to his master, has a sensation of him by scent, or sight; but when seeking him for days in succession, he can have only a perception of him. The animal is confined within the sphere of sensation and perception, and as its sensations are limited to its natural wants, so must be its perceptions. But the perceptions of man are as much more numerous and accurate, as his sensations are more various and acute. And in addition to sensations and perceptions, he has what the animal has not, and which we may express by the term *apperceptions, or thought* (p. 18).

Now Locke did not use perception in our modern sense, but he did not confuse it with a memory or idea, nor would he make apperception (a Kantian term, by the way) equivalent to thought. Rauch's observations on language, on the other hand, are strikingly modern, and hold some value even today.

S. S. Schmucker

In 1842, another, smallish textbook bearing the title *Psychology*, appeared. Its author, Samuel S. Schmucker (1799-1873), was a Lutheran clergyman, trained at the University of Pennsylvania and the Princeton Theological Seminary. Of German origin, he has more in common with Rauch than the use of the same title for a textbook, but his preface is very similar to that of Asa Burton, in which he tells of his disappointment with the existing systems of mental philosophy, both English and German, so that "he then resolved to study exclusively his own mind, and for ten years he read no book on the subject" spending his time in "the examination of his own mental phenomena."

Schmucker was reputed to have been a liberal churchman, in fact so much so that his own son joined the conservative wing of the Lutheran church, but like Asa Burton he espoused psychology in the interests of fundamental Christianity. To him, mental philosophy is the science which discusses the properties of the human soul. He is more scholastic in his definition than Rauch, more dogmatic in his declarations than his contemporaries, always betraying a theological bias, yet is methodical in his presentation and pithy in expression, as contrasted with a man like Upham.

The subtitle "Elements of a New System of Mental Philosophy on the Basis of Consciousness and Common Sense" is scarcely borne out by the contents. His armchair psychology based on "consciousness and common sense" is not novel nor striking, and there are altogether too many references to God as the rationale of our mental operations. The book reeks with subjectivity. Hume is mentioned as "the infidel" (p. 41); "God has so constituted animals that the use of their organs is in itself and for its own sake pleasant" (p. 152); language "is of Divine origin because the nature of these elementary sounds results from the structure of the organs which God gave us" (p. 156).

Peculiar Explanations

Schmucker evidences the foible of the early American divines to resort to God as an all-embracing explanation of every phenomenon, a *machina ex deo* rather than a *deus ex machina* so that almost every other page contains a reference to the Almighty, the great Creator, the Divine Author, the Father, etc. Thus Schmucker reasons on page 163, "If it be asked, *why does the soul engage in active operations at all rather than not,* we reply, the reason is, because the nature of the soul is active. By this we mean, that the Divine Author of our nature has so constituted the mind of man, that, during his waking hours, it is unavoidably and incessantly engaged in some one of these five active processes," and further he accounts for bodily appetite like hunger by saying that "it was designed by the Creator as a periodical motive to urge us to take the necessary food. The same remarks are applicable to thirst, which is nothing else than that peculiar condition of the throat and fauces, occasioned by the want of a liquid, and causing a desire to obtain it, or some other substance, in order to relieve the pain felt; and also sometimes in order to enjoy the pleasure occasioned by the reception of the liquid. The fluid thus taken into the stomach is consumed by the progress of the bodily functions, and its want occasions a painful feeling termed thirst. Both these appetites are the work of God. They are the necessary results of the bodily organization of man, and may justly be considered by Him as clear indications of the Divine will, that they should lead to the course of action by which they are relieved, though under the limitations of reason."

The pietist is so conspicuous in the author that many of

his illustrations revert to religion. "Thus, from the light perceived in the room, the mind of pious habits will revert to the great Father of lights from whom it comes, and to the value of that spiritual light, which constitutes the Christian's greatest and most constant source of happiness on earth and expected bliss in heaven."

Schmucker introduces the term "inspection" as the first operation of the mind or as he calls it "the soul," and defines it as "that active operation in which the attention of the soul is directed to some entity, simple or composite, prospective, present, or retrospective; with a view to acquire some knowledge concerning it," which appears to include introspection as well as judgment, and almost every cognitive process, short of reasoning.

Other mental operations are arrangement and modification.

He is opposed to *a priori* notions, rejecting even the authority of Kant, and, in general, seems to lean to the empiristic or genetic point of view, and nowhere is this tendency so apparent as in the section on speech where he displays remarkable knowledge and insight, at any rate for his time.

Schmucker enjoyed the respect of his contemporaries, and in spite of the small compass of his textbook, it was popular in academies and smaller colleges, perhaps for that reason as well as for its rippling style and its religious atmosphere. It so happened that his grandson taught biology and was an ardent votary of evolution which he expounded enthusiastically in a popular book.

Laurens P. Hickok—Exponent of the Double Aspect

German philosophizing reached something of a peak in Laurens P. Hickok (1798-1888), a Union College theologian, who was nevertheless a vigorous thinker and keen dialectician. The division of psychology into an empirical and a rational part may be said to date from the scholastic period, but Kant and his followers, in a modified form at least, implicitly clung to it, and in Rauch, we find the division followed out in the anthropological and the strictly psychological accounts of mental science.

It would have been natural for one who approached psychology to start with the empirical, and work his way up to the rational, but Hickok did the reverse. In 1848, he managed to bring out a 700-page volume under the title of *Rational Psychology,* which he wisely abridged to 539 pages in the second edition (1861). Evidently there was at least another printing of the second edition, for the title-page on the copy before me bears the date of 1876, from which it would appear that despite the ponderousness of the text, there was a demand for just such a treatment.

Let us bear in mind that a hundred years ago, the empirical was looked down upon as merely a collection of data held to have some connection among themselves because of their figuring in our experience, but not *causally* established. The empiric, in medicine, was supposed to be a man who gathered up certain medical knowledge in a practical but not scientific way, ignorant of the laws obtaining in the physiological sphere, such as the relationship between drugs and certain chemical (toxic) conditions of the body. Hickok, whether influenced by Kant and Hegel, or snapping up his cues "from the air," unlike his contemporaries who talked about laws of feeling and volition, *e.g.*, Schmucker, when they were merely adverting to ordinary facts, was actually searching for ways and means to elevate psychology to the level of science, not aware of the fact that a science cannot be created through philosophical reasoning.

According to Hickok "in this science *i.e.*, rational psychology, we pass from the facts of experience wholly out beyond it, and seek for the *rationale* of experience itself in the necessary and universal principles which must be conditional for all facts of a possible experience. We seek to determine how it is possible for an experience to be, from those *a priori* conditions which render all the functions of an intellectual agency themselves intelligible. In the conclusions of this science it becomes competent for us to affirm, not as from mere experience we may, that this is—but, from these necessary and universal principles, that this *must be*. The intellect is itself investigated and known through the principles which must necessarily control all its agency, and thereby the intellect itself is expounded in its constituent functions and laws of operation.[3]

Eager to Make of Psychology an Exact Science

The author is at pains to prove from the sphere of astronomy and mathematics that a body of measurements cannot produce a science of astronomy or mathematics, but that we

[3] L. P. Hickok: *Rational Psychology*, 2d ed. 1875, p. 14.

must proceed from the phenomenon to the invisible in order to determine what the solar system might be.

Again, I take a body of a triangular form, and by accurate mensuration find that any two of its sides are together greater than the third side. Another triangular body, of different size and proportion of its sides, is also accurately measured, and the same fact is again found. The mensuration of the first did not help to the attainment of the fact in the last, but an experiment only ascertained that so it *is*. Repeated experiments may have been made of a vast number of triangular forms, isosceles, right-angled, and scalene, and of them all, at last, I may make the same affirmation, this is; but from experience I am not warranted to include anything else than so it is, and in so many cases as the experiment has reached. When, however, I construct for myself a triangle in pure space, and intuitively perceive the relations of its sides, I do not need any experiment, but can make this intuition valid universally, and affirm for all possible triangles, so the facts *must be*.

Such everywhere is the distinction between an empirical and a rational process. In the one we have the facts as they appear; in the other, we have the conditioning principle which determines their appearance, and which makes our experience of them possible. And now, the human mind, as an intelligent and free agent, may as readily as any other subject, admit of an investigation under each of these aspects. Facts as given in experience, and those arranged in an orderly system as they appear in consciousness, constitute psychology in that important division which we have denominated *empirical*; and those principles which give the necessary and universal laws to experience, and by which intelligence itself is alone made intelligible, are the elements for a higher psychological science which we term *rational*.[4]

Again, Hickok overlooks the fact that mathematics is vastly different from psychology in this respect that the mathematician *constructs* his world, while the psychologist finds his phenomena *imposed* upon him. The two are incomparable. Let us not forget, however, that Hickok, although he lived

[4] L. P. Hickok: *Loc. cit.*, pp. 16-18.

long enough to see the first psychological laboratories established, had, at the time he wrote his textbooks, no way of anticipating the rise of experimental psychology, and what it would entail.

He deserves, however, a good deal of credit for dwelling on the *problems* of psychology, problems with which William James afterwards grappled, and which were on the borderline of the theory of knowledge (consciousness, the self, space, and time). Just as for Burton and Schmucker, psychology was a springboard for theology, so for Hickok, rational psychology was a foundation for an ontology, which apparently he had never gotten to writing. The last twenty pages of his book, however, dealing with "the facts of a comprehending reason which come within the compass of an absolute personality," afford us an insight into the direction of his thought. This portion of the book is more than a brief for a natural theology.

Even his *Empirical Psychology or the Human Mind as Given in Consciousness* which appeared in 1854 (with a second edition in 1871) is not without its philosophizing, but within the 400 pages, Hickok has not only given the student a large variety of relevant facts, but has exhibited a lucidity and explanatory knack none too evident in the earlier book. Here, in the German tradition, he begins with the so-called anthropological data—race and geographical differences, temperament, aesthetic reflections, etc. He shuns physiology (although he is certainly not ignorant of the sense organs and their structures) because it excludes "all the peculiar endowments and prerogatives of a spiritual life" whereas anthropology, on the other hand, "contemplates man in his *entire being,* physically, intellectually and morally; recognizes the connections of mind with matter, and the influences of one upon the other; and expounds the modifications which mind undergoes, from the action of the external world upon it through the body. The facts attained in such a science have an important bearing upon psychology, where mind is regarded in its own unity, and with all its different faculties and functions of operation relatively to itself."[5]

And it is here that he tells us that the "psychology of angels must differ much from that of man" because of the difference between pure spirit and incarnate spirits, which latter alone

[5] L. P. Hickok: *Empirical Psychology* (2nd edition), p. 28.

can admit of an anthropology. As might have been expected of a metaphysician, the portion devoted to affection (emotions and susceptibilities) covers less than 60 out of 400 pages.

An Operational Issue

That Hickok could adapt his approach and style when writing for students may be judged from the following illustrative passage, as compared with those offered above from his earlier work.

> The genius that first created the idea of a watch, would begin, in the thought, with the moving power at the centre, and carry this force, in its development of forms and connections, outward, till in his completed conception, he had the whole in its unity, from the mainspring to the moving hands over the dialplate. But the discoverer, of how a watch already in experience had been invented, would begin his examination of the hour-index, and go backwards toward the central force in the mainspring. Both get the science of the watch, one *makes* it, the other *learns* it.
>
> In empirical philosophy, we can only be learners. We must study what is, not project what may be. Nature began at the centre and worked outward. She had her vital force in its salient point, and carried that out to the mature development. The germ expanded to the ripened plant; the embryo grew to the adult stature. But the empirical philosopher can take nature's products only so far as already done, and study as he may how has been nature's process. He is shut out from nature's hiding-place at the centre, and cannot say what it is that lies potential there, and determine in the primal cause what the effects must be. He can only learn nature, as she has already made herself to be; and cannot project nature in her primal laws, and thereby determine how she must be.[6]

Hickok rejects the sensualism, as he calls it, of Locke, scoffs at Hume's skepticism, scarcely deigns to mention Berkeley's idealism, looks with suspicion at Reid's realism, which he thinks of as helpless in combat against reason, professes to turn away from Hegel's dialectic movements, and is not altogether certain of Kant's ultimate position, but it is, after all, the old Koenigsberg philosopher, in his more positive

[6] L. P. Hickok: *Loc. cit.,* pp. 71-72.

aspects (what we would now call critical realism) to whom he finds himself closest; and it would appear that what Hickok was aiming at in his more elementary text was to provide the students with a philosophy of life as well as with a number of facts, and especially a methodology, which latter was his forte.

Hickok's twofold division of psychology has not died out. It has had its counterparts at all periods. We may here remind the reader of *Akt* and existential psychologies (see p. 84) as well as of the causal and purposive ledgers of Hugo Münsterberg, and that E. Husserl's search for essential intuitions is, in a sense, a veering from the empirical so as to discover the timeless objective ideas, shorn of their individual subjectivity.

The Merits of Hickok

In spite of the allegedly obscure, and possibly obscurantist, passages in Hickok, there was a modern ring to many of his expressions, and it was he who probably for the first time employed such terms as *introspection, psychographic,* and *conditioned,* in the psychological sense; and if posterity has not given him his due, it was through no fault of his own. We know of at least one ardent disciple who continued Hickok's method, asseverating his allegiance to rational psychology, and speaking almost in contempt of empirical psychology— John Bascom (1827-1911) professor at Williams College, and later president of the University of Wisconsin. His textbook, published in 1869, bore the title which has become associated with a much greater work, from the pen of America's foremost psychologist, *viz., Principles of Psychology.* A dozen years later, a new edition appeared with the title changed to *The Science of Mind,* which was more in keeping with Hickok's view of emphasizing the scientific status of psychology. Since Bascom also wrote the first textbook in "comparative psychology," we shall have occasion to return to him in another connection. In 1882, at the age of 84, Hickok, with the coöperation of J. H. Seelye, President of Amherst College, brought out a revised edition of *Empirical Psychology.*

Asa Mahan (1799-1889)

Asa Mahan, who travelled the road of several of the earlier psychologists in that he was a pastor and college president (Oberlin), and, like Hickok, attained the ripe old age of a nonagenarian, may also be called a rational psychologist, evincing a familiarity with German philosophy which he appears to admire in the abstract and yet often justly criticizes in no uncertain terms. His contribution to psychology comprises an *Abstract of a Course of Lectures on Mental and Moral Philosophy* (1841), *Doctrine of the Will* (1844) and *A System of Intellectual Philosophy* brought out in 1845, and reissued in 1847, with an enlarged edition in 1854. It is the first time that a textbook in psychology is called a system.

Written in a direct and vivacious style, it challenges most of the celebrated names in psychology. Even Kant (not to mention Cousin, Reid, Stewart, Brown, Coleridge, and the post-Kantian transcendentalists) is taken to task more than once. Incidentally, for him "the three luminaries of the first order in the sphere of philosophy" are Coleridge, Cousin, and Kant; an opinion which would evoke a smile today in philosophical circles.

Like another Asa (Burton), he thinks of psychology as a stepping-stone to philosophy and a knowledge of "the Divine authority of Christianity." His *System* is an eclectic arrangement, founded on common sense, his own of course.

Sense must enter into the depth of his own mind, and there notice the real affirmations of his own intelligence, in view of given facts. Such affirmations he may trust in and announce as the real dictates of the common sense of the race. He that will most correctly interpret the real dictates of his own intelligence is the most perfect oracle of the universal intelligence. In retiring, then, from the outward world into the depths of our own minds, and there receiving the real dictates of our own intelligence, we find the true facts and principles of common sense.

* * * * *

We often hear of individuals spoken of as wanting in, or possessed of, a great degree of common sense. The characteristic which distinguishes the latter from the former class, is a well-balanced judgment, particularly in respect to the common transactions of life—a judgment by which they detect and announce at once the real affirmations of the intelligence in the presence of given facts. The mass of men—a fact to which philosophers as a body are by no means exceptions—are so blinded by assumptions, and theories founded thereon, that, in respect to the most important subjects, they do not recognize the real affirmations of their own intelligence. In the presence of given facts, they see in them what all the world sees. Yet under the influence of false assumptions and theories, they disregard what their own intelligence really affirms. Men, on the other hand, distinguished for common sense, in the presence of the same facts and convictions, announce and rely upon, not in their abstract and universal, but in their concrete and particular form, their own judgments, just as they lie in their own intelligence—judgments which all the world really pass in the presence of the same facts; but which, for reasons above stated, philosophic minds especially, in many instances, totally disregard. Of the latter class we say, they are destitute of, or rather do not *use*, their common sense.[7]

From the above quotation one can readily see that Mahan aligns himself with the Scotch school, and not without a certain degree of gratification reveals that he had since come upon a passage of the French philosopher, Jouffroy, which parallels the very thought. Jouffroy, it may not be recalled now, was the French spokesman of the common sense school. In view of Mahan's almost obvious affiliation, for all his cavils at Reid, Cousin, Stewart, and Brown, his professed admiration of the German mind, as set forth in several passages, particularly in regard to the credited emancipation from "blind adherence to authority, to creeds, the decrees of councils, etc," is scarcely in accord with what we know to be the case.

Mahan accordingly wanted to introduce as much of the German doctrine as possible into the United States, but it is strange that a genuine psychologist like Herbert, Kant's successor at Koenigsberg, who died in 1841, before Mahan's *System* was written is not alluded to. Had he known of his theory of apperceiving masses, Mahan would not need to explain the fact of recognizing an entirely new object in terms of the familiar as a result of vivid association.

Fay is not quite just to Mahan when he thinks, "His work added little or nothing to the body of the psychological doctrine so ably enunciated by Upham."[8] The truth is that the former has an epistemological slant and does not cover the same ground. He is more penetrating in general, and is especially of service in differentiating concepts and clarifying hazy points. He deals with fundamentals more than Upham,

[7] A. Mahan: *A System of Intellectual Philosophy*, p. 276.
[8] J. W. Fay: *American Psychology before William James*, p. 118.

although Upham is far more comprehensive so far as coverage of psychological data goes. Thus in Mahan's textbook, there is scarcely anything on the emotions, and even in his *Abstract of a Course of Lectures on Mental and Moral Philosophy,* we find only about a dozen pages, devoted largely to the religious affections, but the concept of consciousness is gone into from all angles.

> I will make a few remarks upon the necessity of relying with implicit confidence upon the testimony of consciousness, as the basis of all conclusions pertaining to the science of mind. The great reason, as I suppose, why many individuals are prejudiced against mental philosophy, as a peculiarly difficult, obscure, and uncertain science, is a secret distrust of the validity of the facts which lie at the basis of the science; in other words, in the credibility of the witness through whom the facts are obtained. In respect to physical science, no such distrust is felt. Mankind generally rest with implicit confidence in the validity of sense, with regard to external, material substances. . . . Of these two sciences, that which is by far of the highest concernment to us, we should not suppose would rest upon the most uncertain basis. If we look also at the real facts of the case, can anyone tell us, or even conceive of the reason, why we should rest with less assurance in the truth of that of which we are conscious, than in that which is perceived and affirmed by the external senses?[9]

Polemicizing against Thomas Brown, pillar of the Scottish school, who taught, as we all understand it today, that consciousness is simply a general term expressive of all the phenomena or states of the mind ("Sensation is not an object of Consciousness differing from itself, but a particular sensation is the consciousness of the moment, as a particular hope, or fear, or grief, or resentment, or simple remembrance, may be the actual consciousness of the next moment.") Mahan presumes to give us an altogether different account:

> I affirm (what is actually true), to myself, or some other individual, that I am in pain. This affirmation implies three things—the existence of the feeling as a state of the sensi-

[9] A. Mahan: *Loc. cit.,* p. 54.

bility—an apprehension of pain in general, together with that of the particular feeling referred to—and a reference of that feeling to myself as the subject, this apprehension and reference being exclusively states of the intelligence. Now this knowledge of the feeling under consideration, with its reference to myself as the subject, is an act of consciousness; . . . The same holds true in respect to all mental exercises. The state itself is one thing. The knowledge of that state, and reference of it to ourselves is quite another. This last exercise of the intelligence is consciousness, an exercise as distinct from the state of which it takes cognizance, as that state is from the object which causes it.[10]

Here we have an intimation of self-psychology, *Akt* psychology, in contradistinction to simple existential psychology, an issue which was later to have precipitated a good deal of controversy (see pp. 201ff).

The Texts of Wayland and Haven

Of the other textbooks, appearing in the decade prior to the Civil War, those of Francis Wayland (1796-1865) published at the time he was President of Brown University, in 1854, and of Joseph Haven (1816-1874) of Amherst College, later teaching systematic theology at the Chicago Theological Seminary, deserves some attention. Of the two, *Mental Philosophy* by Joseph Haven, brought out in 1857 and reprinted several times, (my copy is dated 1872) is the more inclusive and useful, so far as students are concerned, a volume of nearly 600 pages, with bibliographical references, which is something of an innovation on this continent.

Wayland's book, at a somewhat pedestrian pace, laboriously plods over familiar territory, stressing the subject of reasoning (about 75 out of 425 pages), the best portion of which is that relating to testimony and evidence, and taste. In other words, a considerable part of this psychology is devoted to logic and aesthetics, in one form or another. Two letters addressed to the author and a Reverend Raymonds, respectively, in the appendix are of interest in that one, written in 1851, purports to furnish documentary evidence of clairvoyance (extrasensory perception?) witnessed by the writer, while the other letter offers perhaps the first account of a double personality

[10] A. Mahan: *Loc. cit.,* p. 57.

case, in this country, at any rate, written by the patient herself, whose changes started with a series of "fits" as early as 1811.

Requisites of a Textbook

In Haven's textbook on the other hand, we cannot help seeing an advance on previous manuals, with the exception perhaps of Upham's two volumes, which apparently were too much of a load for the average college student, a century or more ago. In 1857, Haven had this to say of the contemporary psychological literature:

> The works on mental science, which have recently appeared in this country, while they are certainly a valuable contribution to the department of philosophy, seem to meet this deficiency in part, but *only* in part. They traverse usually but a portion of the ground which psychology legitimately occupies, confining their attention, for the most part, to the *intellectual* faculties, to the exclusion of the *sensibilities* and the *will*.[11]

What should engage our attention, in particular, is Haven's opinion of the qualities to be sought in a good textbook of psychology. It may well be that the judgment expressed about a century ago is still valid today.

> It is much easier to decide what a work on mental science ought to be, than to produce such a work. It should be comprehensive and complete, treating all that properly pertains to psychology, giving to every part its due proportion and development. It should treat the various topics presented, in a thorough and scientific manner. It should be conversant with the literature of the department, placing the student in possession, not only of the true doctrines, but, to some extent also, of the *history* of those doctrines, showing him what has been held and taught by others upon the points in question. In style it should be clear, perspicuous, concise, yet not so barren of ornament as to be destitute of interest to the reader (p. v).

[11] J. Haven: *Mental Philosophy*, p. iv.

To a large extent, considering the limitations of the age, Haven has fulfilled the promise. He strikes a happy balance in the allotment of space to the scores of topics, and, although a professor of theology, does not make undue propaganda for a Deity. His religious bid, nevertheless, is transparent in other ways, *e.g.*, when he believes that the intelligence of "brutes" differs in kind, not in degree, from that of man. On the matter of prophetic dreams, he declares that "some law, not fully known to us, may exist, by virtue of which the nervous system, when in a highly excited state, becomes susceptible of impressions not ordinarily received and is put in communication, in some way to us mysterious, with scenes, places, and events, far distant, so as to become strangely cognizant of the coming future. Can any one show that this is impossible?" (Pp. 359-360.)

Instinct According to Haven

His remarks on instinct will bear quotation. First his definition is clear and inclusive. "I understand, by instinct, a law of action, governing and directing the movement of sentient beings—distinct, on the one hand, from the mere blind forces of matter, as attraction, etc., and from reason on the other; a law working to a given end by impulse, yet blindly—the subject not knowing why he thus works; a law innate, inherent in the constitution of the animal, not acquired but transmitted, the origin of which is to be found in the intelligent author of the universe. These I take to be the principal characteristics of what we term instinct."[12]

After reviewing the various theories, which even recently have been on the carpet for a "going-over," he can scarcely make up his mind. "Unable to coincide with the merely mechanical theory of Descartes, or with the view which resolves all into mere habit and association, with Locke and Condillac, shall we fall back upon the ancient, and for a long time universally prevalent, view which makes instinct only a lower degree of that intelligence which, in man, becomes reason and reflection?"[13]; for, says he "No amount of training or culture ever brings the animal essentially above the ordinary range of brute capacity, or approximates him to

[12] J. Haven: *Loc. cit.*, p. 330.
[13] J. Haven: *Loc. cit.*, p. 334-335.

the level of the human species."[14] Had he lived in our generation, he might have changed his tune, after taking note of the experiments on primates, at any rate.

Haven's criticism of various classifications of the affections or sensibilities, as they were called at the time, *e.g.*, into natural and moral, or according to the time element, or according to logical categories, is well taken. "The different operations and emotions of the mind must be studied and arranged, not with reference to their *logical or ethical* distinctions, but solely their *psychological* differences," (p. 391). And yet what does he do himself but divide the emotions into instinctive and rational; the affections into benevolent and malevolent; and thus spurns his own precept. His distinction between appetite as a bodily want, and desire as mental craving seems appropriate enough, and among the desires which he briefly outlines are those of happiness, knowledge, power (subdivided into that of superiority and that of possession), the desire of society, and the desire of esteem. It would be possible to include all of these plus the appetites under what are often now listed as wants or needs.

It is in Wayland and Haven that we find, perhaps for the first time, bibliographical references either at the close of the chapter or at the end of the book. The former cites nothing but British works, largely of the Scotch school. Haven is conversant with German works.

[14] J. Haven: *Loc. cit.*, p. 335.

Chapter 8

Impetus from the Natural Sciences

As WE APPROACH the period of the Civil War, psychology seems to be taking a turn in a different direction. It is gradually veering away from the philosophical and purely analytic, and moving toward the scientific. There is no longer the exclusive hold of the Scotch School we found earlier in the century. In Germany, Johannes Müller and E. W. Weber were laying the foundations of experimental physiology. Hermann Lotze through his gigantic works: *Physiologie der Seele* (1844), *Medicinische Psychologie* (1852) and *Mikrokosmos* (1856-1864) produced a system which was scientifically anchored, notwithstanding the idealistic conclusions he had arrived at. Helmholtz had already brought out the first volume of his *Physiologische Optik*, in 1856, while in 1860, there appeared G. T. Fechner's *Elemente der Psychophysik*, and two years later Helmholtz published the companion volume to his great work on physiological optics, his *Tonempfindungen*.

Changes in English Scientific Outlook

In England, the doctrine of evolution was beginning to occupy the centre of attention in scientific circles. Interest in psychology *per se* had shown a decline during the nineteenth century, as compared with the enthusiastic and inspiring efforts of Thomas Reid, Dugald Stewart, Thomas Brown, William Hamilton, and John Abercrombie, in Scotland, to systematize the data of psychology. True, James Mill, and his more illustrious son, John Stuart, had worked out an association psychology with its atomistic implications, which was to last for many decades; and in 1855 both Alexander Bain and Herbert Spencer launched textbooks which were— and this is particularly true of Spencer's, since Bain's handbook on the Emotions and the Will did not come off the press till 1859—monumental, yet it was the impact of men like Alfred Russel Wallace and Charles Darwin, whose *Origin of Species*, published after a long period of watchful waiting, proved so epoch-making, that directed the psychological pursuit into scientific channels. Phrases like "Struggle for Existence," "Survival of the Fittest," "Natural Selection" were soon to become the warp and woof of the fabric which was beginning to take on a semi-materialistic hue. English empiricism, after the middle of the nineteenth century, had crystallized into a search for concrete evidence. H. T. Buckle and Karl Marx, the latter of whom had found a haven in England, were laying the foundations for a materialistic conception of history, and the latter was hard at work on the third volume of his *Kapital*, which was destined to play such an overwhelming part in the global struggle between classes and nations.

Even physicists, chemists, geologists not to speak of physiologists and biologists, began to take a hand in this revaluation of concepts. Tyndall, *e.g.*, a physicist of high standing, joined the group of distinguished Englishmen (Huxley, Romanes, Lewes) who more and more displayed a tendency toward skepticism in metaphysics, agnosticism in religion, although sometimes couched in euphemistic phrases, and epiphenomenalism in the mental sphere. It would be strange if at least some of the waves had not transmitted their undulations across the Atlantic.

Demographic and Historical Upheavals

The American scene had undergone a transformation in other ways during this period. As Fay describes it graphically:

In America, the population doubled between 1860 and 1890, moved further westward, changed still more significantly in ethnic character, and gravitated to the cities. The first five years of the period were completely taken up by the war, and a good part of the next ten was devoted to recovery. Living conditions changed greatly, but the acceleration of pace had not yet brought the vast changes of the twentieth century.

The religious picture changed again through the remarkable growth of the Roman Catholic Church, the rapid development of the Christian Science Movement, and above all by the coming of the Darwinian theory of evolution.

* * * * *

Educational development was checked in the North and practically annihilated in the South by the coming of the

Civil War. The colleges were particularly affected. After the recovery, however, the number of colleges increased by 208, and then began to decline in importance until they were eventually overshadowed by the universities.[1]

That the Civil War did not altogether disorganize education in this country only goes to prove its stamina and vitality. It is true that between 1857 and 1865, nothing of importance had appeared in psychology, aside from a book called *Humanics* by T. W. Collins (1860), J. T. Champlin's *Textbook in Intellectual Philosophy* (1860), I. Ray's first textbook in Mental Hygiene (1863), and two books on the will and freedom of choice (1864), which were really philosophical in character, by R. G. Hazard, an autodidact merchant, and D. D. Whedon, a clergyman, both authors, as we shall presently see, disagreeing with the conclusions of Edwards.

J. T. Champlin's *Textbook in Intellectual Philosophy* (1860) is a suitable outline for elementary students. The author, who was president of Waterville (now Colby) College lays no claim to originality but takes his material from many sources, mainly falling under the spell of William Hamilton. Perhaps that is one reason why nothing is said about the emotions or volition. Apparently the phrase "intellectual philosophy" is taken literally by such compilers.

As to *Humanics* (1860), by T. W. Collins, who was a professor of political philosophy at the University of Louisiana and a former judge, the title alone is interesting because it happens to foreshadow the now fashionable amalgamation of branches of several different sciences. *Humanics* is a potpourri of reflections on life and conduct, with a practical slant, but nothing more.

James Rush (1786-1869) Rebel and Objectivist

Of a different order was the ambitious *Brief Outline of an Analysis of the Human Intellect Intended to Rectify the Scholastic and Vulgar Perversions of the Natural Purpose and Method of Thinking; by Rejecting Altogether the Theoretic Confusion, the Unmeaning Arrangement and Indefinite Nomenclature of the Metaphysician*, by James Rush, which appeared in two volumes, containing over 900 pages, in 1865

---

[1] J. W. Fay: *American Psychology before William James*, p. 130.

(Fay's date as 1885 is either a slip of the pen or a printer's and proofreader's error). In Rush's case, the chief fault of the book lay in its aggressive and pretentious title. Actually there is something refreshing about this Quixotic work; for here we have the antipodes of the dozens of psychologies which stress the metaphysical and theological.

James Rush, brilliant son of a famous father, not only enjoyed the advantages of his good fortune but was subject to the disadvantages which such a relationship entails. The elder Rush was somewhat of an eccentric, but happened to be sufficiently outgoing and public-spirited, being endowed with the social graces which his more impatient and fanatical son did not possess. The latter's early studies with the representatives of the Scotch School, in Edinburgh, left him wholly dissatisfied; and, in 1823, he began to be preoccupied with a *magnum opus* on the human voice, which was completed in 1827, and as the publisher to whom he offered it was reluctant to take the risk in bringing it out, Rush printed it at his own expense, with a simplified orthography, so that "impugn" appeared as "impune," "thought" as "thot," and "plainness" as "plaines." Rush lived to see the seventh steadily enlarged edition in print, which proved that the experienced publisher was mistaken in his judgment. It is not only one of the earliest executions of the simplified spelling project, but constitutes a fundamental system of speech training, which has had many adoptions. And if speech is to be regarded as a phase of psychology, then James Rush has contributed materially to a psychological topic on a physiological and experimental basis, fully half a century before Scripture traversed the same field with better tools.

On a Tack of His Own

It is, however, the primarily psychological work of Rush which deserves our attention here. James Rush, the son of a physician, and himself one, even if he were not a born rebel, could scarcely have been expected to follow in the footsteps of the preachers who seemed to have served almost exclusively as the purveyors of psychology prior to the twentieth century. He had no religious axe to grind.

A prodigy, in an intellectual and professional atmosphere, he developed his talents too precociously to be content with the run of the mill. Whether his stress on the motor phase of the nervous system, which had been neglected by the early psychologists, was due to his red-blooded temperament and mercurial nature, thus preparing him for a prolonged study of the speech mechanism, or whether his sustained interest in the vocal musculature had led him to his behavioristic conclusions is scarcely of consequence. What counts is that his system represents a break from the accepted doctrine that the mind is something like a sponge which soaks up impressions, and that the cognitive processes govern the feelings and volition. For him, the muscles play a very important part, and mind to him, a full century ago, consists of perceiving, thinking, speaking, and acting.

Since we shall have occasion to return to Rush in the chapter on behaviorism, where passages from his now rare work will be cited, it will be enough to say, at this point, that for all the digressions and meanderings in the two volumes, there are nuggets of information and wisdom not to be found in other textbooks. The first volume is mainly theoretical, developing the system of perceptions. The second is along applied lines, dealing with the mentality of various types: the politician, the lawyer, the physician, the businessman, etc. He is also a pioneer in collective psychology; for here, we are given glimpses of human nature, as it manifests itself in the voter, the working of a newspaper, and other institutions. Rush is always at pains to unmask the bigot, or rather the metaphysician, who is to Rush fundamentally a bigot; and he never tires of referring to the mind as "physical." When we consider that this work was written at the age of 70, after he had put aside his notes for 36 years, we must marvel at his perseverance as well as his mental vigor.

Rush's Work a Function of His Personality

James Rush's manner of writing was not conducive to giving him a wide hearing. He was wordy, out of tune with the rest of the authors, addicted to the use of personal references, in which he would predict the ultimate success of his labors and deprecate the attitude of his critics or ignorers. It was evident that he carried a chip on his shoulder and looked down upon his contemporaries as nincompoops who knew how to promote their own ends.

An able publicist, like his father, Benjamin, he was always defending himself by attacking the ubiquitous foe, principally the physiologists and medical men who would not accept his system. These polemic passages often adduce entertaining illustrations from history and biography, but this practice brought him few supporters amongst authorities, and his *Brief Outline . . . of the Human Intellect*, as well as his *Philosophy of the Voice*, was like a voice crying in the wilderness, although in the various prefaces to the latter, he keeps complaining about cases of plagiary on the part of petty individuals. No doubt, he was suffering from a savior complex, even alluding to Judas and the thirty pieces of silver. In connection with his simplified spelling method, he has the following to say: "What is here proposed and exemplified in part will be sufficient to make the hair of the literary formalist and the reviewer stand on-end, at this havoc with their language. Let them calm their horror; it will not tear it up by the roots, to prevent its lying down again, and covering the baldness of their superannuated error.

"The reform here offered will be acceptable to those who dare to use it. Others will stone the innovation as the metaphysical and stiffnecked Israelites served their uncomforming Prophets."[2]

A mild sample of his mood is evinced in the paragraph quoted below, and reproduced in the original orthography.

> As a necesary part of this record, I have unfortunately been obliged, under some prospective views, to notice unoticeable, and to me hapily, unknown individualities: but having on this ocasion taken a nearer view of the ofense than the ofenders, I have, with generic touches only, and with a mitigated reaction on their thõtles inroad, been careful to treat them as many now, and more hereafter may think, with greater kindnes than their cases deserve.[3]

His *Rhymes of Contrast on Wisdom and Folly*, published just before his death, is a sad commentary on an embittered life of one who had turned cynic, without profiting from the humanitarian environment with which his father had surrounded him. Not the least instructive part of this poignant document is the footnote commentary running almost to the full-length page on many of the lines in verse.

[2] J. Rush: *The Philosophy of the Human Voice* (7th ed.), p. XII.

[3] J. Rush: *Loc. cit.*, p. XXVI.

What influence Rush's analysis of the mind, with its behavioristic implications, had had in its day may be inferred from the fact that no copy of this two-volume work is to be found in the world's greatest university library, that of Harvard, which, furthermore, has been the citadel of psychology for more than half a century.

A Colleague with Theological Proclivities

Martyn Paine (1794-1877), in some respects, resembled his contemporary, James Rush. He, too, was a physician and, therefore, had the advantage of a scientific training. His proficiency in physiology is attested by the fact that he was professor in the medical department of the University of New York, and his *Institutes of Medicine* passed through nine editions. Paine undertook everything on a large scale, and he was dynamic in his approach, but unlike James Rush, he possessed the political touch, constantly joining or being elected to learned societies abroad. Still more, however, did they differ in their philosophical outlook; for Paine was the exact opposite of his *confrère*, in that he set himself up as the advocate of the soul, immortality, the vital principle, and of course, a Simon-pure theism; for he was a devout Episcopalian.

The only work that concerns us from the psychological point of view is his *Physiology of the Soul and Instinct as Distinguished from Materialism*, which, starting as a single lecture, in 1848, yielded a small book, even in the enlarged edition of 1849, but by 1872, it assumed formidable proportions.

The work as a whole is a crusade against materialism, in any of its forms, and an extended tirade against the doctrine of evolution, which was then gaining ground, as well as an attempted vindication of the Biblical account of creation, miracles, etc., on a fundamentalist basis. Paine throughout the volume piles Ossa on Pelion to prove that modern scientists who deny the existence of a soul, or who see no difference between the mind of man and that of the ape or lower animals, except in degree, are perverse in their reasoning. He rakes up scores of arguments and illustrations to sustain his position, so that in a sense, this *omnium gatherum* may serve as an anthology of scientific opinion on many vital points during the middle of the nineteenth century.

The distinguished founder of organic chemistry, Justus Liebig, who endeavored to show that thought was simply a special type of chemical (molecular) combination or combustion of oxygen and nerve substance (phosphorus included) is the main target; but dozens of others, the Darwins, Spencer, the Duke of Argyll, Maudsley, Moleschott, Huxley, Ludwig Büchner, Karl Vogt, John Tyndall, William Carpenter, Rudolf Virchow, de Candolle *et al.* come in for a drubbing. On the other hand, men like Newton, Humphrey Davy, Guizot, John Herschel, and those like-minded, are extolled for their theistic beliefs and expressions.

Psychosomatic Observations

Perhaps this whole controversial mosaic need not detain us at this point, although even today there are scientific protagonists in the same tug of war, but there is much material in the fifty-two pages of the second chapter to make us heed, at least, the author's specialized knowledge of the nervous system, which he applies to explain certain psychological phenomena and to entitle him to a place in the history of psychosomatic medicine. Speaking about asthma *e.g.*, he tells us that "in asthma, a stronger irritation is transmitted from the lungs to the brain, and a more intense motor excitement is reflected from that organ upon the muscles of respiration (often including those of the face) than in ordinary breathing, and not unfrequently the will comes to the aid of the irritation propagated to the brain from the lungs. Here, then, it is seen that the prompting of the mind and the physical cause are brought naturally into immediate coöperation in rousing the action of the brain. The physical cause is insufficient for the development of that nervous influence which is necessary to excite the requisite movements of the respiratory muscles, and therefore compels the mind to lend its assistance. Both act in perfect harmony together; nor can any difference be observed in the results of either (which, as we have seen, is also true of involuntary and voluntary respiration), excepting as the mind acts with greater energy in asthma than the remote physical cause, and brings the respiratory muscles of the face into action."[4]

[4] M. Paine: *Physiology of the Soul and Instinct,* etc., 1871, p. 68. The portion dealing with the mental contribution to physical ailments is contained in the early *Discourse,* of 1849, pp. 53-96.

Laughing, yawning, joy, grief, disgust are explained on a similar principle; and one of the corollaries of his philosophy appears to be that nature is a better healer than the physician, and that without its help, no drug is effective.

Despite the repetitions, diffuseness, and meandering course of his so-called "demonstration of the soul," it would be injudicious, as Brett has done in his *History of Psychology* (Vol. III, p. 258), to wave him aside majestically as if he were a pompous tyro. Perhaps the size of the volume, as well as the author's volubility, is hardly in its favor, but even the early small book of 1849, *A Discourse on the Soul and Instinct* has much to recommend it, and is a far more compact approach to the psychophysiological problems than the later turgid elaboration. It is in this little book too, that we have an excellent description of the five temperaments, including the nervous type, all physiologically expounded. Students of the constitutional system known as somatotypology would do well to consult this section.[5] The circumstance that Paine insisted on a sharp cleavage between animal and man, or that he attributed the spontaneity of man to a soul, while the animal to him was only a creature of instinct should not blind us to the many striking passages in his writings pertaining to psychology.

Study of Mind Yields to the Study of Man

The advance of scientific research is indirectly evident in a psychological text which was published in 1878, and was reissued in several printings, and at least one revised edition, by Mark Hopkins (1802-1887) who too, received a medical training, although he practiced but a few months, soon entering the ministry and engaging in teaching at Williams College, of which he subsequently became President. The very title of the book, *An Outline Study of Man; or The Body and Mind in One System* is indicative of Hopkins' progressive trend; for it at once puts us in mind of recent developments in the science. It is not the mind alone, as in previous psychologies, which makes up the totality of the subject, but the organism as a whole. The little volume, which was a boon to thousands of students for nearly two decades, however, had much else to recommend it.

[5] M. Paine: *A Discourse on the Soul and Instinct,* 1849, pp. 216-230.

Hopkins was primarily the inspiring teacher, but he could not have been inspiring unless he had thought out his system in the full confidence that he was contributing something to the mental outlook of his charges. His immediate successor, James A. Garfield's oft-quoted tribute to the man to the effect that his ideal of a college would be fully met by a log in the woods with a student at one end and Mark Hopkins at the other is sufficient proof of Hopkins' prowess as a stimulator of thought; and *that* he did on a tutorial basis. It is as if he were speaking to each reader individually. Hopkins tells us how he wanted to encourage questions from the audience, at his Lowell Institute course, but Mr. Lowell, whom he consulted on that point, did not approve of it. "Then, being averse to saying anything that could not be perfectly understood, and seeing a blackboard behind me, I laid aside my manuscript, and gave three or four lectures on the more abstruse points with the aid of that. This was thought to be a success, and I have so far followed the method since, as to desire to test it further; for if these studies can be popularized, it will be a public benefit."[6]

Thus, we find in the book, which was substantially a "phonographic report" (*i.e.*, really a shorthand transcript of his lectures) the first real attempt by an American to introduce diagrams and charts and tabular schemes to aid the student in grasping psychological and philosophical relations. It is surprising how much Hopkins was able to pack into a book of 300 pages. He includes biological and physiological data, and explains the steps which lead up to man from such properties as gravitation and cohesion through chemical affinity and vegetable life, which prompts both the writer of his sketch in the *Dictionary of American Biography* and Fay in his *History of American Psychology before William James* to see in Hopkins a forerunner of the doctrine of emergent evolution—a suggestion which is obviously far-fetched.

The Feelings Are Stressed

No scholar in the ordinary sense of the word, Hopkins was nevertheless an independent thinker. In most of the psychologies, the intellect, or let us call it cognition, had received practically exclusive attention at the expense of affection and volition. Affection was regarded as a sort of annex to the will.

[6] M. Hopkins: *An Outline Study of Man,* 1891 (Rev. ed.), p. 2.

The mind, as such, was almost equivalent to the totality of sensations, perceptions, memories, images, and all by which we *know* our world. Hopkins rates the intellect lowest in the scheme, and he justifies his attitude thus.

It may, perhaps, seem strange to some that the intellect should be placed lowest, but it belongs there; and the order in which I have presented the different parts of our nature presents, as I suppose, the order of progress of the race when it has been reduced to a savage or semi-barbarous state and would rise again. At first men worship strength of body, physical energy. The man who had the greatest power of muscles was the hero. Even yet there are many with whom physical prowess is the great thing, and who hold those who manifest it in higher esteem than any others. The next step is the worship of intellect. Disputants and intellectual prize fighters become heroes. Great debaters, pleaders, orators, writers, become the great men irrespective of character. This is our present state. No nation has yet gone beyond this. In our literary institutions it is chiefly the intellect that is educated, and in some of them more and more, with little or no systematic regard for the training of the higher powers. No doubt the time will come when this state of things will be looked back upon as we now look back on the ascendency of physical force. Until the intellect is placed by the community where it belongs, and made subordinate to the sensibility and the will, we shall find that mere sharpness, shrewdness, intellectual power, and success through these, will be placed above those higher qualities in which *character* consists, and success through them. The intellect is simply instrumental, and belongs where I have placed it.[7]

This observation, it seems, is remarkably astute, and in advance of his time, in the light of our atomic warfare developments, and the unbalanced political situation we are in today. Non-Aristotelian logicians and general semanticists would probably count him as one of their precursors, if they perused his writings. He draws no sharp demarcation line between intelligence and instinct, but represents the one by the upper triangle and the other by the lower triangle of an oblong diagonally divided:

[7] M. Hopkins: *Loc. cit.*, pp. 2, 58, 59.

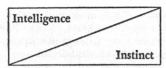

It should be noted, however, that this particular diagram is credited by Hopkins to his successor at Williams, President Chadbourne, who wrote the first American work on instinct, in 1872. Hopkins, nevertheless, goes him one better in that he affirms that "we never reach a point where instinct is wholly absent" (p. 207).

Among the desires, Hopkins lists the desire of continued existence, those of property, knowledge, power, esteem, good, liberty, society. He follows his predecessors in the distinctions between appetites, instincts, desires and affections. "The appetite craves: instinct directs" (p. 205). His definition of appetite as "those cravings of the animal nature that have for their object the well-being of the body, and the continuance of the race" is neat and adequate, but his further earmarks; "as the means of sustaining and continuing the race, they are the condition of all other forms of the sensibility, and so are lower than they; their characteristics are that they take their rise from the body, are periodical, and have a physical limit; and any craving that has these characteristics may properly be called an appetite" (p. 203) clinch his point.

Hopkins had already imbibed a good deal of the evolutionary doctrine, and as a physician, had a broader horizon than many of his theological colleagues, but he too had woven into his text a number of references to the Deity, although he did not, as in the case of others, belabor the issue.

To what extent does a scientific training, that is, *via* laboratory experimentation, help to keep a man within the confines of objectivity? That is something to be yet ascertained. There are paradoxes which are puzzling and which may never be accounted for.

Noah Porter (1811-1882)

That the scientific world was making rapid strides, and causing its impact to be felt even in that sphere which was restricted to intangibles, *viz.*, psychology, may be deduced from the fact that the very divines turning philosophers and eventually psychologists were constrained to take cognizance of the newer developments, although they were loath to give up the soul. One of the most outstanding educators and administrators of his generation, Noah Porter, who later became President of Yale, belongs to this category. At home in all the intricacies of philosophy and psychological theory, he wrote an imposing handbook *The Human Intellect with an Introduction upon Psychology and the Soul* (1868) containing more than half a million words, which, nevertheless, confines itself to the province of cognition alone.

Under the circumstances, it follows in the line of the Scottish tradition, with its emphasis on knowledge, and includes a theory of knowledge as well as a miniature logic, while ignoring the departments of affection and volition. With such limitations, it can scarcely be hailed as the greatest American psychological textbook prior to James's classic, although it does reveal Porter as a scholar abreast of his subject, in the wider sense, and marks a milestone in the expansion of the nascent science. It may readily be conceded that so far as mapping ou the territory of cogentive psychology (sense perception, imagination, memory, reasoning) Porter left no stone unturned in searching every nook and corner of the field. His treatment of memory, years before Ebbinghaus began his memorable experiments, is particularly noteworthy.

It has been claimed by historians of psychology that Porter was eclectic. This opinion must have been due to his numerous quotations from, and references to, philosophers and psychologists of various schools and shades. There can be no question but that Porter is a scion of the Scottish family, and perhaps more zealous than his intellectual forbears, even if the book is dedicated to Adolf Trendelenburg, Hegel's successor at the University of Berlin. There is no gainsaying that Porter possessed an acute and penetrating mind, but his unwillingness to part with some of the basic doctrines or dogmas of the Church, and, worse, his insistence upon forcing them upon the science of mind, proved to be a serious handicap in this connection. Incidentally, about a dozen years after the appearance of his encyclopedic textbook, he strongly objected to the introduction, by G. W. Sumner, of Herbert Spencer's *Principles of Sociology* as prescribed reading at Yale,[8] and he was an inveterate opponent of evolution. No one can quarrel with a man about his religious beliefs, but to inject these into science is an unwarranted intrusion and an attack upon its sovereignty.

[8] *Dictionary of American Biography*, vol. XV. p. 98.

Porter not only employs the term "soul" throughout his volume, but in addition is constantly coupling it with the word "powers." It may naturally be taken for granted that the soul is to him a substance, and as such affects directly the actions of men. Consciousness to him is something apart from sense perception, which comes to the aid and support of consciousness, while the physiological processes are "the essential conditions of the development and activity of the soul."[9]

In an enlightening section of about ten pages, in very fine print, Porter threshes out the issue about the vagueness and inadmissibility of psychology as a science because it permits neither of mathematical formulation nor of experimental verification. He thinks, on the contrary, that it is a science; for otherwise, the authority of all science, which, in the last analysis, rests on consciousness and sense perception, must be questioned; that furthermore, establishing the sequence of operations and the causes of the phenomena is already an *entrée* to the scientific guild.

At times Porter's pronouncements seem too dogmatic to deserve even the consideration of present-day psychology, *e.g.*, when he lays it down "that the soul does know itself, and confides in the knowledge thus attained, will be acknowledged by everyone," but it is more in the regrettable application of terms that we can find fault with him; as for the rest, he has an unusual grasp of the adversary's position, and states it both clearly and carefully. Even the theory of emergent evolution, which Lloyd Morgan much later developed and labelled, finds a place here among the discards (p. 21), and one who wishes to read into Porter some inkling of Freud's doctrine of the unconscious may seize upon such an assertion as; "Now whether or not the life and the soul are one, this certainly must be received as unquestioned, that in addition to the soul's capacities for conscious activities, it is capable also of certain unconscious processes" (p. 37), although a reading of the whole section will disclose that this extent *i.e.*, "beyond the sphere of its conscious activities," does not refer to Freud's unconscious so much as to the physiological occurrences.

Psychology—A Ladder to Heaven

Without naming the doctrine, Porter stands for what was later to be designated as interactionism, *i.e.*, the mutual influ-

[9] N. Porter: *The Human Intellect*, 1868, p. 52.

ence of mind on body and of body on mind. He is also like all of the Scotch School, a staunch intuitionist, believing in first principles, which are implanted in us and by which we gain truth. Neither these attitudes nor his deeply colored theistic philosophy, nor his arguments from design, which he marshals in order to bolster the cause of an omniscient and all-forceful Deity, who plans every detail of the world, including the nervous system of man—none of these characteristics need be taken exception to. What the author is really guilty of amounts to writing a psychology for the glorification of the Lord. Everything set down seems to lead to the Final Cause, the Absolute, who is a *thinking agent*, with the universe as thought as well as extension. "We are not alone justified," he exclaims toward the end of the volume, "we are compelled to conclude an analysis of human intellect with the assertion that its various powers and processes suppose and assume that there is an uncreated thinker, whose thoughts can be interpreted by the human intellect which is made in His image" (p. 662). It is the obtrusion of theological matter, not merely casual references, in a purportedly psychological textbook, as the cornerstone of the whole structure, that renders Porter's vast production suspect. College students, even in the senior year, must have found the work altogether too erudite and controversial; for in it the author appears like a gladiator in the arena, now engaging this opponent and now another, until he fells them all. Perhaps for this reason, he found it advisable to reduce the work to 565 pages of ordinary type. In this abridgement, *Elements of Intellectual Science* (1871), much of the abstruse polemic portion is eliminated. Aside from the device of printing the less elementary passages in fine type, which was an innovation in psychology, at any rate, the index appears as a useful adjunct. At least *that* part was undoubtedly the result of German influence.

Autology and Perceptionalism

If space permitted, perhaps the two Hamiltons would receive some attention in this survey, but since neither D. Howland Hamilton nor E. J. Hamilton made a worthwhile contribution to psychology, although credit is due them for their assiduity in turning out enormous volumes, a paragraph or two will be sufficient to place them on the record.

In the case of the former, citing the title of the ponderous 700-page lucubration is enough to show the drift of his science, even if occasionally a striking utterance does burst through the maze of verbiage. In *Autology: An Inductive System of Mental Science whose Center is the Will and Whose Completion is the Personality; a Vindication of the Manhood of Man, the Godhood of God, and the Divine Authorship of Nature* (1873), we have an illustration of killing three birds with one stone, although the author's aim was presumably to light three objects with one match. The word "autology" *i.e.*, the science of the self should have had more of a chance, in view of the later self-psychologies that were evolved (Mary Calkins) but this earlier autology is saturated with autistic thinking. If D. H. Hamilton were associated with a contemporary school, it would be that of personalism.

Of greater importance was the work of Edward J. Hamilton (1839-1918), who taught at several colleges including Princeton, after serving as a minister during the '60's. Hamilton, despite the fact that he was born in Belfast, Ireland, was affiliated with the Scottish School, notwithstanding his desultory cavils against Reid and other of its representatives. He talks in their language, he dwells almost exclusively on the cognitive, and makes much ado about the intuitions.

Hamilton's first treatise, *The Human Mind* (1883), a large volume of over 700 pages, is marred by awkward, if not altogether faulty, expressions. The author's deviations from the general treatments of the day are a disservice rather than a help, and his reputation for profundity in certain lay quarters was earned by a penchant for the recondite as well as by his energy and boundless self-confidence. To take only one statement: "Intellect is the most prominent faculty of spirit, and is the condition of all physical life, save that of sense only,"[10] can there be anything more muddled than that from our standpoint? Or what psychological enlightenment can be gained from a definition like this one, "Exertion, or action, is an ability in the exercise of which the soul voluntarily uses the mental and physical powers at her command"?

The Human Mind was abridged and published, in 1886, as *Mental Science,* and then it appeared, in 1899, as *The Perceptionalist,* reprinted in 1912. The author was so anxious to have the Germans take notice of his achievement that he took up residence again in Germany, toward the close of his

---

[10] E. J. Hamilton: *The Human Mind,* p. 19.

life, and himself translated his *Perceptionalist* into German, in the belief, apparently, that no native of Germany could be intrusted with the task. Perhaps he felt that the German metaphysical lingo would lend itself more easily to his type of writing.

Chapter 9

Transition Period of the '80's

WE ARE GETTING CLOSER to the fashioning of the new psychology. Intellectual or mental philosophy was beginning to be supplanted by a more characteristic appellation like "mental science" or "psychology." The subject-matter was being sifted, and whatever was metaphysical, or had a theological import, would be set to one side. Thanks to the growing self-assertiveness of the natural sciences abroad, psychology too was to be freed from its bondage, and live a life of its own. This, naturally, was not to be accomplished by an edict from some academy pundit. The liberation was gradual, as German-trained students, now functioning as college instructors in the United States, would begin to look with disdain, if not contempt, at the texts turned out by pulpit psychologists, who, in their turn, were becoming aware of the unsuitability of their double rôle.

In the decade immediately preceding the publication of James's *Principles of Psychology,* a baker's dozen of textbooks on the subject were brought out, some of which had apparently been untouched by the march of intellectual events. Most of them, however, were showing the fruits of the new movement, and it is during this brief period that the foundations were laid for psychology as we understand it today. Of these, three names stand out conspicuously in the annals of scientific psychology: Ladd, Dewey, and Baldwin, while a fourth, that of William James, who had published a portion of his *Principles* in periodicals during the '80's, outshines them all, but even Bowne, McCosh, and Clark Murray, who still belong to the old guard, had profited by the emancipation in general science.

A Personalist at the Throttle

B. P. Bowne (1871-1910) the patron saint—as some will have it, the founder—of personalism in this country, a follower of Lotze, was a valiant champion of the Absolute, and left a large number of disciples who have taken up the cudgels on behalf of an unadulterated idealism. Although his writings comprise a bookshelf, his contribution to psychology consists of a dozen articles critical of the newer trends and an *Introduction to Psychological Theory* (1886) which, however, deals with the philosophical substructure, or perhaps superstructure, of psychology, and in which he makes no bones of his wish to keep psychology in its place as a vassal of philosophy; and, while recognizing the value of physiology *per se*, he is loath to hold out for it any hope of explaining the mysteries of the mind. It is clear that Bowne, a man of tremendous intellectual sweep, is not a psychologist but a dialectician, but even he no longer harps upon the soul, except in his metaphysical works. In his psychological volume, he defines our science as dealing with mental facts and processes.

Last of the Mohicans

James McCosh (1811-1894), however, does rank as a psychologist, in spite of the oblivion which he had fallen into, due partly to the fact that he had in his day usurped so much power in academic spheres, and partly to the school which he was identified with, as its leader in this country. It was evident that the new generation, as in political upheavals, would have no truck with the Scottish School, which held sway for nearly a century.

James McCosh may have been overrated at one time, but at present, he is unduly forgotten; and his name, when mentioned among psychologists, almost always brings up the association of "bosh." Called to fill the Presidency of the College of New Jersey (Princeton) exactly a hundred years after his countryman, John Witherspoon, had received a similar call, he had already established a reputation in Scotland and Ireland, where he had been teaching, prior to coming to the United States, both as a keen philosopher and an able teacher. He was yet to prove his worth as a college administrator; and it may be said at once that in this capacity he did more for Princeton than his more distinguished successor of the twentieth century, Woodrow Wilson.

McCosh had been teaching psychology, or intellectual philosophy as it was then called, for nearly three decades, before he published his compendium on the *Emotions* (1880). Another work on the *Motive Powers* was devoted to the desires, motives, and will. In 1886, there appeared the third part of his trilogy *The Cognitive Powers*. Although Stanley Hall, in the first issue of the *Journal of American Psychology*, which he founded in 1887, damned it with a few left-handed compliments, this book is a readable and well-organized textbook, which, together with the other two books, constitutes as useful a manual of the whole subject as we have had up to the time. Even Porter's hefty volume, more far-reaching in scope and more advanced in its quest of solutions to age-old problems, does not serve the purpose as well. A revised edition of *The Cognitive Powers* was issued in 1892, and there were several printings for both editions. All in all, it is a model of exposition.

True, as Stanley Hall points out, the figures (ten only) are a bit crude, and certainly, as compared with the numerous detailed illustrations in Alexander Bain's *Senses and Intellect* or H. G. Lewes's *Physical Basis of Mind*, they make but a puny impression, but it is, I believe, the first American psychological textbook in which such cuts are introduced, thus proving that McCosh, at least, was ready to adapt himself to new conditions. It was evidently a compromise, since in the preface, he remarks that "in physical science and in literature, they illuminate their books (as in the old missals) by figures. We cannot do this in mental science, as our thoughts have not forms nor colors." It is somewhat sardonic on the part of Hall to take this defense apparently as a cue for the observation that "the woodcuts of brain and sense organs that are inserted are but little more related to the text than the marginal figures with which ancient missals were wont to be illuminated."[1]

Signs of the Times

McCosh arrived in the United States in 1868, which was the year that saw Porter's *The Human Intellect*. Both men had wielded much power not only at Princeton and Yale, of which, respectively, they were Presidents, but their influence radiated to other parts. Of the two, McCosh showed more liberal tendencies. He sponsored the theory of evolution; and in a collaboration with a naturalist, he had already evinced a great interest in vegetative and animal types. That he sought to dam the fresh tide of what seemed to him like materialism may be understood in the light of his training

[1] G. S. Hall: *Amer. Jour. of Psychol.*, 1887, vol. I, p. 147.

under the Scottish masters, but it is apparent that he was prepared to go part way with the "invaders," and a comparison of Porter's and McCosh's books will convince anyone that progress had been made in the approach to psychology, during the brief span which separated their handbooks.

For one thing, in the latter, the terms "soul," "God," "Deity," etc., are used very sparingly. McCosh begins *The Cognitive Powers* with the statement that "Psychology is the science of the soul," but further down the page, he revises this by saying that "Psychology may be more fully defined as that science which inquires into the operations of the conscious self with the view of discovering laws."[2] In view of this definition, it is a bit difficult to understand why McCosh declines to discuss the subject of illusions and hallucinations on the ground that "these belong to physiological psychology rather than to psychology proper." One should think that these phenomena enter into the picture of the self at least as much as ordinary sense perception.

In his decided stand on the intrinsically and independently mental operations in association, as distinct from the physiological processes underlying them, McCosh misunderstands James's pointing up the physical nature of associations and habit, when he naïvely finds fault with the quaint analogy between a lock and a brain, brought in the *Principles of Psychology*.

> Professor James gives a preposterously wide field to habit. He refers to it such acts as, "A lock works better after being used for some time." (*Psych.* vol. i. p. 109). The professor refers all association to physiological causes. But it is certain that there is association of a purely mental character. There is association by resemblance and other relations perceived by intelligence; and surely this cannot be accounted for by brain currents. I regard the physiological action as merely affecting the independent physical laws. I believe a brain perturbed by grief will affect the current of grief. Possibly the exciting and disturbing influence of the secondary laws of association may be produced by brain or nervous action, which, however, has been produced by previous mental ideas.[3]

[2] J. McCosh: *Psychology; The Cognitive Powers* (Rev. ed.), 1892, p. 69.

[3] J. McCosh: *Loc. cit.*, 1906, p. 152, supplementary note.

Obviously it did not occur to McCosh that even association by resemblance could be due to the conduction of nerve impulses along contiguous paths in a common cortical segment. The problem of recognizing resemblances is akin to the perception of relations, despite changed conditions, discussed by the gestaltists.

It is not, however, our purpose here to expatiate on McCosh's views and deficiencies. He deserves a hearing not only as the last spokesman of a very important school, which cradled psychology when it was still an infant, and reared it until it could support itself, but because he did succeed in concatenating and welding an enormous quantity of elusive particles into a more or less solid unit at a time when specialization was not yet in vogue. It may sound out of tune or even an anachronism, on our part, even to suggest it, but possibly, McCosh's volume on the emotions, would, in its plenitude of insights, be more serviceable to present-day students, than the chapters on this topic in many contemporary textbooks with their citations of scores of experimental results, many of which are inconsequential, while the validity of others may seriously be questioned. McCosh's ablest pupil was J. Mark Baldwin, who became one of the leading figures in American psychology during the first decade of the present century.

The Scotch Influence in Canada

Perhaps Canada should be excluded from our survey, if one were to adhere rigidly to political boundary lines. On the other hand, however, it must be considered that a book published in the United States may be regarded as an American production. Furthermore, a certain exchange of instructors has been in process between the two countries for a long time. Lastly, since Canada is so close, and forms part of North America, and is being more and more affected by the culture of the United States, it would be a mistake to ignore Canada's contribution to psychology.

It so happens that when the first volume of Baldwin's *Handbook of Psychology* appeared, the author was the incumbent of a chair at the University of Toronto, where Scottish realism had been strongly intrenched. Baldwin, at this period, was a qualified person to head the department of philosophy, having had his fill of McCosh's teachings, tempered, it is true, by his brief French and German training. Indeed, it may be doubted whether Baldwin ever threw off his Scottish intuitions even when he branched out into experimental psychology and other fields. More will be said of him in a further chapter.

A more indigenous product of Canada was John Clark Murray (1836-1917), who emigrated from Scotland, as a young man, and, after teaching for some time at Queens, in Kingston, became Frothingham professor of philosophy at McGill University in Montreal. His *Handbook of Psychology* was originally published in London, in 1885, but subsequent editions were brought out in Boston, the fifth edition appearing in 1897. Its success was well merited, for it was an unusually informative textbook and, although containing little that could be called original, it was well adapted for the average student. It leaned heavily on the Scottish philosophers, but Clark Murray did not neglect the German developments, and was determined to steer the students in the non-metaphysical path, so that the soul and God, and all the other theological concepts, are avoided, which is not to be construed as proof that Murray was other than devout or that he was not among the most guileless of men. His *Introduction to Psychology* (1904) was a full revision and enlargement of the earlier work.

Dewey's Debut

John Dewey's influence on psychology was more of an indirect sort. Let it be recorded here that it was in this fruitful decade that John Dewey began publishing in psychology. It is not generally known that his doctoral dissertation, at Johns Hopkins, was on the psychology of Kant. Regrettably this had never been published, nor is there a copy extant; for even the University has not preserved the manuscript. In the same year, in 1884, he set forth the chief aims of "The New Psychology," being probably the first to use the phrase in English. In 1886, two of his articles, one on "The Psychological Standpoint" and the other on "Psychology as a Philosophic Method" were published in *Mind*; and in 1887, when he was 26, his 427-page *Psychology* came off the press. Only two years later, in collaboration with J. A. McLellan, he brought out a book on "applied psychology," as they titled it, but the subtitle, *An Introduction to the Prin-*

ciples and Practice of Education reveals the true nature of its contents. Before he was 30, John Dewey had shifted from the theoretical in general to practical psychology, and what can there be more practical, from a social angle, than education?

Surprises and Puzzles

Of what value is John Dewey's *Psychology*? In all candor it must be said that the 26-year-old youth (he may have been 24, at most 25, when he was writing the book) was still groping, and is discovered straddling between two positions. To be sure, the functional viewpoint, which characterizes Dewey's whole philosophy, has already set its impress on the young man, and the knack of framing definitions which require the reader to see something fresh in the relationship of terms is already in evidence; above all, the methodical laying out of the material, with a separate label for almost every paragraph, has never been paralleled in his later works; yet the strange mixture of idealism and down-to-earth empiricism gives it an uncomfortable strabismic appearance.

Students of Dewey's many works will hardly have expected that the grand old man of American philosophy could have defined sensation as the "elementary consciousness which arises from the reaction of *the soul* upon a nervous impulse conducted to the brain from the affection of some sensory nerve-ending by a *physical stimulus*,"[4] although Dewey the instrumentalist is already detectable in the following somewhat roundabout formulation:

The sensation gets significance, accordingly, just in the degree in which the mind puts itself into it. As it puts itself into the sensation it makes it a *sign* of its past experience. Adjustment is the process by which the self so connects itself with the presented datum that this becomes a sign, or symbolic—points to something beyond its own new existence, and hence has meaning. The fact known is not a bare fact, that is, an existence implying no constructive activity of intelligence, but is idealized fact, existence upon which the constructive intelligence has been at work. That which is not thus idealized by the mind has no existence

[4] J. Dewey: *Psychology*, 1887, p. 27.

for intelligence. All knowledge is thus, in a certain sense, self-knowledge.[5]

Nor would he have supposed that Dewey could write that "the true self-related must be the organic unity of the self and the world, of the ideal and the real, and this is what we know as *God*," and that "every concrete act of knowledge involves an intuition of God; for it involves a unity of the real and the ideal, of the objective and the subjective. Stated in another way, every act of knowledge is a realization of intelligence; an attainment of some relation which constitutes truth."[6]

But we must not forget that the author was then torn between two influences, and he was eager to reconcile them. No wonder, Stanley Hall, who may have been his teacher at Johns Hopkins, in the first issue of the *American Journal of Psychology*, good-naturedly ribbed him on his self-assurance, in settling everything in psychology at a time when all was so uncertain. He even charged him with inaccuracies and poor assimilation of his readings. The fact remains, however, that Dewey in this youthful production had already shown promise of an original thinker, and the writing of this textbook was a prodigious feat for a man in the middle twenties. The bibliographical references at the end of each chapter were the most copious yet, but there was no index. Several printings and revised editions were proof that the book, in a decade of close competition, was much in demand.

The wonder is that in the article which appeared earlier, and before the author was 25, we have a strikingly lucid survey of what "The New Psychology" stands for, and a programme is mapped out which is remarkably modern. Written fully 80 years ago, in a prophetic vein, it might still be read with profit today, and from the force of the utterances and the maturity of style, which, in its florid phrasing, savors of a euphuistic William James, one could hardly associate the writer with a youth, who later was to awe the reader with a cumbersome and abstruse form of expression.

The Germ of a Dynamic Psychology

In this essay, one of Dewey's best, in the opinion of one man at least, the trend is toward experience, and away from logic, and an approximation to James's radical empiricism.

[5] J. Dewey: *Loc. cit.*, pp. 142, 143.
[6] J. Dewey: *Loc. cit.*, pp. 244, 245.

He puts his finger on the very flaws of the philosophical psychologists when he lashes at them in the following words:

The old psychologists almost without exception held to a nominalistic logic. This of itself was a matter of no great importance, were it not for the inevitable tendency and attempt to make living concrete facts of experience square with the supposed norms of an abstract, lifeless thought, and to interpret them in accordance with its formal conceptions. This tendency has nowhere been stronger than in those who proclaimed that "experience" was the sole source of all knowledge. They emasculated experience till their logical conceptions could deal with it; they sheared it down till it would fit their logical boxes; they pruned it till it presented a trimmed tameness which would shock none of their laws; they preyed upon its vitality till it would go into the coffin of their abstractions.

The reaction against Hume fell back on certain ultimate, indecomposable, necessary first truths immediately known through some mysterious simple faculty of the mind. Here again the logical model manifests itself. Such intuitions are not psychological; they are conceptions bodily imported from the logical sphere. Their origin, tests, and character are all logical. But the New Psychology would not have necessary truths about principles. It rejects the formalistic intuitionalism for one which has been well termed dynamic. It believes that truth, that reality, not necessary *beliefs about* reality, is given in the living experience of the soul's development.[7]

It is here that he points out the great rôle of the organic conception in dealing with psychological interpretation. "The idea of environment is a necessity to the idea of organism, and with the conception of environment comes the impossibility of considering psychical life as an individual, isolated thing developing in a vacuum."[8]

The social and historical sciences, language, and folklore are bound up with the extension of psychology, in its new frame of reference.

It is probable that this is the first time the term "dynamic" has been employed in a psychological context, and yet it

[7] J. Dewey: "The New Psychology," *Andover Review,* 1884, vol. 2, pp. 287-288.

[8] J. Dewey: *Loc. cit.,* p. 285.

would seem from the phrasing that the word had already been in use before 1884. At any rate, we have here a sufficiently explicit distinction between "psychostatics," another word which appears in the article, and dynamic psychology.

Dewey, the ethical philosopher, is already giving us an inkling of his new direction. "Thus modern psychology is intensely ethical in its tendencies," and at the time he was still looking upward to heaven. "It finds . . . the tendencies of devotion, sacrifice, faith, and idealism . . . upon the altar stairs which slope up to God." Nor is he prone to become overenthusiastic about the promising prospects of physiological psychology as an explain-all of mental phenomena. Thus, the 24- or 25-year-old youth cautions us against too rosy expectations in unmistakable language, and in that tendency he was supported, or perhaps guided, by others, *e.g.*, G. T. Ladd.

> So far as I know, all the leading investigators closely realize that explanations of psychical events in order to explain must themselves be psychical and, not physiological. However important such knowledge . . . may be for physiology, it has *of itself* no value for psychology. . . . Physiology can no more, of itself, give us the *what, why,* and *how* of psychical life than the physical geography of a country can enable us to construct or explain the history of the nation that has dwelt within that country. . . . Psychical events can be observed only through psychical means, and interpreted and explained by psychical conditions and facts (p. 282).

The First Physiological Handbook in English

It was, however, neither McCosh nor Baldwin, neither Bowne nor Dewey, whose book caused a stir in psychological spheres, during this decade, but George Trumbull Ladd's *Elements of Physiological Psychology*, which seemed to be the answer to a psychologist's prayer. Published in 1887, it was brought out in a revised and enlarged edition, with the collaboration of R. S. Woodworth, in 1911, and served as the analogue of Wundt's great work, which it followed in general, in a wise condensation and omission of purely philosophical issues.

The irony, or poetic justice, here was that while heretofore, the doctors of divinity were the dispensers of psychology in a metaphysical mould, and were about to be ignored by the specially trained men, a theologian, who could hold forth on "Divine personality" as theognostically[9] and teleologically as the most dogmatic of the earlier divines, actually was the first psychologist to furnish an explanatory guide for the phenomena which his theological colleagues were treating metaphysically, urging, for the most part, like Porter, Bowne, and others, that physiology cannot help us much to understand the workings of the mind, or, in their language, "operations of the soul." George Trumbull Ladd (1842-1921) demonstrated that a clergyman (from 1881-1905, he was professor of philosophy at Yale) could still enter the ranks of science, without taking recourse to God at every turn; and for a number of years his *Elements of Physiological Psychology* was regarded as a sort of Bible by psychologists of the younger generation.

They were not interested in why the perception, instincts, or appetites were given to man by an omnibeneficent and omniscient Deity, but how they worked. Heretofore, the sense data, emotions, memories, etc., had been tantalizingly elusive, fleeting, and never recurring, once they were experienced, although others would naturally take their place. The clergymen-psychologists took care of this matter by positing a substantial soul from which emanated all the mental or psychic phenomena for the purpose of preserving man and keeping him comfortable, as well as demonstrating the grandeur of the Lord. The researches of Charles Bell, Johannes Müller, Helmholtz, Purkinje, Wundt, and others disclosed the "how," the *modus operandi* of the mental occurrences by studying the neural processes, thus affording them permanent moorings. The emotion, or the smell was momentary perhaps, but the blood vessel or the olfactory nerve was permanent, as were the hypothalamus and the gyrus fornicatus, in the brain. It was reserved for another, this time an original prophet,

[9] The term "theognostic" is coined as a useful label to designate the quality which many philosophers of a theological cast of mind presume to possess, of being able to tell the world all the plans and designs of God as if they were peeping through the keyholes of heaven. Leibniz, in his *Théodicée,* was a typical example but he had a host of predecessors as well as followers. I had thought of a word like "theiscience" but that is a hybrid, while "deiscience" might imply some connection with deism instead of theism. Almost all conservative theologians are theognosticians.

a decade later, to delve again into the "why" of mental phenomena and to discover the motives, not of God in planting such mechanisms, but of the unconscious, which, also, becomes a sort of deity.

A Crucial Instance of Acceptability

Ladd as a psychologist was esteemed despite his theological training and office not because his tenets were accepted throughout, but rather for the reason that he had made no attempt to infiltrate foreign elements into the body of facts with which they were not compatible. It, moreover, proved abundantly that the psychologists, many of whom were of a religious disposition, were not averse to theology in its proper sphere, but were unalterably opposed to laymen—for such the clergy were, in this respect—becoming missionaries on territory which is, by its very nature, closed to that sort of activity. In other words, guests should not try to convince or advise the host on matters which are less familiar to them than to him.

Thus Ladd's *Physiological Psychology,* a sort of *vade mecum* for the newly acquired laboratory, could be regarded as the dividing line between the old and the new approaches, even before William James's *Principles of Psychology* was between covers; for during this period, James had already published several chapters of his great work, and his views, during the '80's, were not unknown. The '80's may have not been the gay decade of the '90's. It was, however, for psychology, a period full of promise, full of excitement; and a few towering men had already begun to leave their impress on the rising generation. The closing decade of the nineteenth century was not at all to be associated with the idea of depression, incident to the *fin-de-siècle,* but was characterized in psychological circles by a feverish activity, by organization and consolidation of results.

Chapter 10

Treatises on the Will

PRIOR TO THE experimental period, there were practically no treatises or monographs on special topics in psychology. Even the emotions, except for the religious affections taken up by Edwards, were not surveyed separately until McCosh published a book on the subject, which formed the first part of his three-volume textbook. S. S. Smith, in 1810, did bring out the nearest attempt at an investigation, when his essay on complexion and figure types appeared, and Chadbourne's book on instinct (1872) was another discussion of a single department, although even this volume is too general as compared with monographs or treatises in other sciences.

One topic alone was more or less successful in drawing attention among the philosophical psychologists of the past two centuries, and that was the will. Fully a dozen volumes, not counting the purely philosophical disquisitions, were devoted to the problems of volition since Jonathan Edwards wrote his classic (1754). The will was singled out by philosophers, theologians, and psychologists as a common stamping ground because it is at the crossroads of several disciplines, and because it is the springboard of action. In Edwards' time, the subject, while not actually new, had a somewhat fresh angle, as nearly all intellectual philosophy had been devoted to cognition.

Edwards, the Predeterminist

In pleading the cause of necessitarianism, as against the freedom of the will, Edwards started the logomachy which was to continue for nearly two centuries in the United States. In psychology, except for Thomistic circles, the problem has ceased to have any significance; and operationally it may be considered a pseudo-problem, and one which has as much chance of being solved as the question in regard to which came first, the chick or the egg. Edwards was by no means the first to uphold predeterminism; for it was a dogma in several creeds, but it was he who had furnished the philosophical support which required a good deal of effort to cope with. Edwards' son, Jona, left a tract on liberty and necessity, which naturally leaned in the direction of his father. The younger Edwards, like a devoted son, seeks to reinforce his father's position by a number of illustrations and contentions.

> The man who is the subject of a certain volition had the power of Will long since, yet it never produced that volition, we may suppose, till this moment. What is the cause or reason that it produces it now and not before? To say it does it, because it will, is to say either that this volition is produced by another preceding, which runs into the infinite series, or that the power of Will, or rather the man in the exercise of that power, is the subject of volition, which is mere trifling. On the whole, the existence of a power of Will in a man will no more account for any particular volition of which he is the subject, than the existence of the *man* will account for the same volition, or the existence of a ship-carpenter will account for the building of a certain ship.[1]

The first prominent divine to take Jonathan Edwards to task was J. Dana, whose *An Examination of President Edwards' Inquiry on Freedom of the Will* appeared anonymously in 1770. His chief argument is that "it makes God the proper author, the efficient cause of all the sins of men and devils." Dana cannot understand how good or evil can be said to lie only in the nature of the act and not in what motivates it. Apparently his little book was so much in demand that a second enlarged edition was brought out before long. It was left for another clergyman, S. West, pastor in Stockbridge, to take up the cudgels on behalf of Edwards. In his *Essay on Moral Agency* (1772) a book of over 250 pages, he attempts to vindicate Edwards and to refute Dana. In 1794, a second edition appeared with an added appendix, dealing with Dana's second *Examination*. The dispute is typical of the eighteenth century and characteristic of preachers who are given to exegetical interpretations. Words are bandied about and the line of reasoning makes little use of the empirical. One of the best passages in West's book is the following:

> But before I finish the section, I beg to be indulged in a conjecture concerning the rise and origin of the notion of

[1] J. Edwards: *Works,* vol. II, p. 332.

this mysterious, incomprehensible power in men. I cannot but apprehend, that the opinion arose from a degree of abstraction, in the ideas of men, of *exercise* from agents; which is a refinement far above vulgar understanding, if not above truth itself. From this abstracted idea of *action*, we have been taught to look upon *the agent* as one thing—his action, as another;—for what can be more absurd, say they, than to talk of an exercise, without something to act? —an *action* without an *agent*? Hence men have been led to consider *an action* and *the agent*, as it were, different substances; the one, the *cause*; the other, the *effect*.[2]

The theologian-psychologists succeeding Edwards, however, did not side with him. They could see the danger of preaching a doctrine of predestination which would kill all hope in man to steer his own ship. They at once recognized the psychological source of Edwards' fallacy, which was to lump desires, motives and emotions, *i.e.*, everything which was not purely cognitive, with the will, and then to proceed, in Aristotelian dialectic manner, to say that if the toper chooses to drink, it is because he cannot do otherwise; in other words, we have here some taste of the principle of excluded middle. Logic alone can not get us very far in the domain of psychology, as we have noted in the portion dealing with early instruction in the colonies. Starting with a wrong premise is sufficient to throw the whole reasoning out of gear.

Edwards Opposed by Upham

It is, however, Thomas C. Upham's *Philosophical and Practical Treatise on the Will* (1834) which, as in his previous texts, brings its author to the fore as the most analytic mind in psychology of his day and as a coördinator of rare quality, who imparts to the whole issue a fresh turn. In the 400 pages comprising the volume, Upham has covered almost exhaustively, for the time, considering especially that the experimental period was only a dream then, practically every angle of the subject; and many a psychologist would do well to look into this forgotten tome, if only to apprise himself of the modernity and freshness with which Upham's conclusions

2 S. West: *An Essay on Moral Agency*, 1794 (2d ed.), pp. 126-127.

are suffused. A list of such propositions and conclusions may be drawn up, yet the very train of argumentation which leads up to them is indispensable to an understanding of the magnitude of his task.

He shows, for instance, that desires differ from volitions in fixedness and permanence, that motives are either internal (what would now be called "needs") or external (in topological terms, *e.g.*, objects in a field with positive or negative valences). External motives derive their efficacy from the mind; for the greatest riches would not attract unless they were the means of enjoyment and gratifying our internal motives (*i.e.*, our needs, in a broad sense). He further argues that the character of motives depends partly on the individual's constitutional traits, a proposition which too few of us nowadays would subscribe to, but many are due to various temporary influences (environment). He digresses into the realm of ethics when he distinguishes between *personal* and *moral* motives. The latter are inherent in faith, and bear an authoritarian coloring. We choose even though it is not for our benefit or that of others. Of course, it would seem *prima facie*, that in all so-called moral motives, we do recognize that, in the long run, believers in eternal reward or punishment might be induced by such considerations, which certainly possess a hedonistic basis. Even those who act on a principle that virtue is its own reward might also be gratifying a need of their own, in the form of a conviction or sentiment. But Upham does not examine the division of the two kinds of motives so closely.

Another observation of his that merits citing is his proposition that though personal and moral motives may be compared in strength within their own division, personal motives cannot be compared with moral, and *vice versa*; for they are radically different from each other.

Jeremiah Day, President of Yale, gave expression to much the same views on the will as Upham. He is more philosophical and less psychological, but his analysis of the will and motives is altogether in a different vein from that of Dana or West in that it does not rest on a wrangling about words. He is concerned with issues, and his directness lends itself to a quicker apprehension of the moot points. He asks many questions, and prepares us for a reservation rather than a final conclusion. His is a sort of epistemological approach to the problems connected with the will. At least the theological coloring is not so saturated as in the case of others who wrote at that time on this perennial subject. A sample of his psychological, or perhaps logical, carriage is afforded by this passage.

> Common sense decides that a man is free, when he does as he will; that is, when his actions are obedient to his volitions. But has common sense taken up this question for adjudication, whether we *will* as we will; whether every volition is preceded by another, on which it depends? Common sense considers a man accountable for what he does willingly, when he is in possession of his reason. But does it find it necessary, before awarding praise or blame, to inquire whether the will always follows the last dictate of the understanding; whether, immediately before acting freely, it must be in a state of equilibrium; whether every volition is preceded by an infinite series of volitions? Does a jury ever undertake to settle these points, before pronouncing on the innocence or guilt of the accused? Would the court allow arguments of this nature to be addressed to them by the counsel? It it said that the common people *take these things for granted*, as self-evident and essential to freedom? How can they take that for granted, which they do not even *think of*, unless some speculating philosopher has made efforts, commonly unavailing, to introduce into their minds some of his finely wrought theories?[3]

Day followed up his *Inquiry* by a larger book in 1841, more directly concerned with Edwards' doctrine.

A Never-Ending Battle

The quarter of a century or so, beginning with 1838 and ending with 1864, saw no less than a dozen books on the will. At a time when psychological works were not plentiful in this country, this seems to be a record for just one topic. Some authors, like Tappan and Hazard, would not rest until they, as they seemed to believe, threshed out the issues once and for all, even if it took three volumes in which to do it. The marathon debate between the necessitarians and the libertarians had its reverberations in England too, but naturally since the great champion of predeterminism was an American,

[3] J. Day: *An Inquiry Respecting the Self-Determining Power of the Will*, 1838, pp. 123-124.

the tempest raged particularly in the New England states, and, curiously enough, it was precipitated by a college president, and, for the most part, participated in by college presidents and other executives. Perhaps it is not so odd, after all, when we consider that it is the will which presumably characterizes the executive, the man of action.

Of these college presidents, who were mainly clergymen too, Asa Mahan, with whom we have become acquainted earlier, in connection with his textbooks, was an influential sponsor of liberty. The chief value of his little book, *Doctrine of the Will* (1846), is in the clear formulation of the *pros* and *cons*. He presents a case, much like a prosecutor, against the teachings of Jonathan Edwards, but at the same time, we are familiarized with the latter's stand in detail. He identifies necessitarianism with fatalism, and asks why anyone should be blamed at all for an act which he cannot help perpetrating, since it has been God's decree. He attributes necessity to the cognitive and affective make-up of man, but liberty to the will alone. One argument which he produces is strangely reminiscent of the ontological proof of the existence of God. It would be best to quote Mahan in order to show the resemblance, and at the same time to reveal the acumen of his scholastic mind.

> I argue the liberty of the will *from the existence of the idea of liberty in the human mind, in the form in which it is there found.*
>
> If the will is not free, the idea of liberty is wholly inapplicable to any phenomena in existence whatever. Yet this idea is in the mind. The action of the will, in conformity to it, is just as conceivable as its action in conformity to the idea of necessity. It remains with the necessitarian to account for the existence of this idea in the human mind, in consistency with his own theory. Here the following considerations present themselves demanding special attention.
>
> 1. The idea of liberty, like that of necessity, is a *simple* and not a *complex* idea. This all will admit.
> 2. It could not have come into the mind from observation or reflection: because all phenomena, external and internal, all the objects of observation and reflection, are, according to the doctrine of necessity, not free, but necessary.
> 3. It could not have originated, as *necessary* ideas do, as the

logical antecedents of the truths given by observation and reflection. For example, the idea of space, time, substance, and cause, are given in the intelligence, as the logical antecedents of the ideas of body, succession, phenomena, cause of the *doing*; but if this I, be regarded as necessitated and events, all of which are truths derived from observation or reflection. Now the idea of liberty, if the doctrine of necessity is true, cannot have arisen in this way; because all the objects of observation and reflection are, according to this doctrine, necessary, and therefore their logical antecedents must be. How shall we account, in consistency with this theory, for the existence of this idea in the mind? It came not from perception, external, or internal, nor as the logical antecedent or consequent of any truth thus perceived. Now if we admit the doctrine of liberty as a truth of universal consciousness, we can give a philosophical account of the existence of the idea of liberty in all minds. If we deny this doctrine, and consequently affirm that of necessity, we may safely challenge any theologian or philosopher to give such an account of the existence of that idea in the mind. For all ideas, in the mind, do and must come from observation or reflection, or as the logical antecedents or consequents of ideas thus obtained. We have here an event without a cause, if the doctrine of necessity is true.

4. All *simple* ideas, with the exception of that of liberty, have realities within or around us, corresponding to them. If the doctrine of necessity is true, we have one solitary idea of this character, that of liberty, to which no reality corresponds. Whence this solitary intruder in the human mind?

The existence of this idea in the mind is proof demonstrative that a reality corresponding to it does and must exist, and as this reality is found nowhere but in the will, there it must be found.[4]

H. P. Tappan, who later became the first Chancellor of the University of Michigan, was so engrossed in the subject of the will that he authored three volumes on it. The first was a review of Edwards' thesis on freedom and necessity, the second is called *The Doctrine of the Will Determined by an Appeal of Consciousness*, and the third is an application of his principles to morals and religion. It is the second of the

[4] A. Mahan: *Doctrine of the Will*, 1846, pp. 50-52.

series which is the most psychological; and furthermore, it is one of the earliest books on psychology containing a chapter on personality. Tappan makes freedom of the will out to be the basis of personality for,

> Personality cannot be conceived of without freedom. When it is affirmed I *do,* the I is truly and properly the in its doing, if its *nisus* be not regarded as really its own determination of another, then it is no more I that *do*—it is no more I that make the *nisus,* it must be referred to some other cause.

> This appears still farther in the use of the personal possessive pronouns. We will take for example the pronoun *mine*. This implies two objects, and the idea of possession. It implies the I, and something which is not me, and the fact that this something belongs to me. But to what do we apply the pronoun *mine*, and on what is possession based? . . . What I cannot govern, regulate, direct, compel, resist, modify or appropriate by will, cannot be mine, but must be *his* or *theirs* who do stand to it in this relation. Lands, houses, and chattels are *mine,* because I have appropriated them by my will, or because I regulate and control them by my will.

> My friends are *mine,* because I can influence them, and bind them to my interests. My enemies are *mine,* either because I have made them such, or because I am engaged in acts of resistance and endeavors to make them yield to my purpose.[5]

Just as Mahan intimated, Tappan, too, finds the laws of reason necessary and immutable, *i.e.,* the laws of logic are universal; and affection too has its own laws, which operate similarly in all, but with the will, Tappan maintains it is different.

> To the will it is all different. Here is a power which, while the whole field of its possible determination is contemplated, retains its absolute contingency and freedom. There are for it no uniform and general laws necessarily governing its determinations, for it governs itself and can violate all law. From the reason it is easy to decide how the will *ought* to act; and for the sensitivity how it would be *most pleasing*

---

[5] H. P. Tappan: *The Doctrine of the Will Determined by an Appeal to Consciousness,* 1840, p. 175.

to act, but it is under no compulsion from one or the other; whatever it does, it does from its own inherent force, in entire freedom. Every volition is its own immediate creation.[6]

Intention, Motive, and Desire

A notable contribution to volition is D. D. Whedon's *Freedom of the Will* (1864) a well-written and closely reasoned work of 438 pages. Although Whedon had the same letters after his surname as before it, the theological argument is reserved for the second part, but even this portion of the book is not without its interest. His definition of the will as "the power of the soul by which it is the conscious author of an intentional act" is simplified into the proposition that volition is "that act of the mind which it performs with intention." To what extent he takes sides in the controversy may be readily inferred from the following passage:

> Every free agent is thus an original creator even out of nothing. But for him and such as he, there would be no guilt in the world. And just so far as the volition is the *necessitated* result, however intrinsically evil, of anterior or surrounding circumstances, just so far the individual stands morally excused.
>
> A moral and responsible volitional act can be performed only by an existent free volitional agent; and once done, by the very necessity of existence, it can never become *not done*.[7]

He takes issue with Locke, Mackintosh and Upham, and one might add here Spinoza, in denying that an emotion (desire, uneasiness, want) must always precede the emotion. He, on the contrary, believes that something may be chosen because it is reasonable, and that is an adequate enough motive.

It is his opinion that there is "volition for every turn of the pen in every letter, so that the pulsations of Will, like the pulsations of sound, fuse into a flow," which according to him, would mean that every stroke of the pen, if the affective theory of Edwards were correct, would be preceded by some

---

[6] H. P. Tappan: *Loc. cit.*, p. 179.
[7] D. D. Whedon: *Freedom of the Will*, 1864, pp. 42-43.

emotion. If will follows only an emotional state, then should not the most emotional be the most determined willers? He rather takes it for granted that, on the contrary, those of unflinching determination are, as a rule, the least emotional.

Whedon, unlike others, does not separate volition, cognition and affection into three separate faculties, but views them as expressions of the whole mind under special circumstances, so that volition is intelligent, and intelligence is volitional. It is, however, in the chapter on uniformities of volition that Whedon appears as a psycho-sociological thinker, first by his definitions of "corporeal," "form," "disposition," "stand-ard-purpose," and "habit"; and then by his consideration of character-formation. "A man can neither be nor do contradic-tory things at the same moment." A sage cannot play the buffoon, because, as Pére Buffier had observed long since, by the very act, he is no sage. "When a volition comes un-expected and *out of character*, we accept it, correct our previous estimate of the man, and add the new fact into the sum-total of which his *visible* character is made" (p. 174).

Determinism has always boasted of an ally in the form of statistics. So often have we heard about the number of crimes in a large city remaining uniform, the number of letters mailed or sent to the dead letter office being proportionally the same, all purporting to prove that necessity, and not a free will, governs our actions. On this argument, Whedon has the following comment:

> But while such statistics show that freedom often operates in the aggregate very much by rule, we are confident there are others which are, or might be kept, which exhibit freedom in its full variations. Accurate Church registers, kept by permanent pastors, show very different numbers of conversions per year. Some seasons surely are remark-able for a much greater religious interest than others. The number of public prayer-meetings in New York City has greatly differed in different years. Other seasons are specially marked by an extraordinary number of burkings or garrotings. Particular periods occur of specially numer-ous suicides, or fires, or steamboat or railroad accidents. If uniformities, thus, prove necessity, these irregularities must equally demonstrate freedom. From all this we con-clude that while it is not to be unexpected that freedom should result in great aggregate uniformities, there are

ample enough varieties to vindicate the will from the imputation of necessity.[8]

Wants, Intelligence and Freedom

R. G. Hazard, although an industrialist who steeped himself in philosophy, did not differ far from Whedon. As a man of affairs, traveling much, he might have been expected to benefit by his broadened experience. Much of what he writes reveals a theological background, but he is somewhat more businesslike in his layout, covering more territory than the clergy writers. He, too, like Whedon, is an opponent of Edwards' doctrine, and furthermore holds that there is no separate will apart from the mind which both thinks and wills. Will is simply the power of the mind for effort. The mind is thus active in one way to attain knowledge, and in another to influence the course of events.

Hazard's *Freedom of Mind in Willing* (1864) is really a system rather than a treatise, in which various psychological topics are discussed in relation to the will: intelligence, want, effort, instinct and habit, freedom, and causation are all explained so as to lead up to his final conclusion that we are as individuals free to act, and that, as a matter of fact, only intelligent beings can be free, God being the cause of all freedom. The second part of the long title of the book mentioned above—*Or every Being that Wills a Creative First Cause* indicates the trend of his argument, *viz.*, that every time we will to do something, we are creating the act. There has been no cause prior to that. Responsibility is attached to an individual only because he errs by knowingly willing what is wrong, and this act emanates from him as a free agent, *i.e.*, had no other cause.

Hazard develops an interesting scheme of wants: primary, referring to goals, and secondary, such as means; physical, aesthetic, moral, and religious types; but these wants are not essential in the direction of the effort. Knowledge alone is the test. Thus we see that he is at the opposite pole to Edwards for whom the desire invariably moves to action. That the want precedes the volition is conceded by Hazard, but it is the knowledge of the act as right or wrong which renders it an act of choice. Otherwise it might be mere animal instinct. Even instinctive action may still be said to involve a free

[8] D. D. Whedon: *Loc. cit.*, pp. 176-177.

effort of the intelligence, although "it precludes the exercise of the rational faculties in devising the mode of effort, or in selecting from different modes already devised by itself or by others." Yet Hazard believes that even such action is free, because the effort is not forced, but rather in such cases, the individual is not restrained from making it (p. 103).

A Question of Semantics?

It would be quite unnecessary to cite other books and authors who have participated in this centuries-old dispute, which, in reality, began in the Middle Ages; and which although it has been flagging of late, has not entirely come to a close. There seem to have been four types of protagonists in this issue: (1) the determinists, like Spinoza, the British evolutionists, Spencer, Huxley, *e.g.* (2) the predeterminists and fatalists (Jonathan Edwards, all Calvinists, mystics in general, Muslims) (3) libertarians (most of the religious class who are neither Calvinistic nor Pauline in their theology) (4) the self-determinists, who meet on common ground with the pure determinists for the purpose of surmounting the difficulty of bridging the gap between the principle of causation and the attachment of responsibility to an agent who is not free to act. In a small obscure collection of verse entitled *Destiny and Desire* (1908), Maryland Watson brings the inconsistency home when she plaintively sings:

> If, as they say, You hold the world
> In the hollow of Your mighty hand,
> And each life that gleams there for a while
> Was fashioned and fated at Your own command.
>
> Then do I come to You—not in prayer
> But only as a weary woman may,
> And this question I fling up to you,
> Why did You put my soul upon this path
> If it was fate that I should lose my way?
>
> How could You never lift a staying hand
> Or still the lilt of my heart's glad song;
> If You placed this passion in my storm-swept soul
> Then, God, why not help me bear the wrong?[9]

[9] Maryland Watson: *Destiny and Desire*, p. 25.

It may seriously be asked whether anything is gained psychologically from the drawn-out discussions on the will. Are they more than a series of metaphysical lucubrations, serving possibly as a fine exercise in mental training? To be sure, it may be replied, there are no experimental results which can be brought to bear upon the problem, but a clarification of the concept employed has been of advantage, no doubt, and even the semantic phase, the meaning of motive, in particular, has been of assistance to the psychologist, as well as to the ethicist and jurist. And if no experimental data have been available and may not be, because of the nature of the subject, many illustrations from everyday life have been introduced to point up and bolster the conclusions on each side. Whatever we think of the proposition, it certainly is provocative to hear that it is only through the experience of willing that we have any notion of causality; in other words, that far from the principle of causation being an intuition derived from associating one event with another, it is really discovered in our actions first, and thence transferred to the external world.

A Transcendental Attempt

Our authors of a century ago did not bother much with German philosophy or psychology. As a rule, they were dominated by either the Scotch or the English school (including Hume). The most important treatise on the will of the nineteenth century came out in 1899, the work of Denton J. Snider, a vigorous and well-rounded thinker who has been all but neglected in the history of both philosophy and psychology in the United States. Snider was the chief emissary of the St. Louis Movement in Philosophy, lecturing in various cities and writing on a variety of subjects, philosophical, psychological and literary, but because of his erratic personality, he appears to have been more or less isolated from the Group in general.

Snider, one might say, is Fichtean in content but Hegelian in form. He takes for his text Fichte's assertion that "Only in so far as I find myself willing do I find *myself*, and in so far as I find myself I necessarily find myself willing." In a sense, this is the counterpart of Descarte's *cogito ergo sum*; only in Fichte's system, it would be changed to *volo ergo sum*. This dictum may sound anachronistic, yet it is at the root of all conative and especially hormic psychologies today. Albert Schweitzer, our most illustrious paragon of self-determination, has also made the will the foundation of his philosophy when he sets down the primary concept as "I am life that wills-to-live in the midst of life that-wills-to-live!"[10] A psychology based on reflexes alone will find the will a more obtrusive fact than is taken for granted, and finally must resort to qualifiers which cannot but countermand the initial order.

Reverting to Snider, the Hegelian turn in his psychology is manifest in his belief that volition and cognition both evolve from the first act of consciousness, the very separation being a volitional process. The stages in the evolution of the will are (a) the undetermined, (b) the determined, and (c) the self-determined will. From another angle, these three stages may be viewed as (a) the universal will, which is abstract and undetermined, (b) the particular, or special, and therefore determined, while (c) the individual will is the universal will becoming concrete or self-determined. In this movement, there is the expression "I am determined to be self-determined." The whole conception has originated with Hegel (*Philosophie des Rechts*).

[10] A. Schweitzer: *Out of My Life and Thought* (Eng. transl.), Epilogue.

PART II

PSYCHOLOGY COMES OF AGE

Chapter 11

The New Psychology

ONLY HISTORICAL EVENTS can be said to have taken place on such and such a day in such and such a year; and even these definite dates tell us little of the brewing process. We say the revolution broke out on that particular night, when someone fired the fatal shot, but the shot was only incidental. How much more difficult is it to establish even the year when a science discloses an altogether fresh angle. Was it Max Planck's publication of his quantum study which ushered in the era of relativity, or should we begin with Albert Einstein's promulgation of his famous theory in that out-of-the-way physics periodical? Similarly may we ask: When did atomic fission come into being? Ernest Rutherford is credited with this exploit, but did not J. J. Thomson have a mighty hand in it?

The history of psychology has nothing so spectacular to offer. No doubt many partisans will start the science with their favorite "ism" and its supposed originator, but such blind votaries are not to be our guide. We can say with certainty that somewhere between 1885 and 1890, American psychology had definitely turned a corner. The turning may have commenced even before then, perhaps as early as 1876, but the uphill pull first had met with some obstacles. The view was still obstructed, and the trail had to be blazed; and it was necessary for more than one to follow in the narrow path before the evidence could be confirmed.

"The New Psychology" is a phrase which has been employed on more than one occasion, in the brief history of our subject. Every time a devotee wished to promote a particular school, he would identify it with the whole of psychology, to the utter disregard of all other points of view, systems, and trends. Thus, in its day, functionalism was dubbed the New Psychology, and behaviorism certainly assumed this distinction. *Gestalt* psychology was not quite so bold, but psychoanalysis made a special bid for this honor; and Tansley was not the only one to call his book *The New Psychology*, and do nothing but expound psychoanalysis, as if everything psychological, prior to Freud, were outmoded.

Possibly the phrase found early currency in France and Germany, but it may have been John Dewey who applied it first, as a youth of 24 or 25, in the article in the *Andover Review*, abstracted in chapter nine. In 1897, E. W. Scripture became the exponent of this new psychology, and in later editions, his book still appears under the title of *The New Psychology*. Both Dewey and Scripture were intent on stressing the departure from the armchair practice of analyzing one's thoughts and feelings, and embarking instead on the experimental method. This was surrounded with other circumstances, which helped to make the break definite and final, and which may be listed as the criteria of the "new psychology."

Some will be disposed to reckon the new era in psychology from the publication date of Ladd's *Elements of Physiological Psychology*, in 1887; others will see in James's *Principles* the guiding star, but these books are only incidental to the general movement which had been initiated in France, Germany, and England, sweeping into America largely through the students who had gone abroad for research. It behooves us, then, to examine the general nature of this fresh gust, which was to make out of psychology a science and not a mere adjunct of philosophy.

Earmarks of Scientific Psychology

In the first place, it is this very separation, which did not become complete—perhaps altogether too much so for its own good—until a quarter of a century later that constituted the new direction. Psychology was no longer to be considered a mere stepping stone to logic, metaphysics, ethics, or theology, but as an end in itself. It now ranged itself with biology or chemistry, and once it threw off the yoke of philosophy, it also discontinued the use of the specifically metaphysical terms, which were generally fraught with a religious connotation. The term "soul" was its first and most important casualty. To employ this word in a psychological textbook, after 1890, signified either being behind the times or adhering to the neoscholastic, *i.e.*, Thomistic, dogma. In the latter case, allowance must naturally be made for the Catholic creed, which dominates all activities in that Church, whereas Protestantism makes provision for scientific pursuit as distinct from religious faith. That many protestants might be tempted to make a special plea for the soul in their works goes without saying. William McDougall is a shining example of this tendency. It is true, nevertheless, that at least no manifest postulate of a mysterious soul greets us now as in days of yore. Like religion, in general, it is a private matter, not to be taken for granted as the fundamental principle of all psychology.

Alliance with Physiology

The weaning away of psychology from philosophy was not wholly achieved without the formation of a new attachment. It would have been another decade before it might be complete master of its domain, and Sigmund Freud was to be the architect of this self-contained structure. For the present, physiology, or neurology, in a stricter sense, was to be the older sister, guiding its fortune. Not only sense perception, but imagination, memory, feeling, emotion, and the higher thought processes, needed a neural basis in order to be integrated; otherwise they could be described only as momentary and nonce phenomena. The next image, memory, or emotion, no matter how similar to the first, is not identical with it. The neural linking bestows on each mental phenomenon a certain permanence so that we might know what to expect from such and such conditions. Psychological laws may be derived or recognized without reference to their physiological counterparts, e.g., after-images and association, but there can be no denying that understanding the neural mechanism affords an insight not to be gained by the observation of the mental processes alone. To be sure, the founding fathers of the new psychology were perhaps too physiologically-minded, but that is to be expected under the circumstances.

Specialization

An important outcome of the break between the old and the new discipline was the special training in psychology which was a requisite, after the '90's. Prior to James and Hall, it was customary for the professor of philosophy to teach psychology, *ex officio*; and the professor of philosophy was usually a clergyman, whose influence as a preacher or as an administrator surrounded him with a philosophical aura as well. It is one of the curiosities of psychology that half of the early writers were college presidents or principals. There were some sixty odd more or less productive psychologists in the

United States during the period between Jonathan Edwards and James McCosh. More than thirty of them were administrators. This in itself is worthy of an investigation; for the proportion is much higher than with any other discipline. Even in our own generation, psychologists yielded a high percentage of college presidents, although not nearly to the same extent as in the past with Edwards of Yale, Johnson at King's (Columbia), Witherspoon, Smith, and McCosh, at Princeton, and Porter at Yale, not to mention the score or more at the lesser colleges. One reason was, of course, that energetic and intellectual clergymen were influential. Their objective in education was philosophy. As philosophers they could not bypass psychology. In fact, they felt more confident in the realm where they could introspect and find justification for their own tenets.

With the shift from philosophy to physiology, and from uncontrolled self-analysis to controlled experimentation, as well as emphasis on problems which could be worked out in the laboratory and that had received scant, if any, consideration previously, special training became a *conditio sine qua non* for anyone teaching psychology in a first-class institution. The first laboratory psychologists had not been allowed to neglect the philosophical pastures. Their instructors were themselves philosophers; and philosophy was still the sea into which all the scientific waters would eventually seek an outlet. In the 17th and 18th centuries, professors might be called upon to teach several different subjects as distant from one another, as Hebrew or Arabic and botany or psychology. In the 19th century, the professor's bailiwick might be logic, ethics, metaphysics, theology, and psychology, in addition to administrative duties as in the case of the college president, and occasional preaching. That James McCosh could, in spite of all his tasks, turn out so many books is a tribute to his physical and mental constitution, but it is evident that his works would have been better, if he had restricted his activities.

It was Goethe who puts into the mouth of one of his characters the utterance "*In der Beschränkung zeigt sich erst der Meister*"—(It is in his limitation that the master is revealed). Goethe, himself, apparently was the type of genius that eluded the force of the epigram, which applies to nearly all. It stands to reason that in our age of "knowing more and more about less and less," we can contribute at least something to a scientific field, whereas knowing less and less about more and more can at most add to our own enjoyment and appreciation of the world. A middle course, as in everything else, is desirable here too, especially as one's own field, say, psychology, grows so enormously that specialization becomes tantamount to examining a pinpoint.

Organization

A consequence of specialization is organization of forces. With the exception of the St. Louis group, headed by W. T. Harris and H. C. Brokmeyer, there had been no society of philosophers, let alone psychologists, in the United States. The St. Louis Philosophical Society, founded by Harris in 1866, was more of a coterie, which had set up Hegel as the figurehead of a cult; and the periodical, edited by Harris between the years 1867 and 1897, by its very title, *The Journal of Speculative Philosophy*, betrayed its special bias. Moreover, the St. Louis Movement was largely an instrument of local percussion, even if some of the lecturers made tours outside the state of Missouri. It was more like the Chautauqua Movement than the American Philosophical Association, even in its infancy. The colleges apparently paid no attention to the small band of zealous inquirers. The society, as well as the Journal, was a monument to Harris, but in the course of American philosophy, it was only an episode.

The academic philosophers, who, as we have seen, were principally recruited from the divinity schools had their church affiliations and councils to consider. It has taken some time for the philosophers to see the purpose of getting together in behalf of a common cause; and since the professors of philosophy also taught psychology, it would have been unlikely for them to make this study the basis for professional organization. The group of young men, however, who had received a special training either in Germany or in France, or even in the United States, were united by the same goals and aspirations, as well as by their critical attitude toward the theologian-metaphysician who passed for a psychologist, and, sooner or later, they felt the need of signalizing their separateness.

The secession from "intellectual philosophy" was marked first by the founding of the *American Journal of Psychology*, in 1887, by Stanley Hall, of whom much more will be said in another chapter, while five years later, came the organization of a small band of psychologists, most of them men of a high order and soon to become famous, into the American Psychological Association. We shall have occasion to note that the year 1892 was the landmark in American psychology, for other reasons too, although a real opportunity for psychology to parade its "new look" came the next year, when the Chicago World's Fair (1893) permitted its promoters to exhibit its wares.

Even during the period of Burton, Upham, and Mahan, when textbooks began to be referred to and reviewed extensively, there was no consciousness of a psychological representation. The works were so many *disjecta membra*. Productivity was an individual matter. No science can thrive unless it is reared in a social atmosphere. The promotion and expansion of any science requires a certain *esprit de corps*, and that emerged only with the organization of the experimentalists and the launching of journals.

Diffusion

The spread of the new psychology was not too rapid, on the whole. In the large universities, however, the older teachings were superseded by courses based on experiments; and psychology was given an independent status on the curriculum. Sometimes conflicts would arise, the old not willing to give up the ghost, but as in all such friction between the generations, youth wins. In a number of cases, the old-guard teachers were ready to make concessions. They tried to familiarize themselves with laboratory methods and results, although not at first-hand, but it would not be long before they just had to yield to a psychologist, and occasionally would enlist the services of a laboratory man, in accordance with the *Zeitgeist*. This bloodless revolution must have had its pathetic, if not tragic, side as when old McCosh, in his bastion of Scottish realism, saw the founding of the Princeton Psychological Laboratory by his most brilliant student, J. Mark Baldwin, but every transition is an ordeal, and growing pains are to be expected in the process of development. Probably each of the larger universities has its story in this connection. The supplanting machinery worked more smoothly in some places than in others, where there was a deep-rooted prejudice against the fresh winds of experimental research, and forces from different faculties clashed before hopeful results could be brought about.

Productivity

Another sequel of the new psychology consisted in the vast avenues that were being opened up for productive research. Instead of the perennial issues of cerebralism, substantiality of the soul, epiphenomenalism, or freedom of the will, which would be argued back and forth with the most futile results, it was now possible for every student to make a definite contribution to the sum of empirical knowledge. Even without the aid of electrical apparatus, chronoscope, kymograph or tachistoscope, one could still acquire data, using only pencil and paper, and a number of observers. The possibilities were unlimited. At every step there was a problem to be solved. True, as time went on, it was evident that many of the investigations were inconsequential; and in many more instances, the methods employed were questionable, or the conclusions were unconvincing, yet the output of even the first few years of experimentation was impressive, and in comparing the scope of psychology with that of physics and chemistry, we might find a favorable balance in the former.

Permanence

What is more, the new psychology had come to stay. It did not consist of a set of new-fangled propositions which would soon outlive their usefulness. Nor was it like a new school, soon to be supplanted by a still newer school. Experimental psychology would be the touchstone of any system propounded by new claimants. Interests may change and techniques may differ, but the experimental method will always reign supreme. Since its inception in the laboratory, it has only grown in importance and extent of application.

To sum up: the new psychology stood for the introduction of experimental methods into the teaching of psychology, which necessitated the founding of laboratories. It further required the removal of religious dogmas from textbook definitions and formulations. It resulted in the specialization of teachers in psychology as distinct from philosophy, and the restriction of theologically-trained and metaphysically-minded instructors to their respective fields. It also, as a matter of course, led to the organization of those engaged in either teaching or research in psychology, and the founding of periodicals, as an outlet for reports of investigations and discussions affecting the science.

Chapter 12

The Psychological Laboratory Comes to America

THE HALLMARK of the new psychology was the creation of the psychological laboratory, and a significant pun may be attached to this; for G. Stanley Hall, who launched the first psychological periodical in this country also started, as he claimed, the first laboratory of experimental psychology in the United States, in 1881, only two years after Wilhelm Wundt founded what was officially accepted as the world's first psychological laboratory, in Leipzig.

A Moot Point

The priority of both Wundt and Hall has been contested by William James and, as in numerous other instances, in the history of science and technology, it is difficult to come to a definite conclusion as to which was actually the first, until we have satisfied ourselves as to what constitutes a psychological laboratory *i.e.*, what is the minimum amount of material and apparatus, and in what respect should it differ from a physiological or anatomical laboratory, in order to come under consideration in our universe of discourse.

William James contended that he had begun instruction in experimental psychology at Harvard either in 1874-5 or 1876, which means at least five years before Stanley Hall opened up his laboratory at Johns Hopkins. We do know of an appropriation James had received "for use in physiology," according to the Harvard treasurer's report for that year, but Stanley Hall described this laboratory of James as a "tiny room under the stairway of Agassiz Museum . . . with a metronome, a device for whirling a frog, a horopter chart, and one or two bits of apparatus."

What Is a Psychological Laboratory?

If this can be called a laboratory, then, of course, it is true that James's was the first psychological laboratory not only in the western hemisphere, but in the world. It can be maintained that it is not the quantity of apparatus which makes the laboratory, but the actual experimentation, and if the vestibular sense of frogs was investigated by means of the "device for whirling a frog," as Hall puts it, and the report even published in the *American Journal of Otology*, then the laboratory was an established fact despite Hall's belittlement. After all, "where the king is, there is the court," as an old English proverb has it.

On the other hand, such questions are only of academic interest, and since this is an academic sphere we are moving in, the whole controversy is even beyond the academic. Even if we accept the Leipzig laboratory as the first psychological workroom to have functioned in the world, which is, at any rate, the official record, is it not true that Fechner must have had a sort of home-made laboratory, in which he nevertheless conducted some interesting experiments, and Helmholtz contributed not a little to our knowledge of sensations? He must have constructed psychological apparatus for the purpose; and what is a laboratory but a collection of apparatus in use?

The physiologist, K. Vierordt, together with his students, carried on much research which would come under the head of experimental psychology today, although with a behavioristic bias; and scanning the titles of the articles in Pflüger's *Archiv für die gesamte Physiologie* of nearly a century ago, we might see something about many of them which bear more than a semblance to our own. The psychological laboratory was only the offspring of the physical, chemical and physiological laboratories, asserting its majority and stressing its own interest.

It may seem curious, but it is nevertheless true that as early as 1877, *i.e.*, before the Leipzig installations, "Dr. Venn and Dr. James Ward urged the need for founding a laboratory of psychophysics at Cambridge. But they fell foul of certain theologically minded mathematicians who were horrified that anybody should even think of measuring the human soul, and nothing was done."[1] Had Venn and Ward been more influential, then the credit for the first psychological laboratory would have accrued to Cambridge and not to Leipzig.

[1] F. C. Bartlett, in *A History of Psychology in Autobiography*, vol. III p. 40. About 40 years later, Bartlett, who had become professor at Cambridge, in a subject which was always regarded with doubtful eyes in England, so much so that professorships in it were restricted to the "radical" University of London, was

On the one hand, then, psychology was emancipated from the grip of metaphysics; on the other, it cut loose from the umbilical cord of physiology. The philosopher who could have picked up his knowledge from books was no longer in any position to instruct a class in the new psychology. It would require some training in the laboratory to speak intelligently on the methods and results of the experiments. It meant that some of the instructors would have to be selected from abroad, until at least the new laboratories in the United States had trained a sufficient number of young research men.

First Professorships in Psychology

In 1887, the University of Pennsylvania (Philadelphia again records a first) established a lectureship, and, in 1888, a professorship in psychology, with J. McKeen Cattell as its first incumbent. Cattell implies that a laboratory was functioning in connection with the courses for undergraduates, but that no research was undertaken as was the case at Johns Hopkins.

The University of Wisconsin was the second in the country to treat psychology as an independent department, but that was on the bold initiative of 25-year-old Joseph Jastrow, who had received the world's first Ph.D. in psychology, in 1886, after graduate study at Johns Hopkins, but could find no post open to him. If being a mere psychologist was a poor recommendation for an instructorship in the average college, where psychology was still under the tutelage of philosophy, and the head of which was likely to be a former cleric, Jastrow's Jewish affiliation would make it doubly difficult for him to obtain a position.

Finally, almost in desperation, Jastrow drew up a list of attractive topics, and sent it around, together with testimonials, to the administration of a selected group of higher institutions, including the University of Wisconsin. In 1888, President T. D. Chamberlain accepted Jastrow's proposal, and appointed him lecturer, and, in the fall of that year, asked him to assume professorial duties. Immediately, Jastrow laid

---

knighted, and became the first titled psychologist in the world (Sir John Adams and Sir Cyril Burt received their titles as educationists), although it must be reckoned that his war service was largely instrumental in the decoration. Perhaps just as unexpected, considering Oxford's attitude toward psychology, was the award of an honorary doctorate to him in 1962.

plans for organizing a laboratory at the University of Wisconsin.[2]

The University of Indiana came next in this progressive series, and W. L. Bryan, who started as an instructor in Greek, and subsequently presided over the fortune of Indiana's State University, inaugurated the new psychology department about this time. At the University of Iowa, G. T. W. Patrick set up a psychological laboratory as early as 1887.

It was during 1890-91 that J. Mark Baldwin established the first psychological laboratory in the British Empire, at the University of Toronto.[3]

Laboratories Spring Up in Rapid Succession

The laboratory which Stanley Hall founded at Johns Hopkins in 1881 was probably an improvement on the pocket-size one started by James in 1875 or 1876, but it was not intended for undergraduate students. Johns Hopkins was the institute for advanced study of the '80's and '90's, and Hall catered to graduate students.

In 1891, however, William James was ready to turn his obscure semi-physiological laboratory into a genuine psychological unit. He was moving up or away from physiology, and his outlook had broadened to such an extent that he felt himself cramped not only in his physiological confines; but even as an experimental psychologist, he was hardly in his element. It was then that he sought out the 28-year-old Hugo Münsterberg, whose daring polemic with the redoubtable Wundt had caught James's fancy, and by 1892, Münsterberg became the *chargé d' affaires* at Dane Hall, which then housed the psychological laboratory. The stalky and energetic young man at once began to purchase and devise new apparatus, especially of the massive type; for the desire to impress was one of the traits of this dazzling psychologist, and from then on, the Harvard psychology department grew to enviable heights.

The Fateful Year—1892

The year 1892 was a year of destiny for psychology in other ways. It seemed as if it then began to blossom in several other institutions. The most important events were the impor-

[2] J. Jastrow in *A History of Psychology in Autobiography*, vol. I, p. 140.

[3] J. McKeen Cattell: "Psychology in America" in *Ninth International Congress of Psychology* (Proceedings), 1929, p. 16.

tation from abroad of Hugo Münsterberg to Harvard, and of Edward Bradford Titchener to Cornell, two young men who were to be influential factors in the development of American psychology. Since much more will be said about them in its proper place, we may proceed to enumerate some of the other achievements for this particular period, which included the establishment of a psychological laboratory at Columbia University, a few months earlier (1891), by J. McKeen Cattell, who, as we shall recall, had been the initiator of the University of Pennsylvania Laboratory.

It was in 1892 that E. W. Scripture organized the Yale psychological laboratory, and in 1893, J. Mark Baldwin, coming from the University of Toronto, began a new laboratory at Princeton University, which he afterwards turned over to his assistant, H. C. Warren.

We thus see that almost as if by a concerted effort, the laboratory was set in as a wedge in the philosophy departments, and in addition to Harvard, Columbia, Yale, and Princeton, there were state universities and even smaller colleges, like Brown, that conspired to make out of psychology a purely experimental science. It was during this year, 1892, that the Second International Congress of Psychology took place in London, which was about the first time that American psychologists had been able to make a showing. Furthermore, the psychologists in the United States were becoming excited over the impending World's Fair at Chicago, which took place in 1893. It was the first opportunity for psychology to make its debut before the public, and both Jastrow and Münsterberg worked feverishly to impress the throngs with the experimental potentialities of the new science. In addition to the exhibit of apparatus, with labels descriptive of their purpose, there was a testing laboratory for such individuals as were curious to know something about their mental capacities and would pay the nominal fee required. Jastrow rigged up the apparatus and Münsterberg wrote up the propaganda booklet—a good team, which, however, did not find favor with men like James, who spoke of the exploit as "Münsterberg's circus."

Nor is it fortuitous that the American Psychological Association was organized in 1892. Apparently that was the year when psychology had become ripe, when twenty-six men gathered at Clark University, at the invitation of Stanley Hall, to discuss mainly problems which had not occurred to the philosophers. Not all of the twenty-six, augmented to thirty-one at the preliminary meeting, had thrown their lot in exclusively with experimental psychology. Philosophy still exercised a hold on the majority, but they were all committed to a certain policy in regard to the teaching of psychology, and with few exceptions, they were familiar with laboratory methods at first-hand.

Although the score of laboratories which had sprung up in the early nineties was astir with enthusiastic students, confident that they were about to make some fresh discovery, bring to light some entirely unknown facts, true for all time, or even formulate some new law, two laboratories had won special distinction; Harvard because of James and Münsterberg, and Cornell because of Titchener. Clark University with one laboratory conducted by Hall for advanced research and the college laboratory, of which Edmund C. Sanford was in charge, ran third in the contest. The problems that engaged Hall's interest were regarded as on the fringe, and the standards were thought to be less rigid than in the other two laboratories, but, in a real sense, Hall was a trailblazer.

In a private communication to the author, Professor Boring has made a welcome contribution to the subject.

Hall had the laboratory at Hopkins. Then Clark started Clark University for him in 1889, and he seems to have had the laboratory at first. Then he turned it over to Sanford in 1892, and had no laboratory himself. Clark grew to hate Hall and died, founding, with his estate, Clark College. The will states that Hall (named) shall never hold a position in the College. The College began in 1902, and I think that Carroll D. Wright was its first president.

In 1909 Wright died and Sanford was made president of the College. Baird came from Illinois to take over the University laboratory from Sanford. There was also a separate College lab., which presently fell to Porter. Baird died in 1917. I succeeded him in 1919. Hall resigned in 1920. The University and College were at last combined. Sanford became a professor again, and Atwood was president. . . . But Hall in his famous seminary had a kind of laboratory. There enthusiasm was rife, and he sent his men to work hard on this topic and that. The papers were then worked up for publication, at first in the *Am. Journal of Psychology*, later in the *Pedagogical Seminary*, whence its name. . . . In his will, Hall identified himself with genetic psychology, but in talk he sometimes spoke of his being a "synthetic psychologist," and he once told my wife he hoped I could succeed him as a "synthetic psychologist."

Laboratory Atmosphere

It did not take long before there developed a certain local patriotism, and even professional jealousy between laboratory heads. Although Hall, Münsterberg, Titchener, Cattell, and Scripture had all been students under Wundt, at Leipzig, at one time or another, it became evident that their personal equation sometimes outweighed their common training. Perhaps their ethnic X had also something to do with it. There was nothing specifically American about this laboratory atmosphere. Germany had its fill of it. The recriminations of Wundt and Stumpf and G. E. Müller, the disagreements between the Leipzig and the Würzburg schools are too well known and need no documentation.

Outside of attaching different interpretations to phenomena observed, like nativism and empiricism (geneticism) in space and time perception, or the perception of melody, there was no cause for any special conflicts. The ramification into schools, so diversified as sometimes to utterly disregard each other's results, had not begun until the following decade. In principle, Münsterberg and Titchener saw eye to eye, but they seemed to be at odds in regard to the methods employed and conclusions arrived at, as well as the philosophical implications, which were strong in Münsterberg; and the phrase "laboratory atmosphere" was wont to be bandied about quite frequently by students. I believe it was Titchener who gave it currency, at least in America.

The mutual criticism which developed, in consequence, was not really detrimental to the development of the new science, for it tended to make researchers more painstaking and circumspect; and since introspection was virtually the sole method pursued in these two laboratories, it required some fillip to keep the overzealous students from straying or overlooking the misses while attention was focused on the looked-for result, perhaps suggested by the director's general point of view or some special theory, if not by an actual hint, inadvertently dropped.

Graduates of these two laboratories "inherited" the atmosphere, so that when they began to direct research they would naturally fall into the same grooves, until new currents rendered them conscious of their master's limitations, or rather the limitations of the period. The *cave*, today, points in other directions; faulty technique, defective apparatus, or statistical errors.

Laboratory Manuals

A new type of textbook came into being as the result of the new trend, *viz.*, the laboratory manual. As early as 1891, Edmund C. Sanford, student, protégé, and, later, colleague of Stanley Hall at Clark University, where he subsequently was made President of the College, had begun to publish serially a *Course in Experimental Psychology*, which ran through volumes 4-7 (1891-96) of the *American Journal of Psychology*, and then appeared as an independent little volume. It was the first of its kind on this side of the Atlantic. C. S. Myers' two-volume *Text-Book of Experimental Psychology*, which was the British analogue, although more elaborate than Sanford's, was not put out until 1909, and was used probably more in the United States and Canada, than in England.

Of E. B. Titchener's magisterial *Experimental Psychology*, published in four volumes, the *Qualitative Manual*, in two volumes (for instructor and student) was brought out in 1901,[4] while the *Quantitative Manual*, also in two volumes, appeared in 1905. There is nothing comparable to this monument of precise planning and careful guidance in the whole field—a veritable Baedeker of the then unexplored territory of *psychologia experimentalis*. The author takes both instructor and student by the hand, although at different times, and points out the snags and pitfalls to be avoided, suggesting more viable routes and means of protection.

The Schools and the Laboratories

The complexity of the psychological laboratory today is perhaps one of its chief features. Certainly there can be no dearth of problems to investigate. Technological expansion

[4] In 1902, there was published Lightner Witmer's *Analytical Psychology*, which was a practical manual, with fifty experiments outlined step by step, and containing excellent charts and illustrations to stimulate the student.

has simplified the work and reduced the number of stumbling blocks for the investigator, but the particular slant of the researcher or director might affect the set-up of the experimenter. The behaviorist will attack a problem with a different technique from that of the gestaltist or the topologist; and occasionally, the different schools, psychologically, will talk different languages.

One great asset of the laboratory, however, compensates for the diversity of experimental approaches, and that is the possible verification or invalidation of the results by repeating the series of experimental trials under controlled conditions. Such checkups have been numerous in the past quarter-century.

Chapter 13

Psychology at Harvard and William James

THE READER must have wondered by this time what had become of Harvard, so far as psychology was concerned, since the 18th century. It might have looked as if the character introduced into a novel with great *éclat*, and described for pages in considerable detail, had suddenly been allowed to take French leave, or perhaps in some mysterious way, had disappeared without causing a ripple. It is curious that while Columbia, Yale, and Princeton played a prominent part in the dissemination of psychological knowledge, and even such institutions as the University of Wisconsin, the University of Pennsylvania, Bowdoin, Oberlin, Amherst, Waterville (Colby), and a dozen more colleges and academies figured on the title pages of textbooks, the oldest, largest, and most famous university in the country, if not on the continent, was apparently non-articulate, and therefore, not productive in a department which should be close to our heart, if the phrase "know thyself" has any significant meaning.

Old Tradition Difficult to Uproot

We have seen that psychology had some place, true, subordinate only to logic, on the curriculum, in the very first years of Harvard's existence. Logic to this day, 1964, is an honored subject in the aulae of this great university. Perhaps the Oxford and Cambridge tradition, deriving from the mediaeval interest in Aristotle's achievement, was partly instrumental in the emphasis. At any rate, both Brattle and Hedge, in their respective logic compendia, devoted some space to the psychological basis of logic. At best, it was a mere show of hospitality or a gesture of charity. Levi Hedge, however, taught psychology, too, at the philosophical level, naturally, and used Thomas Brown's *Philosophy of the Mind*, which he abridged for the purpose, interpolating a good many critical notes as a text.

Hedge's successor, James Walker, like Hedge, was wholly

committed to the Scottish School, and during the three decades which he taught at Harvard, shifting from Stewart's *Elements of the Philosophy of the Mind* to Reid's *Essays on the Intellectual Powers of Man*, he busied himself largely with ethics and metaphysics, apparently on the ground that either psychology or "the philosophy of mind," as it was then called, was too plebeian a subject to spend one's talents on, or, perhaps, the Scottish philosophers had settled matters for all time; and the redaction of Reid's *Essays*, mentioned above, in abridged form, constituted the major portion of Walker's contribution to our embryonic science.

It is in the preface to this edition, which passed through several printings, that we are told of Harvard's attitude toward psychology, and while Walker, who, true to type, was also a doctor of divinity, and became president of the institution in due course, pays lip service to German and other continental developments, he was just as loyal to the Scottish School as his predecessors.

The psychology generally taught in England and in this country for the last fifty years has been that of the Scotch School of which Dr. Reid is the acknowledged head. The influence of the same doctrine is also apparent in the improved state of philosophy of the continental nations and particularly in France. Sir William Hamilton dedicates his annotated edition of Reid's Works to M. Cousin, the distinguished philosopher and statesman through whom Scotland has again been united intellectually to her old political ally, and the author's writing is the best result of Scotch speculation made the basis of academical instruction in philosophy throughout the central nations of Europe . . . The name of Reid therefore historically considered is second to none among the British psychologists and metaphysicians, with perhaps the single exception of Locke.

Enter William James

William James (1842-1910) is the name which symbolizes American psychology. Although he himself aspired to the championship in American philosophy (and in fact the night before he was to be awarded an honorary degree at Harvard, he showed signs of anxiety, his son, Henry, tells us, lest President Eliot would refer to him as a psychologist rather than as a philosopher), that claim has been contested, particularly of late. There can be no question, however, but that he was the foremost psychologist that America produced; and many are even prepared to rank him above Wundt.

What is there about this man who became the figurehead of his science, and not only towers above all the men who labored in this field before him, but is acknowledged to have had no peer in this country in his day or ever since? James himself presents a psychological riddle. Here is a man who did not receive the training prescribed for a psychologist. He had no connection with the philosophical department, where psychology was taught by the same men who lectured on philosophy. He had taken up art, and even spent some time sketching and painting. He then embarked on a technological career at the Lawrence Scientific School, which was cut short after a brief period there. He then enters the medical school, where he obtains his diploma, but does not practice. His earlier travels on the Agassiz expedition to Brazil had turned his attention, although not for long, to natural history. He becomes an instructor in anatomy and in physiology and, under the guise of natural history, makes his way into psychology, operating on the sly, so to speak; and while the official professor in the philosophical department ladles out portions of Cousin, Reid, and Stewart to the students in psychology, the pretender to the throne, in his museum nook, organizes a small band of youths, and drills them on Taine and Spencer, putting into their hands newly-forged weapons, in the shape of experimental research in psychology; and when the representative of the Scottish dynasty abdicates, *i.e.*, resigns, after a forty-year reign, the young assistant professor of physiology steps in and inaugurates a new dynasty, with an entirely different constitution.

Slow Development

His articles in the British quarterly, *Mind,* are scarcely noticed by his colleagues in America, and the administration at Harvard is slow to recognize his worth. He has been coaxed by a large publishing house to complete a textbook in psychology, incorporating his series of articles, but he delays and lingers over the task, until finally in 1890, the long expected *Principles of Psychology* comes off the press; and immediately the name, William James, becomes something to conjure with. Not all the reviewers are delighted with it. Criticism, of course, falls to its lot, too, but the fact that it is discussed by authorities in the most influential psychological, philosophical, and physiological periodicals is, in itself, a triumph; and whatever flaws are discovered in the two large volumes, aggregating some 1500 pages, the freshness of the point of view, the masterly treatment of the main issues, the authority manifest in the handling of scientific data, whether they belong to chemistry, physiology, or anatomy; and, lastly, the inimitable style must have struck the initiates as something of an entirely different order from what they had been accustomed to read.

This work has become the classic in psychology; and yet as a textbook it could hardly compare with Upham's in systematic arrangement and logical development of the subject. Even the abridgement *Psychology: A Briefer Course* did not answer the purpose; despite all that, year in and year out, this condensation was the psychological fare of thousands of students throughout America, for whom the chapters on the "self," "habit," "stream of consciousness," and "the will" offered some slight compensation for the tedious chapters on the nervous system and the abstruse problems taken up in the chapters on space and time perception. Furthermore, the inconsistency of the author in assuming a position and then shifting to its exact opposite, often in the same chapter, must have become apparent even to the bright beginner, let alone the more advanced student, while, to the instructor, it occasionally proved to be the source of mild embarrassment; for it is not easy to explain away contradictions in a textbook purporting to outline a fundamental science. True, the discrepancies did not lie in the facts as such, but in the philosophical aspects surrounding them. Students, however, are not so discerning as to make allowance for the distinction.

Secret of James's Prestige

To understand James's success, in spite of his deficiencies, it is necessary to know more about the personality of the man; for he may have been an outstanding philosopher and a great psychologist, but as a personality he was a genius, if the term can at all be applied in this connection. He was charged with magnetism and charm, and everything he wrote must have been pervaded by this vibrancy. The spontaneity of the man could not but leave its effect on the reader, and willy-nilly, he would be influenced favorably by the buoyant expressions, breathing faith and sincerity, but at the same time fraught with authority, attained through years of specialized reading and contact with the most celebrated scientists of the generation.

James's range or scope was not nearly so extensive as Wundt's, but there was greater sweep and penetration for specific sectors of knowledge, and, of course, a greater understanding of human nature from the inside, as immediacy and not merely as scientific constructs. Wundt would trudge on and on with blinders on his eyes, and would not budge to look around, lest he stray from the beaten path. James, on the other hand, would get into a trotting pace, ever on the alert for some casual event which, although it might slow him up a bit and even divert him, would nevertheless bear on the purpose of his journey. While Wundt would move in a rectilinear direction, and would turn at right angles only after a definite lap had been completed, James did not hesitate to roam about and even retrace his steps, or go back and forth, in order to make sure that he was not taking the wrong road after all.

William James was the Midas of mind. Everything he touched, or rather experienced, was turned into psychic gold. What the world would frown upon as undesirable, or even a failure, James could turn to good account. No doubt, he was regarded as a square peg in a round hole, when he turned from painting to take up engineering; and when he abandoned the Lawrence Scientific School to enter medicine, he must have been thought a flop, but none of these abortive plans, in his case, could be held as a loss of time and energy; for he did not flit about, like the butterfly, but rather, like the bee, extracting nectar and fructifying the flowers. One might go so far as to say that even the nervous disorder which he had endured during his twenties was of advantage to him in his intellectual development; for apart from the fact that the experience in itself was indispensable for a psychologist, and gave him great insight into the assessment of abnormal conditions, especially in dealing with the religious characters which he was to describe and interpret in his *Varieties of Religious Experience*, his trip abroad was the direct result of his desperate search for a cure, which he found in his visits to the various intellectual and artistic centres of Europe.

While teaching anatomy and physiology at the Harvard Medical School, in the '80's, James could still bring himself to invoke the aid of a woman "mind-curer," with whom he has eighteen sittings, during which she "disentangles the snarls" out of his mind.

Let anyone who will, sneer or scoff at the slumming excursions on the part of a scientist like William James. The probability is that he benefited by the conferences, and through him, American psychology has had its grain of profit therefrom.

James's Intellectual Stature

It may well be asked what there was about James which gave him the laurels in psychology. How did he affect American psychology? B. C. Ewer is of the opinion that his "influence upon the subsequent development of academic psychology was, as a matter of detail, not very great."[1] He further holds that only in regard to the raising of its progenitor to the level of a biological science is contemporary psychology beholden to him. In other words, only the changed point of view was a product of James's work, but he contributed little in the way of systematizing ideas, or pointing out new methods or dealing with problems. If we accept this estimate, it is all the more remarkable that James should rank as America's foremost psychologist, especially as half a dozen other psychologists, notably Wundt, had a hand in the transformation of psychology from a philosophical discipline to a biological science. If anything, it might be said that James colored psychology with a philosophical tinge. Without the healthy vitamin which he injected into it, psychology might have spent itself, in the early days, on sterile experimentation with chronoscope, mnemometers, and tachistoscopes.

If we take stock of what is usually associated with the name of James in psychology, we would be forced to admit that, objectively speaking, there was hardly an idea or hypothesis which can be said to have emanated directly from James, although his mental pattern was, no doubt, original.

"His pluralism he discovered in the writings of Renouvier. His pragmatism, even if it is not to be traced to Protagoras, was akin to C. S. Pierce's *pragmatism*, which he generously acknowledges. His greatest work, *The Principles of Psychology*, contains many original *aperçus*, the results of his own transformed experiences, but is there any principle therein which can be called his own, like, say, the Hering and Helm-

[1] B. C. Ewer: *The Personalist*, 1942, vol. 23.

holtz theories of vision, or Lotze's principle of local signs, or the Weber-Fechner psychophysical law, or Johannes Müller's doctrine of specific nerve energies, or Herbart's view of apperceiving masses? Even the organic theory of emotions, which has been most closely associated with his name, was independently formulated by Lange, in Denmark, and Sergi, in Italy, not to mention Lotze's adumbration of it. The motor theory of consciousness was more than hinted at by Stricker and others. Even the distinction between "knowledge about" and "knowledge of acquaintance" does not originate with him."[2]

Was he then an experimentalist who brought to light, as did Pavlov, some new phenomena which would bid us change our notions in regard to the laws of behavior? The fact is that of James's experimental methods, little can be affirmed; for with the exception of his psychical research séances, he relinquished experimental psychology to his successor at Harvard, Hugo Münsterberg. Yet his methodology is apparent in all his works. It consists, briefly, in studying the raw data, and making at least as much of the exceptions as of the rule. In a sense, he foreshadowed the branch of individual psychology. Unlike his colleagues, he was prone to discover some new principle rather than bring a given phenomenon in line with old generalizations through a process reminiscent of Procrustes' bed.

Difficulties Inherent in the Problems

That James's handling of the problems was a slight achievement, however, must be challenged. Certainly, if solution *via* consistency, is our only goal, James has little to offer, but if the understanding of the issues is a desideratum, then it is doubtful whether anyone else has accomplished as much. Even Kant, it will be recalled, face to face with his three antinomies, was obliged to set the arguments *pro* and *con* down in parallel columns, and write them off as insoluble. The one set of arguments calls for belief in the world as finite in space and time, and therefore created, while the other set proves that the world is both infinite and eternal. In the matter of freedom and determinism, there is the same logical impasse. Finally we are in the same quandary, when it comes to decide whether there is any substance which may be called simple.

[2] A. A. Roback: *William James; His Marginalia, Personality, and Contribution*, 1942, pp. 273-274.

Now if Kant, the systematizer *par excellence,* could not cope with problems which are equally balanced, then why must we expect a man who does not care to settle things by hook or crook, so that objections might not be directed against him, to give us satisfactory solutions? Indeed, some of the paralogisms which occupied Kant's attention for years were the very ones which James was grappling with unsuccessfully.

What were these hard nuts which James did not crack, and yet, as if through a fluoroscope, disclosed their content, without relieving our appetite? His dual position, when confronted by the necessity of choosing between two opposite views, has been commented upon almost by every writer on James's philosophy or psychology. He reminded us of the judge who, after listening to one of the litigants, would say "You are quite right," and upon hearing the story of the other, would exclaim again, "You are quite right," whereupon, a colleague asked: "How is it possible for both of them to be in the right? Surely, one must be at fault." "Why, of course," answered the judge, "you are right too." Indeed, James readily saw that it is the business of the scientist to solve problems, not merely to explain or expound them, but he refused to dispose of them at all costs. He was no prestidigitator, and, therefore, if the conditions are such that they defy reason, why, then all we can do is to be understanding and hopeful of the future.

Artist vs. Scientist

James was both a scientist and an artist. The scientist *knew* that every volitional act had its cause, was determined by a preceding event. The artist *felt* that there was a *fiat* which comes from within, which, within limits, can act as an interloper and deflect or refract the laws of causality. The principle of indeterminacy of Heisenberg might have been of some service to William James, had he lived in our generation, to bolster his stand.

As a scientist, pure and simple, he would be drawn to the atomistic theory of mind, and in his chapter on association, he seems to go with the associationists in England and France, yet as an artist, he loathes the very thought of atoms, and sees the complex, the totality, as a unit, which is different from the sum-total of its parts, so that the taste of lemonade is not an addition of the taste of sugar plus the taste of lemon plus the taste of water. The self to the scientist is but a succession of

I—me states, but the artist finds the self a constant, a permanent entity in the life of the individual, which serves as a centre of reference for all other experiences.

As a scientist, he was a strict psychological parallelist, abiding by the thesis that every mental state must have its neural basis, in some physiological process, through a pathway in the tissue, yet as an artist, he could sponsor the interactionist theory, which makes of the conscious a power in itself, partaking of a cosmic consciousness, and protruding from a psychic reservoir of which we, in our normal waking state, are not aware.

We thus see that James was in a sense a double personality, torn between the dictates of his scientific training and the insights gained from his actual raw experience, which to him was just as reliable as its scientific analysis, if not more so. In choosing, he could perhaps give priority to *knowledge gained through acquaintance* rather than to *knowledge about a thing*, scientifically derived, although he must needs have bowed to the imperious demands of methodology. The world to him appeared as one of those equivocal figures, like the duck-rabbit picture or the pattern of two squares with oblique lines running in opposite directions, and inducing retinal rivalry. In connection with this figure, James quotes Helmholtz: "I find that I am able to attend voluntarily now to one and now to the other system of lines; and that then this system remains visible alone for a certain time, whilst the other completely vanishes," adding, "these words of Helmholtz are of fundamental importance. And if true of sensorial attention how much more true of the intellectual variety."[3] The point that both Helmholtz and James are making is that different aspects and relations of any question should be rolled over again and again in one's mind, instead of fixating just one point of view.

Defender of Unregimented Ideas

James was constantly at pains to draw attention to the underdog in ideologies, to the neglected aspect or theory. He sought justice for the obscure concept, and was, therefore, inclined to favor particularly any view which he considered to have had a shabby deal, and to take down a peg the accepted fashions in philosophy and science. These likes and dislikes

[3] William James: *Psychology, A Briefer Course*, p. 227.

ran in syndromes, so that we could almost surmise what his position would be in regard to a certain school of thought. Intellectualism, for example, was repugnant to him. It was riding high at the time, but there were also temperamental reasons for his aversion to it. A corollary of his anti-intellectualism would naturally be his suspicion of any finished system. The classical dictum "Nature abhors a vacuum" might be phrased so far as he was concerned "Nature abhors a finalistic system." It would not be difficult to place James as a pioneer among the non-Aristotelian logicians, although he did not tackle the subject directly.

Now since the substantive was invariably emphasized at the expense of the relational, it should not surprise us that he took sides with the latter, and thus can be recognized as a functionalist, or even a dynamist, as against the structuralist. In his marginalia to Titchener's *Lectures on the Elementary Psychology of Feeling and Attention*, which appeared in 1908, two years before James's death, there is the pencilled notation on page 58 of the book, "shows how different the dynamic point of view is from the structural."[4] In 1908, the word "dynamic" had been very seldom used in a psychological context, although, as we have seen earlier, Dewey employed the term in 1884, but it seems to have fallen by the wayside, in the interim.

It was because the cognitive played such an overwhelming part in the earlier psychology, and because it forms the warp and woof of intellectualism, that James leaned toward the motor. The germ of the ideo-motor principle, as well as of the motor theory of consciousness, seems to be bound up with this partiality; and even the James-Lange theory of the emotions, which insists that there is no special awareness of joy, sadness, fear, or anger, but merely that of the organic sensations incidental to the physiological processes taking place in the blood vessels and muscles at the time we are sad, afraid, or angry—can be linked to the same tendency in James of distributing more equably the jobs of the central and the peripheral systems. "If we fancy some strong emotion, and then try to abstract from our consciousness of it all the feelings of its bodily symptoms, we find we have nothing left behind, no 'mind-stuff' out of which the emotion can be constituted, and that a cold and neutral state of intellectual per-

---

[4] A. A. Roback: *Loc. cit.*, p. 55.

ception is all that remains."[5] In order to carry out this idea, he was compelled to reverse the sequence in the emotional experience. "Common sense says, we lose our fortune, are sorry and weep, we meet a bear, are frightened and run; we are insulted by a rival, are angry and strike. The hypothesis here to be defended says that this order of sequence is incorrect, that the one mental state is not immediately induced by the other, that the bodily manifestations must first be interposed between, and that the more rational statement is that we feel sorry because we cry, angry because we strike, afraid because we tremble, and not that we cry, strike, or tremble because we are sorry, angry, or fearful, as the case may be. Without the bodily states following on the perception, the latter would be purely cognitive in form, pale, colorless, destitute of emotional warmth. We might then see the bear and judge it best to run, receive the insult and deem it right to strike, but we should not actually *feel* afraid or angry" (pp. 375-376).

There was also a practical turn to this motor theory. The emotions must express themselves in action, or else the pent-up steam will cause an inner explosion. There are clinical implications here which may take form in salutary advice to the inexperienced, but may also be applied to the interpretation of historical events through biography. It was a bold step to fly in face of the facts, as we ordinarily have accepted them, whether we be psychologists or not. Nevertheless, the James-Lange theory was treated seriously before it was repudiated by psychologists and even more so by physiologists like Sherrington and Cannon.

Radical Empiricism and Systemlessness

James called himself a radical empiricist. The British empiricists were to him not radical, but artificial. They *constructed* their world of experience, while he wanted us to live our world *in the natural*. It might, therefore, be anticipated that he would defend a nativistic account of space and time as against the genetic theory of Wundt. Nativism does not satisfy us scientifically because it does not explain; it merely asserts that we were born with the capacity to perceive space and time, to be sure, by virtue of certain brain processes; but, on the other hand, to build up our sense of space or time from

[5] William James: *Loc. cit.*, p. 379.

various clues, received through the sense organs, would mean to engage in a sort of mental chemistry, which was taboo for James.

There were certain positive features, then, about James's psychology, from which he would not deviate one iota, but in the main, he would see both sides of the medal with equal clearness. Turning it was all that was needed. Under the circumstances, it is small wonder that opposing camps could claim him as their patron saint. Behaviorism is sometimes traced to his emphasis on the motor side, and psychical research looks upon him as a *defensor fidei*. The personalists interpret his chapter on the self to suit their conception, and the phenomenalists might simply point to his ever changing stream of consciousness in support of their own selfless mind. *Gestalt* psychology should honor him as their herald, but its representatives have minimized the part which James's plea for the indivisibility of the compound has played in fostering the *Gestalt* conception.

Could any other psychologist set up such a double system, which means no system, and "get away with it"? A philosopher like Hegel, who also begat siblings that were disparate from one another, like Karl Marx and D. F. Strauss, after laying his thesis and antithesis side by side, at least, attempted to reconcile them through a synthesis. James was content to expose the gap, and was neither abashed nor afraid to avow his scientific perverseness. Only a year before his death, he wrote to Charles Pierce, "I am a-logical, if not illogical, and glad to be so when I find Bertie Russell trying to excogitate what true knowledge means, in the absence of any concrete universe surrounding the known and the unknown. Ass!" It is true that James could be charged with scientific double talk, but, in reality, he was seeing two irreducible views, which, as in stereoscopy, gave him the actual tridimensional picture. He might, in his turn, claim that the Wundtian schools were suffering from hemianopsia, which allows one to see only one lateral half of the visual field.

The paradox that was William James may be envisaged as the product of his native endowment, his environment, his particular temperament, his artistic bent, his diversified schooling, his nervous ailment, his studies in Germany, his French contacts, and readings, and not least, perhaps, his Celtic origin. All these ingredients became integrated in the personality of James, but it is self-evident that they did not harmonize; in fact, they could not harmonize, considering the contradictory elements. Indeed, it was just because of his even keel that the integration could not proceed on an hierarchical basis, so that either the one constitution or other might prevail at all times.

Intellectual Make-up

James's outlook surely had its genesis, first, in his scientific curiosity and the quest of knowledge, which, we must assume, were biologically grounded, as was his artistic temperament. The Celtic strain perhaps not only helped form the mystic and the poet, but also kept him aloof from the hardheaded Scottish realism, as well as from the English brand of empiricism, which was analytic and inductive. Together with this imaginative predisposition, there was also the influence of his early contacts with Swedenborgianism through his father's friends. His nervous trouble, which sometimes reached an acute stage, would only tend to heighten the mystical outlook, often at odds with his scientific interests and extraordinary training along experimental lines. That he would be drawn toward the French masters with their *esprit* and brilliant flashes of intuition, their understanding of the abnormal states of human nature rather than toward the extremely efficient, but stodgy German professors must be taken as a foregone conclusion. His naturalness, sincerity, integrity, spontaneity, and intellectual courage tell the rest of the story. That, with all his scientific drawbacks, he should be accepted as America's foremost psychologist, if not the greatest in the world, is only a tribute to his mastery of science, his unsurpassed expository talent, including an exquisite style and faultless diction, as well as a charismatic personality which is very rarely found in the academic sphere.

When William James asserted something which did not appeal to our common sense, we still realized that the statement came from a man who had at his command the very best instruments of critical inquiry; for, unlike the psychologists who preceded him, he had worked up to the top from the ground floor, nay, from the basement. Any one who had the opportunity of examining the thousands of books he had read from his youth on could not help admiring the fervor with which he digested and assimilated textbooks and treatises in physics, chemistry, physiology, anatomy, and other medical sciences, mathematics, logic and philosophy, marking passages, adding comments, correlating ideas, and synthesizing facts.

It must become apparent, upon such a casual survey that James read these books not to pass examinations, or by way of consultation, in order to produce a work of his own, nor even to add to the fund of his knowledge, but to understand the world and particularly human nature. That is where he differed from the earlier American psychologists or, to some extent, from a man like Wundt, who seems to have read more than James, but with an eye to incorporating references in his portly works. The divinity-school psychologists absorbed; James assimilated, and made all that he had read his own whether he remembered the exact content or not; it became part of his nervous system. Wundt's mind was more comprehensive. He had an encyclopedic range, but it may be questioned whether he had James's grasp on a number of departments of knowledge. What James knew, he knew well. With all his recalcitrance against discipline, he was accurate.

We now come to the most important question concerning a creative mind, to wit: Was James an original thinker? Let us not tarry to consider the trite observation dating from the age of Ecclesiastes. It will be conceded, on all hands, that originality is a relative quality. So long, however, as the concept has a definite connotation, we are justified in employing the term. In fact, genius is a function of originality. The correlation between the two may even amount to unity.

Although, as we have concluded earlier, there was hardly an idea or hypothesis which can be said to have actually originated with James, it would be a mistake, nevertheless, to place James in the category of a popularizer or exponent of other people's tenets. He was original in his form of expression, in his manner of integrating material, and in his critical oversight of the welter of views. We do not consider Shakespeare any the less original because he appropriated his plots from the *Gesta Romanorum*. The question before us is: What did he do with the stories which were handed down through the ages?

The Permanent in William James

James, too, had taken the cold and lifeless *disjecta membra*, or, rather, assimilating the substance, he animated them with his glow of personality, endowing them with more verisimilitude, and ranging them into a dovetailed whole. The analogy will, no doubt, be frowned upon by many because of the disparity between literature and science. It may even be objected that the introduction of *vraisemblance* implies the very negation of science, that a law is either true or false. But a science, particularly in its early days, is not expounded as a system of laws; and psychology has always been at a disadvantage, to this day, in respect of positiveness. Even in physics, the most fundamental laws and theories have been questioned and subverted. Einstein's relativity doctrine has had its authoritative critics. In psychology, the situation is much worse; for it numbers few conclusions which have not been held up a second time to the experimental touchstone and contested. We have heard a great deal, in the past, of "laboratory atmosphere," offered in explanation of the discrepancy of results reported, supposedly, under the same conditions, in different laboratories.

With this in mind, and in the knowledge that William James realized the scientific predicament psychology was in, we can again point to his achievement in breathing life into the bare and stark facts of the day, investing them with a meaning they did not have, and interrelating them with other bodies of information. That in itself constitutes originality, although not of the highest order. In philosophy, the argument carries still more weight.

A number of James's cherished notions like the "fiat of the will" and the doctrine of the emotions as really organic sensations have been discarded long since. His concern about the "I" and the "me" does not exist for the presentday psychologist. Other problems have been formulated anew so that James would not have recognized them, yet it is incontrovertible that his influence on American psychology has been great and lasting. He invested it with authority, he guided it when it was scarcely out of its swaddling clothes, and he brought credit to it in other lands.

Moreover, James's conception of psychology has permeated many textbooks, and even the most objectivistic of them have not been untouched by the magic wand of the psychological conjuror. Behaviorism, while not directly the product of James's psychology, received some support both from pragmatists (B. H. Bode, H. H. Bawden) and neo-realists (E. B.

Holt), who, in turn, received their impetus, partly at least, from James's radical empiricism.

Whether operationism, which holds together a number of logical positivists and a motley array of scientists, is an outgrowth of instrumentalism, or of pragmatism, cannot easily be decided at present. Since, however, pragmatism preceded the Chicago School, the movement undoubtedly owes a debt to James.

The motor theory of consciousness, which James expounded, has been more fortunate than his more original organic theory of emotions, in that it is still held by many psychologists in a modified form. His rejection of mental atomism in favor of a configurational principle proves him to be a forerunner of *Gestalt* psychology. Strangely enough, he has made no dent in abnormal psychology.

In religious circles, he has been looked upon as a patron saint. To be sure, theologians and religious philosophers showed an ambivalence toward him; for it was with mixed feelings that they accepted his *Varieties of Religious Experience*, which links the divine too closely with the subconscious; and some of his utterances on the erotic sentiments of the saints must have seemed to them fraught with sacrilege. Notwithstanding, James's sympathetic attitude toward religion was too patent; and the crusade against agnosticism and materialism, waged by a scientific authority of his calibre, must have been hailed as a welcome second front.

James was a school philosopher (although decidedly not a scholastic) in the sense that he concerned himself only with trends that were in the air, with perennial issues that were shuttled back and forth between coteries. He was not a lone eagle soaring above the din of slogans and catchwords. Concept and percept; intellectualism and empiricism; monism and pluralism; the finite and infinity—these have been the stock-in-trade of philosophy, under different guises, for many centuries.

Even if James had not contributed a single idea that is now accepted in psychology, he not only tilled the soil but planted the seed. At a time when the search for general laws obscured everything else from view, James was sympathetic to the deviations and exceptions thus throwing his weight on the side of individual differences, and imparting an impetus in new directions. He taught us to read between the lines and note relations, interstices, and blank spaces. He brought the heart into psychology, which previously had been ruled altogether by the head. It was a wholesome influence, and he is not likely to be supplanted as the coryphaeus of American psychology, and the fifteen-story edifice, in construction, to house his behavioral sciences at Harvard University will be a fitting monument to his name.

Chapter 14

G. Stanley Hall and the Genetic Method

GRANVILLE STANLEY HALL (1844[1]-1924) has not been given the recognition due him by his contemporaries, and he has been all but forgotten except by the former Clark students of psychology, but American psychology owes him a deep debt. He has to his credit many first records.

A Record of Firsts

He was the first to receive a Ph.D. in the philosophy department at Harvard. He was the first American student, during the first year of its existence, at the first officially accepted psychological laboratory in the world—at Leipzig under Wundt. He founded the first psychological laboratory in America at Johns Hopkins in 1883, and although, as we have seen, James had already been experimenting in a laboratory of his own, as early as 1876, the label under which it went was "physiology," while Hall made the psychological shingle explicit. Hall, furthermore, launched the first psychological journal in English, the *American Journal of Psychology*, in 1887, since *Mind* in England had been devoted principally to philosophy. He was the first president of Clark University (1888), where he established a psychological laboratory for advanced research, and had E. C. Sanford, as director of the undergraduate laboratory. He was the first president of the American Psychological Association, virtually its organizer, in 1892, and thirty years later, he was elected president, for the second time, of this enormously expanded organization, during the three decades which elapsed. The second psychological journal in the United States, the *Pedagogical Seminary,* which first appeared in 1891, and has continued, after 1927, under the name of the *Journal of Genetic Psychology,* was also his brain child. Other psychological periodicals which owe their existence to him were the *Journal of Religious Psy-*

[1] Some reference works give 1846 as the date of birth.

171

chology, which lasted from 1904 to 1914, the *Journal of Race Development* (1910-1919), which was afterwards known as the *Journal of International Relations*, succeeded by *Foreign Affairs*, and finally the *Journal of Applied Psychology*, the first issue of which came out in 1917. It is hardly known that Hall, after a misunderstanding with his patron, who expected the firstling journal to devote most of its space to psychical research, found himself under the necessity of sinking $8000 of his own[2] in order to keep it going—a veritable fortune for those days. It required not only initiative and enterprise, but self-sacrifice to conduct a journal with nothing but an initial subsidy of $500 and one hundred subscribers.

A Prospector in Science

Hall was born on a farm at Ashfield, near Boston, and even late in life had something of the sturdy and alert farmer in his appearance. Neighborliness is the word which comes to mind when thinking of a characterization for Hall. Tall and well-built, genial yet firm, with a play of mild irony around his mouth, his beard adding to his picturesqueness, he gave the impression of a frontier man during the Civil War period. And a frontier man he was in psychology, as we have had occasion to see. Maturity, rather than precociousness, was his forte, bearing his personal ordeals, as when his child was burned to death, with great fortitude.

Like James, he came to psychology not directly, but through circuitous channels, in his thirties. His education, similarly, had taken a halting and faltering course, but he was not fortunate to have been born into a cultured and prosperous family. His schooling did not come easy, and after graduation from Williams College and the Union Theological Seminary, he discovered that he was not cut out to be a preacher. He had already studied in Germany (Berlin and Bonn), and had taught an assortment of subjects at Antioch College, but the new psychology, as cultivated by Wundt, attracted him; and he was about to leave for a pilgrimage to Wundt, when he was offered a minor teaching post in English at Harvard, where he was able to carry some graduate work under James and Bowen, and at the Harvard Medical School, under Bowditch, receiving his Ph.D. in 1878.

[2] K. C. Dallenbach: "The American Journal of Psychology 1837-1937," *Am. Journal of Psychology*, 1937, vol. 50, p. 491.

Returning to Germany, he specialized in physiology under Kries and Kronecker, then took up work in Wundt's newly founded laboratory, at the University of Leipzig. After giving a series of lectures at Harvard, he was called to Johns Hopkins, first as lecturer (1881) but soon to be promoted to a professorship (1884). It was at Johns Hopkins that he had stimulated a number of students who were to become famous men in philosophy, psychology, physiology, and education. In 1888, he was invited to administer Clark University, which had just been established. Under him, Clark University became a psychological centre, and the University library was one of the best stocked in psychology and allied subjects, and it was only after he retired that the psychological department at Clark began to decline.

Of all the pioneers of the new psychology, Stanley Hall represents best the American point of view and temperament. His German training did not enslave him to the doctrines, methods, and laboratory manners of his teachers. Perhaps one reason for his independence was the circumstance that he had spent his time in four of the principal German universities, and thus did not allow himself to become too much influenced by a single master. When he returned from Germany in 1880, he published a little book, *Aspects of German Culture* (Boston, 1881) in which he could discuss with detachment the question whether German universities were declining, and while he did not think they were, he was not oblivious to some of the evils and drawbacks in the best of them. Hall, unlike James, had no special predilections. He was not given to moods, as was James, and was less the visionary and more the man of vision.

Vision

It may be asked whether Hall could be singled out from among the other pioneers in the halcyon days of American psychology by some one outstanding trait. Granted that he started journals and founded laboratories, would this be a sufficiently great achievement to accord him a significant place in the history of American psychology? Certainly, the fact that he "got in on the ground floor," colloquially speaking, is not his chief claim to the high rank which must be assigned him. What was particularly striking about his type of mind was the degree of vision which he possesssed.

The calibre of the men who were his younger contemporaries, Titchener, Münsterberg, Cattell, Baldwin, and Dewey, not to mention James, who was two years his senior, was of an unusually high order; and yet Hall's vision, in the light of what had transpired, somewhat dims the greater accomplishment, in actual contributions to the science, on the part of any one of his colleagues. It is, of course, a controversial matter, but let his career be followed step by step, and it will be recognized that his projects presupposed a looking ahead into the distant future. He usually did not depend on coöperation. Unlike James, he was not blessed with influential friends and a magnetic personality. He was not an opportunist, making all sorts of bids in order to realize his ambition.

While it is possibly true, as Boring suggests, "Hall was not primarily an administrator. The journals and other organizations were but deposits of his restless mind. It seemed, rather, that he developed a new interest, carried it through the pioneer stage, and then, already caught by the next topic, tried to perpetuate the old by creating for it a new professorship, a journal or an institution,"[3] it must also be taken into consideration that this craving for new interests, which incidentally, were not whims or fads, as will become apparent, this turning from one topic to another evidenced not only the restless mind, but one which is on the alert to perceive new angles, one that will not stay in grooves.

While even James was content to become preoccupied with the issues of the day, Hall allowed his students to spread out along unorthodox lines; and let us not forget that conducting the affairs of a new university does take vision, and furthermore, of all the psychologists who were preëminent during the first decade of the present century, it was Stanley Hall who showed his sympathy toward Freud's psychoanalysis, which was anathema to a man like Münsterberg, and suspect to James and Titchener. Had it not been for Hall, Sigmund Freud might never have visited the United States. Freud's arrival in Worcester, together with his retinue—Jung, Jones, Ferenczi, and others—marks the beginning of the psychoanalytic era, so far as America is concerned. Was Hall interested in Freud only because he was propagating some outlandish doctrine, as it was then thought?

[3] E. G. Boring: *A History of Experimental Psychology* (2d ed.), p. 521.

Hall did not wait for movements or trends to settle before grasping their significance. While Freud was being ostracized in the psychological world, Hall was able to single him out as "the most original and creative mind in psychology of our generation," although he did not believe in the pansexualism to which Freud was then committed.

Hall did not merely flit from project to project and from topic to topic, as the restless mind would, but rather integrated his new experiences and interests so as to form a broader outlook. There was no incompatibility among the constituents, as was the case with James. Consistency meant much to Hall; and when he was confronted with a clash, he would be guided by the system which he had built up, and not by the isolated instance. Perhaps he did show enthusiasm, but it was tempered by a deliberative and prosaic attitude. Even as a young man, he evinced a critical attitude toward the high and mighty. One of his most thoughtful essays is "The Graphic Method" which he wrote in 1879, in his thirties. There he exposes the fallacy of those who suppose that theatrical methods will do wonders for knowledge, that describing curves and instruments and flashing charts will insure the accuracy of a doubtful generalization. The fad of reducing everything to mechanics and motion, which was spreading in the '70's, is deprecated in an ironic vein. He pronounces as "logically and psychologically wrong" the notion that it will become possible "to conceive of self-reproducing machines which can give readings for the whirl of molecules engaged in composing an epic, etc." and that "consciousness will become extinct, since molecular combinations will persist as the most fitting survivals; in a word, all will be action."[4] And is this not just what cybernetics of today is contending?

Hall's Works

Hall's star had declined years before his death. Both Titchener and Münsterberg had stolen the thunder, and graduate students in psychology at Clark University would be rated as scholars, investigators, researchers, and anything one likes, but not as experimental psychologists. Naturally, if the director is easygoing in his standards, it was reasoned, then what might be expected of the flock? His own students, and there were

[4] G. S. Hall: *Aspects of German Culture*, 1881, p. 71.

not a few who rose to the top of their special branch, appraised him as a leading psychologist who substantially affected the course of psychology. The non-Clark Ph.D.'s, as a subsequent detailed questionnaire disclosed, were divided as to his merit. The results, in general, proved, however, that Hall did not fare so poorly in the consensus, as one might have supposed.

Aside from his promotion effort, which of course was a distinct service, he did assemble a large body of data on adolescence, and his two large volumes (about 1300 pages) entitled in full *Adolescence: Its Psychology and its Relations to Psychology, Anthropology, Sociology, Sex, Crime, Religion and Education,* published in 1904, constituted an encyclopedia of useful information which was rather scarce at the time. But this impressive work was not merely a compilation. There was much of Hall, the observer and correlator, in it; and to it all, he brought his genetic method, which will always be associated with his name, but thereby he had also laid under obligation educational psychologists. Several printings, one even as late as 1924, are an indication that there was solid material, much in demand by child psychologists and educators, although the condensed version, which first appeared in 1906, under the title of *Youth, Its Education, Regime and Hygiene,* enjoyed even more issues.

The following year, Hall brought out *Aspects of Life and Education,* a collection of articles, revised, condensed or amplified with up-to-date bibliographies (ed. by Theodate L. Smith). A similar collection had already appeared in German, in 1902 (*Ausgewählte Beiträge zur Kinderforschung und Pädagogie*), and in 1911, two large volumes of *Educational Problems* again pointed to the dominant interest of Hall. In 1912, "an epitome of the published educational writings of President G. Stanley Hall" was published by G. E. Partridge, under the main title *"Genetic Philosophy of Education."*

Many, if not most, of the experiments which were conducted in the Clark laboratory were along the lines of child psychology; and the courses in educational and developmental psychology are the best equipped in Clark University even today. In the early days of Clark, pedagogy and child psychology flourished under men like W. H. Burnham and A. F. Chamberlain. Studies on children's fears, the interpretation of doll life, on jealousy, wonder, etc., were regarded as on the periphery of psychology.

Although Hall wrote hundreds of articles, his works were not numerous, even if some of them were voluminous. In the last decade of his life, Hall's attention turned to biography and autobiography. His *Founders of Modern Psychology* was by no means an adequate work for a man who knew most of the founders personally; and Wundt found slips in regard to his own sketch therein. As he entered the stage of advanced age, his old theological interests beckoned to him, and he became engrossed in a psychological analysis of Jesus—always a hazardous undertaking. The result was a book labelled *Jesus, the Christ in the Light of Psychology*, brought out in 1917, and in spite of the halo in the title, the rather unorthodox expressions did not sit well with his former brethren of the cloth; for here, too, he was applying the genetic method, as in the case of an ordinary person.

His genetic inquiry broadened and deepened as he grew older, and he could thus become a subject or observer for his own self-investigation. The last few years of his life were given over to his own autobiographical writings, which included *Recreations of a Psychologist* (1920) and *Senescence* (1922) in two volumes, which is the first large-scale geriatric survey of a psychological character, in any language. Finally, *The Life and Confessions of a Psychologist* (1923) as an autobiography, is a self-revelatory document offering a good many pointers to students of personality, to say nothing of its value for the history of American psychology. Many details are, of course, controversial, but every autobiography will have its *Dichtung* along with its *Wahrheit*. Even his autobiographical volumes offer a wealth of observations of a psychological nature. After all, not many psychologists can give the world a first-hand account of senescence . . . nor can every aged person, no matter how intelligent and even gifted, with a literary flair, to boot, attack the subject from a psychological angle. Hall's analytical and introspective study rounds out a genetic course pursued throughout life, and falls in line with the new field of geriatrics—another indication of his forward-looking mind.

Specific Contribution

Hall might have been a geneticist, even if he had not worked under Wundt. Indeed, his preface to the earlier English translation of Freud's *General Introduction to Psycho-*

analysis plainly states that Wundt "always and everywhere underestimated the genetic standpoint," meaning, of course, *in its evolutionary phase,* for Wundt *was* a geneticist in his physiological explanations of psychological phenomena, which accords with the bent of British evolutionists to derive the complex from simpler elements, and is to be linked with associationism and the mental chemistry of the Mills. In this point, Hall differed from James, the nativist, and in his experimental work on space perception, he concluded that we perceive space largely by virtue of our muscular sensations.

The elaboration of the questionnaire which Francis Galton had already used in England to gain an insight into the imagery of various individuals was another contribution that Hall has made. The questionnaire was at one time the target for many a joke in the better laboratories; it nevertheless has made good. Münsterberg particularly would poke fun at it by asking what we could tell about a boy's mind if we discovered how many objects he carried in his pocket. Yet the questionnaire became the chief tool in army classification, and is at the basis of all public opinion polls. The Kinsey Report on sex behavior has adopted it. That it has been a necessary addition to the scant psychological methods in vogue fifty years ago can hardly be questioned.

The test of vision can scarcely be applied, as in the case of intuition, during the lifetime of the individual credited with this trait, unless he has been fortunate in the span of his life. With Hall it was beginning to be evident even before he reached the biblical average that his projects were far-sighted, and that what he had undertaken had prospered, but it is his views and interests which best tell the story. The genetic method (both phylogenetic and ontogenetic) with its *evolutionary presuppositions* and anthropological accretions, which concerned him, is as worthy of cultivation today as it was sixty years ago, and Hall's expectations and down-to-earth common-sense slant in psychological theory were more nearly borne out than those of his greater contemporaries, who built up systems and complicated hypotheses that have not survived them. The difference between the scientist, scholar, or artist who has vision and the one who has not is that in the one instance, the world comes around to the issues he was grappling with; in the other, the world passes him by, together with his problems.

In his philosophy, Hall favored the identity theory of mind, and eschewed mystical speculation of any sort. Spiritualism found in him an uncompromising foe, and psychical research had no appeal for him. He made no pretense at evolving a system of psychology, quite content to set a few bricks or stones in place here and there after turning ground (if James could be said to have laid the cornerstone) supervising the early masons, and getting the machinery going.

GEORGE TRUMBULL LADD (1842-1920)

The third of the senior trio that ushered in the new psychology in America, G. T. Ladd, does not quite fit in with the other two, and were it not for his *Elements of Physiological Psychology,* which even in the revised edition of 1911, with the coöperation of Woodworth, has been supplanted by this erstwhile collaborator's up-to-date *Experimental Psychology,* his name would scarcely be remembered, except by the historians in the science. That he was able, in the early '80's, although an ordained clergyman, to see the value of physiological knowledge in dealing with mental facts is in itself a sign of a progressive mind.

While at Bowdoin College, he had already sought to familiarize himself with the experimental method through whatever apparatus he had at his disposal, and when called to Yale in 1881, to fill the chair of philosophy, he took this work more seriously, to the extent of formally founding, in 1892, a laboratory, of which he put E. W. Scripture in charge. Ladd wrote a number of textbooks both in philosophy and psychology. His most valued work was of course *The Elements of Physiological Psychology* (1887) which passed through six printings within less than a decade, but even the abridged version, viz. *The Outlines of Physiological Psychology* (1891) was so widely used that the eighth impression appeared in 1908. His *Psychology, Descriptive and Explanatory* (1894) was a bulky textbook, abridged for elementary classes, in 1898, as *Outlines of Descriptive Psychology,* while his *Philosophy of Mind* was a sort of superstructure corresponding to the earlier rational psychologies. A *Primer of Psychology* (1894) is a condensation of his *Psychology,* for collegiate institutions.

Ladd cannot measure up to either James or Hall. Physically, he resembled, in his quiet dignity, the former, while with Hall, he had the theological training in common, yet that was about all there was in common outside of their teaching the same subjects. Hall, after discovering that preaching was not his *métier*, never bothered about the soul and the divine; and if he did return, in the last decade of his life, to the person of the founder of Christianity, he treated his subject as a psychologist and not as a cleric. Ladd, on the other hand, was more like Burton, Hickok, Porter, and McCosh in that the theological dogma colored his psychological thinking.

Ladd might have helped in showing the way, but he could not wholeheartedly participate in the new movement, which required concentration with no divided loyalties. He had never supposed that the mental phenomena were the results of physiological processes, but that they ran in a parallel series, with the mental possessing greater reality and cohering in a permanent self, which is always functioning and yet adapting itself to the needs of the organism. In consequence of his faith, therefore, he held aloof from the younger set of bustling and buoyant experimentalists: and they, in turn, considered him as someone apart, one who might be a conservative patron but not a fellow-worker.

A Noteworthy Passage of Arms

The difference of opinion came to a head in a critical review of James's *Principles of Psychology,* which Ladd published in the first volume of *The Philosophical Review,* in 1892. The very title of Ladd's review is provocative, and affords us a glimpse into his general attitude toward Wundt's and James's efforts. In this extended review (30 pages), "Psychology—a So-Called 'Natural Science,' " he takes James to task for taking too many things for granted, as if the naturalization of psychology were a *fait accompli,* and charges him with glossing over serious difficulties by physiological explanations, with little regard for logic.

> When, then, Professor James maintains that his oral or schematic descriptions of the nerve processes . . . "show what a deep congruity there is between mental processes and mechanical processes of *some* kind" I must beg his pardon and flatly contradict him. They show nothing of the sort . . . They assume some sort of *unknown* congruity.[5]

[5] G. T. Ladd: "Psychology—a So-Called 'Natural Science,' " *Philos. Review,* 1892, vol. I, p. 37.

Apparently James was so piqued that in his rejoinder, there crept in some sarcasm, which was a rare occurrence with that Nestor, and from even one remark, it will become evident what Ladd was ready to defend, despite his pioneer work (in English). "The kind of psychology," retorts James, "which can cure a case of melancholy or charm a chronic insane delusion away ought certainly to be preferred to the most seraphic insight into the nature of the soul."[6] About Ladd's *Outlines of Physiological Psychology,* James had said in a review in *The Nation:* "His erudition and his broadmindedness are on a par with each other, and his volume will probably for many years to come be the standard work of reference on the subject." Possibly James had no cause to change his mind after Ladd's review of his *Principles,* but that he and Ladd, who, by the way, were born in the same year, did not speak the same language was apparent from this passage of arms in the *Philosophical Review.*

Ladd seems to have forged an instrument which he shows some reluctance about using himself. He is willing to acknowledge a small segment of physiological psychology as forming the nucleus of an independent cerebral study, but the old type of spiritualism, *à la* pneumatology of the 17th century, is inherent in his basic tenets, as may be gathered from his categorical statement in the same discussion of James. "The development of mind can only be regarded as the progressive manifestation in consciousness of the life of a real being which . . . proceeds to unfold powers that are *sui generis* according to laws of its own" (p. 53).

What Ladd Really Represented

In truth, Ladd was a *personalist.* The self is personal, grows and adapts itself in accordance with the bodily needs, ever following an original purpose. Boring in his *History of Experimental Psychology* (2d ed., p. 526) calls Ladd a "functional psychologist," probably because of the tilt between him and Titchener, for whom there could be only two sides, his own, that of structuralism, and his opponent's, which must be functionalism; but to Ladd, the function was not simply adjusting to the environment and fulfilling a need. It was the *activity of the personal will,*[7] which was uppermost in his sys-

[6] W. James: "A Plea for Psychology as a 'Natural Science,'" *Philos. Review,* 1892, vol. I, p. 153.

[7] G. T. Ladd: *The Secret of Personality,* 1918, p. 145.

tem—and Ladd did cultivate one—and whether it was memory, learning, or perception, it is the voluntary aspect which stands out from the rest and makes it human.

Ladd was a prolific writer. In addition to the works enumerated earlier, he published half a score of others, of about 300 pages or more each. These include *A Theory of Reality*, 1899; *Knowledge of Life and Reality*, 1909, second printing 1918; *What Can I Know? What Ought I to Do? What Should I Believe? What May I Hope? The Secret of Personality; The Doctrine of Sacred Scriptures; What is the Bible? The Principles of Church Polity*, besides many articles. It was because of his activity in another domain that psychologists associated him with theology and philosophy, which had a lien on him from the beginning. His fealty to the Church was especially patent in his later works. In *The Secret of Personality*, religion, philosophy, and psychology are all interwoven to produce a personalistic pattern on a voluntaristic principle. The will, which, in modern psychology has been rejected as an element, was to Ladd the cornerstone of his psychology. Thus we may understand, perhaps, why in the year 1942, when James's centenary was observed in the United States with appropriate meetings and publications, Ladd's name was not mentioned, except perhaps at Yale. The senior partner of the firm Ladd and Woodworth, which had produced the avidly read text in physiological psychology, was completely forgotten, although he was the second president of the American Psychological Association, preceding William James in this office.

Chapter 15

Cattell and Baldwin

In many respects, J. McKeen Cattell and J. Mark Baldwin differed widely. The one was essentially a laboratory psychologist with no taste for philosophy; the other was primarily a philosopher, a sociologist with a vast psychological background. Their resemblances, however, were equally great, so that they might be paired off for our purpose. They were both meteors, whose paths crossed for a brief period, and then they took off in oblique directions from the psychological plexus, still displaying a certain brilliance and incandescence, until their eventual extinction, but of a different hue. What unites them is not only the period in which they matured, and the training in Germany (for Baldwin only a year's stay at the Universities of Berlin and Leipzig) but their capacity for organization, their launching periodicals and reference publications on a large scale.

J. McKeen Cattell (1860-1944) was the product of both British and German training, in addition to his undergraduate studies at Lafayette College (where his father was president) and a year of graduate work in Hall's laboratory, at Johns Hopkins. As the first American professor of psychology, first at the University of Pennsylvania, and then at Columbia, he took pains to equip his laboratories with the necessary apparatus for experimentation on the problems which were then occupying the attention of psychologists. He even designed apparatus that had not been used previously, and stimulated his students to be critical of their methods without bothering about theory, which, to his practical mind, was a waste of time.

Cattell's Personal Traits

Had Cattell not been fortunate in the number and status of his students, including E. L. Thorndike, R. S. Woodworth, Clark Wissler, S. I. Franz, and a score of others who later distinguished themselves, it is doubtful whether he would have

183

been accorded more than a few paragraphs in a history of psychology, instead of the ten pages which Boring has devoted to him. This must be said of Cattell: he was earnest and a leader, dauntless in his fight for justice; and his integrity brought him a host of friends and admirers, despite his external grumpiness and even "scrappiness." When, *e.g.*, his close friend, Jacques Loeb, was blackballed at the Century Club, in New York, after he had proposed his name for membership, Cattell resigned from the Club on the ground that it was discriminating against Loeb's ethnic affiliation. On the other hand, at the Ninth International Congress of Psychology at Yale (1929), Cattell was almost insolent to McDougall, whose psychological views, in general, he could not countenance. McDougall was to him reactionary and obscurantist in every way, and, on many occasions, Cattell did not polish his language. His mordant wit was especially enjoyed at conferences and conventions, and his publicistic tone in writing fairly boomed with fervor. In his relations with students and those he got to know more intimately, he was kindly and generous with his time and energy, and in his own circle of friends, he could be the spirit of the party.

Apprenticeship

Cattell had been Wundt's first American assistant, at Cattell's "invitation." During the three years he spent with Wundt, he must have been a great help to him, especially in the construction and manipulation of apparatus. His experiments on reaction time were carried out in a thoroughgoing manner, having earned for the young investigator a considerable reputation as a careful investigator.[1] In 1886, he was graduated from the University of Leipzig as Doctor of Philosophy; and after a year as instructor of psychology at the University of Pennsylvania, he became lecturer at Cambridge University, thanks to his experimental articles in *Mind* and *Brain*. There he met, as he tells us, "the greatest man whom I have known," Francis Galton.

At Leipzig, the formal Wundt apparently had cramped Cattell's style, and the *Verboten* edict, so symbolic of German life, was even clamped on the period of hours which a worker could spend in the laboratory, so that if one wanted to extend

[1] R. S. Woodworth: "J. McKeen Cattell 1860-1944," *Psychol. Review*, 1944, vol. 51, p. 3.

the time, the experiments had to be carried on at home, in an improvised laboratory. Cattell was too American and too dynamic to relish such restrictions. At Leipzig, too, Wundt, who was particularly anxious to safeguard the newly-won status of psychology, as a natural science, would not stand for any puttering with individual reactions. A law deals with phenomena in general, and exceptions cannot be tolerated. Cattell, however, the American individualist, was already groping on the road toward mental testing, which, in contrast to the experiment, standardizes the norms, only with a view to discovering something about the individual.

At Cambridge, Galton who was then at the zenith of his fame, broadened the horizon for the young Cattell. The British titan had tackled so many different problems; some in psychology, others in anthropology, and still others on the borderline of several disciplines. Almost anywhere he applied his divining rod, he struck ore. The inquiry on imaginal types, the investigation of association, the psychometric adventures, the studies in heredity, which led him to the founding of eugenics as a new field, his labors on fingerprints, his experiments on overtones, using the *Galton Whistle,* his invention of composite photography—were more than enough to engage the admiring attention of the scientific world. Cattell could not help being fascinated by all these angles which Wundt, with his blinders, had missed, or perhaps deliberately ignored, in his singleness of purpose to complete a system for all time. Above all, however, Galton's emphasis on statistics and measurements must have made a deep impression on Cattell; for he might be looked upon as the one psychologist, in the early American period, to insist on quantification, ratings, and ranking, in the mental sphere. It was perhaps from him that E. L. Thorndike had received the stimulus for his own proclivity in that direction.

Contributions to Psychology

Cattell's service to American psychology in the early experimental stage was manifold. He continued the reaction-time experiments, but spread out in measuring perception by means of the fall tachistoscope, supporting the educational innovation of teaching the youngsters to read whole words first, rather than letters, on the basis that short familiar words required no more time to read than single letters. Cattell would vary the conditions in such a way as to disclose what happens in special states, *e.g.*, fatigue, marginal attention, etc. After another long series of experiments, Cattell dared to challenge the validity of the Weber-Fechner law in its accepted formulation, and maintained that the error of observation in regard to the intensity of sensation increased not in direct proportion to the magnitude but rather as the square root of the observed magnitude. He also devised a new method for indicating differences between magnitudes or qualities. The order of merit was a valuable addition to the various new devices in measurement.

In 1890, Cattell's attention focused on the project of testing various mental functions, something which Toulouse had done later in France, and Stern, still later, in Germany, on a large scale, thereby adding a new branch, *viz.*, differential psychology. Cattell's curiosity about American men of science was, again, possibly the logical consequence of his association with Galton, whose exploration of hereditary genius in England must have interested this American protégé keenly. Cattell, it may be said, was one of the very few American psychologists, perhaps the only distinguished American, to have segregated American scientists according to their ethnic group, regarding the Jewish representatives as a class, irrespective of what country they hailed from, instead of taking them to be members of a religious sect, as is still absurdly done. The work he had done with Livingston Farrand, the anthropologist, on physical and mental measurements of the students at Columbia University (1896), was, in a measure, a new departure and a harbinger of the avalanche of tests with which we were to be deluged a half-century later.

For all that credit due him as a director of research, Cattell's own output was much less than that of any of his colleagues. In 1944, two volumes appeared posthumously containing all his psychological researches, formal addresses, and publicistic articles. Two volumes in a lifetime of 84 years! Wundt's works, aside from the periodicals which he edited, might fill a bookcase of moderate size. Was Cattell wasting his time? That he certainly was not. We must look then for other activities.

Cattell, the Organizer

As a matter of fact, Cattell was an organizer, a promoter, more than a research man. In 1894, not satisfied with the way Hall was running the *American Journal of Psychology*, he launched together with J. Mark Baldwin, who, as we shall presently see, was no less a promoter, although mainly on his own behalf, a new periodical, *The Psychological Review,* a journal which later was devoted mainly to psychological theory. *Psychological Monographs* and *The Psychological Index* were further undertakings both men were responsible for. The two editors could coöperate only by either assuming all the authority in alternate years. For about a decade this arrangement *faute de mieux* seemed to work more or less satisfactorily, but in 1903, Cattell could no longer bear Baldwin's gradual domination, and by 1904, the *Psychological Review* became Baldwin's property, after a mutual agreement.

That was by no means the end of Cattell's editorial and publishing ventures. If anything, it was only the beginning; for in 1894, he had taken into his hands *Science,* which was ceasing publication for lack of funds, and in 1906, he launched the series of reference works under the title of *American Men of Science,* the eleventh edition of which is in process, followed by *Leaders in Education* and a *Directory of American Scholars. Popular Science Monthly,* established by E. L. Youmans, soon came under his editorship, which, usually, meant that he published it. Later Cattell sold the *title* to a new group, and continued the journal as *The Scientific Monthly,* while a more popular journal resulted from the split. In 1915, he added to his chain of periodicals and serials, *School and Society,* another weekly with a large and influential reading clientele. Cattell was also instrumental in starting the *Archives of Psychology and Scientific Method.*

Organization of Science

He was still a professor at Columbia University, while directing a large publishing plant and, together with members of his family, editing several periodicals, which required a tremendous volume of correspondence. It was natural that his editorial activity and his contacts with hundreds of scientists should raise his prestige in scientific and academic circles, so that he would be consulted on many matters. Probably no one stood as high in the council halls of the educational foundations and learned societies as did Cattell, and many were the offices he held in various associations and academies, beginning with the presidency of the American Psychological Association, in 1896, right after James, then, the vice-presidency of the American Association for the Advancement of Science, and finally the presidency of the same association, with its 25,000 members, in 1924. He was the first psychologist to be elected to the National Academy of Science, in 1901, and, in 1929, he presided at the Ninth International Congress of Psychology, which took place at Yale.

As he became a force in scientific and university organizational matters, it would be inevitable for him to come in conflict with the actual administrators, and, in the first instance, with the powerful president of his own institution, Nicholas Murray Butler, who belonged to the old school of executives. In 1917, the differences came to a head in the dismissal of Cattell, on the ground that he had been disloyal to the Country, in giving vent to a pacifistic sentiment, after war with Germany had been proclaimed. Cattell sued the University and was awarded $40,000 as compensation, but he was not reinstated. Having been out of academic life altogether, he devoted himself, with greater zest, to his publications and the Association for the Advancement of Science, as well as other learned societies; and his influence tended to give psychology greater prestige among the scientists. Despite his pacifistic leanings, his war efforts, largely in the nature of expert guidance to the as yet inexperienced committees which had formed to aid the Government and the Defense department, were of considerable value.

It was in 1921, that Cattell was able to realize one of his great ambitions, which he had already alluded to in his earliest writings, at a time when other American psychologists were busying themselves with "pure" science, reaction-time, imagery, perception, etc., with no thought of their practical applications. The Psychological Corporation came into being as the effort of one person, Cattell, who organized it on the basis of stock purchased by members of the American Psychological Association at $10.00 per share. Naturally, he himself was the largest stockholder, which meant that he had invested thousands of dollars in the undertaking. During the first decade, the Corporation was hardly more than a small research bureau, preparing for the expanded programme which was to follow. In 1942, he donated 600 shares of his Psychological Corporation stock, which now was worth over $50,000, to the Corporation to be used as a fund for the advancement of applied psychology through research and education.

The Prophet of Applied Psychology

The practical interests of Cattell are noticeable in an early article of his, where he tells us that "the mind is the beginning and the end of science. Physical science is possible because the mind observes and arranges, and physical science has worth because it satisfies mental needs,"[2] and in the passage subjoined from the same article we have a miniature programme of applied psychology which the founder of the Psychological Corporation more than a quarter of a century later, had been mulling over. "In laboratories of psychology not only children but every one can be tested, and small defects or changes in the senses and faculties can be discovered. Psychology may thus become an ally of medicine. Degenerations which escape common observation, and even the practiced eye of the physician, can be detected and measured by scientific methods. The overstrained clergyman or man of business can be told when a holiday is necessary, how long it must last, whether rest or amusement be required. As an example of the coöperation of psychology of medicine, surgery of the brain can be given. The part of the brain which is diseased is determined by psychological methods, the skull is opened, the diseased part of the brain is removed, and the patient may be cured. Psychological methods are useful not only in the diagnosis but also in the cure of many diseases. We know much better than formerly how the insane, the vicious, and the criminal should be treated. We know, for example, that social work is far better than solitary confinement. Even diseases not directly dependent on the nervous system may be cured by psychophysical methods—for example, suggesting to the patient in the hypnotic state that he will be cured.

"Those in good health may also profit from an examination in a laboratory of psychology. Valuable traits can be determined as well as defects, and the profession and mode of life most suitable to the person can be indicated.

"It is not necessary to dwell on other applications of psychology. Its relation to the fine arts is evident. The external

[2] J. M. Cattell: "The Progress of Psychology," *Popular Science Monthly*, 1893, vol. 43, p. 779. This paper will be found in *James McKeen Cattell, Man of Science*, 1947, vol. 2, p. 46 ff. (Science Press).

form of art is directly fitted to the senses and its inner essence to the mind. In political economy we need to know more concerning the interest, passions, and needs of the people. Ultimately, we shall be able to determine what distribution of labor, wealth, and power is the best. Indeed, the measurements and statistics of psychology, which, at first sight, may seem remote from common interests, may in the end become the most important factor in the progress of society" (p. 784). This was published in 1893!

Cattell No Behaviorist

It is because of Cattell's impatience with the philosophical and especially the speculative, that his name has been linked with behaviorism, but one of the best arguments against the insistent contention of behaviorism is to be found in the following: "It is often urged as an objection to psychology that the student can observe one mind only, but it is equally true that the student of physics can observe *with* one mind only. Were mental processes so irregular and idiosyncratic as is sometimes assumed, there would be no science of psychology, but physics would be equally out of the question. Psychology is not concerned with individual peculiarities, but with the laws to which all mental processes are subject. Its position is similar to that of physiology, which studies individual organisms in order to learn general truths concerning nutrition, movements, etc. The problems of psychology are evidently complicated by the fact that individual minds differ. But this difference is largely a matter of comparatively unimportant detail. The position of psychology is not very different from that of other sciences. Should astronomy seek to determine the orbits of all the satellites, of all the planets, of all the suns in the universe, it would have a hopeless task; but, if we understand one solar system, we have an astronomy to a large extent universal." Or let us take the utterance in which he tells us that "we know, indeed, more concerning attention, memory, and thought than concerning the cerebral processes which may precede or accompany them" (p. 782). Is it not evident that he has little faith in the promising exploits of a psychology which undertakes to kick consciousness overboard and substitute for it physiological action as the complete story?

PLACE OF J. MARK BALDWIN IN
AMERICAN PSYCHOLOGY

J. Mark Baldwin (1861-1934), who has been mentioned in an earlier chapter, happens to be the first to appear in the series of *History of Psychology in Autobiography* (edited by Carl Murchison) after the fashion of the German *Selbstdarstellungen*.

Like most of the earlier American psychologists, Baldwin was at the outset theologically minded. His training under such a church pillar as McCosh, at Princeton, may have had something to do with it, but, in all probability, Baldwin, himself, had an inclination toward the ministry. Happily, McCosh counselled his young student well in recommending a trip to Germany. After graduation, and when Baldwin returned to Princeton as an instructor, after two semesters at Leipzig and the University of Berlin, the courses which he was simultaneously taking in theology and apologetics, at the Princeton Theological Seminary, were not looked upon as an end in itself.

Baldwin was the founder of two psychological laboratories (University of Toronto and Princeton) and the restorer of the Johns Hopkins laboratory, which had fallen into disuse, after Hall's departure, yet his approach in all he wrote was theoretical and philosophical. As he himself puts it, "The interest in experimental psychology was not subordinate to that in philosophy and theology; but, on the contrary, it increased in force as I took up academic teaching."[3] One other fact ought to be brought out about Baldwin. He was never overawed by the exploits of the German experimentalists. Perhaps there was still a remnant of the Scottish School in his make-up, but what contributed greatly to his outlook was his contact with Charcot, Janet, and Bernheim in France. Later in life, when his academic activity, unfortunately, came to a close in America, he settled in France, and became one of the most vocal advocates for France, particularly during the first World War.

Baldwin's earliest publication in book form was a translation of Ribot's *Psychologie Allemande contemporaine*, which came out in 1886 (the date which appears in Baldwin's own auto-

[3] J. M. Baldwin, in *History of Psychology in Autobiography*, vol. I, p. 4.

biographical sketch is obviously a misprint) when the young psychologist was only 25. At the age of 29, he had already published the first volume of his *Handbook of Psychology*, which was followed, two years later, by the volume on *Feeling and Will*. It was on the strength of this textbook that he was offered a professorship at Princeton, where he stayed for ten years, bringing out, at intervals, the *Princeton Contributions to Psychology*, in addition to editing, with Cattell, as we have already had occasion to note, *The Psychological Review*, and founding *The Psychological Index*, as well as *The Psychological Bulletin*, which was devoted to surveys of the special literature, and book reviews. The Monograph series was probably the most important of these publications, due to Baldwin's initiative.

Three Phases in Baldwin's Progress

In Baldwin's psychological course, there were three strains: (a) the genetic, in which he seems to have approximated, although not coincided with, Hall, (b) the functional, which led him away from the structuralists and elementarists, and (c) the social, which brought him close to the later Chicago school. Baldwin had been nurtured on the theory of evolution, which even his theological teacher, McCosh, espoused. He further had cultivated an interest in the theories of dynamogenesis, which he probably acquired in France. Féré had formulated the principle that any change in the stimulation of a sense organ produces a corresponding effect in altering the tension in the muscles. It so happens that the ideo-motor theory as well as the new postulates of a motor consciousness, advanced by James and Münsterberg, were in keeping with Baldwin's views. Indeed, in 1900, Münsterberg remarked to Baldwin, "you and I are the 'motor men' on the psychological car." While, therefore, the Wundtians in America were engaged on the cognitive process and on reaction-time *per se*, in their experimentation, Baldwin was endeavoring to work out motor interpretations for many of the mental processes through a study of kinaesthesis.

As time went on, Baldwin showed his disappointment in the meagerness of the experimental results, and he began to feel "that there was truth in what James was already lamenting as to the barrenness of the tables and curves coming from many laboratories."[4] He became more and more absorbed in

[4] J. M. Baldwin: *Loc. cit.*

his theoretical work on child and social psychology, where he could propound doctrines unhampered by experimental findings.

Contributions

There were three trends in Baldwin's psychology: (a) the developmental, (b) the affective, in relation to logic, and (c) the axiological, with the aesthetic note the most pronounced. The evolutionary trend was marked by a belief that determinate lines vary as the result of natural selection, in conjunction with spontaneous variations. Thus what Baldwin calls "organic selection," or accommodation, which the individual at an early stage is learning through effort, is a great help in moulding the natural inheritance. Baldwin might have seen an element of truth in the contentions of the Russians, Mitchurin and Lysenko, that the gene does not account for all that is claimed for it. In his *Darwin and the Humanities* (1909) Baldwin attempts to show how the principle of organic selection operates not only in psychology, but in sociology and ethics as well.

His *Mental Development in the Child and the Race* (1894) was one of the most ambitious treatises on child psychology for that period, a pioneer piece of work, stimulated by his fatherly interest in his two little girls. This volume, with its companion, *Social and Ethical Interpretations* (1897) comprises the core of Baldwin's contribution to psychology, as distinct from philosophy. Here will be found experimental, or at least observational, data on right- and left-handedness, on speech, color-perception, suggestion, imitation, all correlated with findings in folk and social psychology. Baldwin's theories on social accommodation, working through circular reaction, and such phrases as "the dialectic of personal growth," the "socius" as the counterpart of the "ego," which develops in the individual from early childhood, were often discussed not only in this country but in Europe, where Baldwin had received recognition through the translation of his works and his frequent trips abroad.

French Influence

The four-volume *Thought and Things or Genetic Logic* was of course a monumental work, but of a nature which is more sociological and epistemological than psychological. In some respects, his treatment of primitive mentality coincides with that of Lévy-Bruhl; and Baldwin's division of thinking stages into the prelogical, logical, and superlogical (which is akin to a high type of mysticism) prepares us for the acceptance of an affective logic, *i.e.,* a logic based on sentiment and motives.

As has already been intimated, Baldwin imbibed at many fonts. He had been brought up on Scotch realism; he had had his apprenticeship in Germany, he was influenced by Darwin, although he did not take kindly to either Spencer or Bain, but above all, there is the impress of French thought in all his work. Charcot, Janet, Ribot, Féré, Tarde and Fouillée seem to have shaped his views. Even his functionalism is not the Chicago product but born of French insight. He was never satisfied to pin his faith, as did practically all of the Wundtians, on cognition. Affection was to him, as to the French, and later the Viennese school, a mighty important item. While Titchener and Münsterberg, rivals as they were, agreed on the primacy of cognition, in the matter of memory, maintaining that affective states cannot be revived without their original stimulus in the form of perceptions, images, etc., Baldwin, drawing his evidence mainly from clinical cases, was certain that emotions and feelings could be reinstated directly.

Thus, Baldwin is led to the conviction that, in addition to the logic of cognition, which is mediated by processes like comparison, generalization, and abstraction, or devices like analogy and substitution, there is an affective logic dealing with interests and values, other than truth, which is the exclusive goal of the logic of cognition. In everyday life, the cognitive and the affective become intertwined; and the products, after curious crisscrossing, are often neither the one nor the other, but mixtures. It is in the fourth volume, *Genetic Theory of Reality,* that Baldwin rounds out his system by developing an aesthetic interpretation of reality—aesthetic, however, in a very catholic sense, which might include mysticism, reverie, and even self-illusionism, but in its highest or crystallized form, it is reached through art and artistic contemplation. This particular philosophy of his, he has dubbed *"Pancalism."*

Assessment

Since Baldwin embodies both the psychologist and the philosopher, it would not be easy to shear him of the one or the other qualification, when assessing his contribution. His influence did not last, largely because he did not have many students, and his academic career in the United States was cut short at a time when he was at the height of his career. His books, after the outbreak of World War I, were mainly political, like *French and American Ideals* (1914), *France and the War* (1916), or *Between Two Wars* (1926) which is autobiographical. We are nevertheless indebted to him for the publication of the first *Dictionary of Psychology and Philosophy* in English (1901-1906). It was a gigantic project; for actually it is more of an encyclopedia than a dictionary, and even though he would occasionally initial articles written by others and revised by himself, his own work in this undertaking must have been enormous, since he not only organized the staff of sixty authorities, but edited the two large volumes. Benjamin Rand's two volumes of bibliography, classified according to subject, are included in the *Dictionary*, and added considerably to its value as a permanent reference work.

Baldwin was a facile writer. He had a vast fund of knowledge, and adapted himself to new currents of thought, but he moved in too large syntheses. One could not quarrel with his aim to coin suitable terms for technical purposes, but often his writings are overcast by a thin mist. His *Story of the Mind* (1898) is a clear presentation of psychology for the layman, and his *History of Psychology*, in two slender volumes (1913) is readable, although altogether too sketchy. Baldwin was the most decorated and most translated American psychologist, with the exception of William James, and he apparently set great store by being elected to, or joining, many learned societies abroad.

Chapter 16

E. W. Scripture—Experimental
Avant-Gardist (1864-1945)

THERE WAS NO CHAPTER or even section devoted to Scripture
in the original edition of this History, largely because he had
become too much of a practitioner and a specialist in one
area—phonetics—but also because as a result of a personal
episode, he had left the United States after a fruitful decade
as Director of the Yale Psychological Laboratory which Ladd
had founded. As an expatriate, he worked in Germany and
Austria, ending his active life in England.

The omission, however, weighed on the present author's
mind, and it is well that, despite possible exceptions that might
be taken, there can be no contesting the fact that Scripture
belongs in a history of American psychology not only by
virtue of his early influences but also for the reason that he
had, through the years of his self-imposed exile, contributed
scores of articles to American journals.

Scripture embodied a tissue of paradoxes from early youth
to posthumous obscurity. His very name, which may have
created a soupçon of promise for the theologically minded
Ladd, when he selected him as director of the Yale Psychological Laboratory, was out of kilter with his general outlook
and rather untraditional behavior. A brilliant experimentalist
and provocative writer who, in a sense, was ahead of his
time, he had been so much out of touch with colleagues that
Who's Who carried his sketch for about a decade after his
death; and what is worse, when he did die, the event seems
to have gone unnoticed, and we learn about it only through
a very casual reference in a footnote by E. G. Boring in
O. G. Ellson's obituary of W. L. Bryan[1]—a curious fate for
a pioneer and one of the twenty-six charter members of the
American Psychological Association, who was productive
up to the beginning of his fifth score of years.

[1] *Amer. Journal of Psychology,* 1956, vol. 69, p. 325. In a card,
Boring tells me that it is "the only published notice of Scripture's
death that I know of."

His opening paragraph in the sketch appearing in the third volume of the *History of Psychology in Autobiography* is arresting and, I think, revealing from a psychoanalytic angle. "How am I to respond," he asks "to an invitation to write the history of my psychological life without committing more indiscretions than anyone would care to be responsible for? And how am I to tell the truth without revealing much that I would prefer to keep to myself?" And after concluding the 31 pages, he appends a note which reads, "I notice a paucity of personal details in my account. I have forgotten most of them and am not interested in the rest; I do not think the reader would be interested either. In order to be dated and placed, I have to state that I was born in 1864, in a village in New Hampshire, U.S.A." It reminds me that when my articles on Münsterberg appeared with the information that he was born of Jewish parents, his widow asked me not to mention the fact if I were to incorporate the essay in a book "as no one is interested in it." Of course, it is only the wish on their part that no one *were* interested—an illustration of the phenomenon involved in "The lady doth protest too much."

Despite Scripture's uncommon reserve to the extent of not even divulging the name of the village in which he first saw the light, he has, willy-nilly, exposed a good deal. It appears that he "foolishly refused an offer" from his father to take up medicine, rectifying his mistake only twenty years later, after academic life had irked him. "After 25 years of active service as a physician, I cannot read the usual book on psychology without being bored." For one who had been among the early American students in Wundt's laboratory (1888) it is again something of a paradox or perhaps an irony. He was even more disgusted with the neurological speculations of the day ("nerve cells tickling one another"). "With the knowledge of neurology acquired at a later date such psychophysiological *Phantasterei* became so repulsive that I now throw aside every book on psychology the moment I see a picture of the brain in it." Nearly thirty years ago he wrote in his credo:

There is not a word of truth in any statement ever made concerning the *nature* of the activity of the brain; the indicator numbers have never been found. . . . When a psychologist attempts to explain mental activity in terms of nerve cells and nerve currents, he is merely trying to cloak psychological ignorance with neurological foolishness.

We can well assume that such an outspoken personality would not win friends or influence people on a large scale. If we examine his portrait, we shall find the tense look of the investigator, impatient to come to grips with the problem at hand, and intolerant of speculative theory. He has the air of a top executive of a national sales organization which he is trying to lift out of the red.

Actually, he belongs to our own period; and as an operationist, although he may not have been aware of it, he would have been more allied to the school of Skinner who, too, flouts theory. What is more, he is the true predecessor of Hull, and his equations are even more formidable than Hull's, although he would never have put all the emphasis on the S-R connection; for he states emphatically, "It is a mistake to treat sensation as depending on any one of the properties of the stimulus alone." Without declaring himself on statistics, factorial analysis, or mathematical models, Scripture contends that "Experimental psychology can never rise above a rather amateurish level till the leaders can handle vectors, Hamiltonians, potentials as well as the representatives of the physical sciences can."

Scripture, who had formed an attachment for German scientific procedure, thought of everything in terms of measurement. He even foresaw possibilities of raising psychoanalysis to the quantitative level. Thus, one can see that Hull was a continuator of Scripture's course at Yale, only he had come there at a more auspicious time. Reticent as he wishes to be, Scripture cannot help complaining of his lot when his popular book *Thinking, Feeling, Doing* created a tempest. His second book, *The New Psychology*, which purported to show how consciousness can be dealt with experimentally and not just theoretically or armchairedly, did not take too well either. The third volume, *Elements of Experimental Phonetics*, was one of the bulkiest publications in psychology about half a century ago. It was truly a monumental work, but it did not make a dent in general psychology, because it was in a peripheral segment and contained numberless tables and records, on smoked paper, and charts. Scripture was putting forth theories of his own which he thought of as laws, based on numerical results, encompassing such topics as articulation, stress, metre, phonetics—all accompanied by shrewd observations, often embellished by sardonic wit, *e.g.*, when he pokes fun at the professors who try to fit Shakespeare's verse into their metric schemes and, failing to make the grade, explain the discrepancy by attributing poetic licence, or even altering the original lines to suit their schemes.

For thirty years Scripture applied the graphic method of analyzing vowel curves, and divided speech into microphonic and macrophonic elements, both consisting of vibrations of the air particles, but the latter made up of puffs of air that emanate from the mouth and die away rapidly.

In 1906, he returned to the United States and became a clinician in the Columbia University Vanderbilt Clinic, where he founded a laboratory of speech neurology, particularly studying epileptic speech. In 1912, he migrated to London, where he founded a laboratory of speech neurology at the West End Hospital for Nervous Diseases.

Scripture passed through four stages of mental development. He started out in adolescence as a naïve Cartesian, then entered the Fechner-Wundt stage of experimentation. Subsequently, Freud caught his fancy, but he wanted to probe into the unconscious via experiments, and finally his acquaintance with the doctrine of relativity acted somewhat like an electroshock. And here he stands, mystified by or at the "great unknown," but bidding the psychologists to discover the methods of measurement so as to be able to handle the data mathematically—an early operationist rather than a factorial analyst. Had he remained in the United States, he would most likely have become one of the pillars of American psychology, wielding great influence in shaping its future course, even if his fiery temper and sharp tongue and trenchant pen might have conduced to lessen his prestige. That the solitary sketch of his life should appear on his centenary is a coincidence that savors of poetic justice.

Chapter 17

The Structuralism of Titchener

IN EDWARD BRADFORD TITCHENER (1867-1927) we have the first European who, for a time, dominated American psychology leaving a lasting impress, not so much on account of his works or systematic principles, as by virtue of his forceful personality and intellect, which awed his graduate students. Titchener was a curious blend in that he enjoyed a thorough education at Oxford, first in the humanities and philosophy, then in physiology, under J. S. Burdon-Sanderson, to whom he dedicated his *Textbook in Psychology*, and after graduation from Brasenose College, Oxford, he came under the direct influence of Wundt, at the University of Leipzig, in 1890, which at the time was a Mecca for scientific pilgrims from every land, and not least from America.

The two years he spent at Leipzig not only decided his own psychological course, but also that of his future students, and to a certain extent, it steered the destiny of American psychology from 1892, when Titchener started, on a very modest scale, to make out of the Cornell laboratory a bulwark of research, until years after his death—perhaps half a century in all. Titchener was 25 then, and had only a summer's experience of lecturing at Oxford, after obtaining his doctorate at Leipzig. During the same year, another graduate from Wundt's laboratory, this time a German (Jew), Hugo Münsterberg, was imported to take charge of William James's laboratory at Harvard, and for the next two decades or more, the keen competition between the two most famous psychological laboratories in the New World was to make scientific history. Both men, of powerful frame, uncommonly energetic and enthusiastic, stood head and shoulders intellectually above their contemporaries in this country. Of the two, Titchener was perhaps the more remarkable, in that he was able to make of a rather humble institution, as Cornell was then, a noted psychological centre.

Neither Titchener nor Münsterberg identified himself with their adopting (more than adopted) country. The former regarded himself as an Englishman till the end; the latter definitely clung to his German ideals. Most psychologists thought of Titchener as the continuator of the Leipzig tradition, or even as the apostle of Wundt on American soil. As one writer puts it, "Only two years at Leipzig had Germanized him. He even looked like a German and was sometimes mistaken for one; the science for which he labored was German to the core."[1] In such a bald statement, there lurks possibly what Titchener himself would have called the "stimulus error." In other words, it's an *ex post facto* reasoning. "Titchener studied at Leipzig; he was in accord with Wundt's system of psychology, *ergo* he must have become thoroughly Germanized; and did he not look unmistakably German?" Actually, he resembled either the English poet and socialist leader, William Morris, or the Russian Prince, Peter Kropotkin, who became the chief theoretical anarchist of his day. Titchener himself was an individualist of high consistency.

Titchener's Mental Constitution

As a matter of fact, Titchener was thoroughly British in temperament, in scientific spirit, and in his motivation. He did not, like Wundt or the other German psychologists, advance philosophical theories, once he settled in his psychological domain; and as for the system which he elaborated, it may have been a legacy from the associationist school as likely as an impress of the Leipzig discipline. It is quite true that at Leipzig, he learned the value of adhering to a system in the most rigorous fashion. The British, or rather the English, are prone to accept it in spirit, rather than emphasizing it to the letter. The content, however, of Titchener's system was British as well as German. It is characterized by a structural form where the elements must fit and dovetail into an even more and more complex unit. It thus differs from the incipient functionalism which was beginning to grow up in other centres, principally in France and the midwest in the United States, as well as from the *Akt* psychology of the Austrian school and, partly, the Ward-Stout faction in England, maintaining, as it did, that the image, *e.g.*, was the product of the act of imagination; the percept brought on by an act of perception, which vaguely suggests an animistic principle as against the Titchenerian view that the mind is

[1] E. Heidbreder: *Seven Psychologies* (1933), p. 114.

only a succession of states, that these states exist as content of which we are aware. When we are not conscious of anything, then the mental state does not exist. Structuralism, as it has been designated (Titchener used the adjective "existential" but not the noun), in contrast to *Akt* psychology, is practically the sequel of Locke and Hume, and it must be remembered that Titchener never cared to follow Wundt into the steep heights of philosophical interpretations of mental phenomena. Boring, who studied with and taught under Titchener, takes exception and considers him very German in outlook. But, then, Boring's forte is not ethnic psychology.

It is hardly correct to say that Titchener was simply a devoted and rigid disciple of Wundt. He was, of course, an admirer of the high priest in Leipzig, who could produce so much outstanding work and embrace a world of information, but he was also interested in and attracted to the Würzburg School, translating one of Külpe's textbooks, and collaborating in the translation of another. If Titchener had not been a student of Wundt's he might still have formulated the same system; for in methodology, he could easily vie with his great teacher. Perhaps on the formal side, he was strengthened by his two years' stay at the University of Leipzig. While the structure which he reared might have been too self-contained, not articulating with other structures, it stood at least solid and shock-proof. Let us then see what were Titchener's scientific assumptions.

Systematic Postulates

Titchener's cardinal psychological postulates may be reduced to at most two or three. Starting out with the definition that psychology is the science of consciousness, he would make certain that (a) anything which is not in consciousness could not come strictly under the head of psychology, and (b) that the only method which could adequately deal with the contents of consciousness would be introspection. Habit, which, to Titchener, was at one time a conscious state later superseded by purely neural processes, could not be assigned more than courtesy space in a textbook. Instinct which, for Titchener, had a similar basis, likewise would be relegated to a cubbyhole, as compared, for instance, with such a central issue as attention, or sensation. In other words, whatever was the object of introspection would receive its due recognition. As soon as it, however, drops below the threshold, it no longer can claim our psychological interest, except in linking up the physiological or biological data with the mental. Thus the old dictum "Nothing is in the intellect which has not been previously in the senses" may now read "Nothing is in the psychological universe of discourse which is not presently in consciousness." Association, or rather the ideas associated, are psychological material, but unconscious association, whether as Lipps expounded it, or as the psychoanalysts, including the secessionists, like Jung and Adler, interpreted it, would not be tolerated by Titchener, or for that matter any Wundtian, not even by Münsterberg. On one point, however, he had to yield, and that was on the matter of meaning, which, emerging as the vanishing point of the imaginal or sensory content, is carried as an attitude, posture, or other behavioral set.

Introspection must be controlled, and only a thorough training could entitle a student to become an investigator. The qualitative aspect of the data had to be supplemented by measurement. The varying of experimental conditions would, of course, require considerable ingenuity in technique, construction of apparatus, and the handling of devices. Accuracy was, above all, the *sine qua non* of experimentation, and the slightest deviation from painstaking effort, to the point of drudgery, would be dealt with severely. Thus, Titchener became the paragon of laboratory meticulousness in American psychology.

Assets and Liabilities of Structuralism

If psychology is to be a science like other natural sciences, it would concern itself with general laws. What happens to the individual is pertinent only in so far as it confirms or tests the law. We are interested in the general mind, not in this or that observer's mind. To be sure, such circumscription tends to brush aside the whole field of individual differences, but for Titchener, the sacrifice was worth while in the cause of scientific psychology. Furthermore, psychology, in order to remain in its scientific orbit should stay "pure," like mathematics or physics. Titchener refused to stray from that path, even when the prospects of applied and abnormal psychology were looming large. This self-imposed restriction was a great pity, and evinced a lack of vision on his part, perhaps also a certain British insularity. Having committed himself to but one school, to but one method, and, in reality, one field, *viz.,* experimental psychology in the normal human sphere, he could not help cutting off from view some important vistas. Small wonder, then, that as new movements and fields began to broaden the science, he would be regarded as a back number by those of the younger generation who were not his students; and some of his distinguished colleagues even saw in his labors a futile attempt to cling to antiquated principles, which could only culminate in sterility.[2]

It might be anticipated that, as a consequence of this fear of rebellion in his own ranks, he would exercise undue authority in the selection of problems for doctoral dissertations. As a rule, the topics were assigned in keeping with the issues which occupied his attention at the time; and as he was building up, so to speak, a systematic skyscraper, the graduate students were expected to work as a collective unit. Thus at one time, attention might be the laboratory issue; at another, perhaps, it would be the determining tendency—a more complex phenomenon—and the problems would be along this line.

Titchener thus erected an ivory tower in which he was to sit aloft and direct the course of what he considered to be the only scientific psychology worthy of the name. Due to this isolation from those of his colleagues who had been forging ahead on new tacks, and certainly from the run-of-the-mill psychologists, his influence could not but wane as time went on. Fortunately, his students, who were obliged to sit with him in this ivory tower, after receiving their doctorates (and, according to Boring, there were fifty-four who received their Ph.D. under him) did spread his ideas after their appointments, usually, to important posts; and, of course, his preëminence as an experimental psychologist could not have been overlooked even by his most captious critics.

Born to the intellectual manor, he was not disposed to brook any opposition in his own estate, although he was gracious about it in handling subordinates, and never having felt even the need of adaptation, let alone, naturalization,

---

[2] It is interesting, however, in this connection that in 1921, Titchener had softened to the extent of accepting office as one of the directors of the Psychological Corporation—an organization avowedly committed to the promotion of applied psychology.

he could not participate in the activities of the American Psychological Association which, to him, was boisterous compared with the quiet Oxford atmosphere or the cool stratosphere of the British Association for the Advancement of Science. To make matters worse, his high principles made no allowance for dillydallying in matters of right and wrong. When he discovered that a member of the American Psychological Association had paraphrased some of his experimental conclusions, palming them off as his own, he demanded the expulsion of the culprit. The Association was not willing to take such drastic measures, especially where it is so difficult to prove actual plagiary; and the result was that Titchener withdrew. It is said that some friends of Titchener, and of psychology, paid his dues for years afterwards, so that his name might continue to grace the membership list.

Personality

Happily for American psychology, as well as for Titchener, a group of psychologists was formed, familiarly referred to as "the Titchener experimentalists," who met at various laboratories from 1904 to 1926, for the comparison of notes in the experimental psychology of the traditional topics, with introspection as its basis. It was a tribute to the Cornell director that even such a rival laboratory as Harvard would be represented by both instructors and students. Thus, among the twenty-five or more who were present at Yale, in 1913, under the auspices of Dean R. P. Angier, one could find H. C. Warren, K. S. Lashley, E. G. Boring, H. P. Weld, as well as the following instructors and graduate students from Harvard: E. B. Holt, H. S. Langfeld (Münsterberg's lieutenant at the time), R. M. Elliott, E. C. Tolman, H. E. Burtt, and A. A. Roback. As fate would have it, of the other five mentioned, Angier had received his doctorate at Harvard, and both Boring and Lashley later accepted professorships at Harvard.

Titchener sat at the head of the table, as if conducting a seminar. There was a genial air about the proceedings. Warren's frequent mirthful laughter, really a social mannerism to set everyone at ease, himself included, did help to relieve the majestic bearing of Titchener. To a young newcomer, Titchener's tic (blinking) would appear as a strange flaw in a great psychologist who is supposed to be, at least, outwardly free from defects, but the personality of the man was so natural and spontaneous, so inwardly unassuming, that even during the very afternoon, the tic would be disregarded and forgotten, and as the acquaintance grew between the older man and the young student from some outside laboratory, the bond would become closer. This is not merely one man's experience. It was general.

The reason, it would seem, lay in Titchener's character, employing the word in the more restricted sense. Some of the foremost psychologists, Wundt among them, could not be said to have been paragons of virtue, or, using perhaps a more explicit, although recently coined term, to have possessed a high degree of "adequacy valence," which comprises three special features (a) insight, (b) sentiment, and (c) independence.[3] Titchener had independence. In addition to his scientific integrity, which emanated from, or was a function of, his independence, his valence of adequacy was what singled him out as the master, so that "where the king was, there was his court." His published books may not display these qualities, but his work as director of a laboratory, as editor, in dealing with contributors, and as correspondent, manifests a good deal of the warmth and sympathy which were often hidden from view by the imposing exterior.

For all his exclusiveness, and inability to enter into professional coöperation with his compeers, Titchener evinced uncommon charitableness and magnanimity toward his famous colleagues, in many cases overlooking their faults and singling out their virtues. He was extremely appreciative of the slightest courtesy, and certainly, in this respect, he typified not the German functionary or educator but the English gentleman. It may be said, incidentally, that some of those he had much praise for were not as generous toward him, in their private communications.

Titchener's Works and Duties

In the 35 years which he spent in the United States, and which represent practically the whole of his productive life, Titchener wrote less than a dozen books. These were *The Outline of Psychology* (1896), the four-volume *Manual of Experimental Psychology*, which has been mentioned earlier,

[3] A. A. Roback: *Personality in Theory and Practice*, chapter 15, "The Criterion of Personality."

Lectures on the Elementary Psychology of Feeling and Attention (1908) and *Experimental Psychology of the Thought Processes* (1909), the *Textbook of Psychology* (1910) which was the most successful handbook for at least a decade, non-philosophical, methodical, literary, and honest, to the extent of telling the students whenever a problem is beyond the solution of the author, a questionable policy in the case of eager youth, *A Beginner's Psychology* (1915) which was the rewritten *Primer of Psychology,* published in 1898, and the slender first volume of *Systematic Psychology,* which was brought out posthumously by his former student and colleague, H. P. Weld. His textbooks enjoyed wide popularity in other countries, some of them having been translated into Russian, Italian, German, Spanish, and French.

These books, however, do not, by any means, give us a total picture of the man's productivity. It should not be forgotten that in directing research and editing his students' dissertations, he was devoting a great deal of the time which he might have employed toward his own writings. For years, too, as successor of Hall, he was editor of *The American Journal of Psychology,* and had been the American editor of *Mind.* Anyone who had ever had dealings with him in his editorial capacity will attest to the fact that Titchener did not perform his duties perfunctorily.

Apart from the many scores of articles and still more minor notes which he contributed to various periodicals, chiefly to *The American Journal of Psychology,* he was a glutton for punishment in the matter of translation. Boring tells us that he had translated all of the third edition of Wundt's *Grundzüge der physiologischen Psychologie,* only to discover that a fourth edition had been completed, which he undertook to translate, but as this was about to go to the printers, the fifth edition of Wundt's *magnum opus* came out, and Titchener withdrew his manuscript, starting work anew on this edition.[4] Finally, the first part of this edition was published. His translation of Külpe's *Grundriss der Psychologie* was another chore which very few scientists of Titchener's

---

[4] Boring, who is so rich in details, seems to be unaware that the second edition of Wundt's *Vorlesungen über die Menschen- und Tierseele* was translated jointly by J. G. Creighton and Titchener. He mentions the English translation, but not the translators, either under Wundt or under Titchener, in his *History of Experimental Psychology.*

standing would have carried out. Titchener probably took a delight in finding apt and felicitous expressions in English for the more awkward ones in German, but unless he felt it incumbent upon himself to set objective value above his own success, he would never have devoted so much precious time and energy to such a thankless self-imposed task.

Self-Realization His Goal

That Titchener was not overambitious to bequeath to the world a library from his own pen, as was his master, Wundt, may readily be inferred from the fact that his hobbies or avocations were never abandoned in deference to his scientific labors. He was the most well-rounded psychologist in the United States. It mattered little to him that thereby he was jeopardizing his lasting fame, without even receiving the glory of the moment, which compensates publicity-seeking educators who digress from their academic pursuits.

Titchener's course in life was self-realization, and if such was to be attained by cultivating the art of music, or even in collecting coins of all times, then this was to be treated as a serious occupation; and indeed to such a degree had Titchener become proficient in music that he substituted at one time for the professor of music at Cornell, and, in addition, it was related, he would conduct a small ensemble at his home every Sunday evening.

His interest in numismatics was not restricted to the mere collecting and classifying. As in his psychology, his thoroughness would manifest itself in mastering the details, certainly the characters on the coins, which entailed learning such remote and difficult languages as Arabic and Chinese, both at opposite poles from English or German. His knowledge of the classical languages may be taken for granted, but he was conversant with half a dozen modern languages as well, including Russian. In one of his letters to A. A. Roback, he writes: "I am afraid that my claims to be counted a philologist go back a quarter of a century; but my interest in that side of the world still persists." It was characteristic of him that he did not part with old associations; he simply added to them, so that he preserved the continuity of his outlook, always broadening, without radically changing, as in the case of other thinkers, like Bertrand Russell, to take one instance.

It is one of the paradoxes that the very man who was so rigid in his one-sided adherence to introspective psychology, who was looked upon as restricted in his point of view by other psychologists as they branched out in various directions, espousing several schools of thought at once, and cultivating three or four different fields, while he was supposed to live in the ivory tower of pure and introspective psychology, should, in the last analysis, have been the most versatile and broadest of contemporary psychologists—biology, physiology, the classics, current fiction, illustrations from which were often introduced in his textbooks, linguistics and philology, music and anthropology forming his cultural horopter. Withal, he stuck steadfastly to a single purpose.

It was the same characteristic—independence and living for the sake of culture rather than in order to produce, at all costs, which led Titchener to carry on a correspondence with hundreds of colleagues and even fledgelings, who were barely out of the graduate school, and who had not been his students, nor were they committed to his system of psychology. His letters were never mere routine; their content was not commensurate with the status of the recipient, but rather in keeping with the urge of the writer and the situation involved. Most of the letters were typewritten by himself, with added material in script. Such voluminous correspondence, especially in editorial connections, must have been very time-consuming. Then, too, few teachers who were creative prepared their lectures as conscientiously as he did. His aim was not only to impart information but to inspire the young students, and his elementary course was said to have been among the all-time highlights at Cornell.

The upshot of all this was that Titchener dissipated a great deal of energy upon things extraneous to psychology. The time spent in such activities, which were always performed in his customary painstaking manner, could have been utilized in developing his system, which necessarily remained in a fragmentary state. In a letter, dated September 21, 1918, he wrote to Roback:

My last seminary gave me, for the first time in my life, a satisfactory answer to the big questions that have been bothering me for a quarter of a century. Now I think I can produce a system of psychology in English, and in several volumes. I have been working for a year on my introductory volume, and it is shaping: slowly and at times a little stiffly, but it is shaping. Once that is done, the actual exposition will be a joy; and though the critics will have their own joy in my extermination, at any rate the framework will be solid enough to give them some real exercise. It is surely time that we had a real system, amply conceived, in the English language. And though with a son in France, it is not altogether easy to concentrate oneself, yet I hope that the result may be even better for the effort that it has cost.

Toward the end of his comparatively short life, it was whispered that Titchener was shifting ground and was yielding to the spirit of the times. He had already made some concession in the matter of meaning, which he thought might be carried in a physiological, and therefore unconscious, setting as context, but he seemed to be irked by such allegations or even expectations. The present writer had once made a casual remark on the possibility, and it is gratifying to have the letter clarifying the issue. In this statement, dated Feb. 1, 1923, Titchener, in his characteristic bluff epistolary manner, spikes the yarn in these words.

Probably some hints of my systematic work are leaking out (as e.g. by way of Ogden's[5] recent papers and are getting misinterpreted (as Ogden has in some measure misinterpreted them). So far as I know, my psychological thought has been continuous since 1890. If the rumours intend that I am heading by the least slant toward behaviourism or dynamism or stimulus-response, I can only say that they lie in their windy throats. If they simply mean that I am giving up 'consciousness,' I can say that never from my earliest infancy have I supposed that Psy. dealt with Cs in their sense of 'awareness,'—that I have tried to hold Cs as an existential term and have failed to get my message over,—and that I dropped the term overtly, with explanation, in my Beginner's book. But why don't the rumour-people read my papers???

Upon Hugo Münsterberg's death, Titchener received a call from Harvard to serve as director of the psychological labora-

---

[5] The Ogden referred to here is not the Cambridge, England, Basic English originator, but R. M. Ogden, of Cornell.

tory, but he declined, although it would have been more advantageous financially and perhaps, too, otherwise, in that he would have had a better selection of graduate students, aside from the prestige of association with the famous university and the department of which William James was the founder. His loyalty toward Cornell and his dislike of new adventures supervened and he remained at Ithaca until his death, of a brain tumor, at the age of sixty.

Chapter 18

Hugo Münsterberg

WHEN WILLIAM JAMES, in 1892, invited Hugo Münsterberg, then 29 years old, to take charge of the Harvard Psychological Laboratory, which he himself was outgrowing, it might have been surmised that the young man had found favor in his eyes because he had dared to challenge the psychological sovereign of the day, Wilhelm Wundt, who was not on the best terms with James. That particular circumstance was only an opportune incident. In Münsterberg, James had picked about the best man for the position; for notwithstanding its director's youth, the Freiburg Laboratory had already attracted a number of research students, some even from the United States, and in both the *Willenshandlung* (1888) and the collection of *Beiträge zur experimentellen Psychologie* (1889-1892), the author showed more than marked promise. Münsterberg, in his twenties, exhibited an extraordinary grasp of the intricate problems which were besetting the new science. He had also published a little book on the origin of morals (*Ursprung der Sitten*) during the Freiburg period.

In addition, Münsterberg was motor-minded *i.e.*, he held the theory that consciousness was not altogether a matter of sensory stimulation involving the afferent nerves, but embraced the motor outlet as well, not successively but simultaneously. James's view of emotion was based on that very principle. In fact, Münsterberg's action theory was the analogue, in attention, of the James theory of emotions. Both were adumbrations, or even phases of, functionalism, which will be discussed in the next chapter, and both were evidence of the practical strain in the two men, although this strain was in two different keys.

Kinship with William James

Münsterberg had more in common with James than was apparent at first blush. They were both philosophers, and in the same quandary as regards the fitting of the values into a scientific framework. It will be remembered that James left himself open to charges of inconsistency, in that he believed in a *fiat* of the will, and yet preached a strict determinism, in accordance with the requisites of physiological psychology. There were other contradictions, as we have seen, in which he became entangled; and yet he made no effort to resolve them. His successor at the Harvard Psychological Laboratory, was more businesslike. He boldly espoused Fichte's idealism in philosophy, while insisting on a strict empiricism or realism in science, and thus, taking the bull by the horns, the dilemma was resolved through a system of double bookkeeping. The values were recorded in one type of ledger, and the facts in another.

Fichte appealed to Münsterberg because of the great stress he laid on action (*Die Tat*). It may have been that Ferdinand Lassalle, who, as Münsterberg once told the present writer, had been a close friend of his father, and an admirer of his aunt, dying in a duel the year after Münsterberg was born, proved the source of his inspiration; for Fichte's philosophy guided Lassalle in his drawn-out campaigns, as an agitator on behalf of the workers. It was action which symbolized Münsterberg's life throughout, and it is not by mere chance that the theory which was chiefly associated with Münsterberg's psychology was named the "action theory."

The Action Theory

There is a curious irony attached to this theory. While working at Wundt's laboratory, Münsterberg, in the course of experiments on willed reactions, took a negative stand toward his master's belief that we are conscious of the amount of effort we are employing, say, in lifting a weight, through the nervous discharge from the central nervous system toward the muscles. Thus, according to Wundt, the will would be to us a direct experience, an element of the mind. Against the authority of his teacher, Münsterberg contended that the sense of effort was entirely due to the sensations coming from the muscles, tendons, and joints (technically known as the kinaesthetic sensations), and had nothing whatever to do with the outgoing current from the central nervous system.

Wundt was placed in a predicament, and, after finding fault with the experimentation, shifted him to another problem, innocuous this time, the investigation of which procured for him his doctorate. Münsterberg, however, was not the man to waste his material and supinely accept his lot. When he became an instructor at Freiburg, he presented the rejected dissertation, in expanded form, as his *Habilitationsschrift*, or inaugural thesis, under the title of *Die Willenshandlung* (Voluntary Action).

The formidable Wundt did not think it beneath his dignity to reply to his young opponent, who had recently been graduated from his laboratory. An animated controversy arose in which Münsterberg won his laurels, but also lost the favor and friendship of his famous teacher at Leipzig. It is even whispered in close circles that Wundt brought his influence to bear in stirring up anti-Semitic feeling among the authorities of the University of Berlin, when Münsterberg's candidacy came up for consideration. It was at this time that the young psychologist was recommended for an appointment at the technical college in Zürich; and three influential German professors were not slow in sending a sheaf of unfavorable comments on the candidate to the governing board of that institution. These were Wundt, Natorp, and G. E. Müller.[1]

The pluck and effective argumentation of the young scholar, however, had already attracted the notice of William James in America. So highly did he esteem the monograph, *Die Willenshandlung*, that he quoted argument after argument from it in his *Principles of Psychology*. In one passage he says: "*Herr* Münsterberg's work is a little masterpiece. . . . I shall repeatedly have to refer to it, and cordially recommend to the reader its most thorough refutation of the *Innervationsgefühl* theory." James believed that the doctrine of innervation received its *coup de grâce* at the hands of Münsterberg; and it was undoubtedly due to the latter's initiative that Wundt himself finally abandoned the view which he had so fervently cherished and defended.

The joke, however, in this controversy, is that Münsterberg's formulation of the action theory harks back to the very innervation principle, which he did so much to destroy; for what does this theory stand for? Actually, it maintains that the strength of our attention, or perhaps better, its vividness, when, *e.g.*, looking at an object, depends on the openness of the motor paths. When these paths leading to the periphery, and, eventually, the muscles, are not wholly clear, the object we are perceiving or the word we are listening to will not

[1] This information comes from the late Ludwig Stein, who, for many years, was Professor of Philosophy at the University of Bern.

register fully in consciousness. To attend will, therefore, require a certain muscular tension or preparedness, and thus, as in the James-Lange theory of emotions, the generally accepted sequence of events is reversed.

Münsterberg has never given a full exposition of the action theory in English. However in the *Grundzüge der Psychologie* (1900; 2d ed. with a memoir by Max Dessoir, 1918) which is probably his chief work, the last chapter of about 15,000 words shows us not only how the nerve processes are involved, down to molecular considerations, but also the *modus operandi* of the theory in various life situations. Throughout the presentation, the details are discussed with a clarity and comprehensiveness that must evoke admiration.

For our purpose, it will not be necessary to translate from the German fundamental work. A few disconnected passages from his textbook, *Psychology, General and Applied*, will serve to illustrate Münsterberg's gift of synthesis and scope and will also bring home to us the reason why this man caught the fancy of leaders in many walks of life.

As long as we try to explain everything only by sense stimulation and association, there are no lights and shades in the picture. The most characteristic features of mental life, vividness and inhibition, remain neglected. The effort to keep house with a mere association theory must therefore be acknowledged as hopeless. An additional principle must be found by which the order and the shading of our mental life may be understood. Not a few psychologists, to be sure, sought a convenient refuge in the introduction of some spiritual principle in the mind, frequently called apperception. It was meant as a power which can intrude into the sphere of ideas and arbitrarily select the one and reject the other, push this forward and suppress that. It was exempt from the chain of causal connections; it broke into the realm of psychical nature like a miracle. Surely no one has a right to say that such a mind power which prefers and inhibits thoughts has no reality, but its reality lies in the world of purposive psychology. We shall find it there as a central energy, but in the sphere of causal psychology it is meaningless. The reënforcement and inhibition must be treated here as processes of the psychophysical mechanism. The theory which we have traced fully satisfies this demand. It overcomes the narrow incompleteness of the association theory and avoids the inconsistency of the apperception theory. In contrast to both, let us call this the *action theory*.[2]

We note that in this paragraph, Münsterberg is opposed to the strict association view of both the Scotch and the English schools, as well as to the voluntaristic or even semi-animistic implications of Wundt, whom he does not mention by name.

It is evident that this formulation of the action theory expresses the principle in its most abstract form. It becomes adjusted to the richness of life only when we consider how extremely complex the motor mechanism is, which, according to the theory, influences the reënforcement and inhibition of the sensory states. Every impulse to movement involves groups of other coördinated or subordinated motor impulses. In the same way the suppression of an antagonistic impulse must have its inhibitory influence on the coördinated and subordinated motor centers. But every one of these aroused motor cells has again its antagonist; every cooperating motor excitement therefore increases the vividness of certain sensory impressions or ideas, and every subdued motor cell group may cut off the chances of certain ideas and impressions.

According to the popular view a world of impressions and ideas exists in us, entirely independent of our actions, and when they are complete and perfect, they send their message to some motor apparatus which carries out the order. Such a fancy must be entirely reversed. In every moment the motor situation decides the possibilities in the sensory sphere. Our ideas are the product of our readiness to act. The little lizard is not aware of thundering noises around him, but when the slightest rustling indicates danger, it perceives it at once and escapes. That slight noise met a disposition to reaction; the loud one is without significance for the system of the lizard's actions. We all perceive the world just as far as we are prepared to react to it. *Our ability to respond is the true vehicle of our power to know*, and all training and habit formation in the sphere of our actions shape and stamp the perceptions and memories and thoughts in our mind.

*　　　*　　　*　　　*　　　*

[2] H. Münsterberg: *Psychology, General and Applied*, 1914, pp. 140-141.

As soon as we have recognized the bearing of the centrifugal action on all the central processes, it seems only natural to consider whether this same principle may not be expanded beyond the sphere of vividness and inhibition. We know that the experience of pleasure leads to one kind of movement, and that of pain to an opposite kind. We know that the stimulus coming from different points in space awakes different reaction movements, that a short or a long or a rhythmical impression awakes motor responses of a very different type. May it not be that in all these cases, too, the character of the process in the motor centres has influence on the preceding sensorial excitement and gives a special shading to the mental impression which leads to those actions? The innervation of the approach movement and the innervation of the withdrawal movement may contribute to the feeling value of the impression, and the innervation of the right or left movement, of the quick or the continued movement, may reflect space value and time value on the sensation. The occurrences in a large railway station cannot be understood as long as only the incoming trains are studied and no attention is given to the outgoing trains which are dependent upon the clearing or blocking of the outward tracks and upon the direction in which they are to start. Whatever goes on in our mental life is dependent upon the clearing and blocking and switching of the tracks for reaction. The whole setting of our centrifugal system influences the flux of our thoughts and feelings, and furnishes all the means for really scientific explanation, while the popular theories refer to the mysteries of a subconscious mind.[3]

It will be evident from these selected utterances that Münsterberg did not uphold elementarism or structuralism, in spite of his German training and affiliation. His reluctance to treat the sensory without regard to the motor impulses at once brings to mind the fact that he anticipated the functionalists. True he did not go so far as to take in the whole organism, or the environment, but in his *Business Psychology*, he does include, in mind, bodily behavior, which was a step toward behaviorism, although we do know he would never have gone farther than that. "Hence 'mind' means for us both that which everyone finds in himself, in his inner private consciousness,

[3] H. Münsterberg: *Loc. cit.*, pp. 142-144.

in which nobody else can directly take part, and at the same time the particular kind of bodily behavior in which the personality expresses itself and which is open to everyone's perception."[4]

The motor phase of any mental process has come to play a part in applied psychology, in that it is recommended to change the attitude in order to obtain better sensory or affective results. Act as if you did not care a rap, and you will be self-assured. A child told to take quinine, as if it were ice cream, will be spared much of the disagreeableness in taste. This principle was injected in education on every occasion by the advocates of the motor consciousness doctrine.

Status and Reputation

Boring, while devoting more than a dozen pages to Titchener, disposes of Münsterberg in a couple of paragraphs, apparently justifying his position on the ground that "there is almost nothing of importance in experimental psychology connected with Münsterberg's name except some of the little experiments in the *Beiträge* of the Freiburg days. What happened was that Münsterberg's mind was too original; his dynamic mind went on at once to still newer psychologies."[5] This is the first time we hear of a man being depreciated because of his originality, although we have known of editors who tell their unsuccessful contributors that their writings are too good for the readers of their journals. Surely originality *per se* could not be a liability; and moreover, a man who directed the research of at least a score of leading psychologists deserves more than two pages in a comprehensive history of experimental psychology. One cannot quarrel with Boring for having given up so much space to his own distinguished teacher, and there is no doubt that as a man of science who is not moved by the *idola fori*, Titchener stands higher in our estimation than Münsterberg, for whom the lure of glamor meant so much, yet let us see what some of Münsterberg's own students said; and their calibre was not inferior to that of the Cornell "brood."

The first expression is from Knight Dunlap who, in his reminiscences, tells us that "there was at least one giant in these days, although his publications do not show it. Münster-

[4] H. Münsterberg: *Business Psychology,* 1918, p. 32.
[5] E. G. Boring: *A History of Experimental Psychology* (2d ed.), p. 428.

berg made no converts to his philosophy. He was not a man to have disciples, but I think the modern trends in American psychology, and especially its experimental interests, are easily traceable to Münsterberg as their father." In the same memoir, Dunlap only confirms what other students of Münsterberg have felt.

In his seminary, he was at his best, and there we got the meat of our work. Never did any loose conclusion or faulty method get by him. I well remember a paper I prepared, which I thought rather good. It was a mass of shreds when he got through with it, and I was perfectly convinced on every point he made. . . .

We were all drawn to Harvard by the same force—it was *the* centre for psychology at the time, and, in spite of the informality and laxness of instruction, we were confirmed in the scientific path. . . . He radiated scientific impulses, and profoundly altered the course of American psychology, even if not into the exact course he would have chosen.[6]

From another leader in American psychology, James R. Angell, we learn that in 1891 (*i.e.*, when Münsterberg was but 28 years old) "It . . . had been my desire to study for a time with Hugo Münsterberg in Freiburg, but before my plans were complete, Münsterberg was invited to go to Harvard."[7]

Mary W. Calkins's estimate may be gathered from the following passage:

Chronologically, third of my great teachers in psychology was Hugo Münsterberg, a man of deep learning, high originality, and astounding versatility, interested alike in systematic psychology, in the setting and solution of experimental problems, and, years later, in the applications of psychology.[8]

But what higher court of appeal is there than Boring's own hero?

In a letter under date of September 21, 1918, Titchener wrote to Roback: "I am especially glad to see the thanks

[6] K. Dunlap in *History of Psychology in Autobiography*, vol. II, p. 42.

[7] J. R. Angell in *History of Psychology in Autobiography*, vol. III, p. 8.

[8] M. W. Calkins in *History of Psychology in Autobiography*, vol. I, p. 33.

rendered to Münsterberg: for, whatever else that we may deplore there was in his make-up, there was beyond doubt a very large dose of the systematic psychologist. He alone of my contemporary friends kept that issue clear. Meumann could never have written a system; Külpe was overwhelmed by a Husserlian theory of knowledge; Kirschmann was incapable; and Frank Angell has definitely turned his back upon systematic questions."

It is obvious from this expression that Titchener did regard Münsterberg as an equal, and as superior to those he named, but it may be hazarded that in the years immediately preceding World War I, Münsterberg rated as the foremost psychologist of his time, barring Wundt, who was scarcely active then. Indeed, even before he was forty, the Harvard psychologist might have been awarded the palm, to judge from his reputation abroad.

From the very beginning of his academic career, Münsterberg was a storm-centre, the object of both vehement attacks and unstinted praise. It was his good fortune, while still in his twenties, to be criticized by older and more established men than himself, such as Wundt, Natorp, and G. E. Müller.

The extent of Münsterberg's influence in the development of psychology will be realized when we consider that in 1904, Chiabra, who is anything but sympathetic to Münsterberg's psychology, wrote that "the two currents of psychological thought now dominant in Italy . . . correspond to the schools of Münsterberg and Wundt."[9]

Let us bear in mind that at the time he and Wundt swayed Italy in opposite directions, he was but forty years old. In Denmark, the aged Høffding singled out Münsterberg's system for discussion in his little book, *Problems of Philosophy*; while in England, Lord Haldane, the former Lord High Chancellor, dwelt on Münsterberg's views in his Gifford lectures. Thus, he was not only well known in his own country, but had actually made a name for himself in the United States, Italy, Great Britain, and Denmark.

Contributions to Psychology

To begin with, calling the *Beiträge* "little experiments," as Boring does, is hardly fair to Münsterberg. It is even worse than understatement. It would require a first class experimentalist to deal with such topics as auditory space-perception, estimation of size, kinaesthesis, association and memory, the influence of drugs (nervina) on mental work, the time-sense, attention, pleasantness. The studies do not consist of a few pages each but occupy practically monographs, and it was all accomplished during the first dozen years of the experimental period in psychology. Nothing comparable had been performed in the United States during that whole decade. Furthermore, in these searching investigations, the problems were considered in perspective, and not merely as a series of experiments on reaction-time or on biliminal touch. As Titchener recognized, there was a systematic trend in everything which Münsterberg tackled.

Boring apparently overlooks, too, the fact that the action theory was a worthy rival of McDougall's drainage theory, since he contends that "McDougall gave the only important physiological theory of attention when he promulgated his drainage theory."[10]

The Two Categories

Münsterberg never tired of harping on the difference between causal and purposive psychology. The former suited the scientist, who seeks to explain the mechanism of phenomena. However, when we are *appreciating* values, when we are *willing* personalities, or wish to *understand* our interlocutors, a new key is required to unlock the secret. The distinction, of course, does not originate with Münsterberg. He picked up the thread of the *Geisteswissenschaften* School, which had among its founders, Wilhelm Dilthey, Wilhelm Windelband, and to a less extent Heinrich Rickert, who probably influenced more directly the subject of our sketch. In dealing with these problems, Münsterberg simply decided to refer the values to another sphere, inaccessible to scientific analysis because not governed by the laws of causality. In this manner, whereas James was forced to change his own personality, according as he approached the one type of phenomena, or the other, his successor at Harvard merely assigned a different place for each series and betrayed no

[10] E. G. Boring: *A History of Experimental Psychology*, (1st ed.), p. 642. This section does not appear in the later edition.

conflict. Orthodox psychology, with a philosophical halo—that is what Münsterberg stood for.

While this manipulation was regarded as a sort of presti-digitation by psychologists in the United States, and the students could never take to it, it had intrigued many of his colleagues abroad, especially those who were still fascinated by objective idealism. In the purposive sphere, there was a possibility of making room for a spiritual principle, and thus the scientist's mystical cravings could be satisfied without doing violence to his rigorous laboratory training. Odd to relate, Münsterberg left no disciples, prepared to carry on his teachings along these lines, and as to the motor trend in his psychology, it was soon absorbed by the nascent functionalist school, without giving him any credit for his pioneer move. Perhaps he was not the trailblazer, like Fechner, Helmholtz, Lotze, or Freud. That he was a pacemaker can scarcely be gainsaid.

The Founder of Applied Psychology

In one important and large field, Münsterberg's service could not be contested, although, even there, it has not received due recognition. It may be said without the risk of serious contradiction that not only was Münsterberg the first champion of applied psychology in the United States but he might well be considered the individual who founded this branch, to the extent that he inspired men like William Stern, Otto Klemm, and Otto Lipmann, in Germany, perhaps too C. S. Myers, in England, to engage in investigations of a practical nature. In the United States, H. E. Burtt has taken on this phase of his teacher's work.

Münsterberg was not content to discuss the theoretical foundations of applied psychology, although his distinction between applied psychology, in the broad sense, and psycho-technics is a useful one, again giving evidence of his lucid mind, but he did field work in a number of segments of this vast territory. He was the first to devise tests for motormen, he took an interest in the test movement in general, he not only wrote on psychotherapy, but actually treated some of the cases which promised to yield fruitful results for science (as a doctor of medicine he was in a position to undertake such therapy without laying himself open to criticism); he made himself conversant with the particulars of the court machinery in criminal prosecution, he would be consulted by industrialists, advertising concerns, efficiency engineers, and his laboratory at Emerson Hall had a number of candidates for the doctorate working on such problems. The so-called *lie-detector, for example, was partly the result of experiments conducted at his instance.*

The Great Popularizer of Psychology

Münsterberg has been generally condemned for writing popular magazine articles and catering too much to the public. Apparently his critics fail to appreciate what his popular articles and lectures meant for the expansion of psychology in this country. We may safely venture to say that if psychology has been able to advance in this country with such a gigantic stride, so that there are actually about twenty-five psychological periodicals published in the United States (not counting the unscientific magazines posing as psychological), while the college curriculum reports show psychology to be the most popular study in a number of our universities, no small share of the credit for giving the propelling force to this vast movement is due to Münsterberg's initiative.

His activities in applied psychology in connection with medicine, law, industrial efficiency, advertising, and various other departments of human endeavor, served to make his science widely known and respected by the physician, the lawyer, the business man, the executive, and others. Much of what he has written on these subjects, it is true, is slipshod and unscientific, if we should take a rigorous stand (*e.g., On the Witness Stand*, which brought him quite an income), but, at least, he was able to enlist the interest of those various practical men in behalf of psychology, certainly not to the detriment of either.

In organizing the International Congress of Arts and Sciences at St. Louis, Münsterberg undertook and completed most successfully a tremendous task. The proceedings of this Congress are presented in a number of large volumes.

The *Deutsch-Amerika Institut*, which he founded with the purpose of promoting good will between this country and Germany, was, as we all realize now, a less successful venture, though it had the hearty support of the last Kaiser, who conferred a Prussian order upon its founder and first director.

As a laboratory director, Münsterberg might have been

highly successful, if he could only give up sufficient time to supervise his students. The problems he assigned were nearly always those which had occupied his mind for years. They were far more diversified than in the case of the Cornell laboratory. There is no question of his ingenuity in suggesting techniques, even if his mechanical knack in the construction of apparatus was below the level of his American colleagues.

He would occasionally tiptoe into rooms where experiments were going on just to show that he was not neglectful, but students were too awed by his extra-curricular activities to bother him; for surely they would not be expected to intrude when he was closeted with the Argentine ambassador, or was serving as host to a German prince, or giving an interview to a metropolitan editor, or advising the head of a detective bureau, or entertaining a wealthy brewer, who might be enlisted as a patron of a projected museum, etc. Not that he discouraged his students. On the contrary, he was genial and friendly, even if he would often indulge in mild sarcasm, the banter of the superior; and he always seemed to be conscious of his station in the cultural world—but such stereotyped expressions as "Well (*ooell*) now Mr. —— you are on the (*zee*) right track, and I expect a fine piece of work from you" could hardly be of any value to one who is groping.

Unlike Titchener, Münsterberg did not prepare his lectures. He could of course draw on his enormous reservoir of ideas, and he was never at a loss for an illustration or analogy, but because of his growing indifference to the routine of teaching, as he was getting more into the limelight as a public personage, he would necessarily become repetitious and at times disjointed, on the lecture platform, especially as he would use no notes.

His Career and Achievement

Hugo Münsterberg was born in Danzig in 1863, the son of a Jewish lumber merchant. After graduation from the Danzig Gymnasium, he studied at Geneva and Leipzig, taking his Ph.D. degree under Wundt. He later studied medicine at Heidelberg, where he obtained his medical degree.

In 1888, he became *Privatdozent* in philosophy at Freiburg, and from then on, his career was phenomenal. Three years later, he was made assistant professor at Freiburg, and the year following, William James effected his appointment as professor of psychology and director of the psychological laboratory at Harvard. In 1910, he was sent to Berlin as exchange professor. It was on this occasion, that he met Kaiser Wilhelm II, and began his political activities. He was vice-president of the International Psychological Congress at Paris, organizer and vice-president of the International Congress of Arts and Sciences at St. Louis, in 1904, vice-president of the International Philosophical Congress at Heidelberg, fellow and vice-president of the American Academy, president of the American Psychological Association, in 1898, and president of the American Philosophical Association, in 1908.

Works

Aside from those volumes already mentioned, particularly the *Grundzüge der Psychologie*, which was written on American territory, there are fully a score of books which might be listed, dealing with aesthetics, philosophy, the criminal, ethics, the teacher, psychotherapy, industrial efficiency, vocational psychology, and a series of popular works consisting, for the most part, of magazine articles, which might come under the head of social psychology (*American Traits* translated by E. B. Holt, 1902, expanded in German, and published as *Die Amerikaner*, 1904 (second edition, 1912), *American Problems*, 1910; *American Patriotism*, 1911, *Psychology and Social Sanity*, 1914; *Philosophie der Werte*, 1907; in English translation, *The Eternal Values* 1909; and his large volume *Grundzüge der Psychotechnik*, which consolidated the data of the several books he had written in English, but was more systematically knit. His books dealing with the World War were publicistic, and did not redound to his credit. In addition to the close to thirty books and monographs he authored, he edited four large volumes of monographs, the production of his laboratory students. The fifth volume of the *Harvard Psychological Studies* contained monographs which were the fruit of experimentation under Münsterberg, but which he did not live to see completed.

It was perhaps because he was so prolific that Münsterberg's works were treated cavalierly by his American contemporaries. With all the popularization and even carelessness, at least four or five of his books contain solid material. Even his textbook should have had a better lot than has fallen to it, after its author had fallen from grace; and here we come to the tragic chapter of his dramatic life, which is punctured by more than one quip of fate. He once remarked to the present author that Ferdinand Lassalle had lost his life on behalf of an adventuress. The same might be said with equal truth about Münsterberg.

A Dramatic Figure

Born a marginal German (in Danzig of Jewish parentage), he was brought up in an assimilatory environment which overglorified Germany and where the Kaiser's birthday was celebrated with a family feast. His great aim was to become a shining light in Germany, but for various reasons, personal mainly, because he had antagonized some of the academic leaders, he found the road steep, despite his industry and brilliance. Eventually (and that, presumably after baptism) he became an instructor at Freiburg, and later was promoted to an assistant professorship at that German university. Münsterberg always had a patronizing attitude toward the Americans or, for that matter, any nationality other than the Germans. In the William James archives, one may come across a letter containing a childish outburst of indignation on the part of the young Münsterberg, threatening not to write in English because of adverse criticism which he received in the British periodical, *Mind*. This must have amused the indulgent James, and Münsterberg learned later to curb his impetuous impulses, but he never lost that attitude of condescension toward America. Not only was he never naturalized, but his investments were made in Germany, so that after the World War, his fortune dwindled to almost nothing.

Elsewhere, I had occasion to make the following observation on that air of superiority:

Those who have had the opportunity of examining the James-Münsterberg correspondence between 1892 and 1895 could not fail to perceive that the younger man's behavior was that of a girl who had her mind set on a prospective husband, indifferent though he might be in his affections, while yet encouraging the attentions of an eager suitor. Münsterberg who was appointed to a post at Harvard in 1892, had returned to Freiburg on a leave of absence, using his Harvard appointment as an argument for advancement in some (or any) German university, which seemed, by reason of his Jewish parentage and the personal animosities brewing underneath, to have become a forlorn hope.

While away, he contrived to have two of his students conduct the laboratory at Harvard, directing them from time to time via long distance.

When finally James and the President [Eliot] could countenance the situation no longer and, after three years, made it clear to him that he would have to choose between returning or being replaced, he became resigned to his fate—directing the Harvard laboratory, in his thirty-second year, at a salary of $4000 (equivalent to at least $15,000,[11] at the present currency level and taxation).

James was not in the least affected by Münsterberg's rebuff in Germany, but welcomed him with open arms, feeling, as he did, that no one was as well qualified to carry on the experimental work at Harvard.[12]

His closer contacts with the mighty in Germany, after his full establishment in the United States, where he sought to cement relations between his "Fatherland" and his "adapted," rather than "adopted" country only made him more attached to Germany, and when the World War broke out, he was certain that the *Vaterland* would win. As, however, it was becoming more and more evident that the United States would be drawn into the struggle, he began to move heaven and earth to prevent the catastrophe. Since he had been mounting the ladder of public affairs and had met many political figures, he began to crusade on behalf of Germany, writing to Theodore Roosevelt and President Wilson and the press, clamoring for a negotiated peace. He even went so far as to write, on the eve of the American declaration of war against Germany, to the then German Chancellor, von Bethmann-Hollweg, telling him of his plans to induce President Wilson, who, in his opinion, was yearning to act the mediator, to offer peace proposals. This letter intercepted, proved Münsterberg's undoing; for it aroused indignation throughout the country, and brought him under a cloud of suspicion. The plea that his letter, as translated, was garbled proved of no avail. Some prospective contributor to Harvard had written to President Lowell that the retaining of Münsterberg on the faculty would cost Harvard ten million dollars. To the credit of the former,

[11] It would have been closer to $20,000 in 1963.
[12] A. A. Roback: *William James*, etc. (1942), pp. 202-203.

it must be said that he had no thought of dismissing the psychologist, but the incident had taken its toll. The story has been circulating that the vacant chair in the famous painting which hangs over the staircase at Emerson Hall, representing William James, Josiah Royce, and George Herbert Palmer at first had, as its occupant, Hugo Münsterberg, but his likeness was blocked out, in consequence of the war scandal,[13] and yet were it not for Münsterberg's efforts to obtain money from his wealthy German friends, Emerson Hall might not have come into being, at least for many years. He not only initiated the plan, but practically designed the laboratory, on the third and fourth floors of the building.

Indefatigable worker that he was, the European war added a new line of activities to his burden that already had been unbearably heavy. "I am working day and night now," he wrote to his friend William Stern.[14]

On December 16, 1916, as he was lecturing to his Radcliffe class, he fell dead, at the age of 53, of a cerebral hemorrhage; and in his case, it seems as if

> *The evil that men do lives after them;*
> *The good is oft interred with their bones.*

Since there had never been established a bond between him and any of his students, nor was he perspicacious enough to appreciate the potentialities or even the merits of some of them, coupled with the fact that he was too worshipful of the meretricious goddess, Success, he left no intellectual heirs, or even executors. Some of the most promising pupils forged out on their own; others followed new trends. His whole make-up had been foreign to them, and now that his siding

---

[13] In a private communication (May 30, 1963) to the present author, Professor W. E. Hocking tells a different story. "The 'empty-chair' painting was definitely not 'painted out.' The point was that Winifred Rieber, who did the painting, and who carefully took private sketches of the four subjects, found Hugo very decided about how he should be painted—he had his own theories of aesthetics—and she felt that she couldn't reconcile them with her own, and so had to omit him."

It is well and fortunate that we still have with us the sprightly nonagenarian; and his statement should scotch the rumor, which had spread even abroad, once and for all.

[14] W. Stern: "Obituary Note on Münsterberg," *Journal of Applied Psychology*, 1917, vol. 1.

with the enemy in an impending war had made him obnoxious, they were even more alienated from him than ever. Despite his shortcomings and ill-considered judgment, he deserved better at the hands of posterity.[15]

[15] I do not recall seeing any notice of the observance of his centenary last year (1963).

Chapter 19

Lightner Witmer, Pioneer in Clinical Psychology

ONE OF THE all-but-forgotten names in American psychology is Lightner Witmer (1867-1956). In general, the University of Pennsylvania psychologists have always been overshadowed by their colleagues at Columbia University. It would be an interesting speculation to consider what Cattell might have amounted to had he stayed in Philadelphia. There was, however, a special reason for Witmer's neglect—his strong individualism and outspokenness, in contrast to Twitmyer's resigned attitude at the same university during that period.[1]

Witmer belongs to the pioneer group of American graduates who continued their studies under Wundt. He obtained his doctorate in 1892. As may be imagined, his first publications were in experimental psychology (laboratory apparatus and procedure), pleasure and pain, spatial aesthetics, but soon his interest shifted to educational problems and child psychology. In 1902, there appeared his *Analytic Psychology*, an

[1] K. M. Dallenbach: "Twitmyer and the Conditioned Response," *Amer. Journal of Psychology,* 1959, Vol. 72, pp. 633-638.

The story of E. B. Twitmyer's neglect is told poignantly by K. M. Dallenbach. According to him, Twitmyer's doctoral dissertation, *A Study of the Knee-jerk,* received scant attention, even when he presented the substance of it at the 1904 meeting of the American Psychological Association, under the presidency of William James. "Not one of his hearers commented upon it after his presentation." Pavlov reported his results on the conditioned reflex in 1904, while Twitmyer had discovered the principle of conditioning at least two years earlier. Dallenbach explains the situation by saying that Twitmyer "had little ability, experience, or inclination along promotional lines, and . . . he could not withstand discouragement." Twitmyer then joined hands with Witmer in the clinical project at the University of Pennsylvania, and his output being small, his name scarcely is seen nowadays in references. Twitmyer's withdrawn personality must have had something to do with his neglect, while in the case of Witmer, there was the disadvantage of being too forward, which was interpreted as arrogance.

excellent first manual to stimulate interest in experimental psychology, novel in its method, and profusely illustrated, something very unusual sixty years ago.

In 1896, Witmer opened the first psychological clinic, thus paving the way for the hundreds of clinics now in operation, and in 1907 he founded the periodical *Psychological Clinic*. In those early days, clinical psychology was not steeped in psychoanalysis or wrapped in existentialism and phenomenology, because the neurotic aspect was not clearly observable. Clinical psychology was restricted to problems of retarded children, mental defectives, delinquents, etc. Later, at about the same time as Lewis Terman, Witmer turned to the study of exceptional children—covering the field of genetic psychology. In 1907 he founded the Witmer School for Psychological Diagnosis and Treatment of Mental Retardation and Deviation.

Witmer did not take to the rising conceptions of the day. A laboratory realist, he sought to help the child handicapped by deafness or reading deficiency, or social maladaptation through methods he considered as based on common sense. Thus, in more influential circles his labors seemed antiquated and out of touch with the spirit of the times. It may be taken for granted, however, that his work led to the growing expansion in the areas of vocational guidance, remedial speech, and education.

His journal, in its constantly changing subtitle and incorporation of new topics and contributors, showed that his outlook was extending, but as a pioneer in his field he wished to adjust the growing branch to his own expanding ideas rather than to change with the times. The final subtitle of the *Psychological Clinic*, which ceased publication in 1937, at the time he became an emeritus, was "Journal of Psychonomic Personeering."

It was Witmer who coined the term "Psychonomic Personeering." In an introductory article in the May 1930 issue, he defines "Psychonomic Personeering" as "the art and science of organizing personal character of surpassing superiority so that men, women, and children, operating as individuals or in groups are able to produce performance that is psychic, *i.e.,* in conformity to law—the creative law of personal and general progress."

Although this definition is hardly in keeping with the tight phraseology of our own day, his formulation of a "personeer" as "one who projects, creates, controls, directs, and perfects this engine of surpassing power" [a personal character of surpassing superiority] is more specific, although the suffix *-eer* would generally be understood in a pejorative sense (*cf.* patrioteer, profiteer, privateer, buccaneer).

Witmer died in 1956, the last of the twenty-six charter members of the American Psychological Association. Outside of his German dissertation and his *Analytic Psychology*, the only other book which he authored, or rather edited, is *Experimental Studies in Personality*; most of his writing consisted of articles appearing in the *Psychological Clinic*. He and J. E. W. Wallin, a younger contemporary, paved the way for the division now known as school psychology; and he was also instrumental in opening up channels that led to the growth of psychiatric social work in which his daughter, Helen, had become a leader.

Characteristic of Witmer was his spirit of defiance as well as his uninhibited critical statements about "the powers that be." In the unpublished correspondence between Münsterberg and James we find the former's indignant reaction and readiness to ask for disciplinary action on the part of the American Psychological Association because of Witmer's negative characterizations of Royce, Münsterberg, and James—the mighty trio at Harvard.

Of James he wrote, among other things,

> Professor James represents to-day the survival of an academic tradition. . . . The spoiled child of American psychology, exempt from all serious criticism, and the beau ideal of a large and cultured circle, Professor James, since the publication of his *Principles of Psychology*, has apparently relaxed the intellectual inhibition which every man should exert over his desires.

James's letter, which follows, is so magnificent in its detachment that it might serve as an example to others who find themselves in a similar situation. It bears the insignia of greatness of mind in its truest sense.

> But, dear Münsterberg, I hope you'll withdraw a second time your protest. I think it undignified to take such an attack seriously. Its excessive dimensions (in my case at any rate), and the smallness and remoteness of the provocation, stamp it as simply eccentric, and to show sensitiveness

only gives it importance in the eyes of readers who otherwise would only smile at its extravagance. Besides, since these temperamental antipathies exist—why isn't it healthy that they should express themselves? For my part, I feel rather glad than otherwise that psychology is so live a subject that psychologists should "go for" each other in this way, and I think it all ought to happen inside of our Association. We ought to cultivate tough hides there, so I hope that you will withdraw the protest. I have mentioned it only to Royce, and will mention it to no one else. I don't like the notion of Harvard people seeming "touchy"! Your fellow victim,   W.J.[2]

[2] A. A. Roback: *William James, His Marginalia, Personality, and Contribution*, pp. 210-212.

PART III

THE SCHOOLS

...whose structure, who was thus... changes in
physiology and biology should not have followed the Darwinians in the direction of educational interpretation. It
would seem, however, for the very reason that I referred to

Chapter 20

The Rise of Functionalism

UP TO ABOUT 1900, psychology in the United States was an undivided science. There may have been differences of opinion on the matter of method or emphasis, but schools had not yet been formed. Furthermore, although they were to bring up a whole generation of American psychologists, neither of the two dominating figures, *i.e.*, neither Titchener nor Münsterberg, wished to be thought of as American. Titchener expressly states in writing: "I am myself very decidedly an English psychologist, if the adjective means nationality; and I hope I am the same thing if it means type of thinking!"[1]

A Puzzle

Before we go any further, let us examine the origin of the word, and the provenance of the concept. Function, from the Latin *fungi*, "to discharge an office" or "perform some special work," is more remotely connected with an Aryan root which means "to enjoy the use of." The concept is primarily a biological one, and has been used in physiology by way of differentiation from the morphological aspect of an organ, or what would correspond, in psychology, to the structural. In fact, in most definitions of objects, we combine both aspects, *e.g.*, when we define a chair in terms of its structure and use.

Boring (*History of Experimental Psychology,* (2d ed., p. 579) is puzzled why Titchener, who was highly trained in physiology and biology, should not have followed the Darwinians in the direction of adaptational interpretation. It would seem, however, for the very reason that Titchener was so well grounded in the subject, that he wanted to draw the line between psychology, as the pure science of mind, and physiology or biology. The time for the convergence of several sciences toward one objective had not yet come; and since Titchener was seeking general laws, he felt that they would not obtain in cross sciences. It is one thing to ascertain how to

[1] In a letter to A. A. Roback (Feb. 1, 1923).

secure practical results and quite another to discover a law. To take another analogy, it is always the linguist, equally at home, say, in French and German, who would not mix the idiom. Those who are not up on the one or the other will often be guilty of barbarisms. It is not unlikely that Titchener, after completing his structural system, had he lived long enough, would have attempted a functional system, but, of course, this is purely conjectural. Titchener's passion for system may have been in reaction to the British customary neglect of it. Certainly, it was not because he was under the spell of Wundt's personality that he became the great exponent of structural or elementaristic psychology.

The Chicago School

While Münsterberg, as we have learned in the last chapter, identified himself with Germany and Titchener claimed to be thoroughly British, the time was beginning to be ripe for the emergence of an American type of psychology; and it was only fit that such should spring up in a region of comparatively recent settlement and far inland, that is to say, about half way from each coast, and therefore relatively free from foreign influences. If one were to plan for the locale of such a school, one would not have hit on a better place than Chicago. The University of Chicago, moreover, was a brand new university, founded only the same year that both Titchener and Münsterberg arrived in America. To this day, this university represents American initiative and enterprise rather than tradition and dignity. The adolescent spirit of the young university pervades almost every department there; and it has advanced in greater strides than any other higher institution of learning. In psychology alone, this university has had almost as many doctorates as Columbia University with the milling millions in its environs.

If the location is typically American, with its bustling packing houses, political machine, etc., the particular brand of psychology which would issue therefrom would be expected to correspond to the American genius, which is characterized by action, utility, practicality; and that is exactly what underlies the new school, labeled functionalism, which was to be found *in embryone,* in William James's *Principles of Psychology,* and more explicitly in Münsterberg's elaboration of the motor-consciousness concept, but came to full expression in Dewey's article "The Reflex Arc Concept in Psychology."[2] However, what seems to have been completely overlooked by writers on functionalism and historians of psychology is that Dewey had already made his stand as a functionalist in his youthful article of 1884, cited earlier, where he definitely asserts, "The idea of environment is a necessity to the idea of organism, and with the conception of environment comes the impossibility of considering psychical life as an individual, isolated thing developing in a vacuum." Here we have the first germ of functionalism years before James published his *Principles*.

Under the Leadership of Dewey

In the 1896 article on the reflex arc, which became the *casus belli* for more than a decade, and a point of departure for the new trend, Dewey merely elaborates on the motor aspect, something which had already been done both by James and Münsterberg. He wishes us to appreciate that stimulus and response do not represent a successive pair, that response bears on the stimulus just as the stimulus calls forth the response; and what is more, the whole reflex arc is not to be considered a closed unit but as a link in a chain of preceding and succeeding arcs, each of which has its rôle to play in the coördination of the organism toward the attainment of a goal. The adaptive process embraces stimulus—response—stimulus —response, and so on, until the uncertain reaction has become a fully fashioned habit. Let us bear in mind, also, that this chain of circuits operates in a setting which involves much else besides stimulus and response. Here we are reminded of the importance James attaches to transitive *vs.* substantive states. Dewey, in his "Reflex Arc Concept," may be said to provide more evidence in substantiation of Münsterberg's action theory, or vice versa: as was suggested in the last chapter, Münsterberg could well be classed with the functionalists, despite his German saturation, or perhaps because he was not a *gen(e)*-uine German. It was because of Münsterberg's leaning toward the functional that he could lay the foundations of applied psychology.

Hitherto, the laboratories were governed by one man. Each laboratory might have been considered a school in itself so far as the problems, methods, and general conclusions were con-

[2] J. Dewey: "The Reflex Arc Concept," *Psychological Review*, 1896, vol. 3.

cerned. For the first time, in Chicago, we could speak of a school, in that several members in the philosophy and psychology departments entertained the same notions. It was in Chicago, that instrumentalism, as a philosophical school, emerged; and the very founder of that school was John Dewey; and as luck would have it, G. H. Mead, and A. W. Moore who, as philosophers, were devoting part of their attention to psychological topics, were independently bolstering the cause of functionalism. It is curious that the later product, semantics, also has its stronghold in Chicago.

Already in 1896, A. W. Moore and J. R. Angell had carried out an experiment on reaction time, which was calculated to refute the Wundtian position that reactions were more rapid whenever the reagent's attention was on the movement to be executed rather than on the sensory stimulus. It was found, e.g., that some subjects needed to put their attention on the signal in order to secure the fastest results. In other words, it was a case of adapting oneself so that the weakest juncture of the coördination would receive most supervision. Here we see how the general law of the structuralists and pure psychologists gives way to another consideration, that of human motivation, thus making allowances for the individual differences, on behalf of which Baldwin was putting up a fight.

Since Dewey had only taken on psychology as an avocation, although his books *How We Think* and *Human Nature and Conduct*, as well as many articles, are part and parcel of the psychological literature, it devolved upon J. R. Angell to crystallize the programme of the functionalists. This he did in his presidential address before the American Psychological Association,[1] where he points out the three objectives of the new trend. In the first place, he and his associates were not so much interested in the mere content of mental experience as in the singling out and *description of the mental operation*. Secondly, the mental state should, when described, contain an account of the *whole setting*; what had called it forth, and finally, we should be looking for *the goal* of the mental process; what it aims to accomplish.

Under the circumstances, in addition to the purely psychical, we shall have to look for the physical as well as the social antecedents, or consequences, of the given mental process. Certainly, this is by no means an easy matter and complicates

[1] J. R. Angell: "The Province of Functional Psychology," *Psychological Review*, 1907, vol. 4.

the inquiry, especially in human psychology, but functional psychology bides its time, and the problems can be divided up. The mind-body relation in functional psychology is insepar- able. Here habit, which, in Titchener's system, is only men- tioned by way of courtesy, receives a prominent position, and social situations which enter into the whole reaction are stud- ied for their pragmatic instrumentality.

Angell gave further expression to his views in an article entitled "The Influence of Darwin on Psychology" and in the chapter on "The Evolution of Intelligence" in the *Evolution of Man*, a symposium. It is not difficult to gather that the functionalists were spreading out and making more contacts with other scientists precisely because they were willing to introduce more or less alien material into their crucible. The net result was greater coöperation.

Titchener Blasts Functionalism

Angell was by no means the only protagonist in the psycho- logical drama of the late '90's and early twentieth century. There were adversaries on the other side of the Atlantic, and there were straggling followers of the Scotch School.

When Titchener published his "Postulates of a Structural Psychology," it was levelled not so much at the American rebels against traditionalism as against the British brand of functionalism, the banner of which was held aloft by Stout. Specifically, it was a reply to W. Caldwell's "Professor Titch- ener's View of the Self" (*Psychological Review*, 1898, vol. 5), an indictment on twelve counts, which Titchener, acting as his own advocate, undertook to annul by outlining the premises of his system. While pleading his case against his Scottish critic, Titchener aimed his darts perhaps more concentratedly in the direction of the young Chicago group. It is true, as Boring observes, that Titchener's article served to publicize the new tendency and make the functionalists more conscious of their separatism. In the first article, Titchener is more con- ciliatory and even leads us to believe that some day in the future, there will be room for a functional psychology too, even though at the present stage, it is still too soon to pin our hopes on it.

> . . . There is reasonable agreement, within the experi- mental camp as to the postulates of a purely structural psychology, whereas there is pretty radical disagreement

among the psychologists of function. . . . The study of function will not yield final fruit until it can be controlled by the genetic, and still more, by the experimental method—in the form both of laboratory experimenting and interpretation of that natural experiment which meets us in certain pathological cases.[4]

The second article[5] was a more explicit attack on functionalism, and a further clarification of his own position; but again neither Dewey nor Angell, nor any other American functionalist, is mentioned. In this pithy defense, the writer once more deals with W. Caldwell, who had submitted a rejoinder to the previous reply by Titchener, and trots out Herrick on the carpet for his suggestion to adopt a "dynamic method." What is of special value here is Titchener's incisive differentiation and convincing argumentation *under the circumstances*. The substance may be summed up as follows: (1) our daily language habits, because of our needs and uses, make for a functional trend, but that does not mean that they have a scientific basis. (2) The structuralist's introspection is observation of an *is*; the functionalist's is that of an *is-for*. Unschooled introspection is extra-psychological altogether, and runs off into channels of "is-for-thought" (meanings, logical functions) and "is-for-conduct" (values, ethics). The most intense introspection can be distorted as when the heroine in fiction is "viewing her mind through an ethical glass," which is really morbid introspection. The logical-function type of introspection is the "besetting sin of the descriptive psychologist."

Here Titchener classifies psychologists and philosophers in accordance with his schema. Herbart and Volkmann introspected on logical grounds, avoiding the *is* for the "should-reasonably-be," and coming to absurd conclusions, in disagreement with the facts. That is true of those who introspect, and find an elementary will process in consciousness. The reason for such a discovery is that will is a desideratum in functional psychology. Here it must be said that American functionalists could hardly come within the bounds of this charge. Titchener, however, was mindful of the British functionalists.

[4] E. B. Titchener: "The Postulates of a Structural Psychology," *Philosophical Review*, 1898, vol. 7, p. 465.
[5] E. B. Titchener: "Structural and Functional Psychology," *Philosophical Review*, 1899, vol. 8.

In the categorization of writers and their approach, Wundt's theory of visual space perception falls within the structural; Lipps's theory within the functional. Külpe inclines toward the structural, while Ebbinghaus's classic on memory belongs to functional psychology, and Hobhouse's treatment of memory takes us into logic. The analysis of attention is analogous to an anatomical section, whereas the doctrine of apperception comes under the head of functionalism.

The criticism that structuralism deals with abstractions—and Angell in his subsequent articles makes much of this—is dispelled by the statement that the concrete experience is translated into its counterpart, without addition or subtraction. The structurally complex must be identical with the elementary constituents in nature (tonal fusion out of tonal sensations); otherwise the passage from the one to the other would be impossible. "Abstractions these elements are, but abstractions from the real, and in so far as participating in reality." In fine, Titchener sees no basic conflict between structural and functional psychology, or even between either and genetic psychology, which, in the future, may be united under one banner. They correspond, respectively, to morphology, physiology, and embryology of biological science.

The Functionalist Platform

In 1903, Angell published his own *credo*, in his early article on functional psychology, where he emphatically declares that "sensation is no discrete psychical entity compacted with other similar entities into the complex we call perception." In this article, Angell stresses mainly the disparity between the concept of structure in biology and psychology. There is no psychological element comparable to the cell. The latter can be isolated and demonstrated, the sensation as such is an artifact when divorced from the whole reality complex. "It is not only in the Hegelian logic, therefore, that the adjective and the adverb reveal a dialectical interplay. In physiological and functional problems the question 'how' is practically identical with the question 'what.' "[6]

Angell, somewhat surprisingly, is far more eager to retain the relationship between psychology and philosophy than Titchener; and he takes pains to show how functional psy-

6 J. R. Angell: "The Relations of Structural and Functional Psychology to Philosophy," *Philosophical Review,* 1903, vol. 12, p. 252.

chology can be of aid to philosophy, in its various subdisciplines. Those were the days when philosophical allies would be useful in the campaign, and since Dewey, Mead, and others who identified themselves with functionalism were primarily philosophers, such a move could very well have been anticipated as calculated to win the philosophical world over to the new school.

Inadequacies of Structuralism

During the next few years, the uprising gathers momentum. Angell becomes president of the American Psychological Association, and his presidential address, in 1906, is the most articulate expression yet of the functionalist stand. It is here that structuralism receives the full onslaught of its opponents. Structuralism is made out to be inadequate in dealing with the problems of body and mind; it is more or less sterile in that it is satisfied with classification instead of extending into the operational sphere, so that it might accomplish results. It is isolated and encourages isolation, which does not conform to reality. Function is something which is constant, while the mental element, say, a sensation or emotion, is unique and fleeting—never the same.

In 1906, Angell discusses the function of consciousness and returns to some of Titchener's arguments. H. C. Warren, the ever genial arbitrator who, while an admirer of Titchener, nevertheless as a student of Baldwin, would have been influenced along adaptational lines, had spoken of cognition, affection, and conation as biological in character. His suggestion that the three phases corresponded respectively to the external, systemic, and kinaesthetic senses, receives a sympathic nod on the part of Angell, but no more. Angell is not eager to make compromises. His quarrel with the "pure" psychologists is too fundamental, and he finally exclaims, "It may be pure science but it is surely purity bought at a great price, *i.e.,* truth to life."

In so far as you attempt to analyze any particular state of consciousness, you find that the mental elements presented to your notice are dependent upon the particular exigencies and conditions which call them forth. Not only does the affective coloring of such a psychical moment depend upon one's temporary condition, mood, and aims but the very sensations themselves are determined in their qualitative texture by the totality of circumstances subjective and objective, within which they arise. . . . The particular sense quality is in short functionally determined by the necessities of the existing situation which it emerges to meet.[7]

In these articles, Angell gave voice to his views far more effectively than in his textbooks, *Psychology,* 1904, and *Introduction to Psychology,* 1918. In fact, the texts are scarcely different from Titchener's except that more space is allotted to language, habit, and social attitudes in general. Functionalism is scarcely ever mentioned, although in one of them, there is a chapter on the function of reason.

Attack and Counterattack

In the many discussions which appeared in psychological periodicals on this subject, the arguments turned round a few central points. The structuralists would hardly dignify functional psychology with the name of science, in the proper sense of the word, but looked upon it as technology, interested in the means of executing a task, regardless of the zone of operation. Thus, to cut across areas like mind and body was considered illegitimate because, though running parallel, they do not form a continuum. It was, furthermore, contended that functionalism implied the injection of teleology, which smacks of the old vitalism, and is inconsistent with the constitution of genuine science. These critics saw no need of going into the "why" of psychological phenomena. The "how" is taken care of by physiology, while what is truly psychological and constitutes the "what" linked up with other "whats" in the same sphere. Titchener endeavored to keep psychology within a definitional framework. The functionalists were not prepared to tie psychology to the apron strings of logic. On the contrary, they were eager to liberate it from all the rigorous shackles of abstraction and bring it as close to experience in the raw as possible.

The dispute began to centre around questions of methodology and usage. Both the Cornell and the Chicago camps voiced their opinions in this controversy. Thus, C. Ruckmick made an extensive survey of the use of the term "function," examining fifteen textbooks, only to find that it had no specific meaning, and that authors showed no consistency. To throw,

[7] J. R. Angell: "The Fundamental Function of Consciousness," *Psychological Bulletin,* 1906, vol. 3.

therefore, all our weight upon a term which permits of equivocation could only lead to confusion. It appeared, too, that teleology is implied in most usages. "In a large number of books . . . mind is still considered an active and purposeful 'organism' of the individual."[8]

K. M. Dallenbach, also, took the concept of function to pieces, and pointed out that functionalism is only an extension of the old faculty psychology, and that, furthermore, it may even be traced back to phrenology, which assigned to the various areas in the brain specific functions, such as memory, reverence, love, mathematical ability. That, of course, was not by any means the view of the Chicago functionalists, but according to Dallenbach, "Phrenology is the matrix from which our term is derived."[9] It is from them that Thomas Brown, he believes, took over.

As Angell became more and more engrossed in his administrative duties as President of Yale University, and Harvey A. Carr (1873) became chairman of the psychology department at the University of Chicago, it devolved upon the latter to take up the cudgels on behalf of the functional school. Carr, as an animal psychologist, saw more of behavior that could not be checked by introspection. In his autobiographical sketch he tells us that "quite early in my career I became impressed with the limitations of the experimental method in the field of human psychology."[10] In 1925, there appeared his textbook *Psychology*, which is more definitely in keeping with the functional point of view than was Angell's. Here we find stress laid on the motor response, adaptive action, and, finally, on motivation. His theoretical position has been presented more elaborately in the chapter on "Functionalism" in *Psychologies of 1930* (ed. by C. Murchison). Like Angell, he adduced instances from other sciences to show that utility is not to be disparaged in science, and that even if the term "function" partakes of two or three meanings, it still represents a well-knit relationship, in that one meaning is an extension or further specification of the other.

[8] C. A. Ruckmick: "Use of the Term 'Function' in English Textbooks of Psychology," *Amer. Journal of Psychology,* 1913, vol. 24.

[9] K. M. Dallenbach: "The History and Derivation of the word 'Function' as a Systematic Term in Psychology," *Amer. Journal of Psychology,* 1915, vol. 26.

[10] H. A. Carr in *History of Psychology in Autobiography,* vol. 3, p. 79.

Service of Judd

A third pillar of functionalism was C. H. Judd (1837-1946), probably the foremost authority on secondary education and practical pedagogy, in the country. Like Angell and Carr, he, too, was an administrator, and when he came to the University of Chicago from Yale, in 1909, functionalism received added momentum; for his influence, as dean of the School of Education, had been great with the students. He was conscientious, solid, and productive. Born in India, of missionary parents, he always retained something of the British leaning toward the adaptive as an explanatory principle. In addition to being a sound theoretician, he was a good experimentalist as well, and his two laboratory manuals were valuable tools in the hands of both instructor and student.

In his textbook, *Psychology* (1907, revised ed. 1917) a deliberate effort is made to bring into focus many of the facts of behavior which had been slurred or neglected in previous texts. On the other hand, other topics hitherto unduly stressed, were set in the background. The chapters on fundamental attitudes, speech as a form of behavior, experience and behavior (treated biologically) and dissociation are among the best in textbooks of that period. It is Judd more than either Angell or Carr who has worked out the implications of a thoroughgoing functional psychology within the covers of a text, giving it a specially biological coloring in an evolutionary or genetic setting.

The Absorption of Functionalism

Intense as was the controversy around functionalism during the first fifteen years of the twentieth century, it seems to bear only a historical interest, now that other psychologies have come to the fore. Since it was the counterpart of structuralism, it lost its significance when structuralism began to ebb through the death of Titchener. True, there are still a few of Titchener's disciples left who are loyal to their teacher and early training, and introspection is still employed as a psychological method in many laboratories, but the inroads by the more recent and aggressive psychologies have played havoc with the more or less basic schools. Functionalism found, at least in the opposition to elementarism, a powerful ally later in *Gestalt* psychology, although the utility phase was absent in the ally.

It paved the way for many experimental investigations, particularly in educational and animal psychology, where the motor response means so much. It encouraged applied psychology, in general, and at first looked sympathetically upon the fighting spirit of the behaviorists, but neither Angell, nor Carr, nor Judd, was willing to give up introspection, and each one expressed a certain aversion for the radical and blustering brand of behaviorism associated with its leader.

In his autobiographical sketch, already cited, Angell tells us that "the subsequent excesses of behaviorism as a cult I naturally could not support and my views were frankly set forth in a paper on this subject published in the *Psychological Review*." Angell here has reference to his article "Behavior as a Category of Psychology" (*Psychological Review*, 1913, vol. 20) in which he questions even Pavlov's epoch-making experiments as significantly affecting the course of psychology. Incidentally, a letter which Angell wrote to the present writer, in 1922, might be offered in evidence, at this point.

YALE UNIVERSITY
New Haven, Connecticut
Office of the President
December 23, 1922

Dr. A. A. Roback
Department of Psychology
Harvard University
Cambridge, Mass.
Dear Dr. Roback:

Some one has sent me the early pages of your forthcoming book on Behaviorism which interests me extremely. Nothing but irresistible pressure of other duties has prevented my trying the same thing myself, for I believe that much of the so-called behaviorism of the present day is psychologically pernicious and philosophically absurd. I am moved to write you, because of wonder on my part as to which of my early sins is responsible for your brief line, in the table of contents, in which you speak of me as sympathetic toward the new movement. I have more than once vigorously attacked its more extreme positions and, while I was undoubtedly sympathetic to the earlier efforts to supplement by objective methods our knowledge of mental process gained by introspection and other subjective forms of attack, I have never for a moment had but one view on the issue as drawn by my former pupil Watson and his followers. I have also been sympathetic to the disposition to find some word like "behavior" which might mitigate some of the needless quarrels over the term "consciousness," but beyond this I have never gone. I shall look forward with great pleasure to a careful reading of your text.

Yours very truly,
JAMES R. ANGELL

The fact that President Angell was impelled to write, intimating that he was sufficiently concerned about the new movement to have had in mind such a critique, is ample proof of the negative feeling toward behaviorism among the functionalist leaders, notwithstanding the frequent claims made by behaviorists regarding their sponsorship.

A similar attitude will be detected in Judd's letter to the author reproduced below.

I think the writers who have recently used the word "behaviorism" to express their spleen against introspection, have run away with a word to which they have absolutely no right. The plain implication of the word behaviorism is that there is in the world something directly antithetical to behavior which needs to be banished from psychology. The psychologist most completely devoted to introspection does not for a moment overlook behavior. The pages of all the early introspectionists confirm this statement. To put behavior and consciousness in antithesis is like putting nutrition and life over against each other. One can have all sorts of vagueness in thinking if one juggles with words in the effort to contrast matters which belong in two wholly different classes.

The true antithesis is between behaviorism and sensationalism as principles of explanation. The early psychologists, misled by the obvious and striking character of the sensory content of experience, sought the explanation of all the facts of human and animal adjustments to environment in sensations and sensation complexes. They were mistaken not because they were introspectionists but because they were misled by the obvious facts which first come to light through superficial introspection.

The break came when James propounded his theory of the emotions. From that date on, behavior took a new place in psychological discussions. The work of James in my judgment is the really significant beginning of behaviorism. The brand of psychology which has since arrogated to itself this name seems to me spurious, temporary, and at times, quite trivial.

If I am at all right in claiming the name behaviorism for that type of psychology which recognizes reactions as fundamental to the explanation of all the phenomena of human experience, then I should certainly class my own work as confirming and extending in certain lines the type of thinking which James first formulated. Possibly it may not be out of place for me to refer in direct support of this statement to my article entitled "Movement and Consciousness" in the 29th Monograph Supplement of the *Psychological Review*.

The reasons why I should not want to be classified with the group who throw introspection aside and call themselves behaviorists are set forth in the address which I read in 1909 before the Psychological Association. If the word behaviorism is destined to mean what it is used to mean by the non-introspectionists, please count me out. If it is used to mean what it ought to mean, I shall be glad to present my credentials of membership. . . .

Very sincerely, for true behaviorism,
CHARLES H. JUDD

Chapter 21

E. L. Thorndike, the Connectionist

THERE ARE, outside of William James and Stanley Hall, the "founding fathers," three who, by virtue of their direct or indirect impact on American psychology, may lay claim to the title of *the* American psychologists: J. McKeen Cattell, E. L. Thorndike, and J. B. Watson. Cattell was the first to be the incumbent of a chair in psychology and, as a professor at Columbia University, he was able to train a number of graduate students who later became prominent in their own right. Watson, as the vociferous promoter of behaviorism, which he was supposed to have founded, and also as an excellent experimentalist, would have earned the title since his type of psychology diverged so far from European conceptions, although behaviorism was suggested both in nineteenth-century France (Comte, Cournot) and in more recent years it has had its sponsors in (Janet and Piéron).

However, neither the one nor the other is acceptable for that honor from our point of view. Cattell was a good teacher and wise mentor, with a number of investigations to his credit, but his production was meagre. He was obliged to quit Columbia University because of his pacifism during World War I, but even before that time, he had become absorbed in educational and academic statistics, in publicistic tasks, in publishing, conferences, projects of a non-psychological nature. Although his interest in psychology continued to his last day, and long after he had been ousted from Columbia he was elected President of the International Congress of Psychology, at Yale, in 1929, it means only that he was an influential figure regarded with respect.

As to John B. Watson, he shone at a time, like a meteor which, however, soon disintegrated and dropped, although the chinks were still being preserved by collectors. Even if behaviorism should be considered a distinctly American product, Watson, in abandoning his original scientific pursuits fairly early in life, has relinquished any claim to high distinction even if his propositions were less unsound, or to put it mildly, less extreme.

Thorndike (1874-1949), on the other hand, is the only one of the pioneers who qualifies for the title of "characteristically American psychologist." At a period when it was customary for every prospective teacher and researcher with high ambitions to imbibe at the font of Leipzig or Würzburg, Thorndike received his entire training in the United States. He was not spoiled in that respect by direct foreign influence and had no conflicts to undergo between former loyalties and original temperamental orientations. His course did not change with the times. His interests widened, and as he advanced in age he tackled new areas of research, always enlisting, in true American fashion, the cooperation of graduate students to carry out some of the experiments and prepare the clerical or statistical material. Furthermore—and this could not be said of his teacher, Cattell—his scientific output bulks large. Several hundred articles and about thirty books were produced in the course of a busy life, much of it devoted to teaching and administrative work, even if he did know how to delegate tasks to assistants.

Personality

Born in Williamstown, Massachusetts, into an originally New Hampshire lawyer-clergymen family and, therefore, to all intents, a native Yankee, Thorndike quickly adapted to the atmosphere of the great metropolis and the cosmopolitan university in which he was to unfold his creative ability and wield his influence over students from the far ends of the world who, in turn, took his teachings to their remote lands. As a New Englander, he might have been expected to follow a conservative trend in his educational activities, but he proved to be more American than New Englander. The progressive spirit which pervaded Columbia under the aegis of John Dewey, Franz Boas, and J. McKeen Cattell fitted in with his own views, if not with his temperament or everyday habits. Outwardly, his reserve and poise, harmonizing with his physique, which might earn him the description of a "big man" could place him in the minds of new acquaintances as the board chairman of a national bank; but the impression of the somewhat bovine exterior would not last long before the warm smile and sophisticated glance would light up his countenance. He never, however, lost his dignity, and there was a tinge of formality in his demeanor.

It is noteworthy perhaps that despite his build he wrote a small hand with a fine pen, indicating, to employ the Jamesian phrase, a tender-minded constitution. In his relations with others, he was inclined to be correct and even accommodating. As the most important figure at Teachers College of Columbia, inspiring hundreds of students each year, he nevertheless displayed no air of authority or semblance of self-importance. He might even be described as shy. It is characteristic—and none of his biographers or eulogists have alluded to it—that of the sixty-odd sketches in the four volumes of *History of Psychology in Autobiography*, his was the skimpiest, containing only eight pages. The median is thirty-three pages and some run to sixty pages. A number of the writers have gone into the details of their life, family events, etc.; others, like Scripture, shun personal particulars while dwelling on their views and writings. Thorndike does neither extensively, as if there were few occurrences of special import to relate ("barren of interest and instruction"), while as to his works, they are there for anyone to read. He does air some observations and opinions which might be of pragmatic value, *e.g.*, he would discourage specialization in reading.

From his meagre self-sketch it is evident that he was a practical man, planning his life in order to accomplish much with as little wear and worry as possible; at saving time, he was a past master even if many of the tasks were imposed upon him by the demands of his station or office. Because of his prestige and position, he experienced no difficulty in placing manuscripts; and invitations to deliver special lectures at other institutions would come thick and fast, although it would seem that he had never been accepted in Europe. His *Principles of Teaching* was translated into Russian and German, and he was, of course, known in France and Germany, but his decidedly American slant appeared radical and perhaps even shallow to psychologists and educationists in the Old Country, who were strong on philosophy.

Training

In the small compass of his miniature autobiography, there are nevertheless some striking facts and aperçus which savor of paradox. Here we have a man who has been one of the most prolific scientists and a pioneer in more than one branch of psychology, yet he cannot recall having heard the term "psychology" until his junior year at college. After graduation from Wesleyan College, he entered Harvard so as to study under James, whose lively style he admired, and took prescribed courses in English and philosophy, but his was not the philosophical mentality.

His first experimental investigation at the Harvard Psychological Laboratory under Delabarre—as Münsterberg was in Germany then, angling for a professorship there on the strength of his call to Harvard—was in the line of operant conditioning. He had youngsters from three to six study his facial expressions in order to guess which of a set of numbers he had in mind. If they guessed correctly, they were rewarded with a bit of candy. The college administration, however, whether for diet reasons or because the children enjoyed it too much, or because guessing was not supposed to be at the time an object of scientific study, soon conditioned, or rather unconditioned, these experiments. Another experiment, with chickens, also struck some snags. Thorndike's landlady understandably objected vehemently to such lodgers, and even William James could not wangle a few feet of space for them in the Agassiz Museum, so he compassionately harbored the chickens in his own cellar on Irving Street.

After acquiring an A.M. from Harvard in 1897, Thorndike applied for a fellowship at Columbia, and in 1898 he received his doctorate, partly based on his thesis *Animal Intelligence*. For a decade, his interests lay in the direction of animal behavior. He experimented on cats, monkeys, chicks, and fishes; it may be said that he was Lloyd Morgan's successor in that domain, but while Morgan was an improvement on Romanes, Thorndike struck out for himself with a strictly controlled technique. His experiments on the intelligence of cats in lifting levers and manipulating latches in order to escape from the box, could, in one sense, be compared with Pavlov's on dogs, carried on at about the same time. To be sure, it lacked the seasoning of the great Russian physiologist, but in common with the procedure of classical conditioning, it kept rigidly to the canons of scientific method, avoiding the pitfalls of theory and popular stereotypes taken over by ordinary researchers.

At heart, Thorndike was inclined to be an iconoclast. He tells us significantly that "although . . . my tendency is to say 'yes' to persons, my tendency seems to have been to say 'no' to ideas. I have been stimulated to study problems to which Romanes, Wesley Mills, Stanley Hall, Alexander Bain,

Kraepelin, Spearman and others seemed to me to give wrong answers, more often than to verify and extend work which seemed sound." As he advanced in years, Thorndike concerned himself more with fresh problems.

In view of his efficiency and success as an experimentalist, it is surprising to read "Young psychologists who share one or more of my disabilities may take comfort in the fact that after all I have done useful experiments without mechanical ability or training and have investigated quantitative relations with very meager knowledge of mathematics"—an admission which hardly anyone would have anticipated.

Associated with the investigation of the delayed reaction is usually the name of W. S. Hunter, whose monograph appeared in 1913, but from Thorndike (autobiographical sketch) we learn that "the delayed reaction experiment (which has proved the most valuable of my methods of studying animal mentality) came to me after two years of work with animals." It would appear then that Thorndike was the pioneer here, and that these experiments must have been conducted at the turn of the century.

Works

Thorndike's early animal experiments actually dealt with learning, and, therefore, when after a year at Western Reserve, he returned at Cattell's invitation to Columbia and took up his life-long teaching responsibilities at Teachers College, what would be more natural for him than to apply the principles gained from his previous investigations to human learning? The nature of intelligence, intelligence tests, individual differences, instinct, measurement—all these subjects occupied his attention for the larger part of his career, but a cursory glance at the hundreds of articles published either independently or jointly with authors will reveal the breadth of his germinating mind. He would never tackle intricate problems, *e.g.*, space perception or the higher thought processes (where he would deal with such, the relationship was tangential or on the surface) but rather issues that had a bearing on possible educational reforms. With John Dewey and Kilpatrick at Columbia, this institution became the world's center for progressive education, training subsequent propagandists of the new educational gospel in the scores, if not in the hundreds.

To list all the books and some of the more important articles authored by Thorndike would take up too much space. *Nulla dies sine linea* seems to have applied to him as it did not to some of his Columbia colleagues. His earliest compendium of psychology in which he possibly wished to emulate William James's *causerie* style, *The Human Nature Club*, is scarcely ever mentioned. It was originally published in 1900 (not 1901 as the *Psychological Register* has it recorded) by the Chautauqua Press and republished, in a somewhat enlarged edition, by Longmans, Green, in 1911 and in 1920. This little book already contains the seed of the general method employed consistently by its author; for although Thorndike broadened his interests and proceeded from area to area, he held fast to his general principles. We shall see presently what this method is and what his principles represent.

Among his major works are *The Elements of Psychology* (1903, 1907), *Principles of Teaching* (1906), *An Introduction to the Theory of Mental and Social Measurement* (1904, 1913), *The Psychology of Arithmetic* (1922), *The Psychology of Algebra* (1923), (with others) *The Measurement of Intelligence* (1926), *Human Learning* (1931), *The Fundamentals of Learning* (1932), *the Psychology of Wants, Interests and Attitudes* (1935), *Human Nature and the Social Order* (1940) constituting the William James Lectures at Harvard, and *Your City* (1939).

Selected Writings from a Connectionist's Psychology (1949), contains his autobiographical sketch, already referred to, plus one and a half pages of supplementary material on his later life, as well as a number of essays not readily available to students such as "Trains of Thought as Symptoms of Interests and Attitudes" from the *Proceedings of the American Philosophical Society*, "Valuations of Achievements, Acts, and Persons" from the *Albert Schweitzer Jubilee Book* (edited by A. A. Roback), and "Darwin's Contribution to Psychology" from the *University of California Chronicle*—a miscellany of topics indicating the diversity of ideas which radiated from his mind.

There were a series of arithmetics, reading scales, writing scales, intelligence tests (the I.E.R. Intelligence Scale—CAVD) word books, and the Thorndike dictionary, but his masterpiece is, of course, his three-volume *Educational Psychology* (1913-1914) of which there was a briefer course also (in collaboration with I. Lorge).

Contribution

Thorndike may be called a functionalist in psychology, alongside of Cattell, Hall, and Dewey, but he chooses to go under the label of "connectionist." At first blush, it may sound very much as if he wanted an individual trademark so as not to be identified with the associationist school of the Mills (father and son). Actually, Thorndike simply wished to stress the physiological connections between cell and cell which mediate the stimulus and response. Every phenomenon, every learning process, is explained in terms of stimulus-response bond.

Why, then, is he not identified as a behaviorist, antedating John B. Watson? As a matter of fact, the behaviorists of forty years ago were disposed to co-opt him as their ally. It was the number 2 behaviorist W. S. Hunter who, in reviewing *Behaviorism and Psychology*, took the author to task for not dealing with Thorndike in the book, and said that his name was among the conspicuous omissions in the chart of sundry behaviorists. I promptly wrote to the latter asking him whether he would consider himself a behaviorist, to which he replied that "I suppose I should be rated a behaviorist and would choose that extreme rather than the other if one must be classified to fit verbal contrasts."

That choice seems, however, to be somewhat undecided when in reply to the next question, "whether you conceive psychology to be the science of stimulus and response rather than the science of mind or consciousness" he tells us that he accepts both. Now a behaviorist would have no truck with consciousness; and certainly a mentalist does not rule out physiological processes as the bases of mental experiences.

The third question, as to whether he would rule out introspection as a method of obtaining psychological data, yielded an unqualified "no." Although Watson and his followers have made some allowance for introspection as a species of behavior, Thorndike did not intend it merely as a stopgap or a makeshift. His emphasis on the questionnaire method would clearly indicate that to him the mind is still a reality and not a delusion. In his annotations, Thorndike referred me to "the chapter on Consciousness and Behavior in my *Animal Intelligence: Experimental Studies* (the book and not the monograph)."

Thorndike's views on individual differences and heredity would be foreign to behaviorism. He questions the results that

Watson sought to foist upon psychologists in general that fear could be induced by *any* stimulus, or that there is no original nature involved in the matter of dominance and submission. In Thorndike's psychology, the genes play a very important part even in mental characteristics. Although he lays due stress on the environment, he cannot shut his eyes to the heredity significance in his own family, when we consider that his brother, Ashley, was a distinguished Professor of English at Columbia—one of the foremost authorities on Elizabethan literature—and that another brother, Lynn, at the same university, ranked as one of the most eminent historians of medieval civilization. In fact, his books are more in use now than his psychologist brother's.

Thorndike's children are all academically engaged. It is curious that his daughter, while a student at Vassar, received the highest score in the *Roback Mentality Tests for Superior Adults*.[1] His son has succeeded to the chair at Teachers College which he had held for a full generation. One may ask, consequently, whether such achievement in a single family can be explained wholly by training and environment. Need we recall here the vaunted challenge of Watson to give him a normally developed infant in the first six months, and he would make anything of it, even a genius? Thorndike was too levelheaded a man to treat such balderdash seriously. He was not as thoroughgoing a hereditarian as Terman, but with Galton as his ideal, and Cattell, his early mentor, he would have gained enough impetus in the geneticist direction to prevent him from falling under the spell of a one-sided environmentalism.

Thorndike's name is most closely associated with his so-called law of effect, which afterward included the state of

---

[1] As a *divertimento*, it may be revealed here that these tests had originated by fluke. At the time the present writer accepted an instructorship at Simmons College, in 1919, the faculty had voted to have the freshman class tested for intelligence. Thorndike had just then published a series of tests for entering freshmen, and they were to be used at Simmons, although they were more achievement tests than indicative of intelligence as such. The price asked, however, was so high that the instructor offered to devise a series of twelve tests the printing of which would be far more economical. The offer was accepted, and within a month or so (since the idea had already been in mind for some time), the Superior Adult Tests were off the press.

readiness and, in simplified form, sets forth that an act which satisfies the agent, whether initiated by chance or deliberately, will, as it is repeated, tend to be stamped in physiologically, as against one which is unpleasant or neutral. In the section on learning, this thesis has been shown to have aroused misgivings on the part of experimentalists, not gestaltists alone. Of wider acceptance is his corollary that punishment is not nearly so effective in learning as reward, because of the side effects, like distraction, resentment, frustration—all of which lead to a certain waste of energy and confusion.

With dogged zeal Thorndike set out to prove that the only basis of learning is frequency of repetition bolstered by satisfaction on the part of the learner. The principle was applied to practically all functions and activities; and to that purpose he would be prepared to rewrite accepted passages in psychological textbooks, even to the extent of denying that primacy was a factor in memory. His arguments were not merely theoretical. They were always based on experiments which either he or his students were conducting. It hardly needs saying that few of his colleagues, outside of Columbia University, were convinced.

One of his pet aversions for the same reason, viz., that it was not exactly compatible with the doctrine of the potency of the stimulus-response bond as an explain-all, was the ideomotor action theory, made popular through William James. On general principles, one would have expected Thorndike to endorse it warmly. For one thing it stressed the motor phase of consciousness and served as a prop for psychological determinism vs. voluntarism (free will). Anything, however, which could be cited as a force in producing action without giving precedence or priority to effect and habit would have to be rejected. Hence his presidential address before the American Psychological Association[2] was devoted to the demolition of this standard tenet. Like Cyrano, he single-handedly takes on Wundt, James, McDougall, Calkins, and others who were important figures, and offers all sorts of reasons for the phenomena which come under that head. One thing is puzzling: McDougall is quoted without a reference as an upholder of the view, but actually he strongly opposed it, as is evident from the following passage in his textbook.

[2] E. L. Thorndike: "Ideo-Motor Action," *Psychol. Review,* 1913, pp. 90-100.

The ideo-motor theory has been widely accepted and may be found dogmatically stated in many recent books. It asserts that every "idea" is not only a state or act of knowing but also a tendency to movement. . . . This ideo-motor theory is most plausible in the case of "ideas" of bodily movement. It has frequently been alleged that, if we think of a movement, that movement inevitably occurs, unless we somehow inhibit it. . . . I cannot discover any substantial foundation for such assertions.[3]

I doubt whether many of the listeners at the Association meeting changed their minds after Thorndike's lucid exhortation. My own typical illustration of the ideo-motor principle is that of involuntarily turning in the direction, whether to the right or left, of the object or person we are referring to, at the time we think of or mention him. The intensity or emotional charge of the state will also be of great importance, as instances from dramatic literature will attest.

Thorndike had greater success in dealing with the doctrine of formal discipline according to which the benefit gained in one type of learning will be carried over to another type, so that whether or not the study of Latin or Greek is desirable in itself, it helps to sharpen the mind. The camps were about equally divided half a century ago, but Thorndike's influence, perhaps more than the experiments which he always brought to bear on the topic, turned the tide; and the public schools adopted a policy of examining the common denominators or factors in any two or more studies which were intended to reinforce one another. Mathematics and music could be of mutual benefit to the pupil only in fostering habits of application or perhaps furthering accuracy.

Specificity

Because of his restrained, never personal, manner in polemic matters, Thorndike was never exactly a storm-center, but he did engage and was engaged in controversy, chiefly by British psychologists. McDougall forever was a foe of simple connectionism, and even indulged in parody, representing an examination in which a number of questions were asked, with the answer *"S-R bond"* occurring for every one of them.

[3] William McDougall: *Outline of Psychology,* 1923, pp. 290-291.

It was on the score of intelligence factors that the disagreement seemed to have been less contained; for here the students of the protagonists had joined in the fray. Thorndike, whose hankering for experimental data was ever present, seemed inclined to look upon intelligence as a segmental affair. His division of intelligence as applicable to three domains: ideas, people, and objects, is not difficult to subscribe to. It is when he breaks up the more abstract or scholastic kind into various abilities that one begins to question the conclusions.

In England, Spearman had developed the theory that there was a general intelligence (G) out of which there emerged specific subtypes. It is sometimes known as a one-factor, or perhaps two-factor, theory. The entire London school of factorial analysis is built around that doctrine, or, it might be better to say, has led up to its birth.

Thorndike's conception, on the other hand, is a multimodal one. Thus, one who is excellent in vocabulary may be poor in mathematics, and vice versa. Neither theory nor factorial computation is to determine the situation, but actual tests and experiments, simple though they might be.

This multimodal tendency has, of course, infiltrated into personality treatment, so that Columbia became known as a specificity plant, where general traits were conjured away. The long-range series of experiments on character traits by May and Hartshorne, which afterward were reported and discussed in three volumes, appeared to substantiate the specificity view, if we did not take a critical stand on the methodology and interpretations. P. M. Symonds, one of a succession of Thorndike aides, even went so far as to make of the trait just a series of similar acts ("confact").

This is one of the questionable advantages of Columbia, viz., that once the chief has adopted a certain theoretical position, the junior department members and graduate students will set their sights for that goal. It would be true of nearly all other institutions, but where a department is not monolithic or single-pillared, there can still be room for differences of opinion.

Thorndike's glottogony (theory of the origin of language) is interesting and in keeping with his "law of effect" and connectionism. Primitive man would babble as babies do. At one point, the act or sensory experience would be accompanied by a certain sound ("guk" or "blin") and the satisfying feeling would tend to produce repetition, with that same experience following in a chain reaction. Then as other humans would come around, they would be hearing that sound and would associate it with the object or act. This "blab-luck" theory has found sponsors among psychologists, but linguists are not impressed, having been exposed to more sophisticated data. Nevertheless, Thorndike's command of the subjects he handles, whether semantics or the psychology of algebra, is truly remarkable; and his realistic, crystal-clear manner of exposition reminds us of the British scientists, like Huxley, Tyndall, and Galton.

It must be said that Thorndike might have attempted to emulate Galton in his tackling so many different problems. There was nothing abstruse or recondite in his treatment any more than there was in Galton's. He did not care to specialize throughout his life, but progressed from one topic to another, covering animal learning, educational psychology, intelligence testing, measurement and its techniques, lexicography and sociology.

His biographers have not noticed that he was very much given to the questionnaire method and that his interest in what people *do* was to him more important than what they *should do*; or perhaps that the former was to decide the norm. Sometimes the questions put were of a hypothetical nature.

In that one respect, the realist turns unrealistic, just as the hardheaded businessman might take stock in some flimsy project. If the questions were to probe the imagination of the interrogated, one could understand the objective, but if serious and significant evaluations are expected of a number of achievements, activities, or acts such as, in imagination, "Eat 4 ounces of cooked human flesh, knowing it to be such," "Marry a Hottentot and live with him or her for a year," "Steal $500 from a rich miser who got it by deceiving the public," "Teaching high school pupils that marriage is a silly custom," then I am afraid that the investigator will obtain only shadows of shadows, as in Plato's cave allegory. There are three or four mental and moral stations to control: (a) imagination, (b) deliberation, (c) candidness, and (d) serious purpose on the part of the participants.

One feature of Thorndike's mentality that has not been adverted to is his penchant for computation. He is constantly taking inventories. He spent, as he tells us, in his sketch of himself over 20,000 hours reading and studying scientific works and journals. There was a *distributive tendency* in his investigative work, and pluralism runs through his system, if it can be called such. His continual expansion and reaching out for new territory was in line with this general trait. The only unitary thread that ran throughout his numerous writings was connectionism, the linking of nerve impulses. As a functionalist and progressive in education, his main concern was *to bring improvement*, not to establish theories.

To what extent his work will live must be contingent upon recent research, some of which, under better facilities and a more elaborate technique, is already puncturing the principle of effect. The exceptions taken to a simple stimulus-response interpretation of human behavior, in the opposing camps, are not to be glossed over. But of one thing we may be certain, Thorndike's contribution to American psychology and education has been both enormous and invaluable; and his straightforward and direct approach to the various problems involved has, in some respects, become a model of exposition. Next to William James, he stands out as the pillar of American psychologists, one who has never been under the direct influence of European teaching.

Chapter 22

Psychology Out of Its Mind

IF FUNCTIONALISM is to be considered the first American school in psychology which broke away from the orthodox standpoint, behaviorism may be regarded as the American brand *par excellence;* for functionalism had its beginnings in Austria (the Graz School), France (Binet), and England (Mackenzie, Stout), before coming of age in the United States with the Chicago school. Functionalism, even in its last stage, may still be considered traditional in that introspection was the basic method, and mind was still the subject-matter of psychology. The revolt against the older school consisted in branching out toward the needs of life, and in pursuing a utilitarian course of investigation. Functionalism would have been content with concessions. Where functionalism was conciliatory, behaviorism became a mortal foe, not only dethroning 'mind,' but negating it. Functionalism merely wanted *Lebensraum,* room to spread out.

Behaviorism Becomes Articulate

Not so behaviorism, as it developed in the second decade of the present century. Its aim was to divorce itself completely from what had come to be regarded as psychology, and it effected a complete revolution in its own province. Indeed, the rift between the "new" psychology of the experimentalists, and the speculative intellectual philosophies of the Scottish School and its offshoots was not as great as between radical behaviorism and traditional psychology, inasmuch as, whether you call the matter "pneuma," "soul," or "mind," you have reference to just one thing, *viz.,* consciousness, whereas behaviorism was intent upon consigning consciousness to the sphere of mythology or the rubbish heap of science.

The chapter heading may seem ambiguous, bordering on the facetious, nevertheless if it is a jest, then its source lies in the very presumptuousness of behaviorism. It has been observed long since that first psychology lost its soul, then it lost consciousness, but no more than an individual who has

264

lost consciousness for all time, can be said to remain a person, can a psychology, without consciousness, exist as such. It can be a branch of physiology—let us call it behavioristics (and this term was actually proposed by Roback in 1922, and has even found its way into the literature, notably in Boring's *History of Experimental Psychology*) but why call a club a spade?

One of the strangest things about this movement is that it has been associated with a single man, who has done actually little in psychology, to begin with, and has stepped out of it completely, abandoning even his so-called brain child. The history of psychology is a remarkable revelation of human foibles, and affords a most interesting commentary on the influence of personality on the shaping of intellectual movements. The iniquity of culture consists largely in the inequity of bestowing credit where it does not belong and cheating the rightful claimants of their laurels. The history of civilization teems with instances of such injustice; and only in some few cases are steps taken to correct the abuse. The cause is due partly to indifference, partly to the routine acceptance of propaganda, and of course mainly to ignorance, born of the other two traits.

The Reputed Founder

John B. Watson (1878-1958) has been credited with the founding of behaviorism. That he has been its promoter, its champion, its leader, or even its high priest, we cannot deny; yes, he has even tacked on the syllable to the word "behavior," turning it into an "ism," a theory, or point of view, technically, but it is little short of a violation of the truth to single him out as the founder, when in 1911, Max F. Meyer (1873-   ) gave us the rudiments of a behavioristic psychology in his *Fundamental Laws of Human Behavior*, followed up by a more systematic exposition in his *Psychology of the Other One* (1921). In 1912, Meyer dealt with the problem of mind and body, and in 1913, he used mechanical analogies in order to prove that the behavioristic conception of nervous function is superior to others. Later, he worked out a scheme of abnormal psychology on a behavioristic basis.

In England, William McDougall published a little book on psychology, defining it as the science of behavior. Watson's behavioristic debut was made with his "Psychology as a

Behaviorist Views It" in 1913 (*Psychol. Review*, vol. 20).
B. H. Bode, from the pragmatist camp, and E. B. Holt, from
the neo-realist angle, had, by that time, made their contribution toward behaviorism. It was not until 1914 that Watson's
Behavior; an Introduction to Comparative Psychology, his
most important, because most solid, work appeared. His
most ambitious and spectacular work, *Psychology from the
Standpoint of a Behaviorist*, came out in 1919. Meanwhile,
A. P. Weiss was supplying the theoretical grounds for behaviorism through a series of articles.

Watson was primarily an animal psychologist. Every one
who has worked with animals, from Romanes and Lloyd
Morgan down to Tolman, is inclined toward behaviorism,
because introspection is, from the nature of the case, ruled
out. In animal psychology, the response, the motor phase,
bulks large, and that is a further stimulant toward acceptance
of the behavioristic philosophy (for behaviorism, in the last
analysis, reduces to an outlook on life). If, however, one
were to cast about for a systematic exposition of behaviorism,
it would be that of Max F. Meyer to merit our attention, even
if it does not possess the foam and sparkle of Watson's.

Comments by Colleagues

Carr in his autobiographical sketch informs us that Watson
"once remarked that it was possible to write a psychology in
purely objective terms—starting with the simple reflexes and
proceeding to the more complex varieties of mental behavior,
and he also added that he intended to write such a book at the
first opportunity. Here were the essential features of his
behaviorism long before he heard of the work of Pavlov and
Bechterev."[1]

Here is another instance of friendly indulgence on the part
of Watson's pupils and associates. Surely it is difficult to believe that at the time Watson was an instructor at the University of Chicago, he had not heard of the conditioned reflex
experiments of Pavlov, reported in 1903.

Dunlap, who was well disposed toward his colleague at
Johns Hopkins, paints a different picture of the situation, and
this was several years later than the period which Carr
describes. From Dunlap it would appear that Watson received

[1] H. A. Carr in *History of Psychology in Autobiography*, vol. 3,
p. 76.

the stimulus of laying the ghost of consciousness from him, and what astonishes us particularly is the tale of Watson's use of visual imagery, after we have been led to believe that visual imagery did not exist (since consciousness was a chimera) and that such alleged imagery is but illusory kinaesthesis (eye movements). Let us now attend to Dunlap.

I had already discarded the old doctrine of "images." Watson, however, still accepted it. He, he said, used visual imagery very effectually in designing his apparatus. Watson had not at that time developed his behaviorism, and his thinking was, to a large extent, along conventional lines. He was violently interested in animal behavior, and was looking for some simplifications of attitude which would align that work with human psychology. Hence, he was interested in the iconoclastic activity I was developing, and was influenced by my views, but carried them out to extremes. I rejected images as psychic objects, and denounced introspection as held by the orthodox psychologists. Watson carried this further, to the excluding from his psychology of everything to which the word "introspection" could be applied, and excluded imagination along with images. I had questioned the possibility of observing "consciousness." Watson carried this to the extreme, also. His first behaviorism, however, was obviously based on the orthodox system by which the mental field was divided into perception, thought, and feeling; and he was merely finding physiological substitutes for these. When I called his attention to this, and urged him to study behavior as behavior, he admitted the apparent Titchenerian basis, but opined that he could get away from that in later writings. He did, eventually, but only after the American psychology generally had moved ahead.[2]

As Boring sizes up the psychological scene in the years following 1910, "Some conservatives were Wundtians, some radicals were functionalists, more psychologists were agnostics. Then Watson touched a match to the mass, there was an explosion, and behaviorism was left. Watson founded behaviorism because everything was all ready for the founding. Otherwise he could not have done it. He was philosophically

[2] K. Dunlap in *History of Psychology in Autobiography,* vol. 3, p. 45.

inept, and behaviorism came into existence without a constitution. Ever since, the behaviorists have been trying to formulate a satisfactory epistemological constitution and thus to explain themselves."[3]

Antecedents of Behaviorism

Boring, too, speaks as if Watson founded behaviorism. In reality, he denied all states of consciousness, but that had already been done by physiologists before him. He merely spread the gospel. He could be represented as an apostle but by no means a founder. For let us make a very brief survey of the psychological negativists. Here is a passage worth quoting. "After 2000 years of psychological pursuit, no one proposition is established to the satisfaction of its followers. They are divided to this day into a multitude of schools, still at variance about the very elements of their doctrine. This introspection gives rise to almost as many theories as there are observers. We ask in vain for any one discovery, great or small, which has been made under this method." Does this not sound as if taken verbatim from one of Watson's books? Yet, the author of this negativistic statement was the father of positivism in philosophy, Auguste Comte, who lived more than a century ago. The critique of introspective psychology was contained in the *Cours de Philosophie Positive,* which appeared in 1842. Cournot had come out with similar strictures against psychology.

What about the biologists? Did they not instigate the radical revolt in the very fort of psychology? Jacques Loeb, *e.g.,* was intent upon reducing all consciousness in lower animals to tropisms; and his ambition was to achieve a measure of success along those lines in the human domain, but that was beyond his level. There were the anti-psychological biologists, like Beer, Nuel, Bethe, and v. Uexsküll, who constantly deprecated any attempt to treat the animal mind as anything but a pure mechanism.

It was the Russian physiologists, most of all, who supplied the basis for American behaviorism, even before Pavlov stirred up the scientific world by his experiments on the conditioned reflex. I. M. Sechenov had been developing a mechanistic

[3] E. G. Boring: *A History of Experimental Psychology* (1st ed.), p. 494.

psychology, and I. P. Pavlov's contemporary and equally able physiologist, Vl. M. Bekhterev elaborated a reflexology which was practically the same as Watson's behaviorism. Did they not test the sensations and perceptions of animals by means of discriminatory responses, and did they not replace association by the conditioned reflex? True, Pavlov, after "achieving" success in throwing consciousness out of the door, invited it in again through the window in the guise of "psychic" reflexes; and his compatriot, Bekhterev went through the same stunt, except that his camouflage took the form of "personal" reflexes.

In Quest of Objectivity

This whole Procrustean operation was performed in the interest of objectivity. Since we are not supposed to know whether animals see, hear, feel, or imagine, and in order to reduce assumption even in the case of humans to a minimum, it soon became fashionable to substitute for such words as sense organs, muscles, etc. technical terms which are more generic or comprehensive, and are applicable to all living organisms. Thus vision becomes *photoreception,* the muscles are known as *proprioceptors,* and the pain spots in the skin are labelled *nociceptors.* This nomenclature invests the subject with an air of objectivity, which is the desideratum of all science, but whether there has been any gain thereby is not certain.

It seems rather as if the physiologists wanted to make sure that all phenomena to be included in their textbooks or treatises, no matter how tangential, could be subsumed under their own rubric. If the particular light organ, say, the photoreceptor, is stimulated by light, and the organism does not see, then the psychologist has no business to treat it as psychological material. However, when a term like *nociceptor* is coined, it still implies that the organ not only is affected by harmful stimuli, but that it registers pain in the individual. It is surely not the harmfulness or harmlessness of the stimulus that is involved, for any and every stimulus can be harmful. Every catabolic process in the nerve is theoretically noxious, and every receptor is therefore a nociceptor, were it not for the fact that some organs are especially adapted to communicate impulses which, when reaching the special cortical centre, yield the sensation of pain.

The Behavioristic Streak in James

As early as 1904, the behavioristic imp manifested itself in William James who had so many facets that we could never know which would begin to glisten under his temperamental whim, when we least expected it to. A decade before Watson "founded" behaviorism, James, in an article, provokingly headed "Does Consciousness Exist?" declares: "The stream of thinking is only a careless name for what, when scrutinized, reveals itself to consist chiefly of the stream of my breathing" together with certain "intracephalic adjustments," and furthermore, he adds, "that entity (*sc.* consciousness) is fictitious."[4] Did James really think that consciousness was a fiction? Of course not. It was only a passing phase with him, a resurgence of that dissociated group of ideas, characterized by doubt and negation, attempting to form an independent little personality, but fortunately appearing very seldom.

For our purpose, however, it is sufficient to show that Watson has not discovered America; and even his theory of thought as implicit behavior *via* sublaryngeal movement was anticipated by S. Stricker, in Austria (*motorische Wortvorstellungen*), V. E. Egger, in France, (*La Parole Intéreure*), and, above all, by E. A. Singer in the United States. The last mentioned, in articles published in 1911 and 1912, tells us what he means by thought, and how we would go about catching it, as it were, when it was not looking. "I should begin," he blandly proposes, "by looking for such movements of atoms as actually moved too slightly for us to notice it[?] —the organs of expression, the tongue principally, and the eyes. Or perhaps I should find part of the movements to be of this nature, part of them such as strained the muscles that inhibited such expression."[5]

There were, of course, many others both among the philosophers and psychologists who were trying to get rid of consciousness by hook or crook, and who had contrived all sorts of devices by which to supply us with *Ersatz* articles in the form of neural arrangements, reflex arcs, adjustments,

[4] William James: "Does Consciousness Exist?" *Journal of Philosophy, Psychology and Scientific Methods,* 1904, vol. 1, p. 49.
[5] E. A. Singer: "Mind as an Observable Object," *Journal of Philosophy, Psychology and Scientific Methods,* 1911, 1912, vols. 8, 9.

muscular contractions etc., but Watson had greater persistence, showed more vehemence in his denunciations, made more enthusiastic promises, and advertized his brand with great *éclat*. If it is true that he set the match to the floating gas which caused the explosion, it is equally true that after the fire was beyond control, he sounded the tom-tom so that the populace might enjoy the spectacle and admire his handiwork.

The First American Behaviorist

Very few psychologists, even of those who are interested in its history, have any inkling as to who might have started the first revolution in psychology, long before Watson was born. It has already been brought out in an earlier chapter that his name was James Rush, the son of the founder of American psychiatry. James Rush was not satisfied with a mind which merely perceives, imagines, and thinks. To him the mind embraces speaking and acting as well. In this pronouncement, we have the basis of later behaviorism, which puts so much weight on the speech organs and the muscles.

It was no mean adventure on the part of Rush to go into the structure and function of speech in all its details, furnishing thereby the theory and technique of that particular branch. The traditional tripartite division of the mind into cognition, affection, and volition was transformed into another threefold schema of human power; (a) the mind, in the stricter sense of observing, comparing, and concluding, (b) the voice to communicate such observations, comparisons, and conclusions, and (c) finally the hand, or other muscular agent, to carry out the aims of the mind and the voice. (*Brief Outline of an Analysis of the Human Intellect,* vol. I, p. 60.) Rush is not oblivious to the obvious objection that speech or sounds are outside of the mind.

"It may here be asked why we include [among?] the parts of the mind those sounds which like other sounds are formed externally to the mind and therefore apparently not a part of it nor in any way to be classed as one of its rudimental parts or constituents."

To make it obvious then, how verbal signs when employed by the mind can be a physical part of it, we have only to consider, how its other four constituents are formed. We endeavored to show; they are respectively primary, memorial, joint, and conclusive perceptions of all the things and objects of Nature and of Art, within the reach of their knowledge and power. Now, the verbal sign we conventionally use is a sound, which is one of the physical things of Nature, formed by the vocal organs. Thus a verbal sign as a physical thing of Nature, may be perceived; or reflected in the mirror of the senses and the brain. That is, we may have through the ear the primary, memorial, joint, and conclusive types of words, as well as of the images or types of color, heat, or any of the other twenty-one elementary things of Nature; and these types of words, appearing in the reflective mirror, under the several forms of the four divisions of perceptions.

To show how the verbal sign is interwoven with the proper working plan of the mind, thereby to justify its being considered a constituent part of it, we must here anticipate a future explanation of our nomenclature.

In the tenth section, on the Qualities, or forms, and degrees, under which the Constituents appear,' we shall learn that perceptions are sometimes Quiescent or silent,' in being known only to the mind of the Percipient; at other times Actionary, in declaring his silent thought by words, or other conventional sign, and transferring to a Hearer, the images and types of his own silent mind. At its origin, in infancy, it appears,' the mind has silent perceptions before it has signs for them,' and silent, before it has actionary signs; since the actionary can represent only antecedent silent perceptions and signs. In this way, the Hearer receives by descriptive language, a transfer of the silent primary, memorial, joint, and conclusive perceptions, which the Percipient had previously derived from the external things and objects of Nature.

But the supposed Percipient and the Hearer, are each alike sentient; alike excitable in all their senses; and alike impressible under all their images and types of the brain. And while the significant words of the Percipient produce by transfer to the Hearer, the working plan of the whole five constituents,' they come back upon the ear of the Percipient himself, producing in him the like primary, memorial, joint, and conclusive perception; with this difference. The Hearer may receive perceptions by the verbal sign that are more or less new to him. What the Percipient communicates, is well-known to himself in the previously silent state of his mind. Thus the former hears what he never heard before; the latter is the hearer of words formed into a significant train of language, within the silent process of his mind,' which when uttered, reacts on the ear of him who uttered it. But as in this process, the silent mind of the Percipient passes over, by its actionary sign, to the mind of the Hearer, and as its verbal sign is returned to the Percipient from his own mouth, they are now on this point, both alike in the communicated knowledge. There are then under our present view, three forms of perception. An actionary or an audible language,' a silent perception,' and a silent verbal sign of it: each condition being properly a part of the mind. But the two latter, being within the mind, and silent, seem to be more particularly part of its constituents. With these three forms of perception,' regarding their application to the working plan of language with thought,' we know,' they are vividly impressed, and readily revived by the audible or actionary sign. And we may here, begin to perceive, that Nature may have provided the same impressive and reviving process, for the use of silent perceptions as they occur in dreams,' by connecting with them, silent verbal signs, to brighten the pictures on the silent mind. Without these silent verbal signs for perception, human thought would be but slightly raised above that of the sub-animal.[6]

An Iconoclast Ignored

James Rush, partly because of his eccentric personality and somewhat unorthodox mode of writing, in addition to the peculiar terminology which he employed, aside from the novel ideas he sought to promulgate, received no hearing on the part of the teachers of psychology. His avowed materialism must have shocked the clergymen, who were mainly the professors of "intellectual philosophy" in those days. His two volumes on psychology are not found even in the Library of Congress, let alone university libraries, and yet the man, with all his longwindedness, repetitiousness, digressions, and rambling, had succeeded in breaking new ground. When he resumed his notes at the age of seventy, after he had put them aside for 36 years, he must have taken out his principal with a considerable accumulation of compound interest.

[6] J. Rush: *Brief Outline of an Analysis of the Human Intellect*, vol. 1, pp. 138-139. (Capitalization and punctuation as in original, except for ; which is supposed to be a pause halfway between , and ;); for "translation" of terms, see p. 176.

Like Watson and his cohorts, Rush, too, is eager to study the animal mind, since it "may be a comparative mentivity throw a varied light on that of the human intellect in showing the relationship of similitude between them." For the fifth sign of the perceptions, he adduces "language and other muscular actions of the body." In other words, he had already noticed then what his successors have been insisting on, *viz.*, that the external manifestations of mental processes are likely to tell us much about them, although he still adhered to the study of perceptions. But what are perceptions to him? How does he envisage thought? As he interprets the phenomena, there is nothing in the mind which is not in matter. Apparently, he stops short at the physiological impressions, which for him are reflections, *i.e.,* physical ones, as in the case of a mirror, and thought is only a complicated series of reflections.

An Original Materialistic System

In the following passage, Rush affords us a glimpse of his own system of psychology which, it must be said, was bold and radical for the '60's of the past century. A word of explanation will be in order, considering the outlandish terms which are often employed. The word "type" has reference to images of a non-visual nature: auditory, olfactory, etc. In his precise use of words, he would not place these on the same level as the visual image. "Mentivity" is simply "mentality" in the technical sense. The "sub-animal" represents just the infra-human organism. As to "primary, memorial, joint and conclusive perceptions," these refer to what we would call perceptions, memory images, judgments, and inference. The term "sensuous" is simply our "sensory," while "actionary" corresponds to the term "motor." And now we can proceed to follow Rush's argumentation for a materialistic psychology.

Let us ask, whether matter can reflect? If to reflect, when understood of the senses and the brain, is to have image or type, represented or impressed upon them, certainly a block of unpolished granite cannot reflect. But as certainly the matter of a mirror can, under this representative meaning. It is the same with the surface of the human retina, which can reflect a measurable image: and when we consider the extreme minuteness, or mere point of reflecting space on the retina of the smallest seeing insect, we find no objection to the admission, that the structure of the brain, however minute, its organic cells or atomic granules, for nature never stops at subtlety, may be clear points for reflecting those images and types of things. Having thus come to the analogical result, that sensuous and cerebral matter under some of its peculiar forms or conditions can reflect or perceive an object; it may be asked; what can reflection or perception of objects of the brain effect? It is readily answered; reflections and perceptions do the important work of Thinking; since we find what is called "thought" is nothing more than those reflected perceptions; for having shown analogically, that the imaged and typical impressions, or what we call perceptions, fulfil all the functions of the mind, they must constitute Thought, which is here only one of the general terms for mind. Perceptions in their primary and memorial form, therefore represent on the senses and the brain, those images and types of external things with their joint, and conclusive comparisons which we call thinking. With regard then to the question, whether matter can think, we might by changing that term to *reflect* and *perceive,* be disposed to admit, that an image and type, being made on the matter of the brain must by reciprocity of action, be material; and that, what is signified by the word "thought" being a reflective or perceptive image and type, must be a resembling function of matter. All this may be a new analysis, seeming to carry us close up to the truth. But it signifies nothing, if it does not touch it, for the whole of our present remarks amount only to analogy; which we conceit to be something that looks like truth.

In the same way, I tried to derive an analogical "argument" from the perception of Pain: and though it seemed to approach it, could not bring its seeming, to the truth. When truth is courted, she is as a mistress; and with an ardent and absent lover, she rises in full and vivid image on the slightest resemblance to her. Who with our views of materiality, can avoid recurring to the mind, on seeing the surface of the foil and the glass laid together, making so perfect a representation of what is set before them? If we were not so familiar with the moving image on a mirror, it might at first sight be mistaken for a function of life. When Narcissus saw a similar effect in the fountain, he died in the belief, he saw an animated being. The fable gives what we would consider a picture of animal perception. But much as we might wish to have sensuous proof, on the subject of materiality, we have only encouraging analogy. All this however, except as hints *at* truth we throw aside; waiting for strict demonstration by the microscope, or other physical means, how the images and types, performing their functions in the brain are not only the proximate cause of thought, but are thought itself. By the preceding views we learn the condition of the whole argument for the claims of the believers respectively in a material and in a spiritual mind. The former from the numerous analogies of the Laws of God and Nature, wishing to believe, that mind is only of the physical instances of those laws. The latter without a speck of analogy, hanging on some antiquated authority of Gods and men, believe, they have the demonstrated fact of Spirit; and that they might if further proof were necessary, plainly see, hear, touch, taste, and scent it. Having therefore the testimony of Gods and men, and if they so believe, of their own five senses, they proceed to persecute, imprison, burn, and crucify the would-be materialist, because he cannot see positively the working plan of either matter or spirit in the human mind.[7]

What Is Radical Behaviorism?

Returning to the Watsonian product of more than half a century later, we can well perceive that the twentieth-century mechanism was superior, thanks to our greater knowledge of reflexes, but the general contour of both Rush's and Watson's system, insofar as an unsystematic series of projections can be called a system, is much the same; it hinges upon the musculature and motor expression of the organism.

Behaviorism, that is to say, the genuine brand, reduces all psychology to a study of movements of limb and muscle or gland, more particularly movements of the body as a whole. Since movements are physical and not mental, it follows that psychology is concerned with physical manifestations alone.

All mental phenomena, in order to be adequately studied,

[7] I derived in childhood, some of the instruction of that period, from a storybook called the *Looking Glass*. Every truth, and unfortunately, every error since learned, has come through that human organization, or physical mirror as I would regard it, of the senses and the brain, reflecting the objects of nature, and the distorted pictures of fiction. In that early play called "Hunt the Slipper," we are said *to burn,* when we come near the place of its concealment. J. Rush: *Loc. cit.,* vol. 1, pp. 54-55.

must, according to a thoroughgoing behaviorism, reduce to movement, secretion, and some observable surface changes like nettling, blushing, electrical responses (behavior). The mental, that state which you identify with yourself, at any given moment of your waking life, is to be disregarded scientifically, with the result that psychology, instead of describing, classifying, and explaining states of consciousness, is transformed into an offshoot of a conglomeration in which physics, physiology, and biology are mixed in unequal parts. This science, taking the place of traditional psychology, is calculated to state what bodily and organic movements will take place upon the slightest change in the environment of a person, or other member of the animal kingdom.

The behaviorist emphasizes external observation at the expense of inner examination of one's states. His method is akin to that of the chemist or physiologist, and his results are of a similar nature.

Behaviorism tends to change the complexion not only of psychology but of all the sciences and disciplines that make use of psychological concepts, as well.

Watson's behaviorism caused a stir in non-psychological circles because it was so radical. Apparently here was an eventful purge of the old paraphernalia, replaced by a fresh set of rules and techniques. Such complete reversals are the delight of the layman and the college youth, who supposes that he stands on the threshold of a new era. There was, besides, a simple aspect to the whole scheme, a push-the-button feature, calculated to explain everything in tangible terms. The "clean-up" season started with the conversion of sensations and perception into discriminatory responses, the reduction of all imagery to kinaesthetic reactions, the "discovery" of the basis of the feelings in the tumescence and detumescence of the genitalia, the referral of association and memory to conditioned reflexes and habits, the casting out of instincts and all congenital tendencies, except for sex, anger, and fear impulses, while retaining the postulate of heredity only in so far as the physical structures were concerned, and the transformation of attention to a matter of selective response. The emotions—and here Watson had the earlier coup of James to go by—were only visceral and glandular reactions to the objectivist, and could be predicted and controlled at will. Thought is, of course, nothing but incipient speech, movement of the vocomotor organs. As to personality, it consists of a large number of habits in constellations, which, in their totality, arouse the conditioned response of either fear (awe, authority, veneration) or love (charm, magnetism) in accordance with the bodily behavior which induces the operation of the reflexes in others, built up in early childhood, as a result of the strict attention of the father and others, who came in contact with the child, or the warm and tender relations of those who indulged the child.

This in a nutshell constitutes the whole of behaviorism. Everything else is just filigree and elaboration. With such an all-embracing plan, Watson began to spread out in all directions. Not alone animal psychology was to benefit from the new procedures, but all that had hitherto been dependent on the classical methods. No wonder so many in the literary world were taken off their feet through sheer enthusiasm when Watson guaranteed to make out of any well-formed and healthy infant a specialist in medicine, law, or art, or even in begging and burglary "regardless of his talents, penchants, tendencies, abilities" etc.[8] It is needless to say that such a boast was never made good in practice. It belongs to the many sanguine utterances which "made a big noise" but were not substantiated by deeds. We have established, on the contrary, that the best education is of no avail in the endeavor to turn a healthy and well-formed infant with no particular talent into a virtuoso or even a tolerable mediocrity. Similarly, it is very doubtful whether you can make of any child a thief or a beggar. The rah-rah technique, however, "went over big," and for a time journalists were plugging that sort of talk, as if it meant the world's salvation.

This is not the place to examine the intricacies of behaviorism and to bring to the surface its tissue of flaws. The author, as mentioned earlier, has already done this during the heyday of the movement. Considering the space at our disposal, it would be advisable to survey the progress of behaviorism since its inception as a school.

Varieties of Behaviorism

In a curious letter which appeared in the *Journal of Philosophy,* in 1922, W. S. Hunter, himself an animal psychologist, a pupil of Carr, but apparently a disciple of Watson, asked what behaviorists there were at the time other than Watson and Weiss. He drew up a formidable list of what he labelled "anti-behaviorists," including the present writer,

[8] J. B. Watson: *Behaviorism*, p. 82.

whom he called "anointed introspectionists" imputing to them a tendency to detect "danger in all objective study." It so happens that about thirty years ago, there were about a dozen staunch behaviorists, including, in addition to the two Hunter cites, Max Meyer, E. B. Holt, E. P. Frost, Z. Y. Kuo, G. A. deLaguna, F. H. Allport, E. A. Singer, and of course himself. There were, in addition, many affiliates from other fields of science. A number of psychologists, it is true, had been sailing under false colors, as behaviorists of one sort or another, because behaviorism was fashionable then. Some have even gone to the length of speaking of "behavior of consciousness," therefore considering themselves behaviorists.

There can, of course, be many different shades of behaviorism. Woodworth discerns four varieties. It would be possible to distinguish a dozen or more nuances. There are semi-behaviorists and quasi-behaviorists, would-be behaviorists, and have-been behaviorists, pseudo-behaviorists and crypto-behaviorists; but there is no unanimity or even consensus of opinion as to what constitutes a behaviorist, or what is to be regarded as the unit of behavior. Mere objectivism in laboratory experimentation is not sufficient to come under the head of behaviorism. Long before the psychological laboratory was founded, Weber, Fechner, Vierordt and Kronecker were conducting experiments in psychology on an objective basis. The writer's own experiments on interference in finger movements and on the graphic mechanism could be classed with behaviorism, since the records on smoked paper, in one case, and on rolls of white paper, in the other, obtained under controlled conditions and quantitatively determined, constitute behavior in the form of muscular contractions. The introspective protocols only served as a further check on the records.

Woodworth, sympathetic to behaviorism, nevertheless does not see a necessary connection between objectivistic experiments and behaviorism. This he has expressed in a letter to the present writer, as well as in an article, which was prompted by the author's questions on this point. As Woodworth put it:

> One would be proud to be the author of only one of numerous investigations made by behaviorists. One need not be a behaviorist to admire them. One need not have been a behaviorist to have made them.[9]

[9] R. S. Woodworth: "Four Varieties of Behaviorism," *Psychological Review*, 1924, vol. 31, p. 264.

Thorndike, who belongs to the half dozen pillars of the "new" psychology, to whom full chapters have been devoted, in a letter to the author preferred to be grouped with the behaviorists, if introspectionism was the other alternative, but he added that he would not rule out introspection as a method of obtaining data. Now, *there*, it would seem to a non-partisan, lies the crux. Behaviorism, to be worthy of the name, must dispense with introspection, either in the manner of Max Meyer and A. P. Weiss, who dealt with the neural correlates of conscious phenomena, or after the fashion of J. B. Watson, in reducing all thought and affection to muscular and glandular action to be analyzed without the aid of introspection, although he later was willing to accept the verbal report as a form of behavior, but behavior of what? If consciousness is either a myth or a mist, then the verbal report is just a meaningless jabbering. If it is representative of what takes place mentally, then it is the actual mental state or process which is significant, and not the communication as such.

Vicissitudes of Behaviorism

After Watson dropped out of psychology (with due regard for his mental capacity, and deference to his indulgent associates and pupils, the fact that a man runs an advertising business successfully does not alone entitle him to be ranked as a psychologist in full standing), W. S. Hunter took over (without the blessing of the Chief, who speaks of him only *en passant*) although there were several others not so thoroughgoing in their anti-mentalist analyses who could have passed as Watson's lieutenants. Hunter designated his brand of behaviorism, "Anthroponomy," and proceeded to work out, with dubious success, a system of human psychology along the lines of animal experimentation. Working with animals, Hunter has given us eight characteristics of thinking, but the essental feature is the ninth, which is missed, of course—the quality of awareness that a process is going on internally, wholly different from other processes. Similarly Kuo's study on inference is a misnomer. The experimenter infers that inference has taken place, but does not validate it.

In spite of these complications, many of the younger generation of psychologists had thrown in their lot with the behaviorists, and some textbooks are definitely of a behavioristic cast. In others, the stock-in-trade phrases of behaviorism:

"reaction-patterns," "stimulus-response," "conditioned reflexes," "adaptive behavior" are copiously scattered throughout, and such slogans as "We think with our muscles" became popular after the first World War.

Writers who were blissfully ignorant of the issues looked to behaviorism as an oracle; and everything or everybody that counted was invested with that distinguishing mark, in some instances, occasioning howlers. A dentist might gladden the hearts of his professional readers by relating the wonders of conditioning children, so that the drill would arouse in them a pleasurable response. Religious writers would make an effort to bring their theological dogmas in line with behavioristic theory, while jurists and medical men would make similar application to their particular spheres of influence. This tendency to hitch one's wagon to a star, whether behaviorism, *Gestalt,* psychoanalysis, or semantics, is one of the most prevalent foibles among enthusiastic drivers who often don't know whither they are bound.

The Palinode

The high tide of behaviorism was reached in the '20's. There has been a steady ebb within the past fifteen years. Even the instincts, which had been generally discarded in psychology, are being courted again, and W. S. Hunter, in summarizing the comments on the heredity-environment symposium, of 1947, has even been defending McDougall's views on instincts. K. S. Lashley, an experimentalist, who was prominently featured by behaviorists, now speaks of instincts in the most matter-of-fact way, and ascribes genetic determination even to the lesser variants in cerebral structure. C. T. Morgan discusses the hoarding instinct without reference to conditioning or learning, and E. C. Tolman, apparently too, has relented on the subject of instinct. "We must suppose that the biological drives, and all of the four types of social techniques are all rooted, to some degree, in 'instinct.' "[10]

Asked to list the behaviorists at the present time, we would be hard put to name a dozen *bona fide* psychologists who have earned the designation. Certainly many are tainted with leanings in that direction. Thus, Clark L. Hull[11] is inclined to attach all goal ideas to habit, attributing all adaptive phenom-

[10] E. C. Tolman: *Drives Toward War,* p. 56.
[11] For a discussion of Hull's system, see Chapter 28.

ena to stimulus and response on a conditioning level, as illustrated by his mechanical gadgets and equations, but he does not go the length of Watson or Hunter. Consciousness is not denied or rejected: it is merely given a place in the background. As to Tolman, he operates with the concepts of psychoanalysis and *Gestalt*, particularly topology, as well as with the premises of behaviorism and hormic psychology. Using rats for subjects, he has no use for introspection, but a thoroughgoing behaviorist would not think of mixing so many unassimilable ingredients in one caldron. It must be added that while Watson is a molecular behaviorist (reflexes, cells, muscles, and secretion, in units which may become organized as bodily behavior),[12] Tolman is a molar behaviorist, dealing with the extra-organismic field as well; and the object out there in space is just as important to his lapidary conception of behavior as the animal movements, if not more so.

---

[12] Cedric A. Larson is working on a definitive biography of John Watson, picking up cues and suggestions from numerous sources. It promises to be a fair and objective evaluation, against a backdrop of the earlier beginnings.

Chapter 23

Dynamic Psychology

DYNAMIC PSYCHOLOGY has sprung up independently in several different countries, and at different periods. As has already been shown, John Dewey, in his youthful essay on the "new" psychology, written nearly eighty years ago, had used the phrase, and spoke as if it were not invented by himself. James employed it in a marginal notation on one of Titchener's books. The school, by no means, originated as Heidbreder supposes, with Woodworth; nor was it born at Columbia University. Neither Cattell nor Thorndike could be called a precursor of dynamic psychology any more than Stanley Hall or Münsterberg. There was probably some kinship between James and dynamic psychology, yet he is not thought of as one of the dynamic pioneers. Certainly Baldwin, as his genetic logic proves, was more of a dynamist than either Cattell or Thorndike.

What Is Dynamic Psychology?

Before we go into the history of this trend in psychology, it behooves us to settle the meaning of the term, even if a formal definition should not be available at this time, because it seems to be a theme with variations, or a current with a dozen different eddies. There are eddies to the right and eddies to the left, and through the centre Freud's psychoanalytic system whirls with fierce intensity. Dynamic psychology did not have its origin in the laboratory. It had its birth in the clinic. It stemmed from the ills and troubles of mankind. Hence, Janet in France, and Freud in Austria, both psychiatrists, were probably each in his own way, the founders of that constellation which came to be known as dynamic psychology; for it is more than a single school when Janet and Freud, almost at opposite poles in one sense, could still be united under the same roof.

Pierre Janet, founder of the dissociation school in abnormal and clinical psychology, stopped just where Freud began. Janet was still interested in causes rather than motives, and his analysis was more description; true, excellent models of detailed observation, but he did not probe deeper. In advanced age, he became more or less of a behaviorist—perhaps by way of reaction to Freud's unconscious. And yet, Janet could not help finding motives, even if he was not seeking them. To take one instance, Janet has often spoken of the maladaptation of psychasthenics as due to flight from reality. Perhaps this is not a motive, in the light of Bleuler's explanation of autistic thinking, and certainly not as the complicated interpretation of psychoanalysis would account for the disorder, but the dynamic note is to be found, nevertheless, not only in Janet, but in Ribot, Binet, Fouillée, Guyau, Le Bon, Dumas, and nearly every French psychologist; for they all had their ear close to the pulse of life, and were concerned with the *affective*; whereas the Germans were engrossed in the cognitive.

Nevertheless, just as in the famous Porson jingle—

> *The Germans in Greek*
> *Are sadly to seek;*
> . . . .
> *All save only Herman[n],*
> *And Herman[n]'s a German.*

—so it may be said that although the German is not a dynamist in psychology, it was Friedrich Herbart who may have been the pioneer, with his *Reals,* or force-centres, which were either positively or negatively charged, and through the supposed clashes of these *Reals,* some of the interrelated ideas would drop below the threshold and exert some influence on the conscious mind. In fact, he even worked out a system of formulae for these attractions and repulsions—formulae which, of course, could not be validated, any more than many of Freud's dynamisms.

The great service of Freud was to plunge into the dynamic whirlpool *ab initio*. He searched for explanations of certain types of behavior. He explored the field of motives. The *how* of the act was subordinated to the *why*, and in place of a thousand and one detached and desultory observations, affirmed and contradicted in turn by different investigators, Freud has given us a system, a system which may be altogether too artificial or too air-tight, but nevertheless a well-organized body of generalizations that seem to illuminate many occurrences in mental life.

Freud, then, if not *the* founder, is at any rate one of the chief pillars of dynamic psychology, which consists in going beyond the mere facts of introspection, so prized by traditional psychology, and allowing for inference as regards what takes place in the subconscious, or better, the unconscious. Ordinarily, we perceive the mental billiard balls collide, move on, or roll back and then fall into the pockets of the table, but the impact has been imparted to the balls by *someone*. Energy has been expended, and even this energy was preceded by an effort, an intention. All these antecedents were scarcely reckoned with prior to Freud.

In the case of human acts we have, of course, conditions obtaining that could not be ascribed to actual ivory balls. Desires, wishes, purposes, motives, intentions—in brief, all that goes to make up the basic mechanism of the so-called *drive*—must be analyzed and related to one another. This is the operating centre of dynamic psychology, and it is here that it shows its advantage over the Wundtian system, which may be characterized perhaps by the dictum *non est in psychologia quod non est in conscientia*. Dynamic psychology, especially that of Freud's brand, would retort to this, "There is more in consciousness and mind than your introspective psychology ever dreamt of."

The Transmutation of Drives

Another feature of dynamic psychology, and one which is frequently lost sight of, is the principle of metamorphosis—the fact that one instinct or drive can be transformed into another. This doctrine is particularly stressed in psychoanalysis, and the concept of sublimation is necessarily based on such a presupposition. McDougall also, to a large extent, makes use of this principle,[1] and Morton Prince, in some of his papers, implies it, although neither subscribes to the well-known *ultima transformatio* of Freud. On the other hand, Woodworth apparently questions the applicability of such a principle in any strict sense. Referring to the concept of *sublimation*, he points out that properly speaking, it should "mean that the tendency toward a certain consummation could be made to drive mechanisms irrelevant or even con-

---

[1] William McDougall: "The Sources and Directions of Psychophysical Energy," *American Journal of Insanity,* 1913, vol. 69, no. 5.

trary to itself," whereas, he continues, "there seems to be really no evidence for this, and it probably is to be regarded as a distinctly wrong reading of the facts of motivation."[2]

Yet the general tendency of dynamic psychology is, presumably, to take it for granted that one drive changes into another without the conscious effort of the individual; and physiologically such a redirection or diversion of energy is readily understandable. By "changes" we do not mean, of course, that one type of energy ceases and is replaced by another, as is the case with, say, electrical or mechanical energy, but that in sublimation, the *libido*, while still operative in its irrepressible and subtle way, evolves, to the "naked eye" at least, something entirely different from its characteristic product. The sex urge, *e.g.*, of the ascetic painter or composer is not wholly lost even during his creative activity, but is exploited by other drives and urges in the interests of society and, besides *providing the impetus* to create, also *flavors* the artistic production. With this qualification, it is, we think, still legitimate to speak of a transformation of the *libido*, referring, in the main, to the different course of the energy and the dissimilarity of the results.

Our metaphor of a billiard ball will, in the light of this metamorphosis, turn out to be altogether inadequate; for the impact of one ball against another does not affect its quality, except after a long series of collisions—and therein lies the danger of introducing physical analogies.

Different Currents in Dynamic Psychology

It has already been intimated that *dynamic psychology* is by no means an integrated whole so that its conclusions would be regulation utterances. Dynamic psychologists are united, indeed, in seeking motives, in analyzing symbols and odd bits of behavior, in accentuating the importance of the affective life and throwing into relief the *motif* of the drives, but there exist nevertheless divergent premises and attitudes amongst the leaders of this school, whose views are colored by their own particular moralistic, sociological, or religious bias.

Every dynamic psychologist evinces a vital interest in the problems of sex, even more so than does the behaviorist, but it is in the actual results and prospects that the differences arise. Dynamic psychology harbors sex radicals—and Freud

[2] R. S. Woodworth: *Dynamic Psychology*, pp. 175, 176.

is not the extremist among them—as well as puritans, who, like McDougall, applaud the rigidity of the law against homosexuals[3] and admonish against flirtation, especially in the case of the married.[4] We have, on the psychoanalytic side, writers like Kempf and MacCurdy; and on the *psychosynthetic* side, Jung and his followers, who are inclined, again, to the ethereal and spiritual; while Morton Prince and Woodworth, representatives of different trends of dynamic psychology, seem to steer clear of the question of good and evil. Adler, thoroughly dynamic in his treatment of human foibles, in his later years, became more and more the educator and less the iconoclast of society. Then, too, there are the sociological and anthropological "dynamists," among whom may be reckoned Flugel[5] and Malinowski. More pronounced still in welding the two branches is Róheim. In fact we should not hesitate to include Stanley Hall "among the prophets," for his magisterial chapter (really a book in length) "The Pedagogy of Sex" in his *Educational Problems*, quite aside from his pioneering work on adolescence, entitles him to a place among the deep probers of human motives.

If we ask ourselves what it is that knits the various psychologists together into a single pattern which we label dynamic, it will be noted that there are four basic elements: (1) the analysis of motives in place of the earlier delving into causes, largely of a physiological nature. In other words, the "how" is discounted for the benefit of the "why," which, in classical psychology, has been sorely neglected; (2) the shifting of interest from cognition to affection, which is further stimulated by (3) the drives, instincts, or complexes, in the psychoanalytic system; and (4) the minimizing of the introspective method in favor of inference from clinical (used in a broad sense) material. We shall see that psychoanalysis offers more basic premises, but the four enumerated suffice to render a specific type of psychology eligible to the claim of dynamic status. In the case of most dynamists, there is a further con-

---

[3] William McDougall: *Introduction to Social Psychology* (12 ed.), p. 417.

[4] William McDougall: *Character and the Conduct of Life* (1927), pp. 32, 307.

[5] Although Flugel is primarily a psychologist, he has through his *Psychoanalysis of the Family,* and other more recent books made a noteworthy contribution to sociology, from the psychoanalytic angle.

viction that any given drive can be transformed into another, and in Freud's system, the libido is the central drive, a sort of final common path or canal, which when obstructed may lead to untoward results.

The Dissociation Theory

If structural psychology revolved around a mental phenomenon or content, and functional psychology represented capacities, both of them more or less static, dynamic psychology deals with forces, energies, tension, all of which imply movement, or at least change of inertia. Latency is one of the underlying features of dynamic psychology. The dynamic concept might be found in germ as far back as the days of Aristotle, but it was only with the psychogenic interpretation of hysteria that its application became apparent, and Janet must be credited with having first given us this theory in some tangible form, although Charcot and Bernheim may have held out hints of it.

The theory took shape in the dissociation formula of nervous and mental disorders, and was obviously derived from the circumstances surrounding the cases of double personality which had come under the surveillance of Janet. That certain elements of the mind would become detached from the general organization and begin a regime of their own was the undoubted conclusion of all who came under the influence of this school. Boris Sidis even thought that each nerve cell had its own measure of consciousness, and that the various mental states would function only in so far as the number of cells involved would be adequate for the occasion. When a large number of cells formed an independent unit, then a secondary personality would emerge. Sidis had been a student of James, and had also come under the influence of Morton Prince.

Prince, the Ideational Dynamist

Morton Prince (1854-1929) had been interested in philosophy sufficiently to write a little book on physical monism when he was scarce out of college. As a physician, he became a disciple first of Weir Mitchell ("rest cure"), but after a short stay in Paris and Nancy, he began to see the subject of nervous disorders in a new light and became impregnated with the ideas of the dissociation school, attaching himself, in principle, to Janet and his teachings. In the United States, at least, Prince may be considered as the pioneer in abnormal psychology, to which he gave a definitely dynamic turn, early in the century. In a sense, he may be regarded as the collaborator of Freud, for whom he entertained a good deal of respect.

Prince's concept of the *coconscious* is not altogether remote from Freud's *unconscious*. His doctrine of meaning, as set forth in the first chapter of his *Clinical and Experimental Studies in Personality*, is the counterpart of Freud's system of complexes, and is one of the most valuable contributions toward the understanding not alone of abnormal phenomena but also of normal occurrences.

His conception of purpose, too, while avowedly akin to McDougall's hormic notion, is more in line with Freud's exposition of the interplay between the individual's *superego* and the experiences which go to make up the *id*, and affect it so powerfully. Prince's reasoning does not sound so novel because he was always endeavoring to employ existing terms and to bring his data in accord with accepted notions.

It is to his credit that in his search for explanations, he would not, even in those early days, move, so to speak, in a psychical vacuum. In spite of his metaphysical commitment that the ultimate essence of matter was psychic (psychical monism) he insisted on a psychophysical foundation in everything pertaining to the mind. His concept of the neurogram, as a system of neural processes (synaptic connections) where dispositions of memories are stored up, which lend themselves to various degrees of activation, is not only interesting, but seems to be a sound principle in accounting for most types of human behavior.

We note then, that Prince was far-sighted enough to sense the direction psychology would take a generation hence, when he rejected the generally accepted tenet that only what is conscious, what we are aware of, is psychological subject-matter, while at the same time, he was realistic enough to ground his inference in physiological, or rather neurological, concepts, often using analogies from physical theory (electron, proton) to clarify his procedure.

In all his professional vicissitudes, Prince managed to steer clear of the mechanistic whirlpool. Not that he believed in the absoluteness of introspection. The observation of objective behavior to him was a *sine qua non* of science, but the patient's testimony surely had to be taken into account. In one sense, he has gone beyond Janet, who, doubtless, influenced his line of inquiry; for he was not satisfied with half-way explanations like "incompleteness" or "exhaustion." Prince was anxious to apply the experimental method to abnormal cases. The result was that in some of his findings, he affords us significant material toward the understanding of personality. In a number of investigations, he had come upon results which show him to be an ally of Pavlov and the conditioned-reflex school. The article on "Association Neuroses," originally published in 1891, gives us the analogue of the conditioned-reflex principle, applied to psychoneurotic patients. Yet the subjective factor, which is excluded by animal objectivists and behaviorists, is not eliminated in Prince's study. On the contrary, it is utilized in integrating hysterical patients whose afflictions appear to be organic.

The artificiality of the division between the normal and the abnormal had been recognized by Prince several decades ago. He dealt with conflict in a truly dynamic manner, making it almost a property of every mental process, similar to inhibition. To be sure, he did not treat it in the grand style of Freud, who was neither hampered by psychological knowledge, nor influenced by his physiological training, but Prince's task was to supply a physical basis for the mental phenomenon.

Prince's catholicity is not the same as eclecticism. He does not *agree* with Freud and with Pavlov, with Janet or McDougall. His position happens to be a sort of intersection of roads. He has not, it is true, explored the roads that others have found. Nevertheless the byways he has taken, leading him into some of the hidden recesses of the human mind—his masterly exposition of multiple personality, his experimental studies of hallucination, visions, and other processes which have been associated with the occult, deserve a place among the prescribed readings for students in psychology. His method is ingenious, his descriptions are vivid, his procedure scientific enough to satisfy the most exacting objectivist, and his reasoning is sound.

Prince and Freud

The question of how Freud has influenced Prince, or what constitutes their chief difference has occurred to many students of abnormal psychology. Sometimes it has been thought that Prince deliberately rejected *ab origine* the psychoanalytic method, viewing with suspicion and alarm the incursion of the Vienna master, and his growing prestige.

To the credit of Morton Prince it must be said that he was a "good sport" not only in games but also in serious matters. While many of his colleagues deprecated the new doctrine, striking at its vulnerable spot—sex, Prince would often, at least tentatively, make use of it, although not apparently with any measure of success. Psychoanalysis was not beneath him. If he could not see eye to eye with its founder, it was because he was trained in a different milieu, and was by nature, too, perhaps an empiricist—in the lineage of Locke, Hume, John Stuart Mill, and Huxley.

Far from decrying Freud's contribution, he has on more than one occasion acknowledged it, "rendering unto Caesar what was Caesar's."

In some cases, Prince pays homage to the genius of Freud. In others, he shows his indebtedness by employing some of his ideas and terms, *e.g.*, secondary elaboration. Here and there a result points to a Freudian mechanism, like condensation. We see there was no repression in that regard; yet there is a marked difference between the scientific attitudes of the two men, although both could be placed in the category of dynamic psychologists.

Freud is primarily an *affective* dynamist, Prince is, in large part, an *ideational* dynamist. The latter recognizes the potency of the instincts and the emotions, but is not willing to relinquish the cognitive claim on our *psyche*. To paraphrase a Kantian dictum, one might say, "Meanings without affects are barren, while affects without meaning are blind." The meanings in this connection need not be envisaged in the light of absolute truth. It would seem that in the field of therapy, at least, Prince is a pragmatist or an instrumentalist.[6]

In the last analysis, Freud's therapy ends with abreaction even though this has later been disavowed in favor of self-understanding (through the breaking up of the repressing forces after getting the resisting *ego* to yield) while Prince's method consists essentialy in re-education, that is to say, in supplying new meanings to the patients, thus arguing for a greater kinship with Jung, so far as ends are concerned.

[6] A. A. Roback: Introduction to *Morton Prince's Clinical and Experimental Studies in Personality,* 2nd ed. (1939), pp. 27-31.

Chapter 24

William McDougall and Hormic Psychology

THE TWO GREAT DYNAMISTS in psychology are Sigmund Freud and William McDougall. Freud was not an American, but the progress of psychoanalysis in the United States will be taken up in a separate chapter. McDougall, however, did reside in this country for about two decades, and although most of his work had already been done in England, where his influence went farther than that of any other psychologist, with the possible exception of Freud, he has contributed sufficiently to the American scene to merit a full chapter.

William McDougall (1871-1938) belongs to the titans in psychology, despite the general belittling attitude toward him on the part of the younger men who were indoctrinated by their teachers and their textbooks. In the first volume, published since his arrival in America, the *Outline of Psychology* (1923), the dedication reads "To the Honored Memory of William James, great Philosopher, great Psychologist and Great Man." This was certainly a fitting and noble gesture under the circumstances, considering that he was filling the chair which James had originally graced. There can be no question, too, that William James was a great personality, an excellent philosopher, and the greatest *American* psychologist, but in the opinion of the writer, McDougall has been and will remain, perhaps for a long time yet, the foremost English-speaking psychologist, with no exception. James may have had greater prestige because of his charming personal qualities and his philosophical contacts, as well as because he was participating in the very delivery of the neonate, but looking objectively into the situation, can it be denied that McDougall has made more independent contributions and in more departments and branches than James? It will be some time before his real status in psychology is established. Already we can note the tide rising in his favor, when an opponent like W. S. Hunter has brought himself recently to admit that McDougall's exposition of the instinct theory had not been fully considered. When James's halo is somewhat dimmed, McDougall will probably emerge in a brighter light.

William McDougall may be regarded as a scion of the Scottish School, although he was reared in the English tradition of Bain, Ward, Stout and Shand. His education at Cambridge, where he received an arts as well as a medical degree, and Oxford (M.A.), interluded by a year at Göttingen and four years' internship at St. Thomas Hospital, gave him an unusual background, but in addition he possessed an adventurous spirit, taking part in various expeditions to such far-off and primitive regions as Torres Straits and New Guinea, where he had been able to get his first glimpse of comparative psychology (used in the older and more appropriate sense), working with such minds as C. S. Myers and W. H. R. Rivers, and later to Borneo, the result of which was a two-volume study of the Pagan tribes of Borneo, published in collaboration with C. Hose.

McDougall As a Scientist

His teaching career began at the University of London, where he had installed a laboratory; and at Oxford, for sixteen years, he was able to initiate a whole generation into the mysteries of a science which was more or less frowned upon in that medieval stronghold of logic and the humanities. In 1920, he received a call from Harvard, where after a while, he began to feel somewhat dissatisfied with the indifference toward him in that atmosphere; and partly due to this circumstance and partly to his growing deafness, he took the opportunity to accept a professorship at Duke University, where the climate was supposed to have rendered his infirmity more tolerable and where his position was not just taken for granted.

Those who have been continually harping upon his obscurantist, mystical, or non-scientific views would give the impression that McDougall was steeped in philosophy or theology, and was unfamiliar with the various facets of science. The truth of the matter is that he was a thorough scientist, well grounded in physiology, and certainly conversant with physics and chemistry. He may have selected certain aspects which would suit his special inclination, but this may be said of him: there was no psychologist who took greater pains to survey the widely differing schools and theories than William McDougall. He was a trenchant critic, but his positive stand was always well documented and, what is more, often bolstered by experimental data.

In the United States, his experimental achievement was depreciated if not deprecated. Perhaps his technique did not measure up to the elaborate and ingenious manipulations of the American experimenters, but to compensate, he had a better perspective and oversight of the problems involved. He was, as a matter of fact, a systematizer, from the beginning; and in this he derives from his Scotch descent, since the English show no particular capacity in this respect, although they may muddle through superbly, whereas the Scots may systematically fall short of the mark. At all events, McDougall's first psychological publication "A Contribution towards an Improvement in Psychological Method" (in *Mind*, 1898) already affords us some insight into the prime interest of the writer, which never waned, although more and more ingredients were being constantly added to the reservoir.

McDougall's experimental work was extensive, varied, and well-knit; and each of his contributions left its mark, whether it was on the color sense or attention, or the sensory acuity of the Torres Islanders, or on the various illusions, the humoral basis of the temperaments, or on the relation of intoxication to introversion and extraversion, or his last important series on the transmission of acquired characteristics, which, however, was practically ignored by the American psychologists, at most mentioned slurringly.

Works

Barring several popular and semi-publicistic books, such as *National Welfare and Decay*, *The Indestructible Union* or *Ethics and Some Modern World Problems*, all his works are marked by a comprehensive grasp of the problems involved and a systematic approach such as is not to be found in William James. His *Primer of Physiological Psychology*, where he already defends a behavioristic definition of psychology (1905) is a model of condensation and exposition and has been the *vade mecum* of many thousands of students not only in the British Empire, but in America too. His *Introduction to Social Psychology* (1908) passed through thirty editions and impressions, and no less, and has been for a long time without a rival in this special field. It is in this textbook that the relationship between instincts and emotions, as well as the development of sentiments, has been elaborated in the most orderly fashion. McDougall was not altogether original in his conception, (Bernard Hollander, unjustly, even accused him of plagiarizing from Gall's phrenological writings) but his analyses and concatenation of the data have never been surpassed.

His *Body and Mind* (1911) has been the most scientific buildup for animism and the most extensive discussion of the mind-body problem to this day, and the little book for the layman, *Psychology, the Study of Behavior*, (1912) was actually heading toward a mild behaviorism, but after the capers which Watson started to cut in his own mischievous way, McDougall repudiated his early definition of 1905 and his stand of 1912 ("Hence I am disposed to say 'If you are going to get on, it's time for me to get off' "[1]) and returned to the older definition of psychology as the science of human nature or mind, apparently not quite satisfied with either. The *Group Mind*, as the sequel of the *Introduction to Social Psychology* (1920), did not meet with the success of the earlier work. In the first place, the author here showed his national bias too openly. Nor did he possess the many-sided learning required for the writing of a collective psychology.

McDougall's American phase was rather inauspiciously timed. It seems as if a black cat had crossed his path on his trans-Atlantic voyage. First, his presidential address before the Society for Psychical Research had appeared just about then. Then his *Group Mind* came before the American academic public, and was regarded by many specialists in anthropology and sociology (particularly those of the Boas school; and who in the United States was not a graduate of the Boas tradition?) as a book of opinion rather than of solid research. Then came another book of questionable value, *viz.*, *National Welfare and Decay* (1921), in which the British author presumes to tell the Americans how to regulate their national life. Such counsel, even when coming from a psychologist, would not conduce to cordial relations. Four years later, *The Indestructible Union*, calculated to cement the Anglo-American bond, only made matters worse for the author, and just about then, behaviorists, mechanists, and sundry sub-schools conspired once and for all to banish the instincts, McDougall's pet project, from the realm of psychology; and the controversy raged for years with considerable acerbity on both sides.

[1] William McDougall: *Outline of Psychology*, p. 38.

On American soil, McDougall continued his productivity. Article after article appeared, now taking Pavlov to book, and now casting his darts against Freud, or the Gestaltists, or whittling Pareto's system down to a mere shadow, or sparring with Watson. There were many papers of a positive nature. McDougall's theories were suggestive but all pointed in one direction, the utter contempt of mechanistic explanations of mental phenomena, and the firm conviction that there is an inner purpose which goads us on to specific action through the instincts. His most important books during his sojourn in America are *The Outline of Psychology* (1923), *Outline of Abnormal Psychology* (1926), *Modern Materialism and Emergent Evolution* (1929), as well as the reports on his Lamarckian experiment. A sidelight of his workmanship is afforded by the fact that the bill for author's corrections on the *Outline* came to one thousand dollars, when printing cost about one-third of what it does to-day. A further characteristic: the left margin in his manuscripts would occupy practically half the page, so that he could fill in afterthoughts.

The Trials of a Psychologist

It is difficult to account for the generally disrespectful treatment which McDougall received in this country after the reverence in which he was held in Great Britain, almost on a par with that of William James in the United States. American psychologists and sociologists looked upon him not only as an outsider, but as a foreigner who wished to impose his views on them. He was considered reactionary and even snobbish, although actually he was unassuming in his demeanor and even somewhat shy. In his mode of living, he was thoroughly democratic and free from prejudice. It is, nevertheless, true that in his semi-political books he preached the aristocratic gospel of castes, and was a votary of eugenics, possibly due to his contacts with Francis Galton at the University of London. Once, when the present writer questioned the attitude of Oxford and Cambridge toward the candidacy of foreign-born teachers, he defended the policy (which it is gratifying to say has been practically changed of late) with the comforting (?) remark that "it takes three generations to make a gentleman."

Perhaps his greatest sin in the eyes of American academic men was his advocacy of animism, which is a euphemism for the belief in a soul, and his sympathetic interest in psychical research, which he was ready to promote, as they thought, at all cost. It was, however, his unalterable opposition to any and every mechanistic, atomistic, or stimulus-response psychology, an opposition often expressed in vehement language, which antagonized many of his colleagues, and led them to think that here was a self-constituted high priest fulminating against them without rhyme or reason.

In the preface of his *Outline of Psychology*, referring to the baleful results of the mechanistic psychology, he employs such an outspoken metaphor as "a most misshapen and beggarly dwarf, namely 'behaviorism,' which just now is rampant in this country." It was evident that McDougall was emotionally involved so far as psychology was concerned. He felt that here was a horde of barbarians bent upon simplifying everything down to stimulus and response, and the system which he had built up at such great pains: instincts, sentiments, and the whole structure of mental organization, was jeopardized by the wicked mechanists, and he would indulge in polemics which would call forth copious animadversions on the other side.

J. McKeen Cattell was especially hostile to McDougall, far more so than J. B. Watson, who would drown any personal animosity which he might have nursed in banter. McDougall was sensitive to criticism, and, contemplating the esteem which he had been accorded in England in comparison with the abuse which many a fledgeling and upstart, instigated by their superiors, would heap upon him, he more than once had cause to regret having severed his British ties. But McDougall was a born adventurer, in the best sense of the word, and was not given to wearing his heart on his sleeve. In the truest Oxford tradition, he could conceal his innermost feelings, and no one could question his stamina and independence. No one who had talked to him the week his son, a lieutenant in the air force, was killed in an air crash could have guessed what a tragedy had befallen the man, who was greatly attached to his family.[2]

Of the celebrated Harvard trio, in succession, McDougall

[2] When McDougall was gibbeted by the press, after being fleeced by a sharper who promised large returns on stock investments, a number of his colleagues could not conceal their *Schadenfreude*. To the general reader of newspapers, a psychologist who allows himself to be deceived thereby discredits his science.

was the most prolific and the most consistent. James was diphasic (or, to employ a more common figure, amphibian) and it depended on the mood he was in whether he could be called a mechanist or a purposivist. At heart, he was probably more of the latter. Münsterberg had another device: one ledger for causal psychology and another for purposive psychology. McDougall alone set out to subsume all phenomena under one type, namely the hormic. All three concerned themselves with psychic research. Münsterberg, who wrote on the occult in his Freiburg period, mainly exposed charlatanry; James, as Roback brought evidence, in his monograph on William James, to prove the fact, was a sympathetic observer but no sponsor, as is generally supposed. McDougall, whose ancestors in the highlands most likely related stories to one another about second sight, was more inclined to believe that there is much to explore in borderland regions; and the parapsychological activities at Duke University have naturally been inspired by McDougall.

What Is Hormic Psychology?

The word "hormic," coined by the educationalist and philosopher P. T. Nunn, from the Greek ὁρμή, "onset" or "impetus" is equivalent to the word "driven" by an *élan*. The central idea seems to be that there is an end or purpose which goads us on to action without any real knowledge of its nature, although a dim or vague foresight or prescience may be there.

The underlying principles of McDougall's system are as follows: (1) Conation, and not cognition, is at the root of all animal activity, cognition serving only as a guidepost or means toward the attainment of the goal. (2) the goal itself is not deliberately set or decided on, in fact, is dimly, if at all recognized. (3) A number of mechanisms or dynamisms, if we wish to steer clear of static concepts, called, variously, "instincts," "urges," and subsequently "propensities" (so as to divert the impact of the general attack on the instinct doctrine in the '20's) presumed to be hereditary in man and animals, but permitting of far greater modifiability in man, impel the organism to act in a specific mode without having learned it. (4) Coupled with each of the major instincts is an affective reaction, *viz.*, the emotion. Thus pugnacity, as an instinct, will produce, on the appropriate occasion, anger;

curiosity will give rise to the emotion of wonder; repulsion will correspond, on the affective side, with disgust. There are some instincts which are not primary or universal, and there are many emotions which are not primary or pure, but derived or compound, such as awe or admiration. (5) Purpose and not pleasure is the mainspring of action, although once the goal has been reached, success is accompanied with a feeling of satisfaction, just as frustration will be accompanied by distress. McDougall never tires of striking at the bogey of hedonism, and the Columbia school, specifically E. L. Thorndike and his law of effect *viz.*, that the satisfyingness of an act stamps it in, come in for constant criticism on his part. (6) Aside from a full discussion of general tendencies (play, suggestion, sympathy, imitation), disposition, temper, temperament and mood, the sentiments are the units of personality, and out of the self-regarding sentiment blossoms forth character. (7) Man has the capacity to determine his own actions, and is thus a free agent. (8) The mind is not a collection of momentary processes, but possesses a permanent organization, which acts upon the physical structure, just as the bodily happenings affect the mind; in other words, there is interaction between body and mind. (9) Teleology enters in as an explanation of the instinctual operations. In order to survive, both as an individual and as a group or as the race, the realization of certain needs and aspirations is a *sine qua non*. The ascent of a high mountain peak may be fraught with danger and all sorts of hardships, if not stark tragedy, yet unless such obstacles are surmounted, progress in the conquest of nature would not be possible.

There are a number of corollaries or side issues, the results of the main principles, which may be inferred, *e.g.*, (1) McDougall's preoccupation with psychic research is bound up very likely with his conception of the mind as a permanent energy, which points to the existence of a soul (if not in the substantial sense, then in some energistic form, constantly functioning in some relation to other souls, a relationship which has not yet been explored; (2) his absorbing interest in, and fervent desire to prove, Lamarck's theory of the transmission of acquired characteristics, devoting a great deal of time to the extended series of experiments with rats of several generations, an objective grounded in the belief that (a) some instincts are the product of adaptation in line with the survival of the fit, (b) we are the architects of our destiny, and if we should discipline ourselves in a given (worthy) direction, then provided our children and grandchildren follow our lead, the stock would, in the long run, improve.

Whether McDougall was a man with a mission, as Boring believes, or not, he takes his place with Freud as the chief dynamist in psychology *i.e.*, the only consistent one. Boring thinks he might have been influenced by Freud,[3] but McDougall was a dynamist before Freud was known outside of his own circle, in Vienna. If McDougall can be considered a missionary, then William James was much of the same sort (*cf.* his *fiat* doctrine, his chapters on habit, the self, and especially the essay on reserves of energy). And may not E. B. Holt be thought of as a missionary, in his own way, *i.e.*, to keep the student from falling under the pernicious influence of the medieval theologian?[4]

At any rate, McDougall fared badly in his American environment. Many of those who cut their psychological teeth on his *Social Psychology* revolted, as psychoanalysis would have seen it, against the father image, nursing an inner aversion for all McDougall stood for. His instincts were not only bowed out of court; they were kicked out. His teleology was given a theological coloring, although he pointed out more than once that he was not concerned about extrinsic supernatural teleology, which refers to the fulfilment of God's purpose, but with the intrinsic teleology inherent in any doctrine of adaptation,[5] and his concept of purpose was turned inside out so that it was now transformed into cause.

Mysticism and Skepticism

It may be that a genuine dynamic psychology is somewhat tinged with mysticism. Psychoanalysis has been criticized after the same fashion, but Freud had developed a system

[3] E. G. Boring: *A History of Experimental Psychology* (2d ed., 1950), p. 718.

[4] Both R. M. Elliot, editor of the series in which Boring's book appeared and E. C. Tolman may remember a visit by the three of us, students then, to the brilliant erratic on Chauncy Street, which ended at 1 A.M., a visit memorable because of Holt's unrestrained remarks on various topics, one of which, as the present writer recalls, uttered with considerable effect, was that "McDougall is a monk in the garb of a psychologist."

[5] William McDougall: "The Hormic Psychology" in *Psychologies of 1930* (ed. by C. Murchison).

which, if not acceptable as science, is fascinating as a masterpiece of art. McDougall's list of instincts does not impress the skeptic. Anyone can make up such a list, it is objected. Furthermore, it has been asked whether there is any other test of an instinct except that the organism acts in such a way as to suggest it. In other words, if the act of fighting implies a pugnacious instinct, and loving points to a parental instinct, etc., then the matter is too simple and affords us no insight into the *modus operandi*.

It would seem, however, that McDougall's opponents see the mote in the other man's theory but are blissfully unaware of the beam in their own hypothesis. Does a complex diagram clinch validity? Is the sequence of operations between stimulus and response so transparent in the higher thought processes, or even, in the case of motivation, in lower animals as to justify self-complacency in divers mechanistic circles? And as to taking a specific activity as an indication that in the particular organism, a certain instinct is aroused, is it any different with talent or capacity? When Mozart was able to play the piano at the age of four and could compose at the age of seven, we were justified in the inference that he possessed a special musical ability which other children, given the same opportunity, did not possess. Why make fish of the one and fowl of the other? What is gravy for capacities should be at least sauce for activities, like fighting, hoarding, mating, etc.

The most vulnerable spot of McDougall's system is probably his conception of mind as a structure, independent of the bodily organization, but interacting with it. Such an assumption does not accord with what is presently known of the principle of conservation. McDougall frankly admits that there is a barrier here, but he manages to draw upon certain passages of eminent physicists, chemists, and physiologists who are equally mystified by phenomena or discrepancies in their more nearly exact sciences. McDougall remains a voluntarist in psychology, and his own industry and self-discipline, as well as courage, constitute an outstanding example of the exercise of will-power, unmotivated by hedonistic considerations. The recent partial vindication of McDougall by some of his erstwhile adversaries goes to prove that his efforts were not in vain after all.

Chapter 25

Woodworth, Lewin, and other Dynamic Psychologists

FOR SOME YEARS, even before McDougall came to America, R. S. Woodworth (1869-1962) has been associated with dynamic psychology. In fact, Boring supposes that it was he who had first used the term in connection with a school. It has already been shown here that the phrase was in use at least eighty years ago.[1] Be that as it may, Woodworth does happen to be one of those to have realized the place of motivation in life, emphasizing the importance of drives in all activity, whether animal or human. He had already done a good deal of work in the sphere of voluntary movement, which would have naturally directed his attention into motivational channels, and also had given some thought to Freudian psychology which did not seem acceptable to him. In 1918, he published his little book *Dynamic Psychology*, and in his *Contemporary Schools of Psychology* (1931) he outlined his general view again. In the *Psychologies of 1925* and *Psychologies of 1930,* we have further statements and expatiations on his particular brand of dynamic psychology.

Woodworth has always tried to take up a safe and sound position. He has never wholeheartedly sponsored the stimulus-response view in its simple behavioristic form, but interposed the organismic conditions of determining factors. On the issue of heredity and environment, his report on the subject[2] savors of the judicial charge to a jury. Every time he senses that one side will receive too much encouragement, he adds a bit of weight to the other side, afraid lest he might commit himself. He reminds us of the duck-rabbit illusion, and in his treatment of dynamic psychology, he displays the same characteristic. At times he appears as the dynamic duck of motivation psychology, but as you look again, he is turned into the

[1] Dewey used it in 1884 with the description "which has been well termed 'dynamic,'" so he was not the coiner.

[2] R. S. Woodworth: *Heredity and Environment* (Social Science Research Council, 1941, Bulletin 47).

mechanistic rabbit which runs a mile at the very sound of purpose. His use of the term "drive," which is really the German *Trieb*, the equivalent of our instinct,[3] is no doubt more in keeping with the dynamic principle, but how has the concept of purpose fared with him?

Purpose—The Touchstone of Dynamic Psychology

It would seem as if purpose were the stumbling block of all mechanistic and physicalistic psychologies and materialistic, positivistic, and neo-realistic philosophies.

Does Woodworth move in a dynamic universe of discourse? Until he recognizes the problem of purpose, we are inclined to agree with Boring that he is just another functional psychologist ("perhaps the best representative of the broad functionalism that is characteristic of American psychology"); for he is still busy, as in his good old days of physiological psychology, seeking the "how," and not the "why" of action. True, he splices the two, but instead of reinforcing the article, he succeeds only in scumbling the surface. For what is the essence of dynamic psychology to him? He may be dwelling on forces and drives, and yet, all the while, he is operating with causes and effects; and purpose itself is viewed as a cause in reverse *i.e.*, the seeking of fame is in itself the cause of an artist's or writer's or scientist's drive to create great works. But that does not account for the so-called cause, *viz.*, the seeking of fame, which, in McDougall's hormic plan, is instinctive (as it is in Adler's individual psychology) or bound up with a specific type of pregenital development, *e.g.*, urethral eroticism, in psychoanalysis. With Woodworth, any mechanism or capacity becomes a drive. To possess a certain talent will eventuate in its cultivation. The means will become an end, and thus no special purpose or horme is required.

It appears plausible that an inborn mathematical ability or a knack for invention will turn the possessor in a mathematical or inventive direction, crowding out other interests. How many times, however, have we encountered the waste of such talents, which lay fallow for years, simply because there was no ambition behind them, while someone else with much less original aptitude forged ahead due to inner drive, whether

[3] In a letter to the present author, in 1959, he wrote, "My purpose was not so much to get rid of the controversial word 'instinct' as it was to mark the importance of 'motivation.'"

born of a wish to outshine others, or for social reasons, or even in order to gratify the desires and needs of a loved wife and children?

Capacity, no doubt, produces interest (although there are not a few with behavioristic leanings who are unwilling to concede this point, ascribing even interest in art, science, etc., to habit conditioning) but interest can lag and wane and become abortive if not nurtured by the native urge, an urge which may at times be latent or, for the time being, diverted, but sooner or later asserts itself when the individual, for instance, is said to have found himself. We must also make allowance for the various fears, anxieties, conflicts, guilt feelings which are often entering wedges in a drive, leading to tracks and trails which are not mapped out by the original capacity. Schopenhauer and Leibniz, Nietzsche and Hegel, Kierkegaard and Fichte—all of them were possessed of a philosophical capacity, and apparently strong conative tendencies to express themselves by writing works, but dynamically they must have all differed; and the difference can scarcely be accounted for in environmental terms.

The Psychodynamics of Kurt Lewin

Kurt Lewin (1890-1947), identified with the *Gestalt* School, is the motivational representative of this influential group, but he has also established a subschool of his own under the name of topology. Like Wertheimer, Koffka, and Köhler, he was a student, although a bit later, at Stumpf's laboratory in the University of Berlin, where he afterwards rose to an assistant professorship, but had the foresight to leave Germany at the beginning of the Hitler regime, teaching and experimenting first at Cornell, then for a decade at the University of Iowa, taking charge of the Child Welfare Research Station which Bird T. Baldwin had built up, and after helping along in the war effort and teaching and directing research for brief periods at various institutions, including Harvard, he was called to organize the newly-founded Research Centre for Group Dynamics at the Massachusetts Institute of Technology. His untimely death two years later cut short a productive and stimulating mind.

Like his colleagues in the *Gestalt* inner circle, Lewin was versed in the physical sciences, having taken mathematics for his model, so that words like topology and vectors, were introduced to fortify the less tangible concepts in psychology. An able experimentalist with a flair for setting problems, and endowed with a dynamic personality and an ebullient temperament which would stand him in good stead in establishing contacts with organizations as well as professionally and academically, he attracted a number of promising students, who worked under his direction, even after they had acquired independent positions.

The Field Theory

Lewin's field theory is not an American product. Experiments on the level of aspiration, or on tension incidental to an uncompleted task had been published by Lewin's students while he was still in Germany, yet the theory had taken hold in this country, and found sponsors among well-known psychologists. In brief, it may be said that Lewin's notion is an extension of the old functionalism, in that it deals with an organism and its environment as constituting one field, which is his *Lebensraum* (space to live in), a rather ominous word, reminiscent of the Nazi slogan.

Now comes the specifically topological angle; for the older functionalists were committed to physiological considerations throughout. Lewin cuts across the mental-physical dimensions by involving forces which operate in both directions. The precipitant is the *tension* in the organism as a result of specific needs or urges. The environment contains the particular objects to relieve the tension. The forces, in the form of vectors, are now called into action, exercising a reciprocal effect on both individual and desideratum. If the object is attainable, the tension is superseded by satisfaction; if there is a barrier, then the positive valence (attraction) which the object possesses might turn to a negative valence (repulsion), or it may bring forth a series of new interactions (*e.g.*, in the case of an intended marriage, prohibited by parents because of different faiths of the lovers, or disparate age, social, or economic status) with a number of vectors of varied proportion and direction interplaying between individual and individual (as object) until a solution works itself out terminating the tension, or else the impasse leads to a definite frustration and its consequences.

Lewin steers clear of such entanglements as purpose. His "life-space" concerns the present. Past and future are without his bounds. The analysis of the actual situation will indubitably have some bearing on the future, but it does not belong to the predictable categories. If we can gauge an individual in terms of his traits and long-standing goals, we are in a better position to foretell future reactions.

Luxury Experiments

The diagrams which Lewin made use of in expounding his field theory were of didactic value. The circles and squares with plus and minus signs and arrows could not fail to impress the visual-minded, and lent an air of simplicity to the exposition. They seemed to implement the premises with which Lewin started out, and to subsume the array of instances under a single constant plan. In the final analysis, it was Lewin's sound intuitions which told the story. The schemata were part of the ritual. In fact, even the experimentation, in many cases, was a sop to the skeptical. Did we not know all along that unfinished business would keep us preoccupied and at times distraught, and did we not hear the most untutored people say, "Well I've got to get this done just to get it off my mind"? Would a common experience of this nature require experimentation just to give the phenomenon a neat frame?

Similarly, the experiment in which groups of boys were organized into clubs, run in the one case by a *Führer* who would dictate the policies and assign the various tasks to each of the members, while in another instance, the boys were left to themselves, without any leadership or government, and, by way of comparison, another group was conducted along democratic lines, determining its own policies but looking to its leader, who was a moderator, for suggestions or arbitration—would turn out just as we expected. Under the democratic system, work (the number of masks produced) was more satisfactory and tension was at a minimum, while in the autocratic group, tension ran high and the organization was a failure. It would have been interesting, however, to have had the conclusions of such experiments as were carried out in Germany in the Hitler days, and in the USSR, at the present time. So far as we are concerned, we could accept Lewin's statements with our eyes shut.

Lewin's topological method is somewhat redolent of Spinoza's *more geometrico* demonstrations. Much as we admired the great philosopher's intellect, we were not convinced by his Q. E. D.'s, but were prepared to accept his theses and corollaries at their face value, because they summed up our own experiences in at least a part of the *Ethica*. An example of Lewin's clear insight will not be amiss here, especially as it is on a problem which occupied the attention of Spinoza and, in fact, which might be said to have involved his own personal life. Discussing the self-hatred among underprivileged minorities, Kurt Lewin presents the case in a direct and sequential manner, which compels our attention and conviction as well.

Motivation in Minorities

Members of the majority are accustomed to think of a minority as a homogeneous group which they can characterize by a stereotype like "the Jew" or "the Negro." It has been shown that this stereotype is created in the growing child by the social atmosphere in which he grows up, and that the degree of prejudice is practically independent of the amount and kind of actual experience which the individual has had with members of the minority group.

Actually, *every* group, including every economically or otherwise underprivileged group, contains a number of social strata. There exists, however, the following difference between the typical structure of a privileged and an underprivileged group. The forces acting on an individual member (m) of a privileged group are directed toward the central layers of that group. The forces acting on a member of an underprivileged group are directed away from the central area, toward the periphery of the group and if possible, toward the still higher status of the majority. The member would leave if the barrier set up by the majority did not prevent him. This picture represents the psychological situation of those members of the underprivileged group who have a basically negative balance. It is the structure of a group of people who are fundamentally turned against themselves.

It is clear that an effective organization of a group becomes more difficult the more it contains members having a negative balance, and the stronger this negative balance is. It is a well-known fact that the task of organizing a group which is economically or otherwise underprivileged is seriously hampered by those members whose real goal is to leave the group rather than to promote it. This deep-seated conflict of goals within an underprivileged group is not always clear to the members themselves. But it is one reason why even a large underprivileged group which would be able to obtain equal rights, if it were united for action, can be kept rather easily in an inferior position.

It is particularly damaging for the organization and action of a minority group that certain types of leaders are bound to arise in it. In any group, those sections are apt to gain leadership which are more generally successful. In a minority group, individual members who are economically successful, or who have distinguished themselves in their professions, usually gain a higher degree of acceptance by the majority group. This places them culturally on the periphery of the underprivileged group and makes them more likely to be "marginal" persons. They frequently have a negative balance and are particularly eager to have their "good connections" not endangered by too close a contact with those sections of the underprivileged group which are not acceptable to the majority. Nevertheless, they are frequently called for leadership by the underprivileged group because of their status and power. They themselves are usually eager to accept the leading role in the minority, partly as a substitute for gaining status in the majority, partly because such leadership makes it possible for them to have and maintain additional contact with the majority.

As a result, we find the rather paradoxical phenomenon of what one might call "the leader from the periphery." Instead of having a group led by people who are proud of the group, who wish to stay in it and to promote it, we see minority leaders who are lukewarm toward the group, who may, under a thin cover of loyalty, be fundamentally eager to leave the group, or who try to use their power outright for acts of negative chauvinism.[4]

Purposive Behaviorism

Closely allied to Lewin's field theory is E. C. Tolman's view of motivation. Tolman (1886-1959) is a behaviorist in that he shies away from mentalistic concepts, and in his work on mice and rats, he would naturally have no use for introspection. The animal's reactions alone interest him, and out of

[4] K. Lewin: "Self-Hatred among Jews," *Contemporary Jewish Record*, 1941, vol. 4, pp. 226-228.

these rodent movements, he would evolve a system applicable to man—thank heavens, with the help of Freudian mechanisms. Under the circumstances, we might still call him a behaviorist; for Holt, too, combined behaviorism and psychoanalysis by supplying a physiological base to the latter, which Freud would surely have repudiated.

Tolman's particular brand of behaviorism is molar, as we have already seen, and is not concerned with the actual physiological processes involved in muscular or glandular activity. Like Lewin, Tolman is fond of employing diagrams or schemata which are calculated to prove the superiority of his system over others. He operates with four independent causes of behavior, viz., the stimulus, heredity, past training, and momentary initiating physiological states. Between these fundamental causes and the actual behavior, he posits a set of intermediate variables called "behavior determinants," such as specific capacities: means-end-readiness, discriminanda- and manipulanda expectations, sign-gestalt-expectations. The feature which Tolman conceives as peculiarly advantageous to his type of psychology is the initiating physiological state, which gives rise to demands on the part of the organism— and one or more of these demands bring about the response, in accord with the means-end-readinesses established through native or acquired media.

But it will be asked why does Tolman call his behaviorism purposive? The answer is that, to his mind, after considerable experimentation, the rat is aware of a goal-object to be sought, and that this particular goal-direction is observable can be externalized in the form of the sign-gestalt-expectation. Tolman speaks of goal-objects as a "demanded to-be-got-to or to-be-got-from internal physiological condition or external environmental object." Does Tolman recognize that he is interpreting the mind, or whatever you want to call it, of the rat in his own anthropomorphic light? Have we any right to infer on strictly behavioristic principles that the rat expects or is bent upon reaching a definite goal? Well, this is the dynamic phase of the system, and so far as we can see, it is hardly in keeping with a non-mentalistic approach.

Tolman, it may be said, not only hunts with the hounds and runs with the hares. He prowls with the wolves and gambols with the lambs; he cavorts with the horses, dances with the bears, and roars with the lions. The fact is that he is accorded hospitality everywhere and bestows his blessings on all. Behaviorism, purposive psychology, psychoanalysis, *Gestalt* psychology, and factorial analysis, all fit into his scheme of things; and, of course, he is an operationist, to boot. Whether Tolman's system is a colorful crazy quilt, or is a clever piece of eclectic dovetailing, or constitutes a consistent and well-integrated plan will be settled only after it is possible to discount the aura or nimbus, as the case may be, in the assessment of cultural contributions.

Tolman, without studied efforts on his part, managed to collect a number of honors during his lifetime. He became a member of the National Academy of Sciences in 1937, a member of the American Philosophical Society in 1947, of the American Academy of Arts and Sciences in 1949, an honorary fellow of the British Psychological Society in 1954. In 1951, Yale University awarded him the honorary degree of Doctor of Science, and in Montreal at the time of the International Psychological Congress, of which he was co-president, McGill University gave him an honorary doctorate. Before his death in 1958, he received an honorary doctorate from the University of California which had suspended him from August 1950 to January 1953, because he led the opposition to the special loyalty oath that the University demanded of teachers. The controversy ended with a legal victory for the rebel professors, and Tolman was reinstated. A painting of him commissioned by his students adorns a wall of the new impressive psychology building in the University, fittingly named Tolman Hall. His biography, by G. W. H. Leytham, of the University of Liverpool, is scheduled for early publication. In 1957, the American Psychological Association presented him, as well as Carl I. Hovland and Curt P. Richter, with a citation for their distinguished scientific contributions. Although not the typical presiding officer, he was chosen as president or vice-president of half a dozen different psychological groups.

During the Montreal International Psychological Congress, I happened to joke, when we were alone, about his phenomenal popularity. With a mock gesture of spitefulness and defiance, savoring of a Victorian debutante's reaction to the teasing of a boy-friend, he grinningly blurted "Yes, I've got a social technique." But if he did have it, no one would have guessed it. His social attitude was so charming because it was completely disarming.

It is little known that after spending the first three years of teaching at Northwestern, he was not reappointed. Apparently the students took his casual teaching manner and diffidence in "laying down the law" as a sign of lack of preparation or inability to clarify an issue. Walter Dill Scott, the pioneer in advertising psychology, and at the time President of the University, was, as he told the present writer then, so aloof that he wouldn't "touch him with a six-foot pole," and I take it that this applied to all other faculty fledglings.

The Dynamics of a Behaviorist

There is no denying that Tolman has brought out new angles in the stimulus-response situation, and that he discerns the assets of various theories. It is difficult for him to commit himself to a full-blooded behaviorism, and yet he cannot espouse a genuinely dynamic psychology, except for his acceptance of psychoanalysis. Tolman's personality and training may furnish some clue as to his views. In the first place, we have in him a man who seems to be amused by everything and, more than all, at himself. One who takes himself so lightly will be taken seriously by his colleagues. A boyish and buoyant air, with perhaps the outgoing naturalness and directness of the finishing school manner, possibly the heritage of his mother, makes him *persona grata* to all. There is never a note of militancy in anything he writes, and his disarming smile is certainly the stimulus for a receptive attitude. In form, his articles remind us of an adolescent who tells his friends of some new boat model he is working on.

By training, Tolman is a technologist, following the family tradition (his brother, incidentally, was one of the foremost physicists in the country). It is the engineer in him who is responsible for the neat figures and diagrams to bolster his theoretical conclusions. Let us bear in mind the cognate origin of *engineer* and *ingenuity*. At Harvard, he was indoctrinated with the neo-realism of E. B. Holt and R. B. Perry, while, in Münsterberg's seminar, he would hear a great deal of purposive psychology. Without his epistemological background he most likely would have remained a crude behaviorist within the confines of his animal laboratory. Fortunately, some fifty years ago, there was enough philosophical discussion even for prospective psychologists, around the seminar table in Emerson Hall, at Harvard; and it was not lost on our subsequent molar behaviorist. Had he been educated at the University of Chicago, his volume would scarcely have been titled "*Purposive* Behavior in Animals and Men." While Tolman, has been taken as one exemplar, to start us off on an exploratory expedition, it may well be that the history of psychology is at least partially a function of the individual personalities that figure in it, and their education.

The particular conjuncture which has shaped the life of our purposive behaviorist has been favorable both for him and psychology; for the very forces which pulled in opposite directions proved a safety valve against falling into the morass of a smug oversimplified mechanism. The echoes of what Tolman had once heard and read, well up from the past and render him less susceptible to the temptations of a Simon-pure "S-R-bond" psychology. He at least is willing to wrestle with the problems which he cannot overlook, and has the courage to differentiate levels and methods of learning, which are usually put into one bag. He has become more sympathetic to the rôle played by heredity, and has renounced his former negative attitude toward instinct as a biological concept, which the "sign-gestalt-readiness" of the animal involves. Oddly enough, while he still spurns a mentalistic conception, or at least minimizes it so as to render it inconsequential, he takes refuge in the Freudian unconscious, when he is called upon to explain other than rodent experiences. It smacks somewhat of the schoolboy who offers to lick anyone in the class, and when taken up on it, he goes home to fetch his big brother.

L. T. Troland

L. T. Troland (1889-1932), who was often confused with Tolman because of their similar-sounding names, was also a graduate of the Massachusetts Institute of Technology, and came practically under the same influences at Harvard as Tolman. Troland, at the time he fell or jumped to his death from the summit of Mt. Wilson, was only 42 years old, but already he had made an enviable reputation for himself both in the academic and the technological world. He ranked as a physicist through his collaboration with D. Comstock on the *Nature of Matter and Electricity*, was well grounded in chemistry and biology, having received the Bowdoin prize for a dissertation in the former, and a degree in public health from the Massachusetts Institute of Technology. He was recognized as a specialist in optics to the extent that at the age of 33, he was elected President of the Optical Society of America. His experimental room at Harvard was filled with apparatus, mainly of his own construction, and his four-volume *Principles of Psychophysiology* would have been a monumental work for a man more mature in years.

At the time of the first World War, he was assigned to the task of developing acoustic devices for detecting approaching submarines; served as chief engineer for the Technicolor Motion Picture Corporation, in which capacity he not only elaborated the process of exhibiting colored moving pictures, but developed methods to promote the manufacture of the film. In October, 1931, the U. S. Patent Office issued to him a patent embracing 234 claims and covering the production of pictures in color, thereby securing for him rights claimed by many contestants since 1921. As if this were not a sufficient range for a single mind, he was also interested in metaphysics and ethical theory.

It is characteristic of the man that he left provision in his will for a fund, "the purpose of which will be the advancement of knowledge with regard to the relationship of consciousness and the physical world."

Unusual Blend of Theoretical and Practical

His mind was an extraordinary combination of the theoretical and the practical. The theoretical scientists respected him because of his technological attainments, while technologists admired him for his vast fund of theoretical knowledge. The only gap in his intellectual inventory was the humanistic segment, including the aesthetic and historical foundations. His practical sense reached out even into the business world, although his ambitions were never high in that direction.

At the time of his tragic death, he had been directing research at the Technicolor Motion Picture Corporation of which he was the Vice-President and inventive genius. Were Troland living today and progressing normally in his career, he would, despite an unimpressive and inexpressive personality, take his place among the first ten American psychologists, so far as achievement goes. Few could rival him in industry and grim determination. Among his notable traits were an even temper, and abiding friendship, and an unpretentiousness rare even in the best-mannered English circles— and Troland was of Scotch-Irish descent, distantly related to his idol, J. J. Thomson.

Synaptic Rate of Conductance

His claim to consideration in this chapter rests on his book, *The Fundamentals of Human Motivation* (1928), which at the time was one of the few works on the subject. Troland was not a dynamist in the contemporary sense of the term; for to him, all had to be explicated in physiological terms. Nevertheless, he had no stomach for behaviorism, even if he was in the habit of employing the objectivistic terminology; beneceptors, nociceptors, neutroceptors (which include all the sense organs that are associated with neither beneficial nor injurious results to the organism). He does not shrink from making use of the instinct theory; his biological training would have given him the proper guidance there. For Troland, "instinct consists not so much in doing the right thing at the right time as in seeking experimentally for an indefinitely foreseen goal, which is nevertheless definitely accepted when found." In this respect, he resembles Tolman, and he could thus be said to belong to the purposive school. His own system is largely structural, but of greater complexity than in the traditional sense. There are dimensions of qualitative variation, and these may form serial constellations; and, of course, there are attributes.

Affection is not an element for Troland, but rather a universal property of consciousness. With such a ubiquitous rôle, one can see that the pleasantness-unpleasantness intensity will be the key to all motivation; for Troland is a hedonist and, unlike McDougall, believes that the goal sought will always reveal a core of pleasantness or the relief of distress. We can understand why the beneceptors and nociceptors are all-important in a scheme like that. The process by which responses are stamped-in or out, in consequence of stimulation, Troland appropriately calls "retroflex" action. In this way, random movements may become definitely fixed. Retroflex action involves both hereditary (instinctive) and conditioned mechanisms, the latter modifying the other. Now although the retroflex sense channels are linked with special subcortical nerve-centres, presumably in a thalamus, which bring about the cortical conditions that are pivotal to the affective situation, actually it is in the synapses of the higher centres that we are to look for the development.

It is the rate of change in the cortical conductances at the synapses which is responsible for our feeling "pleasure" or "pain." When the rate increases, it is the former; when it decreases, it is the latter, and if there is no change, the feeling-tone will be indifference. What will determine the general affective make-up of the individual will be the accumulated fund of retroflexive processes. In other words, not the affective present, so much as the affective past will *retroflexly* shape our disposition to react either positively or negatively to a certain stimulus. Thus Troland gets around the problem of purpose, and thus, too, it may be said his view is in accord with that of Thorndike (law of effect) but his special hypothesis of changing rate of conductance lends it added significance. Whether it is dynamic theory is not clear. Troland is not inclined to infer things. He is too empirical for that, direct experience being his only guide.

Contemporary Dynamic Eddies

G. W. Allport. The dynamic current, nowadays, has left the more general area of learning and motivation and is centering around the problems connected with personality. Among those who have enriched this field, within the past twenty-five years or so, is G. W. Allport, who belongs, with important modifications, to the personalistic school of William Stern, in that he stresses the ultimate and irreducible uniqueness of personality. He differs with the Columbia School in adhering to the view that traits are general bio-physical entities and not merely specific habits bio-socially pigeonholed. The operation of a trait is, for him, "dynamic both in governing the reception of the stimulus and in directing the response." Motives he regards as personalized systems of tension. In each individual, there is not only a distinct pattern of tensions, but this distinct pattern functions differently for various objects and situations, because of past experiences impinging upon the present circumstances.

Allport's definition of personality as "the dynamic organization within the individual of those psychophysical systems that determine his unique adjustments to his environment" shows us at once that its author intends to stay in the dynamic camp. The Yale conception of personality as a social stimulus, depending upon what the individual has done in order to make himself recognized, does not appeal to him. The processes and capacities within him are what count, particularly in the manner they are motivationally regulated, changing, and evolving a new integration with every change.

As to Allport's theory of motivation, the principle of functional autonomy is brought in to take care of activities which are not accountable by original drives. This principle is not unlike that of Woodworth, which rules that every mechanism can become a drive, that the means can turn into a goal. "What was once an instrumental technique," asserts Allport, "becomes a master motive," so that the merchant prince continues to work hard, long after he has accumulated a fortune and the musician will still love his instrument even after he has obtained mastery in playing.[5]

Long a sponsor of religion, G. W. Allport has in such books as *The Individual and His Religion* (1950) and *Becoming* (1955) attempted to find a place for the values in a scientific psychology of personality, espousing more and more a concept like the "self-actualization" developed by Kurt Goldstein. In his recent *Pattern and Growth in Personality* (1961), a reworked edition of his earlier textbook, he has broadened his range by lucid discussions of some of the new cultural movements (extentialism, client-centred therapy) and by an elaboration of his view on motives, without, however, taking up the present author's critique.

Press, Thema, and Regnancy

H. A. Murray's explanation of personality forms another eddy in the general dynamic current. Murray has been influenced largely by Freud, Jung, and Adler, but also by Mc-Dougall, Prince, and Lewin. His list of needs is redolent of McDougall's list of instincts. Murray uses different words, like succorance, harm-avoidance, but it requires little analysis to spot the identity in most cases. For Murray, however, a need is more or less localized, and is definitely a force in the brain region which, through its organizing various intellectual and conative functions in specific ways, brings about a transformation of existing unsatisfying situations. One might have thought that the need is the equivalent of the unsatisfied situation, but we are to understand that it is the force which handles such situations.

Other dynamic concepts which Murray introduces are: press *i.e.*, a directional tendency in an object or situation, and thema *i.e.*, a dynamic structure of an event on a motor level.

[5] G. W. Allport: *Personality; A Psychological Interpretation*, p. 319. See A. A. Roback: *Personality in Theory and Practice*, pp. 148-152, for a critique of this mode of argumentation.

The "press" is hardly more than a Lewinian vector, while the "structure of an event" is a bit obscure. Is the event *in* us or external to us? Is it something like the valence of *Gestalt*, or is it a pattern in our own make-up, which produces certain reactions or attitudes under given conditions? The most characteristic stroke in Murray's sketch is the notion of regnancy, as the totality of processes forming a dominant configuration in the brain. This concept seems to be an outgrowth of Morton Prince's neurogram; and it is apparent that Murray is eager to supply neural bases for mental phenomena, even if they belong to the unconscious. In fact, Murray posits unconscious regnant processes, and there can even be a hierarchy of sub-regnancies. Of course, if the regnancy is only a brain configuration, then it cannot be anything else but unconscious, but if regnancy refers to the experiential counterpart of the brain configuration, then it can be divided into a conscious and an unconscious phase. Regnancy would then connote a segment of personality, psychoneurally considered, dominating the rest at any particular moment. The unconscious regnancies would then be integrated in this or any segment so as to lend it its commanding authority. The cases of multiple personality, it may be recalled, have been interpreted by the dissociation school in much the same way.

Murray's view is, of course, in agreement with dynamic theories, but inasmuch as he wishes to dovetail the mental and the neural, something which Freud did not take it upon himself to accomplish, he succeeds only in beclouding the many terms which he employs, and we obtain the impression that there is much going on, but it is too dark to discern more than a shadowy movement.

The Inferred Self

A sign of the times in a dynamic direction is E. R. Hilgard's plea for a recognition of the continuity of motivational patterns, to satisfy which, there is introduced as a prerequisite, a rather bold construct, viz., the "inferred self,"[6] which draws upon the genotypical ingredients and does not limit itself to what can be fully observed. Hilgard, in addition, is not satisfied with the *integrated* personality, but bids us look to the *integrative* personality as our model. The advocacy of such

[6] E. R. Hilgard: "Human Motives and the Concept of Self," *American Psychol.*, 1949, vol. 4, pp. 379-380.

tenets would be considered as bordering on the mystical a quarter of a century ago, but thanks to psychoanalysis and clinical psychology, the purely mechanical theories, which include not only behaviorism but also the Columbia specificity doctrine, no longer dominate the scene. There is a distinct veering toward the inferential, simply because it comports with the facts better than the so-called observational method, which is also inferential, only surreptitiously so.

Chapter 26

Freud and Psychoanalysis

IN PSYCHOANALYSIS, we have a dynamic psychology with a vengeance. Its originator, Sigmund Freud, whatever we think of his elaborately evolved system, was a genius. Not being a psychologist by training, he was able to start from scratch, unconcerned about the gains of traditional or, for that matter, untraditional psychology. Beginning as a physician, engaged at first in neurology and pediatrics, he found himself in the field of psychiatry, and thence proceeded to revolutionize not only our whole psychological conception but the entire outlook on civilization. There is scarce a nook or cranny in our humanistic structure but which has been somewhat illumined by the psychoanalytic torch; and the prejudices which Freud has had to surmount in order to spread his gospel have been far more intense than those which Copernicus, Galileo, Kepler, and Darwin have had to contend with.

Psychology owes a great deal to the medical sciences. It was Hippocrates, flourishing about 400 B.C., who gave us the first theory of the temperaments, forming the basis for a psychology of personality; and although they lived six centuries apart, his successor, Galen, set it in the humoral framework, which held for more than a millennium. In recent years, most of the shining lights in psychology have had medical degrees: Fechner, Lotze, Helmholtz, Wundt, James, Scripture, Münsterberg, McDougall; and Titchener, while he was not an M.D., received a thorough schooling in physiology and anatomy under Burdon-Sanderson. Of these, none, except Helmholtz, who for a time was a surgeon, and Scripture, who was for a period a psychiatrist, practiced medicine. Freud continued his therapeutic duties until he was forced to flee from Austria.

The biography of Freud does not belong here, nor shall we go into the intricacies of psychoanalysis, which has caught the fancy of thousands of practitioners and millions of lay people. At first, Freud gave credit, for initiating the movement, to his older colleague, Joseph Breuer, who was able to eke out some exasperatingly withheld information from a young woman patient, only in the course of hypnosis. Breuer, however, did not realize the nature of the repression, and abandoned the method, leaving Freud to explore the realm of the unconscious and its obscure operations.

Elevation of the Unconscious

Since Freud was untrammeled by accepted facts and was endowed with a venturesome spirit, as well as with an imaginative mind, which is almost as useful in science as it is indispensable in art, he could bring himself to dispose of the usual notions without qualms or fear that he would be considered aberrant. First, it was essential to find a place for the unconscious in scientific discourse. Orthodox psychology, which was committed to the proposition that there is nothing in the mind unless we are conscious of it, could only see in the unconscious mind a contradiction in terms. At most, a subconscious (or coconscious) state would be admitted. Men like Münsterberg would not even allow the subconscious to be interpreted in mental terms, but held that the goings-on so dubbed could occur only in the brain, as neural processes. Freud bypassed the term "subconscious" altogether, and recognized the *unconscious* as the vast reservoir of mental entities which were forcing their way out, to the conscious, in some disguise, or else through physical outlets.

This involved theoretical difficulties. First, we had always been accustomed to equate the mental with the physiological. How then can we account for this new mental find, the unconscious, without its physiological counterpart? The British psychical researchers, Podmore, Gurney, and principally, Frederick Myers, had encountered a similar obstacle; and William James, in his mystical phase, took refuge in a transmission theory, according to which, a psychic energy pervades the world and affects certain individuals who are attuned to it. Now Freud was far from being inveigled by metaphysical speculations akin to religious inspirations. The unconscious he was dealing with was not cosmic (and therefore, incidentally, Boring is not justified in associating Freud with v. Hartmann, in this connection. Boring: *History, etc.,* 2d ed., p. 714) but strictly individual. It was inferred—and here we have the true dynamic note—from the happenings, which cannot be explained either logically or physiologically.

The Rational Given A Back Seat

With the dethronement of the conscious went the transference to the background of the rational; and the shift to the foreground of the affective and non-rational. Cognition has had its day, and now it was to be relegated to a secondary place. In keeping with this transposition, another great change was to appear, which was to become the trademark, so to speak, of dynamic psychology, *viz.*, the shift of attention from the "how" to the "why." *Motivation,* and not *causation,* was to be our quest; and the answers were not to be sought in the working of the nervous system, but in the dynamism of the mind, chiefly in the unconscious. Such a procedure would entail treating the mind as an altogether independent unit, one that is not moored to a neural apparatus. In other words, the mental was to be explained in mental terms. Determinism was called in for this purpose, but determinism not of a physical but of a mental order, where even overdeterminism was possible, with its own logic that might strain at a gnat and swallow a camel without violating the rules. Under the circumstances, it may readily be perceived that the borderline between the normal and the abnormal is only imaginary. There is really nothing abnormal. "We ask, naturally enough," writes Boring, "whence Freud got his ideas? They were there, ready for him, in the culture. He had only to take them over. One important one, oddly enough, was the theory of the conservation of energy" (*History of Experimental Psychology,* p. 708).

The odd thing about Boring's observation is that Freud's conception of the unconscious and, more especially, his doctrine of conversion hysteria, were in direct contravention of the principle of conservation, and the hitch which confronted McDougall in his interactionism is even more troublesome in the case of Freud. It is notable that both were thoroughly grounded in physiology, and that the latter was not in the slightest degree worried about the discrepancy. For one thing, the "why" enjoyed priority over the "how"; secondly, although the neuron and its appendages are now visible, the actual processes, *when the mind is active,* are just as inferential as the unconscious is. Furthermore, the so-called Freudian mechanisms, like repression, regression, fixation, displacement, condensation, cathexis, rationalization, reaction-formation, identification, etc., were not at the time either in the culture or in the air.

The truth of the matter seems to be that there was only one idea which gripped Freud, and that is the "why" of human behavior; and in the course of finding an answer to the multitude of motives, he stumbled upon other ideas, which formed stations in his long journey. It is futile to suppose, as Boring does,[1] that Freud came upon his pan-sexualism, or pleasure principle, *via* the English hedonists. It was through his clinical practice and his experiences as a student in the Salpêtrière that he came to see the importance of *la chose génitale* in nervous ailments, and its reverberations in every sphere of life. As to his preoccupation with the "why," may there not have been some harking back to the Judaic tradition to account for it? It was largely because the ancient Hebrews were interested in motives that they gave rise to three ethical religions. The Greeks, on the other hand, anchored in the "how," developed a causally-grounded philosophy and science.[2]

In order to understand the vicissitudes and progress of psychoanalysis, it will be best to obtain a very brief, even if oversimplified, summary of Freud's basic tenets. The story begins with the infant and its not so innocent attachment to the parent of the opposite sex. As the child becomes more articulate and sensible, and as the triangle situation becomes more tinged with a sex connotation, the threat of the less loved and, in a sense, hated parent, as well as the guilt-feeling which develops as a result of these contrasted attitudes, begins to take shape as a repressed complex, latent and unrecognized as such, but causing trouble in the form of a neurosis, particularly anxiety, and throwing off occasional sparks, in peculiar distortions, in dreams, slips of the pen and tongue, unintentional acts, accidents, etc., until the foreign body comes to the surface, *i.e.*, to consciousness. "Our therapy," Freud tells us, "does its work by transforming something unconscious into something conscious, and only succeeds in its work insofar as it is able to effect this transformation." The older belief that an abreaction had taken place, similar to an electrical discharge, of the particular trauma was abandoned later in favor of the view that the patient must understand the meaning of the symptoms and be prepared to adjust in the light of the new knowledge. In this respect, then, Freud comes close to the reëducation principle which, as we have seen, was the basis of Morton Prince's method of therapy. To make the patient aware of what is at

[1] E. G. Boring: *A History of Experimental Psychology* (2d ed.), p. 713.

[2] This view was presented in a lengthy paper by the author as a young undergraduate before the McGill Philosophical Society, and was afterwards published as a chapter in his *Jewish Influence in Modern Thought* (1929). Nothing has come forth since to cause the writer to change his original premise.

the root of his trouble requires patience and skill; for often his or her resistance is so great as to drive the analyst to despair. Fortunately, certain devices, like transference, which call forth the same reactions to the physician as were originally experienced in the childhood of the patient, bring about the overcoming of this resistance.

Genital Development

Growing up may signify many things to the person in the street. It means getting bigger, for one thing; equally important is the amassing of information, the acquisition of common sense and understanding, and other gains; but, to a psychoanalyst, what is paramount in the process consists in the successful libidinal organization on the part of the child and youth. As intimated, even the infant is sexually susceptible, although the libido is associated with the mouth (suckling—biting belonging to the later oral stage). The anal stage also with its two periods, comes next, to be followed by the phallic; and finally the genital, which is the graduation point in this instinctual college, climaxes the development. Due to retardation at any one of these stages, various handicaps are in store for the unfortunate—narcissism, sadism, father or mother fixations, homosexuality, and other kinds of what are usually known as perversions, not to mention some of the more severe psychoneuroses and even psychoses.

It is evident that Freud is an environmentalist, although he occasionally drops a hint about constitutional factors.[3] The difference, however, between him and a Pavlov, or the average behaviorist, who ascribes all faults and virtues to habits and conditionings, is that with Freud, *the conditioning can come about through a single experience* (primal scene, *e.g.*, when a very young child has watched the copulation of his parents) which is repressed, only to create mischief later on.

Metapsychology: the Topographical Schema

There is one more significant phase to the psychoanalytic drama—the conflict between the id and the superego, with the ego bearing the brunt as moderator. The infant is all *id*, grabbing everything and offering nothing (except, unwittingly,

[3] Ernest Jones wrote me that "Freud attached great importance to this including inheritance," but if he did, he seldom makes reference to such so that application may be made to his theories.

happiness to doting parents and grandparents). Gradually, the superego develops, first through threats and punishments, and then, as a result of conscience and ideals self-imposed. At the same time, there comes into being the realistic ego, which deals with the outside world, and therefore must seek to mollify both the id and the superego, and adjust so as not to barter away social status or economic advantages for fleeting pleasures on the one hand, or give up the gratification of elementary needs because of an exaggerated remorse and saintliness, on the other. The function of the ego, then, is to keep the mind (both conscious and unconscious) on an even keel, and to iron out differences which might otherwise lead to serious nervous ailments. In later life, Freud began to give more attention to the ego, and less to the id, with its pleasure-principle foundation, but it is hardly accurate to say with Boring[4] that he abandoned this principle. He simply extended his canvas so as to make room for both aspects of human life —pleasure and ambition, thus approaching McDougall's hormic psychology.

If nothing is said about Freud's basic works, like his *Psychopathology of Everyday Life, Interpretation of Dreams, Wit and Its Relation to the Unconscious,* his smaller books like *Civilization and Its Discontents* and *Totem and Tabu,* as well as his numerous monographs, it is because Freud's contributions are not American productions. Nor is it pertinent to declare oneself, in this chapter, either as for or against psychoanalysis. Our task, however, at this point is to trace the progress of psychoanalysis in the United States.

Early Status

Let us first catch a glimpse of Freud's position in the early part of the century. With views such as he had promulgated, making out of the cherub a rival for the libidinal affection of the father or mother, according as it is female or male, and basing his whole system on an incestuous wish, the originator could not expect much encouragement. In his letters to Wilhelm Fliess, he tells of his trials and tribulations in those early days, and of his gratefulness to the members of the B'nai B'rith lodge, in Vienna, for listening sympathetically to his paper on dreams! Most of his colleagues practically shun him, or look at him with scorn. He then succeeds in drawing a few followers, from different walks of life, who were intrigued by

[4] E. G. Boring: *Loc. cit,* p. 714.

the novel ideas, and saw a fertile field in prospect for the dissemination of their own reflections. Fortunately for Freud, such men were attracted as Sandor Ferenczi, Ernest Jones, Otto Rank, Hanns Sachs, Karl Abraham, and Max Eitingon, who, if they did not all remain faithful to their leader, were, at least, influential and brilliant men. Of the group known as the "seven rings," since each had received a ring like the one Freud was wearing, only Jones, Freud's most articulate advocate, and the one who made his escape from Vienna to an open-armed London possible, was the last survivor, but died soon after bringing out his monumental three-volume biography of Freud, on which—he wrote the author—he worked a dozen years.

His "splendid isolation," as Freud reminisced of the days when he met eyes which looked with contempt was not altogether to be deplored. His sense of independence was too great to make of such a thing a tragedy. Soon the contempt turned to scorn or scoffing, but at the same time, there were repercussions of his peculiar doctrine in other countries, and his disciples were growing in number and also in attachment. Freud was an able organizer, and some of his associates acted as apostles. When Eugen Bleuler, in Switzerland, evinced a sympathetic interest in psychoanalysis, Freud was overjoyed; for, with the exception of Jones and maybe one or two others Jung, Hans Blüher, the psychoanalytic coterie consisted of members of his own ethnic group, which was not likely to lend it any prestige in a country where there were definite restrictions against such a minority. Several years later, in 1908, Jung became Freud's heir-apparent, but not for long. He simply did not fit into that circle, and eventually founded his own school of analytical psychology, while Adler had already seceded in 1911, to form his group of individual psychologists. Bleuler never intended to affiliate himself with Freud, and as the latter remarked, his attitude could be described by a word which Bleuler himself had coined, *ambivalent*. Freud still had been able to keep his fold intact, but was not altogether satisfied with the extent of his conquests.

Psychoanalysis Comes to America

Then, in 1909, something happened to indicate that psychoanalysis was on the map. Freud received an invitation from Stanley Hall, whom he playfully refers to as "the kingmaker," to be the honored guest at the twentieth anniversary of the founding of Clark University, and to deliver a series of lectures there.[5] The invitation to lecture at Clark exceeded his fondest daydream, we are told in the autobiographic sketch;[6] especially as Jung was also asked to speak on the occasion. Indeed, one could speak of a retinue; for Ferenczi accompanied them, and Jones came from Toronto to greet the master. Brill, too, was there.

The group picture, taken on the steps of the Clark University library, now well known, shows a number of the most distinguished men, not only in psychology, such as James, Titchener, Stern, Cattell, and Hall, but in other fields as well: Adolf Meyer, in psychiatry; Jennings, in biology; Franz Boas, in anthropology; and Burgerstein, in education. It was truly a gala celebration; and Freud discovered that his teachings were known and discussed in the United States even at that early period. His five lectures were at once translated into English and published in the *American Journal of Psychology*, in 1910, and subsequently in German, Russian, Polish, Dutch, Hungarian, Italian, Danish, French, and Spanish, as well as other languages. Literally, millions of copies have sold of this Freudian product on American soil.

One incident which Freud relates seems to have escaped the attention of all who write on the early history of psychoanalysis. There is an ominous and tragic setting to the occurrence. After one of the sessions, James and Freud went out for a walk, and on this occasion, no doubt, the two intellectual giants were to find out how close they stood to one another in their outlook. Alas, however, James felt an angina attack coming on, and entrusting his briefcase to Freud, he bade him continue, until the crisis had passed, when he would join him. Apparently, the opportunity was gone, and the following year James died. Freud wished that he could face such an ordeal with the same equanimity. Little did he realize then what was in store for him both on account of his buccal cancer and the Nazi fury. What is surprising, perhaps, is that no psychoanalyst has yet come forth with an explanation of unconscious determinism to account for James's onset at the very time when the two might have come to terms.

The Worcester conference led to still greater recognition;

[5] Forty years later, a similar invitation was extended to his daughter.

[6] S. Freud, in *Die Medizin in der Gegenwart in Selbstdarstellungen*, 1925.

for it was there that Freud met James J. Putnam, professor of neurology at the Harvard Medical School, who had been unfavorably disposed toward psychoanalysis, but under the spell of Freud's exposition, and perhaps his personality too, now became a proselytizing votary; and wielding great influence in the Athens of America, he naturally was a powerful ally to acquire. Putnam was really the first of the "Brahmins" to take the hussy ideology under his protection; and the grateful Freud, after Putnam's death in 1918, piously published his addresses on psychoanalysis, with a memoir of the author.

It may be, too, that the young Holt's presence at these meetings was instrumental in the writing of *The Freudian Wish,* the first endorsement of psychoanalysis by an academic psychologist. His rebelliousness against what he considered to be the old-fogeyism of the Harvard philosophical department had already sought expression in his neo-realism, but psychoanalysis would be a Godsend to him; for it was bound to serve as a greater shock, and by combining a behavioristic psychology with Freudianism, he enhanced the deviltry, especially as the two are built on disparate foundations. E. J. Kempf has tried a similar stunt by linking the psychoanalytic mechanisms to the autonomic functions, and in the last analysis, by implication, to endocrine elements, but certainly we know that Freud would have disclaimed such speculations.

On this side of the Atlantic, A. A. Brill became the chief promoter of psychoanalysis through his translations of Freud's books, somewhat shoddily executed though they were.

Spread of Psychoanalysis

Brill and Jones began to spread the psychoanalytic doctrines around 1908, while Morton Prince, who was a member of the dissociation school, nevertheless, was hospitable to the new theory, and his *Journal of Abnormal Psychology* was the first organ to publish steadily articles by Freudians. Among the stalwarts during the first decade of the century were S. E. Jelliffe and W. A. White who formed the most effective team in advancing the interests of the new movement. Jelliffe, the Nestor of American psychiatry, erudite, entertaining, and industrious was managing editor of both the *Journal of Nervous and Mental Disease,* including the monographs, and the newly-founded *Psychoanalytic Review,* while White, who was the psychiatrist-in-chief at St. Elizabeth Hospital, in Washington, was his able coadjutor. Both were well-liked and highly thought of as neurologists and psychiatrists and steered the psychoanalytic ship in this country for decades. Jelliffe, probably taking his cue from Max Groddeck (from whom Freud got the idea of the *id*), even saw in organic diseases, like cancer, psychogenic causes. Of considerable service to psychoanalysis in those days was I. Coriat. Mention might be made, too, in this connection, of the neglected Trigant Burrow, who seems to have fallen between two stools (phylobiology and psychoanalysis).

After 1915, psychoanalysis gathered momentum. Many practitioners found it advantageous to use the method. Patients clamored for it. The literary journals and even newspapers, from time to time, contained at least references to it, if not full articles. From the stage, the platform, and even the pulpit, psychoanalysis would receive at any rate lip-service, and if the American saying that "every knock is a boost" contains any truth, then psychoanalysis had nothing to complain of. At first, Freud was railed at; by 1920, his lot had changed to the extent that more professionals swore by him than swore at him. More psychoanalytic articles began to appear in the psychiatric periodicals, and, what is more important, more psychoanalytic journals came into existence *(Psychoanalytic Quarterly)* but even such media as the *American Journal of Psychiatry, Psychiatric Quarterly*, and especially the *American Journal of Orthopsychiatry* printed more than the expected quota of psychoanalytic articles.

In 1938, *American Imago*, replaced the original *Imago*, with the original co-editor as its founder, *viz.,* Hanns Sachs. *Psychiatry* as an outgrowth of the W. A. White Foundation, would naturally be devoted to psychoanalysis.

The American Psychoanalytic Association was formed about fifty years ago, and became a firmly-knit and exclusive organization. In several large cities, such as Boston, Los Angeles, San Francisco, Topeka, Washington, Baltimore, and Chicago, psychoanalytic institutes came into existence, where courses and seminars have been offered to the profession. What, however, must have been particularly exhilarating to Freud and his associates was that the universities were won over to the new therapy and, of course, with them, the mental hospitals and clinics as well as Foundations like the Judge Baker Guidance Centre, in Boston (Healy) and the Menninger Foundation (in Topeka) in the larger cities. Thus, Paul F. Schilder came to America, in 1925, as professor of psychiatry at New York University. Schilder, a man of great breadth and brilliance, could scarcely be confined to orthodox psychoanalysis, but the basis of most of his multifarious investigations and textbooks was definitely psychoanalytic. Like many of his co-workers in this field, he died comparatively young.

Franz Alexander, coming to the University of Chicago in 1930 as visiting professor of psychoanalysis, was a gain in more than one way. He soon became director of the new Chicago Institute for Psychoanalysis, and while not stepping out of the Freudian compound, he began to take an active part in the building up of psychosomatic medicine, favoring the view that the individual as a whole should be treated. In some respects, his position abuts on Adler's theory of organ jargon, and his cases of hypertension, various gastro-intestinal disturbances or other syndromes, apparently lend themselves to certain attitude-formulations. His use of vectors in interpreting psychosomatic conditions is of a piece with the topological method, except that Alexander circumscribes the field within the organism.

Another triumph for the movement was the coming of Hanns Sachs, a lawyer only by training, to the Harvard Medical School, in 1932, to give a course in psychoanalysis. Since he had been known for his seasoned work in training psychoanalysts in Berlin, his sojourn in Boston stirred up activities there; and the movement thrived there with a growing band of newcomers. To what extent psychoanalysis has expanded in the United States may be gathered from the fact that there are as many as 200 engaged in training physicians for this type of work.

The Dissidents

Although psychoanalysis is a term usually restricted to the orthodox Freudians, one cannot, in a history, afford to exclude the influence of Jung, Adler, and Rank. Jung (1875-1961) it is true, only visited the United States on several occasions, giving no thought to settling here, yet he had made a number of converts to his cause, notably Beatrice Hinkle. Jung's division of mankind into introverts and extraverts was avidly seized upon by the public in general, but his mystical explorations of the collective unconscious meant little to the average psychologist. His vast culture and uncommon energy were appreciated mainly in semi-scientific, religious, and literary circles, through which he made contacts with the wealthy who required treatment or counsel. Harvard honored him at its tercentenary, and the Yale University Press brought out some of his books in English translation, containing his lectures on religion, the soul, and kindred subjects. In England, Jung's psychology had greater luck, partly because of the endeavors of his dynamic votary, H. G. Baynes, who was an institution in himself, dying, however, prematurely.

Alfred Adler (1870-1937) did identify himself with the United States, having spent the last part of his life in this country (although actually he died in Aberdeen, on a lecture tour). He broke away from Freud, in 1911,[7] ostensibly, because he could tolerate no longer the pansexual scope of the school; and, making the goal of superiority, as thwarted by constitutional inferiority and the masculine protest, the basis of neurosis, he proceeded to erect a system of what he called individual psychology, i.e., dealing with the person as a whole and not with diverse impersonal mechanisms. On arriving in this country, Adler set aside much of his earlier scaffolding, and turned from original organ inferiority to home conditions and the style of life for an understanding of the problems involved. Whether one was the oldest, the youngest, or an only child would be of paramount importance; and the attitude of not only parents but brothers and sisters toward the youngster was to be our guide as to the final outcome. Adler's form of theory lent itself, from its very nature, to application to child problems. As Adler would travel extensively, he would set up transient clinics, and lecture in the same city. At first, Adler drew a goodly number of followers, but as he won popularity among the masses for whom the phrase "inferiority complex" had a special allure, he lost prestige in academic and professional circles.

It is evident that Adler stressed the reality principle or the ego, as against the id and superego, in Freud's topographical

---

[7] In *America Imago,* 1951, vol. 8, the dramatic meetings in Vienna at which Adler, the President of the Vienna Psychoanalytic Society outlined his own principles are vividly described from the old protocols. Freud, of course, was not inclined to cede his own points, but he was tolerant, and even gave Adler credit for some new angle. Adler was not ousted by Freud, but most of the members, at the instance of Steiner, felt that with such views, the former would be out of place in that organization, or it would have to be renamed, in order to fit Adler's ideas into its programme and framework.

economy. He also dwelt on the experiences of childhood, but did not limit them so narrowly to the first few years of life. Another difference was Adler's confidence in the conscious and skepticism as to the maneuvers of the unconscious. Adler was more self-deterministic than Freud, so that many educators, and particularly those interested in character education, were more disposed to accept Adler's in preference to Freud's teachings, which, to the uninitiated, seemed altogether too deterministic, if not fatalistic.

Adler made much ado about understanding the patient, instead of being content with manipulating mechanisms. Unfortunately for him, he made no theoretical progress, as did Freud, and many of us have felt that his earlier work was much more original and significant than his later popular books and articles. If some psychoanalysts have of late come closer to the ego principle, it is not because Adler showed the way. It was a natural process which they had to undergo in the course of time. Freud, himself, was passing through the stage at the time he died, and his daughter had taken up the thread from that point.

Adler's work has, nevertheless, found continuators in a small group of energetic clinicians, headed both by his daughter, Alexandra, and on the academic side by H. L. Ansbacher who, as editor of the *Journal of Individual Psychology,* has managed to attract a number of influential contributors from various schools.

Otto Rank (1884-1939) was ousted from the orthodox group, in Vienna, when he erected the birth trauma, which Freud originally suggested in a casual way, into a psychoanalytic fetish. That such an unknowable measure, as regards intensity or potency, could be made the basis of all neurosis is almost incomprehensible, but there were other signs of rebelliousness in the youngest of Freud's heirs; for he advocated a condensed form of analysis which would take only weeks, or at most months, instead of years. Rank was a prodigious worker, endowed with the fervor, somewhat uncontrolled cultural sweep, and power of synthesis usually found in the East European Talmudical scholar. In his large work on the incest motive in literature, he did yeoman's service to his master. All his books, however, are marked by flashes of originality. Inevitably, he reminds us of another Otto—Otto Weininger, who committed suicide at the age of 23, after achieving a phenomenal success with his *Sex and Character.* In his *Myth of the Birth of the Hero* (Nervous and Mental Disease Monographs,

No. 18) Rank is of the opinion that schizophrenia results from a conflict between the masculine and feminine elements in a personality. That is what Weininger might have concluded, had he allowed himself to reach a mature age.

Rank's therapy consisted mainly in causing the patient to re-experience the birth trauma, something which Freud, for valid reasons, could not countenance. In the United States, where Rank spent the last few years of his rather brief span, he found but a slight following. The New York School of Social Work and, particularly, the Pennsylvania School of Social Work were about the only places where Rank's methods were adopted, and where the patient found his task almost one of penance. No wonder his last work was called *Will Therapy*, and that is the name his method goes by among social workers.

Stekel (1868-1942) was known in America through his voluminous writings which were filled with case studies. Several of his works are in two volumes each. Perhaps his *Peculiarities of Behavior* is the most satisfactory of all, yet even his studies on impotence and frigidity, on sexual aberrations, and on sadism and masochism contain a wealth of data, but his far-fetched conclusions, such as that a tendency to tardiness is the unconscious reaction to having been born into a family last, or that collectors are sublimated Don Juans, make us wonder whether he was not more the high-class journalist than the scientist.

Even Stekel, who was no outstanding organizer, formed a group of his own, which, however, did not last long. In the United States, his only promoter was Van Teslaar, who translated most of his works. Several of his European followers have since come to this country. His skill in dream interpretation was acknowledged even by Freud, but his fragmentary segments did not add up to a system; and he remained the wise and sparkling feuilletonist in medical psychology. His widespread appeal lay chiefly in the revelation of bedroom intimacies. Emil A. Gutheil, who died recently in New York, was Stekel's most active disciple in this country.

The Refugee Analysts and Para-Freudians

The annexation of Austria by the Nazi regime and its tightening grip on the Jews in conquered territory sent a new batch of psychoanalysts to the United States. Not only psychoanalysis but all psychotherapy was regarded by the Nazis as Jewish "bunk." Among the émigrés were Otto Fenichel, whose *Psychoanalytic Theory of Neurosis* is encyclopedic in scope, and whose early death deprived the movement of a remarkable systematizer and theorist, E. Hitschmann, one of Freud's early clinical assistants, Geza Róheim, one of the most distinguished of the group, who has applied psychoanalysis to anthropology in actual field work among primitive tribes, and Karen Horney, who, together with Erich Fromm, swerved from the orthodox line, making more of character and the ethical than would be possible on strictly Freudian principles, and launching a more or less independent subschool with a sociological setting. Horney's books, *The Neurotic Personality of Our Time* and *New Ways in Psychoanalysis* were a *défi* hurled at the old guard. The author's vigorous style made an impression on the younger generation. It was clear that Freud's skepticism, pessimism, and disregard of religion and ethics, as hardly anything more than enforced myth, were beginning to be an anachronism in an age which needed a greater support than was necessary at the time that Freud matured. While Freud was active, he could hold such "heresies" in leash, but now that psychoanalysis is without a shepherd, the latent or submerged protests are coming to the fore. Horney has been the ringleader in the new direction, although the instigator seems to have been Fromm, who true to his name has been the pietist in the psychoanalytic sphere. In her latest book, *Neurosis and Human Growth,* Horney attempts a constructive plan, dwelling on the essence of the different selves (real, actual, idealized, and hated) which are inherent in every person. It is really a moral text with a psychoanalytic base. That Freud's position in regard to the id, ego, and superego was far clearer and more precise goes without saying. The Horney-Fromm group has organized into the Association for the Advancement of Psychoanalysis. As might be surmised, a new periodical for psychoanalysis, incorporating the para-Freudian doctrines and harboring such articles as would be possibly suppressed in the more orthodox psychoanalytic periodicals, has been circulating, *viz., The American Journal of Psychoanalysis.* Another newcomer is the veteran, Theodor Reik, who, after years of loyal attachment to the master, is forging out on his own, and the new dissentients are grouping themselves around the National Psychological Association for Psychoanalysis which accepts lay analysts.

Now that Freud is no more, there is likely to be some bickering among the survivors in regard to methods and techniques. Thus Theodor Reik and W. Reich, of whom more will be said presently, are at odds with one another over the question whether the analyst should act like the sun in melting the repressed complexes until they ooze out to the surface or like the wind in forcing them out by breaking the armor with which the neurotic has reinforced himself. Reich has evolved a special kind of technique with ingenious devices to shake up his patient, while Reik, on this matter, tends to defend the method established by Freud, which was more passive, allowing the patient to hit upon the unconscious material himself, with the analyst serving only as a mediator.

Reich has, as a matter of fact, founded an institute of his own, which he designates as the Orgone Institute; and there he applies his special technique. His own species of therapy he calls "character analysis," because, as he claims, the neurotic has surrounded himself with such a hard shell that his character is stunted and impervious. What Reich aims to do is to relax the patient by breaking through this armor. When that is achieved, the orgasm reflex, which is thwarted by the character incrustation, will be liberated, and the individual will feel just as elastic and resilient as a jellyfish, which to Reich, apparently, is the symbol of character.[8] The orgone stuff was pronounced a myth, or denounced as a fraud by law enforcement agencies.

Reich's brilliant mind came to a dismal end in prison, where he had been committed as a result of his failure to desist from continuing the orgone treatment, despite a court order. He, too, has left a devoted band of followers—in nonprofessional circles.

There is no doubt that psychoanalysis is intrenched in the United States. Some years ago, after Austria, and possibly Germany, it was England where psychoanalysis thrived most, but the latter has dropped out of the contest, for more than one reason. Many problems will come up before the psychoanalysts in the near future. Only one of them will affect the future of lay analysis. It may be remembered that Freud was

[8] Cf. A. A. Roback: *The Psychology of Character* (3d enl. ed., 1952), pp. 300-302, for a more extended account of Wilhelm Reich's view.

favorably inclined toward lay analysis, and, indeed, Hanns Sachs, who trained hundreds of analysts, had no medical training whatsoever, but in the United States, the consensus is against lay analysis, and the reason is readily discernible.

Chapter 27

Gestalt Psychology

GESTALT PSYCHOLOGY is not an American brand, but then neither is it German, as it is generally supposed. It developed in Germany, true enough, but how can it be considered a German product if its engineers and fashioners, with one or two exceptions, were candidates for the Majdanek and Auschwitz gas chambers and crematories, precisely because they were singled out as un-German by blood?

A Momentous Digression

Boring speaks of Edgar Rubin as a Dane, and implies that Max Wertheimer, who was born in Prague, was a Czech. On the principle of nativity, even Wolfgang Köhler would have been not a German but an Estonian, for he was born in Reval. Of the other founders of Gestalt psychology, two hailed from Poland (Kurt Goldstein was born in Katowice and Kurt Lewin, in Posen, which for many centuries had been a Polish community and now belongs to Poland). Koffka may have been born in Germany but the German tie is slight in his genealogy. He looked more like a Southern European, and the name certainly sounds Slavic. We might mention a few more: David Katz, Schur, Gelb, v. Hornbostel, Zeigarnik; and the remarkable thing about the list of names is that although their bearers come from various states in Europe, there is one common denominator—they are all Jews, only two of three of them being half-Jews.

What is more, the grandfather of the movement, Christian v. Ehrenfels, despite his exclusive given name, was partly Jewish. Nay more, the man who supplied the philosophical groundwork upon which Gestalt psychology reared its own structure—phenomenology—Edmund Husserl, whose seventy cases of manuscripts had to be spirited away to Louvain lest they be destroyed by the Nazi gang—, was a Moravian Jew; and of little avail was his baptism. Since his death was expected shortly anyway, the then foremost living philosopher in Germany was let off with humiliation and the loss of his assistant. Even the anthropoid station at Teneriffe, where Köhler made his significant observations on chimpanzees to prove his theory of insight, was established by the Jewish-German physiologist, Max Rothmann, Kurt Goldstein's father-in-law.

Köhler was the only one of the Gestalt leaders who might have liven in Berlin unscathed, but his association with so many "non-Aryans," and his courageous letter in a German daily, during the early part of Hitler's regime, made it imperative for him to quit the country. He would have fared badly, had he stayed while the Nazis were consolidating their gains in face of a lethargic world. All the rest of the gestaltists would have been placed in concentration and slave camps, and eventually found their way to the crematories. Yes, even in Denmark, Boring's "Dane," Edgar Rubin, could not have been saved by the valiant late King of Denmark, a credit to royalty; and had he not made his escape in time, he would have doubtless shared the fate of the six million Jews, including Freud's sister, who perished at the hands of the Nazis. As it is, we are told by Rubin's close friend, David Katz, that his death, after a protracted illness, was "brought on in part by the hardships which he suffered in his flight to Sweden during the German occupation of Denmark."[1] That Rubin was politically a Dane, even a true Danish patriot, is incontestable. His cultural environment may have been largely Danish and partly German, but his lineage must surely be taken into consideration; for a dozen or more generations of heredity are more significant for science than the town or state of one's birth. If the latter were to count, then Külpe, who was born in a town in Courland, should be spoken of as a Latvian.

Of all people, the psychologist should be the least concerned with the formalities of the bureaus of vital statistics and naturalization. Let us admit that the studious concealment of minority affiliations is a symptom of discrimination. A man cannot consistently be rated as a Dane or a German when his scientific achievement is assessed, and carted off as a Jew to the extermination camps. A true historian should, of course, treat his figures as political phenotypes (Americans, Englishmen, Germans, etc.) but why ignore the genotypical elements

[1] D. Katz: "Edgar Rubin," *Psychological Review,* 1951, vol. 58, p. 387.

which go to make up the nation as a whole? If the Negroes
have been responsible for the development of a new type of
song, like the spirituals, or a new form of musical expression,
like jazz or swing, why not mention the fact, even though the
over-all credit goes to the United States? Should the Gypsies
not receive a certain mead of recognition for the music which
they have been instrumental in spreading throughout Central
and Eastern Europe, particularly Hungary and Russia? What
purpose does it serve to distort facts so that a whole situation
is misrepresented?

This is not a question of glory for any particular ethnic
group. It is a scientific requisite, which, as in the case of
Gestalt psychology, does not, at least should not, affect the
status of that particular theory, but it may have a bearing
on certain conclusions in social psychology and anthropology.
The very hiding of the facts is, in itself, a phenomenon which
deserves some study. It is an anomaly which points to an
inferiority feeling, on the one hand, and a power attitude on
the other. The minority member who wants his original
stock to be passed over in silence is afraid lest his success
might not be vouchsafed him. The majority member is prepared to fall in with the wishes of the other, since the
achievement will be another undisputed trophy in the cultural
contest of the powers. It is plainly a fascistic gesture which
befits least of all the scholar or scientist, whose aim should
be one of equity and justice to all. Regrettably, in the history
of science, partiality and bias have been just as rife as in
politics. How many Germans, *e.g.*, would have sided with
those who thought that Newton, and not Leibniz, was the
originator of calculus? Similarly, in the various disputes of
priority, it is very seldom, indeed, that a national of one
country upholds the claims of a scientist in another country,
when there is the slightest doubt to be taken advantage of.

In this light, it is understandable that one of the chief
gestaltists himself, whom the writer had confronted with the
noteworthy circumstance of the movement having been
created by Jews, should have entreated him to make no
mention of the fact. In Germany, certainly the Gestalt school
could have lost some prestige on this ground, but it may well
be imagined that there particularly, such "secrets" would be
ferreted out by means of some Semi-Kürschner, or other
reference work of this type. More instructive was the request
by a renowned psychologist's widow for the present author to

refrain from stating her husband's ethnic origin "as no one is interested in it." The request is strange because "the lady doth protest too much." Many things appear which are uninteresting and even dull, but only the reader has a right, in that event, to complain. The very stress laid on such an "uninteresting" point is proof positive that it is very interesting; and we need not be Freudians to perceive the complex which was bothering that, in other respects, very estimable lady. In other words she wished the matter kept *sub rosa* just because it was exceedingly interesting, and, to the genuine historian, a datum of importance. In referring to this very celebrity, J. McKeen Cattell, who admired him in many ways, was sure to mention his nationality as well as his ethnic stock. The present writer, so far as this method is concerned, is following in the footsteps of Cattell and his great teacher, Francis Galton, and is not heeding emotional requests which are incompatible with the requirements of scientific procedure.

Spiking a Defense Argument

The geopolitical slant in learned circles is perhaps the most perverse of the *idola aulae*, and in the case of Jewish achievement constitutes a sort of negative hallucination brought about in part by the hocus-pocus of Franz Boas, who was frightfully Jew-*un*conscious in his lifelong endeavor to compensate for the "misfortune" of his Jewish birth. His enormous contribution to anthropology—he is without a doubt America's greatest anthropologist—does not cover up the blind spot, so that what he did not (wish to) see went equally unperceived for his intellectual children and grandchildren of whom he had many. On the street level of the common man, the Jew is associated with banking, tailoring, the pawnshop, and commerce in general. On the higher level, the scientist usually retorts, with impatient pride, when approached on this question, that he is not concerned with whether a man is a Jew, a Negro, or a Chinaman, but with his work. We find, however, that his treatment will be studded with references to his own compatriots. This is true for England, France, Germany, Russia, Italy, and the United States. Jews are included, of course—how can their contribution be eliminated?—but they are deprived of their genetic affiliation and treated geopolitically. It is the sharecropper's lot that befalls the Jew who, because he has no land of his own,[2] cannot own anything cultural. The separation of state and religion has been effected. We have yet to separate state and science, so that statehood will not be the essential mark of a specific culture.

The biographer's boner (although happily not every biographer is guilty of it) is often defended on the score that the Jews are solely a religious sect, like the Protestants or the Catholics. Even if this were granted, it behooves us as historians to take into account the possible differences in achievement. If the Mennonites, Seventh Day Adventists, or Shakers should have been the dominant factor in the founding of a new school in science, art, or philosophy, it would be our duty to record and discuss it. Indeed, Boring, in his *History of Experimental Psychology* (2d. ed., p. 453), pauses to ruminate on the difference between Catholic Austria and Southern Germany, on the one hand, and Northern Germany, on the other, in respect of psychological attitude and achievement ("Act fits the Church better than content."). In the case of Jewish scientists, religion may play a minimal part, but the culture of three thousand years may not be without its influence in shaping theories or systems. Whether there is a gene linking in this case, or a family tradition, which, even in the most assimilated homes, has not been entirely eradicated (in fact the suppression or repression might have, as in neurosis, led to definite reversions to pristine ethnic outlooks) is not pertinent at this juncture, when all that one demands is a recognition of the ethnic antecedent as a directive agency in the creative élan.

Finally, let us suppose for a moment that the Jews are not an ethnic unit but a conglomeration of groups, varying in their physical make-up from country to country, it would yet be appropriate to set them off for the record in some such meticulously worded *cave*, as this "so-called Jew" or "Wertheimer, descended of a group X, which is singled out by its co-dwellers in any and every country as Jews," or one might even allude to them as "non-Gentiles," for surely they would be that by definition. If, when a Czech, a Pole, a German, a Dane, a Lithuanian, and a Russian all unite to form a school,

[2] The establishment of a Jewish state does not solve the problem, since (a) it is still in its infancy and (b) it harbors but a fraction of the world's Jewry. Politically Jews are American or French or British, but ethnically they are Jews whether they worship or not. Then, too, (c) Israelis are not necessarily Jews.

and it turns out that they are all "so-called" Jews, then it cannot be a mere coincidence, but we must conclude that the Jewish origin has something to do with the event. Forsooth, if this were a coincidence, then the coincidence itself must be a miracle. Surely, the Jews have as much claim to reality as a mirage or an optical illusion, which is at least discussed.

Boring takes issue with me on the Jewish contribution to Gestalt psychology allegedly because I pick out the Jews and leave out of account the non-Jews, and so he brings in all the pre-Gestaltists and phenomenologists since Goethe, but actually we must confine ourselves to the Gestalt sphere, and here we have Wertheimer, the half-Jew Koffka, Lewin, Katz, Rubin, Goldstein, Gelb, Katona, and the half-Jew, V. Hornbostel—all prominent members of the school originating from different countries but ethnically related, whereas Boring puts 1½ Jews against 1½ Gentiles, which is somewhat reminiscent of the procedure of the butcher who advertised 50% horse and 50% rabbit when he used one horse to one rabbit.

Boring concedes only that "the incidence of Jews in Gestalt psychology is greater than in non-Gestalt psychology" (what about psychoanalysis?) and he proceeds to explain his extrapolation "on the ground that Jews trust one another and are more easily influenced by one another, so that you would expect greater community among Jewish psychologists than among psychologists at large" (*Amer. Journal of Psychology,* vol. 66, p. 653).

Well, I declare that this series of assumptions is harder to gulp down than my intimation that the conceptual constitution of the Jews, linked to some basic intelligence and emotional traits, which vary with different ethnic strains just as in the case of breeds of dogs or cats, tends to make the Jews spread out, thus seeing in the whole, in a larger perspective (analysis following), hence their "diasporation" long before the Roman conquest of Judea, their cosmopolitanism, and their special hankering for global and collective systems. The founders of ethnic psychology were Lazarus and Steinthal in Germany, but in France, Durkheim and Lévy-Bruhl founded the so-called French school in sociology, and, in anthropology, the Jews have furnished a preponderant number of researchers from Lombroso, Boas and Sapir and Goldenwieser to Ruth Benedict. That, of course, does not insure the validity of their views. Let me mention, too, that Jews have yielded hardly any behaviorists or parapsychologists.

Boring wonders what there is common to Gestalt psychology and to Jewish culture. One hint has already been dropped; but my contention is that *unless we record the vital data, we shall never be able to go through with an investigation to prove or disprove my view.*[3] Practically all the investigations involving Jews have been centering on such practical problems as how to stem prejudice or anti-Semitism, but the cultural aspects have been entirely overlooked.

It is quite likely that their trimillennial adherence to monotheism is bound up with the same mentality, and that their mastery in interpretation (whether in literature as critics or in music as virtuosi—most of the great pianists, violinists, and conductors, from Hermann Levi at Bayreuth to Mahler and Monteux and Koussevitsky) stems from their global approach.

It has become fashionable of late to attribute everything to culture, *i.e.*, tradition, but I have dealt with this scientific fad, in which there lurks a begging of the questions, elsewhere.[4]

I don't know how the culture theory can explain why the Jew in every country he resides in serves as an enzyme or catalyst, acts as an intermediary between groups, and has frequently been referred to as the nervous system of the social organism. This is a matter neither for pride nor for shame. It is simply a descriptive fact meriting investigation. Why are different strains of mice more important for study than ethnic groups?

The Beginning of Gestalt Psychology

Gestalt psychology is not an American school or movement, but thanks to the Nuremberg laws decreed by the Nazis, the majority of the leaders migrated to the United States, and their books and articles, their students and disciples, form a segment of American culture, even if it is not the endogenous field which behaviorism or functionalism can claim to be.

The seed of the school was planted by C. v. Ehrenfels

[3] A. A. Roback: "Race and Mode of Expression," *Character and Personality*, 1935, vol. 4. The writer has been able to "guess" the Jewish student from examination books in psychology, from which the names have been removed to the extent that the odds against chance-guessing were a million to three.

[4] A. A. Roback: *Present-day Psychology*, pp. 203-209.

(1859-1932), in Prague, who more than sixty years ago, at about the same time when William James was pondering the same question, asked himself how it is possible to recognize the melody of, say, nine notes, played in the key of C, after hearing these played in a different key, let us say G. The conclusion he came to was that there was in addition to the nine sensory elements, a tenth, which is the form-quality or *Gestaltqualität* of the unit of nine tones. It is through this agency that we are able to perceive the resemblance of the two melodies, although every note in the one series is actually different from the corresponding one in the other. Ehrenfels employed the same logic in dealing with the comparison of geometrical figures, and thus derived two kinds of form-qualities, temporal and non-temporal, or spatial.

Ehrenfels merely went so far as to discover that there was an added element involved in the sequence of tones, but it did not occur to him to junk the tones as elements. The form-quality was just another element, and no more. James, when he stated that "the perceptive state of mind is not a compound" and that the "thing perceived is the object of a unique state of thought . . . in no wise 'containing' psychically the identical 'sensations' and images which these currents would severally have aroused if the others were not simultaneously there" was really more radical than Ehrenfels, but James did not stop to analyze and draw up a terminology as did Ehrenfels. With James, it was a direct intuition which brought him close to the latter gestaltists. Ehrenfels still had a summative frame of mind, yet he had begun to undermine the whole foundation of the elementarists.

It would take us too far afield into the realm of epistemology if we wanted to follow the course of the problem and its sequelae through Meinong, Husserl, and the Austrian *Akt* school. It was not until two decades later that Max Wertheimer (1886-1943) who had come to Frankfurt from Prague, tackled the puzzle and suggested a far-reaching solution, which was to cut across into other topics besides perception. Gestalt psychology was born at the University of Frankfurt, and cradled at the University of Berlin. Certainly it would have no chance at Leipzig, which was the bastion of elementarism and empiricism. Stumpf, the nativist and fusionist, although not a gestaltist himself, could not help, human as he was, encouraging the experiments of the youthful group, including Wertheimer, Köhler, Koffka, and v. Hornbostel who were to upset the Wundtian psychological apple-cart. The University of Berlin had been receptive to the more humanistic aspects of philosophy, and the influence of Wilhelm Dilthey, in the formation of the *Geisteswissenschaften* school had carried over into other disciplines, principally psychology, in which he was greatly interested.

Berlin became a centre for the new ideas revolving around phenomena, whether in history, literature, or philosophy; and *understanding* was given more weight than description in terms of analysis. Curiously enough, the *Struktur* subschool which developed out of this is more aligned with Gestalt psychology than with structuralism, by which label the Wundt-Titchener brand was known. The semantic mix-up is doubtless due to the difference between English and German usage, which sometimes leads to confusion, as in the case of *Selbstbewusstsein* and selfconsciousness, which are almost the antitheses of one another. Somehow the Berlin luminaries wrote comparatively little and did not bother to evolve systems. Stumpf, like Dilthey, might be considered indolent beside Wundt, but their *Abhandlungen* and *Anreden* were something like events in learned circles; for they contained flashes of artistic intuition. They were more in the spirit of William James's writings.

Properties of the Gestalt

Max Wertheimer, after leaving Frankfurt and settling in Berlin, fitted well into this atmosphere. He belonged to the semi-genius class. Indeed, it was said that Einstein, who was a close friend of his, and with whom he had certain idiosyncrasies in common, referred to him as a genius. He was not prolific, never made it a point to produce *en gros*, but worked when the spirit moved him, and undertook such tasks only as might be considered diversions. The toy stroboscope and the tachistoscope, rather than the chronoscope or the mnemometer or the ergograph, were the type of apparatus which he employed, and concentrating on the phenomena of movement, afterwards shortened to "phi phenomena," he was able to establish that this perception is not reducible to a compound of sensory qualities, but is a given experience as such. This was supplemented later by the observation of the *pure* "phi"-phenomenon, where nothing but motion is perceived without any trace of color, shape, etc.

The arena of movement seems to have been the place where the elementaristic ogre was expected to be defeated once and for all; but, incidentally, a psychology of movement was being built up on a large scale. After Wertheimer's "phi" phenomenon, Kurt Koffka (1886-1941) and F. Kenkel ventured out on an explanatory research of different types of motion. Eventually, five types of apparent motion were discovered, after Korte and Linke pursued their investigation further. Of the five, perhaps the "alpha" type, in which changes in the size of parts of the figure occur with certain illusion material, as in the case of the Müller-Lyer figure, and its varieties, and the "gamma" type, which consists in the expansion or contraction of a part of the figure, upon sudden exposure, at withdrawal or change in illumination are the most intriguing.

Proceeding from simple experiments, which the person in the street would look upon as play, Wertheimer traversed a large part of the psychological field, and concentrated on the whole-part relationship, which had been taken for granted on the strength of the axiom that the whole is greater than any of its parts; and on this basis it was believed that the whole is nothing but the summation of its parts. That is just what Wertheimer not only questioned but denied. His scornful "and-combination" phrase was echoed and re-echoed in Gestalt publications until it became a Gestalt *cliché*, while the traditional view that every complex consisted of a number of sensations and residues of past experiences was dubbed the "mosaic" or "bundle" hypothesis. Anything which smacked of piecemeal amalgamation was rejected, and the thesis was propounded that "the given is itself in varying degrees 'structured'; it consists of more or less definitely structured wholes and whole-processes with their whole-properties and laws, characteristic whole tendencies and whole determinants of parts. 'Pieces' almost invariably appear 'as parts' in whole processes."[5]

What Wertheimer wished to emphasize here is that there is a whole-determination in the individual parts, which we should not have otherwise supposed. One is too prone to see how the parts make up the whole, but that each part is the whole in miniature in its structure and taxonomy—that did sound a new note. In a sense, it brought us back to the reversal James suggested in the matter of emotional sequence, but here it was not a question of theory. Through a series of ingenious experiments with lines, dots, various patterns and designs, figures and backgrounds, the gestaltists were able to show that a part tends to become a totality in a specific way, that dots and lines group themselves, that figures with loose ends will somehow in perception take on the shape of a closed unit (*closure factor*). It has been found that there are strong configurations, or Gestalten, and weak ones, that Gestalten will range themselves as a hierarchy where the general Gestalt may be weak, and the subforms comparatively strong. There are other properties which recommend themselves to the apprehender. Symmetry is one of them, but Wertheimer takes the trouble to caution us that this characteristic signifies not only homologous or equidistant parts, but rather a logical correctness in the relationship of part to whole, or vice versa.

Equilibrium is another very important feature of the Gestalt —its *Prägnanz*, a term which is difficult to translate into English, and perhaps that is why it is missing in Warren's *Dictionary of Psychology*. Every Gestalt has its own character of definiteness or indefiniteness and seems to waver in quest of attaining equilibrium or homeostasis, which would constitute the normal phase. This stability or regularity, or even simplicity in the sense of plainness rather than indivisibility, may be considered its Prägnanz, quite different from our English word "pregnance." There may be different stages of stability, *e.g.*, when we are unable to say what is out of kilter with a certain Gestalt, although we perceive that is is not quite right. We may speak of "good" and "poor" Gestalten, and even of a "common destiny" factor in the configuration, when a shifted arrangement of dots seems to take a rebellious stand, and ranges itself anew in our sight. In the organization of the Gestalt, proximity or, at times, similarity, may have its share, but it may be a curve which decides its fate. It would appear at first blush that Wertheimer is anthropomorphizing a mere pattern, but to one who is fundamentally a phenomenologist, like Wertheimer, the charge would be almost meaningless.

While Wertheimer was working away at Frankfurt and Berlin, David Katz and, more specifically, Edgar Rubin, at Göttingen, were busy, in their own way, preparing the material which would promote the cause of Gestalt psychology. Katz

(1884-1953) who took refuge in Sweden, where he became Director of the Psychological Laboratory at Stockholm, has been a prolific contributor to various branches of psychology, but his studies on the color sense and his experiments on chickens were particularly of service to Gestalt psychology. In one sense, Katz started to roll the holistic log, which represents configurationism even before Wertheimer, for in 1911, he published his theory of perception as applied to illumination. His researches on the sense of touch brought him even closer to the Gestalt point of view and his analysis of adjustment in hunger dealt with the whole organism. Child psychology was another field Katz cultivated on Gestalt principles. Katz, who, for a year, was visiting professor at the University of Maine, did not belong to the inner sanctum of the Gestalt group, but has since taken a more active part, and has recently brought out an English edition of a little book on Gestalt psychology, in which he goes along with the school, and recounts with characteristic clarity the special advantages of field theory in psychology. As to Rubin, his goblet silhouette has become almost a proprietary article. He, too, was not officially a member of the Gestalt School, but his experiments on visual figures, published in book form, in 1921, were a distinct contribution to Gestalt psychology. His thorough investigation of the relation between figure and ground was an added feather in the Gestalt cap, besides adding to our knowledge of reversive preception. Rubin only visited the United States, in 1929, on the occasion of the International Congress of Psychology at Yale.

The Gestalt Personnel and Division of Labor

It would be possible to envisage the Gestalt group, consisting of only a few leaders, as a sort of government, with Wertheimer, as the president, by virtue of his authority and potential, more than actual, achievement. It must be remembered that Wertheimer inaugurated the school, while both Köhler and Koffka, his juniors, were his able adjutants, and soon became, in this cabinet, respectively the premier and minister of foreign affairs. Köhler also functioned as minister of the interior; for his contacts in Berlin were fortunate, especially after succeeding Stumpf at the University of Berlin, at the age of 35. Köhler had already published his *magnum opus. Die physischen Gestalten in Ruhe und in stationärem*

Zustand was subtitled "an inquiry into natural philosophy," and it certainly deserved the general subtitle; for it is a miscellany of physics and physiology, interlarded with closely reasoned premises, every other one of which might be called in question by opponents.

Why should a psychologist write a book on physics as his most ambitious production? Ostensibly, "because in order to orient itself in the company of natural sciences, psychology must discover connections wherever it can between its own phenomena and those of the older disciples [and] if this search fails, then psychology must recognize that its categories and those of [the] natural sciences are incommensurable,"[6] and further, because "in physics, the mode of thinking suitable for Gestalt problems is induced by *experience* itself . . .; until recently it has been impossible to give conclusive answers to the speculations of additive thinking; now, however, from physics comes evidence to demonstrate the errors of such thinking" (p. 169).

We may, however, look for another motive and that is the thorough training in physics which Köhler received under such teachers as Max Planck, who greatly influenced him. Köhler prided himself on his understanding of physics, and more than once would answer a psychological question by a referral to physics. When he first visited America in 1925, a conference at Clark University on Gestalt psychology attracted a number of psychologists from around Boston. A young instructor, at the close of the session, interposed some objection to a rather complicated explanation on the part of Köhler, which brought the retort, "That's because you don't know physics." The urbane Koffka, sitting beside Köhler, whispered something to his colleague, who later came over to apologize for his brusqueness, or perhaps impertinence, in its etymological and stricter sense.

In Köhler's *Die physischen Gestalten*, which is more ponderous in content than in bulk, we have an attempt to extend the field theory into psychology, and to show that even in physics, always thought to be molecular, in essence, there is a molar superstructure; and furthermore that H_2O is not merely the addition of the properties of hydrogen to those of oxygen, but an entirely new product, a new Gestalt. And from the molar conception of physics, it was easy to make the transition

[6] W. Köhler: *Die physischen Gestalten,* etc., 1920, pp. 10-11.

to a molar aspect of behavior, which differs *toto coelo* from the molecular muscle-gland-reflex behavior of Watson's school, which equated conscious phenomena with its presumed physiological correlates; and upon doing so, dumped the conscious phenomena altogether. The gestaltists developed a theory of isomorphism, according to which the arrangement of the brain processes corresponds in structure to the actual experiences (thoughts, feelings). Hence the whole body-mind problem is bypassed in Gestalt psychology, and the matter-consciousness dichotomy loses its significance in the Gestalt organization.

Köhler's experiments with chimpanzees on Teneriffe, the report of which appeared for the first time, in 1917, then to be translated into English (two editions and several printings) as well as into French and Spanish, sought to prove that primates possessed insight; and since Sultan was able, without fumbling and groping, to fit one bamboo cane inside another, or set one box on top of another to serve as a scaffolding, in order to reach a banana, the consequence is drawn that the ape visualized a certain Gestalt.

Köhler's productivity lagged somewhat after settling in the United States, as Professor at Swarthmore College. Aside from his William James Lectures, which he delivered in 1934 and published, in 1938, under the title of *The Place of Value in a World of Fact*, he gave us a general survey of the school, in his *Gestalt Psychology*, in 1929; and in 1940, he developed some of the special theories in *Dynamics in Psychology*. There is nothing voluminous about his output.

Koffka, on the other hand, was the systematizer of the School. Developmental psychology was his specialty, and his *Growth of the Mind*, which appears to be more than a mere translation of the German work under a similar title, was his first introduction to the academic reader in this country, although it was not his début in English. An all-inclusive exposition of the movement is contained in his chief work, *Principles of Gestalt Psychology*, a book of over 700 pages (1935) which belongs, with some of Titchener's, Baldwin's, Thorndike's, and Troland's work, to the fundamental psychological productions in the United States. Whether we are disposed to accept the system or not hardly matters in this case. There is, for one thing, a mine of information in the book, both historical and constructive, and the keen analysis of many of the problems is refreshing, even if the vigorous argumentation occasionally diverts us from the course pursued.

In our cabinet analogy, Hans Gruhle and Kurt Goldstein, who were the psychopathologists and neurologists of the school might be regarded as the ministers of health. Both served as co-editors of *Psychologische Forschung*. The former's relationship to the School, to judge from his writings —and they were many, largely articles—was not close, and his subsequent status is problematic. Goldstein, however, after migrating to the United States, did not cease upholding the Gestalt position. Both in his book *The Organism; A Holistic Approach to Biology* (1939, originally published in German) and in his William James Lectures, which came out, in 1940, under the title of *Human Nature in the Light of Psychopathology*, he stresses the holistic point of view, adducing evidence, in these volumes as well as in his latest work, *Language and Language Disturbances* (1948), from clinical cases.

Kurt Lewin, who was the youngest of the Gestalt leaders, might have been considered as the minister of justice, as the whole field of personality and motivation was left to him, not that Koffka ignored that segment of experience, but since Lewin had done such a good job on that end of the Gestalt axis, Koffka would try to bring his own results into the framework of Lewin's dynamic system. Lewin, subsequently, while still identified with the Gestalt movement, succeeded in forming a subschool of his own, under the aegis of topology. The "field theory," however, which his subschool goes by, is common to Gestalt psychology as a whole, although it is more appropriate in the sphere of personality than in, let us say, memory.

Rubin and Katz, if not ministers without portfolio, could be envisaged as allies abroad or as ministers plenipotentiary. Katz, moreover, in his compact little volume, *Gestalt Psychology; Its Nature and Significance*, which will have appeared in seven languages, including Finnish, has given us a bird's-eye view of the Gestalt doctrine as applied to most of the departments of psychology and several of its branches. Its greatest virtue is its clarity but it is also comprehensive, even if circumscribed in the specific topics presented.

Division of Labor

The Gestalt School was ideal in that its members coöperated harmoniously, and there was no domination by any one of them. In other words, it represented a strong Gestalt, intrinsically well organized and explicitly articulated, as if by tacit agreement. Wertheimer was the epistemologist of the group, being at home in logic and mathematics. He operated best in the abstract realm; nonetheless his experimental adventures turned out to be very concrete. Köhler had a firm grip on the physical sciences; and his investigations on auditory perception, prompted by Stumpf's longstanding interests, could scarcely have been carried out without a more than bowing acquaintance with physics. But Köhler was also an animal psychologist, and his experiments on apes are more widely quoted than anything else he wrote. He also showed that hens react to relations between greys rather than to specific greys.[7]

Koffka's endeavors lay chiefly in genetic and educational psychology, but, as has already been intimated, he was a systematizer also, conversant with the situation in general, whether it was memory, the self, or group psychology. Both he and Köhler were able polemicists. Of late, Köhler has given up his bouts with opponents and is content with exposition. Lewin was the specialist in the affective field, embracing tensions, needs, desires, the will, and personality as a whole. A deft experimentalist, he and his students would obtain neat results, which were often crystallized in a diagrammatic manner, but, in any case, so lucidly handled as to almost compel acceptance. Lewin may be looked upon as the methodologist of the group and his essay in which he contrasted Aristotle's and Galileo's procedures, showing the superiority of the latter, brought him considerable recognition as an acute discerner of fundamentals. It may be an exaggeration to place him beside Freud in significance, as Tolman did, yet there was something in common about their intuitive grasp, although their systems had no point of incidence, except that they both operated in a dynamic sphere. Goldstein, as a trained neurologist, was in charge of the biological department of the school, and although his clinical cases furnished him much of the material for his books, it was Hans Gruhle, who managed the psychiatric end of the Gestalt School, perhaps not in the zealous fashion of the others; for he may have been a figurehead, like some of the directors or sponsors of a club. Hornbostel was the aesthetician (musical investigator) of the group.

The students and junior associates of the Gestalt leaders

[7] W. Köhler: *Abhandl. d. preussischen Akad. d. Wissensch.* (math.-phys. sect.), 1915, pp. 70-80.

were, of course, assigned problems along the lines of interest evinced in their laboratories or institutions. *Psychologische Forschung*, which circulated from 1921 to 1938, when even Köhler, the "Aryan," began to experience great difficulty in editing it from America, was in the way of eclipsing the older psychological periodicals, when it ceased publication.

The very name *Psychologische Forschung* was something of an innovation; for this substantive was one used particularly by the physical and natural scientists. The whole title was concrete and direct—no *Zeitschrift* or *Archiv* introducing it. Finally, the singular—"Inquiry," instead of the plural, as in the case of other periodicals, which use a similar term, like *Studien, Arbeiten, Untersuchungen,* would imply that there is no division of the task into cut-and-dried elementary units, but that it was to be envisaged as a continuous pursuit of knowledge without any artificial boundaries. The editing of such a journal, running into twenty odd volumes, was an achievement in itself, and the fact that there was no editorial friction, as we have seen it to happen in the early days of American psychological periodicals, is an indication of the smooth collaboration of the Gestalt pioneers.

Affinities with other Schools

Let us now see where Gestalt psychology stands in relation to other, principally American, schools. It has been generally thought by the average psychologist that the chief target of the new school was structuralism or atomistic psychology, and that behaviorism is somewhat closer to it; but, if anything, we might say that it is more at odds with the muscle-gland psychology than with elementarism. For the mere stimulus-response behavior which the American objectivists were constantly appealing to, besides having all the objectionable features of elementarism in Wundt's or Titchener's system, ignores the relational field, which gives meaning to the behavior, and, in addition, deliberately discards the conscious factor which is an essential part of the field. Fully one-quarter of Köhler's *Gestalt Psychology* is devoted to combatting behaviorism and exposing its flaws. At the time the book was in process, behaviorism was riding high on the American campus. It seemed to carry, in its stock-in-trade slogans, the solution to all problems. It was, therefore, incumbent upon Köhler to show up the follies of this purely mechanistic school, which, during those days, was wielding so much influence for various reasons. In the square of opposition, in formal logic, some propositions might be opposed to one another, while others are contradictory. Applied to schools, the analogy would find Gestalt psychology diametrically opposed to behaviorism, but only antagonistic to traditional psychology.

Functionalism, on the other hand, as has been noted in an earlier chapter, is a forerunner of the Gestalt conception; for it, too, placed the organism within a field, *viz.*, the environment. Functionalism concerned itself with individual differences. "If two animals behave differently under similar stimulus conditions," observes Koffka, "then the explanation must be in the animals themselves; they are either by innate endowment or by previous experience so different from each other that the one behaves in one way; the other in another."[8] Koffka here wishes to differentiate between their mere geographical behavior and their molar behavior, *e.g.*, when one ape will use a box as a stool for a footing and the other uses it as a seat, which is a difference not in the geographical but in the behavioral environment. In the last analysis, the geographical type is a physical matter—only a construct, while the behavioral type is one that is fraught with meaning to the animal, a datum or phenomenon, which signifies a something-to-do. There is still another common denominator between the functionalists and gestaltists: they are both willing to annul the gulf between mind and body without compunction. This point will be further referred to in the next paragraph.

Neo-realism is a philosophical rather than a psychological school, although E. B. Holt, a psychologist, was one of its founders. The gestaltists, we must bear in mind, have been greatly encouraged or inspired by certain philosophers, like Husserl, who was genuinely admired by the neo-realists. What finally united the philosophical group at Harvard-Yale-Columbia and the Berlin-Frankfurt-Giessen band was the neutralization of the body-mind territory. At a neo-realist seminar, the uninitiated students would be stunned to hear the statement that when you are thinking of the Andes, then your mind is there, and when you picture the North Pole, the next moment, your mind is at the North Pole. What a stretch to

8 K. Koffka: *Principles of Gestalt Psychology*, 1935 (1st ed.), p. 30.

travel in a second's time, even if the mind could disengage itself from the interior of the skull? But that is just what the neo-realists wished to inculcate into their students, to wit, that the mind is *not* located in the brain. In this connection, then, it is interesting to see that Koffka takes refuge behind a phenomenological screen which was always flaunted by neo-realism, *i.e.*, when it was still alive. Koffka asks, "But in my distinction of geographical and behavioral environment, admittedly equivalent to that of reality and appearance [Koffka should have been more guarded, using terms less deceptive, perhaps such as 'physicality' and 'phenomenon,' to distinguish between the inferred or measured reality of the physicist and the immediately given of experience] have I not smuggled in consciousness through the back door? . . . If we are forced to introduce the concept of consciousness, we have to accept it, whether we like it or not. But it is important to note that the *word* consciousness does not change the *meaning* of our own term, behavioral environment . . . Thus the dog's consciousness in chasing a hare would be 'a hare running through the field,' the ape's consciousness, in trying to obtain the suspended fruit, would be 'a stool standing in that corner.' The field and the hare, the stool and the fruit, by being called conscious, or objects of consciousness, must not therefore be considered as something *within* the animal, if this has the meaning of a behavioral, or experienced, within" (*loc. cit.*, p. 35).

Gestalt psychology may be regarded as a species of dynamic psychology, certainly not less dynamic than Woodworth's brand. Köhler continually refers to it as dynamic, but more as the term is understood in physics. Certainly the whole field theory, with its forces, vectors, valences, *Prägnanz*, etc., gives it the aspect of an energy system. It is in the domain of personality reactions (attitudes, desires, intentions, volitions) that the dynamic character comes to full focus, for tension is the core of it. Yet even Lewin's dynamic structure scarcely abuts on the cathedral which psychoanalysis has built up. In the most comprehensive and bulkiest volume of the whole movement, Koffka's *Principles of Gestalt Psychology*, Freud's name appears but once, and that, too, in a more or less casual connection.

The libido, so vivid and colorful and ubiquitous in the Freudian camp, is so puny here that it attracts no attention among the gestaltists. It is a different child we see through

Freud's colored glasses and through Koffka's and Lewin's frosted spectacles. The unconscious holds neither fascination nor terror for the Gestalt psychologist.

As for hormic psychology, one might see a link between the two schools in the function of the goal-striving, but none of the gestaltists favor the vitalistic principle which is implied in the *hormé*. While gestaltists disclaim the mechanistic label, they would be equally averse to postulating an *élan* of some kind which forces us to do certain things. The instinct theory is grudgingly accepted, in principle, because the stimulus-response-through-conditioning account is, from the nature of common observation, unsuitable, but the gestaltist, in order to avoid investing the organism, especially the animal, with some mystic attribute which drives it in a specific direction, shifts the weight to the provocative or demand character of the object (food, the opposite sex, plaything). Whether that changes the situation is a real question; for it may well be asked: Why should a mink coat, or money, or a book have this demand character for one individual and not for another?

The conditioning theory, while scarcely valid in the majority of cases, at least makes an attempt to explain. That is true of the Freudian analysis. So does the instinct theory, which in addition, has the support of geneticists, but the valence view which adopts neither the one explanation nor the other, it would seem, hangs in midair. The dynamics of the moment, or Koffka's "ego stresses," could rest only on a capricious interplay between organism and object in the dynamic field. It may be added that Gestalt psychology, by way of analogy, comports well with the all-or-none principle which Keith Lucas and E. D. Adrian discovered to operate in the excitation of muscle and nerve fibres, and that the at least partial reversal of the earlier findings of functional localization in the brain, by S. I. Franz and K. S. Lashley, is also a good omen in keeping with the holistic contention of the gestaltists. The law of mass action and the principle of equipotentiality which permits of vicarious functioning are at any rate not incompatible with the isomorphic theory of Wertheimer and Köhler, according to whom, the pattern of processes in the brain corresponds to the phenomenological field pattern. Finally, if we accept the doctrine of formal discipline in education, the totality of the individual's behavior must be a presupposition in the case.

The Status of Gestalt Psychology in America

We now come to the final question of our discussion: to what extent has the movement, a foreign importation, progressed in the United States? That it has had to struggle to gain a foothold may be taken for granted, for in the '20's, behaviorism was riding on a crest of stimulus-response jargon. Anything which savored of a philosophical ingredient—and no one can really fathom the underlying principles of a Gestalt psychology without having had a philosophical training of some sort—was summarily dismissed as speculative or metaphysical; and there was altogether too much argumentation in the writings of Köhler and Koffka, and too little diagrammatic schematization, a mode of exposition to which the younger American psychologists have been accustomed from their college days.

Furthermore, the rows of figures and statistical procedures, which the psychologist of several decades back had so much confidence in, were conspicuously absent in the published investigations of *Psychologische Forschung*; and lacking quantitative treatment, some of the American readers would shrug their shoulders. Add to this the linguistic difficulty, before this country, as a result of the global wars, became somewhat language-conscious. German, it is true, had been a requisite for all Ph.D. candidates, but the Gestalt vocabulary was not easy to grapple with, and secondary sources were few then.

On the other hand, there was something attractive about the novel situations in Gestalt experimentation. The results were suggestive, the interpretation was stimulating. Certainly, there was more creativeness involved in the ingenuity of the technique, simple though it was, than in the elaborate and long drawn-out experiments requiring complicated apparatus and many months of drudgery in the average American laboratory. The pictorial representation of the theory was now furnished by Kurt Lewin, at least, who was able to state his case with great aplomb without indulging in tilts with others. The figures and patterns which comprised the actual material of Gestalt experimentation were, of course, fascinating, and were put into the category of optical illusions and tricks, which are always intriguing even to the scientist. But until Lewin's conational work became known as a phase of the Gestalt design, the purport of the school was missed by most

American psychologists, who supposed that it was dealing exclusively with perception and, after all, one department in psychology would not justify the creation of a new school. It was only after Koffka, in 1935, showed the almost all-embracing nature of its fundamentals that Gestalt psychology was revealed as a complete system on a par with Wundt's.

The Personal Equation and the Course of Events

The school also was fortunate in its auspicious conjunctures. First, there were the contacts made, even during the student days, of gestaltists. A number of American students and professorial visitors to the laboratory of the University of Berlin met or worked under the leaders of the Gestalt school. A definite rapport was established when Koffka arrived in the United States, in 1924, primarily to study the country, and soon found himself engaged in teaching, first at Cornell, then at the University of Wisconsin, and finally winding up as professor at Smith College, where he died. The following year, Köhler came to America as a visiting lecturer. He might have become McDougall's successor at Harvard, if he had his mind set on it, but the Berlin post, in 1926, when McDougall was preparing to leave for Duke University, still meant more than a professorship at Harvard; and the Nazi menace, at the time, was hardly more than a chimera. Now that both Koffka and Köhler, the two most vocal members of the school, were both in this country, going from university to university and addressing conferences, it was inevitable that the new slant should make its appeal in certain quarters, at any rate, and Koffka in particular, made an excellent missionary, even if the proselytes were restricted to a few campuses.

Koffka, who as a child had an English governess and, therefore, spoke English almost without an accent, unless it was British, was a man of wide culture, and had all the marks of good breeding. Polished in manner, he gave the impression of the artist rather than the scientist. In physiognomy, he might have been taken for an Italian, but the family must have come originally from Czechoslovakia, as the name, no doubt cognate with a more famous one in our own day, Kafka, would indicate. There was a feminine delicacy tinged with melancholy in his make-up, although there was nothing effeminate about him, least of all about his style of writing. To look at Köhler, on the other hand, you might think that he was about to click his heels together. At least that was the feeling one got in 1925, when he had just come to this country. His jolliness, however, his *camaraderie*, and his adaptability, not to mention his extraordinary alertness and brilliance as a scientist, soon made him *persona grata* in psychological council halls. He returned to Germany, leaving many friends here, and, as with the rise of Hitler's power, Köhler's associates were to be removed from the university as "non-Aryans," let alone the worse fate that was in store for them and their "non-Aryan" fellows in other walks, no doubt the invitation to deliver the William James lectures at Harvard, in 1934, came in the nick of time, especially as the audacious opinion which Köhler voiced in the Berlin daily, would, however muffled in tone, not have improved his standing with the Nazi gang. The following year, he was appointed to the chair in psychology at Swarthmore College—perhaps a far cry from the Berlin professorship which he had held previously, nevertheless a satisfactory post under the circumstances.

Wertheimer preceded Köhler, and luckily found a haven in the New School for Social Research, although he would have been an ornament in any institution. Wertheimer, too, in addition to his prodigious intellect, possessed fine personal qualities. Gaunt and, in appearance, more the Czech provincial than the German professor, he always seemed somewhat detached and preoccupied, but without a trace of formality, pose, or affectation. It was, in fact, his natural simplicity which endeared him to his students. His output was small but his mental intake and its exploitation must have compensated for it, so far as he was concerned; else he could not have been held in such deference by both Koffka and Köhler. Kurt Lewin, perhaps the least prepossessing of the group physically, seems to have acquired, by virtue of his ebullience, congeniality, and accommodatingness, more close friends than any of his Gestalt colleagues. Probably, too, the most dynamic of them, he expended more energy than the others, always working at high tension. The fourth of the group, Kurt Goldstein, may be characterized as a quiet, unassuming, and helpful man who would naturally be well liked, although, being reserved, he could not obtain the wide hearing which his fellow-gestaltists would be assured of.

Boring is inclined to treat Lewin as apart from the Gestalt group on the ground that he was a dynamic psychologist. That he certainly was, but then so might Köhler and Koffka be designated; for they were constantly speaking of the "mental dynamics" of a situation. Lewin took over the "field theory" from his senior colleagues, and expanded it while applying it to the sphere which he concentrated in, *viz.*, personality and motivation. Naturally, it is here that dynamics operates most typically. The topological subschool which formed around Lewin is nothing other than an extension of the general school into a special department. At no time was Lewin repudiated by his fellow-gestaltists.

With such a quartet in the United States coöperating in a common cause, it is not difficult to understand why Gestalt psychology became widely known throughout the country. It was a splendid team, disciplined from within, and therefore displaying none of the prima donna traits and personal differences which had been the bane of similar undertakings. Had these men been purveyors of Taoism or Rosicrucianism, they would have secured a hearing too, but the article they offered possessed a positive valence, to use their own terminology, for those who had become surfeited with the empty S-R formula; and in spite of the minimizing efforts of both behaviorists and structuralists on the score that there was nothing new in it, the gestaltists succeeded in spreading the gospel even in outlying regions.

Informal Demonstrations

For one thing, they did not confine their methods to the laboratory or the class room. Their principles were demonstrated on all sorts of odd occasions. Just as Houdini did not wait to regale his hosts or guests, as the case might be, until they were members of the audience watching a performance, but would "break off" his thumb and put it together before their eyes and those of the stunned waiter in the restaurant or tea room, while ordering from the menu, so the gestaltists, like the medieval jongleurs, would mystify casual groups with their bag of tricks, improvised nevertheless, and would receive acclaim, at least for the exhibition. So it was with Lewin, who proved, to the satisfaction of his friends, that the waiter, after discharging his duty and with it the tension, could not remember the amount of the check which he knew so well only a very short time ago; and thus Wertheimer, on a more complex and larger scale, brought to the attention of a group of psychologists, standing around between sessions, a phenomenon which must have given them much food for thought, perhaps more than the formally presented papers.

This *divertissement* took place at the Dartmouth meeting of the American Psychological Association, in 1936. The session had come to a close, and a number of the crowd were lingering, or perhaps loitering, in the hall conversing. Without warning, Wertheimer sat down at the piano and played a rather complex and still somewhat familiar melody. He then asked whether any one of the auditors could identify it. It was Haydn's haunting air which is associated generally with *Deutschland, Deutschland über alles.* Any one with a "good ear" for music certainly could have picked out the dominant *motif* from the figuration in which it was encased.

The next demonstration was, from the nature of the case, not so convincing, yet, in a way, more significant. Wertheimer asked three of us to serve as subjects in a matching experiment, with all the rest as observers (*i.e.*, auditors). He played three improvised tunes, each one of which was to characterize a different personality, and he asked for a vote by a show of hands as to which matched which. Most likely, none of the trio was known to Wertheimer and, on the supposition that the external appearance of each could be the only criterion for such correspondence, the majority, including the present writer, who was a subject at the same time, chose the pretty young woman as embodying the most strikingly melodious and lively of the three tunes. Apparently, however, it was not intended that way. It took a whole year for your author to broach the subject in a letter to the founder of Gestalt psychology, whom he had never met personally; and it took another year for Wertheimer to answer the question posed in that communication. Perseveration apparently was strong in both to keep the tension from petering out during such a long interval. Wertheimer's reply is important enough to be cited in a chapter on Gestalt psychology, and as the answers would scarcely be intelligible without the original letter which prompted them, it would be necessary to include it.

Aug. 25, 1937

Dear Dr. Wertheimer:

Ever since your informal demonstration of Gestalt psychology last year at Dartmouth, when you flattered me greatly by matching a very pretty improvised tune against my personality, although I took it to represent the young blooming girl standing next to me, I had been thinking about this little experiment off and on. The following queries have occurred to me.

(1) Does the sight of the individual inspire a certain tune in a musical person?

(2) On subsequent occasions, would the same or a similar tune occur on seeing the same individual?

(3) What criterion of objectivity is there, *e.g.*, if the majority of listeners should vote the correspondence of a given tune with A's personality, who would be the arbiter?

(4) Would the particular make-up of the group have something to do with the relative melodiousness of the improvised tunes? Thus, if A were at first in an inferior group and then placed in a superior group, would there not be a different musical inspiration?

Can you refer me to the literature dealing with experiments of this type? I am interested for more than one reason.

It took me all this time to decide to write, as I was chary about bothering you on a matter which may seem to arise out of personal curiosity.

July 15, 1938

REPLY

Dear Dr. Roback:

I shall *try* to answer the questions of your letter. 1. It sometimes does, especially with regard to some character-qualities of the melody. I mean that often one feels to some degree free in choosing or making the concrete melody, but feels bound or directed toward making a melody with certain character-qualities, somewhat "identical" with the felt character of the person, not on the basis of formulated traits but as the result of "fitting in" to the character of the personality. In most experiments that I did the problem was somewhat easier: if you play three persons in succession for guessing, then *differences* in the character-qualities are often the goal and are often sufficient. The goal is then not to render just this character, but to express differences.

2. *Not* the same melody, unless by chance the first melody was "so good" in itself that it is remembered. Mostly subsequent characterizations differ widely in terms of notes,

etc., but not so in their character-qualities of being gentle, brute, aggressive, energetic, and so on. Sometimes there are some changes in this regard too, which seem to depend upon the changing of the other persons in the group of three, and upon the selection of another side of the character, another *aspect*.

3. There are criteria of different character. First, the goal to get near 100% agreement in the votes, and if not, to try to improve the playing in this direction. Second, a help of clarification: the observers (or the judges) are asked to describe their ideas of the person—see the method in the paper of Arnheim of dealing with "mistakes." Thirdly, I developed several methods to compare objectively the "Gestalt Criteria" of the music, or rhythm played on the one hand (like, for example, simplicity, complicatedness, sudden increases, equality in the passage of time, one-directed increase of the time and intensity, etc.), with similar Gestalt criteria characteristic of the behavior of the person. (Of course, the two sets of judgments were entirely separated.) The ideal criterion (which was reached sometimes very well) is then the question of what I have called "Gestalt-character-identity" in both cases. (See: *Ueber Gestalttheories*.)

4. Yes.

5. For literature, at first I would suggest the book of G. W. Allport. Specifically I could mention only at the moment the papers of Arnheim, Wolff, von Hornbostel, and Klüver.

I am sorry that I did not publish more of my various experiments. I did it only in lectures. Maybe I will get some time to bring them into shape and publish them. I would hope that we would meet sometime soon; then I could tell you more concerning the questions in which you are interested.

I am sorry for the delay, but I was terribly busy.

Yours sincerely,

Gestalt Psychology: Success or Failure—

This caption is the direct result of Boring's opinion that "Gestalt psychology . . . is now dying of its success by being absorbed into what is Psychology" (*History*, etc., 2d ed., p. 600). This raises the question as to what extent the movement is actually dying. Naturally with three of its chief proponents and promoters out of the picture, it has sustained an irretrievable loss, but what constitutes the success of a school or an idea?

The vicissitudes of Gestalt psychology are truly of a fateful character. Had Hitler not come to power during the period when the movement was expanding, and had the Nuremberg laws not been enacted or enforced with such rigorous consistency and efficiency, the impact of the new school might have been no greater than that of the Würzburg school. A number of American students, while in Berlin or Frankfurt, might have become enthusiastic about the new doctrine sufficiently to incorporate it eventually into their textbooks or experimental investigations. Even before Koffka settled in the United States, there might have been one or two Gestalt islands in this country; e.g., at Cornell, in the very stronghold of elementarism, R. M. Ogden was favoring the holistic approach. When, however, a whole school, at any rate its entire leadership, is transplanted and begins to function as a unit, it is no longer an importation, but becomes a domestic product, enjoying all the advantages of the American-born schools.

The advent of gestaltism has been salutary for the course of psychology in our midst. It has served to stem the tide of the plodding and sterile pseudo-simplification we have been subjected to, and, pitting the creative spirit against a stodgy habit-conception of phenomena, it has shed considerable light on the thought processes. The formation of a new organization in place of the retraced past occurrence, as a tenet of the Gestalt school, has been instrumental in opening up new avenues of research, e.g., in memory, it lends support to F. C. Bartlett's conclusion that "remembering appears to be far more decisively an affair of construction than one of mere reproduction,"[9] Similarly there were novel observations in regard to learning, in the application of the Gestalt idea to group psychology, the distinction between the psychological and the sociological group, as also the development of the "ego stress" view in place of the instinct theory.

We can readily perceive that the gestaltian protest has been instrumental in ploughing up the soil anew, injecting fresh

[9] F. C. Bartlett: Remembering; A Study in Experimental and Social Psychology, 1932, p. 205.

vitamins into the soggy parts. It proved an antidote to the unfounded assumptions transmitted from one generation of psychologists to another. Sometimes one hears complaints about the multiplication of schools in psychology. It were a good deal worse, if a traditional line were permitted to perpetuate its errors without the possibility of correction, not merely in regard to a few specific details, but all along the line. That would be analogous to an authoritarian form of government. We are beholden to the theoretical innovators just because, bent upon proving the validity of their theory, they will employ all means at their disposal, both in the formulation of experimental problems and the contrivance of techniques, to substantiate their theories, while putting to the test the ones generally received. What is more, they will have been on the alert to observe phenomena which might not register with those of other schools.

"A new broom sweeps clean" not only because it is fuller and better equipped than the old worn one, but also because the sweeper knows that he has a better tool, and is keener on doing a good job. Every innovator must, of course, have well in hand all that has gone before, and only then is he justified in proposing something new, which ultimately means that he sees better or farther than his predecessor. One asset of the Gestalt school is that its founders have compelled us to examine concepts afresh, and to analyse them in a more or less logical framework. That has often been distasteful to pure experimentalists, who were interested in quantities, and would thus turn to statistics, shunning all qualitative differentiation as quibbling or so much verbiage, and when their conclusions were called in question, on that score, they would not bother considering the objections. The analytic acumen displayed by the chief representatives of the school has been of great service in threshing out issues which ordinarily might be accepted "on principle."[10]

[10] In this connection it is instructive to learn from S. A. Goudsmith's *Alsos* (1951, p. 243) that "another typically German attitude detrimental to their progress was the hero worship of individual scientists. The admiration which his colleagues rightly had for the great physicist, Heisenberg, went so far as to prevent them from thinking critically about his work." The result was, according to Goudsmith, that this deference to authority retarded the work of producing the atom bomb in Germany, while on our side there was a more democratic and coöperative attitude on the part of the collaborators.

If Gestalt psychology is dying, as Boring wishes to have us believe, because it is being absorbed into general psychology, then it is very much alive, for what benefit would there be in remaining a school in the periphery? Is there any school which lives on long enough, without being absorbed, forming the flesh and bone of the science to which it is billeted? To adapt a commonplace from Ecclesiastes,

> *Schools may come and schools may go;*
> *Science lives forever.*

and Gestalt psychology has been but a school. However, the crux of the matter is that it has gained *entrée* into the general body of facts despite the overwhelming antagonism of the old settlers. If American psychology, which is predominantly mechanistic, has adopted only a small portion of the Gestalt system, then it is something of a triumph for the latter. It has had many critics, both abroad and in this country, among them G. E. Müller, in whose laboratory at Göttingen, Rubin and Katz prepared the early experimental material for the school; V. Benussi, E. Rignano, K. Bühler, Wm. McDougall, and others, but its teachings took a firm hold in more than a few American colleges and universities, *e.g.,* Kansas, Duke, the Universities of California and Arizona. At Princeton, H. S. Langfeld, who was a student in Stumpf's laboratory when Koffka, Köhler and v. Hornbostel worked there, has been sympathetic to the school, and at Harvard, G. W. Allport may be said to lean toward it (undivided personality, generality of traits). And, of all places, Cornell, for decades, had a welcome nook for it in Ogden's courses, although, lest we assume that Cornell has capitulated to its old foe, it must be announced that the latest onslaught against the configurationists (to use Titchener's term) has come from one of the younger generation at Cornell, J. J. Gibson, who, in an article in which a dozen different species of forms, divided into three classes, are defined and described, comes to the conclusion that "there is no such thing as form-in-general with the universal characteristics ascribed to it by Gestalt theories," and predicts that "the effort to determine what happens in the brain when one perceives form-in-general will prove to be fruitless."[11]

Gestalt psychology invaded American colleges when behaviorism was in its heyday, and Boring seems to think that

[11] J. J. Gibson: "What is Form?" *Psychol. Review,* 1951, vol. 47, p. 412.

it could only secure a beachhead, but to judge from the number of printings and revised editions which the Gestalt books have had, one would gather that, on the contrary, the gestaltists found a ready public. In seven years, from 1924-1931, Koffka's *Growth of the Mind* passed through two editions and three reprintings, this country furnishing the largest number of consumers. Köhler's *Gestalt Psychology* was reprinted during the month of publication, and even Ellis' *Source Book of Gestalt Psychology*, as late as 1950, was run through the press twice the same year, showing that the demand is still great. It must be remembered that these books are not textbooks but *exparte* treatises which many instructors, for that reason, would prescribe only as collateral reading.

It is too soon to make any predictions with regard to the extent American psychology will have been affected by Gestalt psychology, but that it has had a sobering influence is already clear. To date, there does not seem to be any other school to replace it, although there are, of course, numerous orientations and quasi-schools, like operationism, or factorial psychology, which, however, set up limits and do not cover psychology as a whole, as we shall see in the following chapters.

Latest Phase

Of the original architects of Gestalt psychology, only Köhler remains. Although his early interest has centred in physics, he has, in the course of the last decade, been engrossed in physiological psychology. Gestalt psychology had committed itself to certain propositions which were not generally acceptable. Hence it devolved upon him to try to prove them experimentally. Whether his interpretations of the results carry conviction may be questioned but the results *per se* were worth obtaining.

Köhler is fundamentally a phenomenologist—not in the Husserlian sense—but as a close observer, dwelling upon the thing he perceives, without at once undertaking the reduction of the phenomenon into physicalistic constructs. It is not altogether fair, however, to put him down as a shirker of the scientific task and contenting himself with gazing or straining at some object in order to describe his experience in every last detail.

Working sometimes alone, more frequently with advanced

students, or associates, he has succeeded in catching certain oddities that afford him a peg on which to hang a certain phase of the Gestalt doctrine. It must be said that the mechanistic stimulus-response-bond psychologists who exert so much influence in experimental and physioneurological circles are not altogether happy about his findings upon which they look with misgiving.

Even the older theory of isomorphism, i.e., that there is a structural field (not a localized area necessarily) in the brain which corresponds to the extent of the phenomenon we consciously experience—a doctrine which has become a staple of the school, has had the good fortune of becoming a textbook offering. It smacks apparently of psychophysical parallelism in a new garb. To a neo-behaviorist, it is still physiological speculation; and such infiltration, no matter how qualified, is only grudgingly allowed.

Another Gestalt thesis is equipotentiality, according to which central functions in the brain are not governed by restricted localization but by fields of energy, partly chemical, of which we have as yet little knowledge, but largely electrical, of which we have some experimental evidence—and that is where as a neurophysiologist, Köhler, who in earlier years has written Die physischen Gestalten, proves to be a loyal physicist.

So far as equipotentiality is concerned, Köhler has a powerful ally in Lashley, who has fought the localization principle tooth and nail for years, but the electrotonus hypothesis finds less favor in Lashley's eyes; and in an article, with the collaboration of assistants, based on experiments on the visual cortex of two monkeys, he delivers himself of the Scotch verdict.[12] Köhler naturally does not accept this verdict and questions the technique, but without stopping to argue on both sides, let us see what this electrotonus principle actually represents.

It all ties in with the discovery among Gestalt experimenters that after gazing fixedly at an object, certain anomalies will follow, viz., when we turn to observe test objects in the same region, these will seem to recede from the object we have previously been looking at, as though some hitch had taken place. Figural after-effects are closely linked

[12] K. S. Lashley, K. L. Chow, and J. Semmers: "An Examination of the Electric Field Theory of Cerebral Integration," Psychol. Review, 1951, vol. 58, pp. 123-136.

with what Köhler had called *"satiation,"* which is the tendency for the intensity of a perception to wane after a period of steady observation.

True to Gestalt form, Köhler, in his isomorphic commitment, asks whether we must not look for an obstruction in the nervous system, and sure enough, he alights on a solution, satisfactory to himself. "When a current flows through cells of the nervous system, it affects their surfaces. When it enters the cells, it raises the local impedance and thus blocks its own way. When it leaves the cells, the opposite happens. But since after a short while the former effect becomes stronger, the final result is an obstruction. Thus the current is weakened and the distribution in the tissue changes. . . . Test currents which are now conducted through this region will therefore also deviate from their normal course. They will be weakened where the impedence has been raised. . . . Hence the current as a whole will recede from the affected region just as, in a figural after-effect, a test object recedes from the area previously occupied by an inspection object."[13] Thus Köhler explains the visual phenomenon by what is supposed to be happening in the brain tissues—obstruction for obstruction. The old name in physiological textbooks for such obstructions in the nervous system, Köhler tells us further, is *electrotonus*.

Before closing the supplementary paragraphs on recent Gestalt developments, it would be in place to detail the rift between the functional and the structural camp in regard to what is happening in the brain, even if it has already been intimated that the field theory does not suit the average neurophysiologist. Köhler institutes a division between processes in the peripheral nervous system and those in the higher centers. The impulses along axons from neuron to neuron, in a forward direction, may be taken for granted in both stages, but superimposed centrally, there is a more complex brain action; and here there are all kinds of interacting forces coming into play, compared with which the jogging transverse travel along individual neurons is elementary. To Köhler, the experienced fact is still fundamental; the explanation contingent and receiving its cue from the felt experience.

[13] W. Köhler: "The Present Situation in Brain Physiology," *Amer. Psychologist,* 1958, vol. 13, p. 151.

Chapter 28

Hull and His Behavior System

CLARK L. HULL, born in a log cabin in Akron, Ohio in 1884 and raised on a farm, far from educational facilities, would hardly have been selected to become an outstanding psychologist. Borne down by illness during his adolescence, he was not graduated from college (University of Michigan) until he was twenty-nine. His doctorate at the University of Wisconsin was obtained at the age of thirty-four.

Like Thurstone, Tolman, Boring, and other eminent psychologists, perhaps including even William James (Lawrence Scientific School), Hull exchanged the engineering goal for the psychological as soon as he had acquired a taste for more theoretical problems. Yet, his knack for building things, his motor aptitude, and his mathematical leanings remained with him through life, and he succeeded in combining the theoretical and the practical to good advantage. While still a graduate student at the University of Wisconsin, he gave courses in experimental psychology and stayed on, subsequently directing the Laboratory, until 1929, when he was called to Yale University as Professor at the Institute of Human Relations.

As we survey the articles and books that Hull authored, we are struck with the range of his interests. We find him "all over the place," starting with a short article on "Applied Aspects of Social Psychology" and proceeding to association experiments, turning his attention to aptitudes and testing and then to hypnotism, suggestion, trance, the evolution of concepts, and finally concentrating on a theory of learning which at one time loomed large on the psychological horizon, and bade fair to turn a corner in the matter of predictability of at least animal behavior.

Encouraged by his inventive ability and flair for construction of various working tools that served him in good stead, *e.g.*, an exposure apparatus and a correlation machine, an instrument for summating the oscillations of a line, a mechanical model of the conditioned reflex, he set about to discover

369

quantitaive methods of studying the movements and motivation of rodents, preliminary to making his case for a biological conception of learning, bolstered by a series of posulates, theorems, corollaries, and equations, some of them quite formidable, like $_sE_R = _sE_R - _sO'_R$, which were to indicate the habit strength of the animal in various situations and guide us in predicting the course of behavior not only in rats but eventually in man.

Employing concepts introduced by Tolman—such as the difference between molecular and molar treatments of behavior (actually, as Tolman indicates in his *Purposive Behavior in Animals and Men*,[1] it was C. D. Broad, in *The Mind and Its Place in Nature*, who distinguished the two types) Hull takes, as he supposes, the molar road in dealing with receptors and effectors, stimulus and response sequences, following the classical Pavlovian conditioned reflex methods, which he places in the molar category. But if we read Tolman aright, it will be noted that to him the Watsonian and Pavlovian procedures are really on the molecular scales, while molar represents a global movement within a field, subserving *a goal or purpose*, as a cat escaping from a box, or a child in fright turning to its mother, or a rat rushing toward food. According to Tolman, Hull's own system would be a sample of the molecular type, even if it does not go into the literal molecular structure of the nerves and muscles. Broad's and Tolman's use of the terms is somewhat figurative, as when we say a "pocket" navy or "pea" coal.

Hull is at pains to pattern psychological theory after well-known principles and postulates in physics. Again accepting a Tolman term, *viz.*, "intervening variables," he makes them analogous to the constructs in physics like protons or positrons, which are not observable but which we infer. In this fashion, he deals with drives, habits, and other variables. With technological skill, he erects a deductive structure that is reminiscent of Spinoza's *Ethics*, except that the latter shapes up *more geometrico*, while Hull's develops in an algebraic framework.

A sample of Hull's technique, followed by a theorem from Spinoza will bring home the similarity in method.

[1] E. C. Tolman: *Purposive Behavior in Animals and Men*, pp. 10-12.

Inhibition—Effective Reaction Potential

X. *If a reaction potential ($_sE_R$) has been partially or wholly extinguished, the inclusion of a mild extra stimulus in the conditioned stimulus compounds (S) will result in the strengthening of the effective reaction potentiality ($_s\bar{E}_R$).*

But since $_sI_R$ constitutes only a portion of the total inhibition ($\dot{I}_R$) which weakens $_sE_R$, it follows that disinhibition can only partially restore $_s\bar{E}_R$ to the original value of $_sE_R$; this leads to our eleventh corollary:

X. *When an excitatory habit has been set up by means of well-distributed reinforcements and has then been extinguished, the most effective disinhibitory stimulus possible will never (except through "oscillation") enable S to evoke an R with as great vigor, certainty, or speed as before the extinction occurred.*

From Spinoza's *Ethics*, a sample is here reproduced from Part III.

"Origin and Nature of Emotions"

PROP. XLIX. Love or hatred towards a thing which we imagine to be free must be greater than the love or hatred towards a necessary thing, provided both are subject to the same cause.

Proof.—A thing which we imagine to be free must (Def. 7, Part I.) be perceived through itself without any others. If, therefore, we imagine it to be the cause of the aforesaid pleasure or pain, by that very fact (Note, Prop. 13, Part III.) we shall love or hate it, and that (prev. Prop.) with the greatest love or hatred that can arise from the given emotion. But if we imagine the thing which is the cause of the given effect to be necessary, then (Def. 7, Part I.) we shall imagine it not alone, but together with other things, to be the cause of the given effect: and therefore (prev. Prop.) our love or hatred towards it will be less. *Q.e.d.*

Note.—Hence it follows that men, inasmuch as they consider themselves free, prosecute each with greater reciprocal love or hatred than other things: to this is added the imitation of emotions, of which see Prop. 27, 34, 40, and 43, Part III.

In his zeal to put psychology on a par with the nomothetic (law-formulating) sciences and to quantify the various steps, he resorted to a barrage of technical verbiage which is more impressive than useful. When all is said and done, as we stop to consider the significance of the following postulate and the corollary which Hull deduces therefrom, does it mean any more than just this: With every reaction tendency there is an undetermined inhibitory tendency which will oscillate somewhat from the expected result at any given moment, in accordance with chance, owing to the complexity of the interdependent habit operations in the organism? And if so, then all the very elaborate equations worked out by Hull will hardly be of any avail. At most we might be clinging to an "als ob" ("as if") situation; in other words, a comforting fiction in the psychology of learning.

POSTULATE 10

Associated with every reaction potential ($_sE_R$) there exists an inhibitory potentiality ($_sO_R$) which oscillates in amount from instant to instant according to the normal "law" of chance. The amount of this inhibitory potentiality associated with the several habits of a given organism at a particular instant is uncorrelated, and the amount of diminution in $_s\bar{E}_R$ from the action of $_sO_R$ is limited only by the amount of $_s\bar{E}_R$ at the time available.

From Postulate 10 there follows Major Corollary III:

MAJOR COROLLARY III

Each muscular contraction involved in any increment of habit tendency ($\triangle_sH_R$) oscillates from instant to instant in the reaction-intensity potentiality which it mediates, thus producing a kind of response generalization in both directions from the response intensity originally reinforced.

NOTES

Mathematical Statement of Postulate 10

The mathematical statement of Postulate 10 is given by the following equation:

$$_s\dot{\bar{E}}_R = {_s}\bar{E}_R - {_s}O'_R,$$

(44)

where,

$_s\dot{\bar{E}}_R$ = the momentary effective strength of a reaction potential as modified by the oscillatory potentiality, $_sO_R$,

where,

$_sO'_R = {}_sO_R$ when $_s\bar{E}_R \geqq {}_sO_R$,

and,

$_sO'_R = {}_s\bar{E}_R$ when $_s\bar{E}_R < {}_sO_R$,

where,

zero $\leqq {}_sO_R \leqq 6\sigma$, σ being a constant,

and,

the probability (p) that $_sO_R$ takes on values between zero and 6σ is p,

where,

$$p = \frac{NS}{\sqrt{2}} e^{-\frac{(x-3\sigma)^2}{2\sigma^2}}$$

Hull's table of over 100 symbols alone, clearly explained, is ample evidence of the unremitting labor which he undertook to work out the details of his monumental project. The persistence with which he carried on his investigation, blending theory with experiment, stimulated many laboratory psychologists to follow his course. It was his purpose to rule out consciousness from consideration; so we may call him a behaviorist—but one of a peculiar cast in that he tried to fit the facts to the theory, which he formulated in precise terms. His wish was to establish laws to apply to conditioning.

Hull aimed to be precise and accurate. His goal was to construct a model which could eventually predict behavior—a species of servo-mechanism for psychologists, but he did not figure on the pace of psychology and on the difficulties inherent in such a system, which, instead of simplifying the procedure, complicates it with parallel conveyors that are yet interdependent. It was Hull's ambition to treat all behavior quantitatively, but the variables are often so many, and their weights so uncertain, that it would hardly do to arrange different sets, and arbitrarily assign this or that datum to one or another set of variables.

Hull's faith, enthusiasm, and persistence are to be admired. Several of his students both at Wisconsin and Yale, like C. I. Hovland, Neal E. Miller, and K. Spence have made notable contributions. His ablest student, C. I. Hovland (1912-1962), who succeeded him at Yale as Stirling Professor, seems to have followed in his footsteps, having become interested in the same type of research—learning, computers, and operational problms. In 1957, he received the scientific award of the American Psychological Association, having to his credit an impressive list of important articles, in addition to serving on a number of national commissions.

Chapter 29

Lashley—Iconoclast in Neuropsychology

KARL SPENCER LASHLEY (1890-1958) was not a psychologist who swam in the mainstream. He could never write a textbook on the subject, and would have to be considered a specialist who, for the most part, did not venture out of his area. Yet his work in neuropsychology gave impetus to a good deal of laboratory research and theory, even though he himself was not keen on evolving a system but worked rather piecemeal at various investigations, which had their point of contact in psychology with learning.

Hebb, a physiological psychologist himself, may have tended toward hyperbole in his obituary when he speaks of Lashley's career as "perhaps the most brilliant in the psychology of this century"[1]—but that he performed a great service to both neurology and psychology is undeniable.

Those who are constantly looking for positive results will not concede that Lashley deserved his many awards and honors. But even if by dint of his many ingenious experiments he was able to disprove some of the accepted tenets of the reflexological school, including behaviorism, and puncture the received views of brain localization which seemed so promising, his place in the annals of psychology is securely established.

When McDougall left Harvard for Duke, President Conant was anxious to obtain for the psychological department the greatest psychologist in the world. He settled on or for Lashley to fill the chair which was once graced by William James. Conant, as a chemist, would be partial to someone who was an experimentalist in the natural sciences. There is an irony attached to the appointment because Lashley was inclined to belittle James, who had taught anatomy and physiology in his younger days. Also, Lashley would come to Harvard once or twice a year for a number of days, while his researches were carried on throughout the academic session at the Yerkes Laboratory of Primate Biology in Orange Park, Florida.

[1] D. O. Hebb: "Karl Spencer Lashley," *Amer. Journal of Psychology*, 1959, vol. 72, p. 142.

Born in Davis, West Virginia, in 1890, he was able despite the wandering of the family to California, Alaska and Klondike, to be graduated from high school at the age of fourteen and the University of West Virginia, where he majored in zoology and comparative anatomy, at twenty. At the University of Pittsburgh, where he was a teaching fellow in bacteriology and received his master's degree, he took a course in experimental psychology under another teaching fellow, Karl M. Dallenbach. It was at Johns Hopkins that he obtained his Ph.D. in zoology, working with Jennings, but also to some extent with John B. Watson and Adolf Meyer. During this period he published journeyman experimental papers on various topics from color vision in the hen to handedness in the monkey and the effect of drugs on rat learning.

Coming under the guidance, if not the stricter tutelage, of one of the leading neurophysiologists in America, Shepherd Ivory Franz, at St. Elizabeth Hospital, in Washington, he entered on his lifework—exploring the brain from a functional angle. Here he studied the effect of brain damage, albeit primarily in the rat, but humans too were now accessible to him in the hospital. His instructorship at the University of Minnesota, in 1917, did not last and soon he was doing some work in Washington for the government, together with John B. Watson, on sexual motivation in connection with venereal disease.

Although he was recalled to Minnesota as an assistant research professor and later as full professor with practically no teaching duties, he left for a post in Chicago with the Institute for Juvenile Research in 1926, and thence to the University of Chicago, as a full professor. As he happened to be the President of the American Psychological Association, in 1929, when the Ninth International Congress took place at Yale, he had the opportunity in his presidential address, to show up the weak spots of a pure reflexology.

Honors came to him easily after his Harvard appointment in 1935, and they never added starch to his make-up. He could express himself without too much reserve about celebrities, like any young nuclear researcher on a government project, but his contagious laughter in hearing or telling a story was sufficient evidence that he was not taking himself too seriously. That he would be playing in chamber music ensembles might strike one as odd. I could have imagined Titchener's participation in such sport but hardly Lashley's.

My first impression of Lashley at a meeting of Titchener's

experimental group, at Yale in 1913, is still vivid. I saw a lanky and delicate youth looking like a European intellectual with pince-nez attached to a black cord looped over one ear. He seemed withdrawn, and I felt that he would be more receptive than the others, who were already more or less established. He was still, like myself, a graduate student, but clearly one who had already published. My topic of conversation centered on the neglect of collective psychology in the United States. I can understand now that he cared very little about my complaint, but out of courtesy he agreed with me. Incidentally, about forty years later, he was awarded the gold medal which H. C. Warren, one of the founders of this closed Titchener circle had established as a prize for a distinguished experimentalist. It is also interesting that Lashley later adopted a collective or global view of neurology, in contrast to the stimulus-response or even the reflex-arc connection.

Lashley might have made a skillful surgeon. He was extremely deft with tools and most resourceful in developing techniques. In checking on the work of others, he performed a valuable service; especially to be admired is his willingness to change his views in keeping with his subsequent results. That is not as common as is believed among scientists, who are prone to find some reasons for their exceptions or discrepancies.

Under the influence of Watson at Johns Hopkins, Lashley appeared to have become a staunch behaviorist, but he soon jumped off the smoothly running bandwagon, and we find him defending doctrines that were supposed to have been consigned to the limbo long since, and assailing a portion that had been held sacrosanct in psychophysiology. That address in 1929 must thave come like a bombshell in the ranks of reflexologists and behaviorists, who were then riding high. A few slightly edited excerpts will give the reader an idea of the explicit and emphatic words which Lashley used to convey his meaning.

Both the animal experiments and the clinical material point to the conclusion that a given area may function at different levels of complexity and lesions may limit the complex functions without disturbing the simpler ones.

The limitation of complexity seems to accord with Spearman's view that intelligence is a function of some undifferentiated nervous energy.

No logically derived element of behavior can be shown to have a definite localization; no single sensation, memory, or skilled movement is destroyed alone by any lesion. On the contrary, the various parts of the functional areas seem equipotential for such elements and either a whole constellation of them is affected by the lesion or none at all. In these constellations of activities the grouping is determined, not by associative bonds but by similarities of organization!

The story is told by modes of organization rather than single reactions or conditioned reflexes. The cortex seems to provide a sort of generalized framework to which single reactions conform spontaneously.

Self-regulation of the nervous system takes place, no matter how the anatomical constituents may be disturbed. Turn pieces of the cortex upside down, piece them together getting a random connection of the severed fibres, there could still be a normal capacity for understanding relationships and for dealing with the world of experience.

We are dealing with a complex system in which there is an influence of every part upon every other with all degrees of intimacy in the relations and various degrees of dominance and subordination. Our problem is to discover the means by which these influences are exerted.

We have seen the notion of reflex paths, exerting mutual inhibition and facilitation and conducting nervous impulses over pathways determined by the specific resistance of synapses is not only inadequate to account for the simplest facts of behavior but is also opposed by direct neurological evidence.[2]

At a time when the term *instinct* was treated like a taboo word, Lashley had no qualm about using it and without quotation marks.

How far he is from the environmentalist may be seen from another passage where he frankly espouses hereditarianism.

Some of the more conspicuous structural differences have been shown to be hereditary. . . .

There can be little question that some of the lesser variants in cerebral structure are likewise hereditary.

Even if this is not the case, if the variants are largely th

[2] K. S. Lashley: "Basic Neural Mechanisms in Behavior," *Psychol. Review*, 1930, vol. 27. The excerpts are from pp. 16-21.

result of development accidents, they still present a serious difficulty for the environmentalist. Discussions of heredity and environment have tended to regard the nervous system, if it is considered at all, as a vaguely remote organ, essentially similar in all individuals and largely moulded by experience. Even the limited evidence at hand, however, shows that individuals start life with brains differing enormously in structure; unlike in number, size, and arrangement of neurons as well as in grosser features. The variations in cells and tracts must have functional significance.[3]

Lashley was a psychologist in temperament but a neurologist in technique. He did not, like the average neurologist or physiologist, consider psychology a sort of epiphenomenon of their own science. To him, the subjective experiences were basic. If he did not declare himself on the mentalist issue, it was because his ambit was in a different area, but he did take into consideration the cognitive aspect—motivation for one thing.

In rejecting individual neuron connections as an explanation of behavior and in propounding a theory of equipotentiality of function in the cerebral cortex, he aligns himself in that respect with the gestaltists (Köhler, Koffka) and especially with Kurt Goldstein's organismic views.

His vocal injunctions to be wary of oversimplified explanations have done much to dampen the ardor of the stimulus-response zealots, although, in the absence of positive data which go into the formulation of a definite theory, his most eminent students, while recognizing his stature, do not participate in the rebellion.

Like many an experimentalist, Lashley has not produced large volumes. He has written numerous papers and a few monographs such as *Brain Mechanisms and Intelligence* (1929). Occasionally he published serials in periodicals, and recently a number of his papers were brought together under the title of *Neuropsychology of Lashley* with introductions by F. A. Beach, D. O. Hebb, C. T. Morgan, and H. Nissen —all students of his.

[3] K. S. Lashley: "Structural Variation in the Nervous System in Relation to Behavior," *Psychol. Review*, 1947, vol. 54, p. 333.

Chapter 30

Operationism

IN THE PRESENT chapter, we have largely to deal with outside developments which have affected psychological thought and practice. Operationism is a term which is readily understood. It is a word easy to coin; for all one has to do is to think of "operation" and add "ism," and although that is not exactly what P. W. Bridgman did 35 years ago in his *Logic of Physics,* where he sets forth that any concept worthy of the name scientific must be defined in terms of operations which will establish relations in the form of measurement, it was his constant use of the word "operational" which fanned afresh a movement initiated a long time ago, first by Leibniz in Germany, and then by others in Central Europe, and during the nineteenth century, in England.

History of Movement to Unify Science

Scarcely out of his teens, Leibniz, nearly 300 years ago projected a universal language which would be applicable to all the sciences, and would serve as a sort of calculus, with a common terminology. It is not without a tinge of historical irony that the youth who was engineering such a realistic plan should have later himself become one of the most speculative metaphysicians the world has seen, presuming to tell us so many things about God, in his *Théodicée,* that it would scarcely comport even with the pretensions of a theologian, much less with the aims of a scientist. Yet Leibniz was indubitably a scientist, and his mind was bent on achieving a unity and integration of knowledge, perhaps in a greater degree than in the case of any other polyhistor since Aristotle.

The germ of operationism might be detected in Kant; for did he not, in his antithesis between analytic and synthetic propositions, parallel the formal and empirical dichotomy of present-day operationism? And are his antinomies not a demonstration that so far as scientific procedure is concerned, such problems as infinity, immortality, and freedom are insoluble, and therefore, would come under what Bridgman classes as pseudo-problems?

Comte's positivism, together with the phrase *scepticisme du savant,* which was in vogue during the middle of the nineteenth century, is also a convergent wave in the slow-moving current which carries with it the general scientific float. British empiricism of the same period has added its weight and, of course, the behavioristic activities, beginning with the physiological work in Russia, have lent it special impetus, so that the battle cry of objectivism, which bids fair to drown the voice of introspection in every possible situation, became the slogan of all science.

Pragmatism, which, in effect, is the same stand from a philosophical angle, as the etymology of the word shows, would naturally be considered an ally, and it was James's pet phrase, "the cash value of ideas," which was often heard in scientific circles too. Dewey's instrumentalism at least suggests a closeness to contemporary operationism, even if it is not to be identified with it, as one is so often tempted to see it done.

Operationism may be considered as an outgrowth of the general movement that has given rise to logical positivism, which, officially, stems from Vienna, but has had its beginnings elsewhere. In his *Popular Scientific Lectures,* Ernst Mach includes an important address entitled "On the Principle of Comparison in Physics" which he delivered in 1894. Therein, he tells us that in 1874, Kirchhoff, celebrated both as a theoretical physicist and as an experimentalist, produced something of a furor, to judge from Boltzmann's account, when he defined the "object of mechanics as the description in very simple terms, of the motions occurring in nature."[1] Many thought then that this was altogether too elementary a function for any science to fulfill.

Mach himself seems to have spearheaded this tendency in science, and the Vienna circle, which later came to be known as the logical positivists, were greatly influenced by Mach. It was in the addresss alluded to that he speaks with zeal about the realization in the future of a common ground. "The barriers between the special sciences, which make division of work and concentration possible, but which appear to us after all as cold and conventional restrictions, will gradually disappear. Bridge upon bridge is thrown over the gaps. Contents and methods, even of the remotest branches, are compared." And here we come to a prophetic utterance which, in a

[1] E. Mach: *Popular Scientific Lectures* (Eng. transl. 1898), p. 236.

modest way, has been borne out in a much shorter period than was even hoped for. "When the Congress of Natural Scientists shall meet a hundred years hence, we may expect that they will represent a unity in a higher sense than is possible today, not in sentiment and aim alone, but in method also."

It was not a century, but only forty years later, that a congress such as the one which Mach had in mind took shape, but perhaps it (as well as those that followed) was one which could not satisfy his real disideratum viz., to show unity in content and method, although the unity of aim was certainly manifest.

The Vienna circle consisted of philosophers like Moritz Schlick, who was its leader and whose assassination, in 1936, was a blow to the expanding group; of sociologists, like Otto Neurath, who became the moving spirit of logical positivism after the death of Schlick and who presided at the fifth congress, which took place at Harvard University, in 1939, only two or three weeks before the oubreak of the Nazi War; symbolic logicians, like Rudolf Carnap, who has been concentrating especially on the subject of syntax, and more than his colleagues has sought to prove the tautology of metaphysical statements or indeed of any philosophy; physicists like Philipp Frank, who seems to be at the helm of the rather loose organization (still a circle, in the easygoing Vienna sense) now that Neurath is dead; and mathematicians, like Hans Reichenbach and Richard von Mises, who grapple with the problems of probability in all its applications. Otto Neurath, who conceived the plan of an immense *International Encyclopedia of Unified Science* was the most dynamic and exuberant of the little band, and had he not died so soon after editing the first two or three parts, the huge project might have been on the way to completion.

The Essence of Operationism

It was logical positivism which boldly waved aside any type of research that would not yield empirical results. Propositions which were designated as formal simply were declared as saying the same things in other words. In this endeavor, operationism upholds its earlier contemporary; and as it stems out of the physical laboratory, involving many of the physicists, it actually, did at the outset, demonstrate, by references to and illustrations from physics, the advantage of its claims.

As we can see, operationism does not represent a psychological school. The operationists—and that applies to the logical positivists who extend their activities—form a sort of *over-all committee to restrict investigators who would not or could not fit their data into a physicalistc framework* (which does not mean that they must be regarded as material) *from calling themselves scientists on the same level as themselves.* In other words, it is as if they said, "If you want to play in our yard, you must play our game." Since physicists, chemists, and mathematicians (the latter, of course, recognize the necessarily *formal* constitution of their science) enjoy the greatest prestige, it would be natural for those who would like to hobnob with them to meet their requirements. Sociologists, anthropologists, physiologists, and psychologists would make it a point not only to align themselves with the seemingly new viewpoint, but would be the first ones to blackball those of their colleagues whose terminology and propositions savor of such connotations as essence, substance, rational, values, instinct, etc., which cannot be demonstrated or verified.

In the feverish preparations to become operationally in good standing, the great word was *behavior*; and mentalists who still clung to such antiquated terms as sensations, imagery, feelings, will, or desire were regarded as beyond the pale of science; for they could not bring their conclusions to any empirical outcome. Operationists do not say that logicians, ethicists, aestheticians, or even metaphysicans, have no place in the economy of research and knowledge, but they believe that the subject-matter and treatment come under the head of either *semantics, i.e.,* the field dealing with the relation of a sign to the thing designated, or else *syntactics, i.e.,* the field which takes up the relations between signs and signs (logic, mathematics). Since logicians are among the sponsors of operationism, they, as well as the mathematicians, are quite content to think of themselves as syntacticians or semanticists in the knowledge that they are of the greatest benefit to all others. There is still left a third division of what has been called semeiotics, or the study of signs, in its broadest sense, and that is *pragmatics.* Here, as is implied by the root of the terms, there is an action element, but that is only by way of a rebound from the sign upon the appreciator or understander. Possibly much of psychology, and most of psychoanalysis, might be welcomed here by the operationists.

It is to be understood that not all physicists see exactly eye to eye with Bridgman, although the general bias would be shared by all. H. Margenau, *e.g.*, of Yale, is not sure that an operational clamp can be put on all science, for there is the danger of setting up a scientific world with gaps; and far from achieving unity, the extreme operationists would be plunged into a vast hopscotch sphere, leaping over boundary lines and questionable areas. Margenau adds a *constitutive* type of proposition, which is to be distinguished from the *epistemic* frame of reference.

For Margenau, the epistemic is close to Bridgman's operational definition, showing the relation of a phenomenon or process to some method of measurement. The constitutive definition, however, sets the object or event off in some class and subclass, *e.g.*, time may be defined with reference to clocks and other instruments of measurement, or it may be defined as the independent variable in the laws of motion.

An interplay of both types of definition is necessary so that a given science may not become a stagnant speculative pool of statements, on the one hand, or, on the other hand, is not turned into a mere vast protocol of discrete measurements.[2]

The fragmentary character of an operational method has been adverted to by several others, both philosophers and physicists, and much more will be said on this topic in the course of the critique.

Among psychologists who recognize the advantage of operationism, there are also two camps; a moderate one, exemplified by S. S. Stevens and, it would seem, E. G. Boring, and an extreme one which is peopled by the objectivists, pure mechanists or behaviorists. The latter have no difficulty in securing their credentials; the former are somewhat hard put to prove that an image can be physicalized, so to speak, so that others would be able to agree on its attributes. "Quite contrary to expectation," says Boring, "it turns out that the behaviorist can eat the cake of consciousness and have it too. He may not always know it but he can." One can very well see how exteroceptive sensations or perception can be universalized or externalized through discrimination, but how a shooting pain could be manifested as distinct from, say, a boring or stinging pain, except through description only, and, therefore, the use of symbols, is a poser.

[2] H. Margenau: *Nature of Physical Reality,* 1950, pp. 243-244.

Critique of Operationism

Operationism, on general principles, is a desirable touchstone, which may save a good deal of time by preventing an interminable wrangling between two disputants. It stands to reason that if we reduced all the scientific terminology to fundamentals which could be used *mutatis mutandis,* we should have gained, if nothing else, a certain agreement, but first we must start by agreeing as to what are fundamentals; and thus a new dispute is in progress at the very outset.

Throughout the history of science, a rift will be found between the theorists and the experimentalists. Newton was perhaps the first to place a premium upon operational prospects when he uttered the emphatic triad of words, *Hypotheses non fingo.* Yet he did not abstain from formulating theories, which could not have been absolutely valid, since they were subsequently so qualified and modified as practically to be displaced. The question presents itself as to whether, in our operational zeal, we might not be too hasty in deciding that something of import is a pseudo-problem just because it seems impossible of empirical proof, in one way or another, at this time. Even the psychophysical issue may yet some day be attacked afresh with greater facilities. Only a *contradictio in adjecto* should be entirely relegated to the limbo of historical fads, but we cannot be sufficiently certain even about such stuff as dreams are made of, to make short shrift of it.

Let us consider that out of such a vague and speculative theory as relativity, there grew out the atom bomb, which appears to be that operation which might do away with all human operations. Sixty years ago, the relativity theory, which was beginning to shape itself in the mind of Albert Einstein, would have been looked upon as a grand imaginative conception, with no empirical outlet. Albert A. Michelson, who spent half of his productive years measuring the velocity of light—and surely he, if anyone, was an operationist, before Bridgman was born—did not take kindly to Einstein's theory, which, as a matter of fact, was largely based on Michelson's experiments. In 1911, Arthur Schuster, another famous physicist, referred to Einstein's principle of relativity as an "imagined law." Only two years later Eddington's spectacular expedition confirmed Einstein's assertion as to the curvature of space. Had astronomical appliances not been so precise, we might have had to do more waiting before laboratory experiments could confirm this or that phase of the relativity theory. Similarly, the theory of a space-time continuum, formulated by Einstein's teacher, Hermann Minkowski, and corroborated by his great pupil, would have had small chance with the operationists of that day.

In regard to psychology, there is much more to complain of. It is the old story of assimilative imposition. The physicist is on his high horse and, therefore, would like all his associates to accept his bidding. Physics is tangible; its phenomena are demonstrable; its results are quantitative. "Why, then, let us all talk physics and chemistry. Turn all your psychological data into physical facts, and we can compare notes." That would be the purport of operationist as well as logical positivist; and the mechano-behaviorist would clap his hands in glee —just what he always wanted. But all of nature is not physical or physicalistic. Some of life is, but most of it is not; and the slogan *aut Caesar aut nullus* will play havoc with some of the most essential facts. The operationist in psychology has two alternatives. Either he chooses to disregard all such things as motives, purposes, desires, thoughts, images, and volitions, or else he undertakes to twist them into such monstrous verbal shapes that the Procrustean operation is a matter of child's play compared with it. C. L. Hull's series of postulates and eductions or inferences are extremely ingenious, but what empirical results have come therefrom; and, furthermore, has he dealt with the actual phenomena or with verbal shadows? Psychology can get into the physicalistic state, but only by laying the ghost and becoming depsychologized.

It reminds us of the story told about the fellow who was seen searching on a thoroughfare for a five-dollar bill which he had lost. Some of the passers-by stopped and looked around too. Then one of them said, "Are you sure you lost it around this corner?" "No," replied the searcher, "I lost it in the alley over there, but there is no light there, and this is the only corner which has a lamp-post." If there is no articulation between the lamp of operationism and the coins or bills of the mind which we are trying to recover, then it is a futile, if not fatuous, operation, no matter how luminous it may be.

Have operationists been consistent in the use of their own language? Have they shown that they can steer clear of purposes and desires and wishes? Why, even the physicists frequently betray their helplessness when caught off guard. P. Frank is surely a very competent scientist, and in the vanguard of the operational movement. In his little book *Relativity—a Richer Truth,* which is a model of clear exposition and judicious condensation, he employs the word "instinctive" in a sense which even McDougall would frown on. (". . . and he may long for the help of a professional philosopher in order to have his instinctive vague beliefs bolstered up."[3]) Margenau, in his most recent book, uses the same word in an equally popular sense. Do they believe that beliefs are inherited through the genes? How do they define or analyze "instinct" operationally? In psychology, the foremost operational practitioner is E. C. Tolman, while on the theoretical side, S. S. Stevens is its chief protagonist. Tolman has much to say on purpose, and certainly infers that his experimental rats have desires, but operationally, he has no right to use such terms. What he observes is only a certain type of behavior, and *at no time could purpose be demonstrated. It is only when he looks into himself and begins to draw analogies that he can discover these facts in the rats.* For all the good his carefully worded definitions have done, he might just as well have said, "Now, you and I all know what 'purpose' is, so let us avoid these strained circumlocutions by which we can gain admission to the ringside in the arena of science, and be content with our family circle."

An enlightening demonstration of what might be expected of an operationist regime is contained in S. S. Stevens's thorough and critical survey of the "Science of Science." Taking a passage from J. F. Brown's *Psychology and the Social Order,* which he considers an "important and scholarly work," he analyzes each sentence as to whether it is empirical, or only semantic or syntactical, and, therefore, operationally of no significance. The first sentence reads: "We must first combat the usage of the term personality as a quantitative concept." For Stevens this is a syntactical proposition stating that the word "personality" is not a number-word, or cannot be modified by a number-word.

The clause "Everyone has quite the same amount of personality," again, is only syntactical, merely saying that "personality is a unit-word." Again, the sentence "Personality hence becomes a qualitative rather than a quantitative aspect"

[3] P. Frank: *Relativity—a Richer Truth,* 1950, p. 65.

is syntactically equivalent to "Personality is an expression of kind rather than number." When Brown writes, "We must combat the idea that individual personality is a constant aspect of the individual," Stevens labels the proposition as semantical; for all it does is to deny that the same personality-word goes with the same individual. Even such a statement as "When a normal individual goes insane, his personality changes," Stevens declares to be nothing but a "semantical" proposition.

Well, then what is empirical in the whole passage of sixteen statements? There are exactly three empirical propositions in all the sixteen, but the joke is that they are excruciatingly trivial, a statement like "We shall see later" because that can be verified, or "We as psychologists are not interested in whether the personality is 'good' or 'bad.'" Now here a statement is made about psychologists, which can be verified. The question as to whether personalities are good or bad is operationally a pseudo-problem anyway. Stevens's own conclusion is "We see, therefore, that most of this passage deals with the relation of the word personality to other words (syntactical rules) or to situations (semantic rules). These rules are essentially conventions and can be neither proved nor disproved by appeal to experiment or observation."[4] In that case, we wonder why, if Brown's book consists of mainly synactic or semantic material, it should rate as "important."

Turning the Tables

It would appear that the operationists are often manipulating blocks of words in order to show up the other party, but it is possible to play the game so that the mere psychologist does not come out worsted. Perhaps the empirical proposition, water boils at 100° centigrade, at such and such a sea level, could be turned into a syntactical proposition, especially with the qualifications which the principle of relativity imposes upon all facts in physics. The boiling point may just be a name, as is personality or a psychosis. Those who are acquainted with the rudiments of comparative philology are aware of the grammatical curiosities or anomalies, from our standpoint, to be found there. There is sometimes no real linkage between subject and predicate; and therefore, could we call the statement a proposition? In the Eskimo language

[4] S. S. Stevens: *Psychology and the Science of Science, 1939, p. 39.* Reprinted from the *Psychological Bulletin,* 1939, vol. 36.

the verb is a participial phase of the noun, so that when the Eskimo wishes to say "He loves her," the actual phrasing he employs is "Her being loved by him." Basque presents a similar structure, and in the Dravidian languages, spoken in Southern India, Tibeto-Burman, *e.g.*, "I see" is expressed by "my-seeing," and in Tamil, "We speak" would be represented by "We speech-makers are." Thus the verb is a species of inflected noun. If our operationist is bent upon drawing all the consequences, would he not have to admit that *sub specie aeternitatis,* all the operational information is semantic or syntactic when you come down to the last analysis, and that all the vaunted measurements and standards are valid only under certain conditions? The difference between the private image and the externalized objective bit of behavior is only one of degree, if one should care to make an issue of it. And after all is measurement alone to be our guide in everything? Is not qualitative significance involving judgment, understanding, wisdom, insight, not of some consequence in taking our initial step?

Measurement, to be sure, is our safest resort in every scientific endeavor, and it has been applied in mentalistic psychology no less than in behavioristics. The number of subjects used, the accumulation of protocol material and frequency of common experience and descriptions—all would tend to invest the subjective phenomenon in question with more than a modicum of objectivity, and the results based thereon with a certain validity. Quantification, for all the semantic stigmatization of personality topics, may be introduced into this supposedly hazy field with good prospects. What, for instance, prevents us from measuring the greatness of a personality by the amount of influence he has exerted beneficially on his contemporaries? When we say "this iron rod possesses great strength," is it very far different from the statement: "This character possesses great strength," and can we not measure it by the number and kinds of opportunities foregone, or temptations resisted, in the cause of something more ideal and universally worthwhile?

Our parameters might have to be a little different from those in the physical sciences, but they need not be utterly disregarded because, from the nature of the case, they happen to be on another plane, which leads us to briefly outline another possibility, that some readers may view as a compromise position.

Combinationism

It almost follows from the foregoing that operationism is a sensible approach to all things physical, and that psychology would do well to orient itself accordingly, where possible. If, *e.g.*, the behavioral pattern can give us light where the mental experience leaves us in the dark, there certainly is no harm in examining it carefully. Psychoanalysis in studying slips, symptomatic acts, and even deliberate behavior in order to interpret the mind of the individual, both conscious and unconscious, is doing just that. There are, of course, many cases in which the mental datum remains a private experience. Yet it can be communicated, and thanks to education and a cultural background, the description will not be without its value.

R. Carnap, perhaps the foremost of the logical positivists, believes that we can analyze the statement "A is angry" into a series of physical or physiological events (visible, audible, vaso-muscular behavior, as well as central nerve discharge) so that such a psychological observation is analogous to a proposition like "This beam possesses great strength," both representing, in condensed form, a series of establishable relations which spell anger, in the one case, and strength, in the other, but as R. v. Mises, the humanist of the movement points out, there is a real difference between the two in that when we say "A is angry," there is a reference to an occurrence in one's own self, whereas in the proposition "This beam has great strength," there is no such relatedness.[5] We may even go further than v. Mises and point out that at least the concept "anger," if not "strength," is meaningless without the inner experience which is afforded by introspection. Logical behaviorism, as Carnap's view is often called, is just as pointless as its Simon-pure counterpart, which has been abundantly exposed by the present author.

If we wish to abide by realities, without substituting questionable surrogates, it behooves us, while rendering unto Caesar what is Caesar's to hold resolutely what belongs to us, or in other words, what cannot be evaluated in the domain of Caesar. With the whole physicalistic apparatus at our disposal, motives and purposes, wishes and desires, volitions and interests cannot fit into the operational scheme, without losing their

[5] R. v. Mises: *Positivism: A Study in Human Understanding,* 1951, p. 236.

substance. Of course, we may and should attempt to apply the methods of general science wherever and whenever possible, but as soon as we are confronted by an impasse, rather than transform the phenomenon into a series of non-psychological suppositious parallel elements, we would do well to resort to intuitive methods like understanding, appreciation, or empathy. We may not all agree, but at least we still have before us the article so we can try again and again, but what is the good of consensus about something which is not, or no longer, at issue? When the diamond has fallen out of the ring, then no matter how accurate the appraisal, our chief aim is missed.

Our contention is, then, that only a combination of the two types of methods, the empirical and the intuitive, can yield more or less adequate results. Intuition is required as a control, even in the grasping or perilepsis of the problem, but certainly it is essential in some instances which cannot be approached through a quantitative avenue. This, however, must be set down as a *cave*. It is not every tyro, nor even the mere scholar, who is qualified in this respect. While almost every trained individual can become an experimentalist, the psychologist who is to combine both methods must have had sufficient laboratory experience and, in addition, must have a large fund of humanistic information. Experience in life, seasoning, and what is generally known as sagaciousness or perspicacity could not but be expected in such a one as would undertake to temper the empirical with the intuitive. Otherwise, he would be only tampering with either the one or the other. That is one reason why an observation by a Francis Galton is worth far more than a whole series of experiments by a fledgeling who has taken certain premises for granted which mar the results from the very outset. Physics is the Eldorado of science, but if we cannot enter it as psychologists, then we may as well rest where we are than bask in its reflected glory.

The intuition we have in mind here is not the simple intuition of the common-sense school, but the cultivated understanding which goes with the years of training and reflection. It is not a matter of rejecting the empirical but rather of supplementing it.

It is significant, and probably not too gratifying to physicalists in psychology, that the founder of operationism, at least its original proponent, P. W. Bridgman, a quarter-century later, bids us to gain "mastery in the microscopic world of introspection" (*Scientific Monthly,* July 1954, vol. 79).

Sic transit gloria mundi!

Chapter 31

Boring and His *Zeitgeist*

EDWIN GARRIGUES BORING (1886) at seventy-seven may be described as the dean of American psychologists, and their elder statesman. Hyperkinetic and dynamic, as he walks briskly down a long corridor, his springy gait belies his years, or rather exposes the relative insignificance of chronological age.

In contrast to Scripture, who in his autobiographical sketch rather grudgingly in a postscript reveals the date and place of his birth, restricting his information to his experimental work in the various laboratories, hospitals, and clinics to which he was attached, Boring furnishes us with a veritable family chronicle and acquaints us with his own personality problems in the most candid fashion.[1] Perhaps it was his submitting to psychoanalysis that induced him to be so frank with and about himself. A cynic might find a taint of exhibitionism in his application of the spotlight. But then his objectivism in psychology could well have overstimulated his sense of objectivity toward himself, as if to call forth by virtue of example similar autobiographical analyses among his distinguished colleagues. Be it as it may, we are beholden to him for his communicativeness; for a man's achievement can always better be understood in the light of his personality.

Boring, like a number of other psychologists, was trained as an engineer, although it was physics that had attracted him. While an engineering student, a course in psychology under Titchener, then a name to conjure with, drew him closer to the mind. As he was engaging in graduate work, taking courses in physiology, in educational psychology, and in abnormal psychology, under S. I. Franz, at the Hospital for the Insane in Washington, and publishing all the while, he was clearly on the way to a doctorate, which he received under Titchener, whose acolyte he had meantime become. His instructorship

---

[1] E. G. Boring: *A History of Psychology in Autobiography*, 1952, vol. 4, pp. 27-52. This was reproduced, in expanded form, in his *A Psychologist at Large*, 1962, N.Y., Basic Books.

at Cornell was interrupted by World War I, when he volunteered and entered the Medical Department as a Captain, working under the direction of R. M. Yerkes, who was the chief psychological officer. Subsequently, Boring assisted in the preparation of the huge volume reporting the psychological testing in the Army.

A professorship at Clark University, in 1919, ended in 1922, after his figuring in a rebellion against the reactionary President Atwood, and fortunately he received a call to Harvard, where William McDougall and H. S. Langfeld, who previously served as Münsterberg's right hand, had already been established. McDougall afterward left for Duke University and Langfeld became Director of the Princeton Psychological Laboratory. Boring, too, might have found a new haven at Cornell, succeeding Titchener, but he chose to remain at Harvard for a good reason, as we can understand, but also because, as he rationalizes, "my mission to rescue Harvard psychology from the philosophers was still unfulfilled." There is scarcely any doubt, however, but that in addition to the *Zeitgeist*, his uncommon energy was instrumental in divorcing psychology from philosophy and placing the laboratory on an independent footing.

Boring did not take to electrical engineering, but he has remained an engineer *in spirit* throughout his psychological career. Therefrom stems his efficiency. As to content, he has managed to round out his intellect in various directions, and whatever he has undertaken was well accomplished. As an experimental psychologist, he has published several monographs and articles and could direct research, but there was always something else soliciting his attention. He learned to write with verve, and certainly could rate as a scholar, if only for his monumental *History of Experimental Psychology*, but he has published other works, like *The Physical Dimensions of Consciousness* (1933), *Sensation and Perception in the History of Experimental Psychology* (1942), and has collaborated in a solid textbook, *Psychology: a Factual Textbook*, together with Langfeld and Weld (1935), and did a lot of rewrite work for the collective *Psychology for the Fighting Man* (1943), and published scores of articles, many, as is customary, conjointly with his students.

As a writer, he is incisive, makes his point (although sometimes he will resort to a whimsey, *e.g.*, when he defines intelligence as what the intelligence tests test), and has been constantly at pains to improve his style. After proving himself as a writer, not just an author, Boring, in his restless endeavor to reach out in diverse spheres, made his mark as an editor. He had already been on the editorial board and served as co-editor of several psychological journals, but *Contemporary Psychology*, if not his brain child, has been largely shaped in accordance with his plans. Even after his retirement, the journal still carries his imprint, figuratively speaking. His lucidity of exposition is on a par with his engineering aptitude. He will leave no loose ends around. Precision is his long suit.

In his aforementioned sketch, he declares, "I have come through a period of difficult decisions, but never for a moment have I regretted any one of them," and he asks the rhetorical question: "Is it that my choices were wise, or is it that I was pliant and adjustable?" So far as he himself is concerned, I should think that the answer lies in the fact that his forte is long-range planning and a realistic outlook which will permit of nothing that savors of bohemianism. Another question, however, which Boring does not ask, is whether some of his associates or subordinates or prospective colleagues had reason to be equally satisfied with his choices or, rather, his sometimes exaggerated demands.

It is here that we revert to his own confessions which are decidely germane in the context of psychological history, and even more instructive in the framework of personality assessment. Boring tells us that his outstanding personality traits are the hankering for power and success and need for approval and affection, and that the eternal conflict between the two seemed a source of torment. We are further informed that the lack of security in childhood had flowed over into a sense of inferiority which was with him in late adulthood. He recognizes the fact that he was an authoritarian, domineering, all of which goes to show that he possesses insight into his character and also that he is above board with himself.

It is somewhat of a relief to find that the man himself is aware of a shortcoming which it would be difficult for colleagues to fasten on him. To the man in the street it is simply incredible that one so gifted could be weighted down with a sense of inferiority. Nevertheless, it is true that a power-complex is simply the symptom of an inferiority feeling; and when the truly efficient head of a department will bother and fuss about picayune formalities, it is evident that inwardly he is questioning his own worth.

Hence Boring deserves a good deal of approbation for

deciding to do something about his drawbacks, even after he had become a Harvard professor. It is astounding to read that he had then felt "insecure, unhappy, frustrated, and afraid." What was he afraid of? "I was afraid mostly of not being successful." And he had already published *A History of Experimental Psychology* and other books and was reputed to be one of the foremost in his field. His compulsions were still with him and they were interfering with his work.

Under the circumstances, unless it were a desperate move to stave off a mental breakdown, it was little short of heroic to resort to psychoanalysis; and again he made a wise choice in engaging Hanns Sachs, who, in a sense, was apogeal to him. In an analytic report of the 168 sessions which he spent with Sachs, Boring tactfully expresses his misgivings as to the results.[2] However, whether it was only *post hoc* or *propter hoc*, the bossy Boring of the 1920's and 1930's has given way to a more understanding and mellow superior and associate. We are not sure about the collective *Zeitgeist*, which will be discussed presently, but perhaps the *Zeitgeist* of the individual does accomplish wonders too.

For one thing, we may infer that Boring's level of aspiration is very high. His success was assured, even to the extent of functioning as Honorary President of the 1963 International Congress of Psychology, in Washington, but perhaps he was comparing himself with one of the great pioneers he discussed in his *History of Experimental Psychology*. I am not sure, however, that first-rate scientists are preoccupied with their success. The hedonic paradox seems to apply also in the sphere of achievement. The less we think of success, the more genuine our creativity.

At any rate, Boring's personality traits could have had some effect on the course of American psychology. His compulsiveness may have been a great handicap to him, but although it doubtless has led at times to misunderstandings between himself and colleagues, it must have been a boon to many who were enlightened by his numerous letters. The correspondence on the *History of American Psychology* between reviewer Boring and author Roback—two compulsives, a world apart however, would, in itself, constitute a sizable and enlightening volume.

[2] E. G. Boring: "Was this Analysis a Success?" *Jour. of Abnormal and Social Psychology*, 1940, vol. 35.

It is through the content of such letters, in the thousands, that Boring's impact on American psychology has been far greater than meets the eye. From this angle, it may be observed that a compulsive of this nature is a benefactor. To my mind, Boring is the most dedicated psychologist of our time. There are others, like K. M. Dallenbach, who have committed themselves to serve the cause of psychology, but none, as far as I know, have rendered assistance so generously and spontaneously to individuals.

On the other hand, Boring's insistence on formality, and admiration of *bon ton*, his worship of authority and apotheosis of rule, have led to occasional injustice; and in his leaning backward in order to be objective and fair, he has sometimes overlooked the differential circumstances. He could upbraid and even scold a person of lower rank; he might complain of his peer, but when it comes to rules by which an organization or editor or director is governed, he would never so much as raise a murmur. The Hegelian principle "what is, is right" seems to be *his* motto too. That is probably an emanation of the authoritarian personality, and bespeaks a certain self-discipline; for such an attitude will cause no fracas, will never plead for exceptions, and will make no bid for sympathy or consideration on special grounds. Although Boring comes of Quaker stock, there is a tinge of French (not German) militarism in his make-up—the proverbial martinet.

Moving in a formal and purely scientific atmosphere, Boring misses a large part of life on the lower levels. The seamy side is simply unperceived. He is a man of committees and boards, an organization functionary, who brings to the council halls his engineering skill and practical sense. But with all his perspicacity in self-analysis, he exposes an important lacuna in his make-up, *viz.*, intuition; and lacking it, he deprecates it in others.

His achievement in bridging the usual gap between technology and scholarship is immense, and his creditable performances at writing, editing, administration, and even televised lecturing, are evidence of a versatile mind, but he has never been able to attain to the heights of humanism. Only through intuition can one enter its portals; and Boring is temperamentally averse to it, hence he mentions it in derision, but his intended branding "intuitionist Allport" or "intuitionist Roback" is reminiscent of the philistine who calls the Bach or Mozart votary "highbrow." For, in the last analysis, what does this labeling amount to? Does he mean that we are paying no heed to experimental investigations? But these so-called intuitionists and others have spent years in the psychological laboratory and still repose their faith in experimentation. They are convinced, however, that there are also other avenues to the acquisition of knowledge; and avoidance of them can only lead to the accumulation of pockets of ignorance (with apologies for the Irish bull) on vital topics, such as social psychology, general history, judgment of people, literature, folklore, and many others, even philosophy. Boring has done well to assimilate as much as he has been doing, but there are some disciplines that must be picked up on the ground floor, in the early undergraduate days. Boring's erudition is of a specialized character, as is his undeniable sense of humor.

The difference between the intuitive and the sequential mind is (a) that to the former a certain perception comes in a flash. It then must be corrected or validated. (b) The perception, idea or conception, is generally of a qualitative nature. The sequential mind, on the other hand, must start from a premise, perhaps universally accepted, and then begin to build on it step by step. If the premise is wrong, then no matter how careful the procedure, the conclusion will be invalid. (c) The intuitionist, in his humanistic domain, may not be as careful as the sequentialist,[3] the technologist, knowing that he can revise his view on a second look. The technologist cannot afford such a luxury: 1/100 of a second or 1/16 of an inch off the mark may be the cause of an explosion or collapse.

Nevertheless, the first step is an intuitive one. It is equivalent to what is sometimes referred to as the "pretheoretical model." *It is necessary to take up a position and that requires intuition.* Intuition has been at the root of many discoveries and inventions, and it ill behooves us to spurn it.

A Physicalistic Platform

Now as to Boring's scientific credo, one would naturally expect him to be a physicalist, but his quasi-indenture to Titchener made of him a structuralist until Titchener's death released the moral hold. Boring claims that his basic faith in

---

[3] This term is proposed as an antonym for "intuitionist," *i.e.*, one who goes from step to step.

operationism went back to his paper on the stimulus error. Functionalism, maybe; but one fails to see any sign of operationism therein. On the contrary, it might more easily be taken as a critique of behaviorism. What else could it be when he points out that the only way to emerge from the dark "would be to study the effect of stimulation, of attention, and of criterion by taking hold of these dependent series at their intermediate points thus providing ourselves with a complete knowledge and control of the entire psychological situation. . . . The failure to control the attitudinal factor, implied in the acceptance of a criterion and the attentional factor, again and again results perforce in an equivocal determination of these responses."[4]

Let us not, however, bring up the past. Boring is at present committed to operationism. What is more, he believes that everyone who in psychology does not pursue the same course is behind the times. Since the pros and cons of operationism have already been threshed out, we might as well let it go at that.

Free will, he opines, is a delusion, but a useful and important one required by one's culture even if repudiated by one's intelligence. In this respect, he may be following the "as-if" school of Vaihinger.

As a physicalist he does not bother with mind, repudiating any dualistic implication, yet he believes in the importance of the unconscious in motivation, but when he states that "my unconscious cerebration operates my typewriter and puts down there wiser thoughts and more apt expressions than I ever anticipated when I began," we wonder whether he is alluding to the dynamic unconscious of Freud and Jung or the mere cerebration which is purely physiological. This ambiguity should be cleared up, since Boring has learned "to turn myself over to my unconscious motivations and let them work through me."

In recent years, Boring has made use of a term which was in vogue about seventy-five years ago, *viz., Zeitgeist* (spirit of the times). What is this *Zeitgeist* that is made so much of? Boring cautions us not to attach any mystical significance to it, but we are not sure whether he himself has been able to escape that involvement.

4 E. G. Boring: "The Stimulus Error," *Amer. Journal of Psychology*, 1921, vol. 32, p. 469.

In two well-written essays, afterward reprinted in *A Psychologist at Large*, Boring takes up anew the old issue as to whether the genius is the product of his time or is independently great by virtue of his genes. Thinkers have been divided on this point since antiquity, although it is only within the last century that the problem has been tackled articulately. On the one side range Tolstoi and some of the British empiricists like Herbert Spencer, Andrew Lang, Alfred Russel Wallace, while Carlyle, Emerson, and William James belong to the other camp.

Actually, the issue should be subdivided. To treat it under the label of "great man" controversy brings some confusion into the matter. Let us recognize that there are geniuses and great men. Sometimes there is an overlapping, as in the case of Albert Einstein, but greatness carries something of the ethical, and certainly comprehends personality, while a genius *qua genius* need not be an outstanding personality and may be a reprehensible character, like Francis Bacon.[5]

There are also other sources of confusion to be found in such discussions, as for example, when Boring includes Hitler's name among those he calls great. We may at most regard such as "men of destiny," who were wafted to power through sheer circumstance. Had there been no Versailles Treaty, had Germany been as prosperous during the 1920's as she is now, had the Weimar Government kept Hitler in prison after the *Putsch*, what would he have amounted to? At least Napoleon, although he too benefited by chance happenings, did possess some genius as a commander. Tolstoi in debunking Napoleon's greatness in his famous novel would hardly consider himself to have been an ordinary individual smiled upon by fortune. Tolstoi, Kropotkin, and others of the nobility or royal blood, who cast their lot with the peasants and workers were great because *they did not fit in with the times or their environment,* but *created* the new *Zeitgeist.*

It is evident, however, that Boring is moving in another frame of reference—the world of the scientist, the discoverer of laws, the inventor; and even if that is a circumscribed sphere, let us see just how the *Zeitgeist* applies here. To quote Boring,

Not only is a new discovery seldom made until the times are ready for it, but again and again it turns out to have

[5] A. A. Roback: *William James,* 1942, pp. 240-241, 320-324.

been anticipated inadequately perhaps, but nevertheless explicitly as the times were beginning to get ready for it. Thus the concept of a gradually changing *Zeitgeist* has been used to explain the historical continuity of thought and the observation that the novelty of a discovery . . . appears to be only a historian's artifact.[6]

All this could mean is that in order to make discoveries we must have previous information and also certain instruments. That this takes time to accumulate is simply a truism, but why inject into the time factor a "spirit" or a "ghost," since the German word does duty for both? If Leeuwenhoek had lived in the days of St. Thomas Aquinas, he might have invented his microscope and discovered the "little animals" in the thirteenth century. Roger Bacon did some truly scientific work in the thirteenth century, and the fact that he was condemned to prison because of the obscurantism of his peers so that he could not achieve his goal does not detract from his greatness. In other words, the great man or genius is no less great because fate is against him or because ignorance prevails. If Hitler had had his way, then all art and science would have been crushed; and he lived in the twentieth century!

Does Boring mean that all culture progresses in time? If so, then it may be observed that we have no El Grecos, Raphaels, Titians, Leonardos, or Rembrandts today; no Vivaldis, Bachs, Mozarts or Haydns; no Spinozas, Leibnizs, Humes, or Kants. Was it the period they lived in that made them great?

Our knowledge has advanced, of course, because, to use a common metaphor, we stood on the shoulders of our predecessors, just as they did on others' shoulders; but time here is only incidental. One might as well belabor the thesis that experience comes with age.

Citing several of Ogburn and Thomas's alleged 148 instances of approximately synchronous independent discoveries or inventions, such as Newton's and Leibniz's calculus, Napier's and Briggs's logarithms, Boring thinks this clinches the conclusion, but all it does is to show that great minds often run in like channels. What about the thousands of inventions and discoveries that emanated from individual minds? Where was the *Zeitgeist* then? My own contention is

[6] E. G. Boring: *A Psychologist at Large*, 1962, p. 327. (Reprinted from the *Scientific Monthly*, 1955, vol. 80.)

that before an idea is "in the air" it must have been somewhere "under the hair" first.

Nor does the definition of the *Zeitgeist* as "the sum total of social interactions as it is common to a particular period and particular locale" much help us. Indeed Boring himself asks, "Did the *Zeitgeist* that Newton knew help relativity theory?" And he answers, "No, relativity had to make its way against the *Zeitgeist*." And so did Freud's "unconscious" and the libido doctrine, and others one could mention.

Curiously enough, after piling Ossa on Pelion to build up his *Zeitgeist* hobby, he finally admits that "it is not all the *Zeitgeist*. Some brains are better than others" and "Carlyle was partly right. The History of Civilization is the history of the operation of genius," and he submits that insight and motivation are satisfactory class names for two sets of parameters which are the dimensions along which civilization will be enlarged or lost.[7]

Operationism and Value Judgments

Just as there are syndromes in pathology, there are constellations of attitudes in scientific orientation. An operationist or behaviorist, or physicalist, would naturally be inclined to see in genius or greatness a mere product of environment, training, *Zeitgeist*, and perhaps too *some* ability. This constellation is common to logical positivism; and to both, value judgments are, if not anathema, then just sounds without objectivity, rhyme, or reason.

Boring, an out-and-out physicalist, would expectedly take that position. In his autobiographical essay, he states that value judgments are psychologically prejudices, hence he fears them. Since, however, we cannot live without value judgments, I should think, we ought to learn to reduce the prejudice and, instead of fearing them, begin analyzing them in the light of common sense and the accumulated verdict of the maturely cultured. What else can we do? Should we give as much weight to the judgment of a teen-ager who prefers jive or rock 'n roll to Mozart's *Requiem*? Or should we adopt John B. Watson's measure of counting votes on any painting, so that if a million will prefer a cartoon to twenty-five who will choose the Sistine Madonna, or ten million vote for

---

[7] E. G. Boring: "Great Men and Scientific Progress," *Proceedings of the Amer. Philosophical Society*, 1950, vol. 94, p. 350.

comics like Mutt and Jeff while El Greco's Inquisitor, Cardinal de Guevara, is appreciated by only a few thousand, shall we then accept the comics as superior art?

Tastes will of course differ, but despite prejudices, great art and music will always be recognized, and the creators will live and continue to thrill ever more generations of feeling people, no matter how far the world advances.

Coming back to the more intellectual and even scientific aspects, operationists and their allies scarcely appreciate to what extent value judgments are at the basis of all our operations. We can measure to our heart's content, but unless we first decide as to what to measure and why, all our measurements may be useless. In other words, *we start with a value judgment which does not always stem from a necessity or need.* The thing to remember is that value judgments can generally be corrected or validated in terms of consensus among the *trained in a special field*, not at any given period but *in the course of time*. Its predictive function is not as great as its heuristic usefulness, and eventually its validation by *an enlightened posterity. Per contra*, fear of making or accepting value judgments is likely to breed cynicism and eventually delinquency because the youth is apt to make no distinction between right or wrong, good and bad, or beautiful and ugly. The result is, therefore, worse than throwing out the baby with the bathwater.

Boring's goal, or rather ideal, seems to be *maturity*. In that respect he wavers between descanting on his activities and achievements, on the one hand, and playing down his native endowments, on the other, as if his accomplishments were due to uncommon industry rather than to innate ability. He is even inclined to the belief that, in spite of his present position among his colleagues, he will be forgotten in a decade. There is a great temptation to dilate on the subject of causes of oblivion, but it would require a volume in itself.

Boring's chief mark of maturity comes to evidence in his treatment of opponents toward whom he shows himself eminently fair, even magnanimous.

Chapter 32

Operant Conditioning

A SPECIAL PHASE of operationism is associated with B. F. Skinner (1904-   ) who for the past thirty years has been forging ahead on a program of his own, reaching out in various directions and acting, in a sense, as a missionary, or at least as a social reformer.

With an A.B. from Hamilton College, Skinner came to Harvard where he took his doctorate in experimental psychology in 1931, serving as a research fellow in general physiology. He then joined the faculty at the University of Minnesota and from there he went to the University of Indiana. In 1948, he received a call to Harvard University, where he has been carrying on his various experiments on animals, principally rats and pigeons. His technique in the construction of special equipment has been recognized by workers in animal psychology who have been referring to the "Skinner box" so often that its architect begins to resent the label. He would prefer a more appropriate term, *e.g.*, magazine.

The trademark which suits him best is *operant conditioning*; and his method of procedure is beginning to take hold on a number of campuses and in several nonacademic institutions. Although he has not formed a school in the usual sense, there are operant "islands" throughout the country where the basic principle is to reinforce the initiative of the organism, whether pigeon or human being. Skinner never tires of making a distinction between the classical conditioning of Pavlov, in which the dog or other animal is simply a passive victim or, if you will, subject, and his own method, which rewards the right reaction.

The operant experiments were not perhaps as new as Skinner makes them sound; Thorndike had already tried something of the sort with his pathetic chickens in William James's basement and more successfully taught his cat to manipulate a latch and lever so as to get free or obtain food. But Skinner and his associates, while working on a wartime project, in 1943, succeeded in teaching a pigeon to bowl. That required bold imagination, great skill, and considerable patience. Once the responses were selected for reinforcement so as to approximate the bowling swipe, the result amazed the three experimenters.

Skinner has been steadily refining on his experiments, and some of the reports in the press and popular journals with captions about his training pigeons to play the piano may irk him, but he himself speaks of a pigeon "superstition," which bids fair to encourage newspaper exaggeration.

In his *Behavior of Organisms* Skinner describes an experiment in which a rat "was conditioned to pull a string to get a marble from a rack, pick up the marble with its forepaws, carry it across the cage to a vertical tube rising two inches above the floor, lift the marble and drop it into the tube." I do not know whether its colleague, at Barnard College, Barnabel, showed greater genius, but the man behind the experiments certainly proved to be an ingenious conditioner whose contrivances, both mechanical and electrical, were superior to Thorndike's. For one thing, Thorndike did not have the benefit of electronics and computers and automatic recorders. His cat had to be watched.

In the 1930's, Skinner rated as a promising young man, and in 1964, although no longer a young man, having entered on his sixtieth year, he is still promising, but this time articulately. Indeed, he is perhaps the most energetic propagandist for his psychological causes; for there are several with which his name is identified. These causes are not altogether in the orbit of present-day laboratory trends, and although he is esteemed by his colleagues as an efficient researcher and is sought as a participant in symposia and academic gala affairs, he is thought of as somewhat of a maverick because of his outspoken criticism of accepted traditions and his espousal of scientific and educational policies that are too far right or left of the center.

In the first place, he would have no truck with any views or terminology which smack of mentalism. An uncompromising behaviorist, he is impatient with anyone who straddles, and yet unlike the typical behaviorist, he can appreciate the mentalist who has made a contribution.

Second, he seems to agree with Mephistopheles that

> *Grau, lieber Freund, ist alle Theorie*
> *Grün allein des Lebens gold'ner Baum*

> *Grey, my friend, is all theory*
> *Green alone is life's blooming tree*

Although he looks like anything but a Mephistopheles, he strikes some psychologists as an *advocatus diaboli*; for the psychology of learning is steeped in theory while he not only eschews it but loses no opportunity in laughing it out of court. Usually a man spurns what he is personally not apt in, but that is not true of Skinner; his *Verbal Behavior*, which constituted his William James lectures at Harvard, is not only an extended theory but can be envisaged as a system of linguistic philosophy in which the experimental data are sparse.

Indeed, he may have been under the influence of Whitehead's *Process and Reality* when he was formulating his definitions, classifying his types, and reinforcing his arguments through an abundant supply of illustrative material both from everyday anecdotes and literary episodes, often embellishments for "your reading pleasure," as the radio announcer might put it, rather than relevant evidence. Let us make no mistake, however—at bottom, and weaving through it all, there is Skinner's doctrine of operant conditioning.

"In all verbal behavior under stimulus control," we are told, "there are three important events to be taken into account: a stimulus, a response, and a reinforcement. When a response is characteristically reinforced in a given way, its likelihood of appearing in the behavior of the speaker is a function of the deprivation associated with that reinforcement. The response *candy*! will be more likely to occur after a period of candy deprivation and least likely after candy satiation."[1]

His method in this book is almost scholastic, and his definitions are precise, but we wonder whether the referents of the "tacts" and the "mands" are as clear-cut as he makes them out to be. A "tact," *e.g.,* is "a verbal operant in which a response of given form is evoked or else strengthened by a particular object or event or property of an object or event."[2] It is a bit of behavior which makes *contact* with the physical world, and is represented in speech by such words as mentioning, announcing, stating, naming, or proclaiming. A "mand," on the other hand, is represented by *commands*, requests, advice, exhortation, etc. "Mand" is a verbal operant in which the response is reinforced by a characteristic consequence and is therefore under the functional control of relevant conditions

[1] B. F. Skinner: *Verbal Behavior,* 1957, p. 35.
[2] B. F. Skinner: *Loc. cit.,* p. 8.

of deprivation on aversive stimulation. The response has no specified relation to a prior stimulus. To illustrate, "Fire" may be "(1) a mand to a firing squad, (2) a tact to a conflagration, (3) an interverbal response to the stimulus ready aim . . . , or (4) an echoic, or (5) textual response to appropriate verbal stimuli."

It is apparent that Skinner can theorize as well as the most ratiocinative of psychologists, yet after the "Moor has performed his duty, he can go." He recognizes that "theories are fun . . . but the most elementary preliminary research shows that there are many relevant variables, and until their importance has been experimentally determined, an equation which allows for them will have so many arbitrary constants that a good fit will be a matter of course and cause for very little satisfaction."[3]

Similar utterances, some as *obiter dicta*, will be found in other writings of his, disclosing that he is primarily concerned with generating action. Explanations of what has happened, the construction of models, whether mathematical or physiological, are to his way of thinking a waste of time and energy, because we can never be certain that our assumptions, postulates, or conclusions can be validated. Skinner's thoughts, like the maiden's in *Hiawatha*, are of the future only; and the future of operant conditioning is envisaged in a roseate hue as ushering in a revolution in the whole psychological range.

Whether we agree with Skinner or not, he always enlists our attention. He may write on a case history in scientific method (animal learning) and yet scuff away all technical jargon which makes so many experimental studies dull, if not boresome. Because of his fund of knowledge, he can reach for data from various corners, and for that reason, too, he looms as a doughty champion and lively polemicist, on a dignified level.

There is one sphere, however, in which his behavior thesis is wobbly, and that is *personality*. Skinner seems to avoid the term. Instead he employs the word "self" which, for him, represents "a functionally unified system of responses organized around a discriminative stimulus" and "traits" are "certain conditions of reinforcement and deprivation."[4] It is a case

[3] B. F. Skinner: "Are Theories of Learning Necessary?" *Cumulative Record*, 1961, p. 69.

[4] B. F. Skinner: *Science and Human Behavior*, New York, Macmillan, 1953.

of putting the cart before the horse, because it is the very traits which constitute personality, and the conditions are internal, varying from individual to individual. It is because of this blind spot which is symptomatic of a thoroughgoing behaviorism that he is so puzzled about Albert Schweitzer's motives in spending his life treating African natives instead of working in a medical laboratory discovering some new cures.

Skinner can write on the alliteration in Shakespeare's sonnets and on types of sound-patterning in poetry; and thus he may be accounted a humanist as well as a technologist. In that respect, he has the edge on most of his colleagues, whose ambit is generally circumscribed by their specialized training. It would perhaps be even safe to say that at heart he is a social reformer. His novel *Walden Two* points in that direction; and his rejection of theory and his constant advocacy of action via reinforcement would suggest it. In that capacity, he takes his mission rather seriously, addressing conferences in various parts of the country and traveling abroad, as far as Russia, to make his voice heard.

He is not an *Akt* psychologist in the sense of Brentano, Witasek, or Ach, or even in the tradition of Stout, but an *action* psychologist, in that he seeks to promote action in subjects or charges under his control. It is a peculiarly propitious policy in connection with the psychotics in mental hospitals whose whole life is spent in a sort of vegetative existence only to be "relieved" by spells of anxiety or rage. The idea of getting such patients to press a bar or depress a button, in order to receive a cigarette or candy or an exciting picture, has appealed to investigators and administrators of state institutions. Skinner's skilled adjutant, O. R. Lindsley has been able to rig up a new type of operant conditioning laboratory at the Massachusetts State Hospital in Waltham, Massachusetts, under the auspices of the Harvard Medical School, and has been stirring up something of a rebellion against conventional psychiatrists.

One can understand how Skinner would become engrossed in the matter of teaching machines, for it is governed by the same principle: the facilities are supplied, but the student, like the rodent, regulates the conditions in accordance with the motives and the scheduling or programing. If automation should become a significant factor in teaching, then Skinner will have had much to answer for. Whether it is a Skinner release box for animals, or a teaching box for human reception, or a crate for rearing babies, it is all a contraption minus the impact of personality. Operant conditioning has been of greatest service in the training of animals and in spurring to activity lethargic psychotics. Here personality counts for little. Action alone is the goal; and whatever mediates it is to advantage.

Chapter 33

Factorial Analysis and General Semantics

A. The Era of Statistics

IF OPERATIONISM is the glorification of physicalism, then the factorial school may be regarded as the apotheosis of mathematics in psychology. While the operationists, however, are a restrictive group, barring the psychologists from their sphere until they reduced mentalistic terms to a physicalistic nomenclature, the factorial analysts began by infiltrating into psychology until, like the camel in the fable, they bid fair to dislodge the rightful owner from his domain. From our Greek philosophy days, we may recall how Pythagoras and his disciples sought to deduce everything out of number and harmony. The modern Pythagoras would also settle the most intricate and complicated issues through statistics and quantification.

Prescientific psychology, as we may remember, was woefully lacking in definite results because it did not concern itself with measurement. Then came the experimental period with its stress on reaction time, which involved not only computation, but computation in terms of one-thousandth of a second. It rested on a combination of times and time. The introduction of the Weber-Fechner law gave rise to numerous studies in connection with psychophysical methods, which, again, made a final appeal to mathematical treatment.

Formulas of one sort or another had been used by Herbart, and, in 1876, there appeared a whole book of psychological (really conjectural) formulas[1] of H. Steinthal, organized and explained by one of his disciples, but it was not Germany which gave impetus to psychological statistics. Perhaps Francis Galton, who was the founder of an assortment of scientific movements might be looked upon as the inaugurator of psychometrics, biometrics, and anthropometry about eighty-five years ago. As he formulated it, in his essay on statistical meth-

---

[1] G. Glogau: *Steinthals psychologische Formeln,* 1876.

ods, "The object of statistical science is to discover methods of condensing information concerning large groups of allied facts into brief and compendious expressions . . . The possibility of doing this is based on the constancy and continuity with which objects of the same species are found to vary."[2] The logical pursuits of men, like J. Venn (*The Logic of Chance*) and W. S. Jevons (*The Principles of Science*), too, aided in establishing the new sector of science.

Galton's mind, however, was too versatile to carry on the work beyond the first steps, and the task was bequeathed to his disciple, Karl Pearson (*The Grammar of Science*) who was a specialist, and whose formulas are still extensively used in various connections. Pearson was not a psychologist but a biometrician and general methodologist; and so his statistical work could not be intimately bound up with the mental sciences, but his student, Charles E. Spearman found in the study of intelligence and abilities in general a fruitful field for the development of his factor theory. In England, the psychology department of the University of London, which enjoyed the tradition of Galton, Pearson, and Spearman, became the world centre of statistical psychology, and after Spearman's death, Cyril Burt was left to continue the tradition, while R. B. Cattell brought its influence to the United States; and he has become just as zealous as his teacher in fostering the doctrine, with some modifications, not only in the sphere of intelligence and aptitude testing where it had been originally applied, but especially in the field of personality. Spearman's only rival in England was G. H. Thomson, until his death, professor at the University of Edinburgh.

It must not be thought that psychological statistics was all the while neglected in the United States. Quite the contrary; we must not forget that one of Galton's distinguished students, or perhaps assistants, since Galton accepted no teaching post, was J. McKeen Cattell, the first professor of psychology in America. Not only was he inspired by his idol to dwell on the importance of measurement, but the very nature of differential psychology which Cattell was building up in this country required a quantitative approach. It was, however, not Cattell but his student E. L. Thorndike who became the leader in matters of mental measurement. True, Lewis M. Terman's

[2] F. Galton: *Inquiries into Human Faculty and Its Development* (Everyman), p. 33.

name is the foremost in American testing methods and technique, but the mathematical basis of the testing was scarcely within Terman's scope. Thorndike did surround himself with computers and statisticians and was able, as we shall see, to challenge Spearman's single-factor theory, in the early days of its life. The chief figure in the American field of education, Thorndike, was a man to be reckoned with, but with all his achievement in the sphere of learning, he did not possess the mathematical training requisite in such a progressively complicated domain as statistics, with its newer and newer acquisitions from mathematical theory. He, curiously enough, in his late years, turned to language studies, adding a quantitative slant to the subject (word frequency and syllabification).

It was with Thorndike's student, T. L. Kelley, and the former engineer, L. L. Thurstone that statistical psychology began to take hold, and the latter who, at one time was Thomas Edison's assistant, particularly has broadened the horizon of the factor theory both through the establishment of the psychometric laboratory at the University of Chicago where research along these lines has been accumulating and by his introduction of new principles affecting mental measurement. K. J. Holzinger has been his able coadjutor in his factorial quest, although not always in agreement with him.

The Use of Factorial Analysis

Before going any further, it would be advantageous to learn what actually the factorial analysts purport to do, especially as the term is still often looked upon as something esoteric. As psychologists, we are wont to begin any inquiry with specific postulates based on our everyday observations. Thorndike, e.g., sorted out three types of intelligence: the abstract, the mechanical, and the social. The factor analyst thinks we have no right to decide on such classes before subjecting all items which are included under intelligence to rigid statistical treatment, so as to see by means of the intercorrelations just how the categories range themselves. We can talk about these relationships in terms of x, y, and z, or A, B, and C, without actually committing ourselves on the content. Just as in ascertaining the dimensions of boxes, we need not know what is in the boxes, or separating out certain vitamins and calling them A, B, C, D etc. does not yet prove that we know the function of each of them, so in mental life, the categories are only brought into relation with each other, without further commitment, until subsequent research supplies further details. As the dimensions show certain uniformities, we begin to pair one capacity, trait, or behavior pattern with another, grouping them in clusters perhaps, so as to form a functional unity.

Factorial analysis is, in the first instance, exploratory, whether we set out with some hypothesis which we wish to verify or whether we start without any preconceptions whatever. As we discover some order in the intercorrelations, we may label the factors and find that certain abilities, traits, or neurotic behavior which we treated as fundamentally different are in reality closely related, and vice versa.

It was only natural for the factor theory to be applied to intelligence, after the testing movement had supplied such a vast array of material. Here Spearman, through a series of intercorrelations, found all mental activity to depend on a general factor, which he called G, and which most of us were inclined to identify with general intelligence. In a letter to Roback, Wm. McDougall, who was at one with Spearman on the point, writes, "First I don't see that we need concern ourselves with what intelligence reduces to. Intelligence is, properly speaking, the function of the whole organism, and any analysis which attaches the word *intelligence* to any one factor *reduces* intelligence to that factor. Your difficulty, firstly, arises from insisting on attaching intelligence to 'G' . . . , a procedure which Spearman himself deprecates, and I also." In another letter, McDougall states, "I also feel that I have not answered the difficult question you raised . . . namely: does not my interpretation of Spearman's 'G' make character identical with intelligence? My answer is that I do not identify 'G' with intelligence. It seems to me that almost every one makes the mistake, which Spearman and I avoid, of identifying 'G' with intelligence. 'G' is only one aspect of intelligence, and, in my opinion, that which is most nearly dependent on character formation; which meets your objection that I seem to reduce intelligence merely to power of concentration. I reduce 'G' to that, but not intelligence. If you look at my *Energies of Men*, you will see that I regard the whole system of abilities as factors of intelligence."[3]

[3] William McDougall, in letter to A. A. Roback, Oct. 27, 1935.

General, Specific, and Group Factors

Now that we know what the G factor is not, we may continue with Spearman's subsequent findings. Having satisfied himself that there is a general mental energy, analogous to physical energy in the physical world, he came upon certain results which indicated that there were also specific factors (s) the basis of abilities and talents, which, although in some measure linked to the general factor, are relatively independent. Meeting further obstacles, Spearman introduced another factor, viz., the group factor (g). Thus, every mental activity is composed of at least the G factor, but may, in addition, share some specific and group factor. To test general intelligence, items which would bring out the specific factors are ruled out, and where they persist, it is believed and hoped that they would cancel one another, leaving the field to the G-factor showings. To insure the validity of his claims, he obtained a criterion in the form of a tetrad equation, which yielded further the tetrad difference in each case making t equal zero, if the criterion works. Spearman further introduced three non-cognitive factors, viz., perseveration (p), Will (w), and oscillation (o) as influencing the cognitive factors, unwittingly revealing thereby that the G factor *is* predominantly an intelligence factor, despite McDougall's disclaimer.

Multiple Factors

Thorndike opposed the Spearman factor theory strenuously. He was altogether for a multimodal arrangement which bespeaks a species of atomism in the matter of abilities, not different from J. S. Mill's view of mental chemistry. For Thorndike, any mental activity, any intelligent performance involves a number of fractional elements, incorporated suchwise as to operate for a given purpose. But even Thorndike has thought it expedient to group the vast multitude of elements in such a way as to embrace them in four categories, so far as abstract intelligence is concerned, and thus he has devised a single instrument comprising tests of (a) sentence completion (b) arithmetical reasoning (c) vocabulary, and (d) following directions—the famous CAVD test.

L. L. Thurstone takes a middle course between Spearman's

and Thorndike's, as does G. H. Thomson. Both are experts in this new twig of psycho-mathematics. Thurstone operates with a formidable apparatus. It would take us too far afield, were it even within the competence of the writer, to expound the many devices which he has introduced. The nomenclature alone, the concepts and terms, would require a long chapter in itself. The application of vectors (different from Lewin's use) to mental data, the centroid method of factoring, the treatment of unknown communalities, the matrix formulation of the multiple-factor problem, the concept of simple structure, which has been the butt of much criticism and, above all, the geometrical representation of the subject require concentrated thought in addition to a grounding in mathematical theory. Thurstone traverses the territory which Spearman has covered and exposes the weak spots, all the while arguing on behalf of his multiple-factor theory.

In brief, he holds that there are first-order factors as well as factors of the second order, and that the single-factor, or, as it is generally known, the two-factor theory of Spearman is an unwitting exploitation of these second-order factors, which in Spearman's computations, are confused with the first-order factors.[4] Thurstone further intimates that the selection of the particular battery by the Spearman subschool would likely be determined by the special bias of the single-factorist. At any rate, there is not, for practical purposes, such a gulf between Thurstone and Spearman as might appear at first blush. Spearman, starting with the *G* factor, gathers specific and group factors as he proceeds, while Thurstone, beginning with multiple factors concludes that "a second-order general factor is a part of, and must participate in, the definition of the other factors . . . It is evident, therefore, that a general second-factor is likely to be of more fundamental significance for the domain in question than a general orthogonal first-order factor." In other words, when Spearman strikes snags with residuals, which would not fit into his tetrad differences, he helps himself to some new cards. Thurstone, when he is hard put to explain some results, comes close to perceiving the common factor, albeit not in the first-order but in the second-order class. Thurstone, despite the implication of multiplicity, has succeeded in detecting, by means of his divining rod, only

4 L. L. Thurstone: *Multiple Factor Analysis* (1947), p. 413.

six primary factors in intelligence, which point to the following abilities: number facility, word fluency, verbal meaning, spatial perception, rote memory, and reasoning.

Godfrey H. Thomson's position is that of a moderator between Thorndike and Spearman. He believes that the correlation coefficients may be due to common samplings and combinations of independent factors. He is closer to Thorndike theoretically, but in practice, he leans toward the fiction of "as if," i.e., that it is useful to retain the concept of a general factor inasmuch as where a number of tests draw on a multiplicity of common factors, they will give us a phenotype of a general factor.

The factorial analysts set out to solve some intelligence problems, but soon they were invading the precincts of personality, temperament, character and the neuroses, everywhere correlating and intercorrelating numerical values so as to establish parameters, dimensions, factors, and functions; and through these to shuffle up the traits a bit, exalt the humble and degrade the mighty. What we might have thought to be, on the basis of empirical observation, a very important quality may take a drop to one of the low places, and vice versa. R. B. Cattell has even gone so far as to proclaim the authority of factorial analysis ("internal validation") over actual knowledge from experience in the validation of tests ("peripheral validation")[5] a sort of reversion to Hegel's alleged retort, "So much the worse for the facts," when told that the discovery of a new planet had upset his finalistic cosmology. Factorial analysis is beginning to act almost like that Olympic champion runner who was chasing a thief, but far outstripped the fellow whom he wished to apprehend.

There is a slight irony too in the fact that with all their bustling and effort put in, the factorial analysts are not accepted by the mathematicians. The statisticians certainly do not recognize their achievement, contending, as they do, that mathematics has made advances in recent years which have not been utilized by the factor theorists.

Since the above first appeared, all the architects of factorial analysis have departed, but the differences still remain. The chief representatives are divided along the lines of "the one and the many," or the specific and the general.

[5] R. B. Cattell: *Description and Measurement of Personality*, 1946, p. 546.

For a number of decades, we shall recall, this happened to be the basis of discord between Spearman, in London, and Thorndike, in New York, and now that their pupils or followers have taken over, the geopolitical barrier still separates the two subschools. Both British and American exponents of the movement are convinced of the necessity of untangling through this method the many complex elements that constitute personality, but they disagree on the starting point.

On the basis of a hierarchical model of personality traits, we must recognize that some are specific, others are more general, embracing two or more traits at a lower level. The most concrete events are, of course, the individual reactions, in other words, specific behavior. To a number of these reactions, frequently repeated under various circumstances, we attach a label, *e.g.*, cleanliness, honesty, instability. We may even have higher levels of generality. Where are we to start?

Spearman, assuming intelligence to be an energy, assumed that there was a general factor (G) and a group factor (g) as well as a specific factor (s) like proficiency in music or games. P. Vernon and H. Eysenck, in England, are prone to accept a very limited number of factors within general intelligence, or balancedness *vs.* neuroticism, at the peak of the pyramid, as subsuming a number of related traits. R. B. Cattell, while spending nearly half his life in the United States, is still under British influence in that connection, and adheres to a single-unit factorial analysis, which yields him a restricted number of paired (positive and negative) traits. He thus covers the whole of personality as it were, in a single operation or single set of computations; but when we look at the table, it strikes us that the traits are not of equal weight, some being of a high generality and some of a low generality and, from a phenomenological, *i.e.*, purely empirical angle, there is some overlapping. To take an analogous though somewhat exaggerated instance, if factorial analysis were to prove that a headache is a disease, I, for one, should be loath to take such a conclusion seriously.

J. P. Guilford inclines toward the multimodal view of personality. His strategy consists in beginning with traits of low degree of generality, the more specific ones, because they are closer to observed behavior. It would be on the assessment of these more concrete reactions that traits of a higher generality would be based. Emphasizing the more individual forms of behavior, he would naturally be prepared to make allowance for more factors, while the British bias or tradition is to relate a number of traits and treat them generically as a class.

The cleavage seems to follow the difference of opinion on the validity of the type theory. American psychologists, by and large, are adverse to sponsoring the division of personalities into types, be they temperaments, constitutional categories, or even somatotypes. The European approach is more in keeping with the type doctrine.

At any rate, the factorial controversy is likely to be carried into another decade; and with orientations such as they are, it is doubtful whether the dispute will be settled then. Both sides have something to be said in their favor and both have a weak spot. In the last analysis, it may be a matter of semantics, which will first have to be cleared up before the mathematical tool is applied.

B. General Semantics

If operationism is affiliated with physics, and factorial analysis grew out of mathematical theory, then general semantics is a chip off the logic block. General semantics is not quite the same as the original branch of linguistics which the two Judeo-French philologists, Michel Bréal, who actually coined the word,[6] in 1883, and Arsène Darmesteter founded about eighty years ago. Nor is it to be identified with the field of logic which R. Carnap[7] has been cultivating these past two decades. General semantics should in reality be changed to applied semantics, if it is to be correctly styled; and in the threefold classification of semeiotics, as suggested by C. W. Morris,[8] general semantics would correspond to what he called pragmatics, for it deals with the relation of signs to scientists, that is to say, it asks: What use can be made of the proper understanding of a certain term in matters outside of pure science? General semantics is not a school of psychology. It lies on the outskirts of our science, but because of its application to life, it often meets on common ground with psychology.

[6] M. Bréal: "Les lois intellectuelles du langage; fragment de Sémantique," *Annuaire de l'association pour l'encouragement des études grecques en France*, 1883. A. Darmesteter: *The Life of Words*, 1886.

[7] R. Carnap: *Introduction to Semantics*, 1942.

[8] C. W. Morris: "Foundations of the Theory of Signs," *Intern. Encycl. of Unified Science*, 1938, No. 2.

The man—and here a single individual must receive the credit—who was instrumental in founding this study is Alfred Korzybski (1879-1950), a Polish nobleman, who came to Canada and this country in 1915, on a war mission, and stayed for the rest of his life. Korzybski was an engineer and, of course, was highly trained in mathematics and, to a less extent, in physics and chemistry. His first book, *The Manhood of Humanity*, which was published in 1921, was intended by the author as an essay on human engineering. The transfer of interest from land and water and heavy artillery to human beings and their affections might have been a natural reaction of the war, but it also bespoke a humanistic quality in the man. Always such a conversion carries with it a great deal of fervor which, in an exuberant and ebullient person like Korzybski, exceeds its normal bounds. First of all, it must be said, he believed in his mission; he had faith in his message, and cherished the hope that he could stir up the scientific world by his projects. A good organizer, and not especially fastidious about conventions in the academic world, he began to contact scores, if not hundreds, of well-known authors and scientists; and his ambition was to form a "senate of humanity" which would cure the ills of the world. "If the peoples of the world were told that the best scientists of the world are working on their problems they would settle down and wait, some hope would be restored, otherwise they will not wait." Korzybski was an incorrigible optimist, and although he did not accomplish the larger aim, he did succeed in attracting many brilliant men to his ideas.

The Anthropometer

In order to drive his point home, he devised in the early '20's, a piece of apparatus which looked like a bowl (event) shot through with holes (characteristics of the event), and attached by means of strings to a perforated sphere, through which there runs a rod, and at the bottom is a tag, also containing a series of holes. This tag represents the label or symbol. It stands for an abstraction of the first order, but the sphere represents a higher order of abstractions, and the broken off paraboloid is a still higher order of abstractions and so it goes. In ordinary psychological terminology, we speak of percepts and concepts, but to Korzybski such words are elementaristic and involve a subjective condition. We must get around this, if A is to know what B is thinking of, by means of framing a definition. Without definitions, we are fumbling with relative variables; for even science is different at different ages of man, let alone such vague or indeterminate terms as democracy, justice, the good. If we want a constant, which our label should be, we must have recourse to the definition.

The contraption or gadget which Korzybski employed to demonstrate his newly-discovered truth, he called "anthropometer"—a rather high-sounding name for so simple an instrument, but, if we were to take stock in his promises, we might be inclined to believe that it is not sufficiently honored for its merits; for, let us see what prospects its inventor holds out for it. "With the understanding of the anthropometer, he *must think*; there is no escape for him, and thinking becomes a pleasure to him as well as a necessity." "But with the anthropometer introduced into homes and elementary schools, it is impossible to stop man from thinking . . ." "The anthropometer giving the consciousness that we abstract, brings these issues forcibly home . . ." "Psychiatry as yet, has no preventive methods. The anthropometer is such a preventive educational method against many cases of insanity and different unbalanced states, due to inherited or inhibited [inhibiting? A.A.R.] false doctrines . . ." "The anthropometer should be introduced into elementary schools, and we should start our education with it everywhere . . ." "The modern physico-mathematical discoveries become very simple when explained on the anthropometer."[9]

These and many more virtues of the anthropometer are sung by its maker, and we are to understand also that the insane would come to their senses, once they caught on to the wisdom of this apparatus; for, exclaims Korzybski, "We do not need to doubt human reason, we should distrust our language." But isn't this the rub that we are so built as to distrust the *other person's* language, not our own, and how can we bring the average communist to realize that his use of the terms "freedom," "democracy," "justice" does not comport with the connotations they inherently possess? The difficulty is analogous to the problem for the mice of belling the cat. A paranoiac or megalomaniac may use the anthropometer in

[9] A. Korzybski: *Time Binding; the General Theory*, 1924, *passim*.

order to bolster his own claims that he is being persecuted or that he is Jehovah incarnate.

Korzybski's Road

Korzybski was a propagandist *par excellence*, and a popularizer, in the best sense of the word. He wrote with a punch, and yet he knew enough to antagonize no one in particular. On the contrary, he would try to show that he and whomever he cited belonged to the same ideological or scientific school. With Jacques Loeb, he agreed that life was an electro-colloidal affair. Pragmatism, as a relativistic philosophy, appealed to him, but in general he stood close to logical positivism; and his fundamental thesis is the same as Bridgman's but while Bridgman's operationism is only an episode in his *work*, Korzybski makes out of his few diffuse ideas a system. Perhaps he called it general semantics in order to set it off from philological semantics, and it is possible—who knows the undercurrents of semantic association?—that the military engineer and count needed a general as a sort of *alter ego*. At any rate, it is interesting to follow his development. He began with human engineering, then advanced to the project of a "senate of humanity," an idea which was suggested to him. Later, he conducted a "time-binding" club, and finally found himself when he created the general semantics movement, at the same time establishing the Institute of General Semantics, in Chicago, subsequently transferred to Lakeville, Connecticut.

Purport of General Semantics

Korzybski's great contribution, as he believed, was the discovery that man was time-binding, whereas the infra-human was space-binding. It was hardly an original thought, but Korzybski exploited it in such a way as to impress both a number of the creative minds in the sciences and the popularizers. He was adept at using catchphrases, metaphors, and slogans, and indulged, at times, in play of words, such as "Fido is no *dog*matist, no *cat*egorist," and he might have added, if he had thought of it, no *rat*ifier of hypotheses. Mathematicians, chemists, and psychiatrists patronized him, or at least encouraged him, while younger men, particularly in the department of speech, took to his homely expressions and clichés. A dictum like "The map is not the territory" became a standby among his disciples, and they never tire of repeating it.

After a few years of intense canvassing, Korzybski, with uncommon zeal and remarkable singleness of purpose, set about studying psychiatry and physiology and, in 1941, exactly twenty years after the publication of his first book, his *Science and Sanity*, a large volume, came off the press. In this work, the chief aim was to demonstrate the inadequacy of Aristotelian logic, based on a dichotomy of values, for our present relativistic age. He thus became the chief exponent of a multivalued logical system and the most relentless opponent of the non-identity law, formulated by the great Greek philosopher. As to Korzybski's extensionalism, which is practically the same as physicalism *i.e.*, the principle that the subjective or intensional should become objectified through a suitable definition, carrying general agreement, if it is to become a useful cog in the scientific wheel, it is the nearest step to demonstrating the mental thing in space; and the diagrams employed are of advantage in bringing out the differences among the various levels of occurrence between the happening of the event and the linguistic reaction, which are ordinarily identified in daily life, so that the word is mistaken for the object or feeling. Although he wrote only two books, they were both best sellers among serious books. The *Manhood of Humanity* was reprinted three times in 1921, and a new edition appeared recently, while of *Science and Sanity,* a volume of about 800 pages, over 20,000 copies have sold by this time.

Korzybski was primarily a coördinator. He knew his ground, and was able to draw upon many important recent works in science for illustrations. His disciples came from many fields and walks of life, but, curiously enough, all his efforts were of no avail in mustering academic psychologists for his cause, although a few clinicians might have joined his flock. Heaven knows he tried hard enough. Perhaps we were unduly pigheaded; perhaps we found him too aggressive for a scientist.

But the man settled down to strenuous research later; he mellowed, and became an institution in himself. His successful teaching is attested by the fact that, all told, he had at his various seminars some two thousand mature and, in many instances, trained people from all parts of the country. He lived to preside at three congresses of general semantics, and if all he had accomplished were only to stimulate the writing of several hundred papers on a large variety of topics, such as medicine, law, chemistry, politics, speech therapy,[10] education, the use of words, marital conflicts, social work, all in relation to general semantics, as well as a whole series of books like S. I. Hayakawa's *Language in Action*,[11] Stuart Chase's *Tyranny of Words*, I. J. Lee's *Language Habits in Human Affairs*, and W. Johnson's *People in Quandaries*, as well as Hayakawa's entertaining journal *Etc.*, he would have merited a place in a history of psychology; for actually his object was to effect a *rapprochement* between logic and psychology ("psycho-logic" as he dubbed this segmental combination) on a linguistic terrain.

[10] It is the belief, *e.g.*, of W. Johnson, shared now by many speech correctionists, that at an early age, all children experience difficulty in their articulation, talking too rapidly, repeating words, cluttering their speech, etc., but in the case of some, who are made fun of by chums and classmates or whose parents show visible signs of concern, the difficulty assumes the proportion of a misfortune in the mind of the child, and dwelling on it, he or she begins to stutter, even aggravating the condition as time goes on. To have attached little importance to the early difficulty would have scotched the defect, at the very outset. This would argue against all organic causes of such defects.

[11] An expanded edition appeared in 1949 under the title *Language in Thought and Action*.

Chapter 34

Neo-Scholastic Psychology

THE NEGLECT of Thomistic psychology in the writings of non-Catholic psychologists may be explained in various ways. Perhaps there is no one single reason for ignoring a school that has had the longest record for consistency, which, in itself, may have spelled superannuation to the general psychologist. A school which endures seven centuries, while under the aegis of an authoritarian hierarchy, could not but arouse distrust in outsiders, which in the course of decades, if not centuries, turns into indifference, since they are no longer subject to its authority. In other words, as non-Catholics view the situation, what progress could be expected of scholars, thinkers, and scientists, highly trained though they may be, who are *ab initio* shackled to the hoary dogmas of the Middle Ages, which are regarded as the very antithesis of the scientific spirit? Can we not, under the circumstances, always surmise what the outcome will be, since it must be so—*viz.*, the affirmation of the soul doctrine in psychology and the vitalistic principle in biology, the advocacy of the free will, the combatting of all mechanistic views, and the glorification of man at the expense of all infra-human organisms?

Reason for Neglect

In psychological quarters, it has become almost as disreputable to have any truck with such concepts as the soul as it was blasphemous at one time to express doubt as to its existence; and regardless of what services a man might have rendered to the science, the stigma of a predilection for the soul, as a permanent unifier of mental states, is sufficient to discredit the psychologist for all time. Just as there is a transferred halo which elevates a man above his real worth, so, we have discovered, there is a transferred shadow, which degrades him in the eyes of the professional guild, as we have found it to be in the case of William McDougall, whose animistic bias in *Body and Mind*, also in his primer of *Physiological Psychology*, served to minimize him as a scientist in the eyes of the mechanists of all varieties.

Physicists are not inclined to extend the shadow to other regions, in assessing the achievements of one of their number. Pascal's theorems and laws were not questioned on the ground that the French genius kept in his mind two airtight compartments (religion or theology and science). Nor was J. K. F. Zöllner, the astrophysicist, roundly berated because he was a believer in the occult. Similarly neither William Crookes nor Oliver Lodge lost caste because they were votaries of spiritualism; and Alfred Russel Wallace can still hold his place alongside of Charles Darwin, in spite of his traffic with mediums. Why should a psychologist become a Humpty Dumpty because he sponsors a concept or principle which cannot be proven?

There may be a further element in this not too cordial relationship. Perhaps, there still rankles in the unconscious of the average well-informed psychologist the indignation at the Church for its cruel treatment of Galileo and Copernicus, not to dwell on the burning of Giordano Bruno and scores of lesser minds. Killing its cultural achievements with persistent silence is, therefore, the mildest form which the long-standing vindictiveness could take; and thus the sins of the Fathers of the Church are visited unto the tenth generation.[1]

Little is it realized that intolerance was not peculiar to the Roman Catholic Church. Omitting the ferocious fanaticism of the Moslems, who with fire and sword exterminated all unbelievers, need we mention the overzealous attitude of Luther who brooked no opposition in matters of creed, or the often inhuman austerity of Calvin, which, in no small measure, was indirectly responsible for the hangings of the "witches" in Protestant Salem. The Nazi atrocities are not to be ascribed to any genuine ideological group, but we must not lose sight of the fact that the bulk of those who were guilty of the crimes were Protestants, including intellectuals of a high cerebral order. Furthermore, under the atheistic USSR regime, any teacher or scientist whose results are not in keeping with the dialectical materialism prevalent there, or who favors such heresies as the Ricardian, or indeed, any non-Marxian, system of economics, or who endorses the gene theory of Morgan will

[1] In his lengthy private review, Professor Boring suggested "that it is due to insecurity, that the scientist sets himself to push determinism as the rule of his game, never succeeds in reaching the goal, although always getting nearer." Boring's sense seems to be that the Neo-Scholastic is a distraction to science.

find himself not only excommunicated, *more Bolshevico,* and not only deprived of a livelihood, but is likely to meet with a fate just as dire,[2] even if not so drawn-out in its agony, as did the nonconformist during the days of the Inquisition.

Power is the greatest foe of the idea, perhaps because the genuine idea, the idea motivated by detached scientific curiosity, is the perennial underminer of power, but the sad part of it is that power remains powerful, even if it frequently changes hands, while the idea does not seem to be able to assert itself once and for all; and whereas, prior to World War I, many of us were optimistic about the final victory of the *logos,* we must now accept this principle on wishful faith alone; for too often have our hopes been shattered, even within our own memory. If the Church has been the worst offender in this connection, it is because it has reigned supreme over such a vast territory and through such a long period.

All considered, the Church has undergone a great reformation, if not, transformation. At one time, it burned the books that betrayed the slightest deviation from accepted belief, and occasionally, together with the books, the author too. Later, excommunication took the place of the more drastic punishments. Placing books on the *index expurgatorius* was resorted to in more recent years when the Church wielded less power but still great influence, but in our contemporary period, it was found more expedient to encourage reading and expounding radical views, so as to make it possible to expose the very theories which are taboo in church circles. We shall see presently that Thomistic psychology nowadays may be considered as one of the schools in modern psychology from which it is not to be segregated, as it would have been even in the nineteenth century.

The designation *Thomistic* psychology is probably familiar to most readers, nevertheless it might be advisable to explain at this juncture, that the system, not only of theology and philosophy which rules in Catholic circles, but of psychology as well, has been worked out by that illustrious mind, Thomas Aquinas, whose sobriquet was *Doctor Angelicus,* although physically, with his powerful frame and protuberant paunch, which made it inconvenient for him to sit at table, he must

---

[2] The post-Stalin regime did become somewhat more liberal, but let any teacher be guilty of "idealist" or "revisionist," not to mention "capitalist" views, and his fate is sealed.

have given the impression of a world conqueror. And he might have been a warrior, as most of his family were, and some of them wished him to be, had it not been for the fact that this scion of nobility, and kin to royalty, was possessed of a searching mind and inspiration, as well as of an industrious nature which impelled him, an hereditary count, to don the garb of a Dominican monk and spend his life in tense study, besides lecturing, preaching and giving counsel to high prelates on church matters and to kings on affairs of the state. At his death, in 1274, at the age of 49, he left a long shelf of books behind, principally his voluminous *Summa Theologica*, which has remained the beacon light of the Catholic Church for nearly 700 years.

The Superior Authority of Thomas Aquinas

The question must have occurred to more than one reader just as it has to the writer, how comes it that, of all the medieval theologians who were also philosophers, the Church would elect Thomas Aquinas, whose eponym became a symbol of skepticism—as the proverbial phrase "a doubting Thomas" indicates—to the exalted position he has occupied these seven centuries in ever growing security, after unintentionally dimming the effulgence of his great predecessor, Augustine? There was Thomas's teacher, Albertus Magnus, the only name in philosophy which carried such an honorific; there were Scotus Erigena, Bonaventura, William of Ockham (Occam), Duns Scotus, John of Salisbury, the pupil of the legendary Pierre Abelard, who himself might have been disqualified from consideration because of his soul-stirring and soul-searing romance—and yet they are all merely names, while Thomas Aquinas is still very much alive, the patron saint (the phrase employed for once in its literal sense) of philosophy, whose spiritual presence is felt at meetings and conferences, who inspires writers and lecturers—in short who guides the destiny of the Church, ideologically, if not ecclesiastically. It seems especially puzzling to outsiders who would expect the Church to eye with suspicion any one who leaned on the philosophy of the empirical Aristotle in preference to the idealism of Plato, which would, *prima facie,* harmonize more smoothly with the fundamentals of the Catholic Church.

Therein, however, seems to lie Thomas Aquinas's strength. The man sought not to adapt himself to the trend of the day but, in a most universal spirit, to combine into a reasonable synthesis the best in all thought to which he had access. Thomas Aquinas may, as it is thought by some authorities, have been closer to the early Platonic phase of Aristotle, but the fact remains that he was too much of a realist to believe in the soul as an independent entity to which is attached an encumbrance we call a body. The soul needs the body just as much as the body needs the soul; and in this co-ordination, Thomas Aquinas showed his sense of balance and moderation, which was also the great virtue of the Stagirite. For he seems to have grasped the truth exemplified by the Talmudic dictum "Hast thou seized too much, then thou hast not seized at all" (*tofastah m'rubah, lo tofastah*).

Thomas Aquinas did not have the opportunity of studying the Talmud, although his deductive method of interpretation is akin to the logic employed by the tanaïtes and amorites, but he was conversant with the prince of Jewish medieval philosophers, Maimonides, whom he cites often, referring to him as Rabbi Moses; and it was not beneath him to make himself acquainted with the writings of the Arabian philosophers. Averroës, Avicenna, and others, although two centuries later, he might have found such allusions to infidels, as he indulged in, a rather hazardous practice. It is just because he evinced the true spirit of philosophy and inquired on all sides that he represents catholicity, which, had not the Church deteriorated, through bigoted and corrupt dignitaries for a considerable period of time, might have been coincident with Catholicism.

At any rate, it must be evident to anyone who has familiarized himself with a portion of his writings that Thomas Aquinas, instead of soaring to the stratosphere, had both his feet firmly on the ground. His questions did not pertain to angels on the point of a needle, but were what might be considered practical. If he was not a systematizer, he was a codifier, and were he not a theologian and a philosopher, he might still have ranked high as an interpreter of the law, as an authority on jurisprudence. Like a judge charging the jury, in our own day, he takes up each question explicitly and, brushing aside trivialities and superfluities, deals with objections as if they were brought up by opposing counsel, and then hands down his decision, based on both such symbolic hints as he could find in the Scriptures, or the Church Fathers, and good common sense, which is attached to no particular creed, race, or period.

Even such a rather remote (from our point of view) subject as predestination, which is surely a stumbling block, as we have seen in the case of Jonathan Edwards, to both Calvinists and the majority of Catholic theologians, is deftly turned by the subtle mind of the great scholastic. It is, however, in that part of the *Summa Theologica* which is devoted to marriage that we find the legal, and perhaps, too, logical acumen of Thomas Aquinas at its best. There is scarcely a problem, other than purely domestic ones of incompatibility, etc., which do not occur to him. Incest, frigidity, consanguinity, second marriages, insanity, adultery, divorce, age at betrothal and marriage, impotence, affinity, and a score of other matters are disposed of in his characteristic temperate manner. In Question 55, third article, he asks, *e.g.*, whether unlawful intercourse causes affinity, and after listing the objections on the negative side, which, incidentally, he must have anticipated with a keen eye to potential adversaries, he concludes that "in an unlawful intercourse there is something natural which is common to fornication and marriage, and in this respect it causes affinity," and further in the article, he makes a notable distinction when he decides that "in unnatural copulation, there is no mingling of seeds that makes generation possible; wherefore a like intercourse does not cause affinity."[3]

The Antecedents of Neo-Scholasticism

The method used in the *Summa Theologica* is reminiscent of Abelard's *Sic et Non*, which created such a furore in the twelfth century, but Thomas Aquinas carried it through a score of volumes, and although Abelard might have been more enlightened for the time, without displaying the evidence too boldly, St. Thomas was inconsistently critical, in that he could foresee objections, even if he could not, from the very nature of his beliefs, meet them successfully. Thus, when he asks "whether sacred doctrine is a matter of argument," he rightly sees the dilemma. "If it is a matter of argument, the argument is either from authority or from reason. If it is from authority, it seems unbefitting its dignity, for the proof from authority is the weakest form of proof. But if from reason, this is unbefitting its ends, because according to Gregory (*Homil*. 26) faith has no merit in those things of which hu-

[3] Thomas Aquinas: *Summa Theologica*, Part III, vol. 19, pp. 217-219.

man reason brings its own experience. Therefore sacred doctrine is not a matter of argument."[4] Nevertheless, St. Thomas is inclined to compromise on the question, and allow argument as an auxiliary method, if it stems from outside sources, but only the authority of the canonical Scriptures can serve as incontrovertible proof.

This will suffice as a background for the understanding of neo-scholasticism as applied to psychology. It will be found that it is in the purely speculative parts of the *Summa* that we cannot follow its author, and all theology must, of necessity, be shrouded in speculation; and what seemed almost self-evident to St. Thomas, *e.g.,* that revelation is a higher knowledge than that which we gain through experience, is very far from apodeictic, or even probable, to a non-religious scientist. Modern Thomists naturally, in our own age, recognize the difficulties and are willing to discover new devices to justify their position. The fact of this recognition, *per se,* is an auspicious sign.

It is in this modern spirit that the first recipient of the Aquinas Medal, Jacques Maritain, gave utterance to the following words in acknowledging the award.

> Now I think that the way in which we have to imitate the boldness of the Angelic Doctor has especially to do with the task of sifting out his genuine and perennial philosophical principles from the perishable scientific imagery peculiar to his time, and to apply them to the immense amount of facts and knowledge acquired by modern science, and to the new philosophical problems which are thus constantly arising— so that sometimes we may have to dissent from some particular accidental opinion expressed in the letter of his writings, in order to stick more faithfully to his principles and his spirit. Such a task implies a lot of risks, of course; yet, with a sound critique of knowledge, it is not so difficult, after all, on the condition that we do not expect from modern science more ontological content than it itself claims to possess, and that we realize the inevitably unstable character of any scientific imagery.

*　　*　　*　　*　　*

> The crucial task that Christian Reason has to accomplish in the generations to come will be, I believe, to disengage

[4] *Loc. cit.,* vol. 1, pp. 12-14.

from Thomist theology a complete and articulate body of Thomist philosophy. And this will require the most strenuous and fascinating effort of intellectual pioneering.[5]

The Gist of Faculty Psychology

St. Thomas's psychology rests on Aristotelian principles but is more elaborate and revolves, of course, around the soul and its powers. The soul, united to the body, is known through its powers or faculties. There are three grades: (a) the rational, (b) the sensitive (c) the vegetative. The rational soul is found in man alone. The modes of living engendered by these grades give us (a) the intellectual, in man alone, (b) the locomotive, in most of the animals, (c) the sensitive, in organisms without locomotion, and (d) the vegetative. The genera of powers or faculties are (a) the intellectual, (b) locomotive, (c) appetitive, (d) sensitive and (e) vegetative. Each of the genera, except the locomotive, is subdivided into species. Thus, of the intellectual, the species is cognitive, which operates *as an active agent* for abstractions, but only *passively* for apprehending the "whatness" of things. The appetitive genus or faculty contains an intellectual species, *viz.*, the will, and a sensitive species, which includes desires and aversions. The sensitive genus is composed of an external and an internal species. The former comprises the five senses while the latter consists of (a) imagination, (b) memory, and (c) the ability to assess (*vis aestimativa*), which might correspond to our "insight" into the purpose, use, or intention of an object. In man, the *vis aestimativa* would correspond to a *vis cogitativa*, or an intuitive quality, a reasoning flash which suggests or gives us some clue as to what the other is about. Finally this internal species of the sensitive faculty holds also a *sensus communis*, which unifies the senses and also keeps us from confusing one modality with another. The vegetative genus subdivides into the following three species (a) the nutritive, (b) the augmentative dealing with growth, and (c) the generative or reproductive.

What gives the various operations status or weight? We are told that it is both the act and the object toward which the act is directed which count (*per actus et objecta*). The act of copulation can be considered as spiritual if the purpose is bringing

[5] J. Maritain: *Proceedings of the American Catholic Philosophical Association*, 1951, vol. 35, pp. 7-8.

children into the world, but if the intention is only sensual, then the vegetative faculty which governs it is of a lower order and fulfills only the appetitive nature of man. The object-relation also brings out a different evaluation; for instance, sight is rated higher than hearing or smell, because the source, say, a book, does not change in stimulating the sense organ, nor does the organ change, but in the case of sound, the object must be struck or, in touch, the sense organ is affected by the contact, becoming cold, warm, moist, etc., hence it is not as perfect a state as the undisturbed. Thinking is a higher process because the body is not used for the purpose (Thomas Aquinas could not have known of the nervous apparatus involved in thinking) but the sensory ("sensitive") processes are dependent on bodily sense organs.

The fact that the will is not regarded as a separate faculty but only as a species of the appetitive genus, which contains also the specific desires and aversions, is a pivotal point in the scholastic system. When desires have been passed on by the intellect, we can talk about the will taking over, the will not being attached to any particular material or bodily appetites, but representing the individual as a whole. On the other hand, the various desires, as well as resistances to objects which thwart their attainment, are sense-appetitive because they deal directly with specific objects. It is here, too, that the emotions and feelings are to be found, because they are looked upon as stressed sense-appetites, occurring largely as passions not to be understood as *very* intense, in our sense, but as causing us to undergo some disturbance.

In the scholastic schema, the difference between active and passive, whether as applied to the intellectual or to the appetitive faculties, is quite important and rests on the nature of the particular activity in relation to the object. To use a modern objectivistic analogy, the exteroceptive reaction would be passive, the proprioceptive experience would be active. There are also innumerable accidents in regard to circumstances which have no special bearing on the faculties and their operations. Speculative reason and practical reason are not held to be separate faculties or even species, but only accidents, because they are applications of the same reason to different frames of reference. Here Thomas Aquinas would appear less scholastic than Thorndike, for he did divide intelligence into the abstract, social, and mechanical.

Critique of Faculty Psychology

The criticism of scholastic psychology started with Descartes but reached its peak when Kant's successor, J. F. Herbart, practically demolished the faculty doctrine. Curiously enough, at about the same time that this philosopher-psychologist was advancing his mechanics of *Vorstellungen* and his doctrine of apperceiving masses to account for the operations of the mind, F. J. Gall, in 1810, propounded his system of phrenology, according to which the various faculties were localized in the brain, and for that reason they had to be fixed in number as well as qualitatively determined. Gall did not have the opportunity of classifying and subclassifying his constituents, but parceled off the brain into areas, of various sizes, so that cautiousness would get a larger portion, and color or order would receive a much smaller one. In addition, the higher or lower location might, in some part, correspond to the dignification in the scholastic classification. It will be noted that veneration, in Gall's chart, is at the very top of the brain, with spirituality and hope directly beneath, while amativeness is at the lower back part of the brain occupying a sizeable area. Benevolence, on the other hand, while smaller, is frontally close to veneration. Gall's anatomical investigations did not succeed in proving the truth of phrenology, and his localization of the faculties, which he called propensities, did not help the scholastic cause. If anything it was detrimental to it.

The chief argument against faculty psychology was that it explained nothing; that it was, therefore, a sterile attempt to give information which was of no value. At best, it could serve only as a classifying device, and even there, the basis is too obvious and simple, and for that reason, possibly misleading. For how do we know that there is an intellectual faculty except from the fact that man thinks, or a locomotive faculty, aside from the observation that the animal moves from place to place? In that event, every act should have its own faculty. Other than that, we know nothing about the soul, which is supposed to be the substance from which the faculties originate. It came to such a pass that all one had to do was to state that such and such a view smacked of faculty psychology, and the view at issue would be discredited as antiquated and exploded, as a mere verbal form.

In our own century, the Columbia School, beginning with

the investigation on students in regard to physical and mental correlations, published by Clark Wissler, then of Yale, in 1901,[6] and continuing with the relentless opposition of E. L. Thorndike to any sort of synthetic scheme of abilities or traits, to this very day of specificity-indoctrinated students, has become the bastion of the so-called "anarchic" theory, anarchic, as Spearman has termed it, because none of the mental activities or abilities are supposed to have any relation to one another except through a chance combination of the minute elements which go to make up that specific ability.

Titchener and others were ready at best to tolerate the word "faculty" only as a group label i.e., to designate a useful combination of similar activities which might be subsumed under the same head for practical purposes. It was further shown that the lumping of feelings and emotions with an appetitive faculty, to which is also attached the will, tends to make ducks and drakes of the occurrences as we know them. We have seen how, in the early American textbooks, the soul was bipartite, the residue of the scholastic tradition; and when attempts were afoot to establish the tripartite division i.e., cognition, affection (or sensibility) and volition, Jonathan Edwards brought his whole weight to bear down against the move and still clung to the twofold doctrine which suited his deterministic philosophy.

A Lutheran Scholastic at Columbia

As late as 1800, the scholastic view held its ground at Columbia—true, in modified form, nonetheless fundamentally approaching that of Thomas Aquinas; and its proponent was not a Roman Catholic but a minister of the German Reformed Church. J. D. Gros, a German immigrant, who occupied three chairs at Columbia College, viz., moral philosophy, geography, and chronology, and toward the end of the eighteenth century, brought out, in 1795, a textbook on the "Natural Principles of Rectitude" etc., which was a sort of omnibus on ethics, natural jurisprudence, political economy, government, constitutional, and international law, but contained for its ground-

[6] C. Wissler: "The Correlations of Mental and Physical Tests," *Psychol. Review Monographs,* 1901, No. 3. J. M. Cattell's and L. Farrand's study, "Physical and Mental Measurements of the Students of Columbia University" in the *Psychol. Review,* 1896, vol. 3, was largely methodological in character and had not yet oriented itself in regard to this issue.

work a dozen pages or so on psychology.[7] The scholastic method, which is strong on definition and differentiation, runs throughout the book, but it is not, as Fay supposes, developed *"more geometrico,"* in the style of Spinoza. Fay must have been somewhat misled by the numerous scholia in the book, for the most part, serving as illustrations; but Gros does not proceed to deduce one proposition from another. He simply makes fine distinctions which are well taken, and displays a great deal of good practical judgment.

Gros divides the faculties into cognoscitive and appetitive kinds, each with inferior and superior subclasses. In the cognoscitive inferior, he groups the sensations, imagination, and fancy (like mythological creations, and fictions). Under the inferior appetitive rubric he, like Thomas Aquinas, places the appetites and aversions, which, when strong, become passions, and when they become habitual, give rise to sensuality and form a propensity. Under the superior cognoscitive rubric, he has attention, reflection, understanding, reason and judgment, while under the superior appetitive, he includes volition and nolition, which means that the agent's mind must have adverted to the consequences. It is the motive which determines the will, but where the motives have become long standing, chronic, as it were, attention no longer needs to dwell on the consequences. Two observations in Gros's exposition are noteworthy. He speaks of actions of the soul and of actions of the body. The mutations which seem to explain individual differences stem from the actions of the body, and not of the soul, which constitute the general laws. The other observation is that things are perfect when they are constant (leading up to our principle of homeostasis?).

Faculty Psychology Rediviva

The war on faculty psychology raged on for some years, and subsided after the foe was thought completely vanquished, but, as invariably happens, concepts and principles that are fundamentally ingrained are not so easily uprooted. The deep-dyed are die-hards. The term "faculty" was dropped in non-Catholic circles, and in its place was inserted the term "function." Perhaps a "function'" stands for a more operational or dynamic concept than "faculty" which suggests a stationary

[7] J. D. Gros: *Natural Principles of Rectitude for the Conduct of Man in all States and Situations of Life,* etc. 1795. The book must be rare; for it is kept in the Houghton Library at Harvard.

entity, but like any euphemism, it doesn't take long before the original connotation attaches itself to the new concept. Suppose we take memory for an illustration, then the "faculty" of memory would denote that somewhere in the mind there is a force or power which enables us to remember, no matter what the material, whether figures, objects, meaningless words, or significant ideas, whereas we can distinguish not only between recall and recognition, but it may also be that there is a general memory and many specific memories, dependent on the type of material. The term "function" does permit of a little more latitude in that we ask ourselves whether this result points to a different use or purpose or mental set than another, but in the last analysis, the virtue of the term stems largely from the circumstance that it is something different from the hoary "faculty."

The introduction of factorial psychology by Spearman, and his finding that there is a general factor of ability, has given fresh hope to the faculty psychologists, who are now confined to the scholastic area. At any rate, it is a counterblow to the multifactor thesis of Thorndike and his Columbia progeny; and, given a sufficient number of factors, why can they not be the equivalent of the faculties, differently arranged than of yore? It does seem, however, that too much ado has been made about a word. Call it ability, call it faculty or potentia, or function, or factor, or activity, the chief matter is that there is a *constant somewhere in our make-up,* which, under given circumstances, will bring about certain results, so that we can predict, in large measure, human behavior. That holds in regard to mental abilities as well as for personality and character traits. The cardinal objection to the Thomist conception and classification of faculties is that no consideration seems to have been given to environmental factors, and also another serious obstruction in any conciliation is the persistent belief on the part of neo-scholastics that the higher thought processes transcend the operation of the cortical cells and must, therefore, be grounded in a spiritual principle, to wit, the soul, with its supernatural implications.

Recent Progress in Thomistic Psychology

It is not generally known that the neo-scholastic school developed *pari passu* with experimental psychology, in general, and that the psychological laboratory at the Catholic University of America was founded in 1891, the same year that the laboratories at Cornell, Yale, and Harvard were officially established. The man who was in charge of the department of psychology, E. A. Pace, was, it is true, a priest, but he had studied physiology both at the University of Paris, and at Leipzig, under the celebrated Karl Ludwig, and received his doctorate under Wundt. Thus we can see that the theologian who instituted the new course at the Catholic University of America had imbibed at the same font as Hall and Cattell, and Titchener, and Münsterberg, and the early experiments in that Washington institution, on reaction time and auditory sensations, were no different from those carried on in the other early laboratories; and if he was a theologian, then so were Hall and Ladd. Pace, who afterwards became vice-rector of the Catholic University was a charter member of the American Psychological Association, which formed in 1892, and read papers at its meetings, contributing also to the *American Journal of Psychology* and *The Psychological Review*.

His successor, the Benedictine monk, T. V. Moore, went still further. Not only did he engage in experimental work under Wundt at Leipzig and Külpe at Munich, but spent years as a medical student both at the University of Munich and Johns Hopkins, where he received his M.D. degree, so that he could open a clinic at the Providence Hospital in Washington, later transferred to the Catholic University. Moore, who met Spearman when the two were studying at Leipzig, became one of the leading practitioners of factorial analysis, which he used in most of the experimental work he directed at the Catholic University; and his chief work *Dynamic Psychology,* and the most recent *Driving Forces of Human Nature* (1948) have been on the reading list of first-rate universities, which again goes to show that times have changed. In genetic and educational psychology, P. H. Furfey, at the same university, has made some noteworthy studies on the gang-age, on developmental age, and on social thought, while among other subjects investigated, in the same university, are differences between logical and rote memory; a genetic study of the *G* factor in intelligence, prognostic value of mental symptoms, as well as certain drug effects on the nervous system. *The Empirical Study of Character* by M. R. McDonough (a nun, like many other graduate students in this University) exemplifies both the adequacies of the Catholic University standards—a broad survey of the literature and elaborate statistical treatment of the somewhat meagre results, on the one hand, and a profuse citation of the literature, on the other hand, in lieu of delving into the core of the problem at issue.

Asked which of the other schools, the neo-scholastic attitude leans to, the answer would probably be functional psychology, with a tendency to resuscitate the term "faculty." At the Catholic University, there is also great emphasis laid on factorial analysis, largely because of Moore's training in mathematics, but also for the reason that it is more apt to discover functions or faculties in conformity with the teachings of Thomas Aquinas, *e.g.*, in the distinction between memory (the awareness that something has been experienced) and mere imagination, or meaning (devoid of sensory appurtenances) and imagery, or in cognizing perception as a *knowing* rather than a mere sensory experience.

Of greater import is Moore's acceptance, in large part, of Freudian psychology. Many years ago, he astonished the writer, when he told him that these psychoanalytic concepts were found very useful in his clinical therapy. Who would have believed even fifty years ago that such a deviation on the part of a Catholic would be permitted by his superiors, but Moore is not the only ecclesiastic who has adopted Freud's method and interpretations.

Although the Catholic University of America ranks with the better educational institutions in the United States, Fordham University is a close rival; and, in psychology, it is in a fair way to outstrip it in the not distant future. There are scores of Catholic universities and colleges in this country where psychology is taught in a modern vein, although only a few are equipped with laboratory facilities for advanced research. Some of the colleges are hardly more than academies, glorified high schools, or seminaries, where dogma lords it over scientific inquiry. Astronomy, mathematics, and physics are, in our enlightened day, beyond the cavils of even the most pious, but the social and mental sciences, as well as philosophy of course, are not as well situated because of their possible conflict with time-honored credos (evolution, birth control, eugenics).

The French Canadian Scene

It is, however, in Canada, more specifically Montreal, that something like an implicit revolution, if such is possible, in the attitude of the Church toward psychology is in evidence.

There was a time when we, McGill students, wondered whether the students at the French University in Montreal, then called Laval, had any inkling of modern psychology. Indeed, we looked upon them as backward, steeped in catechism and dogma. Not so many years passed since a magnificent university grew out of the amalgamation of Laval and several other, professional institutions, after a considerable struggle for funds to complete the buildings. The psychological staff of the Université de Montréal, which is the incorporative successor of Laval (the university in Quebec, still called Laval, has progressed too, but less so in psychology) numbers about a score of well-trained men and women, headed by the Dominican, Noël Mailloux, who in addition to his Ph.D. received at Rome (at the Angelicum) has conducted experimental research at the University of Cincinnati.

Similarly, the man in charge of the courses, (Father) Adrian Pinard, studied experimental psychology at Columbia. Others on the staff who hold the doctorate are (Father) J. Beausoleil and G-L. Barbeau, the latter of whom has taken work at Columbia.

It is for this reason that the department at the Université de Montréal is well equipped, and among the doctoral dissertations and master's theses are to be found topics like the psychodynamics of gambling as studied by projective tests; the Rorschach test; the vocabulary of mental deficiency; finger painting in a group of enuretic girls, and familial fantasy in the illegitimate child, while the collective research projects include: (a) a standardization of an intelligence test, in French (just published), (b) a study group of dynamics and ethnic traits, (c) research on the dynamic factors in the adaptation of immigrants, (d) analysis and evaluation of intelligence through the construction of a battery measuring differential modes of intellectual functioning, and others on the same scale. Over 75 courses in psychology (many it is true, brief ones) are offered at this university.

The extensive researches on superior intelligence tests (partly based on the present author's battery) carried out in that Institute should be better known.

Affiliated with the Psychological Institute of the University is an Orientation Centre consisting of a specialized clinic for problem children, a vocational guidance centre, and a training centre for graduate students and interns. A centre of research in human relations, which trains workers in social psychology, anthropology, and criminology is conducted, through the

Aquinas fund, by Noël Mailloux, who is the director of both the orientation centre and the research centre.

It is worth mentioning that while in the past, teachers of psychology in French Canadian institutions would ignore books on sex anomalies or, indeed, the whole Freudian movement, the pendulum has been swinging the other way of late. The Dominicans, who at the time of the Renaissance, were the satirical target of the learned humanists and Reformationists, like Ulrich von Hutten (*Epistolae Virorum Obscurorum*) have advanced in recent years to a high level in recognizing the need of the times and keeping abreast of new developments. In this writer's opinion, there is no better short history of psychology than that by the Dominican, R. E. Brennan, late of the Université de Montréal; and what amazes one is the temperate tone and dispassionate spirit in which it is composed. In the single page devoted to the official psychology of Soviet Russia, the viewpoint of dialectical materialism is not only fairly, though perhaps too briefly represented, but not a trace of animosity or irony creeps into the exposition. The same holds true of his discussion of behaviorism and psychoanalysis. It is cause for congratulation when a Dominican can tell his Catholic students that "Freud's peroccupation with data of this sort shows that he was really working more in line with the tradition of Aristotle and Aquinas than with the heritage of Democritus and Plato. And also it is necessary to approach his system with a respect for its tremendous achievements."[8] Freud did not receive such consideration from some of the general academic psychologists or psychiatrists.

In April, 1952, an article appeared in the bulletin of the Roman Clergy over the signature of Monsignor Pericle Felici, in which Freudian doctrine is not only held to be absurd, but is regarded as coming perilously close to enveloping the believer in mortal sin. Promptly came a disclaimer from official Vatican spokesmen, who made it clear that the Monsignor spoke only as an individual, adding the following significant statement: "Should psychoanalytic treatment be deemed injurious to the spiritual health of the faithful, the Church would not hesitate to take proper measures to denounce it as such. Thus far there is no indication that such measures are about to be taken."

[8] R. E. Brennan: *History of Psychology from the Standpoint of a Thomist*, 1945, p. 248.

It was a former Catholic priest J. S. A. Bois, who furthered the interests of applied psychology in French Canadian Catholic circles, beginning his missionary work about a decade ago, after receiving his Ph.D. at McGill University. Thanks to his good connections both with the clergy and the provincial government (Quebec), he was able to enlist the attention of some high-placed persons in the direction of mental testing, penal reforms, the establishment of mental clinics, etc. During the recent global war, he took it upon himself to prove the value of psychology even to the most lackadaisical officials.

By means of the radio, news letters, and other publicity channels he managed to build up a clientèle among businessmen concerned with problems of personnel and marketing research. More recently, he has become attached to the general semantics movement.

Cui Bono?

Before concluding this chapter, the question may well be asked: What contribution does neo-scholasticism make to psychology in general? For we are likely to be confronted by a dilemma. If dogma prevails in neo-scholastic psychology, then psychology at large cannot accept it, while if its students and workers carry on research without thought of creed or church involvement, then why consider it as a separate school? The various investigators may surely range themselves in accordance with one or another of the several systems already in the field.

If we were to adopt Thomas Aquinas's method, a number of objections might be listed followed by a contrary view, subsequently to be resolved by a decision beginning with "I answer that," in the course of which the objections are countered by ready obviations. But even such emulation would be out of place here, and could pass only as anachronistic imitation. For the sake of brevity, therefore, let it be said that the neo-scholastic viewpoint, whether it is colored by theology or not, is entitled to a hearing just as any other position in psychology. Aside from that, however, the actual contributions, both experimental and theoretical (historical, for example), are a valuable addition to our science. It may be observed quite impartially that many of the Thomistic textbooks and discussions are more readable than our own, and their authors have a better command of English and write with greater clarity and simplicity than their opponents or ignorers. In addition—and that is often overlooked—there is further benefit of *control* which, because of certain commitments on the part of the Thomist, will be vigilantly exercised. Ever on the alert for slips and lacunae in the researches of the mechanists, whether it is in connection with memory, perception, or so-called conditioned behavior, these watchdogs of science will scent the error and will expose the invalidity of the results. If something is taken for granted on inadequate premises, it will be brought to light, and if there is, on the other hand, a possibility which has been slurred by the stimulus-response experimentalists, then it will be adverted to. That in itself is a useful function, since it serves to maintain the balance of power in a terrain which is not as safe as, let us say, physics or chemistry. Such heckling will force us, at times, at least to question, if not to revise, our occasionally too firm convictions.

Nor must it be thought that all neo-scholastic psychologists will agree on all things. Within the framework of Thomism, there are certain differences which one can read between the lines. We cannot help thinking, too, that there is a modicum of rivalry among the various orders. Apparently the Dominicans feel that they are moving more in the tradition of St. Thomas, who was one of them. They look up to Aristotle and, therefore, are more disposed toward the empirical, and perhaps, too, the practical. Some of the other orders may be more Platonic in their outlook, stressing the idea and knowledge. It is the impression of this writer that this constitutes the difference, slight as it might be, between the Université de Montréal and the Catholic University of America.

When Noël Mailloux speaks of T. V. Moore's interpretation of perception as "exaggerated intellectualism," or when another Dominican, R. E. Brennan, at the same university, takes him to task for employing untraditional terms, whether the objections are justified or not, there appears to be in the wind an indication of some slight dissension. As the former puts it: "But discord breaks out when these scholastic psychologists, agreeing with several others on this point dare to offer a description of perception which transcends the data of radical sensationalism. However, it must be noted that certain among them—Moore in particular—seem to incline toward an exaggerated intellectualism."[9] This trend is continued in a further passage, which is somewhat abstract or scholastically technical.

"We are obliged," writes Mailloux, "to admit that the neo-scholastics of our acquaintance who have undertaken the study in reference to contemporary theories have made serious errors on the true nature of sensible perception. Either they seem to have completely ignored (as is the case with T. V. Moore and A. Gemelli) the preponderant rôle the cogitative power plays in intellectual cognition, or else when they have suspected the importance of this intervention, they have (like C. Fabro) confused perception or immediate experimental knowledge with the *experimentum* or discursive experimental knowledge."[10] From the above one might be inclined to call Mailloux a rationalist. The *vis cogitativa,* however, it may be pointed out, is, as we have seen earlier, a sort of practical sense rather than a cogitative function, in present-day usage, which refers to the higher thought process.

It will not be amiss, as a peroration to this chapter, to quote from Jacques Maritain's preface to Brennan's *History of Psychology*; for as usual, the distinguished French philosopher —who would even have been mentioned as a prospective cardinal, which would have been something contrary to tradition— brings to bear upon the problem the results of long years of meditation and analysis.

When the philosopher comes to the end of your book, the great problem with which he is confronted is that modern scientific psychology—all the while tending toward the pure type of scientific knowledge, in which reality is analyzed, conceptualized, and defined, not in terms of intelligible being, but in terms of observable and measurable sense-data, and empirical ways of verification—cannot, nevertheless, undergo full mathematical symbolization and systematization, as physics does, because psychological phenomena, even observed from a merely empiriological point of view, are imbued with the vital unity and totality, dynamism and finality of the ontological reality they express, and cannot be scientifically grasped without at least

[9] Noël Mailloux: "The Problem of Perception." *The Thomist,* 1942, vol. 4, p. 273.

[10] *Loc. cit.,* p. 278.

some indirect consideration of these characters. As a result, scientific psychology, while developing on its own em-piriological level, must take into account, in its own language and by means of some equivalents, the deeper reality which philosophy looks upon from its ontological point of view. Thus we may understand those two facts, that modern psychology has not to use the strictly ontological con-ceptualization of Thomistic philosophy—and even mani-fests an old positivist-minded distrust toward it—and that nevertheless modern psychology, in its general mood and inspiration, makes a kind of growing affinity with this philosophy appear, as you point out at the end of your book. The task of Thomist philosophers will be to bring to light the reasons for this affinity, to make clear the inconsis-tencies of the positivist prejudices, and to achieve, in the psychological field as in the other fields of human knowl-edge, the rapprochement and reconciliation between science and metaphysics.[11]

A Puzzling Attitude

It is somewhat surprising that the authors of *Catholics in Psychology* devote a page and a half to disclaim the implica-tion that Catholic psychologists form a school, as may be inferred from my chapter "Neo-Scholastic Psychology."

They point to the fact (a) that there are differences of opinion among Neo-Scholastics, (b) that Catholics in biology, chemistry, or physiology are not treated separately by his-torians of these sciences, (c) that some distinguished non-Catholic psychologists believed in a soul and held to the doctrine of free-will, (d) that contemporary psychology is no longer divided into distinct schools.[12]

They do admit that Neo-Scholastic psychology as a system of philosophical psychology is based on the principles of the philosophy of St. Thomas Aquinas because in the opinion of Catholic psychologists "it is the best system at present," and also that they will reject behaviorism because

[11] J. Maritain, preface to R. E. Brennan's *History of Psychology from the Standpoint of a Thomist*, 1945.
[12] H. Misiak and Virginia M. Staudt: *Catholics in Psychology*, N. Y., McGraw-Hill, 1954, pp. 279-280.

of its materialistic philosophy and "psychoanalysis because of its psychic determinism and hostility to religion."

If we turn to the dictionary, we find two of the ten senses applicable to the term "school" the following: (a) "The disciples or followers of a teacher, a sect in philosophy, theology, or science, etc., as the Socratic school"; (b) "A group as of painters or musicians under a common local or personal influence producing a general similarity in their work."

It is in the combined sense that we envisage Catholic psychologists as a school; and the fact that they maintain an association of their own and publish a newsletter independent of the American Psychological Association publications would tend to support this opinion. Indeed, the complaint of being treated separately savors of a minority's protest against segregation. In this case, it is hypersensitiveness; for functionalism, psychoanalysis, operationism, and gestalt psychology have also been treated as schools; and none of their respective members have raised their voice against such separation.

Perhaps experimental psychology, pure and simple, is not subject to orientational division, but there is scarcely such a thing as an unadulterated experimental psychology. There is, first of all, the selection of the problem to investigate. The technique is, of course, universal, but the methodology may be affected by the general outlook of the experimenter. The results may, in some cases, be seen a hairline to the right or left, and finally there is the interpretation of the results in the conclusion arrived at.

Although it is true that other than Catholic psychologists have subscribed to the doctrine of a soul, it must be borne in mind that such are also classed together as animists, and their allies in biology are called vitalists and are therefore regarded as a group by themselves. Besides, McDougall, to take one instance, is *led to the conclusion* in his *Body and Mind* that there is a soul, but unlike the Neo-Scholastic, he does not begin with such a postulate.

That Catholic psychologists may be sympathetic to other schools goes without saying. That does not release them from their fealty to church dogma. As the descendants of the original schoolmen, what would be more natural than to consider them as members of a school, at least as well-knit as the behaviorists or Gestaltists? Surely there is no stigma attached to such separate treatment, and therefore any *soupçon* of an inferiority feeling on the part of Neo-Scholastic psychologists is, though perhaps understandable, neither reasonable nor justifiable.

PART IV

GROWTH OF BRANCHES

Chapter 35

Yerkes and Psychobiology

IF ROBERT MEARNS YERKES (1876-1956) has not contributed measurably to the mainstream of American psychology, there is little room for doubt about the place he holds as the chief representative of comparative psychology, although he preferred to be known as a psychobiologist. It was as a fulfillment of his youthful desideratum that he succeeded in being appointed the first professor of psychobiology at Yale, in 1929. It is quite possible that the coinage of the term "psychobiology," and especially the promotion of this inter-discipline, came from Johns Hopkins, where Yerkes (his collaboration with John B. Watson on methods of studying vision in animals was done via letter) for a time had come in contact with the prestigious Adolf Meyer, who was an ardent champion of psychobiology; Meyer influenced his colleague, Knight Dunlap, to the extent of writing a sort of compendium under that name, which, however, was scarcely more than a syllabus of physiological psychology.

Actually, Yerkes was fundamentally the psychobiologist, in the true sense of the word, as we shall presently see. His goal had been to study medicine, and lacking the means, he took a liberal arts course first at Ursinus College and then at Harvard, where he had the opportunity to study under such men as Parker, Davenport, and Castle in biology and zoology, afterward turning to philosophy and psychology under such luminaries as James, Royce, and Münsterberg.

Having obtained his doctorate in 1902, he remained as instructor at Harvard, where he gave courses in comparative psychology and initiated a number of experiments on animals, having already published some of his earlier student papers on entomostraca, the fiddler crab, the turtle, medusa, the crawfish, the frog, tortoises, and other organisms. His first book, an investigation on the dancing mouse, was published in 1907, and his *Introduction to Psychology*, a textbook with emphasis on the comparative method, appeared in 1911. The first inkling in the United States of Pavlov's work on conditioning came through a Russian-Jewish student, S. Morgulis, whom Yerkes set to do the translation. The account was published jointly in 1909 in the *Psychological Bulletin.* Watson's claim that he knew nothing of Pavlov's work while he was elaborating his system of behaviorism, especially as Yerkes and Watson were cooperating on a large project the following year, seems very strange, to say the least.

Yerkes' comparative psychology was extended as a result of his service as a psychologist at the Boston Psychopathic Hospital, under E. E. Southard. That he was not restricting himself to pure animal psychology is evident from the fact that he was interested in a technique for studying the self, and even before he took charge of testing operations for the army, after the outbreak of World War I, he was intent upon devising a more accurate scale for measuring intelligence on the basis of points for individual questions instead of the all-or-none principle postulated by Binet, Simon, and Terman. Despite the many successive workers Yerkes had put on the job, starting with J. W. Bridges and Rose Hardwick in 1912 or 1913, the point-scale was never able to supplant the Stanford-Binet series.

Yerkes did not seem happy at Harvard. His promotion to an associate professorship was not in immediate prospect. Compared to some of the men in the department at the time, Yerkes would be regarded as a second-rater. He could be taken for a pharmacist or perhaps a country physician, and his voice sounded weatherbeaten. As a lecturer he was uninspiring, as if it were all a chore; and he was waiting for the period to end so that he could don his smock and attend to the variety of animals that were probably just as eager to see him. There he was in his element; and when he was telling of the mechanical genius of the monkey, Skirri, who, observing someone hammering nails into a board, proceeded to do the same, his face would light up. The application of the term "genius" to a monkey did cause something of a ripple in the class, but hardly any one of the students then would have supposed that their instructor would play such a prominent part in the annals of American psychology. Least of all, probably President Lowell, who was ever conscious of his Brahmin status and looked down his nose on philosophy and psychology, which to his historico-political mind was all "hot-air"; and after the loss of James and Santayana, he did not even think the air "hot."

If, however, Yerkes gave the impression of being irresolute and vacillating, he must have held his long-range plans in reserve. He resigned in 1917 to accept the chairmanship of the psychology department at the University of Minnesota, but before he could commence the first term, he was, as the then President of the American Psychological Association, commissioned to mobilize the psychologists for the various war activities. Not only was he the highest officer of this group, beginning as major and working in cooperation with the surgeon-general until, toward the end of the war, he was promoted to the rank of lieutenant-colonel, but he soon became one of the leading spirits of the National Research Council, which he helped found, and under his guidance a number of subcommittees were formed to deal with the numerous problems engendered by a global war, *e.g.*, motivation, testing, propaganda, rehabilitation. It was a gigantic task which required level-headedness and foresight; and Yerkes came through with flying colors. Upon returning from Washington a fellow-student under Yerkes said to the writer, "In his uniform, the top brass have nothing on him. He plays his part as if he were a born military man."

In connection with this work, Yerkes, in collaboration, brought out a 900-page quarto volume showing what psychology had contributed to the war service through the testing of 1,700,000 men and officers, the first time such an operation had been conducted on so vast a scale.

It was just about that time that the new President of Yale University, J. R. Angell, himself a psychologist, decided to expand the psychology department; and Yerkes accepted a call to the Institute of Psychology at Yale, in 1924. After spending the interim, since 1919, at Washington, winding up the war work.

At Yale, Yerkes did not have to meet classes. He directed research, of course, and worked hard for the establishment of a primate colony, which was not easy to accomplish, considering that it was his intention to found this "primate Eden" in Florida. It was comparatively simple to arrange for a more or less formal primate laboratory in New Haven, but the chimpanzees and gibbons and orangutans would certainly not care for the academic atmosphere; and aside from cramping their style, the environment and climate would not be conducive to breeding and obtaining significant field results.

The Yale primate laboratory served more as an administrative station.

As it is, the Yale Laboratories of Primate Biology, later named for its founder, yielded a mass of important data. In 1925, Yerkes, together with B. W. Learned, brought out the monograph *Chimpanzee Intelligence and Its Vocal Expression*. In the same year there appeared *Almost Human,* a readable account of the primate research carried on at the Abreu estate, in Havana, with a discussion of anthropoid habits, emotions, intelligence, and even speech, such as it is. The dedication in this book is characteristic: "To all who love truth and seek it diligently irrespective of personal cost."

His *magnum opus,* truly a monumental work, on which his wife, Ada Watterson, collaborated, was a 672-page (double-column) volume entitled *The Great Apes,* published in 1929. This quarto tome would occupy three volumes of ordinary size and print. It is scholarly in its historical portion, comprehensive in its comparative chapters, and withal systematic, so that it is almost encyclopedic in scope, so far as primates go; and the conclusions are carefully considered. Discrepancies among authors are not glossed over. The synopticon alone, in which traits and behavior among the subspecies are compared, is a valuable reference guide.

His Objective—the Study of Man

Yerkes started out as a student of biology or zoology, and familiarized himself with many phases of organic life, but it was the primate that concerned him most. He had gone almost fleetingly from organism to organism: birds and rodents, fish and reptiles, insects and even pigs; but in 1915, we have his study of the maternal instinct in the monkey, and in 1916, he presents his *Mental Life of Monkeys and Apes,* which takes up the question of ideation in man's ancestors.

His collaborated series of papers on the life of the gorilla would make a sizable book, all going as grist into the mill which turned out his and his wife's huge quarto volume on the anthropoid ape. From then on, barring the war years and the consequent involvements, Yerkes never ceased to peer into the mysteries of these anthropoid apes. However, he was not an animal psychologist in the ordinary sense. Nor was he probing into the secrets of learning in order to map out, so to speak, the areas and trace the processes in the brain responsible for the improvement.

If we divide psychologists into phenomenologists and theorists, he belongs to the former. He describes what he sees, compares, supplies data, without bothering to speculate on the neurological goings-on or to set up principles or formulae, making use of formidable equations. He is, notwithstanding, the objective scientist whose evidence supports his conclusions in regard to organic structure and function. Perhaps he empathizes somewhat, and thus is inclined to humanize the chimpanzee or the orangutan, but who is there to prove him wrong? He never tires of intimating that investigating the ape is only a step toward ameliorating the human situation. In that respect, he follows the tradition of American functionalism.

In one passage we read: "Clearly the secret of friendship and intimacy of understanding is the same as between man and man or man and ape. There must always be confidence, sympathy and affection."[1] In another chapter, he almost pleads rhetorically: "Are we humans after all so nearly unique in our flaunted altruism? Are not the fundamentals, and even the essential qualities, of our unselfish feelings and actions existent in organisms which we too long have neglected to study, and too often regarded with abhorrence or disgust? . . . Perhaps the Abreu adventure in the rearing of primates may help to lift us somewhat above ourselves and enable us to see more clearly certain facts which bear on genetic relations, on education, and on social evolution."[2]

One can readily see from such an utterance that the seemingly indifferent class instructor was possessed of more genuine sentiment than many an exuberant teacher, in class, to whom the saw applies "out of sight, out of mind." At times he would select as assistants students who could not pass examinations, but they were crackerjacks with animals— and that determined his choice. He was prompt and businesslike in his correspondence and especially glad to hear from former students who, by the way, might have taken only one course with him. He might even inquire about their welfare, or order a book of theirs, instead of waiting for a presentation copy.

[1] R. M. Yerkes, *Almost Human*, 1925, p. 17.
[2] *Ibid.*, pp. 140-141.

Orientation

In addition to his life-work being given up to uncommunicative organisms, Yerkes served as editor of *Comparative Psychology* and also of the *Journal of Animal Behavior*. In view of this, one might have expected him to be a behaviorist. His collaboration with J. B. Watson might have added to such a surmise, and possibly he could be called a "methodological behaviorist." Yet, when Roback's *Behaviorism and Psychology* appeared in 1923, he was among the first to order a copy and wrote the author afterward, "I suppose you will get a lot of rather hard knocks for your pains, but all the same, I am confident you did a real service by writing the book and will have no difficulty in surviving vicious critics." This expression should be sufficient to answer the question as to whether he was a behaviorist. He could accept the designation "methodological behaviorist," which he was given in the book's chart, but he would not even lean toward the more modern offspring of behaviorism—operationism; for measurement was to him not as important as understanding, insight.

In his detailed study (with B. W. Learned) on Prince Chim, he makes his position clear. It is that of a psychobiologist, an evolutionist. No behaviorist would come to the conclusion that "doubtless there are geniuses even among the anthropoid apes. Prince Chim seems to have been an intellectual genius. His remarkable alertness and quickness to learn were associated with a cheerful and happy disposition which made him the favorite of all, and gave him a place of distinction not only in their regard but in their memories."[3]

It is worth noting that Yerkes is in agreement with Köhler in attributing to anthropoid apes a species of insight lacking in dogs or cats. Pavlov took exception to their findings, which he ascribes to an idealistic dualism. He believes that it is all a matter of quantity and extent of associations, *i.e.*, cortical assembling conditioned by circumstance.

In his autobiographical sketch, Yerkes attributes most of his success to his "love of planning and a degree of prophetic insight therein which sometimes seems to approach genius," as well as to a steady unflagging interest, a constancy of purpose, and a persistence which will not yield to discouragement. He did not work as indefatigably as he was reputed to

[3] *Ibid.*, p. 255.

have, among his colleagues, but he applied himself consistently and with concentration, so that with a fair amount of constructiveness (although not mechanical skill) and ingenuity, he was able to obtain effective results.

Of the two assistant professors in psychology during the early teens at Harvard, E. B. Holt was rated as much the more brilliant, yet how little he had accomplished beside the self-disciplined plodding Yerkes!

Chapter 36

Terman and the Test Movement

LEWIS M. TERMAN (1877-1956) does not belong to the men who helped direct the general trend of American psychology. He held views based on data acquired without special techniques or even factorial analysis, which developed later. The statistics employed by him and his associates or students were of a relatively simple kind, yet he did not fail of his purpose, which was primarily to convince the country that something should be done about differentiating between the dull and the intelligent and raising the standards of education in general on the strength of the empirical results. Theory was not his bailiwick; and besides, once the territory was mapped out and the ground covered, the operation, unlike the field of learning, hardly lends itself to much theorizing.

Terman's name has come to be associated with mental tests in the same way as a household article is designated by the firm which produces or sells it. Terman, however, would not have wished to take all the credit for the advances made in testing on this side of the Atlantic, and there is too much of a tendency for historians, critics, or reviewers to add luster to the most successful and slur, or even ignore, the *proxime accessit.*

Kuhlmann—A Neglected Rival

It is for this reason that it is only fair to say that at the time Terman was doing graduate work at Clark University, Frederick Kuhlmann (1876-1955) had been engaged on similar problems, having obtained his doctorate in 1903, two years earlier than Terman. Kuhlmann became a lecturer at Clark, just as Terman was leaving for a post at a California normal school. After a year as lecturer at the University of Illinois, Kuhlmann settled in Minnesota, where he was employed in the State Department as Director of the Division of Research.

While Terman immediately plunged in *medias res* and began to prepare the material for his life task, Kuhlmann spent a few years on memory experiments, but in 1912, both Kuhlmann and Terman (the latter with H. G. Childs) brought out revisions of the Binet-Simon scale, which made them rivals. Yet, while Kuhlmann was taking the low road exploring feeblemindedness, Terman, through most of his life, was traveling along the high road, spotting, through tests, the upper limits of human mentality. Retardation had already been studied by Witmer and others. It offered nothing spectacular. Dullness could conceivably be the basis of an interesting study, but compared with talent and genius it can hardly make a popular appeal. The drab life in government institutions for the half-witted would be reflected in the mandatory reports and monographs dealing with the subject.

Terman, on the other hand, set out to reform educational methods, and he was an excellent organizer of research, directing a number of associates in their fact-finding. Other factors must also be taken into consideration to account for his success. His academic position, his opportunity in obtaining grants for large-scale investigations and, most likely, too, his attractive personality, his ability to get along with others and win their affection, and, last but not least, his impact on students, many of whom spread his good name as they took teaching or administrative posts in various parts of the country and abroad—all of that must have played a considerable part in the rapid advancement of Terman's ideas.

We must also recognize that while Terman specialized in an applied field of psychology, his scope was broad. He was a voracious reader; furthermore, he would be at pains to revise his revisions at intervals and to follow up his data on gifted children over the years. Small wonder then that he had made his mark as the world's foremost authority on tests and testing, going beyond Binet's orbit, and despite—or if we believe in Adler's theory, because of—his physical handicaps, a tubercular constitution aggravated by some mishaps, Terman had turned out a large number of articles and several impressive volumes.

Although Kuhlmann's revision of the Binet-Simon Test system appeared as a monograph as early as 1912, while Terman's suggestions for revision of the scale were published a year later, the latter received more attention, and when the *Measurement of Intelligence* was brought out in 1916, it was immediately hailed as a standard guide for testing. When the

United States declared war on Germany, in 1917, and R. M. Yerkes, who happened to be then the President of the American Psychological Association, was to take command over all the psychological war efforts, it was natural for Terman to be in charge, as a major, of all the mental testing, which was later reported in a huge volume entitled *Psychological Examining in the United States Army* (1921). It is reasonably certain that the war helped the cause of testing, and incidentally added prestige to Terman, who became an important figure in the council halls and soon was elected President of the American Psychological Association. He was also fortunate in the students who came under him, either as teacher or administrative head of the Department at Stanford University. Several of the fifty-five who received their doctorates during his incumbency of two decades have themselves become eminent and influential. A commemorative volume was presented to him by his students and associates on the occasion of his sixty-fifth anniversary, when he was to become an emeritus.

Collective Projects

Actually, Terman was not a prolific author. Many studies were carried out and prepared for publication conjointly with assistants. It is noteworthy that his chief collaborators were women. Of the four volumes which were titled *Genetic Studies of Genius* (showing the influence of Hall and Clark University) the first, dealing with the mental and physical traits of a thousand gifted children was the product of fifteen participants, including himself, whose long-range planning and organization of the testing were a tribute to his soundness and efficiency.

The following year, in 1926, there appeared the second volume of this collective work, *The Early Mental Traits of Three Hundred Geniuses*. Credit for this volume was given to Catherine M. Cox, who studied the biographies of three hundred illustrious men and women with a view to giving them an intelligence quotient on the basis of their early letters, utterances, products, etc. The results are sometimes startling and dubious. Spinoza, *e.g.*, was known to have been a prodigy among prodigies in the Amsterdam rabbinical school, but he does not fare so well as compared with others in his I.Q., but the method of arriving at quantitative certainties when circumstances are incomparable is so artificial that the chief value of the investigation lies in the collection of data surrounding the mental life of the childhood of genius.

Volume three of the Genetic Studies, *The Promise of Youth* (1930), in the preparation of which Barbara S. Burks and Dortha W. Jensen collaborated, consisted in a follow-up of the thousand gifted children who were selected for the project. The fourth volume (1947), devoted to resurveys of the group, now grown to adulthood and entering middle life, was prepared with the collaboration of Melita H. Oden, who has now completed the project in a fifth volume, *The Gifted Group at Mid-Life,* which was shaping up under Terman when death overtook him in 1956.

The prime gain of this gigantic project was to explode the general notion that precocity was a mark of abnormality and that only the mediocre are well-adjusted and mentally healthy; and that, therefore, the very bright children should not receive any advancement but he kept in classes according to age group, bored though they be with the pedestrian pace. The follow-up has demonstrated that socially and physically the mentally superior children by and large not only have held their own throughout the years but also have exceeded the average type.

That was no mean accomplishment, but, furthermore, the experiment in itself was a boon to the gifted who had a start in life which otherwise would have been drawn out over a decade perhaps. In that respect, because of the so-called progressive point of view—which had overreached itself in the effort to correct the evils of the past, and thus stressed the nonintellectual elements of education—the French government had for centuries been employing various means to select the gifted even from village schools, sending them to higher educational institutions for special training.

Terman was not the man to be content with a job once completed. Just as he felt that the original Binet-Simon device was by no means perfect, he was aware that his own revision could stand improving. All tests are tentative affairs, and only in their administration and application can the various flaws be spotted. He must have received many objections, and he was flexible enough to see the objector's point of view. The present writer once questioned his acceptance as a correct answer a slur on an ethnic group. He replied that this would be changed. At another time, his use of the term "genius" on an intelligence scale was criticized as inappropriate because qualitatively genius and intelligence represent different endowments, hence they are incommensurate. Terman did not take amiss this disapproval. On the contrary, he wrote that it was a mistake in the first place, for which he was sorry.

The second revision of the Stanford-Binet scale was issued in 1937, and in 1960, Maud A. Merrill who had collaborated with Terman in the second revision, completed the third revision, which contains new I.Q. tables. In both the second and third revisions, there are L and M forms, which could be used alternately. It was easy to guess that the L forms were devised by Lewis Terman and the M forms by Maud Merrill.

Two other projects on a large scale must be reverted to: *Sex and Personality—Studies in Masculinity and Femininity* (1936). The team of researchers consisted of nine assistants in addition to the authors, Terman and Catherine Cox Miles. (She was now married to Walter R. Miles of Yale.) In 1938, on the basis of an extended questionnaire as well as personality tests submitted to nearly 800 married couples and 109 divorced couples, Terman published his *Psychological Factors in Married Happiness*.

Perhaps Terman's books are of greater consequence, but it was the Stanford-Binet scale that spread his fame, while the Stanford Achievement Test devised in conjunction with T. L. Kelley and G. M. Tuch (1922, 1930), as well as the Terman Group Test, brought him considerable royalties.

Fundamental Ideas

One might ask why Terman felt called upon to revise the original Binet-Simon scale. The answer is simple. In the first place, some of the questions were not suitable for American children. Then it must be borne in mind that Binet's original scale was in terms of years and months, but it yielded no ortholinear values so that score differences could be seen at a glance for the purpose of comparison. In Germany, William Stern had already suggested something like an intelligence quotient, but he did not specialize, as did Terman. Terman extended from five to six the questions comprising the quiz for a single year—each question representing two months—so that if a five-year-old child answered all the questions for his year, and two questions of the next series, and two questions of the seven-year series, he is five years and eight months old. When we place the mental age as the numerator and the chronological age as the denominator, thus 68/60, we obtain an intelligence quotient of 113 plus, which means that the child is quite bright, although not yet superior.

If tests are to be reliable and valid throughout the years, it must be understood that the quotient is constant. Certain oscillations can be allowed for, and a repeated testing would be in order, but in general, a child retarded at seven or eight will not develop into an intellectual; similarly, a prodigy at nine or ten may not become very distinguished, but certainly will turn out far above normal in intelligence as he or she grows up.

Puzzling exceptions can be found but they are rare, and when investigated will show some physiological or mental disturbance. In the case of W. J. Sidis, whom I have known, I can vouch that at the time he was regarded as mentally regressed he could argue with cogency and was intellectually alert, but he was socially defective because of his schizophrenic make-up. On the other hand, the cretin idiot may approach normality after months of treatment with thyroxin.

Terman's training was along genetic lines, but he seems to have been a hereditarian by temperament. He was too well intrenched in the constitutional position to be affected by the environmentalist movement which was sweeping the country through behavioristic, sociological, anthropological, and progressive-educational propaganda, aided by psychoanalysis and Adlerian individual psychology.

It is understandable then that Terman would become a target of sundry writers who saw in him an old-fogey reactionary, one who could not see that intelligence was affected by living in slums, coming from broken homes, illness, a harsh parent, and so on. When Walter Lippmann, acting as the spokesman of the progressive literary guild and educational circles, undertook to expose the alleged obscurantism of Terman, as setting up castes in an enlightened world, which constituted a threat to democracy, Terman, a model of urbanity, surprised many of his colleagues, some of whom were even shocked, by administering a withering rebuke to Lippmann, couched in the most sarcastic phraseology. His "Great Conspiracy" was printed in *The New Republic* (1922, vol. 33, pp. 116-117) and afterward was expanded into a brochure. The diplomat-psychologists decried the tone as undignified, but the readers of opinion journals would be more likely to learn from a pungent reply than from a "soft answer."

Terman did not follow the general pattern of what is regarded as typical American psychology. In his testing program, he might very well be considered as a functionalist, even as Binet, but he had little use for metal instruments. He could not stomach behaviorism and its offshoots. He believed in innate qualities determined by the genes, and although he would accept a modicum of environmental causality as a factor in mental development, his chief concern was to trace not the repressed complexes nor the interpersonal relations of the child nor the punishment it was subjected to at home, but the antecedents, the mental and physical activities of the child.

Another stand of Terman, which is not typical of the American trend, is his insistence on the unitary form of intelligence. In this respect he could be taken for an ally of Spearman and McDougall. The fragmentation of intelligence in the sense Thorndike taught it was an almost repugnant idea. He could accept the thesis that there are different talents, or perhaps even the division into abstract, mechanical, and social intelligence, but to pile up a load of different categories in abstract intelligence and expect suitable tests for each separate category would play havoc with the entire concept of the intelligence quotient and its constancy.

Several factors have led to Terman's success as the chief authority in the field of testing. Some were circumstantial, of course, like the war, which pressed Terman into service and enabled him to draw on contacts with the "brass hats." His academic status at a first-rate university like Stanford would be another situation in his favor. The rapidly growing demands for mental tests in all types of institutions—educational, penal, and medical—would give him an excellent opportunity to "deliver the goods." But when all is said and done, one can still point to Terman's qualities of mind and heart as the primary reasons for his reputation: (a) a singleness of purpose constantly urging him to keep revising and revising until he could be certain that his norms had reached an unexceptionable standard, (b) clearheadedness in dealing with hundreds of thousands of data where selection and classification are of paramount importance, (c) a reduction of theorizing to a minimum so as not to clutter up the factual framework, and finally, (d) his interest in and responsiveness to people in all walks and of all ages, but especially those in the upper mental brackets, whereas other testers had concentrated on the lower ranges (feeblemindedness).

One of several letters received from Terman will give us a personal glimpse of the man.

Stanford, California
October 27, 1950

Dear Dr. Roback:

Thank you very much for your letter of October 19 and for the book review and the privately printed letter that came with it. I neglected to say in my recent letter that it was your book on "Jewish Influence in Modern Thought" that first interested me so much in the creative productivity of Jews. I have since then had my interest increased by the follow-up of some 88 men and 64 women, Jewish members of the gifted group which I have had under observation now for almost 30 years. As you may have learned, I devoted one chapter in the book, "The Gifted Child Grows Up," published by the Stanford University Press three years ago, to these Jewish members of the group. Now I shall look forward to the forthcoming book "The Jewish Impact on Western Civilization."

You wonder in your letter if I have any Jewish antecedents. So far as I know, I don't. The Termans, whose genealogy in America has been studied for several years by one of my remote cousins, seem to be all descendants of one or more families that came to Virginia from England and/or Scotland early in the 18th Century. The name is spelled in 10 or 12 different ways, including Terman, Turman, Tureman, Tierman, Tearman, and even Thurman. Some branches of the Terman strain that came to Virginia later intermingled with Indians and there is good reason to believe that I myself have some Indian blood. My paternal grandmother was named Jones and was supposed to be of Welsh descent, as most Joneses are. My maternal grandfather was Pennsylvania Dutch (that is, German) and my maternal grandmother was of French Huguenot descent, her maiden name being Deupree.

Under separate cover I am sending you two or three reprints of things I have written in recent years.

Sincerely yours,
LEWIS M. TERMAN

Chapter 37

The Phenomenal Expansion of American Psychology

WE NOW COME to the end of our story begun about 300 years ago in the village which has become one of the country's great university towns, now known as Cambridge, but then called Newtowne. It was a long road to travel, and the turns were few until our own century was reached.

For this reason, the subject was treated longitudinally, or diachronically. How else could it have been approached, when psychology for two and a-half centuries was steeped in theory? It is only within the last fifty years that it has spread horizontally and become diversified into fields, each of which displayed such a luxuriance that nothing short of a companion volume could even begin to do it justice. In the present chapter, only a preview could be attempted, for the area is too large to be covered in a flighty manner.

Harbingers of the new developments very rarely announced themselves, but one swallow does not make summer. In 1863, there appeared Isaac Ray's *Mental Hygiene*, and P. A. Chadbourne's essay on *Instinct*, in 1872, could be regarded as a foundation for animal psychology, but it was theoretical and compilative, as was J. Bascom's *Comparative Psychology,* which was more a genetic approach to the whole problem of intelligence.

Educational Psychology—the First Branch. . . .

As would have been anticipated, educational psychology was the first field to have been cultivated among the dozen or more to have expanded so rapidly within the past half-century. The first manual, for teachers, *Lectures on School-keeping,* was brought out by S. R. Hall, in 1829, and was reproduced by the Dartmouth Press in 1929. A slender book of 136 pages, it contained some professional information of value to teachers, for Hall had opened the first normal school for teachers in the United States. Jacob Abbot's *The Teacher* (1883) a book twice the size of its predecessor was practically without a competitor in the field for a full decade, and its popularity is evidenced by the fact that in a quarter of a century, it passed through 25 editions. The only other textbook to rival it, and soon to outdo it, was David Page's *Theory and Practice of Teaching,* which, since 1847, when it was first published, appeared in numerous editions or reissues.

The first compendium to be actually labelled *"Educational Psychology,"* was a booklet by Louisa P. Hopkins, which came out in 1886. Although containing less than a hundred pages, the outline, for such it was, introduced the psychological applications to education more explicitly than some of the larger volumes. Edward Brooks, who was a pedagogue in the more modern sense, and author of school texts in mathematics, caught the new spirit of teaching in his *Mental Science and Modern Culture,* a book of over 500 pages, which he published in 1883. It could serve as a psychological textbook too, for it treated the very subjects usually found in such works, but the applications to teaching were the chief purpose of the book, and when the author assumed the office of superintendent of the public schools in Philadelphia, his book became the standard text for normal schools and other training institutions for teachers.

The new orientation of experimental psychology is ushered in by John Dewey, in 1889, through his (and J. A. McLellan's) *Applied Psychology* which was at bottom a textbook setting forth the principles and practice of education. Today this label would have been decidedly a misnomer, but at the time, what other applied psychology was there to speak of? His (and McLellan's) *The Psychology of Number* (1895) is again a pedagogical work, a treatise with reference to the teaching of arithmetic. Dewey's later books along the lines of education are of a social and philosophical nature, rather than strictly professional. In fact, a number of books deal directly with education. Such are *Moral Principles in Education* (1909), *Educational Essays* (1910), *Ideals, Aims and Methods in Education* (1922), *Art and Education* (1929), *Contrasts in Education* (1930), *The Way Out of Educational Confusion* (1931), *Experience and Education* (1938) and an even larger number of articles. In fact, all his life he has been preoccupied with this vital subject.

The towering figure, however, in this specialty, one who symbolized Teachers College, is doubtless E. L. Thorndike, who has trained hundreds of educators, among them some of the most eminent in the world. His interest did not lie so much in the mechanics of pedagogy or administration as in the problems of learning. Other outstanding men in educational psychology (exclusive of testers) are C. H. Judd, H. O. Rugg, Wm. H. Burnham, B. H. Bode, W. C. Bagley, V. A. C. Henmon, and M. E. Haggerty. Creditable work has been done by Norma V. Scheidemann, F. B. Knight, P. A. Witty, M. Sherman, J. M. Stephens, S. L. Pressey, A. D. Woodruff, A. I. Gates, and others, whose contributions must wait to be recorded in the horizontal survey of American psychology.

Child and Developmental Psychology

Child psychology is frequently grouped with educational psychology, but it should be given a separate place or else combined with genetic or developmental psychology. Here, the pioneers are G. Stanley Hall and J. Mark Baldwin, but an impressive array of workers may be listed: B. T. Baldwin, A. Gesell, Vernon Jones, H. E. Jones, E. A. Kirkpatrick, Wm. Healy and S. S. and E. T. Glueck, a collaborating couple, who are primarily billeted to criminology (*delinquency problems*), J. E. Wallin, Gladys Schwesinger, Katherine T. Omwake, and Leta S. Hollingworth (*deviates*), Helen T. Wooley, F. L. Goodenough, G. D. Stoddard, Jessie A. Charters, Clara H. Town, (*deviates*), Dorothy W. Baruch, F. K. Shuttleworth, Ada H. Arlitt, Y. S. Nathanson, Beth L. Wellman, L. Carmichael, M. L. Reymert, A. T. Jersild, E. S. Conklin, R. R. Sears, Gertrude H. Hildreth, Margaret W. Curti, Florence Mateer, A. J. Baker (*exceptional children*), J. E. Anderson, W. C. Olson, E. Harms, Elizabeth Hurlock, Luella Cole, C. D. Brooks, Katherine M. Banham, and certainly the new settlers, Heinz Werner and Charlotte Buhler. Problems of old age (*geriatrics*) have occupied the attention of G. Lawton. One of the pioneers in this field has been W. R. Miles (1931). The proportion of women in this field will surely be noted.

Psychometry

Intelligence testing and mental measurement, in general, have had as pioneers and veterans, J. McKeen Cattell, J. Jastrow, Lewis M. Terman, H. H. Goddard, Walter Fernald, F. Kuhlmann (*infant tests, revision of Binet scale*),

T. L. Kelley, W. F. Dearborn, F. N. Freeman (*text*) F. S. Freeman (*text*), L. L. Thurstone, A. S. Otis, C. C. Brigham (*non-verbal tests*), G. M. Whipple, R. M. Yerkes, E. A. Doll, C. L. Hull (*aptitude testing*), O. K. Buros, R. Pinter, C. E. Seashore (*musical ability*), F. A. Moss, Grace Fernald, H. A. Toops, J. L. Stenquist (*mechanical aptitude*), D. Wechsler (*Bellevue Test*), S. P. Hayes (*tests for the blind*), S. D. Porteus (*defectives*), F. L. Wells, M. A. Merrill, M. R. Trabue, Clara C. Cooper, K. M. Cowdery (*vocational*), G. Myers, J. P. Herring (*revision of Binet*), Harriet Babcock (*diagnostic tests*), J. L. Mursell (*textbook*), A. A. Roback (*first superior adult, scientific ingenuity, comprehension, and sense of humor tests*), and J. W. Bridges (*point scale*), J. C. Maller and G. W. Allport (*personality tests*).

To even enumerate all those who have devised some special test would take several pages, and, it may be easily assumed that not a few of the intelligence testers who should have been mentioned will be missed by the reader. On the projective tests almost as much might be said. The Kent-Rosanoff association test, on Jungian principles, might come under this head, but more typical are the Rorschach techniques developed by M. R. Harrower-Erickson, S. J. Beck, B. Klopfer, and D. M. Kelley, the thematic apperception test devised by C. D. Morgan and H. A. Murray, the visual-motor Gestalt test of L. Bender, the play therapy techniques and the finger-painting interpretations. On the theoretical side, we have the discussions, on a very comprehensive scale, by J. E. Bell and, in compact form, by L. K. Frank, also the emphasis on frustration by S. Rosenzweig.

Abnormal and Clinical Psychology

In abnormal psychology, the early contribution of Benjamin Rush has already been referred to, but Rush was a medical man. On the psychological side, there is only the *Outline of Imperfect and Disordered Mental Action* (1840) by T. C. Upham, to report, until the beginning of the present century, when Morton Prince also a medical man, brought to America the ideas of the dissociation school and founded the *Journal of Abnormal Psychology*. Boris Sidis, who took his Ph.D. degree under William James, collaborated with him to some extent, but his egocentric type of writing and far from sociable manner did not obtain the hearing he deserved.

In view of the fact that several fields converge to make up the large territory of abnormal and clinical psychology—criminology, psychiatry, medicine, psychoanalysis, therapeutic counseling, among others, and that the number of fellows and associate members in the division of clinical and abnormal psychology of the American Psychological Association aggregates approximately 3000, it would require something like a booklet to do justice to even the more important men here. Perhaps, then, we might offer only a score of sample names, including those only whose writings appeared in psychological contexts or publications.

The mental hygiene movement was inaugurated by C. W. Beers who "found his mind" and thereupon founded a great institution. We must, of course, not forget the initiator, Lightner Witmer, who started the first psychological clinic, in Philadelphia. Among the better known in the field are K. Menninger, H. S. Sullivan (*interpersonal relations*), C. M. Louttit, R. H. Gault (*criminology*), R. M. Dorcus, M. H. Erickson, R. W. White, D. W. Mackinnon, C. Landis, J. McV. Hunt, R. A. Brotmarkle, C. R. Rogers, S. S. Tomkins, Trigant Burrow, J. L. Moreno, H. Lundholm, D. B. Klein, N. Cameron, D. Malamud, H. Syz, D. M. Levy, D. Rapaport, S. W. Taylor, L. F. Shaffer, J. H. Masserman, E. Weiss, O. E. English, E. S. Conklin, W. E. Galt, W. H. Gantt, D. Shakow, M. A. Seidenfeld, and Anita M. Mühl. This does not begin to afford one an idea as to the extent of the researchers, practitioners, and their activities in this one branch of psychology alone.

A clinician who received his doctorate at Yale at the turn of the century, and who has been most active in founding clinics at various institutions, is J. E. Wallace Wallin, who, in his 88th year, is not thinking of retiring. Indeed, American school children are more indebted to him than to Lightner Witmer, who rated a sketch in this volume.

Ramification of Clinical Psychology

Clinical psychology has, within a quarter-century, spread so rapidly and over such a vast area that it is difficult now to delimit it. It has become so diversified that it may include psychotherapy, counseling, where the patient becomes a "client," the correction of personality flaws, treatment of mild neuroses. The methods and practices may be drawn from various sources: hypnotism, psychoanalysis, experimental psychology, pastoral psychology, which is in itself, a phase of clinical psychology with a religious flavor, individual psychology, analytic psychology, interpersonalism, and several others, or combinations of any two or more.

Since it has been reaching out in all directions, one need not be surprised that clinical psychology has also been affected by existentialism and phenomenology, although these are essentially philosophical schools. The first impetus came from Vienna, where psychoanalysis originated, but oddly enough, existentialism in clinical psychology seeks to reinstate the principle that psychoanalysis, born under a different star, was eager to throw overboard.

Viktor Frankl, a co-ethnic of Freud, and like him a victim of Nazi nefariousness, came to see man not as a bundle of mechanisms or even dynamisms, all determined by experiences in early childhood, but as a self-determining individual whose existence is a series of self-creating acts. While Freud, from his nineteenth-century observation post, would deal with motives only, but could not admit the values into his bailiwick, Frankl goes so far as to state that "man is more than psyche; man is spirit,"[1] and his system of "logotherapy" is intended expressly to lend meaning to one's existence. Frankl's experiences during the Nazi atrocities surely have helped shape his whole conception; and his own daring as a physician, under the circumstances, must have afforded him the insight and confidence that he *could* act in a nonpredetermined manner, unless of course his genes have given him the direction, but even that can be countervailed by force of will.

Like psychoanalysis, which found in the United States its most hospitable haven, existentialism has made more headway in this country than even in Austria. Among its chief representatives besides Frankl are Erwin Straus, another Nazi victim, who has now returned to his rightful academic post in Germany, and Rollo May. Existential psychiatry will, of course, appeal to the clergy, and its newly founded journal contains a number of stimulating articles.

In practice, *i.e.*, shorn of its philosophical moorings, existential psychiatry is kin to Otto Rank's will therapy. In the former, there is a bit more emphasis on the meaning of the individual's existence; in the latter, more stress is laid on self-

[1] V. E. Frankl: *Journal of Existential Psychiatry*, 1961, vol. 2.

discipline. Both are a departure from the passive reproduction of repressed *id* components and the breakdown of the patient's resistance, emphasized by psychoanalysis.

Applied Psychology

The peak of interest and activity in applied psychology (only to be measured in proportion to other branches) was reached about 1920. One would expect it to be a vast field, first, because it includes so many walks of life and, secondly, because of the practical demands in industry and business and, what is more important, the lucrative returns for such services as applied psychologists could offer.

Applied psychology did not come into being until about 1910, when Hugo Münsterberg began to busy himself with the problems arising out of labor and employment, selling, transportation and accidents, the mechanics of legal evidence, etc. Münsterberg had already had some leads in this general sphere, thanks to the pioneer efforts of Frederick W. Taylor[2] whose spectacular results in reducing the expenditure of energy while increasing the output of work had made him a much admired man in the offices of executives. F. B. Gilbreth[3] and his wife, Lillian,[4] who gave birth to twelve children, reared them, and yet found time to collaborate with her engineer husband and continue his work after his death, made some special applications of the Taylor principle. F. Parsons (*Choosing a Vocation*, 1909) was the pioneer in vocational guidance.

It will be noticed that these four were outsiders to psychology. It was Münsterberg, who, as we have seen in the chapter devoted to him, noted the possibilities of welding the scattered data into a system, thus forming a new branch of psychology. Advertising became the most attractive twig in this new branch, and many were the early birds that perched and warbled thereon: W. D. Scott[5] who later became President of Northwestern University, H. L. Hollingworth, Daniel Starch, A. T. Poffenberger; and the volumes published be-

[2] F. W. Taylor: *Shop Management* (1903), *The Principles of Scientific Management* (1911).

[3] F. B. Gilbreth: *Motion Study* (1911).

[4] L. M. Gilbreth: *The Psychology of Management* (1914).

[5] He also published a book on the *Psychology of Public Speaking* (1907).

came more bulky and voluminous as time went on. The *Journal of Applied Psychology* was founded in 1917, and L. R. Geissler, who was then teaching at Clark University, was the appointee, as editor, by Stanley Hall, who most likely was the moving spirit in this successful venture. The founding of the Psychological Corporation by J. McKeen Cattell, as already noted earlier, was another landmark in the annals of applied psychology. The field of applied psychology has a host of cultivators—among the leading ones: W. V. Bingham (*personnel, interview*), D. Fryer (*training techniques*), Lillian Martin (*consulting*), M. S. Viteles (*personnel*), M. Freyd, P. Achilles, and E. K. Strong (*interests*). H. C. Link has built up the marketing research technique. Donald W. Laird has authored a dozen works in almost every department of business and industrial psychology. The Gallup poll is too well publicized to dwell on. The so-called lie detector has been one of the devices used in extra-court investigations. Motivational research in marketing has been conducted by R. Likert. A number of textbooks in applied psychology have appeared recently, the most widely known is probably that by G. W. Crane. H. E. Burtt, a student of Münsterberg, was sufficiently influenced to write a comprehensive manual on the subject, but there are others who brought out texts: N. R. F. Maier, F. A. Moss, and C. Ewer.

Race and Social Psychology

Social psychology was late developing in the United States. It is true that there were treatises and textbooks labelled social psychology, but their authors, E. A. Ross and C. A. Ellwood were sociologists. F. H. Allport's *Social Psychology* (1924) is a behavioristic text, sprinkled with psychoanalysis, and quite out of date now. Among the more recognized race and social psychologists are T. R. Garth (*Indians*), K. Dunlap, S. D. Porteus (*aborigines*), O. Klineberg (*races*), P. Lazarsfeld, H. Cantril (*radio, public opinion*), D. Katz, W. Dennis, S. H. Britt, D. Krech, G. and A. Murphy, G. W. Allport (*social attitudes*), L. W. Doob (*propaganda*), M. Sherif, G. W. Hartmann, R. T. La Piere, S. S. Sargent (*texts*), E. Frenkel-Brunswik (*prejudice*) and A. A. Roback (*folklore and linguistics*).

From anthropology, there were noteworthy contributors, Franz Boas, being the most distinguished of them, but Clark

Wissler and L. Farrand have introduced the test and measurement angle, while E. Sapir, Ruth Benedict, and Margaret Mead, as well as C. Kluckhohn have enriched this branch of psychology with the cultural point of view.

Animal Psychology

The pioneer in American animal psychology was, of course, E. L. Thorndike who, working with cats, gave us the first truly scientific technique, thereby eliminating guesswork and subjective interpretations, but it was Robert M. Yerkes who might be said to have built up this branch. Particularly valuable is his work with primates extending over a period of several decades. What a pity that W. M. Wheeler, who was an older contemporary and made quite a stir with his detailed accounts of ant colonies, is never mentioned in recent books on comparative psychology, let alone texts in general psychology. He was dean at Harvard's Bussey Institution. Margaret F. Washburn, H. C. Carr, J. B. Watson, W. S. Hunter, E. C. Tolman (*rats*), F. A. Beach (*mammals*), C. J. Warden, T. C. Schneirla, B. F. Skinner (*methods*), N. R. F. Maier (*mice*), H. Klüver (*apes*), and O. H. Mowrer (*birds*) have interesting experiments associated with their name. N. L. Munn is more of a comparative coördinator. Nor should we ignore, much as his colleagues are inclined to do, Wm. McDougall's investigation on acquired characteristics in rats.

Naturally, the zoölogists have had much to do with animal psychology, *e.g.*, George Parker and J. S. Holmes. Even the startling work of Jacques Loeb on sea urchins and other low organisms must be considered here. His experiments which gave us the concept of tropism were considered a death blow to the theory of instincts. His research on parthenogenesis is not in our present sphere.

Experimental Psychology

The *chosen* branch of psychology, as may be surmised, is experimental psychology. In the first place, it constitutes the basis for its status as a science. It either proves or disproves the hypothesis presented. It is associated with the founders of the science and carries prestige. It involves more labor, often of a tedious nature, and consumes a great deal of time. The best experimentalists must be gifted, but quite mediocre people can undertake experimentation and obtain valid results, depending upon the nature of the problem. The name of the experimenters is legion. Naturally, experiments may be conducted in every branch of psychology, but in speaking of experimental psychology, one thinks of the various departments such as sensation, imagery, memory, perception, the emotions, volition, abstraction, conditioning and the like. Since a number of the experimentalists have already been alluded to or will figure in branches yet to come, let us confine ourselves to those who, by dint of long devotion to their special field, have received recognition on the part of their colleagues, or at least are worthy of such. There are also those who have been of service in the interpretation of other people's results or in the compilation of experimental summaries. Since there need be no duplication here, once whole chapters or sections were taken up with the early experimenters, Cattell, Titchener, Baldwin, Münsterberg, Woodworth, etc., our roster will include only such names as have been barely mentioned, if at all.

Of the earlier period, let us single out such names as A. Kirschmann (*Toronto*), G. S. Fullerton, A. H. Pierce, E. B. Delabarre, W. L. Bryan, L. Witmer, E. C. Sanford, J. Jastrow, E. W. Scripture, J. W. Baird, G. M. Stratton (*inverted eye image*), K. Dunlap, (*apparatus, habit*), R. Dodge (*eye movements, human variability*), W. R. Miles (*nutrition, biochemical basis of mental states, drugs, geriatrics*), E. B. Huey, and Margaret F. Washburn. In sensation, we have the Ladd-Franklin theory of color vision, introduced by many articles and a book, the long series of experiments of C. E. Ferree and his wife, Gertrude Rand, the studies by L. T. Troland and Selig Hecht; in audition, the important researches of S. S. Stevens (*Harvard*) and of E. G. Wever and C. W. Bray at Princeton, while in learning, there is an array of important studies by S. S. Colvin, G. Katona, C. L. Hull, J. B. Stroud, E. R. Guthrie, E. R. Hilgard, J. Peterson, and R. R. Sears. Other experimenters are K. Dallenbach, H. S. Langfeld, S W. Fernberger, C. A. Darrow, H. Helson, D. G. Paterson, R. R. Willoughby (*genetic issues*), H. B. English (*abstraction*), A. M. Feleky (*emotions*), J. P. Guilford (*tests and measurements*), R. H. Seashore (*methodology*), C. Landis (*emotions*), B. F. Skinner, H. R. Crosland, H. R. DeSilva, J. P. Nafe, J. J. Gibson, F. A. Pattie, J. P.

Seward, P. T. Young, H. Cason, E. Brunswik, L. J. Postman, N. E. Miller, J. S. Bruner (*perception*), H. Schlosberg (*thought*) and G. H. S. Razran (*conditioned reflexes*), A. H. Maslow (*motivation personality*). Among the younger men may be mentioned E. B. Newman, K. W. Spence, and R. L. Solomon, A. G. Bills and W. L. Valentine have brought out textbooks of experimental psychology, H. E. Garrett's survey of great psychological experiments is also a useful text.

If a Rip van Winkle who had fallen asleep in Münsterberg's or Titchener's laboratory, during 1912, were to be awakened in one of the rooms of the Harvard Psychological Laboratory, in 1952, he would, on the assumption that he retained his past memories, be dazed by the amount of large apparatus rigged up in technological fashion; and the constant ticking, clicking, and knocking, with moving recorders registering in red ink every few minutes, would startle him without doubt.

The modern laboratory is geared to deal with long-range experimentation. The experimenter today looks back at the investigations in the past as a bit of exploring, with the researcher nibbling here and there at some problem. The set-up was: a hypothesis, a few simple instruments and pieces of apparatus, a handful of subjects, a series of experiments over the weeks or months, and the results were guaranteed. There was no dearth of problems, and imagination was rife in visualizing possibilities.

At present, this procedure is considered scratching the surface, and no more. The psychologist is more concerned now with rigorous methods in eliminating conditions which could mar the objective results. For this reason, most effort goes into the perfecting of the technique; and each step is taken slowly but carefully. To establish one fact might take years, but then the conclusion is foolproof, and that is in line with the tradition of physics and chemistry. It involves far more tedious work and laborious planning than, say, 25 years ago but there are adequate compensations. In the first place, in the animal experiments, to take one instance, it is no longer necessary to keep watching the subjects to see what progress they are making; for all movements of any account are automatically recorded. Doubts as to what actually went on during the experimenter's absence are thus dispelled, and the necessity of retesting in such cases is dispensed with.

The individual laboratory today will not have such a variety of interesting investigations to offer, and the imaginative knack is spent on technique rather than on the problem itself, but the gain is in terms of validity. The old "laboratory atmosphere" is no longer blamable for discrepancies between results at different institutions. At the same time, it is a pity that in order to achieve some operational result, say in conditioning, the human sphere is almost wholly neglected, and the rodent is still supreme as a subject.

Personality and Character

The department of psychology dealing with personality and character is more like a branch now. It was late in developing. Textbooks prior to 1925 would scarcely mention the term, as if it were nothing but a conversational word. Experiments on isolated traits were being conducted here and there, and tests were being devised for the purpose (W. Fernald in 1912), without unification of the results. A. A. Roback expanded his essay on character and inhibition into *The Psychology of Character* (1927), and published a separate volume as a bibliography of books and articles. Jastrow, it is true in a small book, *Qualities of Men* (1910) and a larger work, *Character and Temperament* (1915), opened up the subject, but it was more a sociological approach, of a rambling nature, though well written. Most of the emphasis was laid on temperament and individual differences.

June Downey was one of the pioneers in that young field, and from the personnel movement around 1917, the subject received some stimulation. Religious bodies and civic organizations became interested especially in problems of character, and it was probably partly due to these activities that P. F. Voelker, in 1921 designed his interesting series of experiments with children, calculated to test their honesty in life situations. V. Cady and W. E. Slaght followed him. It was, however, the Character Education Inquiry, with special reference to religious education, directed by Mark A. May and H. Hartshorne at Teachers College, Columbia, which raised the subject to a new high level. With a staff of forty people, The Inquiry evolved into a sort of institute, lasting from 1923 to 1928. The results were incorporated in three volumes, and tended to confirm the specificity theory, traditional to Columbia.

G. W. Allport's *Personality: A Psychological Interpretation* (1937) was another milestone on the long road; for it contains the steering ideas and basic concepts which many books on personality (and there are many by this time) succeed in eliminating to the advantage of the hundreds of bits of discrete data from various sources. H. A. Murray's *Explorations in Personality,* more or less of a collective volume, is worthy of its title and has been able to excavate some interesting material, which, however, is still in the raw stage. Werner Wolff's studies show originality in the problems tackled. His chief contribution has been in psychodiagnostics. Other investigators are G. B. Watson (not to be confused with the archbehaviorist), A. Angyal, R. Stagner, and G. Murphy. Comprehensive textbooks on personality have recently been published by R. B. Cattell, L. P. Thorpe and by C. M. Harsh, in collaboration with H. G. Schrickel. A. A. Roback's *Personality in Theory and Practice,* and chapters on both personality and character in *Present-day Psychology* (1954), do not have the coverage found in either G. W. Allport's recent *Pattern and Growth in Personality* (1961) or R. M. Dreger's comprehensive *Fundamentals of Personality* (1962). From a much neglected study, personality has become one of the most popular courses on the curriculum.

Physiological Psychology

Perhaps no branch of the science is so exclusive as physiological psychology; for here one must be specialized, and no half-way house will do. It is difficult to know where to begin here; for many physiologists have indirectly affected the course of psychology. Even if the Chicago physiologist, A. J. Carlson, did not bother with the psychological interpretations, his numerous papers on digestive processes and fasting have furthered our knowledge on appetite, hunger and thirst. Somewhat closer to psychology comes G. W. Crile especially in his researches on the endocrine glands and exhaustion, as well as on asphyxiation; for the actual phenomena or inner experiences cannot be bypassed. The physiologist, however, who has advanced the cause of psychology most in this country is W. B. Cannon, whose *Bodily Changes in Pain, Hunger, Fear, and Rage* (1915, 1929) was regarded as "must" reading in intermediate courses. His refutation of the James-Lange theory and his conception of homeostasis figure in most textbooks. In his last book, *The Wisdom of the Body,* he shows again his preoccupation with psychological problems. C. M. Child, although a zoölogist, has been, to some extent adopted by psychologists interested in the nervous system. Child has introduced the concept of gradients, which has been made much of recently, and has written a book on the *Physiological Foundations of Behavior* (1924). C. J. Herrick and G. E. Coghill, who belong to an older generation of biologists and physiologists respectively, have offered important views for psychology.

Two men who have devoted almost a lifetime to the probing of brain localization are S. I. Franz and K. S. Lashley. Franz was the more radical of the two in contesting the accepted doctrine that the various functions are localized. Lashley, although more discreet in his view, also doubts whether we can say anything more than that there are general regions which, if impaired, will affect learning, but even if 50% of the cortical tissue is destroyed in rats, they will still be able to find their way out of the maze. As, however, the maze increases in complexity, a larger number of errors will be shown.

While Lashley's experiments have been on rats, and for this reason, were questioned as applied to humans, the remarkable fact, disclosed by brain surgery in the case of serious melancholias, that the mental functions are not as greatly disturbed as might be expected, would give us cause to weigh the facts of localization anew. However, that the extirpation of certain sensory areas in the brain, like the occipital, would interfere with the sensory function which it governs is not open to doubt.

Of the lesser of younger men who have, nevertheless, done meritorious work, one might mention: L. T. Troland (psychophysiology in four volumes already referred to), H. S. Liddell, A. G. Bills, C. P. Richter, Karl Pribram, F. A. Geldard, C. T. Morgan, L. Carmichael, and D. O. Hebb, F. A. Beach's endocrinological survey has been of considerable service to psychology, more for the sidelights. Of great value, too, is the detailed account of what happens in psychosurgery, as related by W. Freeman and J. W. Watts. W. Penfield (Canada), has gained distinction in tracing cerebral loci of epilepsy.

Psychical Research

There can hardly be a greater contrast than between physiological psychology and psychical research, yet they are both, more or less peripherally, related to psychology, the one as a basis for it; the other as a higher dimension or level. Whether or not we accept its convictions or its methods, it does not behoove us as scientists to dismiss that type of research with a snort.

The history of psychical research in the United States dates back to more than a century ago, even if we exclude such sensational episodes as those which made the Fox sisters the talk of the country after the evening meal. It was in 1842, that a physician by the name of Joseph R. Buchanan claimed to have made the discovery of the peculiar impressibility of the human brain, which enables it to receive cues without the mediation of the senses. He speaks of a certain Bishop Polk, of the Episcopal Church, who afterwards became a general in the Confederate army and was killed during the Civil War, informing him (in 1851) that his own "sensibility was so acute that if he should by accident touch a piece of brass, even in the night when he could not see what he touched, he immediately felt the influence through his system, and could recognize the offensive metallic taste. His cerebral conformations indicated uncommon acuteness of the external senses."[6] Today we might be prone to interpret whatever results such perception showed as due to suggestion, association, and synesthesia.

Buchanan tells of a series of interesting, and even exciting, experiments, the subjects in which were about 80 students and several professors of the Eclectic Medical Institute of Cincinnati, where it turned out that nearly one-half of the students and five of the professors were affected in a definite manner by holding in their hands an envelope containing some drug entirely concealed from view. In the case of an emetic, *e.g.*, (*lobelia*) such sensitive persons could not go on with the experiment because of the urge to vomit. Buchanan concluded that certain subtle influences emanated from the object affecting the acute sensibilities of some nervous systems. He then experimented with living persons, instead of objects, and discovered that by placing the hand on any part of a person, which was in a state of even incipient disease, the observer felt a distinct reaction. Even holding the hand in proximity to a given organ would yield a similar experience, though not in the same degree.

[6] J. R. Buchanan: *Manual of Psychometry* (4th ed.), 1893, p. 17, republished from *Buchanan's Journal of Man*, 1849.

Buchanan, after repeating the experiments on thousands of individuals, named this particular science, as he wishes to dignify it, "psychometry," and was prepared to champion the theory that the electrical properties of the brain (a most original thought about a century ago, when we consider the recency of the electro-encephalographic technique) come in contact with the "mysterious influences" of the object or writing. One is reminded here of the extraordinary exploits of Raphael Schermann in similar experiments. It is worth noting that Buchanan coined the phrase "psychological chemistry" to designate the border territory which explains the connection between the mind and matter.

The founding of the Society for Psychical Research in England which, besides enjoying the participation of men like F. Podmore, E. Gurney and F. C. S. Myers, was patronized by critical and famous men like Alfred Russel Wallace, J. Balfour, H. Sidgwick and Wm. McDougall, led to the establishment of a similar institution in the United States, which at one time was presided over by William James and, subsequently, by William McDougall. The calibre of the men in the American society, otherwise, was not to be compared with that of the moving spirits in England, but the journal which the Society published made some progress among lay people, in this case, including the clergy, "lay," of course, in that particular respect. About 50 years ago, the chief patron of psychical research was J. H. Hyslop, professor of logic and ethics at Columbia University. From 1906 to 1920, when he died, his chief preoccupation was neither logic nor ethics, but human survival after death. During the same period and later, W. F. Prince, a clergyman, was active in the Society, investigating many reported phenomena. As he was studying cases of multiple personality, too, in connection with the supernormal, his namesake, Morton Prince, had cause to be embarrassed more than once when they were confused both because of the common surname and the partial interest common to both.

Of the psychologists who gave their time and energy in pursuit of results, either positive or negative, the following may be enumerated, with indications of their attitude: William James (sympathetic), Hugo Münsterberg, who unmasked Madame Eusapia Paladino and who, even as a young man in Freiburg, was drawn to the subject of thought transference (negative), William McDougall (sympathetic). J. E. Coover obtained negative results in experiments on thought transference; L. T. Troland, after a year on a research fellowship, abandoned the task as useless, C. H. Estabrooks obtained favorable results in experiments with playing cards (color and suit), G. Murphy, in the matter of telepathy, has steadfastly maintained a sympathetic attitude on the basis of experimental data. It was reserved for J. B. Rhine to establish a laboratory at Duke University for the study of extrasensory perception, as he styled it, and to create so much interest in the reported phenomena as to receive sufficient subsidies for various publications including a journal devoted to parapsychology, as the subject is now known, as well as a bulletin. In fact, it may be said that Duke University is the only higher institution of learning which harbors a separate department of this sort.

Systematic and Theoretical Psychology

Since much of this branch has been covered in the portion on schools, it would be appropriate to add only those names which have not yet appeared in that connection. Not all the textbook writers are systematic in the arrangement of their material, let alone being systematizers. A man like W. B. Pillsbury has been a synthesizer in that respect, and his several textbooks, particularly the *Fundamentals of Psychology*, are an indication of the knack requisite for such a specialty. C. R. Griffith, M. Bentley, Max F. Meyer (the theoretician, more than the promoter, of behaviorism), H. C. Warren, E. G. Boring, as well as J. R. Kantor, who, for all his explorations into logic, language, and allied fields, the boundaries of which he delimits expertly, may be charged perhaps with an overdose of systematization, R. H. Wheeler, H. L. Searles, and J. P. Guilford have evinced, through their works, that thair grasp of psychology is fundamental, to the very roots, so to speak. Mary Calkins, belonging to a previous generation, could come into this class, were her system not overloaded with philosophy, bordering on metaphysics. Lundholm's critique of all physicalism (*God's Failure or Man's Folly*) suffers from the same bifurcation in procedure.

Theory, at present, occupies less place in psychology, as compared with the past, and where it does enter, it seems to be confined to some specific account, usually by means of diagrams, of the *modus operandi* of some behavior. Just as in the erection of a building, the wider and the taller the structure, the deeper must we dig, for the foundation to be secure. If theoretical psychology has been sustaining a setback; it is partly for the reason that there is so much divergence of opinion among the theorists, but there is a further reason, and that is the lack of philosophical training among psychologists of the present generation. Even if philosophical issues need not be introduced into psychology, it is essential for the psychologist to be aware of the pitfalls in human thought.

The recent addition of a section of philosophical psychology in the American Psychological Association is a salutary move among some of the members.

Statistics

In the interpretation of experimental results, statistics has now taken the place of theoretical considerations. It may be said that statistics is on the point of dominating all experimental work. In submitting a clean-cut and conclusive piece of experimental research, the writer might hear the verdict "This might have been all right B. S.," which means "before statistics." In other words, the chronology of psychology might as well be divided into a primitive era, B. S., and an enlightened era, of A. S. (after statistics).

In addition to the psychologists cited in the section on factorial analysis, E. L. Thorndike, L. L. Thurstone, R. B. Cattell, T. L. Kelley, K. J. Holzinger, and H. Hotelling, such researchers as H. E. Garrett, I. Lorge, Thelma Hunt, J. P. Guilford, C. E. Kellog, G. F. Kuder, P. Rulon, E. F. Lindquist, A. E. Traxler, Helen M. Walker, B. W. Wood, H. G. Seashore, L. B. Hoisington, and R. L. Thorndike, have had their name in print on many occasions. Statistics has been one of the prerequisites for graduate work in psychology in most universities, and is in the ascendant as a control in every laboratory.

Art (Music) and Aesthetics

Small as the aesthetic division is in the American Psychological Association—no more than 50 fellows, there are nevertheless many more who have given evidence of an interest in that direction, even if they have not joined; J. L.

Mursell, C. M. Diserens, or who are no longer alive, like C. E. Seashore. We may give first place here to Max F. Meyer, veteran worker in audition, with a theory of his own; and in consonance, Max Schoen, M. F. Metfessel, C. C. Pratt, P. R. Farnsworth, and H. T. Moore (*his doctoral dissertation*) have all published sufficiently to deserve our notice here. H. S. Langfeld's book on the *Aesthetic Attitude* deals exclusively with the static or pictorial arts.

We might go on separating the various fields and subfields, for which there are no divisions in the American Psychological Association, alluding to differential psychology, with Anne Anastasi and R. H. Seashore, religious psychology with William James, E. D. Starbuck, J. H. Leuba, G. M. Stratton, H. C. McComas, and a few others; the history of psychology with G. S. Hall, J. M. Baldwin, E. G. Boring, G. S. Brett (*in Canada*), W. B. Pillsbury, S. W. Fernberger (*the chronicler of trends*); and others for their bibliographical achievement (Benjamin Rand) or lexicographical initiative (H B. English, H. C. Warren, and K. Dunlap) or for their editorial service (Carl Murchison, R. M. Elliott, H. C. Warren) or their collections of source books and readings (B. Rand, E. S. Robinson, E. L. Hartley, S. S. Tomkins, Wayne Dennis, and N. H. Pronko), or encyclopedic enterprise (J. M. Baldwin, P. L. Harriman), but it is to be feared that already the lists are cluttering up the presentation; and no doubt more than a few genuine psychologists have not been mentioned.

The Levelling of Achievement

There was a time not so long ago, when it would have been comparatively easy to establish which were the most outstanding psychologists in the country. In the early part of this century, only fifty years ago, no more than a score of men might have been placed on the record, without doing injustice to the others. There was a real gap between men like James, Dewey, Titchener, Münsterberg, or even Baldwin and Thorndike, and the others. We do not find at present that it is possible to place a few contemporary psychologists on a pedestal by themselves. Perhaps it is that we have no intellects like them, or again the reason may be that with thousands of psychologists, the particular specialties of many tend to offset each other. At one time, J. McKeen Cattell adopted the policy of starring the one thousand leading scientists in his *American*

Men of Science, allotting 50 to psychology. This was a questionable procedure even then; but today, it would have caused no end of controversy. Who can take it upon himself to decide which are the foremost psychologists in our midst? How much would personal bias or animus enter in? To what extent would the halo or agreement with an individual view influence our judgment? It would be more practicable to set down the names of perhaps 200 or 300 psychologists as belonging to Class A, and another 300-500 as belonging to Class B.

Synchronic Growth of Psychology

Psychology has grown in the past half-century proportionally more than any other science, not even excepting chemistry. Not only have new branches formed, but the American Psychological Association, which began with a handful of members, has now become an army of very close to 23,000. Thus, the tiny acorn planted in 1892 has grown to the size of a stout oak. If Stanley Hall or William James were to come to life again, in our day, and attend a meeting of the American Psychological Association, with its several concurrent sessions, he would be dazed both by the size of the audience as well as by the variety of the topics, many of which would strike the visitor as strange, not to speak of the technical language which probably would be unintelligible to him. Certainly he would be surprised to find a division of military psychology. At present, if we wished to institute proper divisions, we should have, at least, twenty-five, if not fully thirty. The classification in actual use, as a matter of fact, numbers twenty, yet the basis is not always clear. Why, *e.g.*, should personality be combined with social psychology, when each is a field by itself? And there are fields like differential psychology, history of psychology, etc., which are not sufficiently invested, *i.e.*, which have not had a large enough quota of workers to rate as a division in the Association.

The Social Outlook

One of the encouraging features in the organization is the creation of a division called the Society for the Psychological Study of Social Issues, counting about 900 fellows and members. It is encouraging because it indicates that psychologists are not intent upon merely serving as technologists, professionals, or ivory-tower scientists, shrugging their shoulders when a world issue comes up that deserves their individual or collective attention. It has been the bane of science all along that its votaries, with few exceptions, would be content to do as bidden by the political authorities. Through this division, which corresponds in a measure to the civil liberties union, psychologists have shown their status as citizens; and in our precarious world situation, with evil forces pressing at both extremes in the direction of the levelheaded liberal, such a body within a more powerful body, which the American Psychological Association undeniably has become, is a salutary and auspicious sign. If every scientific organization and learned society had a similar division, perhaps the world would have been in a healthier state today. It might also balance the military division which, ordinarily, would tend to give an unfavorable impression to the peace-loving world.

Fifty years ago, Hugo Münsterberg proclaimed applied psychology to be independent of ethical implications. The man who is consulted on matters of gain must not, he asserted, bother to ascertain whether the practice is consistent with the good of the community, any more than the engineer asks himself whether it is desirable for a projected bridge to be constructed at a certain point. He merely carries out the order of those who employ him. There was only one graduate student who ventured to oppose him in a seminar paper, which was subsequently published, although certainly not at Münsterberg's suggestion.

It is good to know that the committee on professional ethics of the American Psychological Association has adopted the policy of principle, if that is not to be taken as an Irish bull, which that young student championed *vis-à-vis* his over-awing teacher. Furthermore, inasmuch as two decades have now elapsed since Kurt Huber lost his head on the block at the white-gloved hands of the executioner (1943), it will be well for us to take cognizance of the fact that of all the philosophers and scientists in Germany at the time of the Brown Plague, Kurt Huber was the only one to head an open rebellion of students and faculty, in a stirring manifesto, calling the intelligentsia to throw off the yoke of the monster. And, let us mention, Huber was a folk and applied psychologist, which is not only a credit to this much maligned branch of psychology, but to the science as a whole, compensating for the bigoted and cringing attitude of E. R. Jaensch, Hitler's laureate psychologist. There must have been some kindly and liberal physicians in Germany, but all that had transpired at the Nuremberg trials pointed to the inhuman atrocities which many of the foremost in the profession were guilty of, atrocities which brought none of the advantages for science gained in vivisection experiments on guinea pigs. We do not know that a single physician, not even the great surgeon, Emil Sauerbruch, raised his voice, to say nothing about his lifting a finger, on behalf of the victims.

Psychology in Two Wars

It would be incredible to the founders of the science, but psychology received wide acclaim at the time of the first world war. Up to then, it was just beginning to attract attention in the spheres of industry and commerce, but the exigencies of the war made it imperative to press into service all the sciences which would be of the least benefit for the defense of the country. In 1916, the National Research Council was organized, and in 1917, the Council formed a Committee for Psychology, which, in 1919, was replaced by the Division of Anthropology and Psychology. Fostering research projects and co-ordinating activities were the chief aims the Council had in mind; but, as it developed, the war effort required a concentration along different lines.

The dictum "When cannons roar, the poets are mute" has often been quoted. Perhaps it has been true in regard to poetry. We are not certain that the observation holds today, for when cannons roar, the poets may be enlisted to sing paeans to the generalissimo, or they may write their last testaments on the bloody battlefield, inditing such deathless lines as "I have a rendezvous with death," or else, they may trun traitor and broadcast from the land of the enemy, urging their own national troops to desert to the foe. However it be with the poets, the scientists, mainly the engineers, the technologists, have always been called upon to devise facilities for crushing the enemy. The great Leonardo da Vinci, who was aware of the frightful possibilities which science could actualize, was said to have destroyed his model of a submarine that he had invented about 450 years ago. If only scientists were artists, as was this extraordinary genius, even on a small scale, the periodic cataclysms might not take on such terrible proportions.

Shortly after the United States entered the war with Germany, psychology was able to prove its value in practical affairs. Many committees were formed to deal with special problems. The selling of liberty bonds required *propaganda*, which again depended upon *motivation*. The registered men had to fill out a *questionnaire*—a psychological technique, as we have seen in the chapter on Stanley Hall. The drafted men required sorting and a fair proportion of them could be eliminated through *mental tests* without any loss to the fighting forces. There were problems in *vision,* in *audition* (to spot submarines) in the days prior to radar and other precision devices and instruments. *Therapy, re-education, indoctrination* of the men, *personnel* matters, problems of *fatigue, dizziness* while flying, *trade tests* to prevent deception on the part of those who wished non-combatant duties, which they could not perform without hazard, and literally scores of other tasks were handled by the psychologists. The top-ranking psychologist was R. M. Yerkes; and a single report, which dealt with psychological examining in the United States, filled a large quarto volume of nearly 900 pages.

Psychology, the quondam study of modalities and attributes and associations, made good, and was being primed for a greater rôle in the Nazi war, where it was better prepared to take over functions such as have not been thought of before. The whole scientific personnel, this time, was in the hands of a psychologist. During the two decades, between the end of the first world war and the beginning of the second, psychology had made steady progress in all directions, and again emerged with flying colors. True, it could show nothing spectacular like an atom bomb for its pains, but it could fit its wares into the picture both before and after the event, like calming the public mind, reducing panic, and conditioning or unconditioning victims, according to the requirements of the case. Thus the once theoretical science, superciliously treated by the other sciences, has come into its own; and to what extent it has been recognized by the government and the military heads may be gleaned from the fact that a handbook in psychology was distributed to the forces in a million or more copies. Psychology has remained an important cog in national defense. Thanks to the National Research Council which, in the last analysis, means thanks to the war, the science was able to expand, through appropriations and subsidies, and engage in large-scale projects, which had only a tangential relation to war.

Change of Trends

In 1940, J. S. Bruner and G. W. Allport[7] undertook to examine what changes were taking place in the course of the half-century since James's *Principles of Psychology* appeared. In their survey, they detected 37 types of psychological interest and activity, through which were flowing two distinct currents: one was psychology for science's sake; the other was psychology for society's sake. One should think *that* to be a natural divergence, since psychology is, in a sense, created by scientists, who are human beings, and *they* form the two types. Some say "our objective is to discover truth alone and that we shall do, though the world perish" (and from the looks of it, the fantastic hyperbole, in the ancient Latin motto, is more like stark realism) while the others maintain that truth is of no value except for human beings, so that any source of danger to society must inevitably affect the value of truth. Other sciences, like biology and perhaps even chemistry, are in a similar position, although not so decidedly, since psychology, after all, is closer to the desires and motives of man.

In the article on change in American psychology, the writers divided up the period into five decades and characterized each of the decades. Thus, in their opinion, from 1888 to 1898, there were two currents, the physiological and the humanistic running alongside one another, while the next decade may be described as a theoretical one, with the controversies between structuralism and functionalism coming to a head. The methodological era was still in the offing. Behaviorism and objectivistic methods and aims were to have their innings in the next decade, while between 1918 and 1928, the war demands had intensified activities in applied psychology, statistics, and testing techniques. Motivation problems, methodology, and theoretical issues occupied the interest of psychologists mainly around 1930 and in subsequent years, while toward 1940, the trend began to move in the direction of the empirical, mechanistic, qualitative, nomothetic, analytic, and operational. We must surely understand that some of the descriptive words represent, in themselves, opposite tendencies, and therefore we must infer that they are applicable to two different shifts.

[7] J. S. Bruner and G. W. Allport: "Fifty Years of Change in American Psychology," *Psychol. Bulletin*, 1940, vol. 37.

In general, the analysis of Allport and Bruner is acceptable, and if we are to continue this inquiry, it could be shown that the decade 1940-1950 is given over to clinical issues, on the one hand, and a revision of former theoretical conclusions previously accepted. Thus, there is a rejection of radical behaviorism and a sympathetic re-estimate of the doctrine of instincts, as evidenced, most surprisingly, in a recent symposium participated in by veteran psychologists.

There is also a growing tendency to work in coöperation with other sciences. About 25 years ago, psychobiology was the only union of this sort, apart from psychophysics or psychophysiology. At present, there is a much closer bond between psychology and anthropology, psychology and sociology, and even between psychology and chemistry. In the departments and branches of psychology proper, there is also an indication of amalgamation, to the extent that often we are not certain just where the one component begins and the other ends. Personality, for instance, is affiliated with social psychology in the divisions of the Association, and recently, it has been applied to the department of perception. Such applications point up the necessity of collective research, and testify to the magnitude of the task before us; for the first series of combinations will necessarily call forth combinations of a second order, complicating the results, and requiring the most rigid and scrupulous control. The introduction of psychoanalysis, a more or less speculative discipline, into every department and branch of our science has already gone a long way toward enlightening us, in one respect, and obscuring the true facts in another. To take one instance, if we ascribe paranoia to the wrong psychosexual attitude between parent and child, we are shutting our eyes to all other possible causes, and heredity chiefly.

SPECULATIONS ON THE FUTURE

The office of the historian is not only to chronicle and interpret the past. He should also, at least, make an attempt to peer into the future, and this insight into the future can be gained only by reflecting on what has gone on before. It has been remarked recently, presumably because of the frightful events of the second world war, that history teaches us one thing and that is that it can teach us nothing.

Of the psychologists who did the spade work at the turn of the century, only J. McKeen Cattell and G. Stanley Hall envisioned the future to some extent, but even they could not foresee that the modest structure which their blueprint called for would rear itself not so much into a skyscraper, in the vertical direction, but horizontally into a vast many-winged plant, extending into more established plants. The opening up of new avenues is frequently the result of historical events. The two wars, with the imperative needs during the preparations, and still more urgent help required, during and after the war, as a consequence of shock and personality deterioration, have been of the utmost service to the science as a whole, and not only useful to the applied, experimental, and clinical aspects; for although these are now in the forefront, the interrelations with physiological, differential, or social psychology are bound to broaden the latter too, and thence the effect upon theoretical psychology cannot escape us.

Certainly the thousand and one special topics and problems which are now under consideration among the hundreds of productive psychologists could not have been glimpsed, however vaguely, by our precursors. It would be both instructive, as well as entertaining, if the fellows of the American Psychological Association were to submit their conjectures as to what issues would come up and what problems would loom, let us say, in the next quarter of a century. The guess of the proposer is that psychology might become more involved with chemistry and physics, in order to ascertain why one person differs from another, and that the undue stress laid on environmental circumstances and conditioning, with all the propaganda behind it, will give way to a sounder perspective. It may be fatuous, but it has occurred to the author that some individuals may have in their chemical make-up something of the elements which figure so importantly in the construction of the atom bomb.[8] The combination of great intellectual ability, artistic talent, physical energy, and ethical acuity, as well as a superb physique, all in one person would argue against mere conditioning or Freudian interpretation. We should, in particular, be careful not to put all our eggs into one basket, and that is why it is desirable to harbor different views, without clinging to one or another so exclusively as to risk losing some significant clues.

[8] We may remember how startled we were, as youngsters, to learn that there was iron in our body. Perhaps it will yet be found that a speck of uranium, plutonium, or other radioactive substance will reveal the true secret of personality differences.

Another possible development in the not distant future is research on the relation of the agent to the object handled. It may well be, *e.g.*, that the motivation of the photographer might, on an unconscious level, set into readiness such skill as to manipulate the camera in some unusual way, thus producing *effects in keeping with the motive*. Thus far we have assumed that training is all that is necessary in order to bring about certain results. The will has been discounted or even discredited. Now, of course, we are not making here a faculty out of the will, but are content to regard it as an attitude, fashioned out of motives plus effort in realizing the attitude. It may seem mystical, for the present, to suppose that such a person-object relation could exist, but too many facts have been collected by the author to warrant the snubbing of such a general hypothesis, which, if experimentally established, may form another field in psychology.

Present Status

One of the unpredictable happenings in the course of psychology is the status of American psychology at the present time. Gone are the days, never to return, at least in our century, when graduate students, and especially instructors in North American universities, would await with eagerness each issue of the *Archiv f. die gesamte Psychologie*, or the *Zeitschrift*, which always contained some fundamental articles. The German laboratory, the Mecca for American students, prior to the first world war, is now, if at all, patronized more as a matter of curiosity than for any vital gain in knowledge. There is no prestige attached, at this date, to a European doctorate in psychology. It is in the United States, that the largest number of psychologists are found, including many of the foremost in the world, especially since the rise of Nazi power in Europe, when scores of distinguished men and women in Germany and Austria immigrated to this country. The output of psychological books and articles here is greater than the total output in all other countries combined. The slur often heard abroad about *amerikanische Psychologie* is not apt to be repeated for many decades, if ever; and the leadership which has fallen to American psychologists not only invests them with authority but likewise imposes certain obligations upon them to fulfill their function seriously both as individuals and as a collective unit.

Chapter 38

The Past Decade in American Psychology

A DECADE IS A SHORT PERIOD in the course of a science which, in one sense or another, has had a long past. It is not every year that discoveries are made even in physics or chemistry. Rare are the days when a Roentgen comes upon X-rays or a Mendel establishes genetic laws or a Rutherford splits the atom.

Because of its very nature, psychology has been at a special disadvantage, as compared with the physical and natural sciences in that the mind, which has been its universe of operation and discourse, is reachable only through introspection and is therefore subjective or private and, as such, not amenable to measurement, thus lowering and even calling into question its standing as a science.

It was necessary to attach it to a science that dealt with the observable and to some extent measurable, such as physiology. Reflexology, behaviorism, operationism, and other mechanical approaches, were the logical outcome; and experimental psychology, which fifty years ago was wrapped up in introspection, has now become physicalistic to the point of translating the traditional terms into behavioral analogues. It sometimes brashly claims to have started a new conceptual system, uninfluenced by subjective experience.

On the other side of the scale, we do have the clinical terminology, largely of psychiatric and psychoanalytic provenance, and *Gestalt* psychology, which still indicate the need of the mentalistic sphere. There is no doubt, however, that the hard core of American psychology is behavioristic in spirit and functional in its goal. That is not to say that theory is eschewed in the laboratory. Indeed, as we shall see, it is rife and rampant, but with a particular slant.

Growth

Although a science is recognized by quality rather than by quantity, the expansion of psychology in North America has been so extraordinary that the very fact is a sign of the times and a hallmark of our present-day civilization, which in itself requires a disquisition.

If numbers mean anything, then the American Psychological Association, which started just seventy years ago with 26 members and now counts well over 22,000 fellows, members, and associates, doubling its membership in the past decade, is an extremely successful organization. It also shows that there is an attraction for psychology among the academically and professionally minded, and that there are profitable perspectives in some of its branches, such as the clinical, the industrial, and counseling.

The American Psychological Association, while not numerically as important as the American Medical Association, is proportionally better patronized; there are comparatively few bona fide psychologists who are not enrolled as members. It is probably constituted of more divisions than any other learned society, excepting the American Association for the Advancement of Science, which includes many sciences.

As the ramification of American psychology is so little known, a listing of the divisions might be in order: (a) General Psychology, (b) Teaching of Psychology, (c) Experimental Psychology, (d) Evaluation and Measurement, (e) Developmental Psychology, (f) Personality and Social Psychology, (g) Esthetics, (h) Clinical Psychology, (i) Consulting Psychology, (j) Industrial Psychology, (k) Educational Psychology, (l) School Psychologists, (m) Counseling Psychology, (n) Psychologists in Public Service, (o) Military Psychology, (p) Maturity and Old Age, (q) Engineering Psychologists, (r) Psychological Aspects of Disability, (s) Consumer Psychology, (t) Philosophical Psychology.

It will be observed that engineering psychology has been recently added, and the next division to be added is (u) History of Psychology. That this fairly important branch, and one which could have been thought of many years ago, should be the last to form is of itself a commentary on the American scientific temper.

With such a range of interests and activities, it may easily be gathered that specialists, say, in engineering psychology, may know little about social psychology or personality, and vice versa. Both have absorbed the general principles and fundamental information derived from textbooks and a laboratory (or mental-measurement) training and are applying their gains to divergent goals.

With an army of over 20,000 psychologists, most of whom

have either the urge or the task to produce, it is understandable that research papers will be forthcoming annually in the thousands. The last annual convention of the American Psychological Association yielded 1500 reports of investigations. With all states in the Union represented by subsidiary psychological associations, to which must be added regional organizations like the Western, Southern, Midwestern, New England, and Rocky Mountain psychological associations with independent meetings, the number of topics discussed anually aggregates in the thousands; and there are, of course, many articles published which are not read at conventions. Besides, there are allied societies yielding a goodly number of papers that are of a psychological content.

A lay reader is apt to wonder at the multitude of lucubrations. Is it possible to have such an immense number without duplication? Furthermore, how is it possible to find such a quarry of problems to investigate or discuss? Why could we not point to such a plethora a quarter-century back?

Answers to these simple and yet not unjustified questions may vary; still an attempt may be made to explain the situation. First, we may take it for granted that there is some duplication, but that is often a blessing in disguise, for it helps us to evaluate the conclusions. At times, there will be a confirmation, and at other times, the resulting discrepancy will bring to light the flaws in the method, or technique, or fallacies in reasoning.

It may also be conceded that in hundreds of cases the topics are trivial and inconsequential; for what does it matter whether a subject can be conditioned to flex his index finger upon reciting, say, an amphibrachic line of verse? Yet we never can tell what is really trivial until much later. Could even Einstein have imagined that his famous equation, $e=mc^2$, would lead to the manufacture of the nuclear bombs and possibly—*absit omen*—the destruction of the world, a thought that preyed on his mind to the very last?

Such potentiality is not given to psychology, and the picayune problems that are occasionally aired in the journals will only reflect the capacity of the individual psychologist who must have something to show for his academic promotion, or for the grant he has been able to wrangle, or for the professional status he has established in a certain institution.

With the twelve journals published by the American Psychological Association and the twenty-odd periodicals brought out by other institutions and privately, there is still a backlog of publications, which has necessitated in some instances a policy of giving priority to those who pay the printing costs. The motto here might read "Pay as we print" and could be rationalized on the basis that it pays to publish, and special delivery is worth a fee. This might be put in the form of a syllogism (sorites?).

In the past, things were different, because there were fewer journals and relatively fewer psychologists, and the pressure to publish was not so great. Competition was among the score of outstanding men while most of the others did the reading. It is getting so that there will be almost as many writers as readers. When Wayne Dennis[1] tells us that there has been of late a decline in the number of publications as compared with that of other scientific groups, such as chemists and mathematicians, further clarification is needed. He takes it as a danger-sign, but before we begin to worry about it, it is possible to see some good in this circumstance. It may even be too good to be true, for it may well be that instead of putting out several articles, many are busy writing books, especially texts—and hence there is no basis for comparison. Also, unless we have before us the figures of increase and decrease for at least several years in the various scientific groups, we possess no true measure. Mathematics may have been lagging behind so long in that respect that there is now a compensatory productivity while in psychology there is taking place the "pause that refreshes."

At all events, there *is* some advantage in the polygraphy incidental to the legion of psychologists in that there are more types of mind involved and such a plural (not collective) imagination must reach out in nooks and crannies of life that might have remained unexplored were there only a few hundred enrolled. In this respect, while there is also safety in numbers, variety is its chief feature. Goethe has already remarked that *"Wer vieles bringt, wird manchem etwas bringen"* (a plentiful offering is bound to bring something to sundry people).

Scientific Teamwork

This is especially the case in our present decade or two of interdisciplinary mergers and alliances, when the individual

[1] Wayne Dennis: "A Decade in Review," in *Current Trends in Psychological Theory,* 1961, p. 4.

"ologies" are being merged into collectives and, to a certain extent, losing their identity. When Yale established its Institute of Human Relations, there were many who shrugged their shoulders, wondering what this conglomeration represented. Harvard later followed suit with a department of *social relations*, which encompassed sociology, anthropology, and social psychology, including personality. Whereas at one time psychology, except for physiology, was delimited strictly to a particular area, and poaching was considered a violation of departmental etiquette and even of the scientific code, it has now become common university practice, so that courses in linguistic psychology, psychology of literature, or mathematical psychology are figuring in the academic curriculum. When the present writer, on entering the graduate school at Harvard, approached Münsterberg in the hope that he would allow him to work on a problem in connection with the possible origin of language, the towering Director forestalled it with the objection "But there is no one here to validate the results," and set the overawed student to investigate the conflict of will-impulses—one of a series of projects occupying Münsterberg's mind at the time. It was not until forty years later that the original intention was carried out, yielding the volume *Destiny and Motivation in Language*.

Interdisciplinary interests require or presuppose cooperation among researchers in different fields. Thus, there is apt to be greater control if a statistician or factorial analyst will work together with a physiologist, and perhaps, at times, even a pharmacologist as well as an experimental psychologist, on a problem of learning. Such teamwork is facilitated through large grants, which in the early days were rarely expected. Heretofore, a collaboration on joint authorship would be the exception, but it is becoming quite common, perhaps in emulation of procedures in medical laboratories where a task force might be engaged on a single piece of research.

The proliferation of anthologies, readers, and symposia is in keeping with this tendency in the United States. The anthologies are mostly a matter of scissors and paste, reflecting the range of information, tastes, and capacity of one person or perhaps a well-mated couple. Symposia are on a higher level, although mostly, and for obvious reasons, uneven in workmanship. Universities not in the ivy league occasionally will organize a series of lectures with promising and noted psychologists, publishing these as a symposium.

Packaged Research

The functional leaning on the part of Americans may explain, too, why they are seeking packaged wares. Even in labor-management transactions, the term which frequently appears in newspaper items is "package" gains, *i.e.*, consisting of wage increases plus fringe benefits (insurance, longer vacations, fewer hours, etc.).

In American psychology, *learning* is the "package" topic which has been the mainstay of the laboratory and is the chief preoccupation of experimentalists. In Germany, learning would be analyzed into the constituents which go to make it up, with memory as the core. In the United States, the package contains attention, perception, memory, motivation, fatigue, drive, and a few other functions and states. In France, we are beginning to see the equivalent of the American term, learning—*Apprentissage*—in titles of articles. From America, the rat experiments have only recently been taken over. It so happens, too, that objectivism, a mild behaviorism in psychology, has had a foothold ever since the days of Binet, but Janet and Piéron have lent it greater scope and dignity. Indeed, behaviorism (*comportement*) is looked upon sympathetically in French academic circles.

The tradition of learning psychology stems from E. L. Thorndike's experiments on chicks in the cellar of William James's home and his later studies on cats and monkeys (1899-1901). By virtue of his position at Columbia's Teachers College as mentor of thousands of students from all parts of the world, his large volume, *The Fundamentals of Learning*, became the standard work in education for at least a generation; and "the law of effect," which has since been associated with his name, was referred to again and again both in textbooks and in classes, especially as learning was the dominant subject in all teaching institutions, and seemed to have been the stock-in-trade of all animal psychologists as well as the stamping ground of all behaviorists, reflexologists, and operationists.

My own estimate is that the literature on learning is at least triple that on any other topic in psychology. In working with infrahuman subjects, we are bound to get some results in the form of quantitative facts. How telling these facts are, is another story.

"Facts, however, mean little unless they lead to formulae,

laws, or at least, theories that answer whys and wherefores; and so there is a great drive on the part of psychologists to discover these laws or principles. Such questions as: What is happening to the animal or human subject physiologically while he learns? or, Is there some special region in the brain which is affected by learning? or, What are the inner incentives to learning? have been sedulously investigated and discussed, but the avalanche of data and contradictory conclusions put us in mind of Goethe's paradox: *'Das Schlimme ist das alles Denken zum Denken nicht hilft'* (The pity of it is that all thinking does not really help us to think). Paraphrasing it in our present context we may say 'it is unfortunate that fundamentally we learn so little from all the learning experiments!' "

Let us take the locus of learning in the brain. Ever since Fritsch and Hitzig charted the areas of brain functions nearly a century ago, we have been constantly aspiring to discover more specific data on correlation of brain processes and mental operations, but instead of furthering our knowledge, some of the previously acquired knowledge had to be reassessed and even questioned. Even Pavlov's classical results were not necessarily interpreted as he wished it, and curiously enough the British physiologists, who of course accepted the facts of the conditioned reflex, wondered whether there was no mental, *i.e.*, associative middle link in the game.

Barring the experimental control and quantitative treatment, the conditioned-reflex principle had been applied ages ago, *e.g.*, in one of Lope de Vega's plays, a monk, who by way of penance was ordered to eat on the floor where the cats would steal the food almost from his very mouth, taught them a lesson by coughing spasmodically and then throwing the cats into a sack and bashing them against the wall of an arch. It took only a few experiments for the cats to scurry off in panic when he began to cough as the food was brought in. Another story tells of a Knight who, intent upon appropriating his clerical brother's horse, borrowed it for a brief period. He uttered the same words of the missal as the priest would, and dug the spurs into the side of the steed, which caused it to gallop wildly and erratically. This ruse to make the animal useless to the gentle cleric, who had never applied the spur and was not aware of the conditioning by his unscrupulous brother, proved successful. The latter received the horse as a gift.

Thorndike's law of effect, too, was not so novel as the originator thought it to be. The whole philosophy of hedonism implies it. Spencer defined pleasure (gratification, satisfaction) as that which we want to retain. It stands to reason that a feeling of satisfaction would "stamp in" the act which led up to it.

In the preamble to the first chapter of his *Selected Writings from a Connectionist's Psychology* (1949) Thorndike states, "the Law of Effect, that the immediate consequence of a mental connection . . . can work back upon it to strengthen it, is now accepted by most psychologists. It is unnecessary to report here any of the experiments by myself or my pupils which helped to change a heresy into orthodoxy."

By the same token, an act resulting in pain or any kind of punishment would tend to weaken subsequent trials, although not in the same degree as rewards would strengthen further attempts.

Thorndike and his numerous advanced students carried out many experiments to establish his laws, but if it is true that first a proffered thesis is pronounced not new, then it is branded as not true, and then it is accepted, one might add that after acceptance it is frequently given a "double take" and questioned anew, or else so modified that it is scarcely the same.

S. S. Stevens, who has done outstanding work in psychophysics and is an authority on acoustics, has put it neatly when he writes:

> The discovery of a law does not put an end to the nomological pursuit. At least it never has. There seems in fact to exist a meta-nomological principle, a kind of higher law, which says: the announcement of a presumed law in science will trigger prompt and vigorous attempts at its refutation. This higher law holds in all the sciences, but it sometimes appears to enjoy its freshest expression in psychology, where, by precept and performance, we often set criticism above creation.[2]

Not only has Thorndike's law of effect met with opposition among American psychologists, but classical conditioning, which in the USSR has become scientific gospel, is steadily encountering opposition in the United States by experimentalists (Loucks, Hovland, Hilgard, Marquis) whose results do not comport with the Pavlovian conclusions, which appear to be based partly on hypothesis.

[2] S. S. Stevens: *Amer. Psychol.*, 1962, vol. 17, p. 29.

Clark L. Hull has attempted to go beyond Thorndike in an ambitious project to present formulae in which the variables[3] intervening between stimulus and response receive definite values, and instead of the law of effect (Thorndike) Hull has based his own learning theory on the *reduction of need* in the animal.

Like Thorndike, Hull had been impelled to revise his original position. Hull's method of constructing a learning system was to postulate the use of certain constructs, deduce the implications of this assumption in all possible behavior situations, and then accept or reject the hypothesis as the deductions agree or disagree with the empirical findings. His *Principles of Behavior* teems with postulates, propositions, theorems, corollaries, and equations so that no matter how painstaking the author was in his reasoning and computations, every step almost is a scientific hazard where a "miss is as good as a mile."

In 1940, Hull and his students had already published *Mathematico-Deductive Theory of Rote Learning*; there is no question about the intensive energy and thought spent on these studies, but it is not likely that so many mathematically formulated propositions could be valid under the circumstances. About 150 years ago Herbart had already attempted to give us a number of simple formulas which proved to be stabs in the dark.

Certainly experimental psychology had made great strides since, and Hull's learning theory with its formidable quantitative formulations was hailed in certain American circles as a "breakthrough" in this ever so close and yet ever so elusive area. As usual, however, the luminous numbers began to blur and what seemed as clear as day took on a hazy cast so that even Hull's most attached students were tending to veer from the original position, even in the revised version. The precision of the formulas appeared to be too good to be valid.

In 1952, Hull published *A Behavior System*, a more conservative and less complicated version of his learning theory, but it was in the first book that the grind and sweat lay; and it is this one which is usually assigned in classes instead of the later volume.

If it is difficult to say whether K. W. Spence in his *Behavior Theory and Conditioning* only modified his teacher's views on

[3] Tolman is credited with the original use of this term. (C. L. Hull: *Principles of Behavior*, p. 31.)

learning or opposed them, there is no uncertainty about D. O. Hebb's attitude, which may be gathered from a listing of many objections[4] to Hull's system, some on purely logical or semantic grounds, which could have been answered by Hull.

Hebb's *Organization of Behavior* is a significant contribution to the subject of learning as well as of other psychophysical activities. It is clearly written, avoiding the technological phraseology which is often calculated to put a rigorously scientific stamp on the research but occasionally succeeds only in obscuring the issues in a barrage of abstractions. Hebb has set himself the task of establishing what goes on in the cerebral areas, in the groups of brain cells, under various behavioral conditions. His reasoning is acute—one might even say dialectical, but the chief value of this work consists in ploughing up the soil and pointing out flaws and inconsistencies in the results and conclusions of predecessors. More importantly, it brings to the fore many puzzling, paradoxical, and scarcely known facts.

Although critical of Hull and his biological fulcrum (need-reduction), Hebb does not appear to question the soundness of the theorems, equations, and corollaries which revolve around so many intervening variables and slur or even ignore certain "chance" factors emanating from within the organism. In Chapter 17 and toward the end of his book, Hull brings up the matter of "random or chance downward variability," adding that "these fluctuations are believed to be due to a little-understood physiological process which has the power of neutralizing reaction potentials to degrees from moment to moment."[5] He designates this process "oscillation," representing it symbolically as sOR. The causes are supposed to be molecular (neurons) rather than molar; and the oscillation is said to be governed by the laws of probability.

Hull's approach was more operational because of his mathematical orientation and symbolic transformation of all processes; Hebb is intent upon finding the specific *modus operandi* in the nervous system, primarily in the cortex, of our experiences: pain, sleep, emotions, perception, etc. While, then, he is at odds with Hull, he also takes issue with the configurationists and even Lashley, who downgraded the localization principle and found for a pattern of excitation in the brain that did not depend on some special area, such as the occipital

[4] D. O. Hebb: *The Organization of Behavior*, pp. 178-180.
[5] C. L. Hull: *Principles of Behavior*, p. 393.

lobe or the visual cortex, and concluded that a function could be taken over by the cells in some other analogous area (cf. Köhler's doctrine of equipotentiality). Hebb believes that the function inheres in specific cell assemblies, and that the synapses are the crucial points at which, in learning, thickenings or so-called knobs are formed to reinforce the boundaries and thus facilitate further action (*learning*).

Strong on the critical side, Hebb, however, is a bit shaky on the positive side, and on many occasions he becomes conscious of his unsure ground and must admit that he is speculating, that he has little evidence, but is assuming such and such. Well may we say with Faust

> *Die Botschaft hör ich wohl;*
> *Allein mir fehlt der Glaube*

> *your message I indeed hear;*
> *Yet fail to be convinced*

For a time Hebb, who had worked with such a master as Penfield, attracted a considerable following. Anyone versed in neurology is bound to make a fine showing among psychologists; and his critique of other researchers made such good sense that the halo was carried over to the arguments in favor of the hierarchy of cell assemblies, with emphasis on the synaptic knobs[6] even "if there is certainly no direct evidence that this is so, and the postulated change, if it exists, may be metabolic. . . ."

Nevertheless, Hebb's volume, even if it has not succeeded in making many converts or in forming a school, is packed with so much relevant information and is likely to sharpen the wits of student readers by its acumen that it deserved the warm reception it has received among instructors.

Other Splits

Learning theorists are divided on other matters. Ever since Pavlov published his epoch-making report on the conditioned reflex, with the mental or associative link entirely eliminated, he became a target even for his fellow physiologists (Sherring-

---

[6] Hebb's formulation reads: "When an axon of cell A is near enough to excite a cell B and repeatedly or persistently takes part in firing it, some growth process or metabolic change takes place in one or both cells such that A's efficiency as one of the cells firing B, is increased." (*The Organization of Behavior*, p. 62.)

ton, Cannon). His purely behavioristic implication, it was maintained, was not warranted by the facts.

The American stimulus-response experimentalists like Guthrie, to a large extent Thorndike (although the element of gratification in stamping in the effect would surely involve a mental operation), Hull, and Spence—in the earlier stage at any rate—are in this sense connectionists, linemen, as it were, caring nothing about what, if anything, went on in consciousness.

On the other hand, Lashley, the configurationists, Tolman, and those associated with them, inject the cognitive or perceptual process into the learning operation, contending that the animal "expects" or that something sought has some "meaning" for it, or that its purpose is to attain the "goal," or that there is a "perception" of what is learned, and that it is not a matter of mere switchboard activity or a slot-machine affair.

Another source of disagreement lies in the temporal pace of the learning process. The pure mechanists of the stimulus-response school are certain that learning consists in a step-by-step process, in other words, that gradients are involved. The cognitive-perceptive theorists, like Köhler, as is well known from his chimpanzee experiments on Teneriffe, believe with equal conviction that some animals learn in a flash, i.e., do show insight into a situation. Most psychologists are willing to accept both views, reserving the latter for primates and humans.

The question may be asked whether learning is all of one piece. Tolman, who was never afraid to run counter to what might be expected of his orientation, did not flinch from arguing that there was more than one type of learning, thus coming perilously close to the conceptions of Bergson and McDougall in regard to memory.

A further point of contention is the extent of the animal's past experience in shaping the course of the learning process. Here again, experimentalists, who are of course at the same time theorists, take sides in accordance with their general leaning. The pure mechanists place most, if not all, of the stress on the variables in the present environment while the rival camp (configurationists, hormists, field psychologists) makes more allowance for innate and congenital factors as well as past experiences which have become part and parcel of the animal's nervous system.

It will thus be seen that after a half century or more of experimentation on learning, dissension is still rife so far as theory is concerned; and for that matter, even the experimental results are quite often contested. That is what puzzled me far more than differences of opinion. On one of his occasional visits East, I asked Tolman: Why should there not be agreement among experimentalists on observed data when conditions are reproduced. He thought for a moment, wrinkling his brow, and then somewhat falteringly remarked "the hitch is that conditions are not exactly reproduced. There are always certain changes in the procedure among experimenters."

We read of confirmations, too, but the very fact that such confirmations are eagerly flourished like testimonials for an advertisement is a sign of neediness. The real difficulty inheres in the "cussedness of the brute"; or shall we use Hull's technological term "the behavior oscillations"? which are a good deal more whimsical than the meteorological vagaries, which prompted Mark Twain's famous and oft-quoted dictum.

Despite the scientific setbacks and frustrations, however, there is no cause for resignation; for we do know more about the subject now than, say, twenty-five years ago. And, if we are proceeding at a pedestrian pace in a jet age, let us recall Spinoza's salutary advice not to weep, nor laugh, but to try and understand. The contingent of researchers engaged in psychological problems must of necessity engender disagreements, because of individual differences, the personal equation, and exposure to disparate experiences, including the impact of teachers. As the controls are tightened, however, there will eventuate greater conformity and even unanimity in respect of observable and measurable phenomena, as in the case of the sensory field, association, memory, and perception. That cannot be said of a study like philosophy, for example, because the experimental procedure is inapplicable there.

The Hankering after Models

The past decade has seen a curious quest after so-called models. I say "so-called" because the term is more an honorific and hardly stands for more than the word "theory." As in many other cases, psychology, in this connection, is trying to keep up with the physicist Joneses. There is, however, a vast difference between Rutherford's nuclear model of the atom, which led to fission and the awesome sequelae in its wake, or even Avogadro's gas model, exactly a century earlier than Rutherford's, and the various formal and empirical models that one meets within the psychological literature.

Incidentally, I wonder how many of the 22,000 members of the American Psychological Association are aware that the first person to use a true model was a psychologist. It was Etienne Condillac (1714-1780) who more than 200 years ago conceived the notion (which incidentally, he credits to his friend, Anne Ferrand) of tracing the course of sensory development by means of a hypothetical statue. This statue or model (cf. *Traité des sensations*, 1754) starts off with the sense of smell, and proceeding from one stage to another ends in judging and reasoning.

There are models galore now: formal, *i.e.*, mathematical or statistical models, of which the stochastic type, taken over from the more established sciences, takes an honored place, dealing, as it does, with the probabilities or chance occurrences, as in games. But what can be predicted in the inanimate world is hardly predictable even in the case of rats. We know, of course, from empirical evidence that deprivation will increase the activity of the rat, and that rewards will stimulate effort, yet some rats will behave "irrationally," and how much more so the human animal! Even in physics, the principle of indeterminacy in regard to atomic particles has become a real challenge so as to create a certain divisiveness in that field, but the whims generated in the nervous system— the result of so many factors that cannot be pinpointed—make it doubly difficult to forecast events under the best conditions.

R. R. Bush and F. Mosteller, in their *Stochastic Models for Learning* (1955), Estes, in a number of papers, and W. Edwards have been among the most recent investigators to discuss various phases of the problem, and while the diagrams and equations are impressive enough, the complexity of the situation is apt to put a kink into this or that reasoning step.

Actually the term "schema" represents the hypothetical setup more appropriately. Tolman's *sowbug* model[7] is more in keeping with the line of exposition than many other so-called models, which are hardly more than hypotheses or theories, accorded a more concrete status via topological diagrams.

[7] E. C. Tolman: "Prediction of Vicarious Trial and Error by Means of the Schematic Sowbug," *Psychol. Review*, 1939, vol. 46.

H. H. Kendler[8] even favors a pretheoretical model, based on learning, which, so far as I can see, is simply an *orientation* and therefore akin to a specific attitude or leaning. But is that not to be taken for granted without requiring a decision or methodological injunction?

The rift between the formal (statistical, factor-analytic) and empirical models is scarcely mendable. Equations and factorial analysis are superb instruments provided the observable data are taken into consideration. Without them and the implications they point to, mathematical applications must be empty—just shadow manipulation.

Computers As Thinking Machines

With the rise of physicalistic psychology (S-R functionalism, neobehaviorism, operationism) and the spread of engineering tendencies, together with statistical infiltration, the service of computers and electronic apparatus in general has been a distinct blessing, and the answer to a laboratory researcher's prayer. Ordinarily the computer is thought of as a machine to facilitate mathematical operations but the etymological sense of thinking (*puto*), really "to cleanse," has been restored to the term; and we now have in mind a mechanical brain which can do practically everything that a human brain can do, only more efficiently.

In fact, thanks to the tasks assigned to rats and computers, the term "thinking" is becoming obsolete in psychological writing. The new term is "problem-solving." Apparently all other thinking is supposed to be reverie, imagination, fantasy, or day-dreaming; yet I should take more stock in the cerebrations of a La Rochefoucauld or the reflections of an Amiel (even though they were not solving problems, unless supplying their mental needs is solving a problem) than in the solutions of the most intelligent rat or the final answers of the most ingeniously constructed UNIVACS, JOHNIACS, or ILLIACS.

The idea of an automaton is so ancient that it might come under the head of Jung's archetypes, *i.e.*, the elements of the collective unconscious. It occupied the literary mind from the days of the Greeks to Karel Čapek whose RUR (1920) gave us the word *robot* (Slavic stem for "work"). Whether it was the famous Prague Rabbi's *Golem* or the monster that Fran-

[8] H. H. Kendler: "Problems in Problem-Solving Research," in *Current Trends of Psychological Theory*, p. 186.

kenstein was supposed to have created, the sense is the same—some mechanism, usually in human form, fashioned through some mystical formulas, originally designed to serve the creator or the community but almost invariably turning into a threat to humans. In music, Abraham Paul Dukas's *L'apprenti Sorcier* reflects the antics of such a clumsy artifact, defeating the purpose of the fashioner.

The archetype, dream, myth, or legend actually became a reality with the inauguration of the electronic age; and a new branch of science under the name of cybernetics has emerged, participated in by physicists, chemists, engineers, and psychologists.

New Connotation of "Humanism"

The computer has been elevated to human status in certain quarters through the applications of such honorifics as "thinking machines." Its storage capacity has been called "memory." It is even said to be subject to moods and indisposition. We sometimes do not know whether these are meant seriously or whether they are spoken or written with tongue in cheek. I have not yet seen any allusion to the computer's conscience, but I anticipate some discussion of its inferiority complex, despite its glorification as a superhuman brain. In a restaurant, I once picked up a menu on the back of which Norbert Wiener had drawn a complicated diagram of one of these machines. At various spots, indicated by crosses and arrows, were to be found the terms "decision," "purpose." Whether that was intended for the input or whether the machine was to develop these properties, one had no way of ascertaining without asking, and now, alas, it is too late. . . .

There was a time when *humanism* came into use to de-emphasize the theological preoccupation and pursuits. "Humanism" could also serve as a concept in contrast with excessive interest in animals, but with the advent of the thinking machine, a semantic change will necessarily follow so that humanism will now come to mean a frame of reference to set it off against the kingdom of servo-mechanisms erected as thinking entities.

Thus, too, the days when the term *anthropomorphism* was applied to a representation of God in the form of humans, with traits like our own (jealousy, anger, compassion, the need of agreeable odors), seem to be gone. Even the sense of the term applied in the case of animal fanciers and pet votaries who read all sorts of human potentials into cats and dogs is becoming obsolete, but we shall be stressing another and newer development in the concept, *viz.*, the tendency to endow electronic apparatus with human, and even superhuman, intelligence and initiative perhaps. Of one thing we may be quite certain, the thinking machine cannot think of its own accord, and no matter how vastly improved the technique, it will always remain an automaton, *i.e.*, a tool in the hands of the programmer who not only gathers and feeds the data but also directs the course. Speed and accuracy are its only assets, important values, to be sure, but behind it must be the thinking person, regardless of whether the thinking is clear and valid or confused and invalid.

It is only metaphorically that we can ever speak of a computer learning. Learning presupposes physical and mental growth, even if Hering and others have argued for the possibility of memory in all organized matter. A violin can improve with age, and spirituous liquors of an old vintage may taste better, but there is no implication of learning in such melioration, any more than when a floor has been polished or a rock has become smooth through constant moisture. The condition has changed for better or for worse, but learning requires a *genetic process*; and spontaneous growth cannot be said to take place in a machine.

In a contribution to Newman's *The World of Mathematics* (vol. 4), A. M. Turing almost floors us with the very title "Can a Machine Think?" Therein he proposes a test which would answer the question definitively. In brief it is this: If in two separate communication channels a human subject and a computer are quizzed and given tasks by a qualified interrogator who nevertheless is not able to identify which of the reactions emanate from the human subject and which from the machine, then it is assumed that the machine can think. It has been said that some machines have passed the Turing Test, but for my part, I am not inclined to take any one's word for it; and should the claim turn out to be valid, I would urge that the computer receive an honorary Sc.D. or at least an LL.D., which sometimes is awarded these days to many much less deserving.

It was incidentally a pre-Watsonian behaviorist, the philosopher E. A. Singer, at the University of Pennsylvania, who, over fifty years ago, contended that a mechanical sweetheart would be every bit as satisfactory as a living sweetheart. Well, every man to his taste, but I doubt very much whether an electronic sweetheart could be a suitable mate for anyone but a robot.

Types of Computers

Be it as it may, these computers, once they "know their place," are marvelous instruments. They may involve *algorithms, i.e.,* procedures that are entirely technological and for sheer rapidity stagger the imagination, they may follow along a *heuristic* course where seeking new turns is the chief function and, therefore, more in keeping with human modes of thinking, they sift and select means, *but after a previously designed program imposed upon the computer.* In either case, the achievements are of great service as a time and energy-saver, and furthermore the results of the heuristic type are both instructive and entertaining, although the gains for learning theory are of necessity nil.

There are the game players (checkers, chess), the geometry theorem machine, the general problem solvers that followed the logic theorist (Johniac) programmed by A. Newell, J. C. Shaw, and H. A. Simon, probably the chief authorities in programming. Then we have the computers with programs designed for engineering and business decisions, machines dealing with psychological tasks of subjects in the laboratory. We must include here the translating machines, which unlike the more or less heuristic type used in the more selective problem-solving, proceed along algorithmic lines and yield a rough and ready rendering in the case of technical material. It is difficult to conceive a program that would translate Shakespeare adequately. It would prove a flop with idiomatic style between any two languages of different families, say, Hebrew and English.

A computer serviceable in linguistics to indicate the probability in sequence of sounds for various languages has been in operation for some time. In archaeological finds, with some of the text obliterated, such a machine could offer some worthwhile clues.

The ILLIAC, with its programming for musical composition, devised in 1956 by Hiller and Isaacson at the University of Illinois, is perhaps the most intriguing of all; for it is a challenge to human talent or even genius. I daresay that certain machines will be able to turn out compositions comparable with some of the more radically modernistic specimens; and we might expect drawings and other pictorial representations hatched by some ARTAC that might be mistaken for some abstractionist productions by a Klee; but there will continue to be an astronomical distance between a computer and a Bach or an El Greco, just as all the programming of a brain-trust will not yield a single soliloquy of a *Hamlet* or *Life Is a Dream*, athough it would be fun to examine the verse and prose that the laws of probability would treat us to upon elaborate programming.

Carl I. Hovland (1912-1962), Hull's most brilliant student and successor at Yale, who was an enthusiastic researcher in the area of machine programming as well as of learning theory and concept formation, had set his sights for devising means of simulating human thinking in the computer. As he puts it:

Humans, of course, do learn and improve through practice. So the interesting task is to build into the computer this capability as well. Simulation of learning is one of the most interesting potential applications of computer simulation techniques, since the ability to learn is one of the clear-cut differences between human and machine performance. A number of different types of learning are currently being simulated. The first involves stimulus-response learning. It is rather simple to simulate this type of learning with rewards ("reinforcements") given when certain types of behavior occur and not given when other types of responses are made. The probability that the response followed by reward will occur on later trials can then be made to increase. Failure of reward, or punishment, can be made to lead to a decreased probability of response ("extinction").[9]

Hovland supposes that we shall be able to learn a good deal about human thought process through the difficulties experienced in the programming of machines; yet he has to admit that "at present we consider ourselves fortunate if we can simulate on a machine the typical performance of a single individual in solving a particular problem. . . . To date, most simulation has been of the performance of the individual, either real or an imaginary average individual. It may prove

[9] C. I. Hovland: "Computer Simulation of Thinking," *The American Psychologist,* 1960, vol. 15, p. 689.

to be extremely difficult to carry out the next step, that of specifying which characteristics must be known about each individual to be able to simulate the way he varies from the typical pattern." After listing a number of other requirements, such as the effects of experience, drugs, or task pressure (tension?), he concedes that "a long and difficult road lies ahead before we can accomplish successful simulation of a single type of task which has all of these variables programmed."

Norbert Wiener, who in a sense has started the cybernetic movement, is even beset by the fear that the machine will rule and destroy its creator.[10] What, it seems to me, is more disturbing, because more likely to happen, is that man will be apt to lose his very image in becoming so machine-conscious, and humanism, already on the wane, will be nearing the point of what conditionists call extinction!

The Teaching Machine

With UNIVACS, JOHNIACS, and ILLIACS accomplishing wonders, it would have been strange if teaching were not to participate in the general automation movement. We have always known that many outstanding men have taught themselves— to be sure, out of books. Some of these "autodidacts" did more in the way of amassing knowledge than most of their contemporaries who were fortunate in being provided with a private tutor, but the autodidacts we have in mind obtained their knowledge from books and perhaps associates who were more luckily placed. The teaching machine programs "capsuled" information. (Some might call it "canned" information.)

The idea of a teaching machine is not new. Suggestions and hints have been dropped at various times, perhaps more in order "to add to the gaiety of nations," but when S. L. Pressey designed several machines for automatic testing of intelligence he was in dead earnest. That was several decades ago, when automation had not yet taken hold of public fancy. After the cool reception his project received, he dropped it.

It was reserved for B. F. Skinner, a more dynamic psychologist, to make a rather successful attempt not only by employing a different strategy in his persuasive exposition but also by proceeding on another theoretical, or perhaps nontheoretical, line. First, the audio-visual vogue in the educa-

[10] N. Wiener: "Some Moral and Technical Consequences of Automation," *Science*, 1960, vol. 131, pp. 1355-1358.

tional world has been of some service in boosting the teaching machine scheme. The latter after all is only a more advanced phase of the other. Both methods are forms of demonstration, and therefore highly *deictic,* which is a cognate of "teaching," the root of both being *dik*—to show, point out.

The teaching machine—a Greek term like *deiknomaton,* I should think would be more appropriate—certainly has a few advantages not available in the classroom: It can be used at home in the case of illness; it may appeal to a child as a sort of game; it is adjustable to the individual's optimal pace, whereas in a classroom, the brighter students might be bored as the slow learners are trying to keep up with them. In case of a teachers' strike, children might yet continue their education without serious loss of time.

There are, however, questions that to some extent offset the advantages. Will the generally disinterested child by himself give his attention sustainedly on the strength of such reinforcements as gaining information or finding that his answer was correct? If the correct answers were at least rewarded by some edible or toy, the incentive might be sufficient to carry on for some stretch. It would require a studious child to reap the full benefit of the machine in seclusion from others. Above all, the personality of the teacher in molding and otherwise influencing his charges is no slight factor in teaching. While it is true that occasionally there is a temperament clash between teacher and pupil, in which case a transfer is indicated, there can be no denying that the impact of a worthy teacher has frequently been noted by successful men and women as an important feature in their career.

Fundamental to the success of the *deiknomaton* (now that the term has been coined) is of course the quality of the programming. Programmers will have to be trained *en masse;* for, their qualifications are not necessarily those of the teacher, scholar, or researcher. A new profession would come into being—a sort of teaching engineer.

Individual differences will also come in for consideration. Reading a well-written text from which information is gleaned in accordance with one's own peculiar learning habits is one thing; being doled out a word, a definition, or a fact piece-meal is quite another. To the individualist that might become irksome. For one whose grasp is of the global kind, the pecking at a grain of mental pabulum can lead to frustration.

At any rate, it is well that the Fund for the Advancement of Education has sponsored a long-range test of machine instruction at the high school and college level, and Skinner has been able to go through with his project. It is only through experimentation that we can arrive at a valid conclusion. The results will tell the story; and the chances are that automation teaching, as intimated, will work out in special situations. Skinner is diametrically opposed to aversive measures in teaching; and the *deiknomaton* has no punishing device except to show up a wrong answer. "In the light of our present knowledge," he writes, "a school system must be called a failure if it cannot induce students to learn except by threatening them for not learning.[11]

If Skinner can discover a technique for motivating the indolent without any threat, then he will have earned the gratitude not only of millions of school children but also of millions of parents, teachers, and administrators. In our ever tightening civilization, competition itself acts as a threat, which a child realizes soon enough.

In conclusion, it must be brought out that although Skinner is the spearhead of the teaching automation movement, he is not the only participant. As the industry keeps expanding with the adoption of the idea in the more progressive communities, one may predict that a new journal will come into being, together with a new organization in the field of educational psychology.

Information Theory

As psychology was reaching out more and more for scientific status, it would be natural for it to avail itself of all the technological facilities that electronics and automation would bring and employ the engineering methods and terms which make for efficiency.

In this atmosphere there sprouted a new branch or sapling christened "information theory." Sometimes it goes by the name of "communication theory." This segment of science is tangential to many other fields—mathematics, linguistics, traffic, games of hazard, public communication, (radio, TV, telegraphy), servo-mechanism, data processing, encoding—in other words, wherever there is a need to convey a message in

[11] B. F. Skinner: *Cumulative Record*, 1959, p. 177.

any form whatsoever. The most comprehensive and detailed survey in the area of communication which came to my notice was a lengthy article on music, in all its phases—encyclopedic in scope.[12]

Information theory is primarily an engineering matter because its aim is to find the best means for transmitting data so that a maximum of information can be gained in the shortest time and through the least effort. To be sure, that would be expected at all times, information or no information theory. The procedure in the past, however, would be a case of empirical groping, "catching on," as it were. No attempt was made to streamline the implicit postulates and rules so that they could apply in general as basic requirements to all such procedures.

Questions always arise as to how to express oneself so as to achieve clarity without using too many words. Drawing up a contract, composing a telegram or a radiogram, involves information theory—and economics too, for it may affect our wallet. Many of us have been driven to exasperation when we made a long distance call and had to strain our hearing apparatus in order to interpret the sounds at the other end of the line through continuous noise. The noise is additional output in the transmission, but since it is an interference, the input (message to be conveyed) is reduced.

Redundancy is another sample of generosity which does not take; again, because it is a waste and is apt to interfere with our comprehension of the purported communication—a case of "the more, the less." When we are necessarily in doubt, the message is ambiguous. That can be the result of an unstructured statement or unspecific signal, an elliptic or syncopated expression. We must then infer and interpret. If the English alphabet represented each sound uniformly by a single character, our informational gain would be greater.

Actually, in every instance of reconstruction or redaction of faulty texts, in decoding a cryptogram, we are bound to employ principles laid down in information theory. Probably the jigsaw puzzle pieces "fall into place" because every time a chip is correctly added to the body, information is gained which reduces the task of fitting. In all games of hazard, the guessing proceeds along similar lines. A simple cue is often sufficient to start us on a series of leads until the problem is solved. Gaps may be correctly filled in by studying the context. Even an intelligence test or a personality test may be conceived as a communication channel, in that it is calculated to assign a value on a scale for some specific individual.

Where there is a binary choice, *i.e.,* where there are two equally likely possibilities, the "bit" (apparently a portmanteau word, combining *binary* and *digit*) of information of one item is all that is needed, but with three or four items, the dropping out of one leaves a problem still.

Just when the information discussion began is not easy to establish because it seems to be an outgrowth of the work with stochastic models, probability theory, cybernetics, and learning theory. Mathematics certainly must have nurtured it. In 1948, C. E. Shannon presented "A Mathematical Theory of Communication," and then he proceeded in a more practical direction to deal with "Communication in the Presence of Noise." The Harvard Psychological Laboratory became interested in the topic, and we find G. A. Miller, probably under the aegis of Boring, taking up the issues in both articles and a book, *Communication and Language,* and Beebe-Center, shortly before his death, embarked on such research, while E. B. Newman was exploiting a huge computer in order to establish the pattern of vowels and consonants in eleven written languages. As to S. S. Stevens, the Director of the Harvard Psychological Laboratory as well as of the special Psycho-Acoustic Laboratory, a large part of his chosen field—hearing—might be said to contain the seeds of the information theory.

The flurry of activity in that direction, which continued for a few years during the 1950's in psychological circles at Harvard and the Massachusetts Institute of Technology, seems to have waned, although in England it still carries on as a frame of reference and steering point.

Fads and Fancies of Popular Appeal

The results of laboratory experiments may not have been established one way or the other, yet the practical man in business will find a way to exploit the possibilities to his own advantage. Medicine has been in a similar boat. No sooner is a hope in regard to some new drug or technique announced than the public will be duped into buying articles that possess no medicinal value except possibly that of suggestion and belief, dangerous in serious and critical situations.

Subliminal Persuasion

One of the sensations of the past decade had been subliminal advertising, *i.e.*, projecting on the screen suggestions to "buy popcorn" or "drink coca-cola." These messages were flashed either so faintly or for so brief a period, like one-fifth of a second, that the viewers could hardly have been aware, at least, of the content, yet it has been reported that popcorn sales rose more than 50 per cent and coca-cola sales about 18 per cent in the motion picture theaters where the hidden urging took place.

The question of unconscious stimulation had been asked for a full century, perhaps ever since Fechner took the just noticeable difference as the unit of mental measurement. A Russian student, writing in German (Suslova) appears to have been the first to test out discrimination of two-point stimulation on the skin. J. V. McConnell, R. L. Cutler, and E. B. McNeil, in an unusually comprehensive survey of the literature,[13] citing 132 references covering practically every phase of the subject, and dwelling especially on the applied aspect, have found little to recommend in the method or technique or vaunted claims of the advertisers.

There are so many factors to reckon with that adequate control of the experimentation would take years and a large team of researchers. We might well accept some of the conclusions in regard to the perception of stimuli below the threshold of consciousness under certain conditions. Doubt enters our mind as to the efficacy of the suggestion, its persuasiveness. Will those who do not care for popcorn or who drink some cola other than coca-cola be so affected by the below-threshold injunction as to change their habits? Doubt changes to serious misgivings upon consideration of the ethical issue involved here. Should an advertiser be allowed to introduce a force unbeknown to the prospect (or victim) for the sake of gain? What if the coca-cola or popcorn should contain

---

[13] J. V. McConnell, R. L. Cutler and E. B. McNeil: "Subliminal Stimulation: An Overview." *Amer. Psychol.*, 1958, vol. 13, pp. 229-242.

some ingredient which would cause the consumer to splurge all the more? After all, the peanuts (if not the popcorn) may be so salted as to generate greater thirst, and the coca-cola so prepared as to create momentarily a taste for more popcorn or peanuts?

One can understand why the public was somewhat aroused and government agencies became concerned over such intrusion. It was a species of brainwashing in the interest of big business, even if the number of viewers who would be positively affected is much smaller than announced. To what extent the scheme had taken the spotlight in the American discussion spheres may be seen in the fact that Vance Packard's *Hidden Persuaders* had become a best seller.

Learning During Sleep

If subliminal suggestion concerns the public, *unconscious* learning, which had been studied in the laboratory with various results, had its rooters largely among students, for whom it promised to be an Eldorado where application and hard effort were no longer necessary. All one has to do is put on a record or two, and one learns while one sleeps! The idea was by no means new—advertisements could be seen in popular journals some forty years ago of a *psychophone* and pictures of a young and pretty co-ed sleeping peacefully while the phonograph or victrola is "storing" material in her nonwaking mind to be remembered after she woke. At the time there were but few who took this "psychophone" seriously. It was more likely regarded as a "phony psych." However, once a sponsor could be found in a college, matters could change in favor of the contraption manufacturers. The press, which is always willing to bruit about some half-truths that affect the readers and, incidentally, the bank assets of a certain type of publisher, is not above exaggerating the problematic results of an investigation. This is true of medical reports blown up in the daily press. Hopes run high, and while in disease they may have some allaying or alleviating function, in education the false hopes possess no redeeming feature whatever.

After a number of my students confronted me happily with the news item about learning while asleep, I wrote to the psychologist who conducted the research, and received a courteous reply which was not nearly so confident as one might have expected. The confirmation was somewhat hesitant and subject to further experimentation. The shrewd promoters, however, would not wait until the thesis was established, and the selling of recording devices to cram the sleeper's mind with material too dry or dull to learn with an effort went on apace with the gullibility of anxious parents who wanted their Bobby or Billy to make the grade, awake or asleep.

In a lengthy survey of the investigations on sleep-learning,[14] C. W. Simon and W. H. Emmons reviewed ten such studies, half of which turned out to be negative or at least uncertain as to interpretation. Apparently preoccupation with the project began during World War I when every bit of advantage to be gained for the defense program was exploited to the last grain. If the servicemen could learn the easy way, when resistance was ruled out, the whole war machine would naturally function more smoothly. The only one of the major psychologists whose experiments showed up favorably seemed to be L. L. Thurstone, but we must remember that while war stimulates experimentation, its quality is not as good as under peaceful laboratory conditions. Often the wished-for goal influences interpretation.

All in all, whatever the results in the ten investigations surveyed, the methodology leaves much to be desired. Controls are not reported. It is not easy to ascertain whether the subjects were actually asleep when the material was presented via records on tape. The general impression is that either the subjects were awake when they heard the lesson, or if they were sound asleep, learning did not take place.

The Eloquent Dog

A talking bulldog by the name of Mr. Lucky is another of those phenomena that come in for discussion in the Sunday papers. His speaking voice has been recorded by a university speech clinician, but I have been unable to acquire a record on the ground that the reproduction was poor, and therefore I cannot form a reliable judgment. The dog was supposed to have begun with an injunction to his mistress after she stepped into a neighbor's house, which was identified as "Aw come on home now." Other utterances attributed to Mr.

[14] C. W. Simon and W. H. Emmons, "Learning during Sleep," Psychol. Bulletin, 1955, vol. 52, pp. 328-342.

Lucky are: "I want my mama," "Oh dear, oh dear," "I want some," and in the feature article (*Parade*, August 30, 1935) we are told that the bulldog was signed to a twenty-week contract by a Hollywood producer-actor for $1,000 a week. How many educators receive $20,000 for a semester's teaching? Mr. Lucky looks extremely intelligent and even tenderly reflective as he watches over his wife and the nursing puppies, but the legend under the picture, "Mr. Lucky appears to be speechless as he looks at Babe, his wife, and their family," is more hilarious than convincing—a real *tour d'esprit*. In the ten years that have elapsed, we have not heard that Mr. Lucky has addressed meetings or that any of his species have emulated him. Assuming that Mr. Lucky actually did utter the words ascribed to him, can we be certain that he knew what he was saying, or was he simply repeating parrotlike what he had been taught?

Sensory Deprivation

It would have been appropriate to describe a few of the spectacular experiments during the last decade, were there no space restrictions. A couple of samples will have to suffice, however.

In 1956, a team of researchers at McGill University, headed by W. Heron,[15] sought to discover what happened under conditions of sensory deprivation. The only requirement of the subject, hired at $20 a day, was to remain in bed for days. The mattress was soft and comfortable—just right for complete relaxation; and complete quiet in the room, which was sound proof, was sure to induce sleep. Meals would be brought at regular hours, and even at odd times, if the subject so desired and signaled to an attendant sitting outside the room.

Apparently, however, more than food and rest were required to keep the subject content; for the padded goggles placed over his eyes produced a foggy haze, while a dead stillness reigned all around, and if he tried to overcome it by singing or whistling, his own sounds took on an eerie timbre, which was

[15] W. Heron, W. H. Bexton, and D. O. Hebb: "Cognitive Effects of Decreased Variation in Sensory Environment," *Amer. Psychol.*, 1953, vol. 8. E. Z. Levy: "The Subject's Approach Important Factor in Experimental Isolation," *Bulletin Menninger Clinic*, 1962, vol. 26.

more like a muted echo. Since the hands were covered with thick gloves, and to make sure that no object could be touched, a pasteboard gauntlet was superimposed, isolation from the world seemed almost complete.

It took only a couple of hours for some of the subjects to become panicky. After six hours, some started to scream, while to go through this deprivation for forty-eight hours was an endurance test that merited a medal. A complete breakdown was imminent in some cases.

The results were sometimes used to explain the confessions and brainwashing in the communist countries, which seemed to perplex the Western mind. In other words, expose a perfectly normal person to sensory deprivation and he will acquiesce in all that is demanded of him.

In connection with sensory deprivation, it has been experimentally shown[16] that animals brought up in a retarded sensory and social environment behave as though some forms of pain were not noxious and sometimes even court punishment. The greatest tolerance for pain is evinced by "reducers," i.e., those whose perception is reduced in intensity after being stimulated for some time (Köhler's concept of *satiation*). It is also suggested that the extraverts are the better reducers and the more pain-tolerant. Turning to the somatotype schema of personality (William Sheldon), we may recall that the extraverted are found among the endomorphs and mesomorphs, and that the latter make little of inconveniences and pain.

Surrogate Mothers

Another of the more interesting investigations, one which is now presented in the form of a film, was that carried out by H. F. Harlow[17] at the University of Wisconsin. It concerns the behavior of a young monkey, taken from its mother in early infancy and conditioned to regard as its mother a feeding apparatus consisting mostly of wires, but also finding comfort in hugging a cotton wadding surrogate mother. When the monkey was startled by continual banging and intense com-

[16] A. Petrie, W. Collins, and P. Solomon: "Tolerance for Pain and for Sensory Deprivation," *Amer. Journal of Psychology*, 1960, vol. 73, pp. 80-90.

[17] H. F. Harlow: "The Nature of Love," *Amer. Psychologist*, 1958, vol. 13, pp. 637-685.

motion in its surroundings, it would run not to the feeding "mother" but to the cotton effigy for protection. Despite the extrapolation as to the monkey's attitude, sans the benefit of culture, one wonders whether the monkey thinks or feels in terms of a mother. It is quite possible that it spontaneously makes use of the object or doll which fits the particular occasion, irrespective of interpretations.

Is Learning Ingestible?

One of the most interesting experiments in years is that reported by J. V. McConnell.[18] He cut flatworms in half in order to ascertain whether the tail half would learn in some measure comparable to the results obtained with the head half. The surprising feature was that there was very little difference. The tail half in some cases even took fewer shocks to learn its lesson.

More sensational, however, is the finding which seems to be something of a breakthrough, provided the procedure is replicated under special control. McConnell fed a salad of previously trained worms to unconditioned ("ignorant") worms and discovered to his surprise that the cannibal worms had apparently benefited by the training of the worms they had ingested. It means, if the results are verified, that knowledge not only attaches to the soma but can also be assimilated neurally when the physical substance of the conditioned organism is digestively assimilated.

A scientifically-minded high school girl conditioned a number of flatworms to respond to light, which ordinarily requires about 260 shocks. After cutting them up into bits, she fed them to other worms going through a training process by means of a slight electric shock. Control worms, i.e., those that had not been conditioned, were also cut up into segments and fed to the experimental worms. Difficult as it is to believe, the figures showed that the worms which ate their "educated" congeners excelled those that had not been fed likewise, in the ratio of 140 shocks, when fed the conditioned head segment, to 269, when fed an unconditioned tail segment.

Should this conclusion prove valid, it not only might lead to a reconsideration of learning theory but also would force us to admit that the cannibals both of the primitive jungle

18 J. V. McConnell: "Memory Transfer through Cannibalism in Planarians," *Journal of Neuropsychiatry*, 1962, vol. 3.

tribes and of the more civilized peoples who would eat certain organs of their victims in order to strengthen their own powers, associated with these organs, might not have been as far off in their beliefs as we have always supposed; and the well-known pun *Der Mensch ist was er isst* (Man is what he eats), which is perhaps an implicit credo of the historical materialists, contains more truth than jest. Could it perhaps suggest that eating foxes' brains would increase our wiliness? The vista of speculation that such results might open up is almost unbounded.

At any rate, it is important to know that the head part of the worm is not superior to the tail half, and that the learning area is not restricted to the head.

Vision through Touch

Several years ago, a brilliant rodent by the name of Barnabel (trained in the psychological laboratory at Barnard College) made *The New York Times* science section as a result of her skillful manipulations in getting out of a complicated box.

Early in 1964, *The New York Times* and the *Science Newsletter* reported an experiment which Barnard's R. P. Youtz is conducting on a subject (Patricia A. Stanley) who seems to be able to tell colors by the use of her finger tips after being blindfolded. To rule out differences in texture, transparent plastic covers render the material perfectly uniform. No telepathy is claimed, as the colors are presented without the knowledge of the experimenter as to their hue. It is too soon to arrive at a conclusion: whether there is a special ability involved, which can be cultivated so as to help the blind, or whether it belongs to the perennially controversial issues.

Prestige, Awards, and Inferiority Feeling

Psychology—there can be no doubt of it—has grown in prestige, if not among the physical and natural sciences, then at least in the business of American life. To be sure, it is sometimes considered a practical art more like medicine than science; and the medicos, particularly the psychiatrists, are ready to challenge its status, as has transpired at a trial recently where the clinical psychologists have testified to a schizophrenic state on the part of the accused slayer while the psychiatrists opposed this diagnosis and on the witness stand disparaged psychology as a branch of philosophy and metaphysics, which assertion, for one thing, proved that they themselves were not *au courant* with the facts, and apparently were willing to forget that psychiatry is in no position to throw stones at glass houses.

Downgrade, as one would, psychology, its serviceableness in every walk of life cannot be denied. It was during World War I that it was beginning to be taken seriously in official circles. In every department of the armed forces, and in all areas of defense, the psychologist was looked to for advice and testing. The Figaro of all enterprise, from therapy to advertising to theater and church, the psychologist is always resorted to. Every new development in the course of civilization, whether it is astronautics or cybernetics, in the last analysis must deal with human behavior, back of which are mental states and processes like perception, motivation, temperament, complexes, etc.

Psychology has come in for much criticism at the hands of those scientists who feel that their particular discipline has already arrived—the physicist, chemist, biologist, and physiologist. Indeed, from a questionnaire which R. M. Yerkes circulated a number of years ago, there were many who voiced the opinion that psychology was a branch of biology or of physiology. To others who were less charitable, psychology was still an outgrowth of philosophy.

In an eloquent address, really a homily, read before the sixty-seventh Annual Convention of the American Psychological Association, Robert S. Morison, Director of the Medical Sciences at the Rockefeller Foundation, had the following to find fault with in psychology:

> It so happened that that very afternoon I attended a seminar on the relation of the frontal lobes to the delayed response—the first psychological meeting I had been to for some years. As a onetime neurophysiologist, I recalled the original studies done by Carlyle Jacobson in Fulton's laboratory nearly 30 years ago. Naturally, one expected to find that 30 years of work would have brought us precise identification of the variables involved in this obviously simple phenomenon, if not indeed a general theory of frontal lobe function. What then was my surprise to discover that three decades of the most painstaking and in-

telligent investigation by the best minds in psychology had served only to convince us that we have but the foggiest notion of what goes on in the cell assemblies of the frontal lobes between the moment a monkey sees a peanut covered by a small tin can and the time he reaches for it 30 seconds later. Ladies and gentlemen, let us think on this before we set forth to tell mothers how to bring up children, industrial leaders how to abolish delinquency, the staff of the State Department how to negotiate with the Russians, or foundation officers how to detect genius.[19]

Naturally to a neurophysiologist, this ignorance of what happens in the frontal lobe between the stimulus and response in a monkey is enough to discredit the claims or pretensions of psychology, but from other angles, it might be asked whether that knowledge is so crucial, and whether psychology is to blame if the complexity of the situation is so fraught with insuperable difficulties. In the last analysis, would it not be a matter of physics and chemistry rather than psychology or physiology to supply the requisite information? Whether we accept Freud's basic tenets or not, the emancipation of psychology from the dominance of physiology has been a salutary move. Let the two disciplines work hand in hand, but must psychology prove itself by being tied to the apron strings of physiology?

Furthermore, when the eminent neurophysiologist dwells on the fact that scientific method stresses the regularities and uniformities of nature rather than the differences, he seems to overlook Boerhave's epigram about the doubleness of man. Morison, who is conversant with the various schools and the progress of psychology, surely knows that psychology began as a pure science seeking to establish laws. Wundt, Ebbinghaus, G. E. Müller, Titchener, J. McK. Cattell, in the halcyon days, were eager to lift the new science to the pedestal of the natural sciences, but it soon became evident that such a measure leads to sterility, and that, after all, science must consider the needs of man too, and if the atoms and molecules or cells are not burdened with individual differences, it is the physical or natural scientists' good luck. The organism, and especially the higher organism, cannot be studied on the assumption that there are no individual differ-

[19] R. S. Morison: "Gradualness, Gradualness, Gradualness," *Amer. Psychologist*, 1960, vol. 15, p. 187.

ences or that they don't count. In the human sphere it is the exception, the deviate, that sheds light on the norm; and it was William James, trained as a physiologist, who kept that circumstance steadfastly in mind, thus opposing the jolly bandwagon of law-seekers at the turn of the century.

Even those continuing the tradition of the early laboratories like Hull, Hovland, *et alii,* have been impelled to deal with the various types of rats in their learning experiments, although their chief aim had been to formulate laws, principles, and equations.

The strides which psychology has made in all directions are manifest, even if the learning process cannot be physiologically pinpointed. There have been advances made in the study of the sensory processes, in perception, even thought processes. For the first time a scientist billeted to a psychological laboratory in the United States (Harvard) has been awarded the Nobel Prize for his achievement in the area of hearing. G. M. Békésy, Hungarian-born, began as a mathematician, turned to engineering, then physics, subsequently became a physiologist; and specializing in audition, he must willy-nilly be regarded as a psychologist.

Nevertheless, American psychologists do not always act as if they were secure. The *American Psychologist,* very ably edited and generally filled with interesting and important reading matter, reports all sorts of pats on the back after the fashion of a trade organ or a minority group sheet. More symptomatic is the award of a gold medal to the journalist who was commissioned by *Life* to write a series of articles on psychology. Excellent as these articles were, one feels that such recognition could very well be reserved for a score of psychologists who have devoted a lifetime to the science.

Awards have been coming from various organizations, primarily from the American Psychological Foundation to psychologists who have distinguished themselves largely in experimental work. The Warren gold medal is awarded to outstanding experimentalists. Occasionally a government department honors a psychologist for some special service. There are other national bodies and learned or professional groups, like the American Association for the Advancement of Science, offering awards in psychology, and as usual, although the recipients are very worthy, and their accomplishment is meritorious, there are others who are equally deserving. The role of personality, popularity, contacts, seems to play a part in such matters; and psychologists are no exception.

Diversity of Views

The man in the street often supposes that all psychologists are of one opinion on questions concerning the mind or behavior. On the other hand, in scientific circles, psychology is depreciated because there is no unanimity in the results or in the views expressed. Many psychologists, too, deplore the fact that their science is not monolithic.

We have all heard such catty remarks as "what's the difference between philosophy and psychology if you disagree on almost everything in your own ranks?" The physicalistic psychologists are especially exercised over the subjectivity of their colleagues and would have every member of the American Psychological Association committed to a behvioristic or operationistic stand. Somewhere in their id, I fear, there lurks a repressed wish that a totalitarian regime in psychology take over and declass all but their own school. There would then be greater unity and scope for accomplishment (the Nazi *Gleichschaltung*). All investigators would then be oriented in one direction. The heretic would perhaps not be arrested as a counter-revolutionary, but he would be branded as one of the lunatic fringe.

Fortunately we are not all of one mind. The results gained in the laboratory or in the field can be fixed and received by all trained experimenters. Interpretations and theories, however, may vary. That occurs in the best families of science. Biology has its vitalists. In physics (light) the undulatory and corpuscular camps may become reconciled but cannot be fused. Even in mathematics, there are likes and dislikes of certain conceptions (infinite numbers, issues in probability). The neo-Humeian and the neo-Kantian positions are still at odds with one another in regard to the fundamentals of methodology. Nuclear indeterminacy is no less a hitch in understanding the physical sciences than the various "oscillations" or puzzling behavior quirks are in psychology.

So far as empirical psychology is concerned, the facts in the form of experimental results are demonstrable, and where the procedure is impugned, the amended method or technique will straighten out matters. Hardly anyone will dispute the universal preference of praise to criticism or the conclusions gained in memory investigations or the thousands of other useful data acquired in the laboratory. Philosophy does not offer such clean-cut products, and if logical positivism strives to change all that, it is only by turning philosophy into logic and discarding all else as either meaningless or tautological.

That we have no such unanimity in the sphere of interpretation may be deplored, but constructed as we are, there is no way out of it; and perhaps the situation is not so bad as it appears: for mental life or behavior is too complex and comprehensive to be seen through one window, even if it be a bay window. Just because there are so many facets, it behooves us to be stationed at various points to be on the watch for unexpected developments. The worker with rats cannot be expected to see the phenomena that are manifest to the social psychologist, nor can the mental tester appreciate the problems coming up in animal psychology. A different face again looms in the field of personality. Each may require a different approach—all within the province of science, but science in the stream of becoming or expanding, not in the rigid state which bars all considerations that do not fit into the existing mold.

It is thanks to such a program or scientific policy that new and even novel claims may be examined and validated. Freud would never have stood the chance of being even half accepted in psychology, were it not for our diversified mentalities (and of course latitude to recognize them) and we might have missed many an eddy, lost entirely in the authoritarian whirlpool.

As it is, the psychological spectrum, except for the two extremities: mentalism (including those trends based on the unconscious and paraconscious) and behaviorism (stimulus-response mechanism) consists of merging segments. One department or area may favor one view while another department favors another. It does not mean that, therefore, there is confusion. It is only when a certain doctrine becomes an explain-all that we should be on our guard, *e.g.*, when psychoanalysis takes under its wings, nay more, applies the same premise to every phenomenon in human behavior. A properly evolved mosaic may be a more scientific integration than a Procrustean ortholinear unity.

Actually we should be thankful that, although the mechanistic system dominates in the colleges and especially the laboratories, we can still find Köhler clinging to a cognitive point of view and engaged in discovering the flaws in a sure-fire behaviorism and that Tolman, with all his operationistic gusto, could still spurn a purely mechanistic stimulus-response interpretation of even rat behavior. Mowrer, a former President of the American Psychological Association, does not flinch from tracing mental illness not merely to guilt feeling but actually to sin, in a real sense, although Heinroth's similar position over a century ago had been ridiculed by his colleagues in psychiatry. Gordon Allport, another past President of the American Psychological Association, is not ashamed to sponsor a personalistic view, which would affiliate him with some of the idealistic philosophers. Another past President of the American Psychological Association, Gardner Murphy, has identified himself with the parapsychologists having become a patron of psychic research many years since, without veering from his stand. With all the deference to statistical treatment and respect for factorial analysis, Paul Meehl, another past President of the American Psychological Association, has argued effectively in favor of the clinical handling of data independent of statistics (*Clinical versus Statistical Prediction*).

In a recent issue of the *American Psychologist*, we read an account of Brentano, extolling his *Akt* psychology, and fortunately Boring's operationistic *Zeitgeist* is so liberal as to allow him to write a sympathetic foreword to Misiak's and Staudt's *Catholics in Psychology*.

Neo-behaviorism may exult in its dominant status as a force in the shaping of American psychology, but mentalism is beginning to manifest its pristine influence. In a symposium on "Behavior and Awareness," C. W. Erikson opens his contribution with the statement "The past six years have witnessed a marked revival of interest in human awareness and its role and effects upon behavior,"[20] while S. S. Tomkins, at Princeton, has written three volumes in which he develops the thesis that psychology has lost its heart and its mind from fear of methodological impurity, from excessive reliance on primary drives as motivators and from attention to behavior rather than the complex transportations that make behavior possible.

Psychologists are no longer chary of using terms like

[20] C. W. Erikson: "Figments, Fantasies, and Follies; A Search for the Subsconscious Mind," *Journal of Personality*, 1962, vol. 30, No. 2, p. 3, Supplement.

imagery, thought processes, attention, cognition, self, personality, and even instinct, while the stocks of conditioning and stimulus-response have been dropping, after it has become clear that many of the experiments on rats (a) offer nothing conclusive, (b) are inconsequential, and (c) the results are not necessarily applicable to other animals, let alone man. After all, does it really much matter whether a rat copulates umpteen times a day and how many intromissions it takes before he ejaculates, or how many squeaks the female emits during copulation. The first problem for an experimenter with ample facilities is to select a problem of some weight, on a long-range view. Sometimes it would seem as if the investigator's curiosity or sport-need (a species of indoor gaming) is the determining factor in the selection of a given investigation.

What, however, is cause for gratification appears to be the diversified interests and leanings of American psychologists; for it offers corrective measures in the case of exaggerated and lopsided tendencies. A mentalist (or is it "neo-mentalist?") should recognize the claims of neo-behaviorism in a limited segment of behavior, while the operationist or neo-behaviorist might as well be just as magnanimous to the rival; for because of the tremendous complexity of psychology, the subtle counter-reactions to stimulation, the methods of negotiating the vastly differing phenomena, must needs be varied to suit the situation. Even in physics and chemistry, inference takes the place of actual sight or hearing. No one has seen either the alpha or gamma waves; nor is the neutron or positron visible through the most powerful microscope. Evolution as a principle did not require formidable equations to prove its validity, and psychology being a ubiquitous science as well as an art in dealing with human endeavor and flights must cut the sails, or wings, to suit the wind.

Gardner Murphy, in an eloquent recent address at Queens College, has given expression to a similar sentiment

> I am willing to say, though, that a dialectical movement is now perfectly obvious in which, whenever psychology gets itself tightened and hardened, so rigid that it can't move or breathe, something way deep in its insides, something urgent and vital, like the tissues buried far beneath the skin, will begin to wiggle into fresh expression, and there will be a deep breath and the strait jacket will again

burst. In other words, there will be a dialectical movement by which psychology will get more rigid, orderly, scientific, correct, and afraid of saying "boo" to any of the experiences not yet codified. But at the same time, these experiences not yet codified will push and kick until they somehow or other create enough discomfort to prevent rigor mortis from setting in. Psychology will go on tightening and loosening, loosening and tightening, gaining and reaching, codifying and reopening questions. In fact, psychology will go on seething for a long time.[21]

His extrapolation, or prediction, is more important for the elaborate scaffolding than for the minaret built, consisting of the suggested facets to be developed in genetics, neurophysiology, perception research, and ecology, with ecology in the very center.

International Contacts

There was a time not so long ago when American psychology looked up to Germany. Wundt's laboratory, in Leipzig, was for decades the training center for ambitious American psychologists, who, in turn, would send their own brilliant students to the founder of the first psychological laboratory (even though the priority had been under dispute). If it was not to Wundt, then it was to Stumpf, in Berlin, or Külpe, in Würzburg, or even G. E. Müller, in Göttingen, that American students would go for their rounding out, or journeyman's stint before embarking on their teaching career.

All that changed with the advent of the Nazis. Since the Second World War, Germany has been able to get on her feet again economically, but it is doubtful whether she will be able to get on her head for many generations, after ridding herself of the best brains in the country, and losing her prestige as a scientific proving ground.

Some of us can still remember with what zest graduate students and instructors would fall upon each new bulky issue of the German psychological periodicals. At present, I daresay, hardly one in a thousand knows what periodicals are published in Germany, and I have yet to hear of an advanced graduate student going to Germany for earnest laboratory work in psychology.

[21] G. Murphy: "The Psychology of 1975: An Extrapolation. *Amer. Psychol.,* vol. 18, Nov. 1963.

France, except in abnormal psychology and testing, which originated there but seems to have stagnated after Binet's death, while carried on in the United States, has never had an attraction for America. Men like Ribot, Janet, and more recently Piéron, who was co-president of the Montreal Congress in 1955, were highly thought of; Lévy-Bruhl and Durkheim were, of course, studied in the U. S., but they were philosophers with a sociological approach, and not primarily psychologists. French psychology seemed casual and sporadic. American psychology seeks moorings and prizes system. Even French leaning to a species of behaviorism, lacking however the theory and detail of American behaviorism, has not rendered it more palatable to American psychologists.

Of the other countries that could come under consideration, Italy figured somewhat because of Gemelli's laboratory, which turned out a vast deal of experimental work, but the clerical status would be against him, even if the problems investigated had nothing to do with religion. Switzerland has furnished a few well-known men in the allied field, like Jung and Bleuler, but in psychology proper, we now, after Claparède's death, hear only of Piaget, whose books on childhood mentality are extensively discussed with some misgivings about his pat interpretations of the child's logic, reasoning, growth, etc. Belgium's Michotte, at Louvain, is regarded here as a fine experimentalist, naturally with a Thomist bias, which would affect the nature of the problems selected for investigation.

The relation to British psychology has been puzzling. The slow realization in British academic circles that psychology was not merely a pale satellite of philosophy has been the chief factor in American psychologists looking down their nose at the attempts in England to add to their science. Under Myers and Bartlett, the exchange of students occasionally went on, and it was considered prestigious to publish in the *British Journal of Psychology*. Spearman's factor analysis, elaborated at the University of London, too, was of some import, and his G factor in intelligence was debated back and forth by Thorndike and his students, but aside from the controversy it engendered, Spearman's work was little known by the average American graduate student. In developmental psychology, C. Burt's books were often assigned. References to Pear and to Thouless are very sparse in American psychology texts, practically nonexistent.

Strange as it may appear, it is Russian psychology with its

overemphasis of Pavlovian conditioning and its Marxian implications that has fascinated American psychologists, many of whom have made pilgrimages either as individuals or, more frequently, in groups. To be sure, the names of Sechenov, Pavlov and Bekhterev had been known to cognoscenti in the United States for half a century at least; and behaviorism, in all its forms, bears a strong kinship with reflexology, but that does not tell the full story. May it not be that the cold war has, as a reaction, brought about a *rapprochement* on the intellectual side, as if to stave off the imminent catastrophe. In the months preceding the Nazi war, many of the radio stations would be playing Wagnerian music (it would have been more appropriate to play Bach and composers other than Wagner for the occasion) and analogously when the Soviet-American situation became tense, there was a rash of Tchaikovsky, Prokofief, and Shostakovitch or Stravinsky compositions on programs. It apparently is supposed to be the intermezzo that is to calm excited feelings and call to mind the blessings that the Russians have brought into the world.

Aside from such reflections, however, there is the further fact that Russian psychological activities remind one of a beehive, and are conducted under the aegis of the state. In this bustle, everything must be planned, all must click. Nothing haphazard can escape the scrutinizing eyes of the directors and assistant directors; and Americans like to survey a smoothly working machine. The very contrasts intrigue us. How do children fare when both parents are working? How is delinquency treated? How does the individual come into his own, when all attention is centered on the group?

So far as Latin America is concerned, the "friendly neighbor" policy of the Government does not seem to hold here. While it is true that the territory south of California is apparently lacking in scientific enzymes, we must recognize that there is much activity of a psychological nature going on in both Argentina and Brazil, and even in Peru. All three countries could claim one or two well-known names of native psychologists (usually affiliated with psychiatry) but some refugees and possibly even fugitives who had been associated with psychology had settled in South America and broadened the psychological horizon there. Psychoanalysis is especially well represented in Argentina. Perhaps closer contacts will be established when the larger universities there introduce experimental investigations of a long-range type.

As for Canada, its psychologists are generally members of the American Psychological Association and publish in its periodicals, although there is a growing Canadian Psychological Association as well as two periodicals devoted to psychology.

A New Branch of Science

In the last chapter it was suggested that with our fresh insights into the physico-chemical world the gains might yield some valuable information as regards our constitution and behavior. One solitary reviewer laughed out loud at the very thought that radioactive substance in the organism may ultimately explain some of the differences between man and man. It is easier, of course, to poke fun at something than to study its implications, but I can draw up a list of far-fetched hypotheses that are taken seriously today and are applied to therapy, industry, and commerce, *e.g.*, the numerous so-called depth analyses in the field of motivation research.

It is not, however, a general direction that I have here in mind, but rather a new outlet, as it were, of psychology that is being predicted. At a small gathering with E. C. Tolman, during the Psychological Congress in Montreal, a Toronto psychologist asked me about the future of psychology. It was past midnight after a round of cocktails and loud conversation, and the issue was shelved for the time being but not dismissed.

From a retrospective glance at the problems in the fore which occupied the minds of the pioneers, we can at least conclude that much of what, at one time, seemed to have been of paramount importance, hardly is worth while considering now. Our psychological Toynbee might trot out his sleek *Zeitgeist* with no more ado. It is a convenient label that covers a multitude of why's but does not make us any wiser. The spread and growth of laboratories need not be taken as a guarantee that all that is going on there must be of great consequence. In a sense, we have a certain modification of Gresham's law operating here; for often the picayune and indifferent problems would receive so much attention that there was no effort made to discover the more momentous issues. If an individual was engaged in some investigation on his own, without falling in with the majority interest or fashion, he was apt to be addressing himself to a deaf audience, unless he was well established in an institution with graduate students to sit at his feet.

The halo of the positive is so great in all walks, which includes science, that anything smacking of the negative is either unperceived or disregarded. In mathematics, the minus sign or surds were taken account of because they served as components in larger operations, but it took some time before the concept of inhibition assumed any significance. Similarly it is only recently that the cobwebby boundary between nerve cells, the synapse, has been receiving its due share of recognition. William James, and Tetens long before him, made some plea on behalf of *relations*, which were always neglected in psychology to the advantage of the *substantive*.

Small wonder, then, that the whole subject of mistakes has been seen in fragments, sometimes in connection with motor accidents or industrial mishaps or as lapses, in the Freudian system, but never as a whole branch of a science.

It is my prediction that within the next decade a new area will be developed under the head of *science of mistakes*, probably taking its designation, according to tradition, from the Greek *ptaismatology*.[22]

Those who are a bit puzzled at the thought of a science being based on wholly negative phenomena should be reminded that *pathology* is the science of disease—and what an important science it is! It may be observed here that pathology and *ptaismatology* are to an extent related, as often the pathological condition had been induced by a mistake; and also that mistakes in diagnosis could worsen or even end the case.

Naturally, it might be objected that mistakes are of such a variety that they could not be subsumed under one general category, but the fact that they are designated by the same term would indicate that they must all have a common denominator; and it would be the function of the ptaismatologist to set about classifying the mistakes into types and then discovering the motivation behind them, conscious or unconscious, and the circumstances that touch off the motives, or even the neurological structure which favors certain mistakes. The pointing out of mistakes in the various life activities (professional, political, economic, etc.) is certainly not enough. A science of mistakes is definitely part and parcel of the be-

---

[22] The formation πταισμα—a mistake—is from the Greek πταιω, to *stumble*, to *make a false step.* The term *ptaismatology* sounds awkward enough, but so is the act to which it refers. The *pt* phonex suggests a bird, in flight, falling, which is more pathetic than just falling, on the part of an ambulant.

havioral constellation, and it is not too soon to make a start by a systematic classification first.

It is a far cry from a slip of the tongue to a mistake in policy on an international scale, such as Germany attacking Russia while at war with the Allies, but that is true of medicine too when we compare a surface scratch with a metastasized cancer, or an epidemic like the Bubonic plague. Besides, in a totalitarian country, a slip of the tongue or pen, or even a misprint, may spark a conflagration.

Chart of Objectivistic Psychologies

| | | PRE-BEHAVIORISM | | |
Materialists	Positivists	Animal Objectivists[2]	Conditioned Reflex School	American Pre-Behaviorists
Hobbes[1]	Comte[2] Cournot	Beer Bethe von Uexküll Nuel Loeb[4] (*tropisms*)	Pavlov v. Bechterev[5]	Santayana Cattell Dewey Woodbridge

[1] "Sense is some internal motion in the sentient. . . ."

[2] "There can be nothing like scientific observations of the passions except from without."

[3] "There is no comparative [animal] psychology."

[4] "Consciousness is only a metaphysical term for phenomena which are determined by associative memory." Loeb reduces memory, images and other mental facts to physical mechanisms.

[5] "The object of psychoreflexology is the study of the relation of the organism to the external world in connection with the occurring experience, quite independent of the subjective mental state (*Erlebnis*)."

BEHAVIORISM PROPER

Structural — Stress laid on organism and mechanisms				Functional — Stress laid on environment and relations			
Gross	Physiological	Neurological	Formal (non-physiological)	Bio-Sociological	Physico-Social	Philosophical [10]	Dynamic
						Pragmatist / Realist	
Holt [6]	Watson (*emphasis on effectors*)	Meyer, S. B. Russell, Frost (*emphasis on nerve connections*)	Tolman (*stimulus, cue, object, act*)	Parmelee [7], (Paton) [8]	G. DeLaguna [9]	Pragmatist: Bode, Bawden — Realist: Perry, Singer, (Holt)	Holt [11] (*Freudian*), Kempf [12] (*psychoanalytic*), Kantor (*organismic*)
	Weiss	Weiss					

[6] Behavior as specific response. The complete act (eating, swimming) is the unit of behavior, yet Holt inconsistently includes muscle tonus under behavior.

[7] For Parmelee the science of behavior is a sort of super-science including psychology as well as biology and sociology.

[8] Paton is concerned with adjustments, but is unwilling to dispense with the subjective terminology altogether.

[9] "It is only by reference . . . to their function in securing the adjustment of the individual to his environment, physical and social. . . ."

PSYCHO-BEHAVIORISM		NOMINAL BEHAVIORISM					
Psycho-biological	Bi-polar [14]	Heuristic	Methodologic	Genetic	Teleological	Egological	Moto-Mentalist
Dunlap [16]	Hollingworth Warren Pillsbury	McDougall (study of mind more ultimate aim)	Yerkes [15]	Kirkpatrick (*organosis*)	Tawney (*assimation*)	Calkins (relation of self to environment)	The Clark School S. C. Fisher (*behavior of consciousness*) R. F. Richardson ("*behavior of image*")

[10] To some of the philosophical behaviorists, consciousness is a relation between organism and environment; to others it is a brain product or brain function; to still others, the mental fact is identified with the physical fact conditioning it.

[11] The wish in Freud's sense is interpreted in terms of physiological integration.

[12] The decided leaning towards behaviorism in Kempf's "The Autonomic Functions, etc.," is offset by the use he makes of introspective data. Kempf's behavioristic formula is "Affective Craving × Environmental Resistance = Behavior."

[13] Dunlap combats both introspectionism and behaviorism, but adopts the terminology of both.

[14] The bi-polarity consists in making use both of behavior, but while Hollingworth thinks information about consciousness a help to the study of behavior, Warren and Pillsbury believe the two coördinate in value. Of the three, Pillsbury, aside from his definition, is nearest the mentalists.

[15] Yerkes is interested in animal *behavior*, but in human *psychology*. Yerkes is a behaviorist as to method, but his interpretation bears the unmistakable stamp of mentalism.

PHYSICALISM

| operationism
empirical definition
(Bridgman)
(Stevens) | logical positivism
logical behaviorism
(Carnap) [16] | general semantics
extensionalization
(Korzybski) |

[16] Carnap, the most rigorous and most authoritative of the logical positivists, has recently become sympathetic toward introspection, thus following Bridgman's change of attitude, referred to in the text.

Bibliography

In order to avoid useless duplication, the titles listed here do not include the books and articles cited in the text and footnotes. As the present work deals with American psychology, it was deemed advisable to exclude all books authored by non-Americans, unless American psychology is specifically treated therein in historical perspective.

In general, introductory textbooks and collections of readings are omitted. Outstanding texts of a more advanced nature and original symposia (as differentiated from readings) have been cited.

Considering the steady flow of psychological works, only those books published within the last decade or so have been gathered here. The more important ones are indicated by means of an asterisk (*). New editions are listed only if they are considerably revised and enlarged. All references in this section pertain to books, whether hardcover or paperbacks. Many references to articles will be found in the text itself.

* Adorno, T. W., Frenkel-Brunswik, E., Levinson, D. J., and Sanford, R. N. *The Authoritarian Personality,* New York, Harper and Brothers, 1950.

Alexander, F., *Psychoanalysis and Psychotherapy,* New York, W. W. Norton and Co., 1956.

* Allen, R. M., *Personality Assessment Procedures,* New York, Harper and Brothers, 1958.

* Allport, F. H., *Theories of Perception and the Concept of Structure,* New York, John Wiley & Sons, 1955.

Allport, G. W., *Becoming: Basic Considerations for a Psychology of Personality,* New Haven, Yale University Press, 1955.

* Allport, G. W., *Pattern and Growth in Personality,* New York, Holt, Rinehart and Winston, 1961.

* Anastasi, Anne, *Differential Psychology; Individual and Group Differences in Psychology,* rev. ed., New York, The Macmillan Co., 1956.

Anastasi, Anne, *Fields of Applied Psychology,* New York, McGraw-Hill Book Co., 1964.

Appleby, L., Scher, J., and Cumming, J., Editors, *Chronic Schizophrenia,* Glencoe, Illinois, The Free Press, 1959.

Arieti, Sylvano, Editor, *American Handbook of Psychiatry,* 2 vols., New York, Basic Books, 1959.

Asch, S. E., *Social Psychology,* New York, Prentice-Hall, 1952.

Atkinson, J. W., *Motives in Fantasy, Action, and Society: A Method of Assessment and Study,* Princeton, D. Van Nostrand Co., 1958.

Back, S. J., and Molish, H. B., Editors, *Reflexes to Intelligence, A Reader in Clinical Psychology,* Glencoe, Illinois, The Free Press, 1959.

Balint, M., *The Doctor, His Patient and the Illness,* New York, International Universities Press, 1957.

Balser, B. H., Editor, *Psychotherapy of the Adolescent,* New York, International Universities Press, 1957.

Bandura, A. and Walters, R. H., *Adolescent Aggression,* New York, Ronald Press Co., 1959.

Bandura, A. and Walters, R. H., *Social Learning and Personality Development,* New York, Holt, Rinehart and Winston, 1963.

* Bartley, S. H., *Principles of Perception,* New York, Harper and Brothers, 1958.

Berkowitz, L., *Aggression: A Social Psychological Analysis,* New York, McGraw-Hill Book Co., 1962.

* Bonner, Hubert, *Group Dynamics: Principles and Applications,* New York, Ronald Press Co., 1959.

Brown, R., Galanter, E., Hess, E. H., and Mandler, G., *New Directions in Psychology,* New York, Holt, Rinehart and Winston, 1962.

Bruner, J. S., Goodnow, J. J. and Austin, G. A., *A Study of Thinking,* New York, John Wiley and Sons, 1956.

Burrow, T., *Science and Man's Behavior: The Contribution of Phylobiology,* ed. by W. E. Galt, New York, Philosophical Library, 1953.

* Bush, R. R. and Mosteller, F., *Stochastic Models for Learning,* New York, John Wiley and Sons, 1950.

Cameron, Norman, and Margaret Ann, *Behavior Pathology,* Boston, Houghton Mifflin Company, 1951.

Cantril, Hadley, *Human Nature and Political Systems,* New Brunswick, Rutgers University Press, 1961.

* Cattell, R. B., *Personality and Motivation Structure and Environment,* Yonkers, New York, World Book, 1957.

Clark, K. E., *America's Psychologists,* Washington, American Psychological Association, 1957.

Coombs, C. H., *Theory of Data,* New York, John Wiley and Sons, 1964.

Corsini, R. J., *Methods of Group Psychotherapy,* New York, McGraw-Hill Book Co., 1957.

* Cronback, Lee J., *Essentials of Psychological Testing,* rev. ed., New York, Harper and Brothers, 1960.

* Davies, J. C., *Human Nature in Politics,* New York, John Wiley and Sons, 1963.

* Dollard, J. and Miller, N. E., *Personality and Psychotherapy,* New York, McGraw-Hill Book Co., 1950.

* Dreger, R. M., *Fundamentals of Personality,* Philadelphia, J. B. Lippincott Co., 1962.

Eckman, D. P., *Systems: Research and Design,* New York, John Wiley and Sons, 1961.

* Edwards, A. L., *Experimental Design in Psychological Research,* New York, Holt, Rinehart and Winston, 1950.

Ekstein, R. and Wallerstein, R., *The Learning and Teaching of Psychotherapy,* New York, Basic Books, 1958.

Ellis, N. R., Editor, *Handbook of Mental Deficiency: Psychological Theory and Research,* New York, McGraw-Hill Book Co., 1963.

*Feigl, H., Editor, *Concepts, Theories, and the Mind-Body Problem,* Minneapolis, University of Minnesota Press, 1958.

Ferster, C. B. and Skinner, B. F., *Schedules of Reinforcement,* New York, Appleton-Century-Crofts, 1957.

Festinger, L., *Theory of Cognitive Dissonance,* Stanford, California, Stanford University Press, 1957.

Fisher, S. and Cleveland, S. E., *Body Image and Personality,* Princeton, D. Van Nostrand Co., 1958.

Foulquie, P. and Deledalle, G., *La Psychologie Contemporaine,* Paris, Presses Universitaires, 1951.

About a third of the book is devoted to American psychology —about 50 pages alone to various hues of behaviorism, following the lead of Roback's Behaviorism and Psychology but without the polemical approach.

French, W., *Behavioral Goals of General Education in High School,* New York, Russell Sage Foundation, 1957.

Fry, Edward B., *Teaching Machines and Programmed Instruction: An Introduction to Autoinstruction,* New York, McGraw-Hill Book Co., 1963.

*Gagné, R. M., *Psychological Principles in System Development,* New York, Holt, Rinehart and Winston, 1962.

*Gibson, J. J., *The Perception of the Visual World,* Boston, Houghton Mifflin Company, 1964.

Gill, M. M., *Topography and Systems in Psychoanalytic Theory,* New York, International Universities Press, Inc., 1963.

Goodenough, Florence L. and Tyler, Leona E., *Developmental Psychology,* 3rd ed., New York, Appleton-Century-Crofts, 1959.

Gottschalk, L. A., Editor, *Comparative Psycholinguistic Analysis of Two Psychotherapeutic Interviews,* New York, International Universities Press, 1961.

Green, B. F., *Digital Computers in Psychology,* New York, McGraw-Hill Book Co., 1963.

Green, E. J., *The Learning Process and Programmed Instruction,* New York, Holt, Rinehart and Winston, 1962.

*Guilford, J. P., *Psychometric Methods* (2nd ed.) New York, McGraw-Hill Book Co., 1954.

Gulliken, H., *Theory of Mental Tests*, New York, John Wiley and Sons, 1950.

Hare, A. Paul, *Handbook of Small Group Research*, New York, The Free Press, 1962.

Harvey, O. J., Hunt, D. E. and Schroder, H. M., *Conceptual Systems and Personality Organization*, New York, John Wiley and Sons, 1961.

Hebb, D. O., *The Organization of Behavior*, New York, John Wiley and Sons, 1949.

Henry, Jules, *Culture Against Man*, New York, Random House, 1963.

Hochberg, J., *Perception*, Englewood Cliffs, N.J., Prentice-Hall, 1963.

Holland, J. G. and Skinner, B. F., *The Analysis of Behavior: A Program for Self-Instruction*, New York, McGraw-Hill Book Co., 1961.

Hollingshead, A. B. and Redlich, F. C., *Social Class and Mental Illness*, New York, John Wiley and Sons, 1958.

Holt, R. and Luborsky, L., *Personality Patterns of Psychiatrists: A Study in Selection Techniques*, New York, Basic Books, 1958.

Holt, R. T. and Van de Velde, R. W., *Strategic Psychological Operations and American Foreign Policy*, Chicago, Chicago University Press, 1960.

Hoppock, R., *Occupational Information*, New York, McGraw-Hill Book Co., 1957.

*Hull, C. L., *A Behavior System*, New Haven, Yale University Press, 1952.

Hyman, H. H., *Political Socialization: A Study in the Psychology of Political Behavior*, Glencoe, Illinois, The Free Press, 1959.

*Jenkins, J. J. and Paterson, D. M., *Studies in Individual Differences: The Search for Intelligence*, New York, Appleton-Century-Crofts, 1961.

*Johnson, D. M., *The Psychology of Thought and Judgment*, New York, Harper and Brothers, 1955.

Jourard, S. M., *The Transparent Self*, Princeton, D. Van Nostrand Co., 1963.

Kellogg, W., *Porpoises and Sonar*, Chicago, University of Chicago Press, 1963.

Kerlinger, F. N., *Foundations of Behavioral Research*, New York, Holt, Rinehart and Winston, 1964.

Kleemeier, R. W., Editor, *Aging and Leisure: A Research Perspective into the Meaningful Use of Time*, New York, Oxford University Press, 1961.

Klineberg, O., *The Human Factor in International Relations*, New York, Holt, Rinehart and Winston, 1964.

Koch, S., Editor, *Psychology: A Study of a Science*, 7 vols., New York, McGraw-Hill Book Co., 1960-1964.

Leeper, R. W. and Madison, P., *Toward Understanding Human Personalities*, New York, Appleton-Century-Crofts, 1959.

Leighton, A. H., *My Name is Legion: Foundations For a Theory of Man's Response to Culture*, New York, Basic Books, 1959.

Levitt, Eugene E., *Clinical Research Design and Analysis in the Behavioral Sciences*, Springfield, Illinois, Charles C. Thomas, 1961.

Levy, L. H., *Psychological Interpretation*, New York, Holt, Rinehart and Winston, 1963.

Lindzey, G., *Projective Techniques and Cross-cultural Research*, New York, Appleton-Century-Crofts, 1963.

Luce, R. D., Bush, R. R. and Galanter, E., Editors, *Handbook of Mathematical Psychology*, 3 vols., New York, John Wiley and Sons, 1963.

Lysaught, J. P. and Williams, C. M. *A Guide to Programmed Instruction*, New York, John Wiley and Sons, 1963.

Maier, Norman R. F., *Psychology in Industry*, 2nd Edition, Boston, Houghton Mifflin Company, 1955.

Mann, F. C. and Hoffman, L. R., *Automation and the Worker: A Study of Social Change in Power Plants*, New York, Holt, Rinehart and Winston, 1960.

Mansurov, N. S., *Sovremennaya Burzhuaznaya Psykhologiya: Kriticheskii Ocherk (Contemporary Bourgeois Psychology: A Critical Outline)* Moscow, 1962. American psychology is often compared with Marxian-based Russian findings.

Marrow, A. J., *Changing Patterns of Prejudice*, Philadelphia, Chilton Books, 1962.

*Marx, M. H. and Hillix, W. A., *Systems and Theories in Psychology*, New York, McGraw-Hill Book Co., 1963.

Mason, R. E., *Internal Perception and Bodily Functioning*, New York, International Universities Press, 1961.

*May, Rollo, Angel, E. and Ellenberger, H. F., Editors, *Existence: A New Dimension in Psychiatry and Psychology*, New York, Basic Books, 1958.

McClelland, D. C., Atkinson, J. W., Clark, R. A., and Lowell, E. L., *The Achievement Motive*, New York, Appleton-Century-Crofts, 1953.

Mednick, Martha T. and Mednick, S. A., Editors, *Research in Personality*, New York, Holt, Rinehart and Winston, 1963.

Merton, R. K., Reader, G. and Kendall, P. L., *The Student-Physician*, Cambridge, Harvard University Press, 1957.

Messick, S. and Ross, J., Editors, *Measurement in Personality and Cognition*, New York, John Wiley and Sons, 1962.

Mowrer, O. H., *Learning Theory and Personality Dynamics*, New York, Ronald Press Co., 1950.

Mowrer, O. H., *Learning Theory and the Symbolic Processes*, New York, John Wiley and Sons, 1960.

Munn, Norman L., *The Evolution and Growth of Human Behavior: A Revision of Psychological Development*, Boston, Houghton Mifflin Company, 1955.

*Osgood, C. E., Suci, G. J. and Tannenbaum, P. H., *The Measurement of Meaning*, Urbana, Illinois, University of Illinois Press, 1957.

*Osgood, C. E., *Method and Theory in Experimental Psychology*, New York, Oxford University Press, 1953.

Oswald, Ian, *Sleeping and Waking: Physiology and Psychology*, New York, American Elsevier Publishing Co., 1962.

Parnes, S. J. and Harding, H. F., Editors, *A Source Book for Creative Thinking*, New York, Charles Scribner's Sons, 1962.

Pfeiffer, J., *The Thinking Machine: Everyman's Introduction to the World of Electronic Device*, Philadelphia, J. B. Lippincott Co., 1962.

Piotrowski, Z. A., *Perceptanalysis*, New York, The Macmillan Co., 1957.

*Polyak, S., *The Vertebrate Visual System*, Chicago, University of Chicago Press, 1958.

*Postman, L., Editor, *Psychology in the Making; Histories of Selected Research Problems*, New York, Alfred A. Knopf, 1962.

Remmers, H. H. and Radler, D. H., *The American Teenager*, New York, Indianapolis, The Bobbs-Merrill Company, 1957.

Restle, Frank, *Psychology of Judgment and Choice*, New York, John Wiley and Sons, 1961.

Rheingold, Harriet L., Editor, *Maternal Behavior in Mammals*, New York, John Wiley and Sons, 1963.

Rimland, B., *Infantile Autism: The Syndrome and its Implications for a Neural Theory of Behavior*, New York, Appleton-Century-Crofts, 1964.

Roback, A. A., *Destiny and Motivation in Language*, Cambridge, Massachusetts, Sci-Art, 1954.

*Roback, A. A., Editor, *Present-day Psychology; A Symposium*, New York, Philosophical Library, 1955.

Roback, A. A., *Aspects of Applied Psychology and Crime*, Cambridge, Massachusetts, Sci-Art., 1964.

*Roback, A. A., *The Psychology of Character*, 3rd rev. ed., London, Kegan Paul, 1952.

Royce, J. R., *The Encapsulated Man*, Princeton, D. Van Nostrand Co., 1964.

Sarason, I. G., Editor, *Contemporary Research in Personality*, New York, D. Van Nostrand Co., 1962.

*Sears, R. R., Maccoby, E. E. and Levin, H., *Patterns of Child Rearing*, Evanston, Illinois, Row, Peterson and Co., 1958.

Sherif, Muzafer and Hovland, Carl I., *Social Judgment; Assimilation and Contrast Effects in Communication and Attitude Change*, New Haven, Yale University Press, 1961.

Shibutani, Tamotsu, *Society and Personality; An Interactionist*

Approach to Social Psychology, Englewood Cliffs, N. J., Prentice-Hall, 1961.

Shorokhova, E. V., Editor, *Sovremennaya Psykhologya v Kapitalisticheskikh Stranakh (Contemporary Psychology in the Capitalist Countries)* Moscow, Izdatelstvo Akademii Nauk, 1963. Most of the volume is devoted to American psychology with a number of references to the first edition of the present work.

Shubik, M., *Game Theory and Related Approaches to Social Behavior,* New York, John Wiley and Sons, 1963.

*Siegel, S., *Non-parametric Statistics for the Behavioral Sciences,* New York, McGraw-Hill Book Co., 1956.

Siegel, S. and Fouraker, L. E., *Bargaining and Group Decision Making,* New York, McGraw-Hill Book Co., 1960.

*Skinner, B. F., *Cumulative Record,* rev. ed., New York, Appleton-Century-Crofts, 1961.

Skinner, B. F., *Verbal Behavior,* New York, Appleton-Century-Crofts, 1957.

Smith, Ernest A., *American Youth Culture: Group Life in Teenage Society,* New York, The Free Press, 1962.

Spence, K. W., *Behavior Theory and Conditioning,* New Haven, Yale University Press, 1956.

Spiegel, E. A., Editor, *Progress in Neurology and Psychiatry,* vol. 18, New York, Grune & Stratton, 1963.

Stevens, S. S., Editor, *Handbook of Experimental Psychology,* New York, John Wiley and Sons, 1958.

Symonds, P. M. and Jensen, A. R., *From Adolescent to Adult,* New York, Columbia University Press, 1961.

*Symonds, P. M., *Dynamics of Psychotherapy: The Psychology of Personality Change, vol. 3, Procedures,* New York, Grune & Stratton, 1958.

Tallent, N., *Clinical Psychological Consultation: A Rationale and Guide to Team Practice,* Englewood Cliffs, N.J., Prentice-Hall, 1963.

Taylor, C. W. and Barron, F., Editors, *Scientific Creativity: Its Recognition and Development,* New York, John Wiley and Sons, 1963.

Taylor, J. G., *The Behavioral Basis of Perception,* New Haven, Yale University Press, 1962.

Thompson, Laura, *Toward a Science of Mankind,* New York, McGraw-Hill Book Co., 1961.

Thrall, R. M., Coombs, C. H. and David, R. L., Editors, *Decision Processes,* New York, John Wiley and Sons, 1954.

*Tomkins, S. S., *Affect, Imagery, Consciousness,* 4 vols., New York, Springer Publishing Co., 1962-1964.

Tomkins, S. S. and Messick, S., *Computer Simulation of Personality: Frontier of Psychological Theory,* New York, John Wiley and Sons, 1963.

Trow, W. C., *Psychology in Teaching and Learning*, New York, Houghton Mifflin Company, 1960.

Underwood, B. J. and Schulz, R. W., *Meaningfulness and Verbal Learning*, Philadelphia, J. B. Lippincott Co., 1960.

*Watson, R. I., *The Great Psychologists: From Aristotle to Freud*, Philadelphia, J. B. Lippincott Co., 1963.

Watson, R. I., and Campbell, D. T., Editors, *History, Psychology, and Science: Selected Papers by E. G. Boring*, New York, John Wiley and Sons, 1963.

Webb, W. B., Editor, *The Profession of Psychology*, New York, Holt, Rinehart & Winston, 1962.

Werner, H. and Kaplan, B., *Symbol Formation: An Organismic-Developmental Approach to the Psychology of Language*, New York, John Wiley and Sons, 1963.

Wheelis, A., *The Quest for Identity*, New York, W. W. Norton and Company, 1958.

*Wolman, B. B., *Contemporary Theories and Systems in Psychology*, New York, Harper, 1960.

Woodworth, R. S., *Dynamics of Behavior*, New York, Holt, Rinehart and Winston, 1958.

*Zimny, G. H., *Method in Experimental Psychology*, New York, The Ronald Press Company, 1961.

Index of Names

Index of Names

Abbot, Jacob, 464
Abbot, John, 62
Abelard, Pierre, 427, 429
Abercrombie, John, 62, 92
Abraham, Karl, 325
Ach, 408
Achilles, P, 471
Adler, Alfred, 203, 287, 303, 316, 325, 329-331
Adrian, E. D., 355
Alexander, Franz, 329
Allport, F. H., 279, 471
Allport, G. W., 315, 316, 362, 365, 467, 471, 475, 487
Anastasi, Anne, 482
Anderson, J. E., 466
Angell, Frank, 220
Angell, James R., 219, 240-249, 451
Angier, R. P., 205
Angyal, A., 476
Aquinas, Thomas, 426-432, 434, 435, 438, 440, 441
Argyll, Duke of, 99
Aristotle, 30, 72, 154, 288, 351, 427, 428, 440, 442
Arlitt, Ada H., 466
Arminius, 44
Arnheim, R., 362
Augustine, St., 427
Arminius, J., 44
Avicenna, 428

Babcock, Harriet, 467
Bacon, Lord, 33, 37, 40, 53
Bagley, W. C., 466
Bailey, Samuel, 22

Bain, Alexander, 21, 92, 111, 194, 254, 293
Baird, J. W., 473
Baker, A. J., 466
Baldwin, Bird T., 304, 466
Baldwin, J. Mark, 22, 109, 113, 118, 142, 148, 149, 174, 183, 187, 191-195, 240, 244, 283, 349, 466, 482
Balfour, Wallace J., 479
Banham, Katherine M., 466
Barbeau, G. I., 439
Bartholin, E., 30
Bartlett, F. C., 10, 147, 363
Baruch, Dorothy W., 466
Bascom, John, 84, 464
Bawden, H. H., 168
Baynes, H. G., 330
Beach, F. A., 379, 472, 477
Beardsley, E. E., 40
Beasley, Frederick, 65
Beattie, J., 53, 61
Beausoleil, J., 439
Beck, S. J., 467
Beer, T. C., 268
Beers, C. W., 468
Be'ke'sy, G. M., 524
Bekhterev, M., 266, 269
Bell, Charles, 119
Bell, J. E., 466
Bender, L., 466
Benedict, Ruth, 341, 472
Benjamin, 96
Bentley, M., 480
Benussi, V., 365
Berkeley, Bishop, 41, 43, 44, 54, 67
Bernheim, H., 23, 191, 288

549

Index of Topics

Index of Topics